An Introduction to the
Sciences of the Qur'aan

by Abu Ammaar Yasir Qadhi

ISBN 1 898649 32 4

British Library Cataloguing in Publication Data.

A catalogue record for this book is available from the British Library.

First Edition, 1420 AH/1999 CE

Typeset by: Al-Hidaayah Publishing and Distribution

Published by: Al-Hidaayah Publishing and Distribution

                     P.O. Box 3332

                     Birmingham

                     United Kingdom

                     B10 9AW

                     Tel: 0121 753 1889

                     Fax: 0121 753 2422

                     E-Mail: ahpd@hidaayah.demon.co.uk

                     Internet: www.al-hidaayah.co.uk

Printed in Turkey by Mega Printing
export@mega.com.tr

Dedicated to:

Ammi and Abbi,

without whom,
after the blessings of Allaah,
all this would not be possible.

رَّبِّ ٱرْحَمْهُمَا كَمَا رَبَّيَانِي صَغِيرًا

«O My Lord! Bestow your Mercy on them,
even as they reared me when I was young» [17:24]

CONTENTS

TRANSLITERATION TABLE 11

INTRODUCTION 12

1. AN INTRODUCTION TO 'ULOOM AL-QUR'AAN 18
I. Definition of 'Uloom al-Qur'aan 18
II. Benefits of Studying 'Uloom al-Qur'aan 19
III. The History of 'Uloom al-Qur'aan 19

2. THE QUR'AAN 24
I. The Linguistic Meaning of the Word 'Qur'aan' 24
II. The Definition of the Qur'aan 25
   The Breakdown of the Definition 26
III. The Qur'aan as the Speech of Allaah 29
   THE CONCEPT OF THE KALAAM OF ALLAAH 30
   THE QUR'AAN AS THE KALAAM OF ALLAAH 35
   A REFUTATION OF THE ASH'AREES 40
   The Story of Ibraaheem 45
   The Story of Moosaa 46
   Conclusion 52
IV. The Names of the Qur'aan 54
V. The Qur'aan as it Describes Itself 55
VI. The Sunnah as it Describes the Qur'aan 57
   THE STATUS OF THE QUR'AAN 57
   THE REWARDS FOR THOSE WHO RECITE AND PRACTICE THE QUR'AAN 58

3. INSPIRATION – AL-WAHY 61
I. The Concept of Wahy 61
II. The Meaning of Wahy 62
III. The Procedure of Wahy 64
   A. WITHOUT AN INTERMEDIARY 64
   B. WITH AN INTERMEDIARY 67
   The Revelation of the Qur'aan to the Angels 68
   The Revelation of the Qur'aan to the Prophet (ﷺ) from Jibreel 69
IV. The Difference Between the Qur'aan and Hadeeth Qudsee 72

4. GRADUAL REVELATION 75

I. The Stages of Revelation 75

THE FIRST STAGE 75

THE SECOND STAGE 76

THE THIRD STAGE 78

Tampering of the Revelation? 79

THE QUANTITY OF REVELATION 80

II. The Wisdom Behind the Gradual Revelation 81

5. THE FIRST AND THE LAST REVELATIONS 88

I. The First Revelation 89

II. The Last Revelation 91

III. Relative First and Last Verses 95

6. THE MAKKEE AND THE MADANEE VERSES 97

I. The Definition of Makkee and Madanee 98

II. The Knowledge of Makkee and Madanee Verses 99

III. The Attributes of Makkee and Madanee Revelations 100

COMMON THEMES OF MAKKEE AND MADANEE VERSES 100

SPECIFIC CHARACTERISTICS OF MAKKEE AND MADANEE VERSES 102

IV. The Categories of Makkee and Madanee 102

V. The Benefits of Knowing Makkee and Madanee verses 105

7. THE CAUSES OF REVELATION - ASBAAB AN-NUZOOL 107

I. The Definition of Asbaab an-Nuzool 107

Books on Asbaab an-Nuzool 109

II. The Derivation of Asbaab an-Nuzool 109

THE WORDINGS OF ASBAAB AN-NUZOOL 110

III. Multiple Asbaab an-Nuzool for One Verse 111

IV. Multiple Verses for One Sabab an-Nuzool 115

V. A Person as Sabab an-Nuzool 116

VI. The Rulings from these Verses 117

VII. The Benefits of Knowing Asbaab an-Nuzool 119

8. THE COMPILATION OF THE QUR'AAN 124

I. During the Prophet's (☼) Life 125

II. The First Compilation 131

III. The 'Uthmaanic Compilation 135

IV. The Different Mus-hafs 139

A. THE APPEARANCE OF THE MUS-HAFS 139

The Spelling of the Words of the Qur'aan 139

The Script of the Mus-haf 141

The Qur'aan in Print 145

A Warning! 146

B. THE NUMBER OF 'UTHMAANIC MUS-HAFS 147

C. WERE THESE MUS-HAFS THE SAME? 147

D. WHAT HAPPENED TO THE ORIGINAL MUS-HAFS? 149

V. The Verses of the Qur'aan 151

The Necessity of this Knowledge 152

The Origins of this Knowledge 152

The Number of Verses 154

The Arrangement of the Verses 154

The Number of Words and Letters 156

THE BASMALAH AS A VERSE 157

VI. The Soorahs of the Qur'aan 160

The Arrangement of the Soorahs 161

The Number of Soorahs 163

The Names of the Soorahs 164

The Classification of the Soorahs 164

Other Classifications 165

9. THE BEGINNING OF THE SOORAHS 166

I. The Different Categories 166

II. The Disjointed Letters 167

III. The Ending of the Soorahs 170

10. THE AHRUF OF THE QUR'AAN 172

I. The Meaning of the word 'Ahruf' 172

II. The Number of Ahruf of the Qur'aan 173

III. What is Meant by the Ahruf of the Qur'aan? 174

A. THOSE OPINIONS WHICH HAVE NO BASIS WHATSOEVER 176

B. THOSE OPINIONS WHICH HAVE SOME APPARENT BASIS,
BUT ARE WEAK OPINIONS 176

C. THOSE OPINIONS WHICH HAVE STRONG EVIDENCE 177

IV. Are the Ahruf in Existence Today? 179

V. The Wisdom in the Various Ahruf 182

11. THE QIRA'AAT OF THE QUR'AAN 184

I. The meaning of the word 'Qira'aat' 184

II. The History of the Qira'aat 184

III. The Conditions for an Authentic Qiraa'a 187

IV. The Other Types of Qira'aat 191

V. The Authentic Qira'aat and the Qaarees 193

    1) Naafi' al-Madanee 194

    2) Ibn Katheer al-Makkee 194

    3) Aboo 'Amr al-Basree 195

    4) Ibn 'Aamir as-Shaamee 195

    5) 'Aasim al-Koofee 195

    6) Hamza al-Koofee 196

    7) Al-Kisaa'ee 196

    8) Aboo Ja'far al-Madanee 197

    9) Ya'qoob al-Basree 197

    10) Khalaf 197

VI. The Qira'aat Today 199

VII. The Relationship of the Ahruf with the Qira'aat 200

VIII. The Benefits of the Qira'aat 202

IX. Some Examples of the Different Qira'aat 202

12. THE CLEAR AND UNCLEAR VERSES –
AL-MUHKAM WA AL-MUTASHAABIH 207

I. Definition of Muhkam and Mutashaabih 207

  The Qur'aan as Muhkam and Mutashaabih 208

  The Exact Meaning of Muhkam and Mutashaabih 211

    The Attributes of Allaah as Mutashaabih? 211

  Other Categories of Mutashaabih 221

II. The Haqeeqee and the Majaazee 224

    The Attributes of Allaah as Majaaz? 225

III. The 'Aam and the Khaas 228

IV. The Mutlaq and the Muqayyad 229

V. The Mantooq and Mafhoom 230

VI. The Naasikh and the Mansookh 231

13. ABROGATION IN THE QUR'AAN-
AN-NAASIKH WA AL-MANSOOKH 232

I. The Definition of Naskh 232

    The Breakdown of the Definition 233

    The Salaf and the Term 'Naskh' 234

    Books Written on Naskh 235

II. The Proof of Naskh 235

III. The Conditions for Naskh 236

IV. The Categories of Naskh 237

  A. The Sources of the Naasikh and Mansookh 238

    B. The Verse and Ruling in the Qur'aan 240

    C. The Rulings of the Naasikh and Mansookh 243

V. The Blessings of Naskh 244

    Benefits of the General Naskh 245

    Benefits of the Specific Naskh 246

VI. The Benefits of Knowing Naasikh and Mansookh 248

VII. The Difference Between Naskh and Tak<u>h</u>sees 249

VIII. The Number of Naasikh/Mansookh verses in the Qur'aan 250

    The 'Verse of the Sword' 251

    A Last Example 255

    Conclusion 256

14. THE MIRACULOUS NATURE OF THE QUR'AAN – I'JAAZ AL-QUR'AAN 257

I. Definition of I'jaaz 257

    Other Types of Supernatural Acts 258

II. The Proof for I'jaaz 259

    The Challenge! 261

    The Order of the Verses 262

III. The Qur'aan as the Miracle of the Prophet (ﷺ) 264

IV. The Types of I'jaaz 265

    A. The Language and Style of the Qur'aan 267

    B. The Predictions of the Qur'aan 272

    C. The Stories in the Qur'aan 274

    The Purposes of the Stories 275

    D. The Beliefs and Laws of the Qur'aan 276

    E. The Scientific Facts of the Qur'aan 278

    F. The Effect the Qur'aan has on its Listeners 283

    G. The Lack of Contradictions in the Qur'aan 285

    H. The Ease by which the Qur'aan is Memorised 285

V. Intrinsic vs. Extrinsic 286

VI. The Quantity for I'jaaz 287

15. THE INTERPRETATION OF THE QUR'AAN – TAFSEER 289

I. The Definition of Tafseer and Ta'weel 289

II. The Necessity and Importance of Tafseer 290

III. The History of Tafseer 293

    A. The Time of the Prophet (ﷺ) 293

    B. The Period of the Companions 294

    C. The Period of the Successors 296

    D. The Compilation of Tafseer 297

    A Summary 298

IV. The Principles of Tafseer 299

    1) TAFSEER OF THE QUR'AAN BY THE QUR'AAN 300

    2) TAFSEER BY THE SUNNAH 302

    How much of the Qur'aan was explained? 303

    3) TAFSEER BY THE STATEMENT OF THE COMPANIONS 306

    Tafseer by the Statement of the Successors 309

    4) TAFSEER BY ARABIC LANGUAGE AND CLASSICAL POETRY 309

    Linguistic vs. Islaamic 311

    Poetry Prohibited? 312

    Whose Poetry? 314

    5) TAFSEER BY PRE-ISLAAMIC ARAB CUSTOMS 315

    6) TAFSEER BY JUDAEO-CHRISTIAN NARRATIVES 317

    <u>H</u>adeeth Related to Israa'eeliyaat 317

    The Categories of Israa'eeliyaat 319

    7) TAFSEER BY SUBJECTIVE OPINION (RA'Y) 320

    The Two Types of Ra'y 321

    Where is Ra'y Used? 323

    A Divine Blessing 323

V. The Qualifications of a Mufassir 324

VI. The Types of Tafseer 326

    A. TAFSEER BASED ON NARRATIONS 327

    B. TAFSEER BASED ON PERSONAL OPINIONS 339

    C. TAFSEER OF THE JURISTS 332

    D. SCIENTIFIC TAFSEER 333

    E. TAFSEER BASED ON INNER MEANINGS 335

    F. MODERNISTIC TAFSEERS 337

VII. Some Famous Tafseers 339

    'Jaami' al-Bayaan' of at-<u>T</u>abaree 339

    'Tafseer al-Qur'aan al-'Adheem' of Ibn Katheer 340

    'Mafaati<u>h</u> al-Ghayb' of ar-Raazee 341

    'al-Kashaaf' of az-Zamakhsharee 342

VIII. The Dangers of Improper Tafseer 344

16. THE TRANSLATION OF THE QUR'AAN 348

I. The Types of Translation 348

II. The Ruling on Translations 359

    The Conditions of Translation 350

    The Translation as the Qur'aan 351

    THE IMPORTANCE OF ARABIC 353

III. The History of Translation 355
    Translations into Western Languages 356
    English Translation by Muslims 359
IV. The Problems with Translations 361
    A Review of Some Translations 369

17. THE QUR'AAN AND ORIENTALISTS 374
I. The Authorship of the Qur'aan 374
    An Example of the Prophet's (ﷺ) Sincerity 375
    AUTHORSHIP THEORIES 376
    A Poet? 376
    A Madman? 377
    Taught by Others? 378
    Imagination? 381
II. Some Books by Orientalists 383
    'Geschichte des Qorans' of Noeldeke 383
    'Materials for the History of the Text of the Qur'aan' by Arthur Jeffery 384
    'The Collection of the Qur'aan' by John Burton 388

EPILOGUE 392
I. The 'Return' of the Qur'aan 392
II. An Appeal 393

APPENDIX: PICTURE PLATES 397

BIBLIOGRAPHY 415

TRANSLITERATION TABLE

Consonants

ء	'		ض	**d**
ب	**b**		ط	**t**
ت	**t**		ظ	**dh**
ث	**th**		ع	'
ج	**j**		غ	**gh**
ح	**h**		ف	**f**
خ	**kh**		ق	**q**
د	**d**		ك	**k**
ذ	**dh**		ل	**l**
ر	**r**		م	**m**
ز	**z**		ن	**n**
س	**s**		ه	**h**
ش	**sh**		و	**w**
ص	**s**		ي	**y**

Vowels

◌َ	**a**		◌َا	**aa**
◌ُ	**u**		◌ُو	**oo**
◌ِ	**i**		◌ِي	**ee**

INTRODUCTION

All Praise is due to Allaah. We praise Him, seek His help, and ask His forgiveness. We seek refuge in Allaah from the evil of our souls, and the adverse consequences of our deeds. Whoever Allaah guides, there is none that can misguide him, and whoever He misguides, then none can guide him.

I bear witness and testify that there is no deity that is worthy of worship except for Allaah; He is alone, having no partners. I bear witness and testify that Muhammad (ﷺ) is His perfect worshipper, and messenger.

يَـٰٓأَيُّهَا ٱلَّذِينَ ءَامَنُوا۟ ٱتَّقُوا۟ ٱللَّهَ حَقَّ تُقَاتِهِۦ وَلَا تَمُوتُنَّ إِلَّا وَأَنتُم مُّسْلِمُونَ ۝

«O you who have faith! Have *taqwa* of Allaah, as He deserves, and die not except as Muslims» [3:102]

يَـٰٓأَيُّهَا ٱلنَّاسُ ٱتَّقُوا۟ رَبَّكُمُ ٱلَّذِى خَلَقَكُم مِّن نَّفْسٍ وَٰحِدَةٍ وَخَلَقَ مِنْهَا زَوْجَهَا وَبَثَّ مِنْهُمَا رِجَالًا كَثِيرًا وَنِسَآءً وَٱتَّقُوا۟ ٱللَّهَ ٱلَّذِى تَسَآءَلُونَ بِهِۦ وَٱلْأَرْحَامَ إِنَّ ٱللَّهَ كَانَ عَلَيْكُمْ رَقِيبًا ۝

«O Mankind! Have *taqwa* of your Lord, Who created you from a single person, and from him, He created his wife, and from these two, He created multitudes of men, and women. And have *taqwa* of Allaah, through whom you demand your mutual rights, and (do not cut off) the ties of kinship. Verily, Allaah is Ever-Watching over you» [4:1]

يَـٰٓأَيُّهَا ٱلَّذِينَ ءَامَنُوا۟ ٱتَّقُوا۟ ٱللَّهَ وَقُولُوا۟ قَوْلًا سَدِيدًا ۝ يُصْلِحْ لَكُمْ أَعْمَـٰلَكُمْ وَيَغْفِرْ لَكُمْ ذُنُوبَكُمْ وَمَن يُطِعِ ٱللَّهَ وَرَسُولَهُۥ فَقَدْ فَازَ فَوْزًا عَظِيمًا ۝

«O you who you have faith! Have *taqwa* of Allaah, and say righteous speech. He will direct you to do righteous deeds, and He will forgive your sins. And whoever obeys Allaah and His Messenger has indeed achieved the ultimate success» [33:70-71]

As to what follows, then the best Speech is the Speech of Allaah, and the best guidance is the guidance of Muhammad (ﷺ). And the worst of affairs are newly-invented matters, and every innovation is a misguidance, and every misguidance is in the fire of Hell.[1]

In this short speech, which the Prophet (ﷺ) would give every time he spoke, and which he (ﷺ) taught the Companions to give every time they spoke, the Prophet (ﷺ) summarized the essence of Islaam. The words, despite their brevity, are deep in meaning. The speech, despite its lightness, carries great import.

In the first two paragraphs, the Prophet (ﷺ) outlined the fundamentals of faith (*eemaan*). The first paragraph consists of acknowledging the 'Oneness of Allaah in His Existence' (*Tawheed ar-Ruboobiyyah*), and in affirming His unique Names and Attributes (*Tawheed al-Asmaa wa as-Sifaat*). The fact that a person testifies that Allaah is worthy of all types of praise, and that He is the One who is asked in all matters, automatically implies that He exists, and possesses such Names and Attributes that make it deserving and obligatory upon the creation to do these acts.

The second paragraph is the testimony of faith (*shahaadah*), and with it a Muslim testifies that he will worship Allaah, and only Allaah, and that this worship will be based upon the teachings and *Sunnah* of the Prophet Muhammad (ﷺ). This is the essence of the 'Oneness of Actions' (*Tawheed al-Uloohiyyah*); that *all* of a person's acts will be performed with one goal in mind: the pleasure of the Creator.

The three verses that the Prophet (ﷺ) would recite have one central theme: the importance of *taqwa*. The famous student of Ibn 'Abbaas, Mujaahid ibn Jabr (d. 103 A.H.) defined *taqwa* as, "It is that you obey Allaah, so that He is never disobeyed, and you are conscious of Him, so that He is never forgotten, and that you thank Him, so that He is never disbelieved."[2] The *taqwa* of Allaah is the life of the heart; without it all actions are as if dead.

In the last paragraph, the Prophet (ﷺ) summarized the source of all guidance, and the source of all misguidance. Guidance comes only from the two inspirations – the Qur'aan and the *Sunnah*. The Qur'aan is described as the best of all Speech. If this is the case, then it must contain in it the best of all matters in all that is needed by mankind. The *Sunnah*, the best guidance, is superior to all other philosophies and methodologies that mankind has invented, for the *Sunnah* is the perfect example of the worship of Allaah, manifested in the life and actions of the Prophet Muhammad (ﷺ). All that is opposed to the Qur'aan and *Sunnah* – and in this opposition lies the source of all evil – are termed newly-invented innovations, destined to the fire of Hell.

The work that is in the reader's hands is a brief discussion of certain aspects of the first source of guidance – the Qur'aan. It is by no means comprehensive, for there can be no such thing as an exhaustive work on the sciences related to the Qur'aan. It is,

---

1   This speech is a translation of what is called *Khutbat al-Haajah*, which the Prophet (ﷺ) would give whenever he started a speech. See al-Albaanee's '*Khutbat al-Haajah*' (al-Maktab al-Islamee, Damascus, 1980) for details.

2   Reported by al-Maawardee in his *tafseer*, 4/248.

however, an introduction to certain concepts that the scholars of the past have discussed under the topic of *'uloom al-Qur'aan*.

Work on this book began in the summer of 1995, when I had received my acceptance letter to the Islaamic University of Madeenah. I had initially planned to study in the 'College of Qur'aan and Islaamic Sciences' in the University, and, as preparation for the studies ahead, I started reading the few books that I had on *'uloom al-Qur'aan*. This initial research formed the basis of the first draft of this work, which was completed by the time I had arrived in Madeenah. However, due to my limited literary resources (my primary sources for this draft were as-Suyootee's *Itqaan*, az-Zarkashee's *Burhaan*, and Qattaan's *Mabaahith*), I felt the need to critically revise and edit the work.

Even though I eventually did not enter the 'College of Qur'aan' (due to certain factors, I chose to study in the 'College of *Hadeeth*' instead), I was still greatly fascinated by the subject of *'uloom al-Qur'aan*. This fascination was the primary motive that led me to continue editing and revising the work over the next two years. The acceptance of the publication of this work by al-Hidaayah was the final catalyst that was needed to complete the work.

In Madeenah, I had access to and benefited from many references, and the constraints that I had felt whilst writing the initial draft were removed. The primary sources for this book were the general books of *'uloom al-Qur'aan* – both classical and modern. Apart from the three primary works mentioned above, I also particularly benefited from az-Zarqaani's *Manaahil*, and as-Sabt's analysis and critique of az-Zarqaani's work, which he presented as his master's dissertation to the College of Qur'aan and Islaamic Sciences in the University of Madeenah. In addition, for most chapters I also utilized books that were specialized to that chapter's subject. This was done to ensure as much authenticity of the contents as possible.

Not all topics that are found in the works of *'uloom al-Qur'aan* have been discussed in this work. Some have been left out due to the language barrier – certain sciences are so intricately related to the Arabic language that their explanation would be of little use in another language (a cursory look at many of the topics of the *Itqaan* or *Burhaan* will give the reader examples of what I am referring to). Other topics were not dealt with in this edition, and it is hoped that they may be added in later editions, *inshaa Allaah*. Yet other topics were discussed, but not in great detail, primarily due to the fact that their understanding and practicality are dependent on a knowledge of Arabic (example of this are the *'aam* and *khaas*, the *mutlaq* and *muqayyad*, and other word pairs). The science of *tajweed* I purposely avoided, as this is not the place to explain this science, nor is it discussed in the classical works of this field.

Apart from these points, however, I feel confident in stating that the present work will give the reader a general understanding and introduction to the field of *'uloom al-Qur'aan*. The fundamental and important topics related to this science have all been mentioned, in enough detail, *inshaa Allaah*, for an English-speaking audience to benefit from. Although a previous knowledge of certain aspects of *'uloom al-Qur'aan* would help in understanding the concepts in this work, I have purposely ensured that such a knowledge is not a prerequisite to benefit from the work. Therefore, this book is written with the assumption that the reader has not had any previous exposure to *'uloom al-Qur'aan*.

The first fifteen chapters form the main portion of the work, and discuss the standard topics of *'uloom al-Qur'aan*. Throughout the work, the nature of the audience was kept in mind, and concepts were presented and developed in (what is hoped is) a style that is suitable for an English-speaking audience.

The last two chapters in particular have been added with the Western audience in mind: 'The Translation of the Qur'aan', and 'The Qur'aan and Orientalists'. In the first, I have discussed the various topics related to the translation of the Qur'aan from an Islaamic perspective, and given a history of its translation in English. The chapter was concluded with brief reviews of some of the more important translations. In the second, certain views of Orientalists were given concerning the 'authorship' of the Qur'aan, and three important works by Orientalists were critiqued. It is hoped that these two chapters – in particular – are of practical benefit to the audience.

As was mentioned earlier, the initial purpose of writing this book was to benefit myself. As Imaam Muslim ibn al-Hajjaaj (d. 261 A.H.) wrote in the introduction to his *Saheeh*: "... if (the writing of this book) were enforced upon me, and it was willed that I complete it, then the first person who would partake from the benefits of it would be myself in particular, before anyone else of mankind..."[3] And as the Andalusian scholar Ibn Rushd (d. 595 A.H.) wrote in the introduction to his famous work *Bidaayat al-Mujtahid wa Nihaayat al-Muqtasid,* "My purpose in writing this book is so that it may serve as a reminder for myself concerning the opinions of the scholars in the various matters pertaining to the laws (of Islaam)..."[4] The work being written, I cannot help but recall the words of al-'Imaad al-Asfahaanee (d. 597 A.H.), who wrote,[5]

> I have noticed that no author writes a book and finishes it, except that the next day he says, 'If I had only changed this part, it would have been better; and if only I had added this fact, it would have been appreciated more; and if I had only made this section earlier, it would have been easier to comprehend; and if I had only left this section out, it would have been more beautiful.' And this, in fact, is one of the greatest lessons and points to ponder over, for it is a clear indication of the inferiority of the nature of man.

How accurate his observations are! 'Alaa ad-Deen al-Khaazin (d. 741 A.H.), a famous scholar and interpreter of the Qur'aan, outlined the aims of his work when he wrote, in the introduction to his *tafseer*,

> It is appropriate that every author, whenever he writes a book concerning a topic that has already been written about, ensure that his work incorporates five benefits: that it brings forth something new; that it combines

---

3   *Saheeh Muslim,* v. 1, p. 8.
4   Ibn Rushd, p. 1.
5   *Duroos fi at-Ta'beer* (IUM Press, Madeenah, 1986), p. 7.

> information that was previously scattered; that it explains concepts that were previously unclear; that it systematically explains the material; and that it avoids unnecessary and undue elaboration. And I hope that this book of mine is not bereft of any of these characteristics that I have mentioned...[6]

Of course, human enterprise is associated with error, and no work can claim perfection. As Imaam ash-Shaafi'ee (d. 204 A.H.) wrote, "Allaah has refused to allow perfection to any work except His Book."[7]

Therefore, instead of concentrating on the mistakes that are sure to be found in this work, the reader is requested to gloss over the flaws that might exist, and benefit from the rest of the work. In addition, the reader is kindly requested not to be parsimonious in sharing with me his sincere advice, and affording me his constructive criticism, for I am in great need of them, and, 'the religion is the giving of advice'. All comments may be directed care of the publisher.

Of course, no project of this nature can ever be the sole product of one person; there are many that have helped along the way. The book is dedicated to my parents, for it is their upbringing and support (along with the constant blessings of Allaah), that has brought me where I am today. I am honoured by the fact that my teacher, Shaykh 'Abd ar-Razaaq ibn 'Abd al-Muhsin al-'Abaad, took time out of his busy schedule to go over the portions of this book related to 'aqeedah, and to benefit me with his vast knowledge of the subject. I am also indebted to Dr. Muhammad Anwar Sahib for reading over most of the critical portions of this work, despite the fact that he was highly pressed for time, as he was then in the final stages of completing his doctoral dissertation. My friends and fellow students of knowledge, Abu Abdillaah and Abu Sulaymaan, deserve my gratitude for going over the manuscript and sharing with me their valuable advice, as do David Dillon and Abu Sufyaan for their help in proof-reading the final text. Jamaal al-Din Zarabozo also deserves my gratitude for all that I have benefited from him while I was in America, and for his valuable comments and advice on the initial draft of the work. My thanks are also extended to al-Hidaayah Publishing and Distribution for their acceptance of the work. Lastly, I would like to thank the many scholars, students of knowledge, and peers that have helped me with various portions of the work, by answering my questions, giving me advice, or simply encouraging me in my efforts. May Allaah reward all of them!

A note must be added concerning the mention and refutation of certain views of the *Ash'arees*. This group is mentioned, in particular, in the sections concerning the Qur'aan as the *kalaam* of Allaah, the Attributes of Allaah as *mutashaabih*, and the Attributes of Allaah as *majaaz*. Although these refutations are not, in general, found in the works of *'uloom al-Qur'aan*, and are perhaps more relevant to the books of *'aqeedah*, they were nonetheless included in this work for a number of reasons. Firstly, the concepts discussed are not in reality outside the realm of *'uloom al-Qur'aan*, and a discussion and refutation of certain incorrect views regarding these topics will only

---

6   *Tafseer al-Khaazin*, p. 3.
7   cf. as-Sakhaawi, p. 34.

help explain each concept better. Secondly, during the last few years, the ideas of this group have started spreading with renewed vigour and enthusiasm in the West, and their vitriolic attacks and scathing accusations against the *Ahl as-Sunnah wa al-Jamaa'ah* have made it essential that a refutation be written against them. As of yet, no thorough refutation exists in English. Naturally, this book is not meant to be a complete refutation of the *Ash'arees*, and as such the refutations mentioned in this book are not exhaustive. However, it was decided to include in this work those issues which the *Ash'arees* differed with *Ahl as-Sunnah* and were common to *'uloom al-Qur'aan* at the same time, thus affording the English audience a glimpse of such refutations. It is hoped that the brief discussions that are mentioned in this work are enough to caution any person that might have been influenced by this group, and cause him to re-examine the beliefs of the *Ash'arees*. Lastly, the inclusion of these sections will perhaps give the reader an example of how deviation occurs, and the correct Islaamic methodology in solving them.

One last note: the author wishes to make it clear that he is only a student of knowledge – not a scholar, nor a specialist in the field of *'uloom al-Qur'aan*. Therefore, this work does not in any way represent *original* research material; all the views and opinions in it are merely quotations from other scholars . If there is any credit to be given, it is in the collection, editing, translation and presentation of the material, for that is all that the author has done.

All that is correct in this work and of benefit to the readers is from Allaah, and all that is incorrect is from myself and *Shaytaan*.[8]

I sincerely pray that this work helps bring Muslims closer to their religion; that it causes them to grow in their love for the Qur'aan; and that it induces them to further their knowledge of this magnificent and glorious book – the 'best of all Speech' (39:23)! *Ameen!*

Abu Ammaar

27th Ramadhan, 1418 A.H.   (25th January, 1998 CE)

The City of the Prophet (ﷺ) – *al-Madeenah an-Nabaweeyah*

---

8   This statement is based upon a statement of the Companion Ibn Mas'ood, who, after responding to a question, would make this statement. See *Musnad Ahmad*, 6/137.

CHAPTER 1

AN INTRODUCTION TO 'ULOOM AL-QUR'AAN

I. Definition of 'Uloom al-Qur'aan

The knowledge of *'uloom al-Qur'aan*, or 'The Sciences of the Qur'aan', deals with the knowledge of those sciences that have a direct bearing on the recitation, history, understanding and implementation of the Qur'aan. It is, therefore, a vast field of Islaamic scholarship, and one that is of primary importance.

Thus, for example, with regards to recitation, *'uloom al-Qur'aan* deals with the science of pronunciation (*tajweed*), the different methodologies of reciting the Qur'aan (the *qira'aat*), the blessings of reciting the Qur'aan, and the etiquette of its recitation.

With regards to the history of the Qur'aan, *'uloom al-Qur'aan* deals with the stages of revelation of the Qur'aan, the compilation of the Qur'aan, the art and history of writing the Qur'aanic script (*rasm al-maṣaaḥif*), and the preservation of the Qur'aan.

With regards to its understanding and implementation, *'uloom al-Qur'aan* covers the causes of revelation (*asbaab an-nuzool*), the knowledge of the *makkee* and *madanee* revelations, the knowledge of the various forms (*aḥruf*) it was revealed in, the understanding of its abrogated rulings and verses (*naasiḥ wa al-mansookh*), the knowledge of the various classifications of its verses (*muḥkam* and *mutashaabih*, *'aam* and *khaaṣ*, *mutlaq* and *muqqayad*, etc.), the knowledge of the inimitable style of the Qur'aan (*i'jaaz al-Qur'aan*), the knowledge of its interpretation (*tafseer*), the grammatical analysis of the Qur'aan (*'iraab al-Qur'aan*) and the knowledge of those words whose usage has become uncommon over time (*ghareeb al-Qur'aan*).

It has been said that the knowledge of *'uloom al-Qur'aan* is in reality the knowledge that one is required to know in order to properly interpret the Qur'aan. Therefore, to call this branch of Islaamic knowledge 'The Procedure and Methodology of Interpretation' (*'Ilm Uṣool at-Tafseer*) instead of *'uloom al-Qur'aan* would not be far from the truth.[9] However, *'uloom al-Qur'aan* also includes topics that have very little or no bearing on *tafseer*, such as the compilation of the Qur'aan, and the development

---

9   cf. ar-Roomee, Fahd ibn 'Abd al-Raḥmaan ibn Sulaymaan: *Dirasaat fi 'Uloom al-Qur'aan*, Maktabah at-Tawbah, Riyadh, 1994, p. 33, who equates *'Uloom al-Qur'aan* with *Uṣool at-tafseer*.

of the script of the Qur'aan. Therefore, the knowledge of *'uloom al-Qur'aan* is more general then *'Ilm Usool at-Tafseer*.

II. Benefits of Studying 'Uloom al-Qur'aan

There are many benefits to the knowledge of *'uloom al-Qur'aan*. Firstly, it enables the reader to realize the wealth of knowledge and insight that exists with regards to the Book of Allaah. As some of the scholars of the past said, "True knowledge is to know one's ignorance." Only when a person realizes what he does *not* know will he appreciate how little he *does* know. Secondly, it enables the student of knowledge to better understand the Qur'aan, in that he will be familiar with the history of its revelation and collection, and the various aspects that aid its comprehension. When he reads the books of *tafseer*, he will be able to understand the terms used, and benefit from the knowledge in them to a greater extent. In other words, he will be equipped to further increase his knowledge and to learn more about his religion. Thirdly, it increases a person's belief (*eemaan*), because he will realize the beauty of the Qur'aan and the great blessings that he has been given through its revelation. He will not be fooled by the fallacious claims of its enemies, and his heart will be at ease with regards to its authenticity. He will understand the miraculous nature of the Qur'aan, and thus better cherish the greatest Book that mankind has been given. Fourthly, he will be able to defend the Qur'aan against its enemies, since he will be equipped with the true and pristine knowledge of the Qur'aan, unadulterated by the prejudices of its opponents.

It is no exaggeration to say that, once a person learns the essentials of his religion and what is required for him to know, the first knowledge he should turn his attention to is the knowledge of the Qur'aan and its sciences. As Allaah says[10] in the Qur'aan,

$$\text{كِتَـٰبٌ أَنزَلْنَـٰهُ إِلَيْكَ مُبَـٰرَكٌ لِّيَدَّبَّرُوٓا۟ ءَايَـٰتِهِۦ وَلِيَتَذَكَّرَ أُو۟لُوا۟ ٱلْأَلْبَـٰبِ ﴿٢٩﴾}$$

«(This is a) Book that We have sent down to you, full of blessings, so that they may ponder over its verses, and that men of understanding may remember» [38:29]

III. The History of 'Uloom al-Qur'aan

Like all the sciences of Islaam, the knowledge of *'uloom al-Qur'aan* initiated with the Prophet (ﷺ) himself. The Companions used to question the Prophet (ﷺ) about any concept that they did not understand in the Qur'aan. For example, concerning the verse,

---

10   It should be pointed out that the Qur'aan is only in Arabic, and is the speech (*kalaam*) of Allaah, as shall be proved and elaborated upon in the next chapter. Therefore, the unconditional phrase, "Allaah says," when used in this book (or any book), only refers to the Qur'aan. When this phrase is used in a language other than Arabic, it contains an additional implicit clause that should be understood by the audience, and this clause is, "the meaning of which is," since the Qur'aan is only in Arabic. Therefore, this phrase should be understood as, " The meaning of what Allaah has said is..."

اَلَّذِينَ ءَامَنُوا۟ وَلَمْ يَلْبِسُوٓا۟ إِيمَـٰنَهُم بِظُلْمٍ أُو۟لَـٰٓئِكَ لَهُمُ ٱلْأَمْنُ وَهُم مُّهْتَدُونَ ۝

«Those who believe and do not mix their belief with injustice, only they will
have security, and they are the guided»[6:82]

they asked, "O Messenger of Allaah! Who amongst us does not do injustice (to his
soul)?" They had understood that the verse was referring to those believers who did
not commit any injustice, or sin. The Prophet (ﷺ) replied that the injustice referred
to in this verse was *shirk*, or the association of partners with Allaah.[11]

Such was the enthusiasm of the Companions in seeking this knowledge that they
were able to not only explain any verse in the Qur'aan, but also give its history and the
cause of its revelation. Ibn Mas'ood said, "I swear by Allaah, besides whom there is no
other god, there is no *soorah* in the Qur'aan except that I know where it was revealed!
And there is not a single verse in the Qur'aan except that I know the reason behind its
revelation! If there were any person that knew more about the Qur'aan than I did,
and it was possible for me to reach him, I would ride (on my camel) towards him (to
get this knowledge)."[12] 'Alee ibn Abee Taalib told his students, "Ask me! For I swear
by Allaah, there is nothing that you will ask me except that I will answer you. Ask me
concerning the book of Allaah! For I swear by Allaah, there is not a single verse in the
Qur'aan except that I know whether it was revealed at night or during the day, or on a
mountain or on a plain!"[13]

There were many Companions who were famous for their knowledge of the
Qur'aan, among them the four *Khulafaa ar-Raashidoon*,[14] 'Abdullaah ibn Mas'ood (d.
32 A.H.), 'Abdullaah ibn 'Abbaas (d. 68 A.H.), Ubay ibn Ka'ab (d. 32 A.H.), Zayd ibn
Thaabit (d. 45 A.H.), Aboo Moosaa al-Ash'aree (d. 50 A.H.), 'Abdullaah ibn Zubayr
(d. 73 A.H.) and 'Aa'ishah (d. 57 A.H.).

The generation that came after the Companions, the Successors, studied eagerly
under the wise guardianship of the Companions. These students took over their pred-
ecessors' responsibilities, and passed this knowledge faithfully to the next generation.
Ibn 'Abbaas' students, Sa'eed ibn Jubayr (d. 95 A.H.), Mujaahid ibn Jabr (d. 100 A.H.),
'Ikrimah al-Barbaree (d. 104 A.H.), Taawoos ibn Kaysaan (d. 106 A.H.), and 'Ataa'
ibn Rabaah (d. 114 A.H.), were all famous in Makkah; Ubay ibn Ka'ab's students,
Zayd ibn Aslam (d. 63 A.H.), Aboo al-'Aaliyah (d. 90 A.H.) and Muhammad ibn
Ka'ab (d. 120 A.H.), were the teachers of Madeenah; and in Iraaq, 'Abdullaah ibn
Mas'ood left behind his great legacy to 'Alqamah ibn Qays (d. 60 A.H.), Masrooq ibn
al-Ajda' (d. 63 A.H.), al-Hasan al-Basree (d. 110 A.H.), and Qataadah as-Sadoosee
(d. 110 A.H.). These three places, Makkah, Madeenah, and Koofah, were the leading
centres of all the sciences of Islaam, including *tafseer* and *'uloom al-Qur'aan*.

---

11   Reported by al-Bukhaaree.
12   Reported by al-Bukhaaree.
13   ar-Roomee, p. 37.
14   A term that means 'The rightly-guided Caliphs', used to denote the first four caliphs, Aboo Bakr,
'Umar, 'Uthmaan and 'Alee.

Thus the knowledge of the Qur'aan was passed on '..by the trustworthy (scholars) of the *ummah*, who protected it from the alterations of the heretics, the false claims of liars, and the false interpretations of the ignorant.'[15]

Early scholars did not write on *'uloom al-Qur'aan* in general, but rather wrote separate tracts on each science of the Qur'aan. This was due to the fact that, during the early stages of Islaamic history, the oral transmission of knowledge occupied a more important status than the written transmission. In addition, the general level of knowledge was high, and did not warrant the extensive writing down of knowledge.

The first and most important of the topics to be written on was *tafseer*. For example, each of the following scholars wrote a *tafseer* of the Qur'aan, composed of statements from the Prophet (ﷺ) and the Companions: Sufyaan al-Thawree (d. 161 A.H.), Sufyaan ibn 'Uyaynah (d. 198 A.H.), Wakee' ibn al-Jaraah (d. 197 A.H.), and Shu'bah ibn al-Hajjaaj (d. 160 A.H.).

Following his predecessor's footsteps, Muhammad ibn Jareer at-Tabaree (d. 310 A.H.) wrote the monumental *Jaami' al-Bayaan 'an Ta'weel aay al-Qur'aan*, a *tafseer* that all later scholars would benefit from. Other early *tafseer*s were written by Aboo Bakr ibn Mundhir an-Naysabooree (d. 318), Ibn Abee Haatim (d. 328), Ibn Hibbaan (d. 369), al-Haakim (d. 405) and Ibn Mardawayh (d. 410). All of these *tafseer*s were based on reports from the Prophet (ﷺ) and the Companions and Successors, and included the chains of narration (*isnaad*) of the reports.

After the books of *tafseer* followed a plethora of books on the other sciences of the Qur'aan: 'Alee al-Madeenee (d. 234 A.H.), the teacher of Imaam al-Bukhaaree, wrote a book on *Asbaab an-Nuzool*; Aboo 'Ubayd al-Qaasim ibn Sallaam (d. 224 A.H.) wrote two books, one on the science of the *Qira'aat* (which was one of the first of its kind), and one on abrogation in the Qur'aan, *Naasikh wa al-Mansookh*; Ibn Qutaybah (d. 276 A.H.) wrote a book on rare words in the Qur'aan, *Mushkil al-Qur'aan*; Aboo Ishaaq az-Zajjaaj (d. 311) wrote a grammatical analysis of the Qur'aan, *'Iraab al-Qur'aan*; Ibn Darstawayh (d. 330) composed a tract on the miraculous nature of the Qur'aan, *I'jaaz al-Qur'aan*; Aboo Bakr as-Sijistaanee (d. 330 A.H.) wrote another book on the rare words in the Qur'aan, *Ghareeb al-Qur'aan*; Aboo Bakr al-Baaqillaanee (d. 403) wrote his famous treatise, also related to the miraculous nature of the Qur'aan, *I'jaaz al-Qur'aan*; Imaam an-Nasaa'ee (d. 303 A.H.), the author of the *Sunan*, wrote one on the merits of the Qur'aan, *Fadaa'il al-Qur'aan*; Aboo al-Hasan al-Waahidee (d. 468) wrote his famous book on *Asbaab an-Nuzool*; 'Ilm ad-Deen as-Sakhaawee (d. 634) wrote one on the various *qira'aat*, and so on.

It must also be mentioned that, in addition to these books, many of the books of *hadeeth*, such as the *Saheeh*s of al-Bukhaaree and Muslim, included sections on various topics of *'uloom al-Qur'aan*. For example, most of the books of the *Sunnah* have chapters on the *tafseer* of the Qur'aan, the benefits of reciting the Qur'aan, the history of its compilation, and other topics.

---

15 A paraphrase of an authentic *hadeeth* of the Prophet (ﷺ), reported by Ibn 'Adee and Ibn 'Asaakir. The beginning of the *hadeeth* is, 'This knowledge will be carried by the trustworthy of the *ummah*, who will protect...'

Finally, the scholars of the later generations started compiling all of these sciences into one book, and thus began the era of the classic works on 'uloom al-Qur'aan. The first works of this nature were actually meant to be works of tafseer. One of the first works that is reported in later references (but is not extant) is that of Aboo Bakr Muhammad ibn Khalaf ibn al-Marzabaan (d. 309 A.H.), entitled 'al-Haawee fee 'Uloom al-Qur'aan.'[16] Another work, of which manuscript copies of fifteen of a total of thirty volumes are extant, is that of 'Alee ibn Ibraaheem Sa'eed (d. 330), otherwise known as al-Hoofee, which he entitled, 'Al-Burhaan fee 'Uloom al-Qur'aan'. This book is primarily one on tafseer, but also discusses all related aspects of a verse. So, for example, after each portion of the Qur'aan, it includes information about the verses' meaning, its interpretation, its purpose of revelation, its proper method of recitation, the different qira'aat of the verse and how they affect the meaning, where to stop and where not to, and so forth. This work is considered to be the first of its kind in its expansive approach to all the related sciences of the Qur'aan.[17]

There appeared after this, books of a similar nature, until finally Badr ad-Deen az-Zarkashee (d. 794 A.H.) appeared with his monumental Al-Burhaan fee 'Uloom al-Qur'aan (the same title as al-Hoofee's work). This is one of the great classics on 'uloom al-Qur'aan available in print. A little over a century later, another classic appeared, that of Jalaal ad-Deen as-Suyootee (d. 911 A.H.), entitled al-Itqaan fee 'uloom al-Qur'aan. These two works are considered the standard resource works on 'uloom al-Qur'aan, and both have been printed a number of times during the last few decades.

Books on 'uloom al-Qur'aan continued to appear throughout the centuries,[18] and these last few decades have been no exception. The better known books of this era have been Manaahil al-'Irfaan fee 'Uloom al-Qur'aan by Shaykh Muhammad 'Abd al-Adheem az-Zarqaanee; al-Madhkhal li Dirasaat al-Qur'aan al-Kareem by Muhammad Aboo Shahmah; and two books, both of which are entitled Mabaahith fee 'Uloom al-Qur'aan, one by Dr. Subhee Saalih and the other by Dr. Mannaa' al-Qattaan.

Unfortunately, there does not seem to be great interest in English circles concerning this topic. Other topics, such as hadeeth and fiqh, have been given greater attention.[19] In English, the only work present[20] is Ahmed Von Denffer's book, 'Uloom al-

---

16   ar-Roomee, p. 45, quoting Ibn Nadeem's Fihrist, p. 24.

17   az-Zarqaanee, Muhammad 'Abd al-'Adheem: Manaahil al-'Irfaan fi 'Uloom al-Qur'aan, Dar al-Fikr, Cairo. n.d., p. 35 and Qattaan, Manna': Mabahith fi 'Uloom al-Qur'aan, Muasasat al-Risalat, Beirut, 1983, p. 14.

18   See ar-Roomee, pps. 41-48, where he lists the most important works in this field from every century of the hijrah, starting from the second century until the present one.

19   In hadeeth, the best works out for introductory-level students are Hadith Literature: Its Origins, Development and Special Feature by Muhammad Zubayr Siddiqi (Islamic Texts Society, London, 1993), and Studies in Hadith Methodology and Literature by Muhammad Mustafa Azami (American Trust Publication, Indianapolis, 1977); in Usool al-Fiqh, a good work is by Mohammad Hashim Kamali, Principles of Islamic Jurisprudence (Islamic Texts Society, 1991).

20   This is the only book that this author has come across concerning this topic from a Muslim author. There is, however, a translation of Ibn Taymiyyah's An Introduction to the Principles of Tafseer (al-Hidaayah Publishing and Distribution, Birmingham, 1993).

Qur'aan: An Introduction to the Sciences of the Qur'aan.[21] It is a useful book in that it presents a summary of many concepts of *'uloom al-Qur'aan*, and is meant for a young adult audience. However, probably due to the nature of the audience, the author does not go into great detail.

CHAPTER 2

THE QUR'AAN

I. The Linguistic Meaning of the Word 'Qur'aan'

There are a number of different opinions concerning the linguistic meaning of the word 'qur'aan.'

The most popular opinion, and the opinion held by at-Tabaree (d. 310 A.H.), is that the word 'qur'aan' is derived from *qara'a*, which means, 'to read, to recite.' 'Qur'aan' would then be the verbal noun (*masdar*) of *qara'a,* and thus translates as 'The Recitation' or 'The Reading.' Allaah says in reference to the Qur'aan,

$$وَقُرْءَانًا فَرَقْنَٰهُ$$

«And (it is) a Qur'aan which We have divided into parts...» [17:106]

and He says,

$$إِنَّ عَلَيْنَا جَمْعَهُۥ وَقُرْءَانَهُۥ ۝ فَإِذَا قَرَأْنَٰهُ فَٱتَّبِعْ قُرْءَانَهُۥ ۝$$

«It is for Us to collect it and to Recite it (Ar. *qur'aanahoo*). When We have recited it, then follow its Recitation (Ar. *qur'aanah*)» [75:17-8]

On the other hand, Imaam ash-Shaafi'ee (d. 204 A.H.) held the view that the word 'qur'aan' was a proper noun that was not derived from any word, just like 'Torah' or 'Injeel'.[22] He recited the word without a *hamza*, such that 'Qur'aan' would rhyme with the English word 'lawn'. One of the *qira'aat*[23] also pronounced it this way.

Another opinion[24] states that the word 'qur'aan' is from the root *qarana*, which means, 'to join, to associate'. For example, the pilgrimage in which *'Umrah* and *Hajj* are combined is called *Hajj Qiraan*, from the same root word. Therefore the meaning of the word 'qur'aan' would be, 'That which is joined together,' because its verses and *soorahs* are combined to form this book. In this case, the word would be pronounced the same way as Imaam ash-Shaafi'ee pronounced it, without the *hamza*.

---

22   The books given to Moosaa and 'Eesaa, respectively.

23   The *qiraa'a* of Ibn Katheer. See Ch. 11, 'The Qira'aat of the Qur'aan' for more details on the various *qira'aat*.

24   That of Aboo al-Hasan 'Alee al-Ash'aree (d. 324 A.H.), the famous theologian.

A fourth opinion[25] is that 'qur'aan' comes from the word *qaraa'in*, which means 'to resemble, to be similar to'. Hence, the Qur'aan is composed of verses that aid one another in comprehension, and *soorahs* that resemble each other in beauty and prose.[26]

Yet another opinion is that 'Qur'aan' is from *qar'*, which means 'to combine'. It is called such since it combines stories, commands, promises and punishments.[27]

However, the opinion that is the strongest, and the one that the majority of scholars hold, is the first one, namely that the word 'qur'aan' is the verbal noun of *qara'a* and therefore means, 'The Recitation'. The proof for this is that it is named such in the Qur'aan (and most of the *qira'aat* pronounce the word with a *hamza*), and the word conforms with Arabic grammar as the verbal noun of *qara'a*.

It may be asked: how does one explain the fact that some *qira'aat* pronounce the word 'Qur'aan' without a *hamza*, as it is well known that all the *qira'aat* are equally authentic (as shall be discussed in greater detail)? The response to this question is that this particular pronunciation is due to the peculiar rules of recitation (*tajweed*) of those *qira'aat*, and affects many words. In other words, the *qira'aat* that pronounce the word 'Qur'aan' without a *hamza* do not intend to change the pronunciation of the word 'Qur'aan' itself, but rather this occurs due to a particular rule of recitation (*tajweed*) that affects many words in the Qur'aan, including the pronunciation of the word 'Qur'aan.' Therefore, even though the pronunciation of the word 'Qur'aan' is different in these *qira'aat*, the actual word is still the same.

II. The Definition of the Qur'aan

There are many definitions of the Qur'aan, but they differ in wording only. There is no difference of opinion as to what the Qur'aan *is*, but merely what the best way to *define* it is.[28]

One of the more appropriate definitions is as follows:[29] The Qur'aan is the Arabic Speech (*kalaam*) of Allaah, which He revealed to Muhammad (ﷺ) in wording and meaning, and which has been preserved in the *mus-hafs*, and has reached us by *mutawaatir* transmissions, and is a challenge to mankind to produce something similar to it.

---

25   That of Yahya ibn Ziyad ad-Daylamee (d. 207 A.H.), better know as al-Farraa', a famous grammarian from Koofah.

26   For more discussion of these and other opinions, see az-Zarkashee, Badr ad-Din: *al-Burhan fi 'Uloom al-Qur'aan*, Maktabah al-Asriyyah, Beirut, 1972, v.1, p.276-8, and Baazmool, Muhammad ibn 'Umar ibn Saalim: *al-Qiraa'at wa Atharuhaa fee at-Tafseer*, Daar al-Hijrah, Riyaadh, 1996, v. 1, p. 23-27.

27   This is the opinion of Ibn al-Atheer (d. 606 A.H.) in his *an-Nihaayah*, v. 4, p. 30.

28   A good definition must include everything that is essential, exclude everything that is extraneous, and be as succinct as possible.

29   cf. az-Zarqaanee, v. 1, p. 21.

The Breakdown of the Definition

The statement in the definition, *'The Qur'aan is the Arabic...'* implies that the Qur'aan is in the Arabic language. This, therefore, implies that a translation of the Qur'aan into any other language cannot be considered the Qur'aan.[30] Imaam az-Zarkashee said, "Know that the Qur'aan has been revealed in the language of the Arabs. Therefore, it is impermissible to recite it in any other language."[31]

There are eleven references in the Qur'aan that it is in the Arabic language, amongst them the verses,

«...this (the Qur'aan) is in a clear Arabic tongue» [16:103]

and,

وَهَـٰذَا لِسَانٌ عَرَبِيٌّ مُّبِينٌ ۝

«Verily, We have revealed this as an Arabic Qur'aan» [12:2]

and,

وَكَذَٰلِكَ أَوْحَيْنَآ إِلَيْكَ قُرْءَانًا عَرَبِيًّا

«And thus We have inspired you with an Arabic Qur'aan» [42:7]

Since the Qur'aan has described itself as being in Arabic, it is clear that any non-Arabic speech cannot be the Qur'aan.

However, is every single word in the Qur'aan originally from the Arabic language? In other words, does the Qur'aan use words from other languages? There exist narrations from some of the Companions, and many grammarians after them, concerning certain words in the Qur'aan which were claimed to be of non-Arabic origin. Thus, for example, Ibn 'Abbaas claimed that the word *toor* was Syriac for mountain, *tafiqa* meant 'to intend' in the Roman language, *hudnaa* was Hebrew for repentance, *sijl* was Persian for book, *sundus* meant a soft cloth in Hindi (probably referring to Sanskrit), *miskhaat* was a shining lamp in an Ethiopian language, and *sirri* was Greek for a small river.[32] His student 'Ikrimah was also of the same opinion.

This opinion led some later scholars to come forth with numerous examples of words that were claimed to be non-Arabic in origin, yet mentioned in the Qur'aan. As-Suyootee (d. 911 A.H.) compiled a list of over a hundred words in the Qur'aan that were claimed to be non-Arabic in origin, and even versified these words in a poem.[33]

---

30   See Ch. 15, 'The Translation of the Qur'aan,' for a more detailed discussion of this point.
31   az-Zarkashee, v.1, p. 287.
32   Examples taken from az-Zarkashee, v.1, p. 288.
33   as-Suyootee, v.1, p. 181-84.

Other scholars, however, denied the claim that there could be any non-Arabic words in the Qur'aan. Basing their evidences on the Qur'aanic verses quoted above, they held the view that these verses precluded the existence of foreign words in the Qur'aan. Imaam ash-Shaafi'ee (d. 204 A.H.) was particularly strict in this matter, for he wrote concerning some grammarians of his time, "And some have spoken in this topic (of foreign words in the Qur'aan), and had they restrained themselves from speaking it would have been better, and safer for them! For some of them have presumed that the Qur'aan is part Arabic and part foreign! Yet the Qur'aan is explicit that there is nothing in the Book of Allaah except that it is in the language of the Arabs..."[34]

In attempting to refute the opinion that the Qur'aan contains foreign words, at-Tabaree (d. 310 A.H.) claimed that these particular words were used by both of these languages simultaneously, and thus the Companions' claims that these words were non-Arabic only meant that they were also used by other languages as well.[35] However, this is not a satisfactory explanation, as the word must have originated in one of the two languages.

Aboo 'Ubayd al-Qaasim ibn Sallaam (d. 224 A.H.) explained the above narrations from Ibn 'Abbaas correctly when he said,

> The correct opinion with me is that both of the above opinions [meaning that there are foreign words in the Qur'aan, and that the Qur'aan is only in Arabic] are correct. This is because the origin of these words is foreign, like the scholars said [referring to the narrations of Ibn 'Abbaas]. However, these words entered into the Arabic language, and were transformed to Arabic words, and the foreign letters were exchanged for Arabic ones, until they became a part of Arabic. Then the Qur'aan was revealed, and by this time these words had mixed in with the Arabic language. Therefore, he who says that the Qur'aan is only in Arabic is correct, and he who says that there are some foreign words is also correct. [36]

In other words, these particular phrases are originally non-Arabic in origin. However, as is the case with any language, these words were 'borrowed' by Arabic, and were used so commonly that they became a part of the Arabic language. Thus, for all practical purposes, these words became 'a part of fluent Arabic, and were used in poetry... and if an Arab were ignorant of these words, it was as if he were ignorant of other Arabic words.'[37]

Therefore, the correct opinion is that there are no non-Arabic words in the Qur'aan, although there are words that have non-Arabic origins. Due to the continued usage of these words by the Arabs, however, they can no longer be considered foreign.

The next part of the definition of the Qur'aan states that it is the '...*Speech (kalaam) of Allaah...*' The Qur'aan is the Speech (kalaam) of Allaah, that He spoke in a manner

---

34   az-Zarkashee, v. 1, p. 287, quoting from *ar-Risaalah*.
35   as-Suyootee, v. 1, p. 178.
36   az-Zarkashee, v.1, p. 290.
37   az-Zarkashee, v.1, p. 289.

that befits Him. This excludes all speech that emanated from men, *jinn*, and angels. Due to the importance of the fact that the Qur'aan is the *kalaam* of Allaah, and the different philosophies that have evolved concerning this topic, this part of the definition will be discussed in greater detail in the next section.

The next part of the definitions states: '...*which He revealed to Muhammad (ﷺ)...*'. This excludes any other Speech (*kalaam*) of His that He spoke. The *kalaam* of Allaah is infinite, as the Qur'aan says,

«And if all the trees on the earth were pens, and the sea (were ink wherewith to write), with seven seas behind it to add to its supply, still the Words (*kalaam*) of Allaah would not be exhausted. Verily, Allaah is All Mighty, All Wise» [31:27]

Therefore, this part of the definition limits the Qur'aan to the *kalaam* that Allaah revealed to Muhammad (ﷺ), and excludes any Speech that He spoke to other than the Prophet (ﷺ). The Qur'aan is specifically the revelation sent down to the Prophet (ﷺ).

وَإِنَّهُۥ لَتَنزِيلُ رَبِّ ٱلْعَٰلَمِينَ ﴿١٩٢﴾ نَزَلَ بِهِ ٱلرُّوحُ ٱلْأَمِينُ ﴿١٩٣﴾ عَلَىٰ قَلْبِكَ لِتَكُونَ مِنَ ٱلْمُنذِرِينَ ﴿١٩٤﴾

«And truly, this Qur'aan is a revelation from the Lord of the Worlds; which the Trustworthy Spirit (Angel Jibreel) brought down; Upon your heart (O Muhammad) so that you may be among the warners» [26:192-4]

The next part of the definitions states: '...*in wording and meaning...*'. This part of the definition affirms that the words of the Qur'aan are from Allaah, and not from Jibreel or even Muhammad (ﷺ), as some of the innovated sects of Islaam, such as the *Ash'arees*, allege. According to some scholars, this part of the definition also excludes *hadeeth Qudsee*,[38] since, according to these scholars, *hadeeth Qudsee* is only inspired in meaning, while its wording is from the Prophet (ﷺ).

The next part of the definition states: '...*which has been preserved in the mus-hafs...*'. A *mus-haf* is a written copy of the Qur'aan. When used in this definition, it refers specifically to the copies that the Caliph 'Uthmaan ordered to be written.[39] Therefore, it includes one hundred and fourteen *soorahs*, starting with *Soorah* al-Faatihah and ending with *Soorah* an-Naas. The Qur'aan must be written in any one of the *mus-hafs*

---

38   A *hadeeth Qudsee* is defined to be a *hadeeth* in which the Prophet (ﷺ) says, "Allaah says...", attributing the speech to Allaah. This type of *hadeeth* is discussed in more detail in the next chapter, under the heading, 'The Difference between the Qur'aan and *Hadeeth Qudsee*'.

39   See Ch. 8, 'The Collection of the Qur'aan,' for further details.

of 'Uthmaan.

This part of the definition excludes the verses that used to be a part of the Qur'aan, such as those whose recitation was abrogated (the *mansookh*), and those readings that were abrogated by the Prophet (ﷺ) before his death, when he recited the Qur'aan for the last time.[40] The reading must be in at least one *mus-haf* of 'Uthmaan, and not necessarily in all of them.[41]

The next part of the definition states: '*...and has reached us by mutawaatir transmissions...*'. A transmission is called *mutawaatir* when it is reported by a large number of people, such that they could not all be mistaken or intentionally forge a lie. The Qur'aan has reached us through *muttawaatir* chains of narration.[42] In other words, in each generation so many people narrated it that there is no question of its authenticity. There are some readings, however, that have not reached us in *mutawaatir* form (in other words, they are *ahaad*[43]). Such readings are not considered part of the Qur'aan. This point will be further elaborated in a later chapter.

The last part of the definition states:'*...and is a challenge to mankind to produce something similar to it.*' This part of the definition is extraneous in that it does not remove anything that should not be a part of the Qur'aan (unless one believes that *hadeeth Qudsee* is inspired in meaning and wording, in which case this portion would remove *hadeeth Qudsee* as being part of the Qur'aan). This portion is essential, however, in that it mentions the miraculous nature (*i'jaaz*) of the Qur'aan. Allaah has challenged mankind to produce even a chapter similar to it, and this challenge is reserved for the Qur'aan, and not for the *hadeeth*.[44]

It should be mentioned that the word 'Qur'aan' can be used for the whole Qur'aan and for a part of the Qur'aan. Thus, if someone has recited a few verses from the Qur'aan, or has completed the recitation of the whole Qur'aan, it is possible to say in either case, "You have recited the Qur'aan."[45]

III. The Qur'aan as the Speech of Allaah

The detailed discussions of the Qur'aan as the Speech (*kalaam*) of Allaah are typically not found in the books of *'uloom al-Qur'aan*, but rather in the books of *'aqeedah* (faith). However, it was felt that this topic deserved greater attention in this work for a number of reasons: Firstly, due to the importance of this topic, since it deals with some of the Characteristics (*sifaat*) of Allaah, and of the Qur'aan; secondly, this topic

---

40   See Ch.'s 10 and 13, 'The *Ahruf* of the Qur'aan,' and 'Abrogation in the Qur'aan' for an explanation of the *mansookh* and variant readings.

41   The *mus-hafs* that 'Uthmaan wrote were not exactly the same. See Ch. 8 for further details.

42   See 'The Conditions for an Authentic *Qira'aat*' in Ch. 11 for a more detailed discussion of this point.

43   Meaning the *shaadh* readings, and not the '*ahaad*' definition of as-Suyootee; see Ch. 11 for further details.

44   See Ch. 15, which is entirely devoted to discussing the concept of *i'jaaz* in the Qur'aan, for further details.

45   cf. az-Zarqaanee, v. 1, p. 22.

has been the subject of great controversy during the history of Islaam, and great scholars have been persecuted because of it, therefore it deserves some discussion and elaboration; thirdly, there still exist incorrect concepts and ideas concerning the meaning of the *kalaam* of Allaah, primarily amongst innovated sects which claim to be in the fold of *Ahl as-Sunnah wa al-Jamaa'ah*[46]; and, lastly, there does not exist any discussion of this topic in English.[47]

Before discussing the Qur'aan in particular as the *kalaam* of Allaah, it is necessary to understand the concept of the *kalaam* of Allaah.

THE CONCEPT OF THE KALAAM OF ALLAAH

The topic of the *kalaam* of Allaah deals with one of the Attributes that Allaah has described Himself with, namely, that of Speech (*kalaam*). When dealing with the topic of the Names and Attributes of Allaah, two basic principles must be understood.

The first principle is that Allaah has described Himself with the Best and Most Perfect Names and Attributes; Names and Attributes of Beauty, Majesty, Grandeur, Perfection and Excellence; in other words, all Names and Attributes that befit Him. Allaah says in the Qur'aan,

$$\text{وَلِلَّهِ ٱلْأَسْمَآءُ ٱلْحُسْنَىٰ فَٱدْعُوهُ بِهَآ}$$

«And to Allaah belong (all) the Most Beautiful Names, so call on Him with them» [7:180]

In addition to affirming these Names and Attributes, Allaah has also negated all attributes of imperfection from Himself, such as sleep and tiredness (2:255), forgetfulness and error (20:52) and other attributes that do not befit His Glory.[48]

The second principle is that Allaah's Names and Attributes are Unique, and do not resemble the attributes of His creation. Allaah says,

$$\text{لَيْسَ كَمِثْلِهِ شَيْءٌ وَهُوَ ٱلسَّمِيعُ ٱلْبَصِيرُ}$$

«There is nothing that is similar to Him, and He is the All-Hearer, All-Seer» [42:11]

---

46   An expression that translates as 'The Followers of the *Sunnah* and the Right Group,' to differentiate those who do not follow the *Sunnah*, or the Companions of the Prophet (ﷺ). The Prophet (ﷺ) predicted, in a number of *hadeeth*, that his *ummah* would divide into seventy-three sects, all of which would be in the fire of Hell except one. When asked what the characteristics of this saved group were, he (ﷺ) replied, "They are (that group) that follow what I am following today, and my Companions" (Narrated by at-Tirmidhee); meaning the *Ahl as-Sunnah wa al-Jamaa'ah*.

47   However, it should be kept in mind that this is a relatively brief discussion, and it is hoped that perhaps a more detailed explanation of this, and other, concepts of faith be available soon, *Inshaa Allaah*.

48   The affirmation of Allaah's Names and Attributes, in general, occurs specifically; each Name and Attribute is mentioned and affirmed individually. For example, 'The All-Seer', 'The Ever-Living', 'The Bestower of Mercy', etc. As for negation, this occurs in general, unspecific terms (most of the time); for example, 'There is nothing that is similar to Him', 'There is none that is equal to Him', etc. Negation of specific attributes (such as forgetfulness and error) is rare, and only for a purpose.

Therefore, since Allaah's Attributes are unique, it is not possible for mankind to understand the exact nature of Allaah's Names and Attributes, even though it is possible to understand the concept that any Name or Attribute refers to. For example, Allaah has described Himself in the Qur'aan as *al-Hayy*, which means, 'The Ever-Living.' Mankind understands that Allaah is Ever-Living; that He was always with Life, and will always be with Life. He also understands that, even though he himself is 'alive' (*hayy*), the life that he has is very different from the one that Allaah describes Himself as having, for man's life was given to him, and it shall be taken away from him, in contrast to the characteristic of life that Allaah describes Himself with. In addition, man does not have the power to create life, unlike Allaah. So man has the characteristic of life, and Allaah describes Himself as having the characteristic of Life, but the actuality of the two characteristics differ as much as man differs from the Creator. Therefore, mankind understands the concept of Allaah's name *al-Hayy*, but can never understand the actuality of it. The same analogy applies for the other Names and Attributes of Allaah.

It is essential, therefore, when dealing with the Names and Attributes of Allaah, not to deny or distort the meanings of these Names and Attributes, since Allaah has described Himself with these Names and Attributes. Likewise, it is not allowed to try to make these attributes similar to those of the Creation, nor try to delve into the 'how-ness' of His Attributes, since the attributes of the creation are imperfect, whereas the Attributes of Allaah are Perfect and Unique.

With these two basic principles in mind, we now proceed to the concept of the *kalaam* of Allaah.

Allaah, all Praise and Glory be to Him, has described Himself as having the Characteristic of *kalaam* in over two dozen verses in the Qur'aan. Amongst these verses are the following:

وَكَلَّمَ ٱللَّهُ مُوسَىٰ تَكْلِيمًا

«And Allaah spoke directly (*kallama*) to Moosaa» [4:164]

وَتَمَّتْ كَلِمَتُ رَبِّكَ صِدْقًا وَعَدْلًا

«And the Word (*kalaam*) of your Lord has been fulfilled in truth and justice» [6:115]

قُل لَّوْ كَانَ ٱلْبَحْرُ مِدَادًا لِّكَلِمَٰتِ رَبِّي
لَنَفِدَ ٱلْبَحْرُ قَبْلَ أَن تَنفَدَ كَلِمَٰتُ رَبِّي وَلَوْ جِئْنَا بِمِثْلِهِۦ مَدَدًا ۝

«Say, 'If the oceans were ink wherewith to write the *kalaam* of my Lord, the oceans would be exhausted before the *kalaam* of my Lord would finish, even if We brought (another ocean) like it for its aid,'» [18:109]

وَكَلِمَةُ ٱللَّهِ هِيَ ٱلْعُلْيَا

«And the Word of Allaah (*kalima*) is the uppermost» [9:40]

$$سَلَٰمٌ قَوْلًا مِّن رَّبٍّ رَّحِيمٍ ﴿٥٨﴾$$

«(It will be said to the people in the Heavens) 'Peace be on you,' a Word from a Lord who is Most Merciful» [36:58]

Therefore, we affirm what Allaah has affirmed for Himself, namely, that He Speaks when He wishes, and to whomever He wishes. As Allaah says,

$$تِلْكَ ٱلرُّسُلُ فَضَّلْنَا بَعْضَهُمْ عَلَىٰ بَعْضٍ مِّنْهُم مَّن كَلَّمَ ٱللَّهُ$$

«These are the prophets, some of them We have honoured and blessed over others, (and) some of them Allaah spoke to» [2:253]

In addition, the *kalaam* of Allaah is heard by His creation, and consists of words and letters. The fact that the *kalaam* of Allaah can be heard is clearly proven in the Qur'aan and *Sunnah*. For example, in the story of Moosaa, the Qur'aan mentions that Allaah spoke to Moosaa and addressed him:

$$فَلَمَّآ أَتَىٰهَا نُودِىَ يَٰمُوسَىٰٓ ﴿١١﴾$$
$$إِنِّىٓ أَنَا۠ رَبُّكَ فَٱخْلَعْ نَعْلَيْكَ إِنَّكَ بِٱلْوَادِ ٱلْمُقَدَّسِ طُوًى ﴿١٢﴾$$
$$وَأَنَا ٱخْتَرْتُكَ فَٱسْتَمِعْ لِمَا يُوحَىٰٓ ﴿١٣﴾$$

«And when he (Moosaa) came (to the fire), he was called, 'O Moosaa, Verily, I am your Lord...and I have chosen you, therefore *listen* to that which is inspired to you'» [20:11-13]

In another verse, the Qur'aan says,

$$هَلْ أَتَىٰكَ حَدِيثُ مُوسَىٰٓ ﴿١٥﴾ إِذْ نَادَىٰهُ رَبُّهُۥ بِٱلْوَادِ ٱلْمُقَدَّسِ طُوًى ﴿١٦﴾$$

«Have you heard the story of Moosaa? When his Lord *called* him in the sacred valley of Ṭoowa» [79:15-16]

These verses are clear that Allaah spoke to Moosaa and Moosaa heard this speech. The Prophet (ﷺ) also described a meeting between Aadam and Moosaa, in which Aadam asked Moosaa, "Are you the one whom Allaah spoke to, from behind a veil, and there was no interpreter between you, nor was their any messenger?" Moosaa answered, "Yes."[49] The *hadeeth* is explicit in that Allaah's *kalaam* to Moosaa was without any intermediary. In another authentic *hadeeth*, the Prophet (ﷺ) clearly stated that Allaah's *kalaam* is with sound, for he said, "When Allaah decrees a matter in the skies, the angels move their wings in humility for His speech, which sounds like a

---

49   Reported by Aboo Daawood, and others.

chain over a rock..."[50] In this *hadeeth*, the Prophet (ﷺ) gave a description of the sound of the *kalaam* of Allaah, which clearly proves that Allaah's *kalaam* is with sound.

This was also the belief of the *salaf*. Imaam Aḥmad ibn Ḥambal (d. 241 A.H.) was asked by his son 'Abdullaah (d. 290 A.H.), "When Allaah spoke to Moosaa, did He speak with a sound (that was heard by Moosaa)?" Imaam Aḥmad answered, "Yes, indeed! Your Lord speaks with sound, and all of these *hadeeth* (of the *kalaam* of Allaah), we narrate them as we heard them."[51] Imaam al-Bukhaaree (d. 256 A.H.) narrated in his book *al-Adab al-Mufrad* the *hadeeth* of the Prophet (ﷺ) referring to the Day of Judgement, and the reckoning that will occur, and in it is: "...and their Lord will call them with a voice, the one who is close can hear it just as the one who is far can, and He will say, 'I am the King...'"[52] After narrating the entire *hadeeth*, which is also explicit in the fact that Allaah speaks in a *kalaam* that can be heard, Imaam al-Bukhaaree said, "Allaah, all Praise and Glory be to Him, speaks with sound. Those who are close can hear it just as those who are far can, and this is only so for Allaah. And in this is proof that the sound of Allaah does not resemble the sound of mankind."[53]

It is, of course, essential to keep in mind that the Speech of Allaah does not resemble that of His creation, and therefore it is impermissible to ask *how* Allaah speaks, for Allaah says,

$$ لَيْسَ كَمِثْلِهِ شَيْءٌ وَهُوَ السَّمِيعُ الْبَصِيرُ $$

«There is nothing similar to Him, and He is the All-Hearer, All-Seer» [42:11]

The fact that the *kalaam* of Allaah consists of words and letters is something that does not require proof, and can be seen even by the most ignorant person. The Qur'aan (and it is part of the *kalaam* of Allaah, as shall be proven in the next section) consists of words and letters. For example, every Muslim knows that the verse,

$$ قُلْ هُوَ اللَّهُ أَحَدٌ ۝ $$

«Qul hoowa Allaahu aḥad» [112:1]

consists of four words, each word of which consists of a number of letters. It therefore follows that the *kalaam* of Allaah consists of words and letters. The Prophet (ﷺ) himself mentioned that the Qur'aan is composed of words and letters, for he (ﷺ) stated, "Whoever recites one *word* from the Book of Allaah will have ten rewards. And I do not say the *Alif Laam Meem* is (counted as) a word, but rather *Alif* is a word, and *Laam* is a word, and *Meem* is a word."[54] Therefore, the Prophet (ﷺ) divided the

---

50 Reported by al-Bukhaaree. Some groups allege that the sound described in the *hadeeth* refers to the movement of the angel's wings. This can be refuted by a number of ways: firstly, other narrations of this *hadeeth* are explicit that the sound refers to Allaah's *kalaam*, and not the angels' wings (cf. al-Juday', p. 167); secondly, the tense that is used for the sound is masculine, whereas the wings are feminine, so if the wings of the angels were the object of the sound, the tense would have been feminine also.

51 Reported by 'Abdullaah ibn Aḥmad ibn Ḥambal in *Kitaab as-Sunnah*, # 533.

52 Reported by Aḥmad, and al-Bukhaaree in *al-Adab al-Mufrad*.

53 Reported in al-Bukhaaree's *Khalq Af'aal al-'Ibaad*. cf. al-Juday', p. 165.

54 Reported by al-Bukhaaree.

Qur'aan into words and letters.

The *kalaam* of Allaah is not limited to the Arabic language. Allaah revealed the Torah and the Injeel, in Hebrew, and this was also a part of His *kalaam*. As Imaam ad-Daarimee (d. 288 A.H.) wrote, concerning those who deny this concept, "Woe to you! Verily... Allaah is knowledgeable of all languages, and He speaks in whichever language He wishes. If He wishes, He speaks in Arabic, and if He wishes, in Hebrew, and if He wishes, in Syriac, so He has made the Qur'aan His *kalaam* in Arabic, and the Torah and Injeel His *kalaam* in Hebrew, since He has sent the prophets with the language of their peoples."[55] In other words, just as Allaah has sent every prophet to preach in the language of his nation, the *kalaam* of Allaah to any nation (when Allaah revealed a Book to that nation) was also in its language.

Another characteristic of the *kalaam* of Allaah is that it is uncreated. There are clear proofs from the Qur'aan, the *Sunnah*, the statements of the *salaf*, and clear logic for this belief.

The Qur'aan says,

$$ أَلَا لَهُ ٱلْخَلْقُ وَٱلْأَمْرُ $$

«Verily to Him (Allaah) belongs the Creation and the Command» [7:54]

In this verse, Allaah differentiates between the creation, which includes the world and all that is in it, and between the Command, which is His Speech. The Speech is in fact the cause of the creation, as Allaah says,

$$ إِنَّمَا قَوْلُنَا لِشَىْءٍ إِذَآ أَرَدْنَٰهُ أَن نَّقُولَ لَهُۥ كُن فَيَكُونُ ۝ $$

«Verily, Our Word unto a thing when We intend it, is only that We say unto
it: 'Be!'– and it is» [16:40]

Therefore the Speech of Allaah, by the Will of Allaah, is the cause of the creation, so it cannot be created, for if it were created, it would mean that a created characteristic has itself created another object, and this is not possible! In other words, a created object does not have the ability to create another object; only the Creator has this ability. Sufyaan ibn 'Uyaynah (d. 198 A.H.) said, "He has lied (who says that the Qur'aan is created)! Allaah has stated, "To Him belongs the Creation and the Command," so the creation is the creation of Allaah, and His Command is the Qur'aan."[56] Imaam Ahmad ibn Hambal (d. 241 A.H.) also used this verse to prove that the *kalaam* of Allaah is not created.[57]

The Prophet (ﷺ) said, "Whoever dismounts at any place, and says, 'I seek refuge in the *kalimaat* of Allaah from the evil that is created,' nothing will harm him until he moves from his stop."[58] This *hadeeth* also proves that the *kalaam* of Allaah is not cre-

---

55   ad-Daarimee, *ar-Radd*, p. 123.
56   Reported by al-'Aajurree in *as-Sharee'ah*, cf. al-Juday', p. 123.
57   *ibid*.
58   Reported by Muslim and others.

ated, since the Prophet (ﷺ) commanded the believers to seek refuge in the *kalaam* of Allaah from all types of evil. Refuge can only be sought from the Creator (and His Attributes), and not from the creation. Imaam al-Bukhaaree (d. 256 A.H.) stated, "In this *hadeeth* is proof that the *kalaam* of Allaah is not created," and his teacher, Nu'aym ibn Hammaad (d. 228 A.H.), stated, "It is not permissible to seek refuge in the created, nor in the speech of men, *jinn* or angels."[59] In other words, the very fact that a person seeks refuge in the *kalaam* of Allaah proves that it is an uncreated Attribute of Allaah, for it is not allowed to seek refuge in a created object.

A simple logical proof that the *kalaam* of Allaah is not created is as follows: If the *kalaam* of Allaah were created, it would mean that one of Allaah's attributes (that of speech) had a beginning, yet Allaah's attributes do not change with time, for the Qur'aan says,

$$هُوَٱلْأَوَّلُ وَٱلْأَخِرُ$$

«He is the First (i.e., there is nothing before Him), and He is the Last (i.e., there is nothing after Him)...» [57:3]

and His attributes are a part of Him. The *kalaam* of Allaah is an Attribute of Allaah, and all of Allaah's attributes are eternal and uncreated.

THE QUR'AAN AS THE KALAAM OF ALLAAH

In the last section, certain characteristics of the *kalaam* of Allaah were discussed. In this section, it shall be proven that the Qur'aan is a part of the *kalaam* of Allaah. It therefore has the same characteristics that the *kalaam* of Allaah has. Some narrations of the earlier scholars have already been mentioned concerning the fact that the Qur'aan is the *kalaam* of Allaah. However, in this section, this topic will be discussed in greater detail, along with a brief history of the deviations that have occurred with regards to this belief.

The proof that the Qur'aan in particular is the *kalaam* of Allaah is that Allaah Himself has referred to it as His *kalaam*. For example, Allaah says,

$$وَإِنْ أَحَدٌ مِّنَ ٱلْمُشْرِكِينَ ٱسْتَجَارَكَ فَأَجِرْهُ حَتَّىٰ يَسْمَعَ كَلَٰمَ ٱللَّهِ$$

«And if any of the idolaters seeks your protection, then grant him protection, so that he may hear the Word (*kalaam*) of Allaah...» [9:6]

meaning until they hear the Qur'aan. The Prophet (ﷺ) also said, "Verily, the Quraysh have prevented me from spreading the Word (*kalaam*) of my Lord,"[60] meaning that they prevented him from spreading the Qur'aan. The Prophet (ﷺ) also said in refer-

---

59 al-Juday', p. 131, from al-Bukhaaree's *Khalq Af'aal al-'Ibaad*.
60 Reported by al-Daarimee, al-Tirmidhee and others. See Ibn Qudaama, 'Abdullaah ibn Ahmad: *al-Burhan fi Bayan al-Qur'aan*, Maktabah al-Huda, Pt. Said, 1989, p.79.

ence to the Qur'aan, "The superiority of the *kalaam* of Allaah over all other *kalaam* is (like) the superiority of Allaah over His Creation."[61]

The belief that the Qur'aan is the *kalaam* of Allaah was the belief of all of the Companions, and the belief of the scholars of *Ahl as-Sunnah wa al-Jamaa'ah* after them. Hundreds of statements from the scholars of the first three generations exist concerning the fact that the Qur'aan is the *kalaam* of Allaah, and is characterised by the same characteristics as the *kalaam* of Allaah. In fact, no group amongst Muslims actually denied that the Qur'aan was the *kalaam* of Allaah; they only differed concerning the characteristics of this *kalaam*.

As was proven in the last section, the *kalaam* of Allaah is not created. This, of course, implies that the Qur'aan is not created either. Ibn 'Abbaas, in explaining the verse,

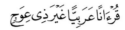

«A Qur'aan without any crookedness» [39:28]

said, "This means that the Qur'aan is not created."[62] 'Amr ibn Deenar (d. 126 A.H.) stated, "I have met the Companions of the Prophet (ﷺ), and those that came after them for seventy years, all of them said, 'Allaah is the Creator, and everything besides Him is created, and the Qur'aan is the *kalaam* of Allaah, from Him it came, and to Him it will return."[63] Imaam Aboo Ḥaneefah (d. 150 A.H.) wrote in his *Fiqh al-Akbar*, "The Qur'aan is the speech (*kalaam*) of Allaah, written in the *muṣ-ḥafs*, preserved in the hearts, recited by the tongues, and revealed to the Prophet (ﷺ)," and in another place he mentions that, "...the Qur'aan is not created."[64] Imaam Maalik (d. 179 A.H.) was asked concerning one who says that the Qur'aan is created, what should be done to him? He replied, "He should be forced to repent, and if he refuses, then his head should be cut off!"[65] Imaam ash-Shaafi'ee (d. 204 A.H.) stated, "Whoever states that the Qur'aan is created is a disbeliever."[66] Imaam Aḥmad ibn Ḥambal (d. 241 A.H.) stated, "It has been narrated from many of our *salaf* that they used to say, 'The Qur'aan is the *kalaam* of Allaah, and it is not created.' This is also what I believe, and I am not a person of philosophy, nor do I think that philosophy plays a part in any (of our beliefs). The only (source) is the Qur'aan, or the *hadeeth* of the Prophet (ﷺ), or a statement of the Companions or Successors. As for anything besides these (sources), then none of it is praiseworthy."[67]

---

61   Reported by Aḥmad and others. For a detailed discussion of the authenticity of the *hadeeth*, see al-Albaanee's *ad-Ḍa'eefah,* #1333, and for the other side, al-Juday', p. 87.

62   Reported by al-Laalikaa'ee, # 355.

63   Reported by al-Bayhaqee in his *Sunan*.

64   *Fiqh al-Akbar*, p. 301, quoted from al-Khamees, p. 14.

65   Reported by al-Laalikaa'ee, # 494.

66   al-Khamees, p. 44.

67   Reported by 'Abdullaah ibn Aḥmad in his *as-Sunnah*, #108.

Imaam at-Tahaawee,[68] in his famous *Aqeedah at-Tahaaweeyah*, wrote:

> The Qur'aan is the Speech (*kalaam*) of Allaah. It originated from Him as an articulated speech in a manner that is not questioned and was revealed to His Prophet (ﷺ) by inspiration. The Believers testify to its revelation. They are certain that it is the actual *kalaam* of Allaah, not created, unlike the speech of humans. Whoever hears it and thinks it is the speech of a man is a disbeliever whom Allaah has condemned and threatened with the Fire of Hell, for Allaah says,

> «I will burn him in the Hell-Fire» [74:26]

> to him who said,

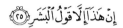

> «This (the Qur'aan) is nothing but the words of a mortal» [74:25]

> (By these verses) we know and are certain that this (the Qur'aan) is the *kalaam* of the Creator of humans, and it does not resemble the speech of mankind.[69]

The narrations from the *salaf* concerning the fact that the Qur'aan is not created has reached and far exceeded the level of *mutawaatir*, and this is a fact that no one can deny. To give one example alone, the great scholar of the *Sunnah*, Aboo al-Qaasim Hibatullaah ibn Hasan al-Laalikaa'ee (d. 418 A.H.) transmitted reports from over five-hundred and fifty scholars of the *salaf*, all of whom stated the same fact: "The Qur'aan is the *kalaam* of Allaah, not created, and whoever states that it is created is a disbeliever." After naming all of these scholars, Imaam al-Laalikaa'ee wrote,[70]

> So these are five-hundred and fifty scholars or more, from the Successors, and the generation after them, and the scholars whom the *ummah* has accepted and are well-pleased with, not including the Companions, from all different places and generations. And of these over a hundred were Imaams, whose opinions and *madh-habs* the people used to follow. And were I to busy myself in compiling the quotes from modern scholars [meaning those after the first three generations](on top of these names), then the

---

68   He is Abu Ja'afar Ahmed ibn Muhammad ibn Salamah al-Azadi al-Tahaawee, d. 321 A.H. In the introduction to his work, he said, "This is the fundamentals of the beliefs of the *Ahl al-Sunnah wa al-Jama'ah*, upon the methodology of the jurists of this *ummah*, Aboo Haneefah Nu'man ibn Thaabit, and Aboo Yusuf... and as-Shaybaanee... (the two primary students of Aboo Hanifah), and their beliefs concerning the fundamentals of the religion." This work of his is an extremely important one in that it gives a clear and lucid explanation of the basics of the belief of the *Ahl al-Sunnah wa al-Jama'ah*. In addition, it clearly shows that the beliefs of Aboo Haneefa were the same as the beliefs of the *Ahl as-Sunnah*; yet, the irony is that many of those who claim to follow this great Imaam in *fiqh* absolutely ignore Aboo Haneefah's beliefs, and instead follow the *Ash'aree* or *Maatureedee* faith! The book has a valuable commentary by Ibn Abd al-Izz al-Hanafee (d. 792 A.H.).

69   *Matn al-Aqeedah at-Tahaawiyah* point # 33, *Sharh Aqeedah at-Tahawiyyah*, p. 168.

70   al-Laalikaa'ee, v. 1, p. 344. For these numerous quotes, see the previous hundred pages (250-345).

> number of names would have reached the thousands... instead, I restricted
> myself to transmissions from these (named scholars); from generation to
> generation, no one refuted or contradicted them, and whoever did so, they
> were forced to repent, or they were commanded to be killed or banished...

The first person to claim that the Qur'aan was created was a person by the name of Ja'ad ibn Dirham (d. 124 A.H.). Ja'ad was one of the leaders of innovation of his time, denying most of the attributes of Allaah, including that of *kalaam*. He was executed by the governor of his time for holding this and other heretical beliefs. However, his student, Jahm ibn Safwaan (d. 128 A.H.), was able to spread his ideas to a much greater extent, and it is after him the group known as the *Jahmiyyah* emerged. This group was considered by the scholars of Islaam to be outside the fold of Islaam for their heretical beliefs. The *Jahmiyyah* claimed, amongst other things, that the *kalaam* of Allaah (and thus the Qur'aan) was created.[71]

Less than a century later, Ahmad ibn Abee Du'aad (d. 240), one of the callers to this belief of the *Jahmiyyah*, even though he himself was of the *Mu'tazilah*, succeeded in converting the 'Abbaasid Caliph Ma'moon (during the year 218 A.H.) to this ideology. Ma'moon then used his power as the *Khaleefah* to begin a relentless persecution of the scholars of his time, forcing many of them to renounce the belief of the *salaf*, and claim that the Qur'aan was created. The most prominent scholars from all over the Muslim lands were ordered to publicly proclaim this ideology. Those that refused were brutally tortured. Only a few brave scholars, led by Imaam Ahmad ibn Hambal (d. 241 A.H.), managed to last through this torture without relenting. Imaam Ahmad was jailed for a number of years, and beaten and whipped so severely that doctors pronounced him on the verge of death.[72] This was one of the greatest trials to ever inflict the Muslim *ummah*, and it was only during the Caliphate of Muttawakil (during the year 237 A.H.) when orthodoxy was finally redeemed.

During this period, due to the great controversy that was generated over this issue, three different groups – besides the *Ahl as-Sunnah* – evolved with regards to the belief of the eternal nature of the Qur'aan.

The first group, comprised of the *Jahmiyyah* and the *Mu'tazilah*[73] claimed that the Qur'aan was created. It was this group that temporarily gained popularity among the people, and due to the power of the Caliph Ma'moon, many scholars were forced to verbally agree with them.

---

71   The *Jahmiyyah* denied all of the names and attributes of Allaah. This led them to believe that Allaah would not be seen in the Hereafter, that Allaah is not above (*istawaa*) His Throne, that He does not have the attribute of *kalaam*, that He does not have the attributes of *yadd* and *wajh* ('Hand' and 'Face'), and so forth. If one examines the belief of the *Ash'arees*, it is clear that, despite their verbal disassociation from the *Jahmiyyah,* in reality many of their beliefs are almost the same as those of the *Jahmiyyah*, as shall be elaborated in the next section.

72   For an interesting account of this Inquisition from an orientalist's perspective, see Walter M. Patton's *Ahmed ibn Hanbal and the Mihna*, Leiden, 1897.

73   The *Mu'tazilah* were a group that tried to harmonise Greek philosophy with Islaam.

The second group were known as the *Waaqifiyyah*. This group did not give an explicit opinion on this issue, and said, "We do not say it is created, nor do we say that it is not created." It should be pointed out that the *Waaqifiyyah* were not ignorant of the status of the Qur'aan, but rather had studied the evidences, and had come to the conclusion that it was unclear whether the Qur'aan was created or not. Since the proofs of the eternal nature of the *kalaam* of Allaah were so clear, and the scholars of *Ahl as-Sunnah* united on this issue, the innovation of the *Waaqifiyyah* was a new innovation, and thus the scholars of their time were very severe in the refutation of this group. One of the *salaf* was asked concerning this group, and he replied, "The Qur'aan is the *kalaam* of Allaah, and it is not created. And can it be other than this? Or can anyone say other than this? We can never have any doubts about it, ever!!"[74] And Imaam Ahmad (d. 241 A.H.) said, "As for the *Waaqifiyyah*, then be in no doubt of their disbelief!"[75]

The last group that formed during this time were the *Lafdhiyyah*. They claimed that the Qur'aan was the *kalaam* of Allaah, and that it was not created, but the recitation of the reciter of the Qur'aan was created. The scholars of Islaam declared that the investigation into this matter was not praiseworthy, since the statement, "My recitation of the Qur'aan is created," can have two meanings, one of which is correct, and the other incorrect. The incorrect meaning, which is what most of the *Lafdhiyyah* intended, is that the actual recitation, meaning the Qur'aan, is created, and thus the *Lafdhiyyah* agreed with the *Jahmiyyah*. However, if the person intended that the sound expelled by the reciter of the Qur'aan was created, then this is a correct meaning, since the voice is created, but the actual recitation (i.e., what is recited) is not.[76]

Imaam Ahmad ibn Hambal (d. 241 A.H.) said, concerning the above three groups, "The *Jahmiyyah* are of three types: One group of them says that the Qur'aan is created; another says that it is the *kalaam* of Allaah, and stop at that; and the third say, 'Our recitation of the Qur'aan is created.' For me, these three groups have the same status (in another narration, he added:) and all of them are of the *Jahmiyyah*, disbelievers. They should be forced to repent, and if they do not do so, then they should be killed!"[77]

After this period, different groups evolved, the most prominent amongst them that of the *Ash'aree*s. Since this group is still present to this day,[78] it will be discussed in greater detail than the other groups.

---

74   al-Laalikaa'ee, #531.

75   *ibid*, #544.

76   For further details, see   al-Lalikaa'ee, pps. 385-399

77   al-Khallaal, v. 5, p. 125.

78   This group, during the fifth and sixth century of the *hijrah*, became extremely popular due to historical reasons, and the effects that this had are still present to this day. Many of the famous scholars of the past were influenced by the *Ash'aree*s, including most of the authors of the classical works on *'uloom al-Qur'aan*. The scholars that follow the *Ash'aree* faith today are many and wide-spread; even such famous institutions such as al-Azhar University, Daar al-Uloom and Deoband are primarily *Ash'aree*.

A REFUTATION OF THE *ASH'AREES*

The *Ash'aree*s are a group that take their *'aqeedah*, and their name, from the teachings of Aboo al-Hasan 'Alee ibn Ismaa'eel al-Ash'aree (d. 324 A.H.).[79, 80]

With regards to the *kalaam* of Allaah, the *Ash'aree*s brought forth an *'aqeedah* that was unknown to the *salaf*. They claimed that Allaah does posses the Attribute of Speech, and that the Qur'aan was the *kalaam* of Allaah, and in this they agreed with the *Ahl as-Sunnah*. However, they explained this attribute in a unique way, for they claimed that Allaah's *kalaam* was an 'internal' *kalaam* – a *kalaam* that could not be heard by anyone. They equated it with the concept of thinking, and stated that, just as the thoughts of men are a type of speech that cannot be heard, likewise the *kalaam* of Allaah is an internal speech that cannot be heard. Therefore, they claimed that Allaah does not speak with sound, and that his *kalaam* does not consist of words or letters. They further stated that Allaah's *kalaam* is not related to His Will; in other words, according to the *Ash'aree*s, Allaah is continually speaking, and will always be speaking – He does not speak when He wishes. They further claimed that the *kalaam* of Allaah is in fact one meaning, and cannot be divided into parts. This led them to claim that the Torah, Injeel and Qur'aan are all in fact 'expressions' of the same *kalaam*, but the actual *kalaam* of Allaah is without any language, and is of the same meaning. Therefore, according to them, the essence of the Torah, the Injeel and the Qur'aan is the same. Since they claimed that Allaah's *kalaam* is an internal *kalaam,* they then followed up this principle by stating that the actual text of the Qur'aan is created, but the *kalaam* of Allaah is not. The Arabic Qur'aan, according to the *Ash'aree*s, is not the actual *kalaam* of Allaah, but rather an 'expression' of the *kalaam* of Allaah.[81]

---

79   It should be pointed out that Aboo al-Hasan al-Ash'aree himself went through three phases during his lifetime. During the first phase, he was a *Mu'tazilee*. However, after the scholars of the *Mu'tazilah* could not satisfy his questions on particular issues of faith, he left them and started teaching the *'aqeedah* of Aboo Muhammad 'Abdullaah ibn Sa'eed ibn Kullaab (d. 240 A.H.). Ibn Kullaab, and al-Ash'aree during this stage, tried to refute the beliefs of the *Mu'tazilah* and defend the teachings of *Ahl as-Sunnah*, but unfortunately the methodology that they used to refute the *Mu'tazilah* was itself greatly influenced by Greek philosophy. Thus, they themselves fell into many errors, especially in the area of the Names and Attributes of Allaah. (Only one of their errors will be elaborated in this section, but it should be kept in mind that a refutation of one point of belief of any group is an *ipso facto* refutation of that group's claim to be *Ahl as-Sunnah*, since the beliefs of *Ahl as-Sunnah* must be perfect.) During the last stage of his life, al-Ash'aree rejected the teachings of Ibn Kullaab, and accepted the *'aqeedah* of *Ahl as-Sunnah*. It was also during this stage that he wrote his book *al-Ibaanah*, in which he defended the *'aqeedah* of the *salaf*, and believed in the Attributes of Allaah, such as *istiwaa* (rising over the throne), *wajh, yad* and other attributes. Therefore, in reality, those who claim to be *Ash'aree* are not truly following Aboo al-Hasan al-Ash'aree, for if they were, they would follow the *'aqeedah* that he had at his death, and not the *'aqeedah* of Ibn Kullaab, which he renounced before his death.

80   It should be mentioned that this section is also a refutation of the sister group of the *Ash'aree*s, the *Maatureedee*s. The beliefs of these two groups with regards to the *kalaam* of Allaah are practically the same for our purposes.

81   These are the primary points of difference between the *Ahl as-Sunnah* and the *Ash'aree*s with regards to the *kalaam* of Allaah. It must be mentioned that some of these points are based upon certain principles that the *Ash'aree*s use to distort many of the Attributes of Allaah. However, due to the brevity of this discussion, these will not be mentioned or refuted. For a full refutation, see Noor's doctoral dissertation on the subject, quoted in the Bibliography.

Aboo Haamid al-Ghazaalee (d. 505 A.H.), one of the leaders and expounders of this 'aqeedah, wrote, "Allaah speaks without words, sounds and letters... and His Speech is the Speech of the mind (i.e., internal speech). Just as the speech of the mind has no sound or words, so His Speech has no sound or words."[82]

The primary principle that led the Ash'arees to distort many of Allaah's Names and Attributes is that they wished to remove all resemblance between Allaah's Names and Attributes, and between those of the creation. This principle, which in essence is correct, was taken by the Ash'arees to an extreme. They used their intellect and logic to decide which of Allaah's Names and Attributes gave some type of resemblance, or anthropomorphic[83] qualities, and those Names and Attributes which did not. Based on this classification, they then interpreted those Names and Attributes which they felt gave anthropomorphic qualities contrary to their literal, understood meanings, thinking that by doing this they were removing any fear of resemblance between Allaah and His creation. In reality, their over-zealousness to free the Names and Attributes of Allaah from resembling those of His creation led them to deny and distort many of His Names and Attributes. They used their intellect as the criterion to understand Allaah's Names and Attributes. Whatever they felt was not befitting to Allaah, even if Allaah Himself had affirmed it, they interpreted until it satisfied their intellect.

As Aboo Haamid al-Ghazaalee, wrote, "All that is found in the traditions (the Qur'aan and Sunnah) (concerning the attributes of Allaah) is examined. Then, if the intellect can agree with it, it becomes obligatory to believe in it... But as for those (attributes) which are deemed by the intellect to be impossible, then it becomes obligatory to interpret what has been found in the traditions (the Qur'aan and Sunnah), for it is not imaginable that the traditions will contain something that contradicts the intellect. As for the hadeeth which contain characteristics of resemblance (of Allaah between His creation), then most of them are not authentic, and those that are authentic are not explicit, but rather can be interpreted."[84]

Therefore, they took their intellect to be their criterion to accept and understand the Attributes of Allaah, so whatever their intellect agreed with, they accepted, and whatever their intellect could not understand, they rejected or re-interpreted. And had they believed in them, without asking, "How?" or "Why?" it would have been better for them. However, they neglected a very crucial point, and that is that Allaah, all Glory be to Him, is more aware of His Names and Attributes than His creation is, and Allaah is more eloquent than any of His creation is. Therefore, it is not appropriate to re-interpret any Name or Attribute that Allaah (or the Prophet (ﷺ)) has described Himself with, merely because our minds cannot comprehend the actuality of an Attribute. They also neglected the fact that it is not possible to compare Allaah's

---

82   cf. al-Ghazalee, Abu Hamid: *Ihyaa 'Uloom al-Din*, Ashraf Publishers, Lahore, n.d., v.1, p.133. It is claimed that Imaam al-Ghazalee, at the end of his life, recanted from the 'aqeedah of the Ash'arees and accepted the 'aqeedah of the salaf.

83   Anthropomorphic: To give an object human-like characteristics.

84   From his *al-Iqtisaad fee al-'Itiqaad*, p. 132. Taken from Noor, v.1, p. 90.

Attributes and to try to understand them by making analogies with the attributes of the creation.

Imaam al-Barbahaaree (d. 329), one of the scholars of the *salaf*, said:

> May Allaah have mercy upon you! Know that speculative speech about the Lord, the Most High, is a newly invented matter, and is an innovation and misguidance. Nothing is to be said about the Lord except what He has described Himself with in the Qur'aan, and what the Messenger of Allaah (ﷺ) explained to the Companions... No one says about the attributes of Allaah, "How?" or "Why?" except one who has doubts about Allaah. The Qur'aan is the *kalaam* of Allaah, His Revelation and Light...[85]

Yet, the *Ash'arees* delved into concepts that could not be understood by men, and tried to reason the actuality of the Attributes of Allaah.

To illustrate this example, with regards to the attribute of *kalaam*, the *Ash'arees* reasoned that the one who speaks must speak with sound and breath, and these are created. In addition, they argued that speech must come from a combination of organs, such as the tongue, throat and mouth, but Allaah is free of these. They also reasoned that words, composed of letters, can never be eternal, since one letter follows another, and has a specific place in each word. Therefore, since each letter is sequential, following the one before it, it cannot have existed from eternity.[86] Therefore, according to them, it was not possible for Allaah's *kalaam* to be with sound, or for Allaah's *kalaam* to be composed of words and letters, for if it were, it would be created.

It can be seen, then, that the *Ash'arees* used their logic to distort clear, explicit concepts in the Qur'aan and *Sunnah*, by first comparing the Attributes of Allaah to those of the creation, and then reasoning that, since Allaah is not like His creation, these Attributes must have a different meaning. Had they only understood that Allaah is Unique, and there is nothing similar to Him, and that it is not possible to understand Allaah's Attributes by comparing them to those of the creation, it would have saved them from falling into the error of denying these Attributes.

As for their belief that the *kalaam* of Allaah is without sound, this contradicts the proofs that were given in the previous section from the Qur'aan, *Sunnah* and statements of the *salaf.* The presumption that sound must come from organs is a presumption based upon the characteristics of humans. Therefore, it is not necessarily true for all objects. Allaah, all Glory and Praise be to Him, has made the Heavens and the Earth speak, for they responded to His Command and said,

---

85   al-Barbahaaree, al-Ḥasan. *Sharḥ as-Sunnah* (Maktabah as-*Sunnah*, Cairo, 1986), p. 28.

86   cf. al-Juday', pps 375-379, and Noor, pps. 517-542, for these and other logical proofs that the *Ash'arees* bring, along with their refutation. The *Ash'arees* also try to prove the fact that the word *kalaam* signifies an internal thought, and not necessarily a spoken word. Their primary proof is a line of poetry attributed to a pre-Islaamic Christian. However, this meaning that they seek to prove contradicts the understood meaning of the word *kalaam* in the Arabic language. In addition, Allaah uses other words besides '*kalaam*' (such as *nidaa*) to denote His Speech, and these words all denote speech with sound. See the above references for a more detailed discussion.

أَتَيْنَا طَآئِعِينَ

«'We come, willingly!'» [41:11]

and Allaah, all Glory and Praise be to Him, will make the skins of the disbelievers speak on the Day of Judgement,

وَقَالُوا لِجُلُودِهِمْ لِمَ شَهِدتُّمْ عَلَيْنَا قَالُوا أَنطَقَنَا ٱللَّهُ ٱلَّذِى أَنطَقَ كُلَّ شَىْءٍ

«And they (the disbelievers) will say, 'Why did you (our skins) testify against us?' They will say, 'Allaah has caused us to speak, as He causes all things to speak...'» [41:21]

Allaah caused these objects to speak, yet these objects do not have the organs that humans need to speak. Is not Allaah, the one who created all things, capable of speaking as He wishes?

Imaam Aḥmad (d. 241 A.H.) stated,

"As for their claim (meaning the claim of the *Jahmiyyah*, which was later taken by the *Ash'arees*) that sound can only occur from a combination of the throat, and lips, and tongue, then did not Allaah say to the Heavens and Earth

ٱئْتِيَا طَوْعًا أَوْ كَرْهًا قَالَتَا أَتَيْنَا طَآئِعِينَ ﴿١١﴾

«'Come willingly or unwillingly!' They both said, 'We come, willingly!'» [41:12]

And did not Allaah say,

وَسَخَّرْنَا مَعَ دَاوُۥدَ ٱلْجِبَالَ يُسَبِّحْنَ وَٱلطَّيْرَ وَكُنَّا فَاعِلِينَ

«And We subjected the mountains and the birds to glorify Our praises, along with (Prophet) Daawood» [21:79]

Do these people presume that they (i.e., the mountains, the Heavens and the Earth) glorified with a throat, and lips, and tongues?! And how about when a disbeliever's limbs will testify against him... Do you think that they will testify with throats, lips and tongues?! Nay, rather Allaah will make them to speak, as He wishes, without any throat or lips or tongues!"[87]

Therefore, to claim that if the *kalaam* of Allaah were with sound, it would entail giving these characteristics to the Creator, cannot be accepted, for it is an analogy of Allaah with man, and this is improper. 'Abdullaah ibn Aḥmad ibn Ḥambal (d. 290 A.H.) said, "My father (Imaam Aḥmad) said, 'The *hadeeth* of Ibn Mas'ood states that when Allaah Speaks, a sound is heard which sounds like (the moving of) a chain over

---

87 *ar-Radd 'ala al-Jahmiyyah*, p. 131; cf. al-Harbee, p. 375.

a rock. And this (*hadeeth*) is denied by the *Jahmiyyah*.[88] These people are disbelievers, they wish to cause confusion and deceive the people. Whoever presumes that Allaah does not Speak is a disbeliever! Verily, we will continue to narrate these *hadeeth* as they came to us!"[89] In this narration, Imaam Ahmad is stating that any person who denies the fact that Allaah speaks with a sound is of the *Jahmiyyah*. In another narration, 'Abdullaah said, "I asked my father: Some people are claiming that Allaah does not speak with a sound." Imaam Ahmad replied, "Nay! Allaah speaks with a sound, and the only people who deny this are the *Jahmiyyah*. They wish to confuse the people and deny (the Attributes of Allaah)."[90]

Imaam ash-Shahrastaanee (d. 548 A.H.), while discussing the historical development of the various sects related to the *kalaam* of Allaah, wrote, "Then (Aboo al-Hasan) al-Ash'aree came, and invented a third opinion, and claimed that all sound must be created. And with this (opinion), he contradicted the consensus (*ijmaa'*) before him, for he claimed that what we recite is not the actual *kalaam* of Allaah. And this (belief) is the essence of innovation."[91]

In addition, if the *Ash'aree*s maintain that the *kalaam* of Allaah is without sound, then the following points must be answered:

1)   If the *kalaam* of Allaah is without sound, then what did Moosaa hear when Allaah spoke to Him? If they respond that Allaah created a sound, and caused Moosaa to hear that created sound, then this means that this created object stated,

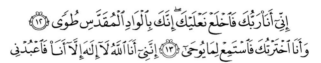

«O Moosaa, Verily, I am your Lord...Verily, I am Allaah, there is not god save
me, so worship Me...» [20:12-14]

Therefore, if they state this, it implies that this created object claimed to be Allaah, and asked Moosaa to worship it! However, if they state that it was the actual *kalaam* of Allaah, then it must be asked, "How then did Moosaa hear it if you claim that Allaah's *kalaam* is without sound?" The scholars of the *Ash'aree*s have not been able to provide a satisfactory response for this.

2)   If the *kalaam* of Allaah is without sound, then what special status do those prophets whom Allaah spoke to gain? In other words, what is the superiority of Moosaa over the other prophets if he did not hear the *kalaam* of Allaah? The Qur'aan mentions that one of the blessings that certain prophets have been given is that Allaah spoke to them directly:

88   This author adds: And the *Ash'aree*s!
89   Reported by 'Abdullaah ibn Ahmad in *as-Sunnah*, # 534.
90   al-Harbee, p. 373.
91   *Nihaayat al-Aqdaam*, p. 313; taken from al-Harbee, p. 365.

تِلْكَ ٱلرُّسُلُ فَضَّلْنَا بَعْضَهُمْ عَلَىٰ بَعْضٍ مِّنْهُم مَّن كَلَّمَ ٱللَّهُ

«These are the Messengers! Some of them We blessed (with a higher status) over others. Some of them Allaah spoke to...» [2:253]

Also, if Allaah speaks to a prophet, but that prophet cannot hear him, then of what difference is this type of inspiration to the other types of inspiration? Allaah says,

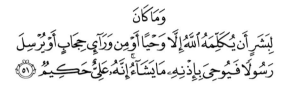

«It is not possible for any human being that Allaah should speak to him, unless it be by Inspiration, or from behind a veil, or (that) He sends a Messenger to reveal what He will by His Permission. Verily, He is the Most High, Most Wise» [42:51]

This verse mentions different types of inspirations. If, according to the *Ash'arees*, the *kalaam* of Allaah cannot be heard, then when Allaah speaks from 'behind a veil,' how is this different from the other forms of inspiration?[92]

3) If the *kalaam* of Allaah is an 'internal' *kalaam*, similar to the 'speech' of the mind, then what is the difference between the Knowledge (*'ilm*) of Allaah, and His Speech. Allaah has described Himself with both of these characteristics in the Qur'aan. If the Speech of Allaah cannot be heard, and is an internal Speech, then this implies that it is the same as the Attribute of Knowledge.

There is another point that the belief of the *Ash'arees* implies, and this is a very dangerous implication: Just as the attribute of speech is a noble attribute, its opposite, muteness, is a characteristic that is not desired, nor is it considered praiseworthy. It is well known that the one who is mute is not like the one who speaks. Therefore, to claim that Allaah does not possess the attribute of speech (or to interpret it away as the *Ash'arees* do) is in reality blasphemous, as this then implies that the Creator is mute, yet Allaah is free of all attributes of imperfection. In fact, this principle of faith was one of the most powerful arguments that the prophets used to deny the worship of other than Allaah! The stories of Ibraaheem and Moosaa clearly show this.

The Story of Ibraaheem

The story of Ibraaheem and the idols is well known: Ibraaheem destroyed all of the idols of his people except the largest one. When his people discovered this, they questioned him as to whether he was the culprit. Ibraaheem answered, as mentioned in the Qur'aan,

---

92   The various types of inspiration will be discussed in the next chapter.

قَالَ بَلْ فَعَلَهُۥ كَبِيرُهُمْ

هَٰذَا فَسْـَٔلُوهُمْ إِن كَانُوا۟ يَنطِقُونَ ۝ فَرَجَعُوٓا۟ إِلَىٰٓ
أَنفُسِهِمْ فَقَالُوٓا۟ إِنَّكُمْ أَنتُمُ ٱلظَّٰلِمُونَ ۝ ثُمَّ نُكِسُوا۟ عَلَىٰ
رُءُوسِهِمْ لَقَدْ عَلِمْتَ مَا هَٰٓؤُلَآءِ يَنطِقُونَ ۝ قَالَ
أَفَتَعْبُدُونَ مِن دُونِ ٱللَّهِ مَا لَا يَنفَعُكُمْ شَيْـًٔا وَلَا
يَضُرُّكُمْ ۝ أُفٍّ لَّكُمْ وَلِمَا تَعْبُدُونَ مِن دُونِ ٱللَّهِ أَفَلَا
تَعْقِلُونَ ۝

«'Rather, this one, the largest of them, did it! (Why don't you) ask them, if they can speak!' So they turned to themselves, and said, 'Verily, you are the wrong-doers (since you left the idols unguarded).' Then they turned to themselves (again) and (responded), 'You know very well (O Ibraaheem) that these (idols) do not speak' (Ibraaheem) replied, 'Do you then worship besides Allaah objects that can neither profit you nor harm you? Fie to you, and upon that which you worship besides Allaah! Have you no sense?!'» [21:63-67]

In these verses, Ibraaheem showed his people that their idols were not worthy of worship, primarily because they could not speak. After they themselves acknowledged this, Ibraaheem rebuked them, and asked them, "Have you no sense?!" meaning, "How can an object that cannot even speak be worthy of worship?" Notice that Ibraaheem was referring to a speech that *could be heard*, for Ibraaheem's people did not answer Ibraaheem with the belief of the *Ash'arees*, "Our god speaks, but a speech that is not heard – an internal speech of the mind!" for they understood what Ibraaheem meant!! This is why they turned to themselves, and realised the foolishness of their actions, and could only reply with the feeble response that everyone knew that their idols could not speak!

The Story of Moosaa

Likewise, when the Children of Israa'eel took the calf that they had built as an object of worship, they were reprimanded in the Qur'aan. Allaah says,

أَفَلَا يَرَوْنَ أَلَّا يَرْجِعُ إِلَيْهِمْ قَوْلًا وَلَا يَمْلِكُ لَهُمْ ضَرًّا وَلَا نَفْعًا ۝

«Did they (those who worshipped the calf) not realise that it (the calf) could *not respond to them with a (single) word*, nor did it have any power to harm or benefit them?» [20:89]

In another verse, Allaah says,

$$\text{وَٱتَّخَذَ قَوْمُ مُوسَىٰ مِنۢ بَعْدِهِۦ مِنْ حُلِيِّهِمْ}$$

$$\text{عِجْلًا جَسَدًا لَّهُۥ خُوَارٌ أَلَمْ يَرَوْاْ أَنَّهُۥ لَا يُكَلِّمُهُمْ وَلَا يَهْدِيهِمْ سَبِيلًا}$$

«And the people of Moosaa made in his absence, out of their ornaments, the image of a calf that made a sound (like the mooing of a cow). Did they not realise that it *could not speak to them*, nor guide them to the (straight) path?» [7:148]

In these two verses, Allaah reprimanded the Children of Israa'eel for worshipping the calf, since the calf was not a perfect object, and one of the clearest indications that it was not worthy of worship was that it could not speak! Even though the calf made noises, it was not capable of intelligent speech.

Therefore, these two stories show that muteness and incoherent speech are attributes that do not befit the Creator, and thus the people of Ibraaheem and Moosaa were rebuked for taking gods that were mute. Yet, the *Ash'arees*, thinking that they were removing all negative attributes from Allaah, in reality equated the Creator with the attributes of these idols, and thus fell into the same error as the people of Moosaa and Ibraaheem did with regards to the attribute of speech! This is why Haaroon ibn Ma'roof (d. 231 A.H.), one of the scholars of the *salaf*, said, "Whoever presumes that Allaah does not speak, then in reality he is worshipping idols."[93]

The *Ash'arees* also claim that the *kalaam* of Allaah is not related to His will, which implies that Allaah does not speak when He wishes to, but rather He is continually speaking. The fact that Allaah's *kalaam* is related to His Will (in other words, Allaah Speaks when He wishes to Speak) is clearly shown in the Qur'aan. Allaah says,

$$\text{إِنَّمَآ أَمْرُهُۥٓ إِذَآ أَرَادَ شَيْئًا أَن يَقُولَ لَهُۥ كُن فَيَكُونُ ﴿٨٢﴾}$$

«Verily, His Command, whenever He intends a thing, is only that He says, 'Be!' – and it is» [37:82]

In this verse, Allaah clearly shows that His *kalaam* is related to His Will, for whenever Allaah intends a thing, He says to it "Be!" which proves that Allaah Speaks when He wishes. Likewise, Allaah states,

$$\text{وَلَمَّا جَآءَ مُوسَىٰ لِمِيقَٰتِنَا وَكَلَّمَهُۥ رَبُّهُۥ}$$

«And when Moosaa came to Our appointed time and place, and his Lord spoke with him...» [7:143]

This verse shows that Allaah spoke to Moosaa after Moosaa had arrived to the meeting point; not before it, nor after it – once again proving that Allaah speaks when He wishes.

---

93   Reported by 'Abdullaah ibn Ahmad, # 209.

The *Ash'aree*s also claim that the *kalaam* of Allaah is all the same meaning,[94] and cannot be divided into parts. This principle then leads them to state that the Qur'aan, Torah and Injeel are in essence the same, and they only differ in their expressions and languages.

If this were the case in reality, then the Qur'aan, Torah and Injeel, when translated into one language, should be the same, since their essence is the same. However, it is well known that each of these three books differs from the other greatly.

In addition, if the *kalaam* of Allaah cannot be divided into parts, and is one whole concept, then this raises a problem that the *Ash'aree*s must solve. The following conversation between one of the scholars of *Ahl as-Sunnah*, Aboo Nasr as-Sijazee (d. 444 A.H.) and one of the scholars of the *Ash'aree*s will prove interesting:[95]

> Aboo Nasr said to the *Ash'aree*, "What do you say when Allaah spoke to Moosaa? Did he understand all of the *kalaam* of Allaah (i.e., if the *kalaam* of Allaah cannot be divided into parts, then did Moosaa hear all of the *kalaam* of Allaah)?"
>
> The *Ash'aree* hesitated a little, and questioned, "What do you intend by this question?"
>
> Aboo Nasr responded, "Forget what I intend, and respond to my question!" but the *Ash'aree* refused to respond until Aboo Nasr told him what he meant by this question.
>
> Aboo Nasr then responded, "What I intend is as follows: If you respond to my question by stating that Moosaa understood all of the *kalaam* of Allaah, then this implies that there is not a single *kalaam* of Allaah except that Moosaa comprehended it, and this is blasphemy and disbelief (for this would imply that Moosaa had been given all of the knowledge of Allaah)... but if you do not say this, then you are forced to state that Allaah made Moosaa comprehend some part of His *kalaam*, and by this statement you have caused yourself to fall into the same thing that you pretend to run away from, and that is the belief that Allaah's *kalaam* can be divided. You also claimed that one who says that the *kalaam* of Allaah can be divided is a disbeliever, yet you have been forced to say it yourself. Therefore, your opponent will be the victor over you, since he believed in what was stated in the Qur'aan and *Sunnah*, (which came) from Allaah and His Messenger (ﷺ), but you refused to submit to them, and instead claimed that it was obligatory to turn to your intellect (to understand these concepts). Yet, your intellect has forced you to agree with the revelation (in that the *kalaam* of Allaah can be divided into parts), and in the process you have humiliated yourself!"

---

94   It should be pointed out that the *Ash'aree* scholars themselves have differed with regards to this point. Some of them claim that the *kalaam* of Allaah can be divided into commands, prohibitions, and facts, others gave different classification, but the majority did not agree with this. This difference of opinion in and of itself is an indication of the people of innovation. The scholars of the *Ahl as-Sunnah* do not disagree amongst themselves in primary matters of *'aqeedah*.

95   Reported in *Dar Ta'aarud al-'Aql wa an-Naql*, 2/90. Taken from Noor, p. 537, with some changes.

The *Ash'aree* responded, "This requires some time for me to think," and left the conversation.

In other words, if the *kalaam* of Allaah is one essence, and cannot be divided into parts, then when Allaah spoke to Moosaa, did Moosaa hear all of the *kalaam* of Allaah? If so, then this implies that Moosaa gained all the knowledge of Allaah, and this is not possible. However, if this is not so, then this implies that Moosaa understood a part of the *kalaam* of Allaah, which is what the *Ahl as-Sunnah* believe.

The final point that will be discussed is in fact the most dangerous consequence of the belief of the *Ash'arees*. Since the *Ash'arees* claimed that Allaah did not actually speak the Qur'aan with a voice that is heard, and that His *kalaam* is not in any language, and not composed of words and letters, they then had to answer a number of questions, including: "Where did the Qur'aan that is present amongst us originate from? And what, then, is the Arabic Qur'aan, with its words and letters?"

In other words, since the *Ash'arees* claimed that Allaah's *kalaam* could not be heard, then where did the Qur'aan come from? And who was the first to recite it? And if, as the *Ash'arees* claim, the *kalaam* of Allaah is not in any language, and neither is it composed of words and letters, then what is the relationship of the Qur'aan, which is in Arabic and composed of words and letters, with the *kalaam* of Allaah?

Concerning this point, the *Ash'arees* were forced to admit that the Qur'aan is not the *actual kalaam* of Allaah (since it is in Arabic, and composed of words and letters), but instead an 'expression' (Ar. '*hikaayah*', or ''*ibaarah*') of the *kalaam* of Allaah. As to who (or what) was the first to actually 'express' it, the *Ash'arees* differed amongst themselves into a number of opinions, all of which are equally blasphemous! Most of them stated that the Qur'aan was first created in the *Lauh al-Mahfoodh* (in other words, the Arabic words of the Qur'aan did not exist until they were created by Allaah in the *Lauh al-Mahfoodh*), thus explicitly claiming that the Qur'aan was created; others stated that Allaah made Jibreel understand the meaning of the Qur'aan, and Jibreel was the first to verbalize it, thus making the Qur'aan the speech of Jibreel; yet others stated that the Qur'aan was inspired in meaning and first spoken by the Prophet (ﷺ), thus making the Qur'aan the speech of the Prophet Muhammad (ﷺ).

In other words, the *Ash'arees* were forced to admit that the Arabic Qur'aan is not the actual *kalaam* of Allaah, and that it is created. This is due to the fact that they differentiated between what they called an 'internal *kalaam*' of Allaah, which is without language, sound and words, and between the actual Qur'aan, which is in Arabic, recited and heard, and composed of words. This 'internal *kalaam*' of Allaah, according to them, is not created, but the Qur'aan, since it is only an 'expression' of the 'internal *kalaam*', and not the *actual kalaam* of Allaah, must be created.

Thus, the *Ash'arees* explicitly state and believe that the Qur'aan is created, even though they then follow up this statement with the phrase, "...but the *kalaam* of Allaah is not." As one of their most famous scholars, Ibraaheem al-Baajooree (d. 1277 A.H.), wrote, "The belief of the *Ahl as-Sunnah* (intending the belief of the *Ash'arees*) is that the Qur'aan, meaning the internal *kalaam* (of Allaah) is not created, but the Qur'aan, meaning the one that we recite, is created."[96]

Therefore, in essence, the *Ash'arees* agreed with the *Jahmiyyah* and the *Mu'tazilah* that the Qur'aan is created.

It must be asked: When all of the scholars of the *salaf* vehemently spoke against those who believed that the Qur'aan was created, and even accused them of disbelief, were they referring to this concept of 'internal *kalaam*' that the *Ash'arees* invented, or where they referring to the Qur'aan that is well known to all Muslims? And when Imaam al-Laalikaa'ee (d. 418 A.H.) quoted over five-hundred scholars of the *salaf* stating that the Qur'aan is the *kalaam* of Allaah, and not created, did any of these scholars differentiate between this 'internal *kalaam*' and the actual Qur'aan, and state that the Qur'aan is only an 'expression' of this 'internal *kalaam*'?

The answer is very clear: none of the *salaf* preached or believed the doctrines that the *Ash'arees* invented, and none of them differentiated between an 'internal *kalaam* of Allaah' and the Qur'aan. What the *salaf* were referring to when they said that the Qur'aan is the *kalaam* of Allaah, and that the Qur'aan is not created, is the actual Qur'aan, and not an imaginary and invented 'internal *kalaam*'. None of them, not even a single scholar (before Aboo al-Hasan al-Ash'aree and his teacher Ibn Kullaab), mentioned this concept of an 'internal' *kalaam*, and differentiated between it and the actual Qur'aan! The *salaf* are all quoted as saying, "The Qur'aan is the *kalaam* of Allaah, and is not created," yet the *Ash'arees* state, "The Qur'aan is only an expression of the *kalaam* of Allaah, and is created"!!

كِتَـٰبٌ أَنزَلْنَـٰهُ إِلَيْكَ مُبَـٰرَكٌ لِّيَدَّبَّرُوٓاْ ءَايَـٰتِهِۦ وَلِيَتَذَكَّرَ أُوْلُواْ ٱلْأَلْبَـٰبِ ﴿٢٩﴾

«Are these two examples the same? *Alhamdulillaah*; but most of them do not know!» [39:29]

In fact, some of the early scholars during the time of the *salaf* explicitly refuted the beliefs of the *Ash'arees*. Ahmad ibn Seenan al-Waasitee (d. 256 A.H.), one of the teachers of Imaam al-Bukhaaree (d. 256 A.H.) and Imaam Muslim (d. 261 A.H.), said in refutation of the belief of Ibn Kullaab (which was later taken by Aboo al-Hasan al-Ash'aree), "Whoever presumes that the Qur'aan is two things (i.e., an 'internal' *kalaam* and an expression of that *kalaam*), or that it is only an 'expression' (of the *kalaam* of Allaah), then by Allaah, besides whom there is no other god, he is a heretic (*zindeeq*) who wishes to destroy Islaam. He is a disbeliever in Allaah. *This* Qur'aan is the Qur'aan that Allaah revealed through Jibreel to the Prophet (ﷺ)..."[97] The scholar Aboo al-'Abbaas Ahmad ibn 'Umar ibn Surayj (d. 303 A.H.), whom Imaam adh-Dhahabi called the 'Renovator' (*mujaddid*) of the fourth century,[98] and because of whom the *fiqh* of Imaam as-Shaafi'ee (d. 204 A.H.) was popularised, wrote,

---

96   Reported in *Kifaayat al-'Awaam*, p. 104. Taken from Juday', p. 398. Al-Baajooree was perhaps the most famous scholar of the *Ash'arees* during the last century. He has an extremely popular explanation to the *Jawharah* (the basic text book of the *Ash'aree* faith), entitled, *Tuhfat al-Mureed alaa Jawharat at-Tawheed*.

97   Juday', p. 436.

98   adh-Dhahabi, *Siyar*, 14/201.

And it has been affirmed and agreed by all the people of this religion, of the *sunnah* and *jamaa'ah*, from the *salaf* that past, from the Companions, and the Successors, and the famous and rightly guided scholars to this time of ours, that all the verses pertaining to the Attributes of Allaah, and the authentic narrations coming from the Prophet (ﷺ) concerning the Attributes...that it is mandatory to believe in them, in each and every one of them, just as they came, and to leave the actuality of them to Allaah...*(and he mentioned some Attributes, many of which the Ash'arees deny, and then said:)*...and to affirm the *kalaam* (of Allaah), with letters, and with sound, and in different languages, and in words, and *soorahs*.... and all of this, we accept it, and do not reject it, nor do we interpret them with the interpretations of the other (groups), or with the anthropomorphism of the anthropomorphists... Rather, we say what Allaah has said, and interpret it as the Prophet (ﷺ) interpreted it, and the Companions, and the Successors, and the scholars of the *salaf*, those who are well known for their religion and character. And we agree upon that which they agreed upon, and do not talk with what they did not talk about (i.e., we do not give interpretations that were not given by them), but rather we accept the apparent meanings of the narrations (of the *hadeeth*) and the verses (of the Qur'aan). *And we do not give for these verses the interpretations of the Mu'tazilah, or the Ash'arees, or the Jahmiyyah, or the disbelievers, or the anthropomorphists... but rather, we accept it (these Attributes), all without any re-interpretation (i.e., we accept the apparent meanings of it), and believe in it without comparing (them to the Creation).* And we state, 'The belief in these (Attributes) is obligatory, and to speak of them is from the *sunnah*, but to try to re-interpret (ta'weel) it (i.e., the way these groups have done) is an innovation!'[99]

In addition, the beliefs of the *Ash'arees* are very similar to the beliefs of the *Lafdhiyyah* (mentioned above), who believed that a person's recitation of the Qur'aan is created. Since the *Ash'arees* believe that the actual text of the Qur'aan is created, this automatically implies that they believe that the recitation of the Qur'aan is also created, for the recitation, according to the *Ash'arees*, is of a created text! Imaam Ahmad (d. 241 A.H.) stated, "The *Lafdhiyyah* are in reality encircling the belief of Jahm (ibn Safwaan), for they believe that Jibreel came with something created (to the Prophet (ﷺ))."[100] In another narration, Imaam Ahmad was asked, "What is your opinion concerning those who say, 'Our recitation of the Qur'aan is created'"? Imaam Ahmad replied, "These people are worse than the *Jahmiyyah*. Whoever believes this, then he believes that Jibreel came with something created, and the Prophet (ﷺ) preached something created!"[101] It should be noted that the belief that Jibreel came with something created, and the belief that the Prophet (ﷺ) preached something created, is exactly the belief of the *Ash'arees*, for they believe that the Arabic Qur'aan is created.

---

99   Juday', p. 438.
100 adh-Dhahabi, *al-Uluww*, p. 191.
101 adh-Dhahabi, *al-Uluww*, p. 212.

Conclusion

The Attributes of Allaah as mentioned in the Qur'aan and *Sunnah* are absolutely Unique. These Attributes are understood literally (in the case of the Attribute of *kalaam*, that Allaah Speaks, whenever He wishes, with a sound, in different languages, and this Speech is composed of words and letters, and is not created), but the actuality and 'how-ness' of these Attributes are not delved into, and any negative similarity between these Attributes and the attributes of the creation are negated (in the case of this Attribute, that the speech of the creation is created, but the Speech of Allaah is not). Understanding these Attributes 'literally' does not mean understanding them in the manner that they are found in the creation, or comparing them with the attributes of the creation; rather, it means affirming the linguistic meaning of that Attribute in a manner that befits the Creator, and will never completely be understood by mankind.

The beliefs and deviations of the *Ash'arees* are all based upon their anthropomorphic understanding of the Attributes of Allaah. If they had only understood that the Attributes of Allaah cannot be compared to the attributes of the creation, nor are they based upon the attributes of the creation, they would not have had to resort to try to 'rationalise' these Attributes to remove this supposed anthropomorphism from them. The *Ash'arees* also failed to realise that, in their over-zealousness to remove this imaginary anthropomorphism that they believed existed in the Qur'aan and *Sunnah*, they ended up comparing Allaah's Attributes with the attributes of inanimate objects.

The *Ash'arees* are an example of how deviation occurs when the proper Islaamic methodology is not followed; they wished to refute the beliefs of the *Mu'tazilah* and the *Jahmiyyah*, and affirm the Attributes of Allaah, but since they were so influenced by the principles of Greek logic and rationalism, they ended up agreeing with the beliefs of the same groups that they sought to refute, and stated that the Qur'aan is created.

In conclusion, the scholar of the *Sunnah*, Imaam Muhammad ibn al-Hasan al-Aajurree (d. 360 A.H.) stated:

> Therefore it is essential that Muslims fear Allaah, and teach each other the Qur'aan... and not argue over it. And they should know that it is the *kalaam* of Allaah, not created. So if a *Jahmee* argues with them, and says, "It is created!" or says, "The Qur'aan is the *kalaam* of Allaah!" and stops at that (i.e., a *Waaqifee*), or says, "My recitation of the Qur'aan is created!" (i.e., a *Lafdhee*), or says, "The Qur'aan is only an 'expression' of what is in the *Lauh al-Mahfoodh*!" (i.e., an *Ash'aree*), then the ruling with regards to such a person is that he be left, and not talked to, nor prayed behind, but rather warned against.
>
> And upon you, O Muslim, are the narrations from the Prophet (ﷺ), and the narrations from the Companions after him, may Allaah be pleased with them, and the statements of the Successors, and the scholars of the Muslims. And leave debating (about the religion by using your intellect), and useless arguementation, and contention! And whoever is upon this path,

then I hope for him all good from Allaah...[102]

---

[102] *ash-Sharee'ah*, v. 1, p. 239. Concerning saying one's prayer behind an *Ash'aree*, it is best to avoid praying behind them. However, if one is forced to pray behind them, the prayer is still valid and need not be repeated. Notice how al-Aajurree equated the beliefs of the *Ash'arees* with the beliefs of the *Jahmiyyah*, and considered it to be one of the sects of the *Jahmiyyah*!!

It should be pointed out that some of the *Ash'arees* claim that the *'aqeedah* of *Ahl as-Sunnah wa al-Jamaa'ah* (part of which was elaborated in this section) is an invention of Ibn Taymiyyah (d. 728 A.H.). They claim that the first person to claim that the Attributes of Allaah are to be taken in their literary meanings was Ibn Taymiyyah, and therefore he was the first to claim that the *kalaam* of Allaah can be heard, and that the Qur'aan is the *actual kalaam* of Allaah. In order to refute this view, this author purposely avoided quoting even one statement of Ibn Taymiyyah throughout the last three sections. This was done to prove that the right to formulate *'aqeedah* does not belong to Ibn Taymiyyah, but rather to Allaah and to His Messenger (ﷺ). In addition, the belief of all of the Companions, Successors, and the scholars of *Ahl as-Sunnah* after them was one, and that is the belief that was elaborated upon and defended above. Every single scholar quoted above lived centuries before Ibn Taymiyyah, therefore how could Ibn Taymiyyah be the first to propagate these views? Instead, it must be asked of the *Ash'arees*, "Can you name even one person before Aboo al-Hasan al-Ash'aree, and Ibn Kullaab, who held the views that you hold? As for us, we have quoted the Qur'aan, and the *Sunnah*, and the statements of the Companions and Successors, and the scholars of the first generations, the likes of Imaam Ahmad, Aboo Haneefah, as-Shaafi'ee, Maalik, al-Bukhaaree, and ad-Daarimee to defend our beliefs. Who is there, before al-Ash'aree, and his teacher Ibn Kullaab, and the innovator Jahm ibn Safwaan, who held the beliefs that you hold?" But if they cannot respond to you – and of a surety they cannot respond to you – then know that they are a people who have turned away from accepting the Qur'aan and *Sunnah*, unless and until it agrees with their intellect and desires!

Another manner by which they seek to confuse the people is by quoting famous and well-known scholars throughout Islaamic history who were *Ash'arees* or influenced to a certain degree by the beliefs of the *Ash'arees*. So, for example, they quote the likes of al-Baaqillaanee (d. 403 A.H.), al-Qurtubee (d. 671 A.H.), an-Nawawee (d. 676 A.H.), Ibn Hajr al-Asqalaani (d. 852 A.H.), as-Suyootee (d. 911 A.H.), Ibn Hajr al-Haythamee (d. 974 A.H.) and many more respected and loved scholars, and claim, "If all of these scholars are misguided *Ash'arees*, then who are the *Ahl as-Sunnah*?!" This may be refuted in a number of ways. Firstly, it is very clearly noticed that all the scholars mentioned lived after the first three generations of the *hijrah*, and these are the generations that the Prophet (ﷺ) himself stated would be the best of all generations! The *Ash'arees* cannot quote even one reputable scholar from the time of the actual *salaf* that was on their beliefs, for the simple reason that there were none. The *Ash'aree* beliefs were founded and propagated during the fourth century of the *hijrah*, and became increasingly popular after that. We are commanded by the Prophet (ﷺ) to take from the first three generations of Islaam, and we consider following them as part of our religion of Islaam. As for the generations and scholars that come after this time, then we look at them individually, and what is good from them we take, and what is incorrect we do not take. Secondly, we do not agree that all of these scholars were pure *Ash'arees*. The likes of al-Baaqillaani and Ibn Hajr al-Asqalaani were influenced by the *Ash'arees*, but at the same time agreed with the *Ahl as-Sunnah* on some points (in fact, as-Suyootee even criticises the belief that *istawaa* means 'to conquer' (*istawlaa*) in his *al-Itqaan*). Therefore it is not accurate to describe them as being pure *Ash'arees*. Thirdly, these scholars were great scholars in their own fields, but we excuse their mistakes in *'aqeedah*, and say that, due to the environment that they were in, they were not exposed to the proper *'aqeedah* and therefore followed the *'aqeedah* of their scholars and teachers, which happened to be the *Ash'aree 'aqeedah*. We consider them as our scholars, and love and respect them, but do not take from them in those matters in which they disagreed with the *salaf*, for the *salaf* are more beloved to us than those who came after them. Fourthly, these names that you quote may be responded to by quoting other names; names of famous scholars that were on the correct *'aqeedah* during the times of these scholars. In other words, not all the scholars of later generations were *Ash'arees*, for the scholars of the correct *'aqeedah* have always existed and will always exist. The likes of Ibn 'Abd al-Barr (d. 463 A.H.), al-Baghawee (d. 510 A.H.), Ibn Qudaamah (d. 610 A.H.), Ibn Taymiyyah (d. 728 A.H.), adh-Dhahabee (d. 748 A.H.), Ibn al-Qayyim (d. 758 A.H.), Ibn Katheer (d. 774 A.H.) and other scholars before them, during their time, and after them, may be quoted. The point is that all these scholars of later generations are not the criterion; the *Ash'arees* may quote famous names, and the *Ahl as-Sunnah* may quote famous names. Rather, the true criterion are the actual scholars of the *salaf*, and those that follow their *'aqeedah*, and not any other generations besides them! May Allaah guide us and the *Ash'arees* to the correct path!

IV. The Names of the Qur'aan

The Qur'aan has referred to itself by a number of names, including:

1) The *Qur'aan* (Recitation): This name is mentioned seventy-three times; thus it should be no surprise that it is by this name that the Book of Allaah is best known. In one verse, Allaah says,

قُل لَّئِنِ ٱجْتَمَعَتِ ٱلْإِنسُ وَٱلْجِنُّ عَلَىٰٓ أَن يَأْتُواْ بِمِثْلِ هَٰذَا ٱلْقُرْءَانِ
لَا يَأْتُونَ بِمِثْلِهِۦ وَلَوْ كَانَ بَعْضُهُمْ لِبَعْضٍ ظَهِيرًا ﴿٨٨﴾

«Say: 'If all of mankind and *jinn* were to gather together to produce something similar to this Qur'aan, they would not be able to produce it – even if they helped one another'» [17:88]

2) The *Kitaab* (Book): This name has been mentioned seventy-seven times in the Qur'aan. This is the Book that Allaah sent down upon His final Prophet (ﷺ), containing all the guidance that they need.

الٓمٓ ﴿١﴾ ذَٰلِكَ ٱلْكِتَٰبُ لَا رَيْبَ فِيهِ هُدًى
لِّلْمُتَّقِينَ ﴿٢﴾

«*Alif Laam Meem*. This is the Book, there is no doubt in it, a guidance for the pious» [2:1-2]

The names 'Qur'aan' and '*Kitaab*' are complementary to one another, since the 'Qur'aan' denotes that which is recited and preserved in the hearts, whereas the '*Kitaab*' signifies the preservation by writing. The Qur'aan, therefore, has been preserved both by memorisation and by writing.[103]

3) The *Furqaan* (Criterion): Allaah has used this name four times in reference to the Qur'aan. The Qur'aan is the Criterion between *tawheed* and *shirk*, truth and falsehood, and good and evil. Allaah says,

تَبَارَكَ ٱلَّذِي نَزَّلَ ٱلْفُرْقَانَ عَلَىٰ عَبْدِهِۦ لِيَكُونَ لِلْعَٰلَمِينَ نَذِيرًا

«Blessed be He Who sent down the Criterion (*Furqaan*) to His Slave (Muhammad (ﷺ)) so that he may be a warner to mankind» [25:1]

4) The *Dhikr* (Remembrance, or Narrative): This name occurs fifty-five times in the Qur'aan. The '*Dhikr*' signifies that the Qur'aan is a Guidance and a Remembrance of the purpose of life, as it describes the purpose of creation, the history of the past nations, and the descriptions of Heaven and Hell. Allaah says,

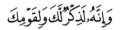

وَإِنَّهُۥ لَذِكْرٌ لَّكَ وَلِقَوْمِكَ

---

103 cf. Daraz, p. 12-13.

«And verily this (Qur'aan) is a Reminder (*Dhikr*) for you and your people»
[43:33]

5) The *Tanzeel* (Revelation): This name, along with all of its derivatives, is used to describe the Qur'aan in over one hundred and forty verses. The root word '*nazala*' signifies the descent of an object from a higher place to a lower place.[104] The Qur'aan, therefore, is a Revelation that was sent down from Allaah to the Prophet (ﷺ). As Allaah says,

«And it is indeed a Revelation from the Lord of the Worlds» [26:192]

This name shows the unique status of the Qur'aan in that it is from Allaah, all Glory be to Him. This name is also one of the many proofs that Allaah, all Glory be to Him, is above His creation, and not everywhere, as some innovated sects claim, as He is the one who 'sent down' the Qur'aan.

There are many other descriptions of the Qur'aan which some scholars have taken as 'names', but it is more appropriate to say that they describe the Qur'aan, and are not 'names' as such. Imaam az-Zarkashee lists over fifty 'names' of the Qur'aan in the Qur'aan, but, as mentioned earlier, these are more descriptive then appellative in nature.[105]

v. The Qur'aan as it Describes Itself

The best and most authentic way to describe the Qur'aan would be to quote what it has to say concerning itself. The number of verses that deal with the Qur'aan are too numerous to mention here,[106] therefore only some of them will be quoted.

The believers are told to rejoice in the revelation that Allaah has sent down,

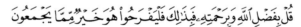

«Say: 'In the Bounty of Allaah and His Mercy, let them rejoice,' this is better than all the (wealth) they can amass» [10:58]

The 'Bounty' and 'Mercy' referred to in this verse have been interpreted by the scholars of *tafseer* to mean Islaam and the Qur'aan.

Some of the verses that describe the Qur'aan are as follows:

---

104 This word is used for three different meanings in the Qur'aan: i) the descent from Allaah to the Prophet (ﷺ), and this is specific to the Qur'aan, ii) the descent from the skies to the earth, such as, "...and We have caused the rain to descend from the sky..." (15:22), iii) the descent of Allaah's mercy and blessings, such as "...and He sent down tranquillity upon them (the believers)..." (48:18). cf. Damishqi, p. 64.

105 cf. az-Zarkashee, v. 1, p. 274-76. Some of these 'names' are quoted in the next section.

106 For one of the best discussions of the names and descriptions of the Qur'aan, see Bulaihi, Ṣaliḥ ibn Ibraaheem: *Al-Huda wa al-Bayan fi Asmaa al-Qur'aan*, [?], 1977, where he lists and discusses over eighty names and descriptions in his book.

$$ يَٰٓأَيُّهَا ٱلنَّاسُ $$

$$ قَدۡ جَآءَكُم بُرۡهَٰنٌ مِّن رَّبِّكُمۡ وَأَنزَلۡنَآ إِلَيۡكُمۡ نُورٗا مُّبِينٗا ۝ $$

«O mankind! Verily, there has come to you a convincing proof from your Lord, and We have sent down to you a Manifest Light» [4:174]

$$ يَٰٓأَيُّهَا ٱلنَّاسُ قَدۡ جَآءَتۡكُم مَّوۡعِظَةٞ $$

$$ مِّن رَّبِّكُمۡ وَشِفَآءٞ لِّمَا فِي ٱلصُّدُورِ وَهُدٗى وَرَحۡمَةٞ لِّلۡمُؤۡمِنِينَ $$

«O mankind! There has come to you a good advice from your Lord, and a healing for the (sicknesses) of the heart – a guidance and mercy for the believers» [10:57]

$$ ٱلۡحَمۡدُ لِلَّهِ ٱلَّذِيٓ أَنزَلَ عَلَىٰ عَبۡدِهِ ٱلۡكِتَٰبَ وَلَمۡ يَجۡعَل لَّهُۥ عِوَجَاۜ ۝ $$

$$ قَيِّمٗا لِّيُنذِرَ بَأۡسٗا شَدِيدٗا مِّن لَّدُنۡهُ وَيُبَشِّرَ ٱلۡمُؤۡمِنِينَ $$

«All Praise and Thanks be to Allaah, Who Has sent down to His slave the Book, and has not placed in it any crookedness (falsehood). (He has made it) Straight to give warning of a severe punishment from Him, and to give glad tidings to the believers...» [18:1-2]

$$ وَنُنَزِّلُ مِنَ ٱلۡقُرۡءَانِ مَا هُوَ شِفَآءٞ وَرَحۡمَةٞ لِّلۡمُؤۡمِنِينَ $$

«And We send down in the Qur'aan that which is a healing and a mercy to those who believe» [17:82]

$$ ٱللَّهُ نَزَّلَ أَحۡسَنَ ٱلۡحَدِيثِ كِتَٰبٗا مُّتَشَٰبِهٗا مَّثَانِيَ $$

«Allaah has sent down the best of statements, a Book, its parts resembling each other in goodness and truth, oft-repeated» [39:23]

$$ إِنَّآ أَنزَلۡنَا عَلَيۡكَ ٱلۡكِتَٰبَ لِلنَّاسِ بِٱلۡحَقِّ فَمَنِ ٱهۡتَدَىٰ $$

$$ فَلِنَفۡسِهِۦ وَمَن ضَلَّ فَإِنَّمَا يَضِلُّ عَلَيۡهَا $$

«Verily, We have sent down to you the Book for mankind in truth. So whoever accepts this guidance, it is only for himself, and whoever goes astray, he strays only for his own loss» [39:41]

$$ وَهَٰذَا ذِكۡرٞ مُّبَارَكٌ أَنزَلۡنَٰهُ أَفَأَنتُمۡ لَهُۥ مُنكِرُونَ ۝ $$

«And this is the Blessed Reminder which We have sent down; will you then (dare to) deny it?» [21:50]

وَكَذَٰلِكَ أَوْحَيْنَآ إِلَيْكَ رُوحًا مِّنْ أَمْرِنَا مَا كُنتَ تَدْرِى مَا ٱلْكِتَـٰبُ
وَلَا ٱلْإِيمَـٰنُ وَلَـٰكِن جَعَلْنَـٰهُ نُورًا نَّهْدِى بِهِۦ مَن نَّشَآءُ

«And thus We have sent down to you an Inspiration from Our Command. You did not know what the Book (Qur'aan) was, nor faith (eemaan), but We made it a light by which We Guide those whom We will» [42:52]

هَـٰذَا بَصَـٰٓئِرُ لِلنَّاسِ وَهُدًى وَرَحْمَةٌ لِّقَوْمٍ يُوقِنُونَ

«This (Qur'aan) is a clear insight and evidence for mankind, and a guidance and a mercy for people who have certain faith» [45:20]

vi. The Sunnah as it Describes the Qur'aan

The importance of the Qur'aan is so great that the Prophet (ﷺ) said, "The best of you are those who learn the Qur'aan and teach it to others."[107] Although this *hadeeth* is most often used in the context of teaching the recitation and memorisation of the Qur'aan, there is no reason not to extend the meaning of this *hadeeth* to include all the sciences of the Qur'aan. After all, of what good is the recitation of the Qur'aan if that recitation is not accompanied by understanding and action?

Again, as with the number of verses about the Qur'aan, there exist numerous *hadeeth* about the merits of the Qur'aan and its reciter. There are many treatises written specifically on this topic, such as the famous one by Imaam an-Nasaa'ee (d. 303 A.H.) entitled '*Fadaa'il al-Qur'aan*', and one by the famous interpreter, Ibn Katheer (d. 778 A.H.), with the same title. Some of these *hadeeth* are as follows:[108]

THE STATUS OF THE QUR'AAN

Jubayr reported that the Prophet (ﷺ) said, "Rejoice! For verily, this Qur'aan – one part of it is in the Hands of Allaah, and the other part is in your hands. Therefore hold on to it, for you will never be destroyed, not will you ever go astray after it!" (Musnad Ahmad).

'Umar reported that the Prophet (ﷺ) said, "Indeed, Allaah will raise (or honour) people (i.e., in this world and the Hereafter) by this Book, and He will debase others by it" (Muslim).

Aboo Maalik al-Ash'aree stated that the Prophet (ﷺ) said, "The Qur'aan is either an evidence (or proof) for you, or against you." (Muslim).

Anas reported that the Prophet (ﷺ) said, "Verily, Allaah has chosen people amongst mankind. The People of the Qur'aan – they are the People of Allaah, and His Chosen

---

107 Reported by al-Bukhaaree.

108 All of these *ahadeeth* have been taken from Muhammad Naasir al-Deen al-Albaanee's *Saheeh al-Jami' al-Sagheer wa Ziyadah*, Maktab al-Islaami, Beirut, 1988, and are graded *saheeh* by him.

ones" (an-Nasaa'ee). The 'People of the Qur'aan' are those who know it and practice it.

Ibn Mas'ood reported that the Prophet (ﷺ) said, "The Qur'aan is an intercessor, and an intercession that is accepted, and a *maahil*,[109] and a credible (book). Whoever puts it ahead of him, it will lead him to Paradise, and whoever throws it behind him, it will drag him into Hell" (at-Tabaraanee).

Nawwaas ibn Sam'aan reported that the Prophet (ﷺ) said, "Allaah has set forth the following as a parable: There is a road which leads straight to the destination. On either side of the road there is a wall in which there are open doors with curtains hanging on them. From the remote end of the road, a voice calls, 'Proceed straight and don't turn to any side!' Whenever someone intends to lift a curtain from the door, another voice calls from above: 'Beware! Don't lift the curtain, otherwise you will be lured inside.' (The Prophet (ﷺ) explained:) The straight path is Islaam; the walls are the limits (*hudood*) of Allaah (which he has placed on actions); the open doors are the things that He has prohibited; the voice which calls from the end of the road is the Qur'aan, and the voice which calls from above is Allaah's monitor in the heart of every believer" (at-Tirmidhee).

Ibn 'Amr reported that the Prophet (ﷺ) said, "The Book of Allaah is the Rope of Allaah which is dangling from the Heavens down to the earth" (Musnad Ahmad).

There is a narration in at-Tirmidhee which is a very eloquent and beautiful description of the Qur'aan; however, it is not an authentic statement of the Prophet (ﷺ), as has been pointed out by at-Tirmidhee himself.[110] Most likely, it is a statement of 'Alee ibn Abee Taalib,[111] and is as follows: "The Book of Allaah – it has the tidings of those before you, and the news of those after you; it is the Judge between you; it is the Criterion; it cannot be taken lightly. Whoever abandons it due to arrogance will be destroyed by Allaah, and whoever seeks guidance by other than it will be misled by Allaah. It is Allaah's strong rope; it is the Wise Remembrance; it is the Straight Path. It is not strayed by (one's) desires, nor are the tongues confused by it. Its wonders never cease, and the scholars never satisfy themselves of it. Whoever speaks with it has spoken the truth; whoever works upon it will be rewarded; whoever judges according to it will be just; and whoever calls to it will be guided to the Straight Path."

THE REWARDS FOR THOSE WHO RECITE AND PRACTICE THE QUR'AAN

Aboo Moosaa al-Ash'aree reported that the Prophet (ﷺ) said, "Part of showing glory to Allaah is to show respect to a white-haired Muslim, and a carrier of the Qur'aan who does not exaggerate in it (i.e., overstep its bounds) nor ignore it (i.e., leave it), and a just ruler" (Aboo Daawood).

---

109 A *maahil* is one who is persistent in his intercession, and goes to all extremes to save a person. cf. *an-Nihaayah*, v. 4, p. 303.

110 cf. *Daeef at-Tirmidhee*, p. 349

111 See al-Albaanee's comments on it in *Sharh Aqeedah at-Tahaawiyyah*, p. 71

'Aa'ishah reported that the Prophet (ﷺ) said, "The person who reads the Qur'aan fluently is with the honourable and obedient scribes (i.e., the angels), and he who reads it with difficulty, (even) he shall get (at least) a double reward" (Aboo Daawood).

Ibn Mas'ood reported that the Prophet (ﷺ) said, "Whoever wishes to love Allaah and His Messenger, let him read the *mus-haf*" (Ibn Nu'aym in his <u>Hilya</u>).

Ibn 'Amr reported that the Prophet (ﷺ) said, "There is no cause to be envious except in two cases: (the first is of a) person whom Allaah has taught the Qur'aan, and he recites it in the day and night, and one of his neighbours hears him and says, 'Woe to me! I wish I had been given what he has been given, then I would do what he is doing!' (The second is of a) person whom Allaah has blessed with wealth, and he spends it in good causes, so a person (who sees him) says, 'Woe to me! I wish I had been given what he has been given, then I would do what he is doing!'" (al-Bukhaaree)

Aboo Hurayrah reported that the Prophet (ﷺ) said, "The Qur'aan will be brought on the Day of Judgement, and it will say, 'O My Lord! Adorn him (the one who read and practised it)!' So he will be adorned with a crown of glory and honour. It will then say, 'O My Lord! Increase this!' So he will be clothed with the clothes of glory and honour. Then it will say, 'O My Lord! Be pleased with Him!' So He (Allaah) will be pleased with him. It will be said, 'Recite! And rise!' and every verse he recites will bless him with a good deed" (at-Tirmidhee).

Ibn 'Amr reported that the Prophet (ﷺ) said, "It will be said to the companion of the Qur'aan after he has entered Paradise, 'Recite, and rise!' For every verse he recites, he will rise one level (in Paradise), until he recites the last verse with him (i.e., in his memory)." (Aboo Daawood).

Ibn Mas'ood reported that the Prophet (ﷺ) said, "Recite the Qur'aan, for verily you will be rewarded for it. I am not saying that *Alif-Laam-Meem* will count as a word, but rather that *Alif* has ten (rewards), *Laam* has ten (rewards), and *Meem* has ten (rewards), so this is thirty (rewards)." (Khateeb al-Baghdaadee).

'Ismah ibn Maalik reported that the Prophet (ﷺ) said, "If the Qur'aan is enclosed by skin (i.e., if a person memorises the entire Qur'aan),[112] then Allaah will never burn it in the Fire (of Hell)" (al-Bayhaqee).

Aboo Hurayrah reported that the Prophet (ﷺ) said, "Never do a group of people gather together in one of the houses of Allaah, reciting the book of Allaah and pondering over it, except that peace descends upon them, and mercy surrounds them, and the angels encircle them, and Allaah remembers them in His gathering" (Aboo Daawood).

---

112 This is one of the two interpretations that classical scholars have given to this *hadeeth* (cf. *an-Nihaayah*; *Majma' Bihaar al-Anwaar*, v. 1, p. 136). This author also asked a number of scholars concerning this *hadeeth*, and they stated that this interpretation is an acceptable understanding of the *hadeeth*. The other interpretation of the *hadeeth* is that if the *mus-haf* was wrapped in a leather skin during the lifetime of the Prophet (ﷺ), then thrown in a fire, it would not be burnt, so the *hadeeth* is an indication of one of the miracles of the Qur'aan. There is no contradiction if both of these meanings are understood from this *hadeeth*, and Allaah knows best.

Aboo Moosaa al-Asha'aree reported that the Prophet (ﷺ) said, "The believer who recites the Qur'aan is like a citrus fruit – its fragrance is pleasing and its taste is sweet. The believer who does not recite the Qur'aan is like a dry date – it has no fragrance but its taste is sweet. The hypocrite who recites the Qur'aan is like a basil – its fragrance is sweet, but its taste is bitter. The hypocrite who does not recite the Qur'aan is like a colocynth – it has no smell, and its taste is bitter" (Muslim).

CHAPTER 3

INSPIRATION — AL-WAHY

I. The Concept of Wahy

Since the creation of mankind, Allaah has communicated with them by choosing some of them as prophets and messengers, and inspiring them with His message, to guide mankind from the darkness of *shirk* to the light of Islaam, and from the immorality of their desires to the purity of worship. Allaah said when He sent Aadam down to Earth,

فَإِمَّا يَأْتِيَنَّكُم مِّنِّي هُدًى فَمَن تَبِعَ
هُدَايَ فَلَا خَوْفٌ عَلَيْهِمْ وَلَا هُمْ يَحْزَنُونَ ﴿٣٨﴾

«...then whenever there comes to you (mankind) Guidance from Me – and whoever follows My Guidance, there shall be no fear on them, nor shall they grieve» [2:38]

In another verse, He stated,

يَٰبَنِيٓ ءَادَمَ إِمَّا يَأْتِيَنَّكُمْ رُسُلٌ مِّنكُمْ يَقُصُّونَ عَلَيْكُمْ ءَايَٰتِي فَمَنِ
ٱتَّقَىٰ وَأَصْلَحَ فَلَا خَوْفٌ عَلَيْهِمْ وَلَا هُمْ يَحْزَنُونَ ﴿٣٥﴾

«O Children of Aadam! If there comes to you messengers from amongst you reciting to you My verses, then whosoever becomes pious and righteous, on them shall be no fear, nor shall they grieve» [7:35]

In fulfilment of these promises of messengers, Allaah says in the Qur'aan,

۞ إِنَّآ أَوْحَيْنَآ إِلَيْكَ كَمَآ أَوْحَيْنَآ إِلَىٰ نُوحٍ وَٱلنَّبِيِّـۧنَ مِنۢ بَعْدِهِۦ
وَأَوْحَيْنَآ إِلَىٰٓ إِبْرَٰهِيمَ وَإِسْمَٰعِيلَ وَإِسْحَٰقَ وَيَعْقُوبَ
وَٱلْأَسْبَاطِ وَعِيسَىٰ وَأَيُّوبَ وَيُونُسَ وَهَٰرُونَ وَسُلَيْمَٰنَ
وَءَاتَيْنَا دَاوُۥدَ زَبُورًا ﴿١٦٣﴾ وَرُسُلًا قَدْ قَصَصْنَٰهُمْ عَلَيْكَ
مِن قَبْلُ وَرُسُلًا لَّمْ نَقْصُصْهُمْ عَلَيْكَ وَكَلَّمَ ٱللَّهُ مُوسَىٰ
تَكْلِيمًا ﴿١٦٤﴾ رُّسُلًا مُّبَشِّرِينَ وَمُنذِرِينَ لِئَلَّا يَكُونَ
لِلنَّاسِ عَلَى ٱللَّهِ حُجَّةٌۢ بَعْدَ ٱلرُّسُلِ وَكَانَ ٱللَّهُ عَزِيزًا حَكِيمًا

«Verily We have inspired you (O Muhammad) as We inspired Nooh and the prophets after him; And We inspired Ibraaheem, and Ismaa'eel, and Ishaaq, and Ya'qoob and the Tribes (of the Children of Israa'eel), and 'Eesaa, and Ayyoob, and Yoonus, and Haaroon and Sulaymaan, and to Daawood We gave the Psalms (*Zaboor*). And there are messengers whom We have mentioned to you before, and messengers whom we have not told you about – and to Moosaa, Allaah spoke directly. Messengers (who came) as bearers of good news, and as givers of warning, in order that mankind should have no plea against Allaah after the messengers. And Allaah is Ever-Powerful, All-Wise» [4:163-65]

In fact, this inspiration of Allaah to His prophets has been so common, that when the disbelievers of Makkah were amazed at the prophethood of Muhammad (ﷺ), Allaah revealed,

أَكَانَ لِلنَّاسِ عَجَبًا أَنْ أَوْحَيْنَآ إِلَىٰ رَجُلٍ مِّنْهُمْ

«Is it a cause of wonder for mankind that We have sent Our inspiration to a man from among themselves...» [10:2]

This has been the only way that Allaah has communicated with mankind as a whole: that of inspiring one of their own with the message of truth.

The final recipient of any revelation from Allaah, and the last of the prophets that was ever to be inspired by Allaah, was Muhammad, the son of 'Abdullaah, the Arab, the Qurashee, (ﷺ). When he (ﷺ) was called by his Lord to return to his eternal resting place, his servant Umm Ayman was found crying. She was told, "Do not grieve; Verily he (ﷺ) is now in a better place than where he used to be." She responded, "(I am not crying because of his death, for) indeed I know that what he (ﷺ) has received from his Lord is better for him (than this life). I am crying because now Allaah has stopped His revelation to mankind!" When she said this, Aboo Bakr and 'Umar started weeping with her.[113]

II. The Meaning of Wahy

'*Wahy*' means to inspire, or to communicate in a manner that is not obvious or apparent to anybody else, in a swift manner. The word '*wahy*' in its linguistic meaning has been used in a number of places in the Qur'aan to denote the following:

1) The natural order and laws of nature. For example, Allaah says,

فَقَضَىٰهُنَّ سَبْعَ سَمَٰوَاتٍ فِى يَوْمَيْنِ وَأَوْحَىٰ فِى كُلِّ سَمَآءٍ أَمْرَهَا

«Then He completed and finished their creation (as) seven heavens, and He inspired in each heaven its affair» [41:12]

This can be considered as the natural laws of nature, such as the orbits of the planets and the rotation of the earth, etc.

---

113 Reported by Muslim.

2) Natural animal instinct. For example, Allaah says,

$$وَأَوْحَىٰ رَبُّكَ إِلَى ٱلنَّحْلِ$$
$$أَنِ ٱتَّخِذِى مِنَ ٱلْجِبَالِ بُيُوتًا وَمِنَ ٱلشَّجَرِ وَمِمَّا يَعْرِشُونَ ۝ ثُمَّ كُلِى$$
$$مِن كُلِّ ٱلثَّمَرَٰتِ فَٱسْلُكِى سُبُلَ رَبِّكِ$$

«And your Lord inspired the bee, saying, Take as habitations mountains, and in the tree and in what (mankind) builds. Then, eat of all fruits, and follow the ways of your Lord...» [16:68-69]

This signifies the natural animal instinct that every creature is endowed with; bees, for example, instinctively build their hives and search for nectar from flowers.

3) Human intuition and emotion. This type is also called *ilhaam*. Allaah said,

$$وَأَوْحَيْنَا إِلَىٰ أُمِّ مُوسَىٰٓ$$
$$أَنْ أَرْضِعِيهِ فَإِذَا خِفْتِ عَلَيْهِ فَأَلْقِيهِ فِى ٱلْيَمِّ وَلَا تَخَافِى$$
$$وَلَا تَحْزَنِىٓ$$

«And we inspired the mother of Moosaa, 'Suckle him! But when you fear for him, then cast him into the river and fear not, nor grieve'» [28:7]

In this case, the mother of Moosaa knew that if she were to leave her baby to float on the river, Allaah would protect him, since she had received this *ilhaam* from Allaah. This type of inspiration, however, does not make its recipient a prophet.

4) Signals or gestures to communicate. When Allaah forbade Zakariyyah from speaking for three days,

$$فَخَرَجَ عَلَىٰ قَوْمِهِۦ$$
$$مِنَ ٱلْمِحْرَابِ فَأَوْحَىٰٓ إِلَيْهِمْ أَن سَبِّحُوا بُكْرَةً وَعَشِيًّا ۝$$

«...he came out unto his people, and inspired them (by gestures and signs) to glorify Allaah's praises in the morning and afternoon» [19:11]

In this verse, the gestures that Zakariyyah did to his people have been called an 'inspiration' since he did not verbalise his intent.

5) Evil whispers from Satan. Allaah says,

$$وَإِنَّ ٱلشَّيَٰطِينَ لَيُوحُونَ إِلَىٰٓ أَوْلِيَآئِهِمْ لِيُجَٰدِلُوكُمْ$$

«...and of a certainty the devils inspire their cohorts (amongst mankind) to dispute with you...» [6:121]

and again,

$$وَكَذَٰلِكَ جَعَلْنَا لِكُلِّ نَبِيٍّ عَدُوًّا$$

$$شَيَاطِينَ ٱلْإِنسِ وَٱلْجِنِّ يُوحِى بَعْضُهُمْ إِلَىٰ بَعْضٍ$$

«And thus We have appointed for every prophet an enemy – devils among mankind and *jinns*, inspiring one another...» [6:112]

We are also told to seek refuge in Allaah from the Satans who,

$$ٱلَّذِى يُوَسْوِسُ فِى صُدُورِ ٱلنَّاسِ ۝$$

«...whisper in the breast of men» [114:5]

6)   Guidance to the angels from Allaah. Allaah says,

$$إِذْ يُوحِى رَبُّكَ إِلَى ٱلْمَلَٰٓئِكَةِ أَنِّى مَعَكُمْ فَثَبِّتُوا۟ ٱلَّذِينَ ءَامَنُوٓا۟$$

«(Remember) when your Lord inspired the angels, 'I am with you, so keep firm those who have believed'»...[8:12]

7)   The inspiration to the prophets. This category is the subject of discussion of this chapter, and is the meaning of the word '*wahy*' when used in the context of Islaamic sciences.

The primary verse that discusses the types and categories of *wahy* is Allaah's statement:

$$وَمَا كَانَ$$

$$لِبَشَرٍ أَن يُكَلِّمَهُ ٱللَّهُ إِلَّا وَحْيًا أَوْ مِن وَرَآئِ حِجَابٍ أَوْ يُرْسِلَ$$

$$رَسُولًا فَيُوحِىَ بِإِذْنِهِ مَا يَشَآءُ إِنَّهُۥ عَلِىٌّ حَكِيمٌ ۝$$

«It is not possible for any human being that Allaah should speak to him unless it be by Inspiration, or from behind a veil, or (that) He sends a Messenger to reveal what He wills by His Permission. Verily, He is the Most High, Most Wise» [42:51]

These categories shall be the topic of discussion of the next section.

III. The Procedure of Wahy

Wahy can occur in two ways: without an intermediary, and with an intermediary.

A. WITHOUT AN INTERMEDIARY

In this case, Allaah reveals His message directly to His servant. This can occur in two forms:

1) By way of dreams.

This is the first type of inspiration that the Prophet (ﷺ) received. 'Aa'ishah reports, "The commencement of the divine inspiration upon the Prophet (ﷺ) was in the form of good dreams; he never used to dream about anything except that it came true like the rising of the sun."[114] In other words, before the Prophet (ﷺ) received his mission of prophethood, he (ﷺ) would see dreams of events which would eventually come true, just like the sun rises every morning.

The dreams of all the prophets are an inspiration from Allaah. In these dreams, the prophets are either shown some event of the future, or given commandments by Allaah. This is proven by the dream in which Ibraaheem saw himself sacrificing his son Ismaa'eel. Ibraaheem understood that this dream was a command from Allaah, directing him to sacrifice his son.

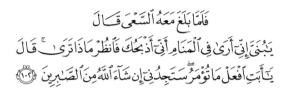

«And when he (Ismaa'eel) was old enough to walk with him, he said, O my son! I have seen in a dream that I am slaughtering you, so what do you think?' (Ismaa'eel) said, 'O my father, do what you have been commanded! Verily, you will find me, *inshaa Allaah*, from amongst the patient'» [37:102]

Ibraaheem understood that this was a command from Allaah, as did Ismaa'eel, even though it was in the form of a dream.

Another example of this is the Treaty of Ḥudaybiyah. The Prophet (ﷺ) had been shown a vision in which the Muslims were performing the rites of 'Umrah, and the Companions set out with the Prophet (ﷺ) from Madeenah to Makkah hoping to perform the 'Umrah. The pagans of Makkah, however, did not allow the Muslims to enter Makkah, and a treaty was enacted between the Muslims and the pagans, later to be known as the Treaty of Ḥudaybiyah. One of the conditions of the treaty was that, in the following year, the Muslims would return and complete the rites of 'Umrah. As the Muslims returned sad-heartened to Madeenah, Allaah revealed,

$$لَّقَدْ صَدَقَ ٱللَّهُ رَسُولَهُ ٱلرُّءْيَا بِٱلْحَقِّ لَتَدْخُلُنَّ ٱلْمَسْجِدَ ٱلْحَرَامَ إِن شَآءَ ٱللَّهُ ءَامِنِينَ مُحَلِّقِينَ رُءُوسَكُمْ وَمُقَصِّرِينَ لَا تَخَافُونَ$$

«Indeed, of a surety shall Allaah fulfil the dream which He showed His Messenger; you shall enter the *Masjid al-Ḥaraam*, if Allaah wills, secure, with your heads shaved or trimmed (after performing the rites of pilgrimage), fearing none» [48:27]

---

114 Reported by al-Bukhaaree.

The following year, the Muslims performed the 'Umrah as per the terms of the agreement. The dream that the Prophet (ﷺ) had seen eventually came true.

The Prophet (ﷺ) never received any Qur'aan in this manner,[115] but he did say, "Nothing is left of prophethood except 'mubashiraat' (glad tidings)." When he was asked what this was, he replied, "A true dream."[116] In other words, the only type of inspiration that is left after the death of the Prophet (ﷺ) is in the form of true dreams to a believer. In another narration, he (ﷺ) said, "A true and pious dream is one out of forty-six parts of prophethood."[117]

2) Direct speech from Allaah.

This is the second way in which Allaah communicates to the prophets directly. This is the meaning of the verse,

$$\text{وَمَا كَانَ لِبَشَرٍ أَن يُكَلِّمَهُ ٱللَّهُ إِلَّا وَحْيًا أَوْ مِن وَرَآئِ حِجَابٍ}$$

«It is not possible for any human being that Allaah should speak to him unless it be... from behind a veil...» [42:51]

Allaah speaks directly to the prophet, but the prophet does not see him.

An example of this was when Allaah spoke to Moosaa on Mount Ṭoor,:

$$\text{وَلَمَّا جَآءَ مُوسَىٰ لِمِيقَٰتِنَا وَكَلَّمَهُۥ رَبُّهُۥ قَالَ رَبِّ أَرِنِىٓ أَنظُرْ إِلَيْكَ قَالَ لَن تَرَىٰنِى}$$

«And when Moosaa came at the time and place appointed by Us, and his Lord spoke to him, (Moosaa) said, 'O My Lord! Allow me to look at you!' (Allaah) said, 'You will not see Me...'» [7:143]

This method of *wahy* occurred once with the Prophet (ﷺ), when he went on his journey of *al-Israa wa al-Mi'raaj*.[118] The Prophet (ﷺ) did not see Allaah, since there was a veil of light between them. Aboo Dharr asked the Prophet (ﷺ), "Did you see your Lord (on the journey of *al-Israa*)?" The Prophet (ﷺ) replied, "Light – how could I see Him?"[119] meaning that there was a veil of Light that was between the

---

115 Although some researchers claim that the Prophet (ﷺ) did receive some Qur'aan in this manner, the evidence that they use is not explicit. The particular narration is on the authority of Anas ibn Maalik, who stated that once the Prophet (ﷺ) was sitting amongst them, when he dozed off. He then raised his head and smiled. They asked him, "What makes you smile, O Messenger of Allaah (ﷺ)?" He replied, "A *soorah* has just been revealed to me..." (Reported by Muslim). This is not explicit evidence since the narration does not mention that the revelation occurred *during* the Prophet's (ﷺ) sleep. It is possible that the inspiration could have occurred before the Prophet (ﷺ) dozed off. It is also possible that the Prophet (ﷺ) was not actually asleep, but the Companions presumed him to be so. Therefore, it is not possible to use this narration as evidence against other stronger and clearer proofs to the contrary.

116 Reported by al-Bukhaaree.

117 Reported by al-Daarimee from al-Nawwaas ibn Sama'aan. Some commentators have explained the fraction as being the time that the Prophet (ﷺ) received true dreams before his prophethood (six months) over the total time of his prophethood (23 years); hence one out of forty-six, and Allaah know best.

118 The journey which occurred during the late Makkan stage of the Prophet (ﷺ), in which he (ﷺ) was taken from Makkah to Jerusalem, and then to the Heavens.

119 Reported by Muslim.

Prophet (ﷺ) and Allaah. In fact, seeing Allaah before the Day of Judgement is not possible for any human.[120]

Some scholars claim that the last two verses of *Soorah* al-Baqarah were revealed in this manner (i.e., the Prophet (ﷺ) received them from Allaah, without an intermediary, during the night of *al-Israa wa al-Mi'raaj*). However, there is no authentic, explicit proof for this opinion, therefore, it cannot be accepted.

B. WITH AN INTERMEDIARY

This is the primary and most common method of inspiration. This method of *wahy* is when Allaah sends an angel to inspire His Messenger. This is the meaning of the phrase,

وَمَا كَانَ لِبَشَرٍ أَن يُكَلِّمَهُ ٱللَّهُ إِلَّا وَحْيًا أَوْ مِن وَرَآئِ حِجَابٍ أَوْ يُرْسِلَ رَسُولًا فَيُوحِيَ بِإِذْنِهِ مَا يَشَآءُ إِنَّهُ عَلِيٌّ حَكِيمٌ ﴿٥١﴾

«It is not possible for any human being that Allaah should speak to him unless... He sends a messenger, so He inspires him with what He wills...» [42:5]

This messenger was sometimes seen by the Prophet (ﷺ) and sometimes hidden. The messenger whom Allaah chose to communicate with His prophets was the Angel Jibreel. Allaah says,

مَن كَانَ عَدُوًّا لِّجِبْرِيلَ فَإِنَّهُ نَزَّلَهُ عَلَىٰ قَلْبِكَ بِإِذْنِ ٱللَّهِ

«Whoever is an enemy to Jibreel (let him perish), for indeed he has brought this (Qur'aan) down to your heart, by Allaah's permission» [2:97]

In another verse,

وَإِنَّهُ لَتَنزِيلُ رَبِّ ٱلْعَالَمِينَ ﴿١٩٢﴾ نَزَلَ بِهِ ٱلرُّوحُ ٱلْأَمِينُ ﴿١٩٣﴾ عَلَىٰ قَلْبِكَ لِتَكُونَ مِنَ ٱلْمُنذِرِينَ ﴿١٩٤﴾

"And truly this (the Qur'aan) is a Revelation from the Lord of the Worlds; which the Trustworthy Spirit (Jibreel) brought down; Upon your heart (O Muhammad) that you may be among the warners» [26:192-194]

When the Prophet (ﷺ) saw Jibreel for the first time, his wife Khadeejah took him to her uncle, Waraqah ibn Nawfal, who had converted to Christianity, and was knowledgeable of the Torah and Injeel. After the Prophet (ﷺ) informed him of what he had

---

120 For the proofs of this, see *Sharh 'Aqeedah at-Tahawiyyah*, p. 196-7.

seen, Waraqah told him, "This (angel) is the same one, the *Naamoos* (Keeper of Secrets), whom Allaah sent to Moosaa!"[121]

When discussing this concept of *wahy*, it is essential to discuss two types of inspirations: firstly, how Allaah inspires Jibreel with the Qur'aan, and, secondly, how Jibreel inspired the prophets, and specifically the Prophet Muhammad (ﷺ).

The Revelation of the Qur'aan to the Angels

In the last chapter, the Qur'aan as the *kalaam* of Allaah was discussed, and the fact that Allaah spoke the Qur'aan in a manner that is befitting Him, not similar or comparable to the speech of humans, was proven. It was also discussed that the *kalaam* of Allaah can be heard, contrary to the beliefs of some of the innovated sects. Therefore, the belief of the *Ahl as-Sunnah wa al-Jamaa'ah* is that Jibreel heard the Qur'aan directly from Allaah, as the *kalaam* of Allaah.

The Prophet (ﷺ) said, "Whenever Allaah desires to inspire a matter (to His servants), He speaks with the inspiration, and (because of this) the heavens themselves shake out of fear of Allaah. When the people of the Heaven (i.e., the angels) hear of it, they fall down in a swoon and prostrate to Him. The first one to raise his head is Jibreel, and Allaah speaks to him with the inspiration that He wishes. Then Jibreel passes by the angels; whenever he goes by any heaven, the angels of that heaven ask him, 'What did our Lord say, O Jibreel?' He answers, 'He has Spoken the Truth, and He is the Most High, the Most Great.'"[122] This *hadeeth* is explicit in that "...Allaah speaks to him with the inspiration."

Apart from the proofs from the Qur'aan and *Sunnah* that were quoted above (in the section concerning the *kalaam* of Allaah), there exist narrations from such scholars as Imaam ash-Shaafi'ee (d. 204 A.H.), Imaam Maalik (d. 179 A.H.), and al-Bukhaaree (d. 256 A.H.) concerning this point.[123] Imaam Ahmad (d. 241 A.H.) was also very explicit on this point, for he said, "Jibreel heard the Qur'aan from Allaah, and the Prophet (ﷺ) heard the Qur'aan from Jibreel, and the Companions of the Prophet (ﷺ) heard the Qur'aan from the Prophet (ﷺ). Therefore, the Qur'aan is uncreated."[124]

Imaam al-Bayhaqee (d. 458 A.H.), said in explaining the verse,

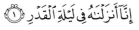

«Verily, We have revealed it in the Night of Decree» [97:1]

---

121 Reported in al-Bukhaaree.

122 Reported by al-Bukhaaree, Ibn Khuzaymah, at-Tabaraani, and others. This *hadeeth* is in reference to the verse, "Until, when fear is removed from their (the angel's) hearts, they say, 'What did your Lord say?' They answer, 'The truth, and He is the Most High, the Most Great'" [34:23].

123 cf. Bulaihi, pps. 139-147, where he quotes over a dozen scholars on this one issue.

124 Reported by al-Khallaal, # 1779.

This verse means – and Allaah knows best – 'We made our angels hear it and understand it, and revealed with him what he heard, and so the angel descended with the revelation from a higher place (the skies) to a lower one (the earth).'[125]

However, some scholars claimed that Jibreel took the Qur'aan from the *Lauh al-Mahfoodh* (The Protected Tablet).[126] Those who follow this opinion use the verses in the Qur'aan that allude to the *Lauh al-Mahfoodh* (which will be discussed in the next chapter). These evidences, however, do not explicitly mention that Jibreel took the Qur'aan from the *Lauh al-Mahfoodh*. Other scholars, primary those of the *Ash'arees*, claimed that Jibreel was inspired the meaning of the Qur'aan, but the wording is either from Jibreel or Muhammad (ﷺ). This opinion is rejected outright, for its adherents deny what Allaah has affirmed for Himself, namely that the Qur'aan is His *kalaam* that He Spoke in a manner and way that befits Him. To say that the wording of the Qur'aan is from Jibreel or Muhammad (ﷺ) denies the whole concept of the *kalaam* of Allaah, and of the miraculous nature of the Qur'aan. In fact, this type of inspiration is for the *Sunnah* of the Prophet (ﷺ) only, and not for the Qur'aan, as shall be explained shortly.

The Revelation of the Qur'aan to the Prophet (ﷺ) from Jibreel

After Jibreel heard the Qur'aan from Allaah, he communicated this to the Prophet (ﷺ). This occurred in one of two ways.

1) The revelation came to the Prophet (ﷺ) in a very severe manner, like the ringing of a bell. This was the hardest for the Prophet (ﷺ), and it is reported that he used to break into a sweat, even on very cold nights, when he was being inspired. After this state passed, the Prophet (ﷺ) remembered what was inspired to him. As the Qur'aan says,

$$ إِنَّا سَنُلْقِى عَلَيْكَ قَوْلًا ثَقِيلًا $$

«Verily We shall send down to you a heavy speech» [73:5]

2) Jibreel took on the form of a man and came to the Prophet (ﷺ). This type of inspiration was easier for the Prophet (ﷺ).

The proof for these two methods is found in the *hadeeth* of 'Aa'ishah, in which she stated that Haarith ibn Hishaam asked the Prophet (ﷺ), "O Allaah's Messenger! How is the divine message revealed to you?" He (ﷺ) responded, "Sometimes it comes to me like the ringing of a bell. This form is the hardest on me, and this state passes off after I have grasped what is inspired. Sometimes the angel comes to me in the form of a man and talks to me, and I grasp what he says."[127]

---

125 Damishqi, p. 62
126 See Ch. 4, under 'The Stages of Revelation', for a more detailed discussion of the *Lauh al-Mahfoodh*.
127 Narrated by al-Bukhaaree

Therefore, in the first case, the angel would remain in its angelic form, and the state of the Prophet (ﷺ) would change so that he (ﷺ) could communicate with the angel, and this state was difficult for him. In the second case, the angel would change from his angelic being to a human form, and communicate with the Prophet (ﷺ). Since the Prophet (ﷺ) remained as he was, this type of inspiration was easier for him.[128] However, in both cases, the Prophet (ﷺ) explained that he clearly understood the inspiration, for he (ﷺ) said after explaining each of the two types of inspiration, "...and I grasp what he says."

In the beginning of his prophethood, the Prophet (ﷺ) was fearful of forgetting the verses that Jibreel recited to him, so he (ﷺ) used to quickly repeat after Jibreel, even before Jibreel had finished his recitation. At this, Allaah revealed,

«Do not move your tongue with haste concerning (the Qur'aan); it is for Us to collect it and Recite it. After we have recited it to you, then follow its recital» [75:16-18]

The Prophet (ﷺ) was assured that he would not forget the Qur'aan, so there was no need for him to hasten in repeating after the angel:

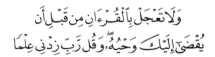

«And do not be in haste (in taking) the Qur'aan (from the angel) before its inspiration is completed to you, and say, 'My Lord! Increase my knowledge!'» [20:114]

There are no reported incidents where Jibreel came in the form of a man and inspired the Prophet (ﷺ) in front of the Companions or any other bystanders. Although the Companions saw Jibreel on a number of occasions in the form of a man, he never inspired the Prophet (ﷺ) with the Qur'aan on these occasions. Thus it may be surmised that when Jibreel came to the Prophet (ﷺ) in this form, with the *wahy*, only the Prophet (ﷺ) could see him.

Jibreel also came to the Prophet (ﷺ) in his natural form, without taking on a different shape. This occurred three times; once in the Cave of Hiraa' when the first revelation came down, once shortly afterwards (probably the second or third revelation) and once on the Night of *al-Israa wa al-Mi'raaj*.[129] The Prophet (ﷺ) reported

---

128 cf. Qattaan, p. 39. The scholar Ibn Khaldoon (d. 808 A.H.) is also quoted on this point of communication. However, it should be kept in mind that the exact nature of this communication will never be known to mankind, and as such the investigation into, and commentary on, this subject should be kept limited.

129 Cf. Ubaydaat, p. 34-36. Some scholars claim that the Prophet (ﷺ) saw Jibreel in his natural form only twice, and this is based on an authentic report.

that Jibreel had six hundred wings, and that Jibreel was so large that he reached the heavens in height.[130]

It might be asked: Was Jibreel the only angel that the Prophet (ﷺ) communicated with? The answer is that the Prophet (ﷺ) communicated with a number of different angels, but the only angel whose name is mentioned with regards to the revelation of the Qur'aan is Jibreel. For example, Ibn 'Abbaas reports that once Jibreel was sitting with the Prophet (ﷺ), when they heard a sound from above. Jibreel said, "This is (the sound of) a door from the skies, it has never opened until today." An angel came down to them, and Jibreel said, "This angel has come down to the earth, it has never come down before today." The angel gave his *salaams* to them, and said to the Prophet (ﷺ), "I give you glad tidings of two lights that you have been given, which have not been given to any prophet before you: The Opening of the Book (i.e., *Soorah* al-Faatihah), and the last verses of *Soorah* al-Baqarah, you shall not read any word in it except that you will be granted it."[131] Also, there are narrations in which the Prophet (ﷺ) informed the Companions that the angels had whispered in his heart certain statements. Therefore, although Jibreel was not the only angel whom the Prophet (ﷺ) communicated with, to the best of our knowledge he is the only angel that came with the Qur'aan. This agrees with the description that is given of the Qur'aan,

$$ وَإِنَّهُۥ لَتَنزِيلُ رَبِّ ٱلْعَٰلَمِينَ ﴿١٩٢﴾ نَزَلَ بِهِ ٱلرُّوحُ ٱلْأَمِينُ ﴿١٩٣﴾ $$

«And this (Qur'aan) is a Revelation from the Lord of the world; which the trustworthy Angel (Jibreel) has brought down» [26:192-193]

In other words, Jibreel brought down all of the Qur'aan.

The effect that the revelation process had on the Prophet (ﷺ) has been recorded in a number of *hadeeth*. 'Aa'ishah narrates, "Sometimes the revelations would descend upon the Prophet (ﷺ) on a very cold morning, and his forehead would glisten with sweat."[132]

'Ubaadah ibn as-Saamit reported that whenever the *wahy* descended upon the Prophet (ﷺ), the significance and importance that he gave (to the inspiration) could be seen, and his face became slightly pale. Also, the Prophet (ﷺ) would lower his head during the inspiration process, and the Companions, due to their love for the Prophet (ﷺ), would also lower their heads, until the revelation had ended.[133]

The Companions were eager to witness the revelation upon the Prophet (ﷺ). It was only natural that they would be so curious about witnessing such a rare phenomenon. Safwaan ibn Ya'la ibn Umayyah reported that his father, Ya'la ibn Umayyah used to say (during the Prophet's (ﷺ) lifetime), "How I wish I could see the Prophet (ﷺ) while the *wahy* comes down to him!" So, one day, the Prophet (ﷺ) was at (a

---

130 cf. Ashqar, *'Aalim al-Malaa'ikah*, p. 11.
131 Reported by Muslim.
132 Reported by Muslim.
133 Reported by Muslim.

place called) Ji'raanah, when a person came to him and said, "O Messenger of Allaah! What is the ruling for one who enters into the state of *ihraam*[134] while his clothes are soaked in perfume?" So the Prophet (ﷺ) waited for a while, until the inspiration came to him. 'Umar ibn al-Khattaab motioned to Ya'la, "Come quickly!" so Ya'la came and stuck his head into the Prophet's (ﷺ) tent to see him! He saw the Prophet (ﷺ), his face was red (due to the inspiration), and he stayed like that for some time, then it was lifted off from him, and he called the questioner and said, "As for the perfume on you body, then wash yourself three times, and as for your clothes, then replace them (with non-scented ones)..."[135] This narration shows the extreme desire that the Companions had to see the Prophet (ﷺ) during this state, and also demonstrates the difficulty of the revelation process on the Prophet (ﷺ).

To summarise the various types of inspiration, it is appropriate to quote Ibn al-Qayyim's (d. 758 A.H.) classification of the types of *wahy*: [136]

1) True dreams, such as those experienced by the Prophet (ﷺ) before his prophethood.

2) The inspiration that used to be whispered into the Prophet's (ﷺ) heart by the angels, such as his (ﷺ) statement, "Verily, the Holy Spirit has whispered in my heart that a person will never die until his (preordained) time comes..."[137]

3) The angel used to come to him in the form of a human and speak with him.

4) The inspiration used to come to him like the ringing of a bell.

5) He (ﷺ) used to see the angel in the original form that the angel was created in.

6) What Allaah inspired in him (ﷺ) directly, when he was above the seven skies in his journey of *al-Israa wa al-Mi'raaj*.

7) What Allaah Spoke to him directly, just like He spoke to Moosaa, and this also occurred in his (ﷺ) journey of *al-Israa wa al-Mi'raaj*.

The revelation of the Qur'aan occurred by the third, fourth and fifth methods only.

IV. The Difference Between the Qur'aan and Hadeeth Qudsee

A *hadeeth Qudsee* is a *hadeeth* in which the Prophet (ﷺ) narrates a statement from Allaah. For example, the Prophet (ﷺ) said, "Allaah said, 'O My servants, I have made injustice *haraam* for Me, and have made it *haraam* between you also, so do not be unjust to one another.'"[138]

---

134 The state that a person who desires to perform the major or minor pilgrimage must enter. During this state, it is not allowed to perfume the body, hence the reason for the question.

135 Reported by al-Bukhaaree.

136 Ibn al-Qayyim also mentions an eighth category, and that is the inspiration from Allaah to the Prophet (ﷺ) without any barrier between them, but this category is one that has never occurred. cf. *Zaad al-Ma'ad*, v.1, p. 18.

137 Ibn Nu'aym in his *Hilya*, see *Saheeh al-Jami'*, #2085.

138 Reported by Muslim.

There are a number of differences between *hadeeth Qudsee* and the Qur'aan:

1) The primary difference that is given by most scholars is that the Qur'aan is the Speech of Allaah, revealed to the Prophet (ﷺ) in meaning and wording. Thus, the Qur'aan is from Allaah even in wording. *Hadeeth Qudsee*, according to many scholars, is only from Allaah in meaning.[139]

   Therefore, the Qur'aan is attributed directly to Allaah. It is said, 'Allaah said...' with regards to a verse of the Qur'aan, but this cannot be used for a *hadeeth Qudsee* without adding the phrase, 'The Prophet (ﷺ) said that Allaah said...'.

2) The Qur'aan has been put forth as a miracle that can never be imitated in its style, prose or content. It is an open challenge for all of mankind to produce even a chapter similar to it. A *hadeeth Qudsee*, on the other hand, has no miraculous nature in it.

3) Allaah has promised to preserve the Qur'aan, whereas no such promise exists for the *hadeeth Qudsee*.

4) The Qur'aan has reached us in *mutawaatir* chains of narration. There is no difference of opinion over the Qur'aan; all scholars are in agreement as to what its verses and letters are. *Hadeeth Qudsee*, on the other hand, mainly exist in the form of *ahaad* (i.e., non-*mutawaatir*) *hadeeth*. There are authentic, weak and even fabricated *hadeeth Qudsee*,[140] for it is still a *hadeeth* that must be checked with all the rules of the scholars of *hadeeth*.

5) It is an act of worship to recite the Qur'aan, whereas this is not the case for a *hadeeth Qudsee*. The person who reads *hadeeth Qudsee* will be rewarded for seeking knowledge, just as if he read other *hadeeth*. The recitation of the Qur'aan, on the other hand, is an act of worship in and of itself.

   This point also implies that a *hadeeth Qudsee* cannot be read in prayers, and if done so then such a prayer will not be valid. Only the Qur'aan may be recited in prayer.

---

139 This is the opinion that almost all authors of *'uloom al-Qur'aan* quote. Some scholars, however, say that even the wording of *hadeeth Qudsee* is from Allaah, and this is the opinion that this author inclines towards. The reason is that most of the authors of the works of *'uloom al-Qur'aan* have been *Ash'arees*, and the opinion that *hadeeth Qudsee* are inspired in 'meaning' and are not the actual *kalaam* of Allaah reeks of the *Ash'aree* faith. There is absolutely no proof to show that the words of the *hadeeth Qudsee* are not from Allaah. When the Prophet (ﷺ) says, "Allaah says...", it should be held upon its literal, apparent meaning; namely, that Allaah actually spoke these words, and the Prophet (ﷺ) was inspired these words; and Allaah knows best. However, the *wordings* of the *hadeeth Qudsee* have not been promised to be preserved by Allaah (in contrast to the Qur'aan); only their *meanings* have been preserved. Therefore, the same *hadeeth Qudsee* is found in different works of *hadeeth* with different wordings. The Qur'aan, on the other hand, has been preserved in wording *and* meaning.

140 There have also been attempts to fabricate Qur'aanic recitations (see Ch. 11 for further details), but the difference is that these rejected recitations of the Qur'aan are agreed upon by all the scholars. Certain *hadeeth Qudsee*, on the other hand, are subject to a difference of opinion over their authenticity, just like other *hadeeth*.

It should be mentioned that all of the *hadeeth* of the Prophet (ﷺ), whether they are *Qudsee* or not, are a type of inspiration sent down to him. As the Qur'aan says,

$$ وَمَا يَنطِقُ عَنِ ٱلْهَوَىٰٓ ٣ إِنْ هُوَ إِلَّا وَحْيٌ يُوحَىٰ ٤ $$

«And he (ﷺ) does not speak of his own desires; rather it is only a revelation
sent down to him» [53:3-4]

This verse does not speak only of the Qur'aan but also of the *Sunnah*. The Prophet (ﷺ) said, "Verily, I was given the Qur'aan and something equivalent to it (i.e., the *Sunnah*)!"[141] Since the Prophet (ﷺ) said, '...I was given...' this implies that his (ﷺ) *Sunnah* is also a type of inspiration.

The difference, therefore, between the Qur'aan and the *Sunnah* is that the Qur'aan is the Speech of Allaah, inspired to the Prophet (ﷺ) in wording and meaning, whereas the *Sunnah* is the speech of Muḥammad (ﷺ), inspired only in meaning. Even though the *Sunnah* is an integral part of Islaamic belief and law, and its meanings safeguarded by Allaah, the Qur'aan is superior to it since it is the actual *kalaam* of Allaah.

---

141   Reported by Aboo Daawood, at-Tirmidhee and Aḥmad.

CHAPTER 4

GRADUAL REVELATION

The Qur'aan was revealed gradually over a period of twenty-three years. The procedure of the *wahy* that the Prophet (ﷺ) received was discussed in the previous chapter. This chapter now seeks to explain the piece-meal revelation of the Qur'aan to the Prophet Muhammad (ﷺ). This topic includes the various stages of revelation of the Qur'aan, and the wisdom behind its gradual revelation.

Before discussing the revelation of the Qur'aan to the Prophet (ﷺ), it should be mentioned that the revelations to the previous prophets were not gradual like the revelation of the Qur'aan. Rather, each previous Scripture was given to the particular prophet all at once. This is why the people at the time of the Prophet (ﷺ) were surprised that the Qur'aan was being revealed piece-meal, as the Qur'aan says,

«Those who disbelieve ask, 'Why is not the Qur'aan revealed all at once?'
Thus (it is sent down in parts) so that We may strengthen your heart, and
We have revealed it to you, gradually, in stages» [25:32]

Another proof for this fact is that Moosaa was given the Torah all at once, as mentioned in the Qur'aan (7:144-154).[142]

I. The Stages of Revelation

The vast majority of scholars hold the opinion that the process of revelation occurred in three distinct stages:

THE FIRST STAGE

The Qur'aan, the Speech of Allaah,[143] was written on the *Lauh al-Mahfoodh*, or the Preserved Tablet, which is with Allaah, all Praise be to Him. The *Lauh al-Mahfoodh*

---

142 cf. Baazmool for a more detailed discussion, v.1, p.40-42.

143 See 'The Qur'aan as the Speech of Allaah' in Ch. 2. Note the difference between this point, and the belief of the *Ash'arees*. The *Ash'arees* claim that the Arabic Qur'aan did not exist until it was written and created in the *Lauh al-Mahfoodh*, whereas *Ahl as-Sunnah* claim that the Qur'aan existed without any beginning (from eternity) as the *kalaam* of Allaah, and was written in the *Lauh al-Mahfoodh* before the creation of the Heavens and earth.

is the Tablet upon which all of the things that will happen from the creation of the Heavens and Earth, until the end of time, are written. The Prophet (ﷺ) said, "The first thing that Allaah created was the Pen. He said to it, "Write!" It responded, "O My Lord! And what shall I write?" Allaah said, "Write the destiny of all things, until the Day of Judgement."[144] This writing occurred and was preserved on the *Lauh al-Mahfoodh*.

Therefore, included in the *Lauh al-Mahfoodh* is the text of the Qur'aan. The method of this writing, and when it occurred, is known only to Allaah. The fact that the Qur'aan is written on the *Lauh al-Mahfoodh* is mentioned in the Qur'aan itself:

$$ بَلۡ هُوَ قُرۡءَانٌ مَّجِيدٌ ۝ فِى لَوۡحٍ مَّحۡفُوظِۭ ۝ $$

«Nay! This is indeed a Glorious Qur'aan! (Inscribed) in the *Lauh al-Mahfoodh*» [85:21-2]

and also,

$$ إِنَّهُۥ لَقُرۡءَانٌ كَرِيمٌ ۝ فِى كِتَٰبٍ مَّكۡنُونٍ ۝ $$

«And this is indeed a Noble Qur'aan; In a Book well-guarded (i.e., the *Lauh al-Mahfoodh*)» [56:77-78]

Part of the wisdom of this stage is to prove to the believers the authenticity of the Qur'aan, as it was written down even before its revelation, in a place that guarantees its safety. This is also a manifestation of the infinite knowledge of Allaah, as the *Lauh al-Mahfoodh* has written on it all the commands and decrees of Allaah. The Qur'aan describes the *Lauh al-Mahfoodh* as having everything – small or big – recorded on it (54:53).

The second stage

From the *Lauh al-Mahfoodh*, Allaah revealed the Qur'aan to the lower heavens, in a place called "The House of Honour" (*al-Bayt al-'Izza*). This revelation occurred in Ramadaan, on the Night of Decree (*Laylat al-Qadr*). The proof for this is found in some verses of the Qur'aan, and the statements of the Companions.

The Qur'aan states,

$$ شَهۡرُ رَمَضَانَ ٱلَّذِىٓ أُنزِلَ فِيهِ ٱلۡقُرۡءَانُ $$

«The month of Ramadaan is the month in which the Qur'aan was revealed...» [2:185]

and it also states,

$$ إِنَّآ أَنزَلۡنَٰهُ فِى لَيۡلَةٍ مُّبَٰرَكَةٍ $$

---

144   Reported by Aboo Daawood. See *Sharh 'Aqeedah at-Tahaawiyyah*, p. 264, for further details.

«We have sent it (the Qur'aan) down, on a Blessed Night» [44:3]

The Qur'aan later specifies this Blessed Night as,

$$ إِنَّآ أَنزَلۡنَٰهُ فِى لَيۡلَةِ ٱلۡقَدۡرِ ۝ $$

«We have sent it down in the Night of Decree» [97:1]

These verses specify that the entire Qur'aan was sent down in the month of Ramadaan, and specifically on the Night of Decree.

Explaining these verses, Ibn 'Abbaas said, "The whole Qur'aan was sent down to the lower heavens on the Night of Decree. Then, whenever Allaah wished to inspire something (from the Qur'aan), He would inspire it,"[145] and in another narration, "...it was then revealed piece-meal over a period of twenty years."[146] Other narrations from Ibn 'Abbaas mention that the place the Qur'aan was revealed to is called Bayt al-'Izza, or, 'The House of Honour.'[147]

It is seen that, in this revelation, the whole Qur'aan was sent down in one night. The famous scholar, Imaam Aboo Shaamah, (d. 665 A.H.) wrote,[148]

> If it were asked: What is the secret of the revelation of the Qur'aan to the lower heavens? The response is: In its revelation is a sign of the eminence and excellence of the Book, and of the one whom it was revealed to. This is because it is an indication to the inhabitants of the heavens (the angels) that this Book is the last of all books (to be revealed), revealed to the last of all prophets, to the best of all nations. It has been made close to them so that it can be revealed to them. And were it not for the fact that the Wisdom of Allaah was not to reveal the Book at once, it would have been revealed all at once, just as the previous Scriptures were revealed all at once, but instead Allaah decided to honour the Prophet (ﷺ), and differentiate between him and the other prophets (by causing the Qur'aan to be revealed piece-meal). Therefore, (by this initial descent to the lower heavens) Allaah combined the two matters together: He made the Prophet (ﷺ) similar to the other prophets (in the sense that the Qur'aan was revealed at once to the lower heavens, like the previous books), and He honoured him (ﷺ) (by causing it to be revealed piece-meal after that).

In other words, this initial descent of the Qur'aan to the lower heavens was similar to the revelation of the previous Scriptures, since it was done at once; therefore in this aspect the Prophet (ﷺ) shared the same procedure of revelation as the other prophets had. Yet, the Prophet (ﷺ) also had the superiority of having the Qur'aan revealed piece-meal over a period of twenty-three years.

---

145 Narrated by at-Tabaree and al-Haakim.

146 Narrated by al-Haakim, al-Nasaa'i and al-Baihaqee.

147 Dr. Subhi Salih, in his Mabahith fi 'Uloom al-Qur'aan, p. 51, denies these two stages, stating that since these narrations do not go back to the Prophet (ﷺ), we cannot accept them. However, this knowledge cannot be derived through ijtihaad (personal reasoning), therefore Ibn 'Abbaas must have heard this from the Prophet (ﷺ), and this narration takes on the status of marfoo' (a hadeeth that has originated from the Prophet (ﷺ)).

148 Baazmool, p. 44.

THE THIRD STAGE

The final stage of revelation was alluded to by Ibn 'Abbaas in his previous narration. In this stage, Jibreel brought those portions of the Qur'aan which Allaah commanded him to bring. The Qur'aan refers to this revelation in many verses. In one verse, Allaah says,

«And truly this (Qur'aan) is a revelation from the Lord of the Worlds; Which
the trustworthy Spirit (Angel Jibreel) has brought down; Upon Your heart
(O Muḥammad), so that you may be one of the warners» [26:192-4]

The procedure by which the Qur'aan was inspired to the Prophet (ﷺ) has already been discussed in the previous chapter.

This gradual revelation occurred over a period of twenty-three years, according to the strongest opinion. Some scholars hold this period to be twenty years, and yet another group twenty five. The reason for this difference is the fact that the age of the Prophet (ﷺ) is itself a subject of dispute; the narrations state it variously to be sixty, sixty three, or sixty five years. All scholars, however, agree that he spent ten years in Madeenah, and that his prophethood began when he (ﷺ) was forty. The difference, therefore, revolves around how many years he stayed in Makkah before the *hijrah*. However, the strongest opinion, and the opinion that is widespread among the Muslims, is that he (ﷺ) passed away at the age of sixty-three, which would then imply that the period in which the Qur'aan was sent down was twenty-three years.

It should be remembered that the Qur'aan is the Speech of Allaah, as has been elaborated and discussed in the previous chapter. Therefore, it is incorrect to use the narrations of Ibn 'Abbaas which allude to the *Lauh al-Maḥfoodh* to negate the fact that Jibreel heard the Qur'aan from Allaah. These narrations do not mention that Jibreel took the Qur'aan from the *Lauh al-Maḥfoodh*; in fact, the narration is explicit in that Allaah would '...inspire' the portion of the Qur'aan that He wished to reveal. The process of inspiration to the angels was discussed, and it was shown that Jibreel heard the Qur'aan from Allaah. In other words, what Jibreel recited to the Prophet (ﷺ) were the words that Allaah Spoke to him.

Some scholars, however, have inferred from these narrations that Jibreel took the Qur'aan from the *Lauh al-Maḥfoodh*. As for the *Ash'arees*, most of them claimed that this was the *only* method by which Jibreel received the Qur'aan. This opinion is rejected immediately, as this denies the whole concept of the Qur'aan being the actual *kalaam* of Allaah. However, other scholars stated that Jibreel heard the Qur'aan from Allaah *and* took the Qur'aan from the *Lauh al-Maḥfoodh*. Whether Jibreel also took the Qur'aan from the *Lauh al-Maḥfoodh* or not, is, as az-Zarqaanee stated, "...not of great importance, as long as we are sure the source of revelation is Allaah alone."[149]

---

149 az-Zarqaanee, p. 49.

Tampering of the Revelation?

The possibility that the revelation of the Qur'aan might have been tampered or changed during the revelation process is ruled out by Allaah, so no doubt can remain with regards to its authenticity.

Firstly, the trustworthiness of Jibreel has been guaranteed by Allaah. Allaah describes the angels in general as,

«They do not speak until He has spoken, and they act on His Command» [21:27]

meaning that they do not disobey Allaah. Allaah then praises Jibreel in particular, and calls him the

«trustworthy Spirit» [26:193]

meaning that Jibreel was trustworthy in revealing the Qur'aan to the Prophet (ﷺ).

Secondly, as the Prophet (ﷺ) was chosen by Allaah to be the recipient of the Qur'aan, Allaah assured him that he (ﷺ) would not forget or miss any verse. When the Prophet (ﷺ) used to hurriedly recite the verses from Jibreel, in fear that he might forget, Allaah revealed,

«Move not your tongue concerning (the Qur'aan) to make haste therewith. It is for Us to collect it, and to give you (O Muhammad) the ability to recite it.[150] And when We have recited it to you, then follow its recital» [75:16-8]

The Prophet (ﷺ) was instructed to be patient, and allow Jibreel to finish his recitation before he (ﷺ) should start reciting.

Thirdly, after having ensured that the Prophet (ﷺ) memorised the revelation, Allaah then ordered him to convey the revelation that he (ﷺ) had been given, and told him that a failure on his part to do so would mean a failure in his mission as a Prophet:

«O Messenger! Proclaim (the message) which has been sent down to you from your Lord. If you do not do so, then you have not conveyed His message!» [5:67]

Fourthly, Allaah even ruled out the possibility that the Prophet (ﷺ) might tamper with the message deliberately, for He said,

---

150 This verse can also read, "It is for Us to collect it and Recite it to you."

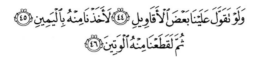

«And he (Muhammad) does not speak from his own desires; it is only an inspiration that is inspired» [53:3-4]

«Say (O Muhammad): 'It is not for me to change it (the Qur'aan) from my own desire. I only follow that which is revealed to me'» [10:15]

In another verse, a severe punishment is promised for forging any revelation:

«And if he (Muhammad) had forged a false saying, attributing it to Us, We surely would have seized him by his right hand, and then certainly have cut off his life artery!» [69:44-6]

Therefore, the Qur'aan has been preserved safely, and no doubt can be cast on its authenticity. The Qur'aan – as the *kalaam* of Allaah – existed from eternity. It was then written in the *Lauh al-Mahfoodh*, in a protected, well-guarded Tablet. During the month in which the Prophet (ﷺ) began his mission, the Qur'aan was sent down to the lower heavens. The trustworthy Angel Jibreel, after he had heard the Qur'aan from Allaah, then revealed it to the Prophet Muhammad (ﷺ), who preserved it faithfully, without any alteration, and who then passed it on to mankind.

The Quantity of Revelation

A question that arises is the quantity of Qur'aan that Jibreel used to come with to the Prophet (ﷺ) in each revelation. As-Suyootee (d. 911 A.H.) discusses this question and concludes:

> It can be inferred from (combining) the authentic narrations, and other evidences that the (quantity) of the Qur'aan revealed would depend on the particular situation; five verses, or ten verses, or more, or less. The revelation of ten verses during the story of 'Aa'ishah has been authenticated... as has the revelation of a small part of a verse

«...except those who are disabled...» [4:95]

> As for those narrations that explicitly mention only five verses, such as the report in Ibn 'Asaakir that (the Companion) Aboo Sa'eed al-Khudree would teach his students five verses in the morning and five in the evening, and say, 'Jibreel used to bring the Qur'aan five verses at a time,' and the report in al-Bayhaqee that 'Umar ibn al-Khattaab said, 'Learn the Qur'aan

five verses at a time, for Jibreel used to come to the Prophet (ﷺ) with five verses at a time,'...the meaning of these reports is that Jibreel would quote the Prophet (ﷺ) five verses at a time so that he (ﷺ) could memorise them, then he would quote him the rest of the revelation, five verses at a time. This is explained by the narration in al-Bayhaqee in which Khaalid ibn Deenar said, 'Aboo al-'Aaliyah told us to learn the Qur'aan five verses at a time, for the Prophet (ﷺ) would take from Jibreel five verses at a time.'[151]

Yet another question is whether the frequency of revelation was the same throughout the Prophet's (ﷺ) life, or did it change?

Towards the end of the Prophet's (ﷺ) life, the revelation increased greatly, so much so that the last years of the prophethood were the years in which most of the revelation occurred. Anas ibn Maalik narrates, "Allaah increased the *wahy* upon the Prophet (ﷺ) before his death, until before his death, the *wahy* was more than it ever was, then the Prophet (ﷺ) passed away."[152] Al-Haafidh Ibn Hajr (d. 852 A.H.), commenting on this phenomenon, said,[153]

> This shows that the time frame in which the Prophet (ﷺ) passed away was the time frame which had the highest frequency of revelations. And the reason for this is that, after the Conquest of Makkah, the delegations that were sent from other tribes to the Prophet (ﷺ) increased, and so did the number of questions pertaining to laws. Therefore, the *wahy* also increased in frequency (to respond to these questions). And this is in contrast to the early period, for, during the beginning of the prophethood, the *wahy* would come occasionally, with breaks in between the revelations. This gradually increased (with time). During the period of Makkah, hardly any of the long *soorahs* were revealed. Then, after the *hijrah*, most of the longer *soorahs* were revealed, and these contained most of the laws (of the *sharee'ah*). And the last part of the prophethood witnessed the highest frequency of revelation, for the reasons outlined above.

II. The Wisdom Behind the Gradual Revelation

If Allaah had willed, the Qur'aan would have been sent down in its entirety to the Prophet (ﷺ) at the beginning of his prophethood, just like the previous Scriptures. However, this was not the case. The Qur'aan in fact refers to its gradual revelation in many verses, and from these verses some of the merits and benefits of this piece-meal revelation can be understood.

Allaah says,

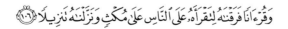

وَقُرْءَانًا فَرَقْنَٰهُ لِتَقْرَأَهُۥ عَلَى ٱلنَّاسِ عَلَىٰ مُكْثٍ وَنَزَّلْنَٰهُ تَنزِيلًا ﴿١٠٦﴾

---

151 as-Suyootee, v. 1, p. 57. The translation has been paraphrased at places.
152 Reported by al-Bukhaaree.
153 *Fath al-Baaree*, v. 9, p. 8.

«And it (is a) Qur'aan which We have divided (into parts), in order that you
might recite it to mankind at intervals. And verily, We have revealed it by
stages!» [17:106]

When the disbelievers mocked the gradual revelation of the Qur'aan, and challenged the Prophet (ﷺ) to bring forth the Qur'aan in its entirety, Allaah revealed:

$$ وَقَالَ ٱلَّذِينَ كَفَرُوا۟ لَوْلَا نُزِّلَ عَلَيْهِ ٱلْقُرْءَانُ جُمْلَةً $$
$$ وَٰحِدَةً ۚ كَذَٰلِكَ لِنُثَبِّتَ بِهِۦ فُؤَادَكَ ۖ وَرَتَّلْنَٰهُ تَرْتِيلًا ﴿٣٢﴾ $$

«And those who disbelieve say, 'Why is not the Qur'aan revealed to him all
at once?' Thus (it is sent down in parts) that We may strengthen your heart
thereby. And We have revealed it to you gradually, in stages» [25:32]

Thus the gradual revelation was considered a blessing that Allaah gave to the
Prophet (ﷺ), and to his *ummah*.

Some of the benefits of the gradual revelation are as follows:[154]

1) To strengthen the resolve of the Prophet (ﷺ) against the disbelievers.

The Prophet (ﷺ) was anguished and distressed by the attitude of his people towards his message. They ridiculed and mocked him, and claimed that he was a sorcerer, a madman, or that he was possessed by the *jinn*. Allaah reminds him,

$$ وَلَقَدْ نَعْلَمُ أَنَّكَ يَضِيقُ صَدْرُكَ بِمَا يَقُولُونَ ﴿٩٧﴾ $$

«Indeed, We know that your heart is straitened by what they (the disbelievers) say» [15:97]

By the continual revelation of the Qur'aan to the Prophet (ﷺ), he was reaffirmed
in his determination and zeal. This is what Allaah alludes to when He discusses the
graduality of the revelation,

$$ كَذَٰلِكَ لِنُثَبِّتَ بِهِۦ فُؤَادَكَ $$

«Thus (it is sent down in parts) that We may strengthen your heart thereby»
[25:32]

This can also be seen in the content of the earlier revelations in Makkah, where
the stories of the prophets of old are told, and how the prophets dealt with the hard-
ships and torments that they faced from their peoples. In *Soorah* Hood, after mentioning the stories of many prophets, Allaah concludes,

«And all that We relate to you (O Muḥammad) of the news of the messengers is in order that We may make your heart strong and firm!» [11:120]

---

154 cf. Baazmool, v. 1, p. 45-46, Ubaydaat, 99-101, Qattaan, 107-117.

There are a number of ways in which the Prophet (ﷺ) was helped by these stories. The Prophet (ﷺ) was told to learn from the lessons of the previous prophets,

فَٱصۡبِرۡ كَمَا صَبَرَ أُوْلُواْ ٱلۡعَزۡمِ مِنَ ٱلرُّسُلِ

«Therefore, be patient (O Muhammad), like the messengers of firm resolution (before you did)» [46:35]

He (ﷺ) was told that the plots of the disbelievers, and all their mockery of Islaam, will do no harm to Allaah's Plans,

فَلَا يَحۡزُنكَ قَوۡلُهُمۡ إِنَّا نَعۡلَمُ مَا يُسِرُّونَ وَمَا يُعۡلِنُونَ

«So let not their speech grieve you, for verily, We know what they conceal and what they reveal» [36:75]

He (ﷺ) was promised help from his Creator,

كَتَبَ ٱللَّهُ لَأَغۡلِبَنَّ أَنَا۠ وَرُسُلِيٓ

«Allaah has ordained, 'Verily, it is I and the messengers who will be Victorious'» [58:21]

And, he (ﷺ) was reassured by the warnings given to the disbelievers by Allaah,

سَيُهۡزَمُ ٱلۡجَمۡعُ وَيُوَلُّونَ ٱلدُّبُرَ ﴿٤٥﴾

«Verily, their multitudes will be put to flight, and they will show their backs (in retreat)» [54:45]

This gradual method of revelation also helped to strengthen the determination of the Companions. These same verses inspired the Companions with courage and patience, and gave them the stamina they needed to withstand the persecution of the idolaters. The Qur'aan says, as was quoted above,

وَكُلّٗا نَّقُصُّ
عَلَيۡكَ مِنۡ أَنۢبَآءِ ٱلرُّسُلِ مَا نُثَبِّتُ بِهِۦ فُؤَادَكَ وَجَآءَكَ فِي هَٰذِهِ
ٱلۡحَقُّ وَمَوۡعِظَةٞ وَذِكۡرَىٰ لِلۡمُؤۡمِنِينَ ﴿١٢٠﴾

«And all that we relate to you (O Muhammad) of the news of the messengers is in order that We may make your heart strong and firm! And in this has come to you the truth, *as well as an admonition and a reminder for the believers*» [11:120]

2) To simplify its memorisation and understanding by the Companions.

The piece-meal revelations of the Qur'aan made it easier for the Companions to understand, memorise and implement the portions that were revealed. If the Qur'aan had been revealed all at once, it might have been very difficult for the Companions to understand all of its verses properly. Yet, with gradual revelations, the Companions understood and implemented the Qur'aan correctly.

The Companions adopted the procedure of teaching the Qur'aan to the Successors gradually, even after its revelation had been completed, and its compilation finished. Aboo 'Abd al-Rahmaan al-Sulamee (d. 70 A.H.), a very famous Successor, narrates that whenever the people who taught them the Qur'aan, like 'Abdullaah ibn Mas'ood, 'Uthmaan ibn 'Affaan, and others, would learn ten verses of the Qur'aan, they would not proceed onwards until they had learnt whatever concepts and regulations those verses contained. They used to say, "We learnt the text of the Qur'aan, and studied its ideas and injunctions all together."[155] Another Successor, Aboo Nadrah (d. 109 A.H.), related, "We used to learn from Aboo Sa'eed al-Khudree five verses in the morning, and five in the evening, for he told us that Jibreel used to bring (on average) five verses at a time."[156] Thus, even after the complete revelation of the Qur'aan, the Companions adopted the same gradual approach in teaching it to the later generations. They had learnt the benefits of teaching the Qur'aan gradually from the piece-meal revelation of the Qur'aan.

It can also be said that, had the Qur'aan been revealed all at once, in book form (as the Torah was revealed), it might have led to a feeling of complacency with regards to the preservation of the Qur'aan. Instead, due to the fact that verses were revealed occasionally, there was a strong incentive to ensure that the verses were memorised and written. This was crucial for the preservation of the Qur'aan.

3) To prove the truthfulness of the Prophet (ﷺ).

The idolaters and the People of the Book used to ask the Prophet (ﷺ) questions in order to outwit him, but every time Allaah would reply to their queries. As Ibn 'Abbaas said, "Whenever the disbelievers brought a new question to the Prophet (ﷺ), Allaah would reveal to them an answer (through the Qur'aan)."[157] The Qur'aan itself refers to this aspect of the revelation,

$$ وَلَا يَأْتُونَكَ بِمَثَلٍ إِلَّا جِئْنَاكَ بِالْحَقِّ وَأَحْسَنَ تَفْسِيرًا ٣٣ $$

«And no example or similitude do they bring (to oppose or to find fault in you) except that We reveal to you the truth (against this similitude), and the better explanation thereof» [25:33]

There are many examples of such verses; when the idolaters demanded miracles from the Prophet (ﷺ), Allaah revealed,

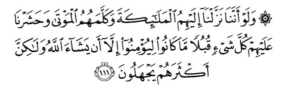

---

155 Ibn Taymiyyah, *Principles*, p. 12.
156 Qattaan, p. 110.
157 ibid., p. 110.

«And even if We had sent down unto them angels, and the dead had spoken to them, and We had gathered together all things before their very eyes, they would not have believed unless Allaah willed, but most of them behave ignorantly» [6:111]

Included in this category are the answers that the Prophet (ﷺ) gave to the problems that the believers faced. Whenever a situation or crises arose, the Qur'aan would clearly lay out the solution. For example, when Khawlah bint Tha'labah complained to the Prophet (ﷺ) that her husband had made himself unlawful to her,[158] Allaah revealed,

$$قَدۡ سَمِعَ ٱللَّهُ قَوۡلَ ٱلَّتِى تُجَٰدِلُكَ فِى زَوۡجِهَا وَتَشۡتَكِىٓ إِلَى ٱللَّهِ وَٱللَّهُ يَسۡمَعُ تَحَاوُرَكُمَآۚ إِنَّ ٱللَّهَ سَمِيعُۢ بَصِيرٌ ۝١$$

«Indeed Allaah has heard the statement of she who disputes with you concerning her husband, and complains to Allaah. Allaah hears the argument between both of you; verily, Allaah is All-Hearing, All-Seeing» [58:1]

'Aa'ishah reports, "All praise be to Allaah, whose Hearing encompasses all voices! The woman came complaining to the Prophet (ﷺ), and I was sitting in the corner of the room, straining to hear what she was saying (in one narration, 'I could hear some of it and some of it I could not'), and immediately Allaah's revelation came down, 'Indeed Allaah has heard the statement of she who disputes with you concerning her husband, and complains to Allaah...'"[159] Even though 'Aa'ishah was sitting in the same room, she was not able to hear the entire conversation, yet Allaah, all Praise be to Him, heard it from above the seven heavens, and immediately sent down these verses to solve the problem between them, and also between all future spouses who face the same problem.

Therefore, the fact that the Qur'aan came down immediately to cater to the questions and problems of the people proved that it was in fact the word of Allaah, revealed through the Prophet (ﷺ).

4) To prove the miraculous nature of the Qur'aan.

Indeed, one of the most outstanding miracles of the Qur'aan was that it was revealed over a period of two decades; it answered many questions from believers and idolaters, it catered to a plethora of situations, it solved a wide variety of problems, it frequently commanded the Prophet (ﷺ) and the believers to a course of action, and yet not a single of its six thousand plus verses is contradicted by another! A human-authored book of this size and nature, even if written instantaneously, is invariably

---

158 The Arabs had a custom known as *dhihaar*, in which a man would tell his wife, "You are to me like the back of my mother." This statement meant that the man had taken a vow upon himself not to approach his wife sexually. It was as if the woman had been put in a 'suspended' state: neither was she divorced so that she could remarry, nor was she a proper wife to the husband. After this particular incident, the Qur'aan prohibited this act (cf. 58:1-10)

159 Narrated by al-Bukhaaree.

bound to contain errors and contradictions; how much greater the miracle of the Qur'aan when it is revealed over a period of twenty-three years! To add to its miraculous nature, the order and arrangement of the verses was not done chronologically – rather, the Prophet (ﷺ) would instruct his Companions of the location of any new verses. The Qur'aan was literally assembled out of the fragmental revelations. It was as if an intricate puzzle was perfectly pieced together during a period of over two decades to form a flawless masterpiece.

The Qur'aan challenges,

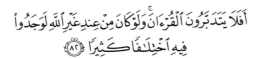

«Do they not ponder over the Qur'aan? For indeed, had it been from other than Allaah, they would surely have found many contradictions in it» [4:82]

5) To reveal the laws of Islaam – the *Sharee'ah* – in a gradual manner.

Among the blessings of Allaah to the Companions is that He revealed to them the laws of Islaam gradually, and thus made it easier for them to adopt these laws. Initially, there were no specific laws of *halaal* and *haraam*.[160] The Companions during the Makkan stage were being trained spiritually so that they could form the nucleus of the future Muslim state in Madeenah. Once they had passed this stage, Allaah then completed the revelation of the *sharee'ah* in gradual steps, so that they could adapt to the lifestyle of Islaam.

It can be seen that the first revelations warned against *shirk*, and proved the existence of Allaah through His Creation. These verses called upon the pagans to worship the one true God, and not to call upon others for help and aid. They elaborated the unique concept of *tawheed*, and instilled in the early Muslims the strong faith that they needed to overcome the persecution of the idolaters. Soon after this, revelations came down establishing the basics of worship, and warning against the major sins.[161]

This fact was stated by 'Aa'ishah when she commented, "The first revelations only mentioned Heaven and Hell (i.e., the basics of *'aqeedah*). Eventually, when the people were firm in their conviction of Islaam, Allaah revealed the *halaal* and the *haraam*. If the first verse revealed was, 'Do not drink wine,' they would have responded, 'We will never give up wine!' And if the first verse revealed was, 'Do no fornicate,' they would have responded, 'We will never give up fornication!'"[162] Thus, the laws of Islaam were revealed gradually, to ease the process of conversion upon the early Muslims.

6) To ease the revelation process on the Prophet (ﷺ).

The process of inspiration, or *wahy*, was a difficult one for the Prophet (ﷺ), as was mentioned in the last chapter. At times, he used to sweat profusely, even on a cold

---

160 See Chapter 6, "The *makkee* and *madanee* Verses," for further details.
161 For further details on this, see Zarqaanee, v. 1, p. 57.
162 Narrated by al-Bukhaaree.

night, because of the severity of the inspiration. Had the Qur'aan been revealed all at once, it might have been too difficult for the Prophet (ﷺ) to bear.

To summarise the concept of the gradual revelation, it is appropriate to quote the great scholar and interpreter of the Qur'aan, Aboo al-Fidaa Ismaa'eel ibn 'Umar (d. 774 A.H.), otherwise known as Ibn Katheer, who stated:[163]

> And all of this (meaning the concept of the gradual revelation) only shows the concern, and the high status that was given to the Prophet (ﷺ), since the revelation would come to him continually, morning and evening, night and day, at home or while travelling. And every time the angel would come to him with the Qur'aan, unlike the previous prophets, who would be given their books at once. So the status of the Prophet (ﷺ) was greater, and higher, and more magnificent from all of his fellow prophets – may Allaah send His blessing and Mercy to all of them.

> The Qur'aan is the most honoured book to be revealed by Allaah, and Muhammad (ﷺ) is the most honoured prophet that was sent by Allaah. And Allaah combined in the revelation of the Qur'aan the two procedures: He first revealed the Qur'aan all at once, from the *Lauh al-Mahfoodh* to the lower heavens, and He then revealed it to earth gradually, to cater to the situation and needs of the people.

---

163 *Tafseer Ibn Katheer*, 3/318.

CHAPTER 5

THE FIRST AND THE LAST REVELATIONS

The changing point in the life of the Prophet Muḥammad (ﷺ) – and for all of humanity afterwards – was the occurrence of the first revelation that Allaah communicated to him. From this point onwards, he (ﷺ) had a mission the like of which no human before him had:

لِّنُنذِرَأُمَّ ٱلْقُرَىٰ وَمَنْ حَوْلَهَا

«so that you may warn the Mother of Cities and all that surrounds it » [42:7]

meaning the entire world, or as Ibn Katheer puts it, "all lands east and west"[164]! In no unexplicit terms, the Qur'aan lays out the monumental task of the Prophet (ﷺ):

قُل
يَـٰٓأَيُّهَا ٱلنَّاسُ إِنِّي رَسُولُ ٱللَّهِ إِلَيْكُمْ جَمِيعًا ٱلَّذِى
لَهُۥ مُلْكُ ٱلسَّمَـٰوَٰتِ وَٱلْأَرْضِ

«Say, 'O Mankind! Verily I am sent to you all as the Messenger of Allaah, to Whom belongs the Dominions of the Heavens and the Earth...'» [7:158]

The Prophet (ﷺ) was to be the recipient of the Creator's final Revelation to Mankind:

«And truly, this (Qur'aan) is a Revelation from the Lord of the Worlds; Which the trustworthy Spirit (Angel Jibreel) has brought down; Upon Your heart (O Muḥammad), so that you may be one of the warners» [26:192-4]

But what was the first revelation that the Prophet (ﷺ) received? And what was the last?

I. The First Revelation

There are four opinions concerning the first verses that the Prophet (ﷺ) received.

1) The first five verses of *Soorah* al-'Alaq:

$$\text{اقْرَأْ بِاسْمِ رَبِّكَ الَّذِي خَلَقَ ۝ خَلَقَ الْإِنسَانَ مِنْ عَلَقٍ ۝ اقْرَأْ وَرَبُّكَ الْأَكْرَمُ ۝ الَّذِي عَلَّمَ بِالْقَلَمِ ۝ عَلَّمَ الْإِنسَانَ مَا لَمْ يَعْلَمْ ۝}$$

«Read! In the Name of your Lord, Who has created (all that exists). Has Created man from a clot. Read! Verily, your Lord is the Most Generous. Who has taught (the writing) by the Pen. Has taught man that which he knew not» [96:1-5]

The proof for this opinion is the *hadeeth* narrated by al-Bukhaaree from 'Aa'ishah, in which she said, "The commencement of the divine revelation to Allaah's Messenger was in the form of good dreams which came true, like the bright daylight. Then, the love of seclusion was bestowed upon him (ﷺ). He used to go for seclusion to the Cave of Hiraa', where he used to worship Allaah continuously for many days, before his desire to see his family (caused him to return). He used to take with him food for the stay, and then come back to Khadeejah to take his food again, until the truth descended upon him while he was in the Cave of Hiraa'. The angel (Jibreel) came to him, and asked him to read. The Prophet (ﷺ) responded, 'I do not know how to read!'

The Prophet (ﷺ) added, "The angel grabbed me (forcibly) and pressed me so hard that I could not bear it any more. He then released me and again asked me to read, and I again replied, 'I do not know how to read!' Thereupon he caught me for the second time, and pressed me until I could not bear it. He then released me and asked me to read. I again responded, 'I do now know how to read' (in another narration, 'What shall I read?'). Thereupon, he caught me for the third time, and pressed me, and then released me and said,

$$\text{اقْرَأْ بِاسْمِ رَبِّكَ الَّذِي خَلَقَ ۝ خَلَقَ الْإِنسَانَ مِنْ عَلَقٍ ۝ اقْرَأْ وَرَبُّكَ الْأَكْرَمُ ۝}$$

«Read! in the name of your Lord, who created. Created man from a clot. Read! And your Lord is the Most Generous!» [96:1-5]

This *hadeeth* clearly shows that this was the first revelation that the Prophet (ﷺ) received, and it is the correct opinion.

There is also a narration in at-Tabaraanee from Aboo Raja al-Uthaardee (d. 105 A.H.), who said, "Aboo Moosaa al-Asha'aree used to recite the Qur'aan to us, and we used to sit around him in a circle (to listen to him). He used to wear two white garments. When he came to '*Iqra..*' (96:1) he said, 'This is the first *soorah* to be revealed to the Prophet (ﷺ).'"[165]

---

165 az-Zarqaanee, v. 1, p. 94.

2) *Soorah* al-Muddathir. The proof for this is based on another *hadeeth* in al-Bukhaaree, in which Jaabir ibn 'Abdillaah was asked, "What part of the Qur'aan was revealed the first?" He replied, "

يَٰٓأَيُّهَا ٱلْمُدَّثِّرُ ۝

«Say: O You Enveloped (in garments)» [74:1]

was revealed first." The questioner then said, "I was informed that it was

ٱقْرَأْ بِٱسْمِ رَبِّكَ

«Read! In the Name of your Lord.»[96:1]"

Jaabir replied, "I am only telling you that which I heard from the Prophet (), for he said, 'I was in the mountain of Hiraa', and when I came down to the valley (I heard a voice), so I looked to the right, and to the left, and in front of me, and behind me. Then I looked to the skies, and I saw him – meaning Jibreel – and a great fear overtook me! So I returned to Khadeejah, and told her to cover me. Allaah then revealed,

يَٰٓأَيُّهَا ٱلْمُدَّثِّرُ ۝

«Say: O You Enveloped (in garments)» [74:1]'"

This *hadeeth* has been explained by saying that Jaabir told the questioner which *soorah* had been revealed in its entirety first, since *Soorah* al-Muddathir was revealed in its entirety before the remaining verses of *Soorah* al-'Alaq. Alternately, some scholars have claimed that Jaabir was not present when the Prophet (صلى الله عليه وسلم) began narrating the above *hadeeth* in which he (صلى الله عليه وسلم) described his encounter with Jibreel, but entered while the Prophet (صلى الله عليه وسلم) was mid-way in his narration. Therefore, Jaabir only heard the last part of the *hadeeth*. This opinion is supported by another narration of this *hadeeth*, in which Jaabir stated that the Prophet (صلى الله عليه وسلم) said, "While I was walking, I heard a voice from the sky. I looked up and saw the same angel who had visited me at the cave of Hiraa' sitting on a chair between the sky and the earth..."[166] In this narration, Jaabir mentions that the Prophet (صلى الله عليه وسلم) had already seen Jibreel before this incident, which proves that the first revelation had already occurred.

Whatever the case might be, the *hadeeth* which describes the encounter with Jibreel (the first *hadeeth*) is explicit that the first five verses of *Soorah* al-'Alaq were revealed first, and that the next revelation was *Soorah* al-Muddathir. Therefore, this second opinion is the weaker one.

3) *Soorah* al-Faatihah. There is a narration in al-Bayhaqee that states that the first revelation was *Soorah* al-Faatihah. However, this narration is not authentic, therefore, it does not hold any weight.

4) The *Basmalah*. Another *hadeeth*, reported by al-Waahidee, states that the first

---

166 Reported by al-Bukhaaree.

verse revealed was the *basmalah*, "In the Name of Allaah, the Ever Merciful, the Bestower of Mercy," but this report too is not authentic, and cannot be taken as proof.[167]

II. The Last Revelation

There are a number of opinions concerning the last revelation that the Prophet (ﷺ) received. This is because there is more than one *hadeeth* which discusses this subject, each one of which gives a different verse. Also, unlike the first revelation, there does not exist any *hadeeth* in which the Prophet (ﷺ) himself states what the final revelation was. There are eleven opinions concerning the last revelation, as follows:[168]

1) Al-Bukhaaree and at-Tabaree narrate from Ibn 'Abbaas that the last verse revealed to the Prophet (ﷺ) was,

$$ وَٱتَّقُواْ يَوْمًا تُرْجَعُونَ فِيهِ إِلَى ٱللَّهِ ثُمَّ تُوَفَّىٰ كُلُّ نَفْسٍ مَّا كَسَبَتْ وَهُمْ لَا يُظْلَمُونَ ۝ $$

«And fear the day in which you will return to Allaah. Then everyone will be paid what he earned, and they will not be dealt with unjustly» [2:281]

Ibn 'Abbaas added, "The Prophet (ﷺ) lived nine nights after this verse was revealed, then he (ﷺ) passed away."

2) Another narration, also by al-Bukhaaree from Ibn 'Abbaas, states that the last verse revealed was the 'Verse of Interest',

$$ يَٰٓأَيُّهَا ٱلَّذِينَ ءَامَنُواْ ٱتَّقُواْ ٱللَّهَ وَذَرُواْ مَا بَقِيَ مِنَ ٱلرِّبَوٰٓاْ إِن كُنتُم مُّؤْمِنِينَ ۝ $$

«O you who believe! Fear Allaah, and give up what remains from your interest, if you are indeed Believers» [2:278]

3) At-Tabaree reported that Sa'eed ibn al-Mussayyib (d. 90 A.H.) narrated, "The final verse revealed to the Messenger (ﷺ) was the 'Verse of Loaning',

$$ يَٰٓأَيُّهَا ٱلَّذِينَ ءَامَنُوٓاْ إِذَا تَدَايَنتُم بِدَيْنٍ إِلَىٰٓ أَجَلٍ مُّسَمًّى فَٱكْتُبُوهُ $$

«O you who believe! If you contract a debt for a fixed time, write it down» [2:282]

4) Al-Bukhaaree and Muslim report from al-Baraa' ibn 'Aazib that the final verse was the verse of *kalaalah* (a person who does not leave ascendants or descendants),

---

167 Both of the above narrations are weak since the name of the Companion who narrated each *hadeeth* is missing; cf. Zarzur, p. 96.

168 cf. Ubaydaat, pps. 80-84; Qattaan, pps. 69-71; Zarzur, pps. 97-100.

$$ يَسْتَفْتُونَكَ قُلِ ٱللَّهُ يُفْتِيكُمْ فِى ٱلْكَلَٰلَةِ $$

«They ask you for a legal verdict. Say: Allaah directs thus about *kalaalah*...»
[4:176]

5)   Al-Haakim reports from Ubay ibn Ka'ab that the final revelation comprised of the last two verses of *Soorah* at-Tawbah,

$$ لَقَدْ جَآءَكُمْ رَسُولٌ مِّنْ أَنفُسِكُمْ $$

«Verily, there has come unto you a Messenger from amongst yourselves...»
[9:128-9]

6)   Muslim reports from Ibn 'Abbaas that the final *soorah* revealed was *Soorah* an-Nasr,

$$ إِذَا جَآءَ نَصْرُ ٱللَّهِ وَٱلْفَتْحُ ۞ وَرَأَيْتَ ٱلنَّاسَ $$
$$ يَدْخُلُونَ فِى دِينِ ٱللَّهِ أَفْوَاجًا ۞ فَسَبِّحْ بِحَمْدِ رَبِّكَ $$
$$ وَٱسْتَغْفِرْهُ إِنَّهُۥ كَانَ تَوَّابًۢا ۞ $$

«When the Help of Allaah comes to you, and the Conquest (of Makkah)...»
[110:1-4]

7)   Al-Bukhaaree reports from Ibn 'Abbaas that the verse,

$$ وَمَن يَقْتُلْ مُؤْمِنًا $$
$$ مُّتَعَمِّدًا فَجَزَآؤُهُۥ جَهَنَّمُ خَٰلِدًا فِيهَا $$

«And whoever kills a Believer intentionally, his recompense is Hell, to abide therein forever...» [4:93]

was the last verse revealed, and no verse after it abrogated it.

8)   Ibn Mardawayh narrates from Umm Salama: "The final verse revealed was,

$$ فَٱسْتَجَابَ لَهُمْ رَبُّهُمْ أَنِّى لَآ أُضِيعُ عَمَلَ عَٰمِلٍ مِّنكُم مِّن ذَكَرٍ أَوْ أُنثَىٰ $$

«So their Lord answered them (their prayers, and said), "Never will I allow to be lost the work of any of you, be he male or female. You are (members) one of another...»'[3:195]

This (verse was revealed) because I asked, 'O Messenger of Allaah! I see that Allaah always mentions men (in the Qur'aan), but not women!' So Allaah (first) revealed,

$$ وَلَا تَتَمَنَّوْا۟ مَا فَضَّلَ ٱللَّهُ بِهِۦ بَعْضَكُمْ عَلَىٰ بَعْضٍ لِّلرِّجَالِ $$
$$ نَصِيبٌ مِّمَّا ٱكْتَسَبُوا۟ وَلِلنِّسَآءِ نَصِيبٌ مِّمَّا ٱكْتَسَبْنَ $$

«Do not wish for those things which Allaah has made some of you to excel over others. For men there is a reward for what they have earned, and for women there is a reward for what they have earned...»[4:32]

and then He revealed the verse,

$$\text{إِنَّ ٱلْمُسْلِمِينَ وَٱلْمُسْلِمَٰتِ وَٱلْمُؤْمِنِينَ وَٱلْمُؤْمِنَٰتِ}$$
$$\text{وَٱلْقَٰنِتِينَ وَٱلْقَٰنِتَٰتِ وَٱلصَّٰدِقِينَ وَٱلصَّٰدِقَٰتِ وَٱلصَّٰبِرِينَ}$$
$$\text{وَٱلصَّٰبِرَٰتِ وَٱلْخَٰشِعِينَ وَٱلْخَٰشِعَٰتِ وَٱلْمُتَصَدِّقِينَ}$$
$$\text{وَٱلْمُتَصَدِّقَٰتِ وَٱلصَّٰٓئِمِينَ وَٱلصَّٰٓئِمَٰتِ وَٱلْحَٰفِظِينَ}$$
$$\text{فُرُوجَهُمْ وَٱلْحَٰفِظَٰتِ وَٱلذَّٰكِرِينَ ٱللَّهَ كَثِيرًا}$$
$$\text{وَٱلذَّٰكِرَٰتِ أَعَدَّ ٱللَّهُ لَهُم مَّغْفِرَةً وَأَجْرًا عَظِيمًا ﴿٣٥﴾}$$

«Verily, the Muslim men and women, and the believing men and women... Allaah has prepared for them forgiveness, and a great reward» [33:35]

and finally He revealed,

$$\text{أَنِّى لَآ أُضِيعُ عَمَلَ عَٰمِلٍ مِّنكُم}$$

«Never will I allow to be lost the work of any of you...» [3:195]

Therefore, it was the last verse revealed."

9) At-Tirmidhee and al-Ḥaakim narrated from 'Aa'ishah that the last *soorah* revealed was *Soorah* al-Maa'idah.

10) At-Tabaree reported that Mu'aawiyah ibn Abee Sufyaan claimed that the last verse revealed was the last verse of *Soorah* al-Kahf (18:110).

11) It has been said that the last verse revealed was,

$$\text{ٱلْيَوْمَ أَكْمَلْتُ لَكُمْ دِينَكُمْ وَأَتْمَمْتُ}$$
$$\text{عَلَيْكُمْ نِعْمَتِى وَرَضِيتُ لَكُمُ ٱلْإِسْلَٰمَ دِينًا}$$

«Today I have perfected your religion for you, and have Completed My Favours upon you, and have chosen for you Islaam as your religion» [5:3]

A cursory look at these opinions removes many of them, since each Companion was narrating the last verse to be revealed concerning a particular topic. Al-Baraa' ibn 'Aazib was referring to the final verse revealed concerning the laws of inheritance; Umm Salama was referring to the last verse revealed concerning the relative status of men and women; concerning 4:93, Ibn 'Abbaas' statement, 'And no verse after it abrogated it,' shows that he was referring to the last verse revealed concerning the laws of manslaughter; and Ibn 'Abbaas' report concerning *Soorah* al-Naṣr talks about the final complete *soorah* revealed, not the final verse revealed. The report of 'Aa'ishah that the last *soorah* to be revealed was *Soorah* al-Maa'idah means that this was the last *soorah* to be revealed which contained any legal rulings, as other narrations show.

As for the first three opinions, all of these verses are from the same passage in the Qur'aan, viz. 2:278-82, therefore there is no contradiction among these three opinions, as it is possible that all these verses were revealed together. As-Suyootee stated, "As for these three (opinions), then I do not see any contradiction between them, for it seems as if these verses were revealed at the same time, and their position in the *mus-haf* is also the same."[169]

The remaining narrations deal with very late revelations, but not the last.

The strongest opinion is the first one, since it explicitly mentions that hardly a week remained between its revelation and the Prophet's (ﷺ) death. The meaning of the verse also strengthens this opinion, as it refers to death and the Day of Resurrection:

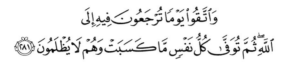

«And fear the day in which you will return to Allaah. Then everyone will be
paid what he earned, and they will not be dealt with unjustly» [2:281]

As for the last opinion, this is what is commonly believed by most Muslims to be the last verse revealed:

اَلْيَوْمَ أَكْمَلْتُ لَكُمْ دِينَكُمْ

«Today I have Perfected your religion for you...»[5:3]

However, this is definitely *not* the last revelation. This verse was revealed on the Day of 'Arafah, at the Farewell Pilgrimage, a number of months before the Prophet's (ﷺ) death. Since it refers to the completion of the religion of Islaam, many Muslims have thought that this signified the end of the revelation. What is actually meant by this verse, however, is that all the verses dealing with the rulings of Islaam (*halaal* and *haraam*) have been revealed. (This also explains 'Aa'ishah's opinion that the last *soorah* to be revealed was al-Maa'idah, for this verse is in *Soorah* al-Maa'idah, and it was the last *soorah* dealing with legal rulings.) It is clear in the *hadeeth* of Ibn 'Abbaas that the revelation of the Qur'aan continued to the Prophet (ﷺ) until only days before he (ﷺ) died. In fact, no major scholar ever held the view that this was the last verse of the Qur'aan to be revealed.[170]

---

169 *Itqaan*, v. 1, p. 36.
170 cf. Abu Shahbah, pps. 125-127.

III. Relative First and Last Verses

The first two sections dealt with the first and last revelations of the Qur'aan in general. The scholars of Islaam have also divided the subject of the first and last revelations conditionally, into separate categories, defining the first and the last revelations dealing with particular topics.

For example, there are a number of verses in the Qur'aan that deal with intoxicants. These verses have been arranged chronologically by the scholars of Islaam. The first verse to mention intoxicants was:

$$يَسْـَٔلُونَكَ عَنِ ٱلْخَمْرِ وَٱلْمَيْسِرِ قُلْ فِيهِمَآ إِثْمٌ كَبِيرٌ وَمَنَـٰفِعُ لِلنَّاسِ وَإِثْمُهُمَآ أَكْبَرُ مِن نَّفْعِهِمَا$$

«They ask you concerning intoxicants and games of chance. Say: In them is great harm, and (also) some benefit to mankind, but the harm (that is caused) is greater than the benefit (that is gained)...» [2:219]

The next verse that was revealed restricted the consumption of intoxicants, such that they could only be drunk after the 'Ishaa prayer:

$$يَـٰٓأَيُّهَا ٱلَّذِينَ ءَامَنُوا۟ لَا تَقْرَبُوا۟ ٱلصَّلَوٰةَ وَأَنتُمْ سُكَـٰرَىٰ$$

«O You who believe! Do not approach the prayer in a state of drunkenness...»[4:43]

The last verse revealed concerning intoxicants prohibited any amount of consumption:

$$إِنَّمَا يُرِيدُ ٱلشَّيْطَـٰنُ أَن يُوقِعَ بَيْنَكُمُ ٱلْعَدَٰوَةَ وَٱلْبَغْضَآءَ فِى ٱلْخَمْرِ وَٱلْمَيْسِرِ وَيَصُدَّكُمْ عَن ذِكْرِ ٱللَّهِ وَعَنِ ٱلصَّلَوٰةِ فَهَلْ أَنتُم مُّنتَهُونَ$$

«Satan only wants to excite enmity and hatred between you with intoxicants... so will you not then abstain?» [5:91]

Another topic for which the first and last verses have been defined are the verses that deal with the lawful and prohibited foods. The first verse revealed was during the Makkan stage:

$$قُل لَّآ أَجِدُ فِى مَآ أُوحِىَ إِلَىَّ مُحَرَّمًا عَلَىٰ طَاعِمٍ يَطْعَمُهُۥٓ إِلَّآ أَن يَكُونَ مَيْتَةً أَوْ دَمًا مَّسْفُوحًا أَوْ لَحْمَ خِنزِيرٍ فَإِنَّهُۥ رِجْسٌ أَوْ فِسْقًا أُهِلَّ لِغَيْرِ ٱللَّهِ بِهِۦ$$

«Say: I do not find in that which has been inspired to me anything forbidden to eat by one who wishes to do so, except if it be a dead animal, or blood poured forth, or the flesh of swine – for that is surely impure – or the impious meat that has been sacrificed to other than Allaah» [6:145]

After this, 16:114 was revealed, and this was followed in Madeenah by 2:73, and lastly by 5:3, which classified the various types of dead meats that are forbidden.

A similar examination of the verses pertaining to *jihaad* have also been made.[171]

The knowledge of this chronology is essential in differentiating the abrogated rulings from the applicable ones. It also enables the scholar to understand and appreciate the history of the evolution of Islaamic law, and it demonstrates the care with which the knowledge of the Qur'aan has been preserved.

---

171 cf. Abu Shahbah, pps. 129-130.

CHAPTER 6

THE MAKKEE AND
THE MADANEE VERSES

The Muslims started out weak and powerless in Makkah, and yet within a few decades they managed to unite all the tribes of Arabia in the worship of Allaah. The turning point in this period was the *hijrah* of the Prophet (ﷺ) from Makkah to Madeenah. It was after the *hijrah* that the Muslims finally had a state in which they could practice their religion without any fear. Therefore, it is not surprising to find that the Qur'aan catered to the specific needs of the Muslims in Madeenah in a different way than it had done in Makkah. There is a marked difference in the verse content, style and syntax of these two periods, reflecting the different circumstances that the Muslims were in. It is this topic that is the subject of the *makkee* and *madanee* verses.

The Qur'aan has been preserved to an extent that is unrivalled by any other book. This is no surprise to a Muslim, for Allaah Himself has promised to safeguard it. The Qur'aan says,

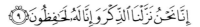

«Verily, it is We who have sent down the Remembrance, and of a surety, We will guard it (from corruption)» [15:9]

The Qur'aan has been preserved so carefully that not only has the actual text been safeguarded, but also all related knowledge that is needed to understand it. Among these aspects is the science of categorising those verses and *soorahs* which are *makkee* and those which are *madanee*.

The Prophet (ﷺ) did not specifically remark whether a verse was *makkee* or *madanee*, but the Companions understood the importance of this topic and carefully preserved this knowledge, as it is essential in understanding the Qur'aan. Ibn Mas'ood said: "I swear by Allaah, besides whom there is no other god, there is no *soorah* in the Qur'aan except that I know where it was revealed. And there is not a single verse in the Qur'aan except that I know the reason behind its revelation. And if there were any person that knew more about the Qur'aan than I did, and it was possible for me to reach him, I would ride (on my camel) towards him (to get this knowledge)."[172]

---

172 Reported by al-Bukhaaree.

It is because of this enthusiasm of the Companions that all external information concerning a verse's revelation was preserved. The scholar Aboo Bakr al-Baaqillaanee (d. 403 A.H.) said,[173]

> This (preservation) is based upon the strong enthusiasm of the Companions and Successors. Just like the students (of a certain scholar) follow up on the works of their teacher, and memorize his speeches and books, and keep a record of what he wrote first and what he wrote last, so too the Qur'aan was (preserved) – in fact to an even greater extent, for the eagerness for it was even stronger.

Thus, it is not uncommon to find a Companion narrating external information concerning a verse's revelation – information that might at first seem irrelevant. Such information included the time and place of revelation, and sometimes even the circumstances the Prophet (ﷺ) was in. For example, al-Bukhaaree narrates that verse 9:118 was revealed at Tabook during the last third of the night, when the Prophet (ﷺ) was with Umm Salamah. Ibn Mas'ood said, "Once, we were with the Prophet (ﷺ) in one of the caves of Mina when Allaah revealed,

«By the winds sent forth...»" [77:1].[174]

And the verse,

وَٱللَّهُ يَعْصِمُكَ مِنَ ٱلنَّاسِ

«Allaah will protect you from mankind» [5:67]

was revealed 'at night when the Prophet (ﷺ) was in a tent, surrounded by bodyguards.' When Allaah revealed this verse, the Prophet (ﷺ) lifted the covering of the tent and said to his bodyguards, "O people! You may leave, for Allaah has promised to protect me."[175] After this, the Prophet (ﷺ) never took any bodyguards.[176]

First, it is essential to discuss the definition of *makkee* and *madanee* verses.

I. The Definition of Makkee and Madanee

There are three methodologies by which the *makkee* and *madanee* revelations are defined.

The first definition relies upon the time of revelation, taking the Prophet's (ﷺ) *hijrah* as the division factor. According to this definition, if a verse was revealed before the *hijrah*, it is considered *makkee*, and if revealed after the *hijrah*, it is considered *madanee*. This definition ignores the actual place of revelation. Therefore, those verses revealed at the Farewell Pilgrimage (8 A.H.), or the Conquest of Makkah (10 A.H.),

---

173 az-Zarkashee, v. 1, p. 191.
174 Reported by al-Bukhaaree.
175 Reported by at-Tirmidhee and al-Haakim.
176 For other examples of this nature, see Zarzur, pps. 136-138.

would be considered *madanee* by this definition, even though the actual place of revelation was Makkah. The criterion according to this definition, once again, is the *time* of revelation, not *place*. This is the strongest of the three definitions, since it is the most beneficial, and is therefore the one primarily utilised by the scholars of Islaam.

The second definition relies upon the place where the verse was revealed. If a verse was revealed in Madeenah, it is *madanee*, and if it was revealed in Makkah, it is *makkee*. Therefore, the verses revealed at Makkah during the Farewell Pilgrimage would be considered *makkee*, even though they were revealed after the *hijrah*. The criterion here is not the *time* of revelation, as in the first definition, but *place*. A flaw with this definition is that those verses revealed neither in Makkah nor Madeenah (for example, the verses revealed at Tabook) would not be classified as either *makkee* or *madanee*, as this definition cannot take such verses into its classification scheme.

The third definition depends upon the addressees of the verse. If the verse is meant for the Quraysh and the polytheists of Makkah, it is considered *makkee*, and if the verse is addressing the Muslims or hypocrites in Madeenah, it will be considered *madanee*. One of the flaws in this definition is that there are many verses in the Qur'aan where the addressees are not specifically Makkan or Madeenan. Sometimes, the Qur'aan addresses a specific portion of mankind, such as the People of the Book, and at other times, it addresses all of the creation.

It is also possible to combine these three definitions when dealing with a verse or *soorah* and to say, for example, that the verse is *madanee* with regards to time and place, yet *makkee* with regards to whom it is addressing. An example of this is *Soorah ar-Ra'ad*, which was revealed after the *hijrah* in Madeenah, but addresses the polytheists of Makkah.

It should also be mentioned that certain modern authors[177] have divided each of the Makkan and Madeenan periods into three stages: early, middle, and late revelations. They then attempted to show that each of these three stages has a unique style and specific subject. Despite the ingenuity of this classification, there does not seem to be a very fine line that discerns these stages from one another.

II. The Knowledge of Makkee and Madanee Verses

There are two ways of knowing whether a verse or *soorah* is *makkee* or *madanee*. The first way is by relying upon reports from the Companions; in other words, a Companion specifically states the place and/or time of revelation, or gives some external information from which the time of revelation can be inferred. The second way is by personal reasoning, or *ijtihaad*. In this method, a scholar will take the verses' meaning and style into account and try to 'presume' whether the verse is *makkee* or *madanee*. These two methods are not equivalent in acceptability.

---

177 cf. Saleh, pps. 185-223.

If there exist reports from the Companions stating that a particular revelation occurred at a certain time and place, this knowledge is taken as undisputed fact.[178] This is because the Companions were present at the time of revelation, and were the only eye-witnesses to the actual revelation process.

If, on the other hand, the ruling that a certain verse is *makkee* or *madanee* was derived by the *ijtihaad* of a scholar, then this ruling may be accepted or rejected. The scholar applies the known characteristics of *makkee* and *madanee* revelations (which shall be discussed next) to arrive at this verdict, but it is possible that such a verdict may be incorrect.

III. The Attributes of Makkee and Madanee Revelations

One of the aspects of *makkee* and *madanee* revelations is that they each have unique attributes. This is because each type of revelation catered to a different need. The state of the Muslims differed greatly before and after the *hijrah*. In the early stages of revelation, Islaam was still a relatively new religion, and the beliefs of Islaam still had to be established. In addition, the Muslims were oppressed and had very little power, and thus needed continual moral encouragement. In the second period, however, the Muslims had their own state and were relatively established. The beliefs of Islaam had been revealed, and now the Muslims were in need of divine guidance in their daily and social lives. They also needed to know the rules and conduct of *jihaad*, and the laws of inter-religious conduct.

In other words, as the needs of the *ummah* varied according to its situation, so did the style and content of the revelation.

The attributes of the *makkee* and *madanee* revelations are divided into two categories: the common themes of each type of revelation, and the specific characteristics that have been observed of each type of revelation. It should not be presumed that every *makkee* or *madanee* verse is indicative of these particular characteristics and themes; rather, these are general trends that are applicable to most *makkee* and *madanee* verses. [179]

COMMON THEMES OF MAKKEE AND MADANEE VERSES

The *makkee soorahs* have as common themes:

1) The call to the pure worship of Allaah (*tawheed*), by affirming His Names and Attributes, and rejecting all false deities and idols. The fact that there is only one true god is proven in these verses. Many *makkan* verses also stress the necessity of purifying one's worship to Allaah, and that this is the logical consequence in the belief of one god.

---

178 Unless there exist statements to the contrary by other Companions. There are a number of methods of inspecting the various reports by Companions to arrive at the strongest conclusion, but these are beyond the scope of this book.

179 For these attributes, see: az-Zarkashee, 1/187-191; as-Suyootee, 1/22-23; Qattaan, 63-64; Ubaydaat 114-117.

2) The establishment of the *'aqeedah* (beliefs), by affirming belief in prophethood, the angels, the previously revealed scriptures, and the Day of Judgement. The *makkee soorahs*, therefore, elaborated upon the stories of the previous prophets, the description of the Day of Resurrection, the descriptions of Heaven and Hell and the rewards and punishments in them, and other aspects of *'aqeedah*.

3) The establishment of morality. For example, *makkee* verses called for good conduct, respecting orphan's properties, and treating female infants properly (as there was a custom amongst the Arabs of female infanticide). At this stage, only a broad basis of morality was established; specific laws (concerning fornication, drinking, etc.,) were not revealed.

4) The stories of the previous generations. The *makkee soorahs* emphasised the stories of the previous prophets, and the trials and tribulations that the believers faced at the hands of the disbelievers. These *soorahs* repeatedly warned the idolaters of the punishment that the earlier nations had received.

As for the *madanee* revelations, their common themes are:

1) The perfection of the rituals of worship. In the *madanee* verses, the detailed laws of prayer,[180] charity, fasting and pilgrimage were revealed.

2) The establishment of a system of laws governing individual, familial and societal relationships. Included in this are laws for *jihaad*, marriage, inheritance, the laws concerning the relationship of the Islaamic state in war and peace, the relationship of the Muslims with other religious groups, and the punishments for specific crimes (*hudood*).

3) The discussion with the Jews and Christians concerning their religions, and an exposition of their faults and shortcomings. The *madanee* verses sought to invite the Christians and Jews to Islaam, primarily by exposing the corruption in their books and beliefs, and by explaining the true teachings of Moosaa and 'Eesaa. The *madanee* verses also discussed in detail the history of the Children of Israa'eel, and how Allaah dealt with their faithlessness and treachery.

4) The exposition of the plots of the hypocrites. The Madeenan phase witnessed a new phenomenon that was unknown to the Muslims of Makkah – that of hypocrisy. For the first time, it was socially and politically advantageous to be considered a Muslim, and this led to a new breed of people, those who professed belief but in reality were nothing more than pretenders! Thus, the *madanee* verses mentions the hypocrites and their plots, in order to warn the Muslims against their evils, and caution the Muslims not be become like them.

---

180 Prayer had already been established in the Makkan stage, but it was in Madeenah that the number of *raka'ats* were changed and specified for all later generations.

Specific Characteristics of Makkee and Madanee verses

Some specific characteristics of *makkee* revelations are:

1) Every *soorah* that has the oath, "Nay (*kalaa*)!" is *makkee*. This oath only occurs in the last half of the Qur'aan, in over fifteen *soorahs*.

2) All *soorahs* that begin with disjointed letters (*al-muqatta'aat*),[181] such as *Alif-Lam-Meem*, and *Ha-Meem*, are *makkee*, with the exceptions of al-Baqarah and Aali-'Imraan.

3) All *soorahs* which have a verse of prostration (*sajdah at-tilaawah*) are *makkee*.

4) All *soorahs* which mention the stories of the previous prophets, and the story of Aadam and the creation, are *makkee*, with the exception of *Soorah* al-Baqarah.

5) Generally, the verses in *makkee* revelations are short and succinct, using strong words and frequent oaths.

Some specific characteristics of *madanee* revelations are:

1) Every verse that mentions a punishment for a crime (*hudood*) is *madanee*.

2) Every *soorah* that mentions the hypocrites is *madanee*, except *Soorah* al-'Ankaboot.

3) Every *soorah* that addresses the Jews and Christians is *madanee*.

4) Every *soorah* that mentions *jihaad* is *madanee*.

5) Generally, *madanee* verses are longer than their *makkee* counterparts.

IV. The Categories of Makkee and Madanee

There is more to the knowledge of *makkee* and *madanee* verses than whether a particular verse was revealed before or after the *hijrah*. The scholar Aboo al-Qaasim Hasan ibn Muhammad an-Naysabooree (d. 406 A.H.) wrote:

> Amongst the most noble of Qur'aanic sciences is the knowledge of its revelation, and its classification into *makkee* and *madanee*, and that which was revealed at Makkah yet is *madanee*, and that which was revealed at Madeenah yet is *makkee*, and that which was revealed at Makkah concerning the people of Madeenah, and that which was revealed at Madeenah concerning the people of Makkah, and...(*nineteen other categories*). These are twenty-five different categories in total; whoever does not know them and cannot distinguish between them is prohibited from explaining the Book of Allaah![182]

Some of the more important categories are mentioned below:[183]

---

181 See Ch. 9, 'The Beginning of the *Soorahs*'.
182 az-Zarkashee, v. 1, p. 192.
183 See az-Zarkashee, p. 187-205 for most of these examples, and as-Suyootee, 1/11-31.

1) The *makkee soorahs*. These are the *soorahs* whose verses, or most of whose verses, were revealed before the *hijrah*.

2) The *madanee soorahs*. These are the *soorahs* whose verses, or most of whose verses, were revealed after the *hijrah*.

3) Those *soorahs* in which there is a difference of opinion, so that it is unsure whether they are *makkee* or *madanee*.

The *madanee soorahs* are: al-Baqarah, Aali-'Imraan, an-Nisaa, al-Maa'idah, al-Anfaal, at-Tawbah, an-Noor, al-Ahzaab, Muhammad, al-Fath, al-Hujuraat, al-Hadeed, al-Mujaadalah, al-Hashr, al-Mumtahinah, al-Jumu'ah, al-Munafiqoon, at-Talaaq, at-Tahreem, and an-Nasr. These are twenty *soorahs* of the Qur'aan.

The *soorahs* in which there is a difference of opinion are twelve in number: al-Faatihah, ar-Ra'ad, ar-Rahmaan, as-Saff, at-Taghaabun, al-Muttafifeen, al-Qadr, al-Bayinnah, az-Zilzaal, al-Ikhlas, al-Falaq and an-Naas.

The rest of the eighty-two *soorahs* are *makkee*.

4) *Makkee* verses in *madanee soorahs*. As was alluded to earlier, even though a *soorah* might in general be *madanee*, it is possible that certain verses are *makkee*.[184] For example, *Soorah* al-Anfaal is *madanee*, yet verse 64 in particular is *makkee*, "O Messenger (ﷺ), Allaah is Sufficient for you and for the believers who follow you!"

5) *Madanee* verses in *makkee soorahs*. In a similar manner, *Soorah* al-An'aam is *makkee* except for three verses which were revealed after the *hijrah*, verses 151-153, which begin, "Say: Come, and I will recite to you what your Lord has forbidden for you..."

6) That which was revealed at Makkah yet is *madanee*. In other words, those verses that were revealed after the *hijrah* at Makkah. An example of this is the verse

$$ ٱلۡيَوۡمَ أَكۡمَلۡتُ لَكُمۡ دِينَكُمۡ وَأَتۡمَمۡتُ عَلَيۡكُمۡ نِعۡمَتِي وَرَضِيتُ لَكُمُ ٱلۡإِسۡلَٰمَ دِينًا $$

«Today I have perfected your religion for you, and have completed my favours upon you, and chosen Islaam as your way of life» [5:3]

This verse was revealed at the Farewell Pilgrimage, yet since it was revealed after the *hijrah*, it is considered *madanee*.

7) That which resembles the *madanee* revelations in content and style yet is *makkee*. For example,

$$ وَأَقِمِ ٱلصَّلَوٰةَ طَرَفَيِ ٱلنَّهَارِ وَزُلَفًا مِّنَ ٱلَّيۡلِ $$

«And offer prayers perfectly at the two ends of the day and in some hours of the night...» [11:114]

---

184 The actual arrangement of the verses was not chronological. See Ch. 8 on the arrangement of the *soorah*s and verses.

This verse was revealed at Makkah and alludes to the five daily prayers, yet the prayer with all of its laws was not completely established until after the *hijrah*.

8) That which resembles the *makkee* revelations yet is *madanee*. For example,

$$وَإِذْ قَالُواْ ٱللَّهُمَّ إِن كَانَ هَٰذَا$$
$$هُوَ ٱلْحَقَّ مِنْ عِندِكَ فَأَمْطِرْ عَلَيْنَا حِجَارَةً مِّنَ ٱلسَّمَآءِ$$

«And when they (the disbelievers) said, 'O Allaah! If this is indeed the truth from You, then rain down stones on us from the sky...'» [8:32]

This verse seems to be *makkee* since it discusses the idolaters of Makkah, but was in fact revealed after the *hijrah*.

9) That which was revealed in Madeenah addressing the Makkans. There are many verses like this, such as *Soorah* ar-Ra'ad in its entirety, and the first few verses of *Soorah* Tawbah, and *Soorah* al-Mumtaḥinah.

10) That which was revealed at night. For example, the first verse of *Soorah* al-Ḥajj, and the whole of *Soorah* Maryam. The verse revealed at Aboo Ṭaalib's death:

$$إِنَّكَ لَا تَهْدِى مَنْ أَحْبَبْتَ وَلَٰكِنَّ ٱللَّهَ يَهْدِى مَن يَشَآءُ$$

«Indeed, you will not guide whom you love, but rather Allaah guides whom He wills» [28:56]

was revealed when the Prophet (ﷺ) was in his bed. However, as 'Aa'ishah narrated, most of the Qur'aan was revealed during the daytime.[185]

11) That which was taken from Makkah to Madeenah. The first *soorah* to be taken from Makkah to Madeenah was *Soorah* Yoosuf. 'Auf ibn 'Afra was among the eighty Anṣaar who embraced Islaam at the hands of the Prophet (ﷺ) in Makkah (at the second covenant of al-'Aqabah). He returned to Madeenah after he had memorised *Soorah* Yoosuf, and recited it to the people of Madeenah, which led to the conversion of many people. After this, more and more *soorahs* were taken from Makkah to Madeenah.

12) That which was taken from Madeenah to Makkah. There were a number of verses that were sent by the Prophet (ﷺ) to the people of Makkah after the *hijrah*. For example, the verse,

$$يَسْـَٔلُونَكَ عَنِ ٱلشَّهْرِ ٱلْحَرَامِ قِتَالٍ فِيهِ$$

«They ask you (O Muḥammad) about fighting in the Sacred Months.....» [2:217]

was revealed when the Muslims of Makkah were being attacked by the pagans during the Sacred Months. These Muslims asked the Prophet (ﷺ) whether they were allowed to fight back, and Allaah revealed the answer in this verse. Also in this cat-

---

185 az-Zarkashee, v. 1, p. 191.

egory is the verse that prohibits interest (2:278), and the verse that informs the Muslims of Makkah who were unable to perform the *hijrah* that it is possible that Allaah would forgive them (4:99). Another example is *Soorah* at-Tawbah (also called al-Baraa'ah). The Prophet (ﷺ) sent this *soorah* to Aboo Bakr while he was performing Hajj, so that he could recite the *soorah* to the polytheists of Makkah.

13) That which was revealed during the *hijrah*. On the way from Makkah to Madeenah, during the *hijrah*, Allaah revealed these verses to console the Prophet (ﷺ):

$$إِنَّ ٱلَّذِى فَرَضَ عَلَيْكَ ٱلْقُرْءَانَ لَرَآدُّكَ إِلَىٰ مَعَادٍ$$

«Verily, He Who has given you (O Muhammad) the Qur'aan will return
you back to the place of return (i.e., Makkah)» [28:85]

14) That which was taken from Makkah to Abyssinia. These verses were sent by the Prophet (ﷺ) to Ja'far ibn Abee Taalib when he was debating with the Negus of Abyssinia:

$$قُلْ يَٰأَهْلَ ٱلْكِتَٰبِ تَعَالَوْا إِلَىٰ كَلِمَةٍ سَوَآءٍ بَيْنَنَا وَبَيْنَكُمْ$$
$$أَلَّا نَعْبُدَ إِلَّا ٱللَّهَ$$

«O People of the Book: Come to a word that is just and fair between us and
you, that we worship none save Allaah....»[3:64]

15) That which was revealed while the Prophet (ﷺ) was travelling. Most of the Qur'aan was revealed when the Prophet (ﷺ) was not travelling. However, some of the Qur'aan was revealed during battles or travels away from Makkah or Madeenah. For example, *Soorah* al-Fath was revealed at Hudaybiyah, when the Muslims were barred from performing *'Umrah*.

There are other categories of *makkee* and *madanee*, but these are the more important ones, and will suffice for the present discussion.

v. The Benefits of Knowing Makkee and Madanee verses

Some of the benefits of the knowledge of *makkee* and *madanee* verses are:

1) This knowledge is essential in arriving at a proper understanding and interpretation of the Qur'aan, as it is a key to understanding the reason behind the revelation of a verse or *soorah*.[186] The fact that the verse,

$$إِنَّ ٱلَّذِى فَرَضَ عَلَيْكَ ٱلْقُرْءَانَ لَرَآدُّكَ إِلَىٰ مَعَادٍ$$

«Verily, He Who has given you (O Muhammad) the Qur'aan will return
you back to the place of return (i.e., Makkah)» [28:85]

was revealed during the *hijrah*, for example, helps in understanding that Allaah is consoling the Prophet (ﷺ) that he will eventually return to Makkah.

---

186 See Ch. 7, 'The Cause of Revelation.'

2) This knowledge helps differentiate the abrogated verses from the non-abrogated ones. For example, if two verses deal with the same topic and give different rulings, but one is *madanee* and the other is *makkee*, the ruling is taken from the *madanee* verse.[187]

3) It gives an insight into the life of the Prophet (ﷺ). For example, in the *makkee* verses, the Prophet (ﷺ) is told by Allaah to bear patiently the torments of the polytheists, while in the *madanee* verses he (ﷺ) is told to beware of the plotting of the hypocrites. In each case, the reader gains a better understanding of the life of the Prophet (ﷺ), and of the Companions.

4) It gives the history of the gradual revelation of the *sharee'ah*. The first and most important topic, that of *'aqeedah* (Islaamic beliefs), was the primary subject of the *makkee* revelations. In these *soorahs*, the Qur'aan talks about *tawheed* (monotheism), belief in the prophets, angels, the Day of Judgement, Heaven, Hell and other crucial topics. In the *madanee* revelations, on the other hand, the Qur'aan primarily talks about laws for the individual, family and state. The graduality by which different Islaamic laws were implemented is appreciated when one gains an understanding of *makkee* and *madanee* verses.

5) It lays out the procedure and methodology of calling to Islaam (*da'wah*). The *makkee* and *madanee* verses have different methods and characteristics in calling to the religion of Allaah, depending on whom the verse addresses. The polytheists are given different arguments than the Jews or Christians, for example. The caller to Islaam should use the same methodology when addressing these groups. No matter which group is being addressed, however, emphasis is always given on the importance of *tawheed* – of directing all forms of worship, from love, fear, trust, hope, prayer, sacrifice, and vows only to Allaah. Likewise, all *da'wah* should begin with this same theme.

6) Lastly, it proves the care and detail with which the knowledge of the Qur'aan was preserved. A person cannot help but marvel at the miracle of the preservation of each and every intricate detail of the Qur'aan. If the knowledge of where, when and how a verse was revealed has been preserved, then how is it possible that the actual meaning and intent of the verse has not been preserved?

---

187 See Ch. 13, 'Abrogation in the Qur'aan.'

CHAPTER 7

THE CAUSES OF REVELATION - ASBAAB AN-NUZOOL

I. The Definition of Asbaab an-Nuzool

The *sabab an-nuzool* (plural: *asbaab an-nuzool*) is defined to be the event or occurrence that was the direct cause of revelation of a particular verse or *soorah* of the Qur'aan. Therefore, all the verses of the Qur'aan may be divided into two categories with respect to *asbaab an-nuzool*, as follows:

1) The verses revealed without a *sabab an-nuzool*. Most of the verses of the Qur'aan were revealed without a particular incident occurring before their revelation. The primary purpose for the revelation of the Qur'aan was to

«guide mankind out of the darkness into the light» [14:1]

but this does not qualify as a *sabab an-nuzool* for the revelation of the Qur'aan, as shall be discussed later.

As for the statement of Ibn Mas'ood quoted earlier, "...and there is not a single verse in the Qur'aan except that I know the reason behind its revelation...," this does not imply that every verse had a specific cause of revelation, but rather that when such a cause existed, Ibn Mas'ood was aware of it.

2) Those verses revealed in response to a question, or because of an incident or occurrence. It is these verses that are the subject of this chapter.

The *sabab an-nuzool* must be a specific incident, occurrence or question that was a direct cause of revelation of a particular verse or verses. In addition, it must have occurred shortly before the revelation. In other words, the verses must have been revealed in response to the occurrence, and give an answer or ruling pertaining to that occurrence. An example of this are the verses pertaining to inheritance,

«Allaah commands you with regards to your children's (inheritance)...» [4:11]

These verses were revealed when the Prophet (ﷺ) visited Jaabir ibn 'Abdillaah while he was sick, and he asked the Prophet (ﷺ) how he should divide his money among his children.[188] Therefore, the *sabab an-nuzool* of this verse was the question that Jaabir asked the Prophet (ﷺ).

As was mentioned, the *sabab an-nuzool* must be a specific incident; therefore it cannot be claimed that the *sabab an-nuzool* of the Qur'aan was to guide mankind, since this is not a specific incident. This is not to say that the guidance of mankind is not the purpose of the revelation of the Qur'aan, but rather that such a purpose does not qualify as *sabab an-nuzool*. The *sabab an-nuzool* must also have occurred shortly before the revelation of the verse. Therefore to claim that the *sabab an-nuzool* of *Soorah al-Feel* ("Have you not seen how your Lord dealt with the owners of the elephants?" (105:1)), was the attacking of the Ka'bah by Abrahah, is incorrect. Abrahah set out with an army of elephants to destroy the Ka'bah, but this occurred before the Prophet's (ﷺ) birth. Even though this incident explains the meaning of the verses, it does not qualify as *sabab an-nuzool*, since it did not occur immediately preceding the revelation of this *soorah*. Also excluded from *sabab an-nuzool* are the histories of the previous nations, and the knowledge of the unseen.

There is an occurrence that some authors have discussed under *asbaab an-nuzool*, but a little inspection shows that it does not come directly under this topic. This is when the verse precedes the actual occurrence; for example, a verse mentions a prediction that eventually comes true, or a later occurrence clarifies the meaning of a verse. An example of this is the verse,

$$\text{لَا أُقْسِمُ بِهَٰذَا ٱلْبَلَدِ ۝ وَأَنتَ حِلٌّۢ بِهَٰذَا ٱلْبَلَدِ ۝}$$

«I swear by this city! And you are a free (man) in this city...»[90:1-2]

This *soorah* was revealed in Makkah, yet the Prophet (ﷺ) was not completely a 'free' person in Makkah until after the Conquest of Makkah. Another example is the verse,

$$\text{سَيُهْزَمُ ٱلْجَمْعُ وَيُوَلُّونَ ٱلدُّبُرَ ۝}$$

«Their multitude will be put to flight, and they will show their backs» [54:45]

This verse was revealed at Makkah, and some of the Companions understood it to have been a prediction of the Battle of Badr, since during this battle the pagans of Makkah were 'put to flight' and thus 'showed their backs'.[189] However, it seems strained to say that the Conquest of Makkah was the *sabab an-nuzool* of the first verse, or that the Battle of Badr was the *sabab an-nuzool* of the second. Rather, these verses were predictions that came true.

---

188 Narrated by al-Bukhaaree.
189 cf. Abu Shahbah, p. 256, for these and other examples.

Books on Asbaab an-Nuzool

There have been many books written specifically on the topic of *asbaab an-nuzool*. The first person to write a book exclusively on this topic was 'Alee al-Madeenee (d. 234 A.H.), the teacher of Imaam al-Bukhaaree.[190] The classics that are available in this field are the works by Abul Hasan 'Alee al-Waahidee (d. 487 A.H.), entitled *Asbaab an-Nuzool*, and Jalaal ad-Deen as-Suyootee (d. 911 A.H.), entitled *Lubaab an-Nuqool fi Asbaab an-Nuzool*. Al-Haafidh Ibn Hajr (d. 852 A.H.) also authored a work on this topic. In this era, one of the most comprehensive works is by Khaleefah Aleeway, entitled *Jami' an-Nuqool fi Asbaab an-Nuzool*,[191] and one of the most authentic is by the famous scholar of Yemen, Shaykh Muqbil ibn Haadee al-Waadi'ee, entitled *Saheeh al-Musnad min Asbaab an-Nuzool*.[192]

II. The Derivation of Asbaab an-Nuzool

From what has been discussed earlier, it is clear that the *sabab an-nuzool* is a particular occurrence in the lifetime of the Prophet (ﷺ). Therefore, there is no room for personal reasoning (*ijtihaad*) in determining the *sabab an-nuzool* of any verse. It is necessary to rely on the people who were present when the verse was revealed to ascertain the *sabab an-nuzool*.

The sources for *asbaab an-nuzool*, therefore, are *hadeeth* from the Prophet (ﷺ), or statements from the Companions. Al-Waahidee (d. 487 A.H.) said, "It is not permitted to speak about *asbaab an-nuzool* except by transmitting reports from those who witnessed the revelation of the Qur'aan."[193] Since the Companions witnessed the actual revelation of the Qur'aan, their testimony of *asbaab an-nuzool* is accepted.

The scholars have differed with regards to the testimony of the Successors, or the students of the Companions: should their reports of *asbaab an-nuzool* be accepted? Some scholars say that such testimony from the Successors must have come from the Companions, therefore these narrations must be accepted. Other scholars respond by claiming that this reasoning can be used for accepting a narration for *sabab an-nuzool* from any generation, since it would have come from the generation before it, all the way back to the Companions.

Perhaps the safest opinion is to say that reports concerning *sabab an-nuzool* will be accepted from only those Successors who were well known for their association with the Companions and their knowledge of *tafseer*, such as Mujaahid ibn Jabr (d. 103 A.H.), 'Ikrimah (d. 104 A.H.), Sa'eed ibn Jubayr (d. 95 A.H.), and Qataadah as-Sadoosee (d. 110 A.H.).[194]

---

190 Unfortunately, this work has been lost, and is only known through later references of it. See the masters dissertation entitled *Imaam 'Alee al-Madinee wa Manhajuhu fi Naqd ar-Rijal* by Ikraam Allaah al-Haqq, Umm al-Qurra University, Makkah, 1984, p. 220.

191 Published by *Matabi al-Ashaa'*, Riyadh, 1984. This work combines all narrations, authentic and otherwise, concerning *asbaab an-nuzool*. Therefore, it is essential to differentiate the authentic narrations from the inauthentic ones before quoting any material from it.

192 Unfortunately, the publisher's name, city and date of publication are not mentioned.

193 Al-Waahidee, p. 8.

194 as-Suyootee, 1/42.

The Wordings of Asbaab an-Nuzool

It is essential to discuss the different wordings that the Companions used in narrating the *sabab an-nuzool* of particular verses, and how these wordings are to be interpreted. This is because, occasionally, the Companions intended to imply that a particular act came under the ruling of a verse, and not necessarily that it was the *sabab an-nuzool* of that verse. At other times, they conveyed their own uncertainty in the *sabab an-nuzool* (i.e., 'I think this verse came down regarding...').

There are two primary ways or wordings that the Companions used in narrating such incidents. The first manner of phrasing that is found in the statement of the Companions is clear and unequivocal concerning the *sabab an-nuzool* of the verse; for example, the statement: 'The reason this verse was revealed was...,' or, 'The Prophet (صلى الله عليه وسلم) was asked concerning such-and-such, and so Allaah revealed...' If the *sabab an-nuzool* is narrated in such a manner, then there is no doubt or ambiguity in accepting it.

The second type of phrasing, however, is not explicit and unequivocal in nature; for example the statement, 'This verse was revealed concerning such-and-such an act.' Scholars have differed with regards to the acceptance of this type of report as *sabab an-nuzool*. This is because this type of statement does not necessarily imply that the particular act mentioned was the *sabab an-nuzool* of the verse. It could imply that the ruling of the verse applies to that case, or it could also imply that the act was the *sabab an-nuzool*. In other words, due to the ambiguity in the wording of the statement, it does not give certain knowledge, and can be interpreted either way.

In such a case, Imaam al-Bukhaaree (d. 256 A.H.) took these reports as equivalent to a *hadeeth* of the Prophet (صلى الله عليه وسلم), and accepted them as *sabab an-nuzool*. On the other hand, Imaam Muslim (d. 261 A.H.), Ahmad ibn Hambal (d. 204 A.H.) and az-Zarkashee only accepted such reports to mean that the ruling of the verse applied to that situation, but the situation was not the *sabab an-nuzool* of the verse.[195]

It is possible that there exists more than one narration concerning the *sabab an-nuzool* of a particular verse. This occurrence will be discussed in greater detail in the next section. The point that is wished to be understood in this section is that, if one of the reports is narrated in an unequivocal, clear manner (i.e., the first type of phrasing), and the other report is not (i.e., the second type of phrasing), then the former is taken to be the *sabab an-nuzool* of the verse, and the latter as coming under the meaning of the verse.

Perhaps an example will better clarify this point. The particular example is the verse:

$$نِسَآؤُكُمْ حَرْثٌ لَّكُمْ فَأْتُواْ حَرْثَكُمْ أَنَّىٰ شِئْتُمْ$$

«Your wives are a tilth for you, so go into your tilth (i.e., have sexual relations with them) as and when you wish...» [2:223]

---

195 Ubaydaat, p.68.

The verse has two narrations concerning its *sabab an-nuzool*. Ibn 'Umar narrated, "This verse was revealed concerning anal intercourse (i.e., to prohibit it)."[196] On the other hand, there exists another narration from Jaabir ibn 'Abdillaah in which he stated that this verse was revealed in response to a question from the Ansaar. The Jews of Madeenah used to claim that if a person had intercourse with his wife from the back[197] then the child would be born with a deficiency. When the Ansaar asked the Prophet (ﷺ) about this superstition, Allaah revealed this verse, instructing them that such intercourse was allowed.[198]

In this example, it is seen that there are two narrations for the *sabab an-nuzool* of the verse. The narration of Ibn 'Umar is of the second type of wording. It could imply that the verse was revealed in response to the question, "Is anal intercourse allowed?" (in which case it would be the *sabab an-nuzool* of the verse), or it could imply that the verse prohibits anal intercourse (in which case this is one of the points that can be derived from the verse, and has no relation to its *sabab an-nuzool*). The report of Jaabir, however, is explicit in its wording, in that the verse was revealed in response to a particular question from the Ansaar.

Faced with these two narrations, both of which are narrated in al-Bukhaaree, the explicit one takes precedence, i.e., the verse was revealed in response to the question of the Ansaar. The narration of Ibn 'Umar shows that this verse also prohibits anal intercourse, and therefore he said, 'This verse was revealed concerning anal intercourse.'

III. Multiple Asbaab an-Nuzool for One Verse

There are many instances where there exists more than one narration concerning the *sabab an-nuzool* of a particular verse. One such example concerning verse 2:223 has just been mentioned.

When there exist multiple narrations concerning *asbaab an-nuzool* for a single verse, the following guidelines are used:[199]

1) If one of the narrations is weak, and the other is authentic, then the weak one is rejected and the authentic one accepted.

For example, there are two reports concerning the *sabab an-nuzool* for *soorah* 93,

$$ وَٱلضُّحَىٰ ۝ وَٱلَّيْلِ إِذَا سَجَىٰ ۝ مَا وَدَّعَكَ رَبُّكَ وَمَا قَلَىٰ ۝ $$

«By the Forenoon! And by the Night when it is Still! Your Lord has neither Forsaken you nor Hated you!» [93:1-3]

Al-Bukhaaree and Muslim narrate that once the Prophet (ﷺ) did not receive inspiration for a few days, so one of the women of the Quraysh ridiculed him, saying,

---

196 Reported in al-Bukhaaree.
197 In other words, if he had normal intercourse with his wife with her back towards him.
198 Reported in al-Bukhaaree.
199 cf. Ubaydaat, p.70-73, Qattaan 87-91.

"O Muḥammad, I think your Satan has left you." Allaah then revealed these verses in response to her. On the other hand, there exists a narration in at-Ṭabaraanee, stating that the Prophet (ﷺ) did not receive inspiration for a few days, so he started worrying about this. This caused the servant of the Prophet (ﷺ) to clean the house, and she discovered a dead puppy under the bed. When she removed it, this *soorah* was revealed. Since this narration is weak,[200] it is rejected as *sabab an-nuzool*.

2)   If both narrations are authentic, then it is investigated to see if there are any grounds for preferring one narration over the other.

For example, if one of them is narrated in a clear manner as being the *sabab an-nuzool* (i.e., the first type of phrasing mentioned in the previous section), whereas the other is not, then the former narration is accepted, as with the story of the Anṣaar above.

Another reason that one narration is preferred over another is if one of the narrations is reported by a Companion who witnessed the *sabab an-nuzool* of the verse and was present at the time of the revelation, and another that is based on second-hand information. In this case, the eyewitness report is accepted.

The verse,

$$\text{وَيَسْـَٔلُونَكَ عَنِ ٱلرُّوحِ قُلِ ٱلرُّوحُ مِنْ أَمْرِ رَبِّى}$$

«They ask you concerning the Spirit. Say: 'The Spirit is from the command (or knowledge) of my Lord...'»[17:85]

has two reports concerning its *sabab an-nuzool*. The first one is reported by Ibn Mas'ood, who said, "I was walking with the Prophet (ﷺ) in Madeenah, and he was leaning on a stick. We passed by a group of Jews, who whispered to one another, 'Why do you not ask him something (to try to outwit him)?' Then they asked, 'Tell us about the Spirit.' I saw the Prophet (ﷺ) stand for a while, raising his head, so I knew he was being inspired. When the inspiration finished, he (ﷺ) read,

$$\text{وَيَسْـَٔلُونَكَ عَنِ ٱلرُّوحِ قُلِ ٱلرُّوحُ مِنْ أَمْرِ رَبِّى}$$
$$\text{وَمَآ أُوتِيتُم مِّنَ ٱلْعِلْمِ إِلَّا قَلِيلًا ﴿٨٥﴾}$$

«They ask you concerning the Spirit. Say: The Spirit is from the command (or knowledge) of my Lord,' and of knowledge, you have only been given little'» [17:85].[201]

The second report is from Ibn 'Abbaas, who said that the polytheists of Makkah asked the Jews to give them a question that they could ask the Prophet (ﷺ), in order to baffle him. The Jews told them to ask about the Spirit, and when they did, Allaah revealed these verses. In this report, it is the Quraysh who are asking the Prophet (ﷺ), and not the Jews.[202]

---

200 There is an unknown narrator in its chain. See Ibn Ḥajr's comments in *Fatḥ* (v. 8, p. 671).
201 Reported in al-Bukhaaree.
202 Narrated in at-Tirmidhee.

Faced with these two reports, precedence is given to the first one, since Ibn Mas'ood was present at the time of revelation, whereas Ibn 'Abbaas was not.

3) If both reports are equivalent in authenticity, and there does not exist any means of giving preference to any one of them, then this implies the verse was revealed in response to both of the incidents.

Ibn Hajr (d. 852 A.H.) said, "There is nothing to prevent there being more than one cause of revelation."[203]

This stance is taken when it is possible that these incidents occurred during the same time frame. An example of this is the 'Verse of *li'aan*' (24:4), which deals with the case of a husband who accuses his wife of adultery without the necessary four witnesses.

Al-Bukhaaree narrates that Hilaal ibn Umayyah accused his wife of adultery. The Prophet (ﷺ) said, "O Umayyah! Either bring your proof (the four witnesses), or else we will have to punish you (for slander by whipping you with eighty lashes)!"[204] Umayyah responded, "O Messenger of Allaah (ﷺ)! A man sees his wife with another man; does he need to go and seek other witnesses!" But the Prophet (ﷺ) repeated what he had said. Umayyah responded, "I swear by Him who has sent you! I am truthful, and Allaah will reveal to you (concerning my innocence) to free me of the punishment!" Thereafter, Jibreel came down with the following verses,

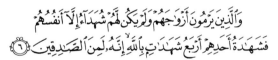

«As for those who accuse their wives, but have no witnesses except themselves, then let them testify four times, swearing by Allaah that they are indeed truthful...»[24:6]

However, another narration in al-Bukhaaree states that 'Uwaymir saw his wife with another man, and he came to the Prophet (ﷺ) and asked him, "O Messenger of Allaah (ﷺ)! A man sees his wife with another man, should he kill him, and then himself be killed (for murder), or what should he do?" The Prophet (ﷺ) responded, "Allaah has revealed verses concerning you and your spouse." He then recited the verses of *li'aan*.

Faced with these two authentic reports, it is concluded that both of these incidents occurred in a similar time frame,[205] and the verses of *li'aan* were revealed in response to both of these cases.

4) If both reports are equally authentic and the time frames are known to be far apart, then this implies that the verse was revealed more than once.

---

203 Aleeway, p. 15.

204 Up to this time, the only verses governing accusations stated that an accuser had to bring four witnesses to prove his accusation, or else he would be whipped for slander.

205 However, it seems apparent that the incident of Hilaal occurred slightly before 'Uwaymir's, since when 'Uwaymir came to the Prophet (ﷺ), the Prophet (ﷺ) could immediately respond to his question.

In other words, if there exists more than one report of *asbaab an-nuzool*, all of which are authentic, and none of which can be given preference over the others, and it is inconceivable that all of these incidents occurred simultaneously, then this implies that the verse was revealed on all of these occasions. As az-Zarkashee stated, "It is possible that a verse is revealed twice, to signify its importance, and to remind people of it... And the wisdom behind all of this (meaning the multiple revelation of a single verse), is that it is possible that a certain incident or question should be the cause of the revelation of a verse, but a verse has already been revealed before it that gives the ruling concerning that incident. Therefore, the same verse is re-revealed to the Prophet (ﷺ), so that the people can be reminded of it, and to show them that the verse also contains the ruling of that incident."[206]

An example of this type of plural revelation is of the verse,

مَا كَانَ لِلنَّبِيِّ وَالَّذِينَ ءَامَنُوٓاْ أَن يَسۡتَغۡفِرُواْ لِلۡمُشۡرِكِينَ

«It is not proper for the Prophet and those who believe to ask forgiveness for the polytheists and pagans...» [9:113]

There are three reports concerning the revelation of this verse, all of which are equally authentic. In addition, it is not possible for all of these incidents to have occurred simultaneously. The first report is that of at-Tirmidhee, who reports from 'Alee ibn Abee Taalib that a person asked forgiveness for his parents, even though they died as pagans. When the Prophet (ﷺ) was informed of this, these verses were revealed. The second report is from al-Haakim who narrates from Ibn Mas'ood that once the Prophet (ﷺ) sat next to a grave, and started crying. Then he (ﷺ) said, "This grave is the grave of my mother. I asked Allaah's permission to pray for her, but He forbade me." He (ﷺ) then read the above verse. And lastly, al-Bukhaaree narrates that when Aboo Taalib was on his death bed, the Prophet (ﷺ) tried to convince him to become a Muslim. However, Aboo Jahl taunted him, saying, "O Aboo Taalib, are you going to turn away from the religion of (your father) 'Abdul Muttalib?" Therefore Aboo Taalib died upon the religion of his father. The Prophet (ﷺ) said, "I will continue to seek forgiveness for you as long as I am not prohibited from doing so." At this, Allaah revealed the above verse.

Faced with these three authentic narrations, it is concluded that it was revealed three separate times, on each of these occasions.

It should be mentioned that some scholars deny that any verse of the Qur'aan was revealed more than once. They claim that once a verse was revealed, there was no need to reveal the verse again.[207] Therefore, when it comes to reports on *asbaab an-nuzool* such as these, they will try to find which of these reports is the strongest (so, for example, with regards to the above story, they will prefer the narration in al-Bukhaaree, since this is the most authentic book of *hadeeth*). However, most scholars do hold the

---

206   az-Zarkashee, v. 1 p. 29,31.
207   For example, see Qattaan's opinion, in his *Mabaahith* p. 91.

view that it is possible that certain verses were revealed on more than one occasion, saying that this is an indication of the importance of such verses.[208]

IV. Multiple Verses for One Sabab an-Nuzool

It is also possible that a number of verses were revealed in response to one occasion or question, thus making one *sabab an-nuzool* the cause of revelation for a number of different verses.

For example, Umm Salamah, one of the wives of the Prophet (ﷺ), asked, "O Messenger of Allaah! I see that Allaah always mentions men (in the Qur'aan), but not women!"

In response to her comment, Allaah revealed three verses: firstly, the verse,

$$\text{وَلَا تَتَمَنَّوْا مَا فَضَّلَ ٱللَّهُ بِهِۦ بَعْضَكُمْ عَلَىٰ بَعْضٍۚ لِّلرِّجَالِ نَصِيبٌ مِّمَّا ٱكْتَسَبُوا ۖ وَلِلنِّسَاءِ نَصِيبٌ مِّمَّا ٱكْتَسَبْنَ}$$

«Do not wish for that which Allaah has made some of you to excel over others. For men there is a reward for what they have earned, and for women there is a reward for what they have earned...» [4:32]

secondly, the verse,

$$\text{إِنَّ ٱلْمُسْلِمِينَ وَٱلْمُسْلِمَٰتِ وَٱلْمُؤْمِنِينَ وَٱلْمُؤْمِنَٰتِ وَٱلْقَٰنِتِينَ وَٱلْقَٰنِتَٰتِ وَٱلصَّٰدِقِينَ وَٱلصَّٰدِقَٰتِ وَٱلصَّٰبِرِينَ وَٱلصَّٰبِرَٰتِ وَٱلْخَٰشِعِينَ وَٱلْخَٰشِعَٰتِ وَٱلْمُتَصَدِّقِينَ وَٱلْمُتَصَدِّقَٰتِ وَٱلصَّٰئِمِينَ وَٱلصَّٰئِمَٰتِ وَٱلْحَٰفِظِينَ فُرُوجَهُمْ وَٱلْحَٰفِظَٰتِ وَٱلذَّٰكِرِينَ ٱللَّهَ كَثِيرًا وَٱلذَّٰكِرَٰتِ أَعَدَّ ٱللَّهُ لَهُم مَّغْفِرَةً وَأَجْرًا عَظِيمًا ٣٥}$$

«Verily, the believing men and women, and the Muslim men and women, and the obedient men and women... Allaah has prepared for them forgiveness and a great reward» [33:35]

and lastly, the verse,

$$\text{أَنِّي لَا أُضِيعُ عَمَلَ عَٰمِلٍ مِّنكُم مِّن ذَكَرٍ أَوْ أُنثَىٰ ۖ بَعْضُكُم مِّنۢ بَعْضٍ}$$

«Never will I allow to be lost the work of any of you, be he male or female. You are (members), one of another» [3:195]

---

208 cf. az-Zarkashee, v.1, pps. 29-32, where he has a whole section devoted to such examples.

There are a number of different narrations in which Umm Salamah asked the Messenger of Allaah (ﷺ) this question, and each narration gives one of these verses. Therefore, it is concluded that all of these verses were revealed because of this one *sabab an-nuzool*.[209]

v. A Person as Sabab an-Nuzool

The Companions used to record which verses were revealed concerning them, as this was a source of honour and distinction for them. For example, Sa'ad ibn Abee Waqqaas stated, "Four verses of the Qur'aan were revealed concerning me (or because of me). (The first one was due to the fact that) my mother promised not to eat or drink until I leave the Prophet Muhammad (ﷺ). Therefore, Allaah revealed,

وَإِن جَٰهَدَاكَ عَلَىٰٓ أَن تُشۡرِكَ بِى مَا لَيۡسَ لَكَ بِهِۦ عِلۡمٌ فَلَا تُطِعۡهُمَاۖ وَصَاحِبۡهُمَا فِى ٱلدُّنۡيَا مَعۡرُوفٗاۖ

«But if they (your parents) try to force you to join in worship with Me partners of which you have no knowledge, then do not obey them, but treat them in this world with kindness...»[31:15]

The second verse was revealed concerning the booty we had captured in war. There was a sword that I really liked, so I asked the Messenger of Allaah (ﷺ) to give it to me. Allaah revealed,

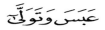

«They ask you concerning the spoils of war...»[8:1]

The third verse was revealed when the Prophet (ﷺ) visited me when I was sick. I asked him, 'O Prophet (ﷺ)! I wish to distribute my wealth, should I give away half of it?' He answered, 'No!' I then asked, 'A third?' He did not respond to this, so from then onwards (a bequest) of a third was allowed.[210] And the fourth one occurred when I was drinking wine with a group of the Ansaar. One of them hit me on my nose (because he was drunk), so I went to the Prophet (ﷺ) (to complain), and then Allaah revealed the verse prohibiting wine."[211]

'Umar ibn al-Khattaab also reported a number of verses that came down because of him. He stated, "I agreed with my Lord (i.e., my judgement agreed with my Lord's) in three matters: (The first was that) I asked the Prophet (ﷺ), 'If only we were to take the 'Station of Ibraaheem'[212] as a place of prayer?!' So Allaah revealed,

---

209   The revelation of the first verse in response to Umm Salamah's question is narrated by at-Tirmidhee, the second verse is narrated by Ahmad, and the third by al-Haakim. See Qattaan, p. 92.

210   Sa'ad was probably referring to 2:180, 'It is written for you when one of you approaches death to leave a will for his parents and kin...'

211   az-Zarkashee, v. 1, p. 33.

212   This is the stone that Ibraheem stood on while he was building the Ka'abah. It used to be right in front of the Ka'abah, but during the Caliphate of 'Umar ibn al-Khattaab, it was moved to its present location, a few metres in front of the door of the Ka'abah.

$$\text{وَٱتَّخِذُوا۟ مِن مَّقَامِ إِبْرَٰهِـۧمَ مُصَلًّى}$$

«And take the Station of Ibraheem as a place of prayer» [2:125]

(The second was when) I told the Prophet (ﷺ), 'Verily, both pious and impious people enter (your house and see) your women. Why don't you order them to seclude themselves?' So Allaah revealed,

$$\text{يَـٰٓأَيُّهَا ٱلَّذِينَ ءَامَنُوا۟ لَا تَدْخُلُوا۟ بُيُوتَ ٱلنَّبِىِّ}$$

«O you who believe! Enter not the Prophet's (ﷺ) houses...»[33:53]

(Thirdly,) once the Prophet's (ﷺ) wives complained to him, so I told them, 'If Allaah willed, the Prophet (ﷺ) could divorce all of you and replace you with better women.'"[213]

In fact, sometimes the Prophet Muhammad (ﷺ) was himself the *sabab an-nuzool* of a verse. For example, al-Bukhaaree reports that once the Prophet (ﷺ) asked Jibreel, "Why do you not visit us more often?" Allaah then revealed,

$$\text{وَمَا نَتَنَزَّلُ إِلَّا بِأَمْرِ رَبِّكَ}$$

«And we (the angels) do not descend except by the command of your Lord...»[19:64]

In this case, the Prophet's (ﷺ) question was the *sabab an-nuzool* of the verse.

VI. The Rulings from these Verses

If the *sabab an-nuzool* of a verse is known, should the verse only apply to the particular case for which it was revealed, or should it be extended to all cases that the wording implies? In other words, is the ruling restricted to the specific circumstances in which it was revealed, or is it applied according to the generality of the wording of the verse?

To quote an example, the oft-quoted verse,

$$\text{وَمَآ ءَاتَىٰكُمُ ٱلرَّسُولُ فَخُذُوهُ وَمَا نَهَىٰكُمْ عَنْهُ فَٱنتَهُوا۟}$$

«And whatever the Messenger gives you, take it, and whatever he forbids you, abstain from it...»[59:7]

was revealed concerning the booty of war. Is this verse then understood to apply only to the spoils of war, or does it apply to everything the Prophet (ﷺ) commanded or forbade, since the wording of the verse implies this?

The majority of scholars hold the view that the rulings from such verses are applied to every case that the wording of the verse covers. In other words, the ruling is

---

213 Reported by al-Bukhaaree. The verse that 'Umar is referring to is 66:5, 'It may be that if he divorced you, his Lord will give him, instead of you, wives better than you...'

not restricted to the *sabab an-nuzool*, but rather to every case that comes under the wording of the verse. In fact, one of the popular legal maxims in *fiqh* is, "The consideration for a ruling comes from the generality of the wording, and not the specificity of its circumstance of revelation."

So, for example, the verses of *li'aan* – despite the fact that they were revealed for particular persons (the Prophet (ﷺ) even said, "Allaah has revealed verses concerning you and your spouse," to 'Uwaymir) – are applied to every husband who accuses his wife of adultery without bringing any witnesses. This is because it is not possible to restrict the ruling to the circumstances of its revelation, for the Qur'aan was revealed as a guidance for all the nations until the Day of Judgement, and not just for the Companions.

However, there are a very small number of verses that are specifically meant to apply only for the *sabab an-nuzool* for which they were revealed. These verses cannot apply to the Muslims in general. When this is the case, an inspection into the *asbaab an-nuzool* enables the researcher to know whether these verses should be applied in general, or whether they are an exception. For example, the verses of *li'aan* were revealed concerning a certain circumstance (i.e., that a husband accuses his wife of adultery without bringing forth the necessary witnesses). It makes sense to apply this ruling to every similar case. However, the verses that came down to clear 'Aa'ishah of the false charges that were impugned on her[214] are obviously meant only for her, and not for the Muslims in general.

This practice (of taking the ruling from the generality of the verse and not from the specificity of the *sabab*) was the one practised by the Companions and those who followed them, and by the majority of the jurists. The other opinion – that of applying the verse only to its *sabab an-nuzool* – was held by a small group of jurists, and is definitely the rejected view. According to these jurists, in order to extend the ruling of the verse beyond the *sabab an-nuzool*, analogy (*qiyaas*) must be resorted to, as the verse cannot be taken to apply to a later case.

Therefore, going back to the initial example of the verse, "And whatever the Messenger gives you, take it...," even though the verses were revealed with regards to the booty of war, since the wording of the verse implies every command and prohibition from the Prophet (ﷺ), this verse is applied based on the generality of the wording.

This fact is also proven by the Companions, who used this verse as evidence for obeying the Prophet (ﷺ) in commands and prohibitions not related to the spoils of war. For example, a woman came to 'Abdullaah ibn Mas'ood, and said, "I have heard that you curse those ladies who tattoo themselves or tattoo others, and those ladies who get their facial hair removed, and those ladies who create gaps between their teeth (to look more beautiful), thereby changing the creation of Allaah!" He answered,

---

214 'Aa'ishah was accused by some hypocrites of committing adultery, and this accusation spread amongst the people of Madeenah. In response to this false charge, Allaah revealed the first twenty verses of *Soorah an-Noor*, which cleared 'Aa'ishah of this accusation, and promised the culprits a severe punishment.

"And why should I not curse them, when the Prophet (ﷺ) has cursed them, and they are cursed by Allaah's Book?" She replied, "I have read the whole Qur'aan from cover to cover, and yet did not find this (curse)!" He answered, "Indeed, had you really read it, you would have found it. Did you not read the statement of Allaah,

$$ وَمَآ ءَاتَىٰكُمُ ٱلرَّسُولُ فَخُذُوهُ وَمَا نَهَىٰكُمْ عَنْهُ فَٱنتَهُواْ $$

«And whatever the Messenger commands you, take it, and whatever he prohibits you from, abstain from it?»" [59:7]

In this case, 'Abdullaah ibn Mas'ood used the verse according to the generality of its meaning (that the Qur'aan commands the Muslims to obey the Prophet (ﷺ) in all matters), and did not limit it to its *sabab an-nuzool*.

In fact, in an even more explicit report, it was the Prophet (ﷺ) himself who showed that the ruling from a verse is to be taken from the generality of the wording, and not the specific circumstances. Once, a man came to the Prophet (ﷺ) and said, "O Messenger of Allaah (ﷺ)! I have kissed a woman that was unlawful for me to kiss, so do with me as you please!" 'Umar chided him, "Allaah hid your sin, if only you had done the same!" The Prophet (ﷺ) remained silent, and did not respond to the man. After a while, the man left the gathering. The Prophet (ﷺ) ordered that he be called, and when he came, the Prophet (ﷺ) recited a verse that had just been revealed to him:

$$ إِنَّ ٱلْحَسَنَٰتِ يُذْهِبْنَ ٱلسَّيِّئَاتِ $$

«Verily, good deeds remove evil deeds» [11:114]

In other words, the Prophet (ﷺ) commanded him to follow up this evil dead with good deeds in order for him to be forgiven. The man asked him, "O Messenger of Allaah (ﷺ)! Is this verse only for me?" He (ﷺ) responded, "No, rather it is for all of mankind."[215] Even though this person was the *sabab an-nuzool* of the verse, the application of the verse was not limited to him.

VII. The Benefits of Knowing Asbaab an-Nuzool

Some of the benefits of this knowledge are as follows:

1) To arrive at a proper understanding of the verse, and remove any misinterpretations or doubts concerning the verse's meaning.

This by far is the primary purpose of the knowledge of *asbaab an-nuzool*. Concerning this topic, al-Waahidee (d. 487 A.H.) said, "It is impossible to properly interpret a verse without reflecting over its *sabab an-nuzool*." Shaykh al-Islaam Ibn Taymiyyah (d. 728 A.H.) said, "The knowledge of *asbaab an-nuzool* aids in understanding the verse, for knowledge of its cause of revelation produces knowledge of its application." Ibn Daqeeq al-'Eed (d. 702 A.H.) stated, "Knowing *asbaab an-nuzool* is

---

215 Narrated by al-Bukhaaree.

a powerful tool in understanding the meaning of the Qur'aan." So important is this knowledge that one who is deprived of it is prohibited from interpreting the Qur'aan.[216]

Some examples will help illustrate the importance of this topic.

'Urwah ibn az-Zubayr read the following verse,

$$إِنَّ ٱلصَّفَا وَٱلْمَرْوَةَ مِن شَعَآئِرِ ٱللَّهِ$$
$$فَمَنْ حَجَّ ٱلْبَيْتَ أَوِ ٱعْتَمَرَ فَلَا جُنَاحَ عَلَيْهِ أَن يَطَّوَّفَ بِهِمَا$$

«Verily, (the mountains of) Safa and Marwa are from the signs of Allaah! So
it is not a sin on one who performs _Hajj_ or _'Umrah_ to the House (of Allaah)
to pass between them»[2:158]

The walking between Safa and Marwa is an integral aspect of Hajj and 'Umrah, yet 'Urwah could not understand how these verses implied this obligation, since the verse says, '... it is not a sin... to pass between them.' From the apparent meaning of the verse, there is no sin if one walks between Safa and Marwa, but neither is it obligatory. He went to his aunt, 'Aa'ishah, and asked her concerning these verses. She then explained that this verse was revealed to clear up some doubts that the Muslims had. In the days before Islaam, there used to be two idols, one on Safa and the other on Marwa, and the pagans of Makkah used to walk between Safa and Marwa for the sake of these idols. When the Muslims conquered Makkah, they destroyed these idols, but were concerned about this 'pagan' ritual that used to be performed between Safa and Marwa. Therefore, Allaah revealed to them that there was no sin on them for walking between these mountains. The verse clarified that the walk between Safa and Marwa was an Islaamic practice and had nothing to do with the practice of the pagans of old. The _sabab an-nuzool_ of the verse shows that the verse was not revealed to explain the legal status of the act of walking between Safa and Marwa, but rather to remove any doubts that the Muslims had with regards to its relationship with the pagan custom of old. After 'Aa'ishah explained the _sabab an-nuzool_ of this verse, 'Urwah was able to understand its meaning.[217]

Another example is of the following verse,

$$وَلِلَّهِ ٱلْمَشْرِقُ وَٱلْمَغْرِبُ فَأَيْنَمَا تُوَلُّوا۟ فَثَمَّ وَجْهُ ٱللَّهِ$$

«And to Allaah belongs the East and West! So wherever you turn your faces
(in prayer), you will find the Face of Allaah» [2:115]

This verse might lead a person to believe that it is not a requirement of the prayer to face the Ka'bah. However, the _sabab an-nuzool_ of the verse shows this to be an incorrect meaning; the verse was revealed concerning a group of Muslims who did not know which direction the Ka'bah was, so they prayed in different directions. After they reported what they had done to the Prophet (ﷺ), this verse was revealed, imply-

---

216 Quotes taken from Ubaydaat, p. 62 and as-Suyootee, _Labaab an-Nuqool_, p. 5.
217 Narrated by al-Bukhaaree and Muslim.

ing that in circumstances where it is not possible to ascertain the *qiblah*, Allaah will still accept the prayer.[218] According to other reports, this verse was revealed concerning the voluntary prayer of the traveller, which may be prayed in any direction. Ibn 'Umar said, "This verse was revealed concerning the traveller on his mount. Wherever he faces (his prayer is acceptable)."[219] In either case, the *asbaab an-nuzool* clarifies the misconception that the apparent meaning of the verse might cause.

Yet another example is concerning the verse,

$$
\text{لَيْسَ عَلَى ٱلَّذِينَ ءَامَنُوا۟ وَعَمِلُوا۟}
$$

$$
\text{ٱلصَّٰلِحَٰتِ جُنَاحٌ فِيمَا طَعِمُوٓا۟ إِذَا مَا ٱتَّقَوا۟ وَّءَامَنُوا۟ وَعَمِلُوا۟}
$$

$$
\text{ٱلصَّٰلِحَٰتِ}
$$

«There is no sin on those who believe and do righteous deeds concerning
what they eat, if they fear Allaah, and believe, and do righteous deeds» [5:93]

The apparent meaning of this verse caused one of the Companions, Qudaamah ibn Madhoon,[220] to believe that drinking wine was allowed. He used this verse to interpret that a pious person was allowed to eat or drink anything, and would not be held accountable for his diet. However, had the *sabab an-nuzool* of this verse been known to him, he would not have come to this conclusion. This verse was revealed in response to a question by some Muslims concerning those people who had fought and died before the drinking of alcohol was prohibited; would Allaah punish them for drinking alcohol, or accept their martyrdom? This verse was then revealed, answering them that Allaah would not hold them accountable for what they had eaten or drank in the past, since these actions had occurred before the prohibition of intoxicants.

It can be seen from these three example that without the *asbaab an-nuzool*, it would be very difficult, if not impossible, to fully understand these verses.

2) To understand the circumstances in which a verse was revealed.

There are many verses in the Qur'aan which would be impossible to understand if the *sabab an-nuzool* were not known. An example are the first twenty verses of *Soorah al-Noor*. These verses were revealed to clear 'Aa'ishah of the false charges that were used to disparage her honour. If the *sabab an-nuzool* of these verses was unknown, it would be impossible to understand what the verses were referring to.

---

218 al-Waahidee, p. 30.

219 az-Zarqaanee, v. 1, p. 110.

220 Almost all authors quote the name of Qudaamah ibn Madhoon's brother, 'Uthmaan ibn Madhoon, when they refer to this incident. This is because az-Zarkashee, in his *al-Burhaan* (v. 1, p. 28), incorrectly mentions 'Uthmaan as the Companion who held this opinion, and almost all later authors (including as-Suyootee) followed him in this error. However, a cursory look at any book of history will show the inaccuracy of this. 'Uthmaan ibn Madhoon died after the Battle of Badr, in 2 A.H. (cf. *al-Isaabah fi Tamyiz as-Sahaabah*, # 5469), whereas his brother Qudaamah ibn Madhoon died in the year 36 A.H. In fact, Ibn Hajr clearly mentions that it was Qudaamah who held this opinion, and 'Umar ibn al-Khattaab had him flogged during his Caliphate for drinking wine, and informed him of the error of his interpretation of the verse (cf. *al-Isaabah*, # 7103, and Abu Shahbah, p. 138).

Likewise, it is necessary to know the *sabab an-nuzool* of the verse,

$$\text{قَدْ سَمِعَ ٱللَّهُ قَوْلَ ٱلَّتِي تُجَادِلُكَ فِي زَوْجِهَا}$$

«Verily Allaah has heard the woman who has come to you complaining about her husband,» [58:1]

in order to understand its meaning.

3)   To apply the verses in a proper manner.

There are certain verses that were revealed concerning particular, exceptional cases. A knowledge of the *asbaab an-nuzool* enables the researcher to know when the verses are applied in general, and when they are specific to the case for which they were revealed. In the previous example of the verses in *Soorah* al-Noor, it is obvious these verses are in reference to 'Aa'ishah and her accusers only, the verse reads,

$$\text{إِنَّ ٱلَّذِينَ يَرْمُونَ ٱلْمُحْصَنَٰتِ ٱلْغَٰفِلَٰتِ}$$
$$\text{ٱلْمُؤْمِنَٰتِ لُعِنُوا۟ فِي ٱلدُّنْيَا وَٱلْأَخِرَةِ}$$

«Verily those who accuse chaste women... are cursed in this life and the Hereafter...»[24:23]

This verse did not allow any repentance for those who accused 'Aa'ishah; however, repentance is still accepted from those who accuse other women.[221] By knowing the *asbaab an-nuzool*, it is possible to know when to apply the verses according to the generality of the wording, and when to apply it specifically to the case it was revealed for.

4)   To know the person who caused the revelation of the verse.

When a Companion was the cause of revelation, this is an honour for him. On the other hand, if the cause of revelation was a disbeliever, this is a further disgrace for him. For example, the verses instructing believing women to cover themselves was revealed after 'Umar ibn al-Khattaab asked the Prophet (ﷺ) to instruct them to do so. This is an honour for 'Umar, since the revelation supported the opinion of 'Umar. On the other hand, the verses that were revealed concerning Aboo Lahab,

$$\text{تَبَّتْ يَدَآ أَبِي لَهَبٍ وَتَبَّ ۝}$$

«Perish the two hands of Aboo Lahab, and may he perish too!» [111:1]

are a further humiliation for him.

The knowledge of *asbaab an-nuzool* also prevents the application of the verse to the wrong persons. For example, when Mu'aawiyah wanted to nominate his son Yazeed for the position of the next caliph, he instructed all of the governors to make this announcement. The governor of Madeenah, Marwaan, called the people and asked them to give allegiance to Yazeed, and he said, "This is the custom of Aboo Bakr and

---

221 Qattaan, p. 80.

'Umar." 'Abd ar-Ra<u>h</u>maan ibn Abee Bakr said, "Nay, rather the custom of Caesar and Heraclius!" Marwaan tried to capture 'Abd ar-Ra<u>h</u>maan, but he entered the house of his sister 'Aa'ishah. Marwaan then said, "I swear by Allaah, he is the one this verse is referring to,

$$وَٱلَّذِى قَالَ$$

$$لِوَٰلِدَيْهِ أُفٍّ لَّكُمَآ أَتَعِدَانِنِىٓ أَنْ أُخْرَجَ وَقَدْ خَلَتِ ٱلْقُرُونُ مِن$$

$$قَبْلِى وَهُمَا يَسْتَغِيثَانِ ٱللَّهَ وَيْلَكَ ءَامِنْ إِنَّ وَعْدَ ٱللَّهِ حَقٌّ فَيَقُولُ$$

$$مَا هَٰذَآ إِلَّآ أَسَٰطِيرُ ٱلْأَوَّلِينَ ۝$$

«'But he who says to his parent, Woe to you! Do you hold on to the promise
that I shall be raised up (on the Day of Judgement), when the generations
before me have perished.... these are nothing but tales of the ancient!'»[46:17]

To this, 'Aa'ishah replied, "I swear by Allaah, he is not the one; if you wish I can tell you the name of the person this verse is referring to." Therefore, 'Aa'ishah's knowledge of *asbaab an-nuzool* enabled her to prevent the application of this verse to one whom it did not refer to.[222]

---

222 az-Zarqaanee, v. 1, p. 114 (cf. *al-Isaabah*, #5165).

CHAPTER 8

THE COMPILATION OF THE QUR'AAN

The compilation of the Qur'aan is a unique phenomenon that is peculiar to Islaamic history, for no other religious book can claim to be anywhere near as authentic as the Qur'aan. The New Testament was authored over a century after 'Eesaa's death, and the Old Testament's authors are shrouded in mystery, as are the authors of the Hindu scriptures.[223] Only the Qur'aan can be claimed to have been preserved in its original form.

And how can it not be preserved, when Allaah has taken it upon Himself to guard it and protect it? For He says,

إِنَّا نَحْنُ نَزَّلْنَا ٱلذِّكْرَ وَإِنَّا لَهُۥ لَحَٰفِظُونَ ٩

«Verily, We have sent down this Remembrance (the Qur'aan), and We are of a surety going to protect it (from tampering)» [15:9]

And when the Prophet (ﷺ) was fearful of forgetting its verses, Allaah revealed,

لَا تُحَرِّكْ بِهِۦ لِسَانَكَ لِتَعْجَلَ بِهِۦٓ ١٦ إِنَّ عَلَيْنَا جَمْعَهُۥ وَقُرْءَانَهُۥ ١٧

«Do not move your tongue with haste concerning it! For it is for Us to Collect it and give you the ability to recite it» [75:17]

Allaah describes the Qur'aan as,

وَإِنَّهُۥ لَكِتَٰبٌ عَزِيزٌ ٤١ لَّا يَأْتِيهِ ٱلْبَٰطِلُ مِنۢ بَيْنِ يَدَيْهِ وَلَا مِنْ خَلْفِهِۦ تَنزِيلٌ مِّنْ حَكِيمٍ حَمِيدٍ ٤٢

«...an honourable and respected Book. Falsehood cannot approach it from in front of it or from behind it; it is a revelation from One who is All-Wise, Worthy of Praise» [41:41-42]

This is one of the unique blessings that this *ummah* – and the Prophet (ﷺ) – has been favoured with over other nations. The Qur'aan is the only divinely-revealed Scripture whose preservation has been promised by Allaah. The responsibility of pre-

---

223 Khaleefah, p. 9.

serving earlier Scriptures had been placed upon its recipients, without any divine aid. Allaah mentions, concerning the earlier Scriptures,

$$وَٱلرَّبَّـٰنِيُّونَ وَٱلۡأَحۡبَارُ بِمَا ٱسۡتُحۡفِظُواْ مِن كِتَـٰبِ ٱللَّهِ وَكَانُواْ عَلَيۡهِ شُهَدَآءَ$$

«...and the rabbis and the priests (judged according to their Scriptures), *for to them was entrusted the protection of the Book of Allaah*, and they were witnesses to it...» [5:44]

Thus, the earlier nations were given the responsibility of protecting their scriptures, in contrast to the Qur'aan, whose protection was the responsibility of the Creator.

An unbiased researcher, whether he believes in the prophethood of Muḥammad (ﷺ) or not, must conclude that the Qur'aan that is present today is the same Qur'aan that the Prophet (ﷺ) taught to the Companions. It therefore behoves Muslims when making such bold claims to investigate the history of its compilation, and examine the manner in which it was preserved.

There are three distinct stages of the compilation of the Qur'aan. The first is the preservation of the Qur'aan during the lifetime of the Prophet (ﷺ); the second, the compilation of the Qur'aan by Aboo Bakr; and the third, the compilation of 'Uthmaan. All that occurred after the compilation of 'Uthmaan is not related to its preservation, and will not be discussed in as much detail.

I. During the Prophet's (ﷺ) Life

The Prophet (ﷺ) was sent to an illiterate nation, as the Qur'aan itself alludes to:

$$هُوَ ٱلَّذِى بَعَثَ فِى ٱلۡأُمِّيِّـۧنَ رَسُولًا مِّنۡهُمۡ يَتۡلُواْ$$
$$عَلَيۡهِمۡ ءَايَـٰتِهِۦ وَيُزَكِّيهِمۡ وَيُعَلِّمُهُمُ ٱلۡكِتَـٰبَ وَٱلۡحِكۡمَةَ وَإِن كَانُواْ$$
$$مِن قَبۡلُ لَفِى ضَلَـٰلٍ مُّبِينٍ ۝$$

«He is the one Who has sent amongst the illiterate ones a Messenger from amongst themselves, who will recite to them His signs, and purify them, and teach them the Book, and the Wisdom; and before this, they were indeed in manifest error» [62:2]

Not only was the nation that the Prophet (ﷺ) was sent to illiterate, but so was the Prophet (ﷺ) himself. Allaah commands mankind in the Qur'aan:

$$قُلۡ$$
$$يَـٰٓأَيُّهَا ٱلنَّاسُ إِنِّى رَسُولُ ٱللَّهِ إِلَيۡكُمۡ جَمِيعًا ٱلَّذِى$$
$$لَهُۥ مُلۡكُ ٱلسَّمَـٰوَٰتِ وَٱلۡأَرۡضِ لَآ إِلَـٰهَ إِلَّا هُوَ يُحۡىِۦ وَيُمِيتُ$$
$$فَـَٔامِنُواْ بِٱللَّهِ وَرَسُولِهِ ٱلنَّبِىِّ ٱلۡأُمِّىِّ$$

«Say (O Mu<u>h</u>ammad (ﷺ)): 'O Mankind! Verily, I am sent to you all, as the Messenger of Allaah, to Whom belongs the dominion of the heavens and earth. There is no god except He!' So believe in Allaah, and His Messenger, who can neither read nor write...» [7:158]

In another verse, Allaah describes the believers as,

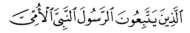

«Those who follow the unlettered prophet...» [7:157]

The fact that the Prophet (ﷺ) could neither read nor write was meant to be one of the greatest proofs that the Qur'aan was not from him, but rather from the Creator Himself. If Mu<u>h</u>ammad (ﷺ) was illiterate, then from where did he bring forth the literary masterpiece of the Qur'aan? The Qur'aan itself says:

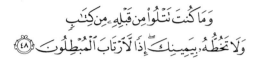

«Neither did you (O Mu<u>h</u>ammad) read any book before it (i.e., the revelation of the Qur'aan), nor did you write (any book) with your right hand! In that case, indeed, the followers of falsehood might have doubted» [29:48].[224]

In other words, if the Prophet (ﷺ) had been a writer, and one whom the people knew to be an eloquent author, this might have given reason to doubt the Prophet's (ﷺ) claim of prophethood; but since the Prophet (ﷺ) was illiterate, and well-known to be so, then such a doubt could not exist!

The fact that the Prophet (ﷺ) and the nation that he was sent to was illiterate does not imply that the Arabs had no experience in the art of composition and rhetoric. On the contrary, the Arabs of the Prophet's (ﷺ) time had a very strong oral tradition of poetry, and the various tribes of Arabia used to compete with one another in producing the most eloquent poems. The annual fair of 'Ukaa<u>dh</u> was the time when every poet would try to compete for the honour of having his poem posted on the door of the Ka'bah. What is known, however, is that the knowledge of reading and writing was minimal. It is said that, at the time of the advent of Islaam, only seventeen people knew how to read and write in Makkah.[225] Thus, the Arabs were forced to pass on most of their history and poetry orally, and because of this, they became well known for their strong memories. This was the literary situation of the people that the Prophet (ﷺ) was sent to.

---

224 It should be mentioned that a small number of classical scholars believed that the Prophet (ﷺ) eventually learnt how to read and write. They claimed that, after the miracle of the Qur'aan and his (ﷺ) illiteracy was established, there was no need for the Prophet (ﷺ) to remain illiterate, and thus Allaah taught him how to read and write. However, the proofs for this are not explicit, and this opinion is rejected by the majority of scholars. In addition, these 'proofs' clearly contradict the Qur'aan's description of the Prophet (ﷺ) as being illiterate, and therefore cannot be accepted. See az-Zarqaanee, v. 1, pps. 364-367 for an in-depth discussion of this point.

225 Azami, p. 1

With these facts in mind, it is doubtful that the Qur'aan was written down during the very early Makkan period, meaning the first two or three years. However, due to the modest number of *soorahs* revealed, it would have been very easy to memorise this quantity. The prayer (*salaat*) had already been made obligatory before the Prophet's (🕌) journey of *al-Israa wa al-Mi'raaj*,[226] so the Companions would have had to memorise the *soorahs* in existence at the time to recite in their prayers.

The earliest record that exists of the Qur'aan having been written down is during the sixth year of the prophethood (seven years before the *hijrah*), when 'Umar ibn al-Khattaab accepted Islaam. The story of 'Umar's conversion mentions that his sister had a *saheefah* (parchment) that one of the Companions, Khabaab ibn al-Arath, had brought with him to teach her family. Khabaab would secretly come to the house of 'Umar's brother-in-law with this parchment, and teach them the Qur'aan. This parchment had the first few verses of *Soorah Taa Haa* written on it. After 'Umar read it, he said, "How beautiful and eloquent is this speech!"[227] and realised that the Qur'aan was a revelation from Allaah and accepted Islaam. This story indicates that the Qur'aan was being recorded and taught to others even during the early stages of the Prophet's (🕌) mission, when the Muslims were still being persecuted.

The Prophet (🕌) was also very concerned about the preservation of the Qur'aan. He (🕌) used to be fearful of forgetting the verses that Jibreel recited to him, so he used to start repeating the verses even before Jibreel finished. Allaah then revealed, to reassure him,

$$لَا تُحَرِّكْ بِهِۦ لِسَانَكَ لِتَعْجَلَ بِهِۦٓ ۝ إِنَّ عَلَيْنَا جَمْعَهُۥ وَقُرْءَانَهُۥ ۝$$

«Move not your tongue with haste, to recite it. It is for Us to collect it and give you the ability to recite it» [75:16-17]

Also, the Prophet (🕌) used to spend large portions of the night reciting the Qur'aan. The Qur'aan mentions,

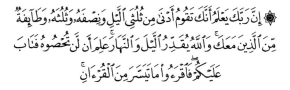

«Verily, your Lord knows that you stand (to pray) a little less than two thirds of the night, or (sometimes) half of it, or (sometimes) a third of it, and so do

---

226 This is the journey of the Prophet (🕌) in which Allaah took him to Jerusalem, and from thence to the Heavens. At this occasion, Allaah obligated the prayer five time a day. Before this, the prayer had been twice a day, and according to the strongest opinion, had been obligated the second year of his (🕌) prophethood. See Mubarakfooree, *Raheeq al-Makhtum*, p. 89.

227 See Mubarakfooree, p. 122-4 for further details on the conversion of 'Umar. Although some scholars point out that the *isnaad* of this story is not authentic, in the details of the *seerah* and other aspects of history, it is not essential that each incident have a perfect *isnaad*. This is because no law or belief is based on these stories.

a group of (believers) with you.... so recite as much of the Qur'aan as easy for you...»[73:20]

In later years, when larger portions of the Qur'aan had been revealed, the Prophet (ﷺ) used to recite, in one *rak'ah*, *Soorah* al-Baqarah, Aali-'Imraan, and an-Nisaa' (around a sixth of the Qur'aan).

The concern that the Prophet (ﷺ) showed in teaching the Qur'aan is shown by the following narration: 'Ubaadah ibn as-Saamit reported, "Whenever a person migrated to Madeenah, the Prophet (ﷺ) would assign him to one of us so that we could teach him the Qur'aan. Eventually, the *masjid* became so noisy because of all of this recitation of the Qur'aan that the Prophet (ﷺ) ordered us to lower our voices so as not to distort the meaning (by mixing all of these verses)."[228] Therefore, the Prophet (ﷺ) would ensure that each new Muslim had a teacher to teach him the Qur'aan.

Such was the concern of the Prophet (ﷺ) in teaching the Qur'aan to the new Muslims that he would even send Companions to other cities to ensure that the Muslims in those cities could memorise the Qur'aan. Even before the *hijrah*, the Prophet (ﷺ) sent two Companions, Ibn Umm Maktoom and Mus'ab ibn 'Umayr, to teach the Muslims of Madeenah the Qur'aan. After the *hijrah*, the Prophet (ﷺ) sent Mu'aadh ibn Jabal to Makkah to teach the Qur'aan to those who had not been able to perform the *hijrah*.[229]

The Companions shared the Prophet's (ﷺ) concern for the preservation of the Qur'aan. They would recite and memorise as much of the Qur'aan as possible. Those who were famous for having memorised most if not all of the Qur'aan were Aboo Bakr, 'Umar ibn al-Khattaab, 'Uthmaan ibn 'Affaan, 'Alee ibn Abee Taalib, Hudhayfah ibn al-Yamaan, 'Abdullaah ibn Mas'ood, 'Abdullaah ibn 'Amr, 'Abdullaah ibn 'Abbaas, Ubay ibn Ka'ab, Mu'aadh ibn Jabal, Zayd ibn Thaabit, and others. During the incident of *Bi'r Ma'oonah*[230] alone, which occurred in the fourth year after the *hijrah*, seventy reciters (memorizers) of the Qur'aan were killed, and a similar number were killed in the Battle of Yamaamah (12 A.H.). This shows that many of the Companions had memorised most, if not all of the Qur'aan.

There are some narrations, however, that seem to imply that only a certain number of people memorised the Qur'aan during the Prophet's (ﷺ) lifetime. For example, a narration in al-Bukhaaree mentions Anas ibn Maalik as saying that only four people memorised the Qur'aan before the Prophet's (ﷺ) death: Ubay ibn Ka'ab, Mu'aadh ibn Jabal, Zayd ibn Thaabit and Aboo Zayd (his name was Qays ibn as-Sakan). Another narration, also in al-Bukhaaree, states that the Prophet (ﷺ) said, "Learn the Qur'aan from four people: 'Abdullaah ibn Mas'ood, Saalim, Mu'aadh ibn Jabal, and Ubay ibn Ka'ab."

---

228 Ubaydaat, p.120.

229 Mubarakfooree, p. 170.

230 The Prophet (ﷺ) had sent these seventy Companions to teach certain tribes that had pretended to show an interest in Islaam, but in reality were disbelievers. When these Companions reached the Well (*Bi'r*) of Ma'oonah, they were massacred. cf. Mubarakfooree, p. 345.

The meaning of these narrations, as Imaam adh-Dhahabee (d. 748 A.H.) mentions, is that these Companions were the ones who were the foremost in the memorisation of the Qur'aan, and it is through them that the chains of narration of the Qur'aan go back to the Prophet (ﷺ). In other words, these Companions were the most famous in their knowledge of the recitation of the Qur'aan, and the most prominent in teaching it to the next generation. Imaam adh-Dhahabee said, after mentioning the names of the seven Companions[231] who were the most famous as having memorised the Qur'aan, "These are the ones whom we know to have memorised the Qur'aan during the lifetime of the Prophet (ﷺ), and the Qur'aan was taken from them directly, and from them originate the chains of narrations (isnaad) of all ten qira'aat.[232] The Qur'aan was also memorised by other Companions, but their recitations have not reached us (through any isnaads)."[233]

During the later periods, the Prophet (ﷺ) also made sure that the Qur'aan was written down, and not just memorised. Al-Bukhaaree reports the following story:

> When it was revealed:
>
> $$\text{لَّا يَسْتَوِى ٱلْقَٰعِدُونَ مِنَ ٱلْمُؤْمِنِينَ غَيْرُ أُو۟لِى ٱلضَّرَرِ وَٱلْمُجَٰهِدُونَ فِى سَبِيلِ ٱللَّهِ}$$
>
> «Not equal are those believers who sit at home and those that strive in the cause of Allaah...» [4:95]
>
> the Prophet (ﷺ) said 'Call Zayd ibn Thaabit for me, and tell him to bring the ink-pot and the scapula bone (i.e., paper and pen).' When Zayd came, the Prophet (ﷺ) told him, 'Write: "Not equal are those believers who sit at home and those...(to the end of the verse)"'.

This incident shows the haste with which the Prophet (ﷺ) recorded the Qur'aan to ensure its preservation. Not only did the Prophet (ﷺ) ensure that the Qur'aan was written down, but he (ﷺ) also checked whether it was written correctly. Zayd narrates, "I used to write the Revelation (the Qur'aan) for the Prophet (ﷺ), and he would dictate it to me. When he finished, he would command me: 'Read it (back to me)!' So I used to recite back to him (what I had written)..."[234]

The parchments on which the Qur'aan was written were so common that Zayd ibn Thaabit reported, "During the lifetime of the Prophet (ﷺ), we used to compile the Qur'aan from scraps of cloth."[235] In other words, they used to form the various soorahs and join the verses scrap by scrap. The writing materials included cloth, stones, date-palm leaves, saddles and shoulder blades of animals. According to the Tabaqaat of Ibn Sa'ad, twenty-four different people acted in the capacity of scribes for the Prophet (ﷺ), among them the four caliphs, and Zayd bin Thaabit.

---

231 These were: 'Uthmaan ibn 'Affaan, 'Alee ibn Abee Ṭaalib, 'Ubay ibn Ka'ab, 'Abdullaah ibn Mas'ood, Zayd ibn Thaabit, Aboo Moosaa al-Ash'aree and Aboo ad-Dardaa.

232 See Chapter 11 'The Qira'aat of the Qur'aan' for details on the qira'aat.

233 adh-Dhahabee, p. 42.

234 al-Ḥamad, p. 98

235 Reported by al-Ḥaakim.

The Companions also had their own personal copies of the Qur'aan. The Prophet (ﷺ) had commanded the Companions, "Do not write anything from me except the Qur'aan. Whoever writes anything besides the Qur'aan should burn it."[236] So common, in fact, were these *mus-hafs* that the Prophet (ﷺ) had to issue an order prohibiting the Companions from travelling to enemy territories with copies of the Qur'aan, for fear that these *mus-hafs* might fall into enemy hands and thus be disrespected.[237]

Those Companions who were famous for their *mus-hafs* were Ubay ibn Ka'ab, 'Abdullaah ibn Mas'ood, 'Umar ibn al-Khattaab, 'Alee ibn Abee Taalib, and some of the wives of the Prophet (ﷺ), amongst them 'Aa'ishah and Hafsa. Some sources have listed over fifteen Companions who were recorded to have written down most of the Qur'aan.[238] These were not complete copies of the Qur'aan, nor was the arrangement of the *soorahs* in them the same as the later arrangement. For example, Ibn Mas'ood had one hundred and six *soorahs*, and the order of the *soorahs* was not the order which is present today. Ubay ibn Ka'ab also had less than one hundred and fourteen *soorahs* and, in addition to the *soorahs* that he had, the prayer for *qunoot*[239] and a *hadeeth* are also found.

'Scholars' who try to cast doubts on the authenticity of the Qur'aan use such narrations to try to prove that these additions were actually 'verses' that were left out of the Qur'aan, but it should be remembered that these copies were for personal use, and as such the Companions could have written any knowledge besides the Qur'aan that they wished to preserve. Az-Zarqaanee writes:

> To summarise, some Companions who used to write the Qur'aan in personal *mus-hafs* sometimes wrote material that was not a part of the Qur'aan. This (material) might be interpretative clauses for certain obscure phrases in the Qur'aan, or prayers (*du'aas*), or other similar things. They were fully aware that these additions were not a part of the Qur'aan. However, because of the scarcity of writing materials, and since the *mus-hafs* were for personal use, they wrote these additions in the *mus-haf* since there was no fear of them mixing the additions that they had written with the text of the Qur'aan. Those people of little intellect fail to take these factors into account, and assume that these additions were actually a part of the Qur'aan, even though this was not the case.[240]

It was the practice of the Prophet (ﷺ) to recite the Qur'aan to the Angel Jibreel every year, during the month of Ramadaan, and Jibreel would also recite it back to him. Faatimah, the daughter of the Prophet (ﷺ), reported that the Prophet (ﷺ) confided in her, "Jibreel used to recite the whole Qur'aan to me every Ramadaan, but this year he has recited it to me twice. I do not see (any explanation for this) except that

---

236 Reported by Muslim. This command was later abrogated by him, for he later allowed the Companions to write down *hadeeth* also. See Azami, p. 22-25.

237 Ibn Abee Daawood, p. 179.

238 Jeffery, p. 14.

239 A prayer that is meant to be recited in the *witr* prayer.

240 az-Zarqaanee, v. 1, p. 271. This point will be discussed in greater detail in Ch. 17.

my time (of death) is near."[241] In another narration, 'Aa'ishah added, "The Prophet (ﷺ) used to meet Jibreel every night of Ramadaan, and recite to him the Qur'aan."[242] Therefore, the Prophet (ﷺ) used to recite the Qur'aan to Jibreel, and used to hear Jibreel's recitation also, and the year that he (ﷺ) died, he recited the Qur'aan twice to Jibreel, and heard it from Jibreel twice. During this last recitation, Zayd ibn Thaabit was present.

The Prophet (ﷺ) did not compile the Qur'aan in one book during his lifetime, nor did he command the Companions to do so. He made sure that the Qur'aan was written down in its totality, but he (ﷺ) did not order for it to be compiled between two covers. There are a number of reasons for this:

1) There was no pressing need during the lifetime of the Prophet (ﷺ) to compile the whole Qur'aan in one book, since the Qur'aan was not in any danger of being lost. There were numerous Companions who had memorised all of it, and each Companion had memorised various portions of it.

2) During the lifetime of the Prophet (ﷺ), the Qur'aan used to be continually revealed. Therefore it would not have been feasible to compile all of it in one book, since it had not been completely revealed yet. The last verse was revealed only nine days before the death of the Prophet (ﷺ).

3) The arrangement of the verses and *soorahs* was not chronological. Verses that were revealed years after the *hijrah* could be placed, by the command of the Prophet (ﷺ), in the midst of *makkan* verses, and vice versa. Therefore, the Prophet (ﷺ) could not have compiled the Qur'aan in the correct order until all its verses had been revealed.

4) There were some revelations that used to be a part of the Qur'aan, but Allaah abrogated their recitation.[243] During the lifetime of the Prophet (ﷺ), this abrogation could occur at any time; therefore it was essential that the *wahy* be terminated before the Qur'aan be compiled.

To summarise, when the Prophet (ﷺ) passed away, the entire Qur'aan had been memorised by many of the Companions, and existed in written form, but it had not been compiled between two covers. Rather, it was scattered in loose fragments that were owned by different people. Some Companions also had substantial (yet incomplete) copies of the Qur'aan.

II. The First Compilation

After the death of the Prophet (ﷺ), the Companions chose the best of them to be their leader, and Aboo Bakr took over the affairs of the Muslims. The first issue that Aboo Bakr had to deal with was the issue of apostasy. Some 'Muslims' had accepted

---

241 Reported by al-Bukhaaree.
242 Reported by al-Bukhaaree.
243 See Ch. 13 'Abrogation in the Qur'aan' for further details.

Islaam during the lifetime of the Prophet (ﷺ) for political reasons, and immediately after the death of the Prophet (ﷺ), refused to give allegiance to the new Islaamic state. Many of these 'Muslims' had given their allegiance to people who claimed to be prophets. Aboo Bakr then undertook a series of wars that became known as the 'Wars of Apostasy' against these people, in order to consolidate the Muslim *ummah*.

During one of these battles, the Battle of Yamaamah (12 A.H.),[244] around seventy Companions who had memorised the Qur'aan were martyred. The death of such a large number of *qurraa'* (memorizers of the Qur'aan) alarmed 'Umar, and he went to Aboo Bakr and said, "Many of the memorizers of the Qur'aan have died, and I am scared lest more die in later battles. This might lead to the loss of the Qur'aan, unless you collect it." 'Umar not only realised the danger of this great loss, but also proposed a solution.

Aboo Bakr replied, "How can I do that which the Prophet (ﷺ) did not do?" Aboo Bakr, the one whom the Prophet (ﷺ) trusted the most in all his affairs, could not even think of undertaking a project that the Prophet (ﷺ) had not done, nor ordered to be done. He was worried that such a project might be considered an innovation in the religion.

But 'Umar continued to convince him, exhorting him of the merits of such an idea, and proving to him that such a project was in no way an innovation. 'Umar realised that this act did not qualify as an innovation in the religion, since the compilation of the Qur'aan was not a religious act *per se*, but rather an act that was of general benefit (*maslaha*) to the Muslims. He continued to convince Aboo Bakr until Aboo Bakr understood 'Umar's arguments and agreed to the project. They both decided to put the Companion Zayd bin Thaabit in charge of collecting the entire Qur'aan in one manuscript. Aboo Bakr told him, "You are an intelligent young man, and we do not doubt you. You used to write the revelation for the Prophet (ﷺ), so we want you to collect the Qur'aan."[245]

They chose Zayd because he was the person best suited for the job, for the following reasons:

1)   He was the primary scribe of the Prophet (ﷺ), and it was because of this that Aboo Bakr said, "You used to write the revelation for the Prophet (ﷺ)." This is also shown by the above-mentioned narration in al-Bukhaaree in which the Prophet (ﷺ) ordered for Zayd to be called. Once, after the Prophet's (ﷺ) death, some people entered in upon Zayd and asked him, "Narrate to us something from the Prophet (ﷺ)." He responded, "And what can I narrate to you? (or, "And what should I narrate to you?") I used to be a neighbour of the Prophet (ﷺ), so whenever any inspiration came to him, he would call me to write it..."[246] Zayd,

---

244   This was an attack on Musaylamah the Liar, who had claimed to be a prophet. It was one of the bloodiest of the 'Wars of Apostasy.'

245   The incident of the compilation of the Qur'aan is reported by al-Bukhaaree, and others.

246   Ibn Abee Daawood, p. 3.

therefore, was the one whom the Prophet (ﷺ) had entrusted with the writing of the Qur'aan.

2) He had memorised the entire Qur'aan during the lifetime of the Prophet (ﷺ). Anas ibn Maalik said, "Only four people memorised the Qur'aan before the Prophet's (ﷺ) death: Ubay ibn Ka'ab, Mu'aadh ibn Jabal, Zayd ibn Thaabit and Aboo Zayd."[247]

3) He was relatively younger than the other Companions, and thus his memory was sharper. He narrates concerning himself that when he was eleven years old, and the Prophet (ﷺ) had just arrived in Madeenah, "I was brought to the Prophet (ﷺ), and the people said, 'O Messenger of Allaah (ﷺ)! This is one of the boys of (the tribe of) Banee an-Najjaar, and he has memorised seventeen *soorahs*.' So I recited to the Prophet (ﷺ), and he was well pleased with that."[248]

4) He was present at time of the Prophet's (ﷺ) last recitation to Jibreel in the Ramadaan before he (ﷺ) died. The famous successor, Aboo 'Abd ar-Rahmaan as-Sulamee (d. 70 A.H.), said, "Zayd witnessed the last recitation (of the Prophet (ﷺ) to Jibreel), and because of this, Aboo Bakr relied upon him in its compilation, and 'Uthmaan put him in charge of writing it (during the second compilation)."[249]

5) He was one of the most knowledgeable Companions with regards to the recitation of the Qur'aan. Sulayman ibn Yasaar (d. 100 A.H.) said, "Neither 'Umar nor 'Uthmaan preferred anyone over Zayd ibn Thaabit when it came to the laws of inheritance... and the recitation of the Qur'aan." 'Aamir ibn Sharaheel ash-Sha'bee (d. 103 A.H.) said, "Zayd ibn Thaabit overwhelmed and conquered the people with his knowledge of the recitation (of the Qur'aan), and his knowledge of the laws of inheritance." Such was his stature among the Companions that 'Umar, 'Uthmaan and 'Alee all appointed Zayd to be one of the main judges and reciters of Madeenah, and he remained in this post until he passed away in 45 A.H. The day he died, Ibn 'Umar said, "May Allaah have mercy on him! He was a scholar amongst the people...'Umar sent out scholars to take over the judicial posts all over the Muslims lands, but he kept Zayd in Madeenah so that he could give verdicts amongst its inhabitants!"[250]

Thus, it is of little surprise that Aboo Bakr and 'Umar both thought of Zayd as the person who should be given this monumental task, for he had in him all the qualities that were needed for this undertaking. But Zayd too was reluctant, and it was only after both Aboo Bakr and 'Umar convinced him that he agreed to do the task. "It would have been easier for me to move a mountain than do that which they told me to do," he said.

---

247 Reported by al-Bukhaaree. The meaning of this narration was explained earlier.
248 al-Hamad, p. 112.
249 az-Zarkashee, v. 1, p. 237.
250 All quotes taken from al-Hamad, p. 113.

He set about collecting the various fragments of the Qur'aan from 'the pieces of wood and the chests of people'. He required at least two people (besides himself) who had learnt the verses from the Prophet (ﷺ) directly, and at least one written copy of the verse written under the supervision of the Prophet (ﷺ), to merit its acceptance into his final compilation. 'Umar ibn al-Khattaab stood up in the mosque and proclaimed, "Whoever has learnt any Qur'aan from the Prophet (ﷺ) then let him bring it forth."[251]

At this, the people brought him the scraps and parchments upon which they had written the Qur'aan. Aboo Bakr told them, "Sit at the door of the mosque. Whoever brings you two witnesses (for a verse), then write it down."[252] Some scholars have interpreted this as meaning two witnesses and two written copies were required.

Zayd reports, "I collected the Qur'aan, until I found the last two verses of *Soorah* at-Tawbah with Khuzaymah ibn Thaabit al-Ansaaree:

$$لَقَدْ جَآءَكُمْ رَسُولٌ مِّنْ أَنفُسِكُمْ$$

«There has come to you, from amongst yourselves, a Messenger...»[9:128]

I found these verses with him only."[253] This report does not mean that only Khuzaymah had heard the verse from the Prophet (ﷺ), but rather that he was the only one that brought a parchment that had these verses written on it. In fact, when Khuzaymah came, 'Uthmaan ibn 'Affaan said, "I testify that these verses have been (revealed from) Allaah!"[254]

The strict criteria employed by Zayd ensured the authenticity of the compilation. Even though Zayd had memorised the entire Qur'aan, and could have written it from his own memory, he still made sure that there were at least two other memorizers of the verse, and a written copy of the verse, written under the direct supervision of the Prophet (ﷺ). The narration of Khuzaymah, mentioned above, indicates that Zayd was looking for the last two verses of *Soorah* at-Tawbah, since he had heard them from the Prophet (ﷺ), but nobody else had brought forth written copies until Khuzaymah came. Another narration adds, 'I could not find a verse that I used to hear from the Prophet (ﷺ), until I found it with a person from the Ansaar, and I did not find it with anybody else,

$$مِّنَ ٱلْمُؤْمِنِينَ رِجَالٌ صَدَقُوا۟ مَا عَـٰهَدُوا۟ ٱللَّهَ عَلَيْهِ$$

«Amongst the Believers are men who have fulfilled their covenant with Allaah» [33:23],'

so I put it in its proper *soorah*."[255] This narration also proves the fact that Zayd knew what was part of the Qur'aan and what was not, since he mentioned that he was

---

251 Ibn Abee Daawood, p. 10.
252 *ibid.*, p. 10.
253 Reported by al-Bukhaaree.
254 Ibn Abee Daawood, p. 11.
255 Ibn Abee Daawood, p. 8.

searching for a particular verse, and could not find it. It also proves that the arrangement of the verses was known to the Companions, because he put the verse 'in its proper *soorah*.'

Now, for the first time, the Qur'aan was in one book. Barely two years after the death of the Prophet (☀), when all of the major Companions were still alive, the Qur'aan had been compiled. The written copy of the Qur'aan was called a *mus-haf* (literally meaning a collection of loose papers) and remained with Aboo Bakr and, after his death, with 'Umar, then with Ḥafsah, the daughter of 'Umar and a wife of the Prophet (☀).

The *mus-haf* that Aboo Bakr ordered to be collected was not meant to be an official copy that the whole *ummah* had to follow. Rather, it was meant to preserve the Qur'aan in its entirety, and ensure that none of its verses were lost. In this, Aboo Bakr accomplished a momentous task. 'Alee ibn Abee Ṭaalib remarked, "The person with the greatest rewards with regards to the (compilation) of the *mus-haf* is Aboo Bakr. May Allaah's mercy be on Aboo Bakr, he was the first person to compile the Book of Allaah."[256]

There is some difference of opinion over the arrangement of the *soorahs* in Aboo Bakr's *mus-haf*. Most of the scholars are of the opinion that Aboo Bakr's *mus-haf* did not concern itself with the proper order of the *soorahs*, for it was not meant to be an official copy that was binding upon the *ummah*. Others allege the *soorahs* were in the same order as that of 'Uthmaan. Also, it is alleged that this *mus-haf* was written to preserve all the *ahruf*[257] of the Qur'aan. In reality, it is of no great consequence whether the *mus-haf* of Aboo Bakr was in the same arrangement of *soorahs* as that of the 'Uthmaanic one or not, or whether it was written with the intent of preserving all the *ahruf*; the primary purpose of this compilation was to serve as a basis for the 'Uthmaanic compilation, and it is this compilation that is linked directly to the *mus-hafs* that are present in our hands today.

III. The 'Uthmaanic Compilation

After the death of Aboo Bakr, 'Umar ibn al-Khaṭṭaaab took over the leadership of the Muslims. Under his auspicious caliphate, the territories of the Muslims expanded five-fold what they had been. When he passed away, the Muslims controlled the remnants of the Persian Empire, Egypt, Syria and parts of the then-defunct Byzantine (Eastern Roman) Empire.

After 'Umar's death, 'Uthmaan took over the caliphate, and continued the great legacy of his two predecessors. The Muslims were successful in waging *jihaad* for the cause of Allaah, and spreading the religion of Islaam. One of the places where this

---

256 Qattaan, p. 128. As for the claim by certain Islaamic sects that 'Alee was the first to compile the Qur'aan, this narration from 'Alee himself shows it to be false. Also, the narration which mentions 'Alee as being the first is weak, cf. Ibn Abee Daawood, p. 10.

257 See Ch. 10, 'The *Ahruf* of the Qur'aan', for further details.

was occurring were the territories of Armenia and Azerbaijan. Muslims from different parts of the *ummah* had joined forces to fight against the enemy.

Unfortunately, the Muslims started differing amongst themselves with regards to
the recitation of the Qur'aan. The Muslims from Syria were reciting the Qur'aan
differently than the Muslims from Iraq.[258] They began contending with each other,
each regarding his recitation superior to his brother's. These Muslims were not Companions, and therefore were not trained in the proper manner and etiquette of the
recitation of the Qur'aan. One of the Companions who was present amongst them,
Hudhayfah ibn al-Yamaan, could not believe what was happening. He advised them
to leave this argumentation, but realised that some action must be taken to prevent
this occurrence on a larger scale. He therefore left Azerbaijan for Madeenah, to report
to the caliph 'Uthmaan.

"O Commander of the Faithful!" Hudhayfah pleaded to 'Uthmaan, "save this
ummah before it disagrees about its Book, like the Jews and Christians did before
it."[259] Hudhayfah told 'Uthmaan what had occurred amongst the new Muslims in
Azerbaijan. 'Uthmaan, alarmed by this news, convened a gathering of the leading
Companions. He informed them of what Hudhayfah had told him, and requested
their advice on this matter. The Companions, in return, asked 'Uthmaan what he
thought the best plan of action was. 'Uthmaan told them his opinion: Official copies
of the Qur'aan should be written and sent to all the provinces, and all other copies
destroyed, so that the *ummah* would have one standard Qur'aan. Therefore, this standard version would serve to unite the Muslims upon one recitation.

'Alee ibn Abee Ṭaalib said concerning this incident, "O People! Do not say evil of
'Uthmaan, but only say good about him. Concerning the burning of the *mus-hafs*, I
swear by Allaah, he only did this after he had called all of us. He asked us, 'What do
you think (should be done) concerning these recitations (in Azerbaijan)? For it has
reached me that each party is claiming that their recitation is better, and this (attitude) might lead to disbelief.' We asked him, 'What do you suggest we do?' He responded, 'I think we should consolidate the Muslims on one *mus-haf*, so that there
not be any disagreements or disunity.' We said, 'Verily, this idea of yours is an excellent
idea.'"[260] The action of 'Uthmaan was agreed upon by all of the Companions.

Therefore, after the Companions agreed to his idea, he requested Ḥafsah, the
daughter of 'Umar ibn al-Khattaab, to loan him the *mus-haf* that Aboo Bakr had
ordered to be compiled, which she did. He then chose a committee of four people,[261]
namely Zayd ibn Thaabit, 'Abdullaah ibn az-Zubayr, Sa'eed ibn al-'Aas and 'Abd al-

---

258   The reason why the recitations of Syria and 'Iraq differed from one another will be understood after
one reads Ch. 10 on the *ahruf*.

259   This incident is reported in al-Bukhaaree. Other narrations imply that such a disagreement had also
occurred in Madeenah, and when Hudhayfah informed 'Uthmaan of the situation in Azerbaijan, this further alarmed 'Uthmaan, and caused him to convene a gathering of the Companions.

260   Ibn Abee Daawood, p. 22.

261   According to another opinion, twelve people, but this is the weaker opinion. Cf., Ibn Abee Daawood,
p. 26.

Ra<u>h</u>maan ibn al-<u>H</u>aarith to rewrite the *mus-<u>h</u>af* of Aboo Bakr. He chose Zayd ibn Thaabit for the same reasons that Aboo Bakr had done before him, and Sa'eed ibn al-'Aas was known for his knowledge of the Arabic language. Imaam adh-Dhahabee (d. 748 A.H.) said, "Sa'eed ibn al-'Aas was one of the members of the committee whom 'Uthmaan chose to write the *mus-<u>h</u>af*, due to his eloquence, and because his (Arabic) style was very similar to the Prophet's ()."[262] The other two members were respectable Companions, knowledgeable of the Arabic language and of the Qur'aan.

Apart from Zayd, the other three committee members were from the Quraysh. This was done on purpose; 'Uthmaan told them, "If you (three) and Zayd differ (on how to spell a word), then spell it in the dialect of the Quraysh, for verily it was revealed in their dialect."[263] 'Uthmaan said this in response to a difference that arose amongst them concerning the writing of the word '*taboot*' (in 2:248); should they write the word in the Qurayshee style of '*taboot*' or the Madanee style of '*tabooh*' (i.e., with a *taa marbootah*)? 'Uthmaan answered them that they should write it as *taboot*, since this was the style of the Quraysh.

This incident shows that the committee consulted the other Companions concerning even such minor details as the spellings of certain words. At times, when there was a difference of opinion, they even called that particular scribe (if it happened to be other than Zayd) who had written the verse for the Prophet (), so that they could ask him how he had spelt the word.[264]

After the committee finished its task, 'Uthmaan ordered that one copy of this *mus-<u>h</u>af* be sent to every province, and ordered the governors of each province to burn all the other copies of the Qur'aan in their provinces. This was a drastic step, but it was necessary if the unity of the Muslims was to be preserved. Every Qur'aan written after this time had to conform letter for letter to 'Uthmaan's *mus-<u>h</u>af*. By his wise decision, 'Uthmaan provided a copy of the Qur'aan that would serve as a model for all future *mus-<u>h</u>afs*. And, as 'Alee pointed out, 'Uthmaan did this with the approval of the Companions.[265] In fact 'Alee ibn Abee <u>T</u>aalib said, "If I were in charge (of the affairs of the Muslims) when 'Uthmaan had been, I would have done the same as he did."[266]

Not only did 'Uthmaan send the actual *mus-<u>h</u>afs* to each province, he also sent Qur'aanic reciters to teach the people the correct recitation of the Qur'aan. He kept Zayd ibn Thaabit in Madeenah; with the Makkan *mus-<u>h</u>af*, he sent 'Abdullaah ibn Saa'ib (d. 63 A.H.) ; to Syria was sent al-Mugheerah ibn Shu'bah (d. 50 A.H.); Aboo 'Abd ar-Ra<u>h</u>maan as-Sulamee (d. 70 A.H.) was sent to Koofah; and 'Aamir ibn 'Abdul

---

262 adh-Dhahabee, *Siyar*, v. 3, p. 449.

263 Reported by al-Bukhaaree.

264 cf. al-<u>H</u>amad, p. 126-7 for examples.

265 Although there are some reports that initially 'Abdullaah ibn Mas'ood did not agree with 'Uthmaan's decision, it is also reported that he later changed his mind; cf. Ibn Abee Daawood, pps. 13-18. According to the famous historian, Ibn Katheer, 'Uthmaan wrote to Ibn Mas'ood advising him to follow the consensus of the other Companions, which he agreed to do; cf. *al-Bidaayah wa an-Nihaayah*, v. 7, p. 207.

266 az-Zarqaanee, v.1, p. 262..

Qays to Basrah (d. ~ 55 A.H.).[267] All of these reciters were well-known for their recitation of the Qur'aan, and it is in fact through them that most of the *qira'aat* are preserved.

'Uthmaan's compilation occurred in the year 24 A.H., or according to others in the early part of 25 A.H.[268]

Aboo Bakr's compilation of the *mus-haf* differed from 'Uthmaan's compilation in the following:

1) The reason that each of them compiled the Qur'aan was different. Aboo Bakr compiled the Qur'aan in response to the large number of deaths of those who had memorised the Qur'aan, and in fear of its being lost. 'Uthmaan, on the other hand, compiled the *mus-hafs* in response to the inauthentic recitations that newcomers to Islaam, who were ignorant of the Arabic of the Qur'aan, were reciting. He wished to unite the Muslims on the proper recitation of the Qur'aan, and therefore ordered the eradication of all other *mus-hafs*, so that the people would have only one *mus-haf* in their hands.

2) The number of people who were in charge of the two compilations was different. Aboo Bakr relied on the person who was the best suited and most qualified to do so, namely Zayd ibn Thabit. 'Uthmaan, on the other hand, used the services of Zayd but also had three of the major Companions, all of whom were known for their knowledge of the Qur'aan, to help him.

3) The number of *mus-hafs* Aboo Bakr ordered to be made was only one, whereas 'Uthmaan ordered several.

4) Since Aboo Bakr did not face the problem of inauthentic recitations of the Qur'aan, he did not have to take the step that 'Uthmaan did in destroying all other written copies of the Qur'aan. 'Uthmaan's decision ensured that all future copies would have to rely upon the original 'Uthmaanic ones.

5) Aboo Bakr compiled the Qur'aan from '...date-palm leaves, wood and the hearts of people...' whereas 'Uthmaan ordered the rewriting of Aboo Bakr's *mus-haf* in the writing style of the Quraysh.

6) Aboo Bakr's *mus-haf*, according to one opinion, did not concern itself with arranging the *soorahs* properly; only the verses of each *soorah* were arranged. 'Uthmaan, on the other hand, arranged the *soorahs* and verses in their proper arrangement.

7) According to some,[269] the *mus-haf* of Aboo Bakr was written to preserve all seven *ahruf*, but the *mus-haf* of 'Uthmaan only included one *harf* and left out the other six. This opinion, however, does not have any basis to support it.[270]

---

267 az-Zarqaanee, v.1, p. 404.

268 cf. Aboo Sulaymaan, p. 28. However, the *Taareekh* of Khaleefah ibn Khayyaat (d. 240 A.H.) lists the battles of Azerbaijan as having occurred in the year 28 A.H. cf. *Taareekh,* p. 160.

269 az-Zarqaanee, v.1, p. 253.

270 cf. al-Hamad, p. 145.

To summarise, the eminent scholar of Islaam Ibn Taymiyyah (d. 728 A.H.) said, "...so in the year that the Prophet (ﷺ) passed away, Jibreel went over the Qur'aan with him twice, and this last rehearsal is the recitation of Zayd ibn Thaabit and others, and it is the recitation that the *Khulafaa ar-Rashidoon*, Aboo Bakr, 'Umar, 'Uthmaan and 'Alee ordered to be written in *mus-hafs*, and Aboo Bakr (was the first) to write it. Then 'Uthmaan, during his caliphate, ordered it to be written (again), and he sent it to all of the provinces, and the Companions all agreed to this."[271]

IV. The Different Mus-hafs

A. THE APPEARANCE OF THE Mus-hafs

The Spelling of the Words of the Qur'aan

The spelling of the words of the Qur'aan is not the same as the spelling of modern-day Arabic. There are certain peculiarities of the 'Uthmaanic script that are not present in modern Arabic. Among these peculiarities in the writing of the *mus-haf* is that the 'Uthmaanic script eliminated certain *alifs* (for example the word '*rahmaan*' is written without an *alif*); added certain silent letters (for example the word '*salaat*' is written with a silent *waw*); merged particular words (for example when the word '*min*' is followed by '*maa*' it is usually written as one word '*mimaa*'); and occasionally spelt the same word that occurred in different places differently.[272] Some of these peculiarities were common of the Arabic and specifically Qurayshee script of that time, but later Arabic grammar changed these rules.

Another peculiarity was that when their existed two recitations of a particular word, the word was written such that both recitations would be preserved. For example, the word '*maaliki*' in (1:4) is written without an *alif*, since there is an alternate recitation '*maliki*.' Had the *alif* been written on this word, the second recitation would not have been possible from the *mus-haf* of 'Uthmaan; however, by writing it without an *alif*, both recitations are possible. The nature of the Arabic script and manner of writing allows for this, in contrast to Latin-based languages.

Due to these peculiarities of the *mus-haf* of 'Uthmaan, later scholars differed over the legitimacy of changing the spelling of the *mus-haf* to conform to later Arabic. This difference of opinion was primarily based upon the origin of the spelling: was it from the Prophet (ﷺ) himself, or was it by consensus of the Companions? Or, was the spelling of the Qur'aan not based upon either of these two factors, but upon the popular custom of that time? The various opinions can be summarised as follows:

---

271 Aboo Sulaymaan, p. 31.
272 This discussion has purposely been left short, since it requires a knowledge of Arabic writing. For further detail, see Ubaydaat, pps. 143-45; az-Zarqaanee, v.1, pps 369-373. Some scholars have attempted to 'read in' the wisdom behind such subtle changes, but in reality these attempts are based more upon imagination than certain knowledge. cf. as-Sabt, v. 1, pps. 403-413.

1) The spelling of the Qur'aan cannot be changed, and the spelling of the *mus-haf* of 'Uthmaan must be adhered to.

The proponents of this opinion differed over *why* the spelling could not be changed into two groups. The first group claimed that the spelling of the Qur'aan was the *Sunnah* of the Prophet (ﷺ), and that he had ordered the Qur'aan to be written in the manner with which it was. Therefore, because the Prophet (ﷺ) ordered this spelling, it is not allowed to modify it. In other words, the spelling of the Qur'aan was with the approval of the Prophet (ﷺ), and cannot be changed.[273]

This opinion is contradicted by the incident in which 'Uthmaan said to the committee that compiled the Qur'aan, 'If you differ in the spelling of a word, then write it in the spelling of the Quraysh.' Had the script of the Qur'aan been decided by the Prophet (ﷺ), then this committee would never have differed about the spelling of any word.

The second group claimed that the spelling of the Qur'aan was not from the Prophet (ﷺ) but from the Companions. Since the Companions all agreed to the spelling of 'Uthmaan, this constitutes *ijmaa'* (consensus), which later generations are not allowed to change.

Both of these groups, however, concluded that the spelling of the 'Uthmaanic *mus-haf* was obligatory upon later generations to conform to. This ruling was the opinion of the vast majority of the *salaf*.

Imaam Ahmad (d. 241 A.H.) was asked concerning the deletion of certain letters that were not pronounced (such as the *waw* in '*salaat*'). He answered, "It is forbidden (*haraam*) to differ from the writing of 'Uthmaan in (the letters) *waw*, or *yaa*, or *alif*, or any (letter) besides these."[274] Imaam Maalik (d. 179 A.H.), when asked whether the Qur'aan could be written in newly invented styles and methods, replied, "No! It may only be written the way it was written first!"[275] In fact, Aboo 'Amr ad-Daanee (d. 444 A.H.) said, "I do not know of any scholar who disagrees with Maalik in this issue!"[276]

Imaam al-Bayhaqee (d. 458 A.H.) said,

> Whoever writes the *mus-haf* must preserve its letters and not change anything of what (the earlier) generations wrote, for they were more knowledgeable than us, and had purer hearts and tongues, and were more trustworthy. Therefore, we should never presume ourselves to be greater than them.[277]

2) The spelling of the Qur'aan depends upon the custom of the time.

In other words, the only reason the Companions wrote the Qur'aan with the spelling that they did was because that was the procedure of writing at the time. Since this

---

273 As for those reports in which the Prophet (ﷺ) supposedly commanded the scribe how to write certain letters, they are very weak or forged. cf. az-Zarqaanee, v.1, p. 377.

274 Qattaan, p. 148.

275 Qattaan, p. 147.

276 az-Zarqaanee, v.1, p.329.

277 az-Zarqaanee, v.1, p.380.

has changed, the Qur'aan may be written to conform with these changes, as long as the recitation is still exactly the same. This is the opinion of Aboo Bakr al-Baaqillaanee (d. 403 A.H.), and al-'Izz ibn 'Abd as-Salaam (d. 660 A.H.). As proof, they use the fact that the Companions were not instructed by the Prophet (ﷺ) to conform to a particular spelling, but rather wrote in the manner that they knew. Thus, if the rules of spelling were different in their time, they would have written the *mus-haf* differently.

In weighing the two opinions above, the first opinion must be conceded to in light of the fact that almost all the scholars of the *salaf* were of this opinion. In addition, if the door were opened to change the spelling of the *mus-haf*, this might lead to playing with the Book of Allaah, since the rules of spelling change with time. The *mus-haf* must not be affected by the passage of time, and the 'Uthmaanic *mus-haf* must retain its sanctity.

Therefore, it is concluded that it is obligatory to adhere to the spelling of the *mus-haf* of 'Uthmaan, since this spelling was accepted and agreed upon by the Companions and the generations after them.[278]

The Script of the Mus-haf

The script in which the 'Uthmaanic *mus-haf* was written was the old *Koofee* script.[279] This script is almost incomprehensible to modern-day Arabic readers. The *mus-hafs* were written without any *hamzah*s, dots (*nuqat*)[280] or vowel marks (*tashkeel*).[281] This was the traditional manner of writing at that time. Therefore, for example, a straight line could represent the letter *baa*, *taa*, *thaa* and *yaa*, and each letter could have any of the vowel marks assigned to it. It was only by context that the appropriate letters and vowels could be differentiated. The Arabs at that time were accustomed to such a script, and would substitute the appropriate letter and vowel depending on the context.

The 'Uthmaanic *mus-haf* was arranged in the order of the *soorahs* present today. There were no indications signifying the ending of the verses, and the only sign that a *soorah* had ended was the *basmalah*.[282] There were also no textual divisions (into

---

278 In fact, al-Azhar released a *fatwa* in the year 1355 A.H. stating that it was not permissible to print a *mus-haf* or re-write the Qur'aan in modern Arabic. They stated that the spelling of the *mus-haf* must conform to the 'Uthmaanic spelling. cf. al-Hamad, p. 609.

279 The *script* of the Arabic is the style of writing of the various letters. For example, the font with which this text is written differs from the font of the chapter title. The *script*, then, is the style with which the letters are written. This is to be differentiated from the *spelling*, which was the topic of the previous section.

280 The *nuqat* are the dots that are used to differentiate between different letters that have the same base structure; for example, the only way to differentiate between the letters *yaa* and *taa* is by the dots: if two dots are above the line, it is a *taa*, and if they are below, it is a *yaa*.

281 The *taskheel* of the Qur'aan are the diacritical marks of the *fathha*, *kasra*, and *damma* (in Urdu, the *zeer*, *zabar*, and *pesh*), and other marks (such as the *shadda*) that are used to pronounce the particular letters correctly.

282 The phrase '*Bismillah al-Rahmaan al-Raheem*', which appears at the beginning of each *soorah* except the ninth.

thirtieths, sixtieths, etc.). This was done so that the Qur'aan be preserved with the utmost purity; only the text of the Qur'aan, unadorned with later embellishments, was written.

This was the appearance of the original 'Uthmaanic *mus-hafs*. As is well-known, however, the appearance of modern *mus-hafs* is strikingly different from the simple 'Uthmaanic one. The process of this change was gradual.

The first change to occur was the addition of the diacritical marks – the *tashkeel*. There are varying reports as to who the first person to add *tashkeel* into the Qur'aan was.

The name that is most commonly mentioned is that of a Successor by the name of Aboo al-Aswad ad-Du'aly (d. 69 A.H.), who was also the first to codify the science of Arabic grammar (*nahw*). According to one report, 'Alee ibn Abee Taalib asked him to make the *mus-haf* easier for the people to recite, but he initially declined to do so, since he did not believe it was necessary. However, he once heard a person recite the verse,

$$\text{أَنَّ ٱللَّهَ بَرِىٓءٌ مِّنَ ٱلْمُشْرِكِينَ وَرَسُولُهُۥ}$$

«Allaah and His apostle break off all ties with the pagans» [9:3]

as "Allaah breaks off all ties with the pagans and His Apostle." This drastic change in meaning occurred by changing only one vowel (i.e., pronouncing *rasooluh* as *rasoolih*). Said Aboo al-Aswad, "I did not think the state of the people had degenerated to this level!" Recalling the advice of 'Alee ibn Abee Taalib, he went to Ziyaad ibn Abeehee, the governor of Iraq under 'Alee ibn Abee Taalib, and requested him to supply him with a scribe. Aboo al-Aswad told the scribe, "If I pronounce (the vowel) *a*, then write a dot above the letter. If I pronounce it as *u*, then write a dot in front of the letter. If I pronounce an *i*, then write it below the letter."[283] Aboo al-Aswad was reacting to the problems that had arisen amongst non-Arabs who had embraced Islaam and were new to the Arabic language. They had difficulty reading the script of 'Uthmaan, without *tashkeel*. Thus, Aboo al-Aswad started the rudimentary art of *tashkeel*.

Other reports give the names of Nasr ibn 'Aasim (d. 89 A.H.), Yahya ibn Ya'mar (d. 100 A.H.), al-Hassan al-Basree (d. 110 A.H.) and Muhammad ibn Seereen (d. 110 A.H.). However, some of these reports qualify Nasr and Yayha as adding the dots (*nuqat*) for the first time, and not the *taskheel*. Yet another report states that it was Aboo al-Aswad who was the first to do this, but at the command of Hajjaaj ibn Yoosuf (d. 95 A.H.), the infamous governor of Iraq under the fifth Umayyad Caliph, 'Abd al-Malik ibn Marwaan, and not under the caliphate of 'Alee.

In combining all of these reports, the strongest series of events seems to be as follows: Aboo al-Aswad was the first to add the *tashkeel* into the *mus-haf* on an official

---

283 al-Hamad, p. 492. According to other reports, Ziyaad ibn Abeehee purposely had a person mispronounce the verse in front of Aboo al-Aswad so that he would realise the necessity of adding the *tashkeel*, cf. al-Badawee, p. 328.

basis, during the caliphate of 'Alee, and his students Yaḥya ibn Ya'mar and Naṣr ibn 'Aaṣim were the first to officially add dots (nuqat) during the reign of 'Abd al-Malik ibn Marwaan (d. 86 A.H.). They were not the first to do so, however, as both al-Ḥassan al-Basree and Muḥammad ibn Seereen had preceded them in this endeavour. However, al-Ḥassan al-Baṣree and Muḥammad ibn Seereen had added the nuqat on their private mus-ḥafs, whereas Aboo al-Aswad and his two students were the first to add the tashkeel and nuqat on an official basis into the mus-ḥaf. This sequence of events takes into account all of the narrations, and is the one that most of the researchers in this field have concluded.[284] Az-Zarqaanee writes,

> May Allaah have mercy on these two scholars (Yaḥya ibn Ya'mar and Naṣr ibn 'Aaṣim), for they were successful in this endeavour (of adding nuqat to the Qur'aan), and completed the addition of the nuqat for the first time. They conditioned upon themselves not to increase the number of dots of any letter above three. This system spread and became popular amongst the people after them, and it had a great impact in removing confusion and doubts concerning (the proper recitation of) the mus-ḥaf.[285]

Thus, Aboo al-Aswad was the first to add the tashkeel into the Qur'aan, and Yaḥya and Naṣr were the were the first who differentiated the various similar letters of the Arabic alphabet by means of dots. They did this during the reign of the Ummayad Caliph 'Abd al-Maalik.

Aboo al-Aswad died in 69 A.H., and 'Abd al-Maalik's reign ended in 86 A.H., which means that less than three-quarters of a century after the Prophet's (ﷺ) death, while some of the Companions were still alive, the Qur'aan had been written down with a rudimentary version of tashkeel and nuqat.

In the beginning, scribes used to write the nuqat in black and the tashkeel in red to distinguish it from the actual text of the Qur'aan. There are hundreds of mus-ḥafs dating from the first two centuries of the hijrah still present with this type of tashkeel system.

There are some narrations from the salaf concerning their disapproval of these additions. It is narrated from Ibn Mas'ood, an-Nakhaa'ee (d. 96 A.H.), Qataadah (d. 117 A.H.) and other scholars of the first two generations concerning the prohibition of adding these dots to the mus-ḥaf. Other scholars, however, such as al-Ḥasan al-Basree (d. 110 A.H.) and Ibn Seereen (d. 110 A.H.), did not see a problem with the addition of these dots.[286] Imaam Maalik (d. 179 A.H.) was asked concerning the addition of tashkeel and nuqat in the Qur'aan. He replied, "The people continued to ask me concerning the addition of dots in the Qur'aan, so I say: As for the major mus-ḥafs, I don't think they should be dotted, nor should anything be added that is not in them. As for the minor mus-ḥafs – the ones that the children learn from – then I don't see any problem with it."[287] Therefore, Imaam Maalik was of the opinion that the Qur'aan

---

284 az-Zarqaanee, v.1, p. 406 and al-Badawee, pps. 329-331.

285 az-Zarqaanee, v. 1, p. 407.

286 cf. al-Ḥamad for these quotes, p. 516.

287 al-Ḥamad, p. 517.

should be left the way that it was written, and the only exception were the *mus-hafs* that children learnt from. This strictness was due to the concern felt by these scholars to keep the script of the *mus-haf* of 'Uthmaan pure from all additions.

However, later scholars of the *salaf* became less strict concerning the addition of the *taskheel* and *nuqat*. This was due to the benefit that was gained, for it aided the average person in properly reciting the Qur'aan. Khalaf ibn Hishaam (d. 229 A.H.) reports, "I used to sit in the gathering of al-Kisaa'ee (the famous *Qaaree*), and the people would add (*taskheel*) based upon his recitation." Ad-Daanee (d. 444 A.H.) writes,

> "I happened to come across an old copy of the *mus-haf*, written during the beginning of the Caliphate of Hishaam ibn 'Abd al-Maalik. Its date (of writing) was written on the last page: 'Written by Mugheerah ibn Meenaa, in Rajab, in the year 110 A.H.' It had *taskheel,* the *hamzahs...* and the dots (*nuqat*) were in red."[288]

Both these quotes show that, eventually, the addition of *tashkeel* and *nuqat* was accepted as a part of the writing of the *mus-haf*.[289]

During the next few centuries, further developments occurred, such as the writing of the *soorah* names at the beginning of the *soorah*, and the separation of the verses by special symbols and numbers. Initially, the verses were distinguished by placing three dots at the end of a verse. After every five verses, the word '*khams*' (five) was written, and after every ten, '*ashr*' (ten), after which the numbering would start from the beginning, until the end of that particular *soorah*. Soon afterwards, the word *khams* was abbreviated to the letter *khaa*, and the word *ashr* to a the letter *ayn*, both of which were written in the margin of the *mus-haf*. Eventually, the verses were indicated by a circle at the end of each verse, and the sequential number of the verse was written in the circle, as is present in the *mus-hafs* of today.[290]

During the first century of the *hijrah*, the primary material upon which the *mus-haf* was written was parchment. After the Muslim conquest of Trans-oxania in the early part of the second century of the *hijrah,* the Muslims learnt from Chinese crafts-men the art of paper-making, and thus paper became the primary material upon which the *mus-haf* was written.[291]

The sixth Ummayad caliph, al-Waleed ibn 'Abd al-Maalik (ruled 86-96 A.H.), was the first to officially order the beautification of the Qur'aan. He ordered the cal-ligrapher Khaalid ibn Abee Hayyaaj to write the Qur'aan in *Koofee* calligraphy. Dur-

---

288 Both quotes from al-Hamad, p. 518.

289 The College of Qur'aan and Islaamic Sciences in the Islaamic University of Madeenah embarked on its 'Qur'aan Project' in 1982. The goal was to print a *mus-haf* that would be a copy of the 'Uthmaanic one in its script, and include *nuqat, tashkeel,* verse numbers, and *soorah* names in a different colour, to differentiate between the actual text of Uthman and later additions. Unfortunately, due to certain problems, the project collapsed, but not after it had written a portion of the Qur'aan. To see an example of their work, see *Majallah Kuliyyah al-Qur'aan al-Kareem*, Islaamic University of Madeenah, 1983, v. 1, pps. 355-362.

290 al-Badawee, p.337.

291 James, David. *Qur'ans of the Mamluks*. Alexandria Press, London, 1988. p. 6.

ing the Abbasid era, Khaleel bin Ahmad (d. 170 A.H.), one of the teachers of the famous Arabic grammarian Seebawayh, also beautified it and made it simpler. He was also the first to introduce the present system of *taskheel*: a straight line above the letter for the vowel *a*, a line below the letter for *i*, a *damma* for *u*, a *shaddah* for showing assimilation, and a small *khaa* without the dot to indicate that the letter had no vowel but was not silent.[292]

However, the greatest change in the style of writing came in the third century of *hijrah* by Ibn Muqlah (d. 327 A.H.), who is regarded as the founder of the calligraphy of the Qur'aan. He introduced the *Naskhee* script, which totally replaced the former *Koofee* script, and upon which the style of writing of the Qur'aan today is based. Ibn Muqlah also established rules for the writing of each letter. Ibn al-Bawwaab (d. 413 A.H.) also played a vital role in the spreading of the *Naskhee* script. In the seventh century of *hijrah*, 'Aamir 'Alee Tabreezee introduced *Khat an-Nastaleeq*, another popular script.[293]

The Qur'aan in Print

With the advent of the printing press, the *mus-haf* changed accordingly. The first Qur'aan that is known to have been printed with movable type techniques was done in 1694 CE, in Hamburg, Germany. It was edited by a Jew, Abraham Hinkellmann, and contained many errors. Al-Hamad criticises it as follows:

> There are major errors (in this print), and on almost every page the reader will find manifest examples of these... which only proves the poor level of knowledge the editor had of the Arabic language and its rules.[294]

In 1841, Gustav Fluegel released another printed *mus-haf*, in which the verse numbering differed from traditional *mus-hafs*. This *mus-haf* was actually a reproduction of a famous Turkish *mus-haf*, written by Haafidh 'Uthmaan (d. 1110 A.H.).[295] This was published in Leipzig, and became a standard version for Orientalists for the next two centuries

The first *mus-haf* done by Muslims in this style is reputed to be the one done in St. Petersburg, Russia, in 1787 CE. These were followed by *mus-hafs* printed in Kazan (in 1828 CE), Persia (in 1833 CE), Istanbul (in 1877 CE) and Cairo (in 1890 CE). A more common one, which took on the role of a 'standard printed version', is one that was ordered by King Fu'aad of Egypt, in 1925. It was written by a committee of scholars from al-Azhar University, under the supervision of Sheikh Mohammad 'Alee Khalaf al-Husaynee.[296]

---

292 The origin of these five symbols are the letters *alif, yaa, waw,* the letter *sheen* to represent the word *shaddah* (double letter), and the *khaa* without a dot to represent the word *khuluw* (empty), respectively. cf. al-Badawee, p. 330.

293 For one of the most fascinating accounts of the development of the script of the *mus-haf*, see al-Hamad's dissertation (*op. cit.*) on this topic.

294 al-Hamad, p. 602.

295 al-Hamad, p. 604.

296 cf. Von Denffer, p. 65, al-Hamad, pps 601-606.

Since then, literally hundreds of other printed *mus-hafs* have followed. One of the more beautiful ones is the 'Madeenah *mus-haf*,' recently printed in Saudi Arabia, in the King Fahd Complex for the Printing of the Holy Qur'aan in Madeenah.

All of these have been in the *qiraa'a* of Hafs *'an* 'Aasim.[297] There are also printed copies of the Qur'aan in the *qiraa'a* of Warsh *'an* Nafi' (printed in Algeria and Morocco, and very recently also by the King Fahd Complex), and in the *qiraa'a* of Qaloon *'an* Nafi' (printed in Libya).

In the present age, almost all *mus-hafs* follow one of two scripts: either *Naskhee* (most of the Arab countries), or *Farsee* (the Indian sub-continent). The *mus-hafs* printed in the *qiraa'a* of Warsh, however, are typically written in *Maghribee* script, which is very unique and confusing for the unaccustomed eye. For example, the letter *qaaf* is represented with one dot above a circle (vs. two dots), and the letter *faa* with one dot below it (vs. above it)!

Not only has the *mus-haf* been printed in different *qira'aat* and scripts, it has also been printed in Braille! The Ministry of Religious Affairs in Saudi Arabia released a three-volume Qur'aan written in Arabic Braille. Each Arabic letter is represented by a special set of dots, and each diacritical mark also has its special code, and, just like in other *mus-hafs*, is either written above or below the letter. Not only that, but the various signs for stopping (*wuqoof*) are also included in the *mus-haf*, as are the verse and *soorah* numbers!

A Warning!

Before completing this section concerning the evolution of the script of the *mus-haf*, it is very relevant to quote the *hadeeth* of the Prophet (ﷺ) in which he said, "When you decorate your mosques, and beautify your *mus-hafs*, then destruction will be upon you!"[298] This *hadeeth* can be taken as a factual statement, or as a warning. In other words, if taken factually, the Prophet (ﷺ) is informing his *ummah* that when mosques and *mus-hafs* are decorated and beautified, this will be a time of destruction for the Muslims. However, the stronger opinion is that this *hadeeth* is a warning to the Muslims,[299] in which case any unnecessary and excessive decoration of the *mus-haf* is to be discouraged. This is one of the indications of the austerity and simplicity of Islaam, such that even its places of worship and its Sacred Book must be absent from all types of embellishments, which typically is an indication of arrogance, and a love for this world. Rather, such religious symbols should be examples of modesty and humility.

---

297 See Ch. 11, The Qira'aat of the Qur'aan, for further details.

298 Reported by Ibn Abee Shaybah in his *Musannaf*; cf. *as-Saheehah* # 1351.

299 Due to the fact that there exist other authentic narrations forbidding Muslims to decorate their mosques. Therefore, it makes sense to understand this *hadeeth* as a warning and prohibition rather than a factual prophecy.

B. The Number of 'Uthmaanic Mus-hafs

There are five opinions concerning the number of original *mus-hafs* that 'Uthmaan compiled:

1) Imaam az-Zarkashee follows Aboo 'Amr ad-Daanee's (d. 444 A.H.) opinion that the number of *mus-hafs* was four; 'Uthmaan kept one in Madeenah, and sent the other three to Koofah, Basrah and Shaam (Syria). Ad-Daanee writes in his *Muqni'*, "The majority of the scholars hold that when 'Uthmaan wrote the *mus-haf*, he ordered four copies to be written, and he sent one to each of the major provinces."[300]

2) As-Suyootee, in his *Itqaan*, and Ibn Hajr (d. 852 A.H.), state that there were five copies, which were sent to the above four cities and Makkah.[301]

3) Some scholars maintain that there were six copies, the sixth one having been the one 'Uthmaan commissioned for his personal use, different from the *mus-haf* of Madeenah.[302]

4) Aboo Haatim as-Sijistaanee (d. 255 A.H.) stated that there were seven copies, one of which was kept in Madeenah, and the rest sent to Makkah, Syria, Basrah, Koofah, Yemen and Bahrain (another opinion maintains that the last of the seven was sent to Egypt, and not Bahrain).

5) Lastly, some maintain there have been eight copies; in addition to the above seven, they include the personal *mus-haf* of 'Uthmaan.

It is not of very great concern to know the exact number of *mus-hafs* that 'Uthmaan ordered to be written, for regardless of the number of original *mus-hafs*, all future *mus-hafs* were written as exact copies of these.

However, if forced to choose between these opinions, the second one is probably the strongest, since it has the strongest historical evidence. At the time that the *mus-hafs* were commissioned, Yemen, Bahrain and Egypt would probably not have merited having a special *mus-haf* sent to them, and it does not seem too unrealistic to venture that the 'personal' *mus-haf* of 'Uthmaan was none other than the *mus-haf* of Madeenah, which 'Uthmaan would have kept in his possession.

C. Were these Mus-hafs the Same?

Did the 'Uthmaanic four or eight *mus-hafs* match each other letter for letter? Surprisingly, contrary to popular opinion, the evidence indicates otherwise.

The different copies that 'Uthmaan ordered to be written differed from each other in a few letters. There is no extra verse in any one of the *mus-hafs*, but there are additional or different letters in some of the *mus-hafs*. This was not done accidentally or by

---

300 az-Zarkashee, v.1, p. 240.
301 as-Suyootee, v. 1, p. 80.
302 az-Zarqaanee, v.1, p.406.

chance. Rather, these slight changes were done in order to accommodate the various recitations of a particular verse (the *ahruf*). If the Prophet (ﷺ) had recited the verse in a number of ways, and it was possible to accommodate all of these recitations in one particular spelling, then the word was written with that spelling. The example of '*maaliki*' and '*maliki*' has already been given before. However, if the recitations could not all be accommodated in one spelling, then it was written with one of the recitations in one *mus-haf*, and another recitation in another *mus-haf*. The Companions did not write both recitations in one *mus-haf* for fear of confusion between the two.[303]

The fact that the 'Uthmaanic *mus-hafs* differed is known by two ways:

1) The *qira'aat*: Between the various *qira'aat*, there occur changes in letters and sometimes words that cannot be attributed to one script, even if this script were without dots and vowel marks. For example, some of the *qira'aat*[304] read 91:15 as '*wa laa yakhaafu...*' This is the recitation that most of the readers will be familiar with. On the other hand, other *qira'aat*[305] read it as '*fa laa yakhaafu...*', changing the *waw* to a *fa*. This letter change can not be attributed to the same script, and must indicate a difference in the *mus-hafs* of 'Uthmaan.[306] Another example is the *qiraa'a* of Ibn 'Aamir, who read 3:184 as '*wa bi zuburi wa bil kitaab*' whereas the rest of the *qira'aat* read '*wa zuburi wal kitaab*' (i.e., without the two *bas*). Ibn 'Aamir was Syrian, and it is known that the *mus-haf* that 'Uthmaan sent to Syria had the two extra *bas* in it, whereas the other *mus-hafs* did not. In this example, an actual word is added in one of the *mus-hafs*.

2) Visual Inspection: The second way that it is known that these *mus-hafs* differed from one another is by comparing them. Since the various *mus-hafs* are not present any more, reports must be taken from those who were fortunate enough to have read more than one of the original *mus-hafs* of 'Uthmaan, or at least knew and reported from those who did. In fact, a number of scholars had written books specially on this topic.

Some authors have mentioned at least ten scholars of the first four centuries of the *hijrah* who had written specific tracts on this topic, amongst them, al-Kisaa'ee (d. 189 A.H.), and al-Farraa' (d. 207 A.H.).[307] Unfortunately, the only book that remains of these classical works is the work authored by 'Abdullaah ibn Abee Daawood (d. 316 A.H.), the son of the famous scholar of *hadeeth*, Aboo Daawood (d. 275 A.H.), which he entitled *Kitaab al-Masaahif*.[308]

---

303 az-Zarqaanee, v.1, p.262.
304 Those of 'Aasim, Kisaa'ee, Hamza, Abu 'Amr and Ibn Katheer.
305 That of Naafi' and Ibn 'Aamir.
306 This point will be better understood after one reads Ch. 11 on the *qira'aat*.
307 cf. Introduction to Ibn Abee Daawood, p. 10.
308 Unfortunately, the first (and only) person to edit and publish it was the famous Orientalist scholar Arthur Jeffery (published in Cairo, 1936), as part of his famous work *Materials for the History of the Text of the Holy Qur'aan*, which is discussed in greater detail in Ch. 17.

Khaalid ibn Iyaas (d. *circa* 150 A.H.) reported that he read the *mus-haf* of 'Uthmaan, and found that it differed with the *mus-hafs* of Madeenah in twelve verses, which he quoted.[309] The first of these was 2:132 '*wa wasa...*' instead of '*wa awsa...*' meaning that the first was without an *alif*, whereas the second was with an *alif*. This is in the actual script of the *mus-hafs*, and is reflected in the differences between the *qira'aat*. Of the ten *qira'aat*, Naafi' and Ibn 'Aamir read it with the *alif*, whereas the rest do not. In the same way, all of the other differences in the script of the *mus-haf* are still found in the differences between the *qira'aat*.

There are more than just twelve differences, though. Khaalid ibn Iyaas only compared the *mus-haf* of 'Uthmaan with the *mus-hafs* of Madeenah. The other *mus-hafs* differed from the Madeenah *mus-haf*, as for example in verse 3:184, the *mus-haf* that 'Uthmaan sent to Syria had the extra letters, but the others did not.[310]

These differences, as noted earlier, are only with regards to certain letters and words. There are no verses or phrases that are present in some *mus-hafs* without the others.

Actually, if one reflects over this phenomenon, he will be even more certain that the Qur'aan has been preserved even to the minutest detail. This is so because all of the differences that originated in the different *mus-hafs* of 'Uthmaan are still found scattered in the various *qira'aat*, showing that the scriptural differences are not accidental, but rather intentional. The Prophet (ﷺ) used to recite the Qur'aan in all of these ways, as will be elaborated upon later.

Therefore, the purpose behind having these trivial changes between the *mus-hafs* was to preserve the various *ahruf* of the Qur'aan, even to the most minute detail.

D. WHAT HAPPENED TO THE ORIGINAL Mus-hafs?

It is of great historical importance (and curiosity) to know what happened to these original *mus-hafs*.

As for the *mus-haf* of Aboo Bakr, after he passed away it was given to 'Umar. On his death-bed, 'Umar did not nominate any one successor after him, but rather a committee of six people. Therefore when 'Umar passed away, there was no immediate Caliph present, as was the case when Aboo Bakr passed away. The *mus-haf* was then naturally inherited by Hafsah, his daughter and a wife of the Prophet (ﷺ). According to a report from Ibn Abee Daawood's *Kitaab al-Masaahif*, Hafsah was very protective of the *mus-haf*, and even refused to give it 'Uthmaan until he assured her that he would return it.[311] During the caliphates of 'Uthmaan and 'Alee, it remained with Hafsah.

---

309 For these and many more differences, see Ibn Abee Daawood, pps. 37-49.
310 See al-Hamad, pps. 695-702, where he lists around sixty differences between the various *mus-hafs*.
311 Ibn Abee Daawood, p. 9.

After the caliphate of 'Alee, Marwaan ibn al-Hakam (d. 65 A.H.) became the governor of Madeenah. Marwaan wanted to eliminate this *mus-haf*, since the 'Uthmaanic *mus-haf* was sufficient for the Muslims, but Hafsah refused to hand it over. Marwaan had to wait until Hafsah passed away in 41 A.H. before destroying the *mus-haf*.[312] He said, "The only reason I did this was because all that is in this *mus-haf* (of Aboo Bakr) has been written and preserved by the *mus-haf* (of 'Uthmaan), so I feared that after some time people would doubt the veracity of this *mus-haf*, or they would say that there was something in it that had not been written down. (Therefore, to prevent these doubts I burnt it)."[313]

As for the 'Uthmaanic *mus-hafs*, Ibn Katheer (d. 774 A.H.), of *Tafseer ibn Katheer* fame, wrote in his monumental history, *al-Bidaayah wa an-Nihaayah*, that he had seen one of them. It had been sent from Palestine to Damascus, and it was 'very large, in beautiful clear strong writing with strong ink, on parchment, I think, made of camel skin'.[314] Some say this copy made its way to England via Leningrad, but this does not seem likely. Another opinion states that it was burned in a fire that occurred in the Grand Mosque of Damascus, in the year 1310 A.H. (1893 CE). Ibn al-Jazaree (d. 832 A.H.) also reported seeing the *mus-haf* of Syria.[315]

Ibn Battuta (d. 779 A.H.), the famous Muslim traveller, reports seeing many *mus-hafs* that were copied directly from the *mus-haf* of 'Uthmaan. As for the Madeenah manuscript:

> Ibn Jubair (d. 614 A.H./1217 CE) saw the manuscript in the mosque of Madeenah in the year 580 A.H./1184 CE. Some say it remained in Madeenah until the Turks took it from there in 1334 A.H. / 1915 CE. It has been reported that this copy was removed by the Turkish authorities to Istanbul, from where it came to Berlin during World War I. The Treaty of Versailles, which concluded World War I, contains the following clause:

> 'Article 246: Within six months from the coming into the force of the present treaty, Germany will restore to His Majesty, King of Hedjaz, the original Koran (*sic*) of the Caliph Othman, which was removed from Medinah by the Turkish authorities and is stated to have been presented to the ex-Emperor William II.'

> The manuscript then reached Istanbul, but not Madeenah.[316]

This copy is now on exhibit at the Topkapi Museum in Istanbul, Turkey, for all to see.

There is also a copy of a *mus-haf* in Tashkent (former USSR) that is alleged to be an 'Uthmaanic copy, although some say that it is a copy of the original. If this is an 'Uthmaanic *mus-haf*, it might actually be the *mus-haf* that 'Uthmaan kept for himself,

---

312   In fact, he ordered for it to be destroyed the very hour that Hafsa was buried!
313   ibid., p. 25.
314   Qattaan p. 134, Von Denffer, p.62.
315   az-Zarqanee, v. 1, p. 403.
316   Taken from Von Denffer, p. 62.

and the one he was reading from when he was murdered. It came to Samarkand (after the Umayyads had taken it from Madeenah to Morocco) in 890 A.H. (1485 CE), and remained there until, in 1869, the Russians took it to St. Petersburg. They returned it to Samarqand (close to Tashkent) in 1924, and it has remained in Tashkent since. The Russian authorities had made facsimiles of the *mus-haf*, and because of this the *mus-haf* is available through this medium at a number of leading universities and private collections.[317]

Therefore, there exist at least two *mus-hafs* that are reputed to be official 'Uthmaanic *mus-hafs*. Even if they are not originals (and this is very difficult to disprove), they are at worst copies of the original, since the style of writing conforms to the first few decades after the *hijrah*.

v. The Verses of the Qur'aan

By 'verse' is meant what is known as an '*aayah*'. This word, linguistically, has a number of meanings to it, including:

1)   A sign or indication. Allaah says,

$$ وَقَالَ لَهُمْ نَبِيُّهُمْ إِنَّ ءَايَةَ مُلْكِهِۦ أَن يَأْتِيَكُمُ ٱلتَّابُوتُ $$

«And their prophet said to them (the Children of Israel), 'The sign (*'aayah*) of his Kingdom is that there shall come to you a wooden box...»[2:248]

2)   An admonition or lesson. Allaah says,

$$ إِنَّ فِى ذَٰلِكَ لَـَٔايَةً لِّقَوْمٍ يَتَفَكَّرُونَ $$

«In this there is a lesson (*aayah*) for those who give thought» [16:11]

3)   A miracle. Allaah says,

$$ سَلْ بَنِىٓ إِسْرَٰٓءِيلَ كَمْ ءَاتَيْنَٰهُم مِّنْ ءَايَةٍۭ بَيِّنَةٍ $$

«Ask the Children of Israel how many miracles (*aayah*) we gave them» [2:211]

4)   A verse or sentence. Allaah says,

$$ وَإِذَا بَدَّلْنَآ ءَايَةً مَّكَانَ ءَايَةٍ وَٱللَّهُ أَعْلَمُ $$
$$ بِمَا يُنَزِّلُ قَالُوٓا إِنَّمَآ أَنتَ مُفْتَرٍ بَلْ أَكْثَرُهُمْ لَا يَعْلَمُونَ $$

«And when We change a verse (*aayah*) (in the Qur'aan) in place of another – and Allaah knows best what he sends down – they say, 'You (O Muhammad) are but a forger.' Nay, (but) most of them are ignorant!» [16:101]

---

317 Al-Hamad describes this *mus-haf* in great detail, and concludes that it is the strongest candidate for being an original *mus-haf* of 'Uthmaan. As for the other copies in Egypt that are reputed to be 'Uthmaanic *mus-hafs*, he concludes that this is very unlikely, as they have *nuqat* and *tashkeel* marks. Even less likely candidates for the 'Uthmaanic *mus-hafs* are a number of *mus-hafs* of Iran and Iraq which are claimed to be Alee's personal *mus-haf*. al-Hamad, 191-3.

When used in Islaamic sciences, it is defined to be a part of the Qur'aan composed of sequential letters and words, separate from what is before it and after it, with a beginning and end, occupying a specific place in a specific *soorah*.[318]

Combining the above linguistic meanings, an *aayah* is a verse of the Qur'aan, and a miracle from Allaah (since it is inimitable).[319] It contains lessons for mankind to benefit from, and admonitions for the believers and disbelievers.

The Necessity of this Knowledge

The knowledge of where a verse begins and ends is essential for a number of reasons, including:[320]

1)   The acceptability of the prayer. Some scholars state that, if a person has not memorised the *Faatihah*, he must recite seven other verses of the Qur'aan instead of it, and this cannot be done unless one knows the beginning and end of a verse. Most scholars also encourage the recitation of three short or one long verse after the *Faatihah*, and this recitation is also dependent upon this knowledge.

2)   The proper recitation of the Qur'aan. It is preferable – but not mandatory – to pause at the end of every verse, and many scholars have stated that this is the Prophet's (ﷺ) *Sunnah*. Likewise, it is not encouraged to start or stop a recitation from the middle of a verse; any recitation should be started from the beginning of a verse, and concluded at the ending of one. In addition, certain rules of recitation (*tajweed*) depend upon the location of the end of a verse.

3)   The acceptability of the Friday sermon. Some scholars have stated that it is obligatory for the Friday sermon to include at least one full verse in it.

4)   The ease in finding particular passages in the Qur'aan. The finding of a particular passage is simplified by the knowledge and numbering of the verses of the Qur'aan.

The Origins of this Knowledge

There are two opinions as to how the location of the beginning and ending of a verse is known.

The first opinion is that all of this knowledge is from the Prophet (ﷺ) – in other words, the beginning and end of every single verse was taught to the Companions by the Prophet (ﷺ). As proof, the adherents of this opinion bring forth the numerous *hadeeth* in which the Prophet (ﷺ) clearly mentions particular verses in certain *soorahs*. For example, the Prophet (ﷺ) said, "Whoever memorises the last ten verses of *Soorah al-Kahf* will be saved from the tribulation of Dajjal,"[321] and, Verily, there is a *soorah* in

---

318   cf. az-Zarqaanee, v. 1, p. 339.
319   See Chapter 15 under 'The Quantity for *i'jaaz*' for a discussion of the inimitability of a verse.
320   Moosaa, 'Abd ar-Razaaq. *Murshid al-Khalaan*, IUM Press, Madeenah, 1990, p. 30.
321   Reported by Muslim.

the Qur'aan composed of thirty verses that interceded for its companions until he was forgiven. It is,

$$تَبَـٰرَكَ ٱلَّذِى بِيَدِهِ ٱلۡمُلۡكُ$$

«Blessed be He in Whose Hands is the Dominion» [67:1]

(i.e., *Soorah* al-Mulk),[322] and, "Read the last two verses of *Soorah* al-Baqarah, for indeed I was given them from under the Throne (of Allaah),"[323] and, "...and in it (*Soorah* al-Baqarah), there is a verse which is the Queen of all other verses. (It is) the 'Verse of the Foot-Stool.'"[324] These narrations show that the Qur'aan had already been divided into verses by the Prophet (صلى الله عليه وسلم).

The second opinion, and perhaps the stronger one, states that most of this knowledge is from the Prophet (صلى الله عليه وسلم), and some of it is based upon the personal reasoning (*ijtihaad*) of the scholars of the *salaf*. Those who hold this opinion give as proof the fact that there exists a difference of opinion over some 'verses' in the Qur'aan (as shall be discussed below). Thus, taking into account this fact, and the above narrations from the Prophet (صلى الله عليه وسلم), they claim that most of the locations for the breaks between the verses were well-known, and from the Prophet (صلى الله عليه وسلم), whereas some locations were arrived at based upon *ijtihaad*.

The reason that certain locations are subject to a difference of opinion is explained as follows: When the Prophet (صلى الله عليه وسلم) used to recite the Qur'aan, he would stop at particular places. Those places where he continually stopped whenever he (صلى الله عليه وسلم) recited that passage are taken as verse breaks, without any difference of opinion. The difference of opinion occurs at those places where he (صلى الله عليه وسلم) sometimes stopped and sometimes did not; some scholars took this to be a stop for breath, and thus did not count it as a verse break, whereas other took this to be the beginning of a new verse. Moosaa writes:[325]

> The reason for the difference of opinion over the verse (breaks) is that the Prophet (صلى الله عليه وسلم) would stop (while reciting the Qur'aan)...The locations upon which the Prophet (صلى الله عليه وسلم) always stopped, and never connected, are agreed upon as verse breaks, and there is no difference of opinion over them. Then there are locations upon which the Prophet (صلى الله عليه وسلم) never stopped, but rather always continued his recitation, so these too are agreed upon that they are not verse breaks. And then there are other locations upon which the Prophet (صلى الله عليه وسلم) sometimes stopped, and sometimes did not; these locations are the reason for the difference of opinion, and where (the scholars) performed *ijtihaad*.

Of course, even when *ijtihaad* was resorted to, there were certain rules that these scholars employed to discern the exact location of the break. Of primary importance

---

322 Reported by Aboo Daawood.
323 Reported by Ahmad.
324 Reported by at-Tirmidhee.
325 Moosaa, p. 32.

was the context of the verse; what was the average length of its sister verses? what was the rhythm and rhyme of the passage? what was the ending sound and note of the verses before it and after it?[326] Thus, they compared the particular verse with its sister verses, and established its beginning and end based upon them.

It should be emphasised again that the actual arrangement of the words and phrases is the same – the difference of opinion occurs only where one verse ends and the next verse begins.[327]

The Number of Verses

With this in mind, how many verses are there in the Qur'aan?

As mentioned above, most of the verse breaks are agreed upon, and some are subject to a difference of opinion. Thus, the scholars of the Qur'aan (to be more precise, the scholars of the *qira'aat*) were divided with regards to this question into seven opinions. Each city (and therefore each *qiraa'a*) had its own verse-number. The scholars of Koofah held the view that there were 6236 verses (and this is the numbering that is present in the *mus-hafs* written in the *qiraa'a* of Hafs *'an* 'Aasim). The scholars of Basrah considered there to be 6204 verses. In Damascus, the scholars agreed that the verses were 6227 in number, whereas in Hims (Palestine) they held that there were 6232 verses. In Makkah, 6210 verses was the common opinion, whereas in Madeenah the earlier scholars said there were 6217 verses, and the later ones held there to be 6214 verses.[328]

Again, the difference occurs only in where to stop one verse and start another. What might be one verse for the scholars of Koofah might be considered as two by the scholars of Madeenah, and so on. So, for example, some of the *qira'aat* consider the last verse of *Soorah* Faatihah to start from '*Siraat aladheen an'amta'a* ...' whereas others consider it to start from '*Ghayr il-maghdoobi*...', thus breaking the last 'verse' into two verses.

The Arrangement of the Verses

Even though there is a difference of opinion over the actual verse numbering, there is no difference of opinion over the fact that the arrangement and order of the verses in each *soorah* is from the Prophet (ﷺ) himself. The scholars of Islaam have agreed (*ijmaa'*) on this point. Aboo Ja'far ibn Zubayr (d. 807 A.H.) said,

> "The arrangement of the verses in the *soorahs* is a matter which is from
> the command of the Prophet (ﷺ) and we cannot question it (i.e., exercise
> *ijtihaad* in it). This is a matter in which there is no difference of opinion
> among the Muslims."[329]

---

326 cf. Moosaa, pps. 34-38 for more details and examples.

327 The only 'verse' in the Qur'aan over which there is a difference of opinion concerning its status is the *basmalah* at the beginning of each *soorah*, and this difference will be elaborated on in a separate section.

328 ad-Daanee, p. 9, Moosa, p. 27.

329 Qattaan, p. 139.

The Prophet (ﷺ) used to mention to the scribe writing the verse where to put the verse in the Qur'aan. He (ﷺ) did not used to do this by his own judgement, for Jibreel used to tell him, and Jibreel was inspired by Allaah with this knowledge.

'Uthmaan ibn Abee al-'Aas reported that he was once sitting by the Prophet (ﷺ) when he noticed that the Prophet (ﷺ) raised his eyes and fixed his gaze (an indication that he (ﷺ) was being inspired), then he said, "Jibreel came to me and commanded me to put this verse at a certain place in this *soorah*,

إِنَّ ٱللَّهَ يَأْمُرُ بِٱلْعَدْلِ

«Allaah commands you with justice....»[16:90].[330]

In other words, the Prophet (ﷺ) was told not only in which *soorah* to place the verse but also in which portion of the *soorah* to do so.

'Abdullaah ibn az-Zubayr was reading the Qur'aan when he came across this verse,

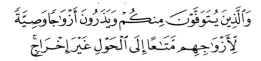

«And those of you who die and leave behind their wives should bequeath for them a year's maintenance and residence, without turning them out...»[2:240]

He went to 'Uthmaan ibn 'Affaan, and asked him, "This verse has been abrogated by the verses after it, so why do you write it?" He answered, "O my nephew, I will not change anything from its place."[331] In this narration, 'Uthmaan signified that he knew the place of the verses, but he was not willing to leave anything out that the Prophet (ﷺ) had not ordered him to.

Apart from these proofs, the fact that the Prophet (ﷺ) used to recite complete *soorahs* in the prayer, and to the Companions individually, shows that the arrangement of the verses must have been taught by the Prophet (ﷺ) to the Companions. In all of the prayers in which the recitation is aloud, the Prophet (ﷺ) would have had to recite various *soorahs*. There are reports, for example, that he (ﷺ) recited *Soorah* Sajdah in Fajr, and he (ﷺ) recited al-Baqarah, and Aali-'Imraan, and Nisaa', and A'raaf, and many more *soorahs* in the prayer,[332] and he recited *Soorah* Qaaf more than once during the Friday sermons. In addition, the Prophet (ﷺ) used to recite the entire Qur'aan during the month of Ramadaan, and this was witnessed by Zayd ibn Thaabit. Therefore, the Companions must have heard the various verses put together to form the *soorah*.

This is why as-Suyootee said, "The recitation of the Prophet (ﷺ) in front of the gatherings of the Companions proves that the arrangement of the verses is from him,

---

330 Reported in *Musnad Ahmad*.
331 Reported by al-Bukhaaree.
332 cf. az-Zarqaanee, v. 1, p. 347.

and the Companions could not change the order of the verses from what the Prophet
(ﷺ) recited. Therefore, the knowledge of the order of the verses is *mutawaatir*."[333]
This is reflected in the fact that there is absolutely no known difference of opinion in
the arrangement of the verses for each *soorah*.

The Number of Words and Letters

There are 77,437 words in the Qur'aan, and 323,671 letters, with difference of
opinion in both of these numbers. The reason this difference of opinion exists is due
to the fact that certain *qira'aat* pronounce letters that are not written in the script, and,
as mentioned earlier, the *mus-hafs* of 'Uthmaan were not identical to one another.

For example, Hajjaaj ibn Yoosuf (d. 95 A.H.), the infamous governor of Iraq, called
the scholars of Basrah, and he chose al-Hasan al-Basree (d. 110 A.H.), Aboo al-'Aaliyah
(d. 90 A.H.), Nasr ibn 'Aasim (d. 89 A.H.) and two more scholars, and commanded
them, "Count the number of words in the Qur'aan." So they stayed four months
counting the letters and words, and they concluded that there were 77,439 words, and
323,015 letters in the Qur'aan.[334] Other opinions give different numbers, but they are
in the same range as the examples cited. Imaam as-Sakhaawee's (d. 643 A.H.) statement should be kept in mind in such discussions. He wrote, after mentioning the
various opinions, "And I don't see any benefit (in all of these numbers). For, if it had
any benefit, it would be for a book that is possible to be added to or subtracted from.
As for the Qur'aan, this is not possible."[335] Also, the Companions and those after them
agreed that these numbers have no Islaamic significance or valid esoteric interpretations whatsoever.[336]

The longest verse is the 'Verse of Loaning', 2:282. The shortest verse is 93:1, '*Wa
ad-duha*' and 89:1, '*Wa al-fajr*'.[337] Both consist of six letters in writing, but only five in
pronunciation.

The longest continuous string of related letters is '*fa-asqaynaakumoohu*', in 15:22,
which consists of eleven letters.

---

333   as-Suyootee, v. 1, p. 82.
334   az-Zarkashee, v. 1, p. 249.
335   as-Sakhaawee, p. 231.
336   cf. Qattaan, p. 356.
337   This is according to the *qiraa'a* of Hafs. Some of the *qira'aat* consider the disjointed letters to be a
separate verse, which would make these letters the smallest verse in the Qur'aan, for these *qira'aat*.

THE BASMALAH AS A VERSE

The *basmalah* is the phrase that occurs at the beginning of each *soorah* of the Qur'aan, except for *Soorah* at-Tawbah, and reads, as every Muslim knows,

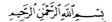

'Bismillaah ar-Rahmaan ar-Raheem'

(In the Name of Allaah, the Ever-Merciful, the Bestower of Mercy).

There is a difference of opinion amongst the scholars of the Qur'aan over whether this phrase is to be considered as a verse at the beginning of each *soorah*, in particular *Soorah* al-Faatihah, or whether this is merely a phrase said for blessings between the *soorahs*, and is meant to identify where one *soorah* ends and the next begins.

The scholars are agreed that the *basmalah* does not form a part of *Soorah* at-Tawbah, and that it is a verse of the Qur'aan in 27:30 (which reads, إِنَّهُۥ مِن سُلَيْمَٰنَ وَإِنَّهُۥ بِسْمِ ٱللَّهِ ٱلرَّحْمَٰنِ ٱلرَّحِيمِ ۝ "Verily, it (the letter) is from Sulaymaan, and it (reads): In the Name of Allaah, The Ever-Merciful, the Bestower of Mercy!"), but disagree as to its status at the beginning of the other *soorahs*. There are five opinions on this matter, as follows:[338]

1) The *basmalah* is a separate verse at the beginning of every *soorah*. This would imply that the *basmalah* is the first verse of every *soorah*.

2) The *basmalah* is only a part of a verse at the beginning of every *soorah*. In other words, the *basmalah* is the first part of the first verse in every *soorah*, and not a separate verse.

3) The *basmalah* is a verse only at the beginning of *Soorah* al-Faatihah, and not for other *soorahs*.

4) The *basmalah* is a separate verse, not a part of any *soorah*, that has been placed at the beginning of the *soorah*. In other words, the *basmalah* is not to be counted as a verse in any *soorah*, but is a verse of the Qur'aan.

5) The *basmalah* is not a verse of the Qur'aan, but rather a phrase which is used to distinguish one *soorah* from another.

It can be seen that the above opinions can be divided into two main categories: those who claim that the *basmalah* at the beginning of the *soorahs* is a verse in the Qur'aan, and those who claim that it is not.

The scholars who claim that the *basmalah* at the beginning of the *soorahs* is a verse of the Qur'aan, such as Imaam ash-Shaafi'ee (d. 204 A.H.), Imaam Ahmad (d. 241 A.H.), and others, use as evidence the fact that the *mus-hafs* that 'Uthmaan ordered to be written all contained the *basmalah* at the beginning of the *soorahs* (except for the ninth *soorah*, *Soorah* at-Tawbah). This, according to them, automatically implies that the *basmalah* at the beginning of the *soorahs* is a verse in the Qur'aan, since the Companions only wrote in the 'Uthmaanic *mus-haf* what was agreed to be the Qur'aan,

---

338 cf. Ibn Katheer, v. 1, p. 17.

and did not write anything besides it. In addition, they also use as evidence those narrations in which the Prophet (ﷺ) recited the *basmalah* at the beginning of certain *soorahs*, such as the narration in which the Prophet (ﷺ) smiled with pleasure, and said, "Last night, a *soorah* was revealed to me:

«*Bismillaah ar-Rahmaan ar-Raheem.* Verily, We have given you the [Fountain) of *Kawthar*...»"[108:1-3]

In this narration, the Prophet (ﷺ) started the *soorah* with the *basmalah*, and it can be inferred that it was revealed with the *soorah*.

However, those that do not hold the *basmalah* at the beginning of the *soorahs* to be a part of the Qur'aan, such as Imaam Maalik (d. 179 A.H.), Aboo Haneefah (d. 150 A.H.) and others, use the fact that the purpose of the *basmalah* is to signify where a new *soorah* starts, as the following narration of Ibn 'Abbaas indicates. Ibn 'Abbaas said, "The Prophet (ﷺ) did not know where a *soorah* ended until the *basmalah* was revealed to him."[339] Another narration that this group uses is the *hadeeth* in which the Prophet (ﷺ) said, "Allaah has said, 'I have divided the prayer between Me and My servant, so when he says,

«All Praise is due to Allaah» [1:1]

I respond, "My servant has Praised Me."...'"[340] In other words, in this narration, which mentions the entire *Soorah al-Faatihah*, the *basmalah* is not mentioned, thus implying that it is not a verse. An even more explicit narration is the one reported by Aboo Hurayrah, who said that the Prophet (ﷺ) said,

«All Praise is due to Allaah» [1:1]

is the 'Mother of the Qur'aan' and the 'Mother of the Book' and the 'Seven oft-repeated verses.'"[341] In this narration, the Prophet (ﷺ) started *Soorah al-Faatihah* without reciting the *basmalah*, showing, according to these scholars, that it is not a verse of the Qur'aan.

Based on this classic difference of opinion, the *qira'aat* themselves differed over whether the *basmalah* was a verse in *Soorah al-Faatihah* and the other *soorahs*. Among the *Qaarees*, Ibn Katheer, 'Aasim and al-Kisaa'ee were the only ones who considered it to be a verse at the beginning of each *soorah*, whereas the others did not.

---

339 Reported by Aboo Daawood.
340 Reported by Muslim and Aboo Daawood.
341 Reported by al-Bukhaaree and others.

To resolve this difference of opinion, some scholars claimed that the *basmalah* was revealed in some of the *ahruf* of the Qur'aan, and left out of others![342] This opinion would perhaps resolve the difference of opinion, were it not for the fact that the *basmalah* is written in all the *mus-hafs* of 'Uthmaan. Had the *basmalah* been a verse in some *ahruf* and not in others, it would have been written in some of the *mus-haf* and left out of others.

Perhaps the strongest opinion amongst these, however, is the opinion that the *basmalah* is a part of *Soorah* al-Faatihah, and not a part of the other *soorahs*. For the other *soorahs*, the purpose of the *basmalah*, as the narration of Ibn 'Abbaas mentions, is to differentiate between the ending of one *soorah* and the beginning of the next. The strongest proof for this opinion is an authentic narration that leaves no room for any doubt. Aboo Hurayrah reported that the Prophet (ﷺ) said, "When you recite,

«All Praise is due to Allaah» [1:1]

then recite (with it), '*Bismillaah ar-Rahmaan ar-Raheem*' for verily it (i.e., the *Faatihah*) is the 'Mother of the Qur'aan' and the 'Mother of the Book' and the 'Seven oft-re-peated verses'; and '*Bismillah ar-Rahmaan ar-Raheem*' is a verse of it."[343] This narra-tion is explicit in that the *basmalah* is a verse of *Soorah* al-Faatihah, and since the narrations that are used to prove that the *basmalah* is not a verse are all based on implicit reasoning, this narration must take precedence.[344] However, there is no strong proof that the *basmalah* is a verse at the beginning of the other *soorahs*, for there exist narrations that the Prophet (ﷺ) used to mention other *soorahs* without reciting the *basmalah*. For example, the Prophet (ﷺ) said, "Verily, there is a *soorah* in the Qur'aan composed of thirty verses that interceded for its companions until he was forgiven. It is,

$$تَبَارَكَ ٱلَّذِى بِيَدِهِ ٱلْمُلْكُ$$

«Blessed be He in Whose Hands is the Dominion...» [67:1].[345]

This narration shows that the *basmalah* is not a verse of the *soorah*, as this *soorah* is composed of thirty verses without the *basmalah*.

The issue of whether the *basmalah* is a verse at the beginning of the *soorahs* or not is not of significant importance, since the difference of opinion is not over whether the *basmalah* is an actual *verse* (the scholars are agreed that it is a part of the verse in

---

342 cf. al-Banna, p. 358. For a discussion of the *ahruf*, refer to Chapter 10.

343 Reported by ad-Daraqutnee; cf. *as-Saheehah*, # 1183. This *hadeeth* is narrated through a number of different chains, most of which make this a statement of Aboo Hurayrah, and not a *hadeeth* of the Prophet (ﷺ). This is why some scholars stated that this *hadeeth* is not authentic (meaning that it is a statement of Aboo Hurayrah, and not a *hadeeth*).

344 cf. ar-Raazee, Muhammad ibn 'Umar Fakhr ad-Din: *Ahkaam al-Basmalah*, ed. Majdi Ibrahim, Maktabah al-Qur'aan, Cairo, n.d., pps. 29-34, for an explanation of the previous 'implicit' narrations.

345 Reported by Aboo Daawood.

27:30), but rather, *where* is it a verse; is it only in verse 27:30, or at the beginning of all the *soorahs*, or only of *Soorah* al-Faatihah? Therefore, the issue of whether the *basmalah* forms a part of the *soorah* as a verse or not is the only area in which difference of opinion is permitted. As such, it occupies a unique status in that a person who denies the *basmalah* as a verse of the *soorah* is not to be considered a disbeliever. Contrary to this, to deny any other verse of the Qur'aan is considered to be disbelief. Az-Zarkashee writes, "There is no difference of opinion among the Muslims that a person who denies the *basmalah* as a verse in the Qur'aan (at the beginning of the *soorahs*) is not to be considered a disbeliever."[346]

To conclude, the *basmalah* is counted as a verse at the beginning of *Soorah* al-Faatihah, but is not a verse at the beginning of any other *soorah*, and Allaah knows best.

As for the fact that *Soorah* at-Tawbah does not begin with the *basmalah*, there have been many interpretations seeking to explain this. There are narrations from 'Alee ibn Abee Taalib to the effect that the *basmalah* was left out of at-Tawbah since the *basmalah* signifies peace and mercy, and at-Tawbah was revealed as a warning and threat for the pagans. Other weak narrations mention the story that the Companions did not know whether at-Tawbah and al-Anfaal were two *soorahs* or one, so they purposely left the *basmalah* out at this place.[347] The strongest opinion, however, is as al-Qushayree says, 'The correct reason that the *basmalah* is not at the beginning of it is because Jibreel did not reveal it with (the *soorah*)."[348]

VI. The Soorahs of the Qur'aan

The word '*soorah*' means an enclosure or a fencing, such as the walls around a city. It is also used to denote an elevated plain.[349]

When applied to Islaamic sciences, it signifies a specific group of verses in the Qur'aan, arranged in a specific manner. Combing its linguistic meaning to the Islaamic meaning, a '*soorah*' has 'enclosed' certain verses, and is elevated in status over all other speech. Ibn Katheer (d. 774 A.H.) writes, "The scholars have differed over the linguistic meaning of '*soorah*.' Some say it is from the root word that signifies elevation... so it is as if the reciter of the Qur'aan rises from one level to another, or due to its (the *soorah*'s) high status.... And it is also possible that '*soorah*' signifies the combining of various verses, just as the walls of a city (Ar. *soor*) combine and enclose its inhabitants..."[350]

346 az-Zarkashee, *Bahr*, p. 472.
347 This narration will be discussed in the next section.
348 az-Zarkashee, v. 1, p. 263.
349 Ubaydaat, p. 136.
350 *Tafseer Ibn Katheer*, v. 1, p. 9.

The Arrangement of the Soorahs

The scholars of Islaam have agreed (*ijmaa'*) to the fact that it is obligatory to follow the arrangement of the *soorahs* in the writing of the *mus-haf*, and that it is recommended (but not obligatory) to follow this arrangement in the recitation of the Qur'aan, whether this recitation occurs during the prayer or outside of it. However, they have disagreed concerning the origin of this arrangement into three opinions.

1) The first opinion states that the arrangement of the *soorahs* was from the *ijtihaad* of the Companions. In other words, when Zayd compiled the official *mus-haf*, he employed his own *ijtihaad* in the arrangement of the *soorahs*, and the other Companions agreed to this. This is the opinion of Imaam Maalik (d. 179 A.H.) and Aboo Bakr al-Baaqillaanee (d. 403 A.H.).[351]

The proof that is given for this opinion is the fact that the different Companions had different arrangements of the *soorahs* in their respective *mus-hafs*. For example, 'Alee's *mus-haf* was arranged in chronological order, starting with *Soorah* al-Iqra', then al-Muddathir, and so on. Both the *mus-hafs* of 'Ubay ibn Ka'ab and Ibn Mas'ood started with al-Baqarah, then an-Nisaa, then Aali-'Imraan. These differences, according to the proponents of this opinion, show that the arrangement of the *soorahs* was not from the Prophet (ﷺ), for had it been so, these Companions would have written their *mus-hafs* with the proper arrangement of the *soorahs*.

However, this is the weakest of the three opinions, since the *mus-hafs* of the Companions were personal, and were not meant for others to read. Most of them were in fact incomplete, and as such do not constitute any proof. Apart from that, these *mus-hafs* were written during the lifetime of the Prophet (ﷺ), when the revelation of the Qur'aan had not even been completed. Therefore, it would not even have been possible for these *mus-hafs* to have been arranged in the correct order.

2) The second opinion claims that part of the arrangement was done by the Prophet (ﷺ), and part by the *ijtihaad* of the Companions. The followers of this opinion, however, have disagreed as to how many *soorahs* were arranged by the Prophet (ﷺ) and how many by the Companions.

The most common opinion amongst this group is that all the *soorahs* were arranged by the Prophet (ﷺ) except for *Soorah* at-Tawbah and al-Anfaal. As proof, they use the following narration:

Ibn 'Abbaas narrates that he asked 'Uthmaan, "Why did you pair al-Anfaal, even though it is from the *mathaani*[352] with at-Tawbah, which is from the *mi'een*. And why did you not write the *basmalah* between them, and put both of them in the *tiwaal soorahs*?" 'Uthmaan answered, "The *soorahs* used to be revealed to the Prophet (ﷺ), so whenever something was revealed he would call a scribe and tell him, 'Put this verse in the *soorah* in which such-and-such is mentioned.' *Soorah* al-Anfaal was one of the first *soorahs* to be revealed in Madeenah, and *Soorah* at-Tawbah was one of the

---

351 as-Suyootee, v. 1, p. 82.
352 For a discussion of the *mathaani*, *tiwaal* and *mi-een*, see the last section of this chapter.

last parts of the Qur'aan revealed, and its story was similar to it (i.e., *Soorah* at-Tawbah resembled *Soorah* al-Anfaal), so I thought that it was a part of it. The Prophet (![]) passed away before I could ask him concerning this issue, so because of this, I put the two of these together, and did not write the *basmalah* between them, and put them amongst the seven *tiwaal soorahs*."[353]

This narration would be a very explicit proof for those who hold this opinion, if it was not for the fact that the above narration is weak.[354] Therefore, this narration cannot be taken as proof in this matter.

This opinion, that all of the Qur'aan except for at-Tawbah and al-Anfaal was arranged by the Prophet (![]), was held by as-Suyootee (who claimed that this was the opinion of the majority of scholars), al-Bayhaqee (d. 458 A.H.) and others.

It should be pointed out that the proponents of both of the above opinions claim that the present arrangement must be followed, since the Companions all agreed to it (*ijmaa'*).

3) The last opinion states that the *soorah* order was from the command of the Prophet (![]). In other words, the arrangement of the *soorahs* was understood by the Companions since the Prophet (![]) taught them this, and this is why 'Uthmaan arranged the *soorahs* in the present arrangement.

This is perhaps the strongest opinion on the matter. This is because the Prophet (![]) used to recite the *soorahs* to the Companions in a specific order, and he (![]) mentioned the order of some of them in certain *hadeeth*. For example, he said, "Recite the two bright ones: al-Baqarah and Aali-'Imraan,"[355] and he (![]) said, "I have been given in place of the Torah the seven *tiwaal*, and I have been given in place of the Psalms the *mi'een*, and I have been given in place of the Gospel the *mathaani*, and I was honoured over the others with the *mufassal*."[356] This *hadeeth* will be discussed in the next section; however, it clearly shows that the Qur'aan had been arranged into some order by the Prophet (![]).

Also, when the Prophet (![]) recited the Qur'aan to Jibreel every year, he (![]) must have recited it in a particular order, and Zayd was present when he recited it. When 'Uthmaan compiled the *mus-haf*, Zayd would have used the same order that he had heard from the Prophet (![]). Another proof is that none of the Companions objected to this order. Therefore, the arrangement of the *soorahs* must have been known to the Companions, and that is why they agreed to it (*ijmaa'*).

Perhaps the strongest proof is the narration of Hudhayfah at-Thaqafee (d. 42 A.H.), in which he said, "I asked the Companions (during the lifetime of the Prophet (![])), 'How do you divide the Qur'aan?' They replied, 'We break it into three *soorahs*, then

---

353   Reported by Aboo Daawood and others, cf. Qattaan p. 143.

354   In its chain is Yazeed al-Farsee, whom al-Bukhaaree mentioned in his *ad-Du'afaa*. Ahmad Shaakir said of this *hadeeth*, "It has no basis." See Qattaan, p. 144.

355   Reported by Muslim.

356   Reported by at-Tabaranee in his *Kabeer*; cf. *as-Saheehah* # 1480.

five, then seven, then nine, then eleven, then thirteen, then the *mufassal* from Qaaf to the end.'"[357] In other words, the Companions would recite the Qur'aan in a specific order so that they could finish it every week. This narration shows that the arrangement of the *soorahs* was known to all the Companions even during the life of the Prophet (ﷺ).

Imaam al-Karmaanee said, "The arrangement of the *soorahs* is from Allaah, and the Qur'aan is written in the *Lauh al-Mahfoodh* in this arrangement. It was recited to Jibreel by the Prophet (ﷺ) in this order every year, and he (ﷺ) recited it twice the year he died." Aboo Bakr al-Anbaaree (d. 328 A.H.) said, "The whole Qur'aan was revealed to the lower heavens, then it was revealed gradually, over a period of twenty or so years. A *soorah* would be revealed in response to an occurrence, and a verse in response to a happening. Jibreel used to inform the Prophet (ﷺ) of the arrangement and place of the verses and *soorahs*, so the arrangement of the *soorahs* is like the arrangement of the verses and words – all of it is from the Prophet (ﷺ). Therefore, whoever changes the arrangement of a *soorah* to a place before or after what it should be has ruined the arrangement of the Qur'aan."[358] Al-Hamad writes, "The proofs given (by the proponents of the second opinion) are not explicit, and the possibility remains that the Companions took this arrangement from the Prophet (ﷺ), and this is the correct view..."[359]

In fact, many of the scholars have discussed the wisdom behind the present arrangement of the *soorahs*. The majority of *tafseers* also discuss the relationship between the *soorahs*. In fact, as-Suyootee wrote a multi-volume work solely on this topic, entitled *Tanaasiq ad-Durar fi Tanaasub as-Suwar*.[360]

The Number of Soorahs

There are 114 *soorahs* in the Qur'aan, and this is the view held by almost all the scholars. A very small minority held the opinion that *Soorah* al-Anfaal and at-Tawbah are in fact one *soorah*, and thus consider there to be 113 *soorahs*. Imaam az-Zarkashee said,

> And know that the number of *soorahs* of the Qur'aan, by consensus of those in authority,[361] is 114, as is present in the *mus-haf* of 'Uthmaan, the first of which is al-Faatihah and the last of which is an-Naas. Mujaahid (d. 100 A.H.) said that there were 113, combining al-Anfaal and at-Tawbah as one... but this is refuted by the fact that the Prophet (ﷺ) named each of them separately.[362]

---

357 Reported by Aboo Daawood.

358 Both quotes from az-Zarkashee, v.1, p. 259. What is meant by changing the arrangement is not to recite one *soorah* before the other in prayer, for this was occasionally done by the Prophet (ﷺ), but rather to consider a *soorah* as having a position that is not consistent with the present arrangement.

359 al-Hamad, p. 122.

360 Published by 'Aalim al-Kutub, Beirut, 1987.

361 Ar. *Ahl al-Hall wa al-'Aqd*.

362 az-Zarkashee, v. 1, p. 251.

The Names of the Soorahs

As for the names of the *soorahs*, many of them have been given by the Prophet (ﷺ), such as the *hadeeth* quoted above that mention the names of al-Baqarah, Aali-'Imraan and al-Kahf. However, the names of all the *soorahs* are not found in the *hadeeth* of the Prophet (ﷺ). Some names were given by the *salaf* as well, and thus it is possible that a *soorah* has more than one name (although there are some who hold that even the names of the *soorahs* are from the Prophet (ﷺ)).[363] For example *Soorah* at-Tawbah is also called al-Baraa'ah, and *Soorah* al-Ghaafir is also called al-Mu'min. A *soorah* was typically named for a story, theme or word in it.

The longest *soorah* is *Soorah* al-Baqarah, and the shortest is *Soorah* al-Kawthar.

The Classification of the Soorahs

The *soorahs* of the Qur'aan are grouped into four categories, the *tiwaal* (long) *soorahs*, the *mi'een* (hundred) *soorahs*, the *mathaani* (oft-recited) *soorahs* and the *mufassal* (disjointed) *soorahs*.

These categories are based on a *hadeeth* of the Prophet (ﷺ) in which he said, "I have been given in place of the Torah the seven *tiwaal*, and I have been given in place of the Psalms the *mi'een*, and I have been given in place of the Gospel the *mathaani*, and I was honoured over the others with the *mufassal*."[364]

1) The *tiwaal soorahs*: These are the first seven *soorahs* in the Qur'aan after the *Faatihah*. Some have added at-Tawbah as included in the *tiwaal* since there is no *basmalah* that separates it from *Soorah* al-Anfaal. They have been called *tiwaal* because they are the longest *soorahs* in the Qur'aan.

2) The *mi'een*: These are the *soorahs* that have over or around a hundred verses, hence their name.

3) The *mathaani*: These *soorahs* are the oft-repeated ones since they are recited in prayers more often than the longer ones. They occur after the *mi-een*.

4) The *mufassal*: These *soorahs* are called disjointed or broken because of the frequent occurrence of the *basmalah*. They start, according to the strongest opinion, from Qaaf (or, according to another opinion, al-Hujuraat) and finish with an-Naas.

As for the particular *soorahs* that qualify as the *mi'een* and *mathaani*, there does not appear to be any consensus. Some have said that the *mi-een soorahs* ends at *Soorah* Faatir.

This would then imply that the *tiwaal* are the *soorahs* from al-Baqarah to at-Tawbah; the *mi-een* from Yoonus to al-Faatir; the *mathaani* from Ya Seen to al-Hujuraat and

---

363 See az-Zarkashee, v. 1, p. 270, where he himself expresses his doubt over the divine origin of the *soorah* names, although it seems that he also leans to this opinion.

364 Reported by at-Tabaaraanee in his *Kabeer*; cf. *as-Saheehah* # 1480.

the *mufassal* from Qaaf to an-Naas. Again, this classification is not agreed upon by the scholars.[365]

Other Classifications

The Qur'aan has also been divided into sections to facilitate reading. These divisions have been adopted to assist the completion of the Qur'aan in a certain number of days. The ones that are more common in the *mus-hafs* of today are as follows:

1) *Manzil*: The Qur'aan is divided into seven *manzils*, so that if a person wishes to finish the Qur'aan in one week, he may read one *manzil* a day.

Most of the Companions used to finish the Qur'aan in one week. The narration quoted earlier from Hudhayfah shows this: "I asked the Companions of the Prophet (☼) how they used to divide the Qur'aan (for reading purposes). They responded, 'Three *soorahs*, then five *soorahs*, then seven *soorahs*, then nine *soorahs*, then eleven *soorahs*, then thirteen *soorahs*, then the *mufassal* from Qaaf to the end.'"[366] In other words, the first day of the week they would recite al-Baqarah, Aali-'Imraan and an-Nisaa; on the second day, the next five *soorahs*; and so on, so that the recitation of the Qur'aan would be finished weekly.

In the *mus-hafs* of today, the *manzils* are different from this narration. This division of the Qur'aan into *manzils* is not present in most *mus-hafs* printed in Arab countries.

2) *Juz*: The Qur'aan is also divided into thirty parts, each of which is called a *juz*. This is done in order to facilitate its reading in one month. In certain non-Arab countries, this division is also called a *sipaara*.

3) *Hizb*: The *mus-hafs* printed in Arab countries are typically divided into *hizbs*. The Qur'aan is composed of sixty *hizbs*, and thus every *juz* contains two *hizbs*. The beginning of each *juz* is also the beginning of a *hizb*, and the middle of a *juz* is the beginning of another *hizb*. Each *hizb* is further divided into quarters called *ruba'*. Thus, each *juz* contains eight *ruba's*.

4) *Ruku*: The *mus-hafs* printed in the Indian subcontinent are typically divided into *rukus*, each equivalent to one or two paragraphs of text. The *ruku* is accompanied by three numbers. The top number denotes the number of the *ruku* with respect to that particular *soorah*. The middle number indicates the number of verses in that *ruku*. The bottom number indicates the number of the *ruku* with respect to the *juz* in which it occurs.

---

365 Although Tarhooni in his work does not hold that it is necessary for the *soorahs* in each of the different categories to be sequential. So, for example, he holds that the *tiwaal* are from al-Baqarah to al-Aaraf, and Yunus, placing al-Anfaal with the *mathani*, and at-Tawbah in the *mi'een*!

366 Reported by Aboo Daawood.

CHAPTER 9

THE BEGINNING OF THE Soorahs

I. The Different Categories

The beginning of the *soorahs* may be divided into ten categories, into which all the 114 *soorahs* may be classified.[367]

1) The Disjointed Letters (*al-Muqatta'aat*). For example, *Alif-Laam-Meem*, *Kaaf-Haa-Yaa-'Ayn-Saad*, *Haa-Meem*, etc. These are twenty nine *soorahs* in number. This category shall be discussed in greater detail in the next section.

2) The Glorification of Allaah. This is divided into two sub-categories.

The first category is the glorification by means of Praise, and by attributing Names and Attributes of Perfection. For example,

الْحَمْدُ لِلَّهِ

«All Praise is due to Allaah...» [1:1]

and,

تَبَارَكَ ٱلَّذِى بِيَدِهِ ٱلْمُلْكُ

«Blessed be He in whose Hands is the Dominion» [67:1]

The second category is the glorification by means of negating attributes of weakness and imperfection. For example,

سُبْحَٰنَ ٱلَّذِىٓ

«Glorified and Exalted be He (i.e., He is Exalted over all evil that is attributed to Him)» [17:1]

and,

سَبِّحِ ٱسْمَ رَبِّكَ ٱلْأَعْلَى

«Glorify the Name of your Lord, the Most High» [87:1].[368]

---

367 az-Zarkashee, v. 1, p.164-181.

368 This distinction will be better appreciated if one understands the different meanings of 'Subhaan Allaah' and 'Alhamdullilaah'. The latter has the connotation of praising Allaah because He possesses the Most Perfect Names and Attributes, whereas the former has the connotation of negating from Allaah any attributes of imperfection, and thus affirming only Perfect Attributes.

There are a total of fourteen *soorahs* that begin with glorification; half of them are in the first category and half are in the second.

3) A Call. For example, يَـٰٓأَيُّهَا ٱلَّذِينَ ءَامَنُوٓا۟ "O You who Believe" (5:1 and others); يَـٰٓأَيُّهَا ٱلنَّاسُ "O Mankind" (22:1 and others); يَـٰٓأَيُّهَا ٱلنَّبِىُّ and "O Prophet" (33:1 and others). There are ten *soorahs* that fit into this category, five of which address the Prophet (ﷺ).

4) A Statement of Fact. For example, قَدْ أَفْلَحَ ٱلْمُؤْمِنُونَ "Successful indeed are the Believers" (23:1), or عَبَسَ وَتَوَلَّىٰٓ "He frowned and turned away" (80:1). This occurs in twenty-three *soorahs*.

5) An Oath. For example, وَٱلْعَصْرِ "By the Time!" (103:1), or وَٱلنَّجْمِ إِذَا هَوَىٰ "By the Star when it goes down" (53:1). This occurs in fifteen *soorahs*, all of which are Makkan.

6) A Condition. For example, إِذَا جَآءَ نَصْرُ ٱللَّهِ وَٱلْفَتْحُ "When the Help of Allaah Comes, and the Conquest" (110:1), or إِذَا وَقَعَتِ ٱلْوَاقِعَةُ "When the Event Befalls" (56:1). This occurs in seven *soorahs*.

7) A Command. For example, ٱقْرَأْ بِٱسْمِ رَبِّكَ ٱلَّذِى خَلَقَ "Read, in the name of your Lord!" (96:1), or قُلْ هُوَ ٱللَّهُ أَحَدٌ "Say: He is Allaah, the One!" (112:1) There are six *soorahs* that fit into this category.

8) A Question. For example, عَمَّ يَتَسَآءَلُونَ "What are they asking about?" (78:1) or أَرَءَيْتَ ٱلَّذِى يُكَذِّبُ بِٱلدِّينِ "Have you seen him who denies the Recompense?" (107:1). This also occurs in six *soorahs*.

9) An Invocation. For example, وَيْلٌ لِّلْمُطَفِّفِينَ "Woe to those who give less in measure and weight!" (83:1), وَيْلٌ لِّكُلِّ هُمَزَةٍ لُّمَزَةٍ "Woe to every slanderer and backbiter!" (104:1), and تَبَّتْ يَدَآ أَبِى لَهَبٍ وَتَبَّ "May the two hands of Aboo Lahab perish, and he (along with them)!" (111:1). These are the only three *soorahs* where this occurs.

10) A Reason or Cause. There is only one *soorah* where this occurs: لِإِيلَٰفِ قُرَيْشٍ "For the taming of the Quraysh!" (106:1).

II. The Disjointed Letters

The disjointed letters, or the *muqatta'aat*, occur at the beginning of twenty-nine *soorahs* in the Qur'aan. These letters, fourteen in number, comprise exactly half the letters of the Arabic alphabet. Three *soorahs* begin with only one letter, ten with two letters, twelve with three letters, two with four letters, and two with five. The most common letter is *meem*, in seventeen *soorahs*. The least common are *kaaf* and *noon*, which both occur only once.

There have been numerous interpretations as to the meaning and purpose of these letters, ranging from the ludicrous (some Orientalists claim that these letters are the initials of the scribes who wrote the Qur'aan for the Prophet (ﷺ)), to the sensible. Some of the more common interpretations and opinions are discussed below:

1) These letters are from the *Mutashaabih*,[369] and only Allaah knows their meanings. This opinion is a very common one, and it is definitely the safest opinion. Aboo Bakr as-Siddeeq is reported to have said, "Every book has secrets in it, and the secret of the Qur'aan is in the beginning of the *soorahs* (in the *muqatta'aat*)."[370]

However, even though this opinion is the safest one, it does not rule out the possibility that these letters have some purpose and meaning. Fakhr ad-Deen ar-Raazee (d. 606 A.H.) said, commenting on this view, "It is not possible that Allaah would include something in His Book that His Creation would not understand, because Allaah is the one who has commanded us to reflect over this Book, and seek guidance from it. This cannot be achieved except by understanding its meanings."[371]

2) These letters are from the names of Allaah. There are reports from Ibn 'Abbaas to this effect, such as '*Alif-Lam-Meem*' indicates the three names: Allaah, *Lateef* and *Majeed*, all of which are amongst the names of Allaah. However, all these reports are not authentic. Other weak reports state that these letters are the greatest name of Allaah (*al-Ism al-'Adham*), but these reports must be rejected too.[372]

3) Allaah has sworn by these letters. In other words, these letters have the same purpose as the other oaths in the Qur'aan, such as "By the Dawn" (89:1). This view is refuted since this is not the proper way the Arabs used to swear, and therefore this opinion does not seem to have much weight.

4) These letters represent numerical values. This opinion is rejected outright, as all such numerical interpretations are unfounded in the Qur'aan or *Sunnah*. Certain fabricated *hadeeth* support this view.

5) They stand for specific meanings. In other words, they are acronyms for phrases. For example, '*Alif-Laam-Meem*' stands for *Ana Allaahu 'Alam* (I, Allaah, Know), or Allaah, Jibreel and Muhammad. Again, there is no proof for this.

6) Esoteric Interpretations. These are usually given by certain extremist *Soofis* and other heretical groups. Needless to say, all of these opinions are baseless since there is no proof from the Qur'aan or *Sunnah* to support them.

7) They are from the names of the Qur'aan. Most of the scholars have rejected this view, as the Qur'aan is not referred to as '*Alif-Lam-Meem*,' or any of the other letters.

8) They are meant to baffle the disbelievers. The disbelievers used to say,

$$\text{لَا تَسْمَعُوا لِهَٰذَا ٱلْقُرْءَانِ وَٱلْغَوْا۟ فِيهِ لَعَلَّكُمْ تَغْلِبُونَ}$$

«Do not listen to the Qur'aan, and make noise (i.e., babble) in the midst of it, so that you may overcome (the Qur'aan)» [41:26]

---

369 See Ch. 12, 'The Clear and Unclear Verses'.
370 az-Zarkashee, v. 1, p. 173. It is essential, however, to verify if this actually *was* the statement of Aboo Bakr, as az-Zarkashee reports it without an *isnaad*.
371 az-Zarkashee, v. 1, p. 173.
372 Ubaydaat, p. 208.

Thus, Allaah revealed these letters to bewilder the disbelievers. This opinion is a plausible one, but again there does not seem to be any strong proof in support of it. This was the opinion of ar-Raazee in his famous *tafseer*.[373]

9) They are the names of the *soorahs*. Thus, it is possible to say *Soorah* Ya-Seen, *Soorah* Ṭaa Haa, etc. Although this might be one of the purposes the *muqatta'aat* can be used for, it does not really explain the meaning of the *muqatta'aat*. Also, less than a third of the *soorahs* actually begin with these letters, therefore this cannot be their primary purpose.

10) They are meant to demonstrate man's limited knowledge. By including the *muqatta'aat* as the first verse of the Qur'aan after *Soorah* al-Faatiḥah, man is being reminded of his limited knowledge, and the infinite knowledge of his Creator.

11) They are a reference to the other half of the alphabet. In other words, the Arabs are being reminded that this Qur'aan is composed of their letters, and the words are the same as their words, and yet it cannot be imitated in its style and prose. Thus, these letters seek to display the miraculous nature of the Qur'aan.

To add weight to this explanation, it is noticed that, in almost all *soorahs* where these letters occur, the very next verse mentions the Qur'aan. For example,

«*Alif-Lam-Meem*. This is indeed the Book, there is no doubt in it, a guidance for the pious» [2:1-2].[374]

This last opinion was the opinion of az-Zamakhsharee (d. 538 A.H.) in his famous *tafseer*.[375] Imaam al-Baaqillaanee (d. 403 A.H.) said, "These letters are exactly half the alphabet, as if it is being said, 'Whoever presumes that the Qur'aan is not a miracle, let him take the other half and form a speech that can compete with the Qur'aan!'"[376]

12) They are used to attract attention. The *muqatta'aat* are not a phenomenon started by the Qur'aan; the Arab poets of *Jaahilliyah* occasionally used disjointed letters at the beginning of their poetry to attract attention to the poem that was to follow.

Also, the Arabs at the time of the Prophet (ﷺ) never questioned the *muqatta'aat*, despite the fact that they tried everything to disparage the Prophet (ﷺ), and the Companions never asked the explanation of these letters from the Prophet (ﷺ), despite their thirst for knowledge. This shows that they were not puzzled by these letters, since they were accustomed to its use in the poems of *Jaahilliyah*. Thus, according to this opinion, the *muqatta'aat* are used to attract attention to the *soorahs*, and to prove to the disbelieving Arabs that the Qur'aan was a revelation from Allaah, since even

---

373 *Tafseer ar-Raazee*, v.1, p.17.

374 The only *soorahs* where this does not occur are al-'Ankaboot and ar-Room, but even these mention the Qur'aan in the middle of the *soorahs*.

375 *al-Kashaaf*, v. 1, p. 17.

though the *muqatta'aat* were used by the poets of old, the Qur'aan's style of 'poetry' is inimitable.

In a topic of this nature, it is impossible to authoritatively say which of these opinions is the correct one, since there does not exist absolute proof for any of them (hence, in a way, this aids the first opinion!). Many can be eliminated as baseless or weak (opinions two through seven).

Opinions eight, nine, and ten, although are plausible ones, do not seem to be the primary purpose of the *muqatta'aat*. They may, however, be secondary purposes.

This leaves three opinions, the first, eleventh and twelfth. As for the first, as was pointed out earlier, it is true that only Allaah knows for certain the meanings of these letters, but this does not rule out the possibility that they may have meanings that are possible to grasp. Concerning the last two opinions, there does not seem to be any grounds for rejecting either of them. It seems likely, therefore, that they both are the strongest opinions, and Allaah knows best.

It is concluded, then, that the actual purpose of the *muqatta'aat* is known only to Allaah; but it does not seem too unreasonable to claim that their purpose is to prove the miraculous nature of the Qur'aan, both by showing the Arabs that the Qur'aan – despite its inimitability – was composed of their letters and words, and by using the techniques of the *Jaahilliyah* poets to challenge and prevail over the eloquence of the poems of old.[377, 378]

III. The Ending of the Soorahs

Just as the beginning of the *soorahs* have a certain unique style, so too do the endings of the *soorahs*. The last part of a speech is the part which the reader will leave with, therefore it must have certain characteristics that make it stand out above the rest of the speech.

The endings of the *soorahs* are typically very comprehensive and forceful, leaving a strong impact upon the reader. An example is the ending of *Soorah* Ibraheem:

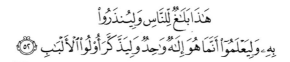

---

377 Zarzur, p.157.

377 Also see the opinion of Aboo Bakr al-Jazaa'iree in his *tafseer*, v. 1, p. 7.

378 The Committee of Permanent Scholars (*al-Lajnah ad-Daa'imah*) of Saudi Arabia was asked concerning these letters at the beginning of the *soorahs*. In response to this question, they issued a *fatwa* (# 6395; v. 4, p. 144 of their *Fataawa*) which states: "The scholars have differing opinions concerning this issue, but the correct one – and Allaah knows best – is that these letters at the beginning of the *soorahs* are an indication of the *i'jaaz* of the Qur'aan, and that the creation is incapable of bringing forth something equivalent to it, despite the fact that it is composed of these same disjointed letters (i.e., the Arabic alphabet) that they talk in. And this opinion is the one that Shaykh al-Islaam Ibn Taymiyyah defended, and Aboo al-Hajjaaj al-Mizzi agreed with." The Committee members were: 'Abdullaah ibn Qa'ood, 'Abdullaah ibn Ghudayaan, 'Abd ar-Razaaq Afeefi, and 'Abd al-'Azeez ibn 'Abd Allaah ibn Baaz.

«This (Qur'aan) is a Message for mankind (and a proof against them), in order that they may be warned thereby, and that they may know that there is only One God who is worthy of worship, and that men of understanding may take heed!» [14:52]

Another example is the comprehensive *du'aa* that forms the last two verses of *Soorah* al-Baqarah. *Soorah* Aali-'Imraan ends with the exhortation of being patient and persevering in the cause of Allaah; *Soorah* al-Maa'idah and al-Hashr end with the praise and glorification of Allaah; *Soorah* at-Tawbah ends with a beautiful description of the Prophet (ﷺ), and so forth.

An important aspect of this topic is the relationship of the beginning of a *soorah* with its ending. For example, *Soorah* al-Mu'minoon starts off with the phrase,

$$قَدۡ أَفۡلَحَ ٱلۡمُؤۡمِنُونَ$$

«Indeed, of a surety the believers are successful!» [23:1]

and ends with,

$$إِنَّهُۥ لَا يُفۡلِحُ ٱلۡكَٰفِرُونَ$$

«Surely, the disbelievers will not be successful...» [23:117]

The relationship of the ending of a *soorah* with the beginning of the next one is also a topic of great importance. Typically, the beginning of a *soorah* is related to the ending of the previous one, either by meaning, or wording. For example, the ending of *Soorah* al-Faatihah is a request to Allaah to guide us to the Straight Path, and the beginning of *Soorah* al-Baqarah describes the Qur'aan as a guidance, as if in answer to the prayer. Likewise, the ending of *Soorah* Aali-'Imraan exhorts the believers to be patient and fear Allaah, and the beginning of *Soorah* an-Nisaa' commands mankind to fear Allaah, and fulfil the ties of kinship; the ending of *Soorah* an-Nisaa' contains the laws of being just amongst relatives with regards to the laws of inheritance, and the beginning of *Soorah* al-Maa'idah reaffirms these commands by commanding the believers to be just in fulfilling their promises and obligations.

An example of a relationship in wording is the ending of *Soorah* at-Toor,

$$وَمِنَ ٱلَّيۡلِ فَسَبِّحۡهُ وَإِدۡبَٰرَ ٱلنُّجُومِ$$

«And in the night-time, glorify (Allaah's) praises, and at the setting of the stars» [52:49]

and the beginning of *Soorah* an-Najm,

$$وَٱلنَّجۡمِ إِذَا هَوَىٰ$$

«By the star when it goes down» [53:1]

both the ending and beginning mention the word 'star.'[379]

---

379 For this section, cf. az-Zarkashee, v. 1, p. 186.

CHAPTER 10

THE AHRUF OF THE QUR'AAN

1. The Meaning of the Word 'Ahruf'

The word *ahruf* is the plural of *harf*. Linguistically, '*harf*' has a number of meanings, including:

1) 'A letter or a word.' *Al-huruf al-abjadiyya*, for example, means the letters of the alphabet.

2) 'The border, the edge of something, the brink.' For example, Allaah says,

$$وَمِنَ ٱلنَّاسِ مَن يَعْبُدُ ٱللَّهَ عَلَىٰ حَرْفٍ$$

«And among mankind is he who worships Allaah (as it were) upon a *harf* (i.e., upon the very edge, or in doubt)» [22:11]

3) 'To swerve from the truth, to distort.' Allaah says concerning the Jews,

$$يُحَرِّفُونَ ٱلْكَلِمَ عَن مَّوَاضِعِهِۦ$$

«... they have displaced (lit., *yuharifuna*) words from their right places...» [4:46]

Its exact definition in Qur'aanic sciences is the subject matter of this chapter, and therefore cannot be defined at this point. However, a temporary definition may be given as follows: The *ahruf* are the various ways that the verses of the Qur'aan are read. Imaam al-Qurtubee (d. 671 A.H.) said, "Every variation of a word in the Qur'aan is said to be a *harf*. So, for example, when we say the *harf* of Ibn Mas'ood, it means the way that Ibn Mas'ood used to recite that verse or word."[380]

Most English authors translate *ahruf* as 'modes' or 'dialects.' However, in this book the word will be left in Arabic since the meaning is broader than these translated words.

---

380 Ubaydaat, p. 153.

II. The Number of Ahruf of the Qur'aan

The Qur'aan was revealed in seven *ahruf*. The proof for this is found in many narrations from the Prophet (ﷺ), so much so that it reaches the level of *mutawaatir*.[381] Jalaal ad-Deen as-Suyootee lists twenty-one companions who narrated that the Qur'aan was revealed in seven *ahruf*.[382] Some of these narrations are as follows:

1) Ibn 'Abbaas reported that the Prophet (ﷺ) said, "Jibreel recited the Qur'aan to me in one *harf*, and I recited it back to him, but I requested him to increase (the number of *harf*) and he continued to increase it for me, until we stopped at seven *ahruf*." Ibn Shihaab az-Zuhree (d. 124 A.H.), one of the narrators of the *hadeeth*, said, "It has reached me that these seven *ahruf* are essentially one (in meaning), they do not differ about what is permitted or forbidden."[383]

2) 'Ubay ibn Ka'ab reported that the Prophet (ﷺ) was once on the outskirts of Madeenah (near the tribe of Banoo Ghifaar) when Jibreel came to him and said, "Allaah has commanded that you recite the Qur'aan to your people in one *harf*." The Prophet (ﷺ) replied, "I ask Allaah's pardon and forgiveness! My people are not capable of doing this!" Jibreel then came again and said, "Allaah has commanded you to recite the Qur'aan to your people in two *ahruf*." The Prophet (ﷺ) again replied, "I ask Allaah's pardon and forgiveness! My people are not capable of doing this!" Jibreel then came a third time and said, "Allaah has commanded you to recite the Qur'aan to your people in three *ahruf*." The Prophet (ﷺ) replied for a third time, "I ask Allaah's pardon and forgiveness! My people are not capable of doing this!" At last, Jibreel came for the fourth time, and said, "Allaah has commanded you to recite the Qur'aan to your people in seven *ahruf*, and in whichever *harf* they recite, they would be right.[384]"

3) 'Umar ibn al-Khattaab narrated, "I was sitting in the *masjid* when I heard Hishaam ibn Hakeem recite *Soorah* al-Furqaan. I was almost about to jump on him in his prayer, but I waited until he finished, and then grabbed him by his garment and asked him, 'Who taught you to recite in such a manner?'" He replied, 'It was the Prophet (ﷺ) himself!' I responded, 'You are mistaken, for indeed I learnt this *soorah* from the Prophet (ﷺ) and it was different from your recitation!' Therefore, I dragged him to the Prophet (ﷺ) and complained to him that Hishaam had recited *Soorah* al-Furqaan in a manner different from what he (ﷺ) had taught me. At this, the Prophet (ﷺ) told me to let go of Hishaam, and asked him to recite *Soorah* al-Furqaan. Hishaam recited the *Soorah* in the same way I had heard him before. When he finished, the Prophet (ﷺ) said, 'It was revealed this way.' He then asked me to recite the same *soorah*. When I had finished, he (ﷺ) said, 'It was (also) revealed this way. Indeed, the Qur'aan has been revealed in seven different *ahruf*, so recite whichever one is easy for you.'"[385]

---

381 A *mutawaatir hadeeth* is one that is reported by a large number of narrators in every stage of the chain, so much so that they could not all be mistaken or agree upon a lie.

382 as-Suyootee, vol. 1, p. 45.

383 Narrated by al-Bukhaaree and Muslim.

384 Narrated by Muslim.

385 Narrated by al-Bukhaaree and Muslim.

4) In a story similar to 'Umar's, 'Ubay ibn Ka'ab also heard two people reciting the Qur'aan in a manner different from what he had learnt. After some discussion, both parties went to the Prophet (ﷺ) and recited the same portion to him. He (ﷺ) approved of both parties' recitations. At this point, Ubay narrates, "...there occurred in my mind a sort of denial and doubt that did not exist even in the time of *Jaahilliyah* (before Islaam)! When the Messenger (ﷺ) saw how I was affected, he struck my chest, whereupon I started sweating, and felt as though I were looking at Allaah in fear! Then the Prophet (ﷺ) said, 'O Ubay! A message was sent to me to recite the Qur'aan in one *harf*, but I requested (Allaah) to make things easy on my nation. A second message came that I should recite the Qur'aan in two *ahruf*, but I again made the same request. I was then ordered to recite the Qur'aan in seven *ahruf*.'"[386]

5) Ubay ibn Ka'ab narrates that once the Prophet (ﷺ) met Jibreel, and said, "O Jibreel! I have been sent to an illiterate nation. Among them are old and young men and women, and those who have never read any writing!" Jibreel answered him, "O Muhammad, the Qur'aan has been revealed in seven *ahruf*!"[387]

There are many other *hadeeth* that confirm that the Qur'aan was revealed in seven *ahruf*, but these narrations will suffice for the present discussion.

III. What is Meant by the Ahruf of the Qur'aan?

Before discussing the answer to this question, it would be useful to mention some points that can be inferred from the above narrations:

1) The different *ahruf* are all directly from Allaah, and not from the Companions. In all the narrations where the Companions differed from each other, it was clear that each one had been taught directly from the Prophet (ﷺ), who was inspired by Allaah. This is why the Prophet (ﷺ) said to each one of the *ahruf* recited by 'Umar and Hishaam, "It was revealed this way."

2) The reason the Prophet (ﷺ) requested the number of *ahruf* to be increased was to make the memorisation and recitation of the Qur'aan easier for his *Ummah*. The Prophet (ﷺ) prayed to increase the *ahruf* because in his *ummah* were "... old and young men and women, and those who have never read any writing." Therefore, the limitations of the Qur'aan being in only one *harf* have been removed by Allaah as a blessing for this *Ummah*.

3) The Prophet (ﷺ) used to teach the different *ahruf* to different Companions, depending on the condition and situation of that Companion. It can be assumed that the Prophet (ﷺ) chose the particular *harf* to recite to a Companion depending on which one would be the easiest for that particular Companion to memorise, since the purpose of the *ahruf* was to simplify recitation and memorisation. The Prophet (ﷺ) did not teach all the *ahruf* to all the Companions, for 'Umar and Hishaam did not know about the existence of the different *ahruf*. Also, the

---

386 Narrated by Muslim.
387 Narrated by at-Tirmidhee.

cause for Ubay's doubts was the fact that he was unaware of these *ahruf*, and the Prophet (ﷺ) had to pray to Allaah to remove his doubts.

4) The differences between these *ahruf* were not so great as to prevent recognition of what was being recited. In other words, even though Hishaam was reciting the Qur'aan in a different *harf* than 'Umar, 'Umar could still recognise that Hishaam was reciting *Soorah* al-Furqaan, thus showing that the *ahruf* were not radically different from each other. Also, the narration of Ibn Shihaab shows that the basic meaning of all these *ahruf* was the same.

5) Each one of these *ahruf* is complete in and of itself. The proof for this is the statement of the Prophet (ﷺ) "...so whichever one of them they recite, they are correct." This is not to say that the *ahruf* do not complement one another in meaning, but rather that the recitation of the Qur'aan in one *harf* is sufficient.

6) The number of *ahruf* is exactly seven – not more, not less. The Prophet (ﷺ) asked Jibreel to increase the number of *ahruf* until Jibreel reached seven *ahruf*; therefore interpretations to the effect that 'seven' indicates an unspecified plurality (this was the opinion of Qaadee 'Iyaad (d. 504 A.H.)) are false.

However, one narration in the *Musnad* of Imaam Ahmad states that the Qur'aan was revealed in three *ahruf*, and yet another narration states that it was revealed in ten *ahruf*. Some scholars have tried to explain the first narrations as meaning that, in the Makkan stage, the Qur'aan was revealed in three *ahruf*, whereas in the Madeenan stage, Allaah increased this to seven *ahruf*. Other scholars have given different interpretations to reconcile these *hadeeth*.[388] However, there is no need to resort to such explanations, since both of these narrations are weak.[389] Therefore, the Qur'aan was revealed in exactly seven *ahruf*.

7) The revelation of the Qur'aan in seven *ahruf* started in Madeenah, after the *hijrah*. In one of the narrations, the phrase, "...while the Prophet (ﷺ) was on the outskirts of Madeenah," indicates that this occurred after the *hijrah*.

8) A last benefit that can be inferred from these *hadeeth* (although this is not relevant to the *ahruf*) is the concern shown by the Companions in the preservation of the correct recitation of the Qur'aan. In all the cases quoted above, the Companions were not content with listening to recitations that were different from theirs – despite the fact that these recitations were said to have been learnt from the Prophet (ﷺ) – until they had taken the matter to the Prophet (ﷺ) himself.

As for what is meant by these seven *ahruf*, there is a great deal of difference on this issue. Ibn Qutaybah (d. 276 A.H.) recorded thirty-five opinions on this issue, and as-Suyootee listed over forty. Ibn Sa'adan (d. 231 A.H.), a famous grammarian and reciter of the Qur'aan, even declared that the true meaning of the *ahruf* was known only to Allaah, and thus to attempt to investigate into this issue was futile! On the other hand, Imaam Muhammad ibn al-Jazaree (d. 832 A.H.), perhaps the greatest scholar

---

388 cf. Itr, pps. 78-80.
389 cf., al-Albaanee, *Da'eef al-Jaami'*, # 1335 and 1339.

of the *qira'aat* after the era of the *salaf*, said, "I have sought to discover the meanings of these *hadeeth* (about the *ahruf*), and have pondered over them, and contemplated this topic for over thirty years, until Allaah opened my mind to that which is the correct answer in this matter, *Inshaa Allaah!*"[390]

The reason that such a great difference of opinion exists concerning the exact meaning of the *ahruf* is due to the fact that there does not exist any explicit narration from the Prophet (ﷺ), or the *salaf*, concerning the exact nature of the *ahruf*; these various opinions are merely the conclusions of later scholars, based upon their examination of the evidences and their personal reasoning (*ijtihaad*).

Therefore, it should be understood from the outset that to arrive at one specific conclusion, and claim with certainty that it alone is correct and all else is wrong, is pure folly. What is desired, however, is to narrow down the various opinions and eliminate as many as possible based upon the evidences.

All of these opinions can be divided into three broad categories, which are discussed in the following sections.[391]

A. THOSE OPINIONS WHICH HAVE NO BASIS WHATSOEVER:

In this category fall those opinions which do not have any *hadeeth* to support them, nor do they make logical sense. Some of these are:

1) Seven different categories of texts. For example: constrained and unconstrained, general and specific, literal and metaphoric, *naasikh* and *mansookh*. Other categories include those given by grammarians and linguists, specifying different verb forms.

2) An esoteric interpretation by certain *Soofi* groups, claiming that there are seven levels of knowledge, or seven degrees of meanings to each verse.

3) Seven different branches of knowledge, such as *tawheed*, *sharee'ah*, etc.

All these opinions contradict the purpose of the *ahruf*, namely to make the recitation of the Qur'aan easier for the *Ummah*. Also, there is no proof for these opinions, and they contradict common sense.

B. THOSE OPINIONS WHICH HAVE SOME APPARENT BASIS, BUT ARE WEAK OPINIONS:

Included in this category are the following opinions:

1) These *ahruf* are seven different ways to pronounce the words, without actually changing the letters. However, this opinion contradicts the variations in words that occurs in the *qira'aat*.

---

390 Itr, p. 10.
391 cf. al-Hamad, pps. 133-144; az-Zarqaanee, v.1, pps. 137-191; Itr, 122-190.

2) The *ahruf* are seven types of verses in the Qur'aan: apparent, command, recommendation, specific, particular, general and parable. There is a weak *hadeeth* to support this.

3) Similar to the above, and also based on a weak *hadeeth*, the different types are: commands and prohibitions, promises and occurrences, *halaal* and *haraam*, clear and ambiguous.[392]

4) The seven *ahruf* are the same as the seven *qira'aat*. This is contradicted historically, as there are more than seven *qira'aat*, and the collection and codification of the *qira'aat* occurred four centuries after the Prophet's (🕌) death.[393] None of the major scholars of Islaam held this view, as Ibn Taymiyyah (d. 728 A.H.) said, "There is no difference of opinion among the scholars that the seven *ahruf* are not the same as the seven famous *qira'aat*."[394]

Unfortunately, most of the Muslim masses understand the *hadeeth* of the *ahruf* to refer to the *qira'aat*.

C. THOSE OPINIONS WHICH HAVE STRONG EVIDENCE:

These opinions are the ones that are worthy of serious inspection, as they have strong evidence historically and from the meanings of the *ahaadeeth*. There are three opinions in this category.

1) The seven *ahruf* refer to the seven dialects (*lughaat*) of the Arabs prevalent at the time of the Prophet (🕌). Each of these dialects belongs to a tribe among the Arabs, namely, the Quraysh, Hudhayl, Tameem, Hawaazin, Thaqeef, Kinaanah and Yemen (other scholars gave the names of other tribes). Thus, under this opinion, various verses would be pronounced according to the pronunciation of that particular tribe, and words from one dialect would be replaced by other words used by that particular tribe.

Some scholars say that these seven dialects are spread throughout the Qur'aan, meaning that part of the Qur'aan is in the dialect of Quraysh, other parts are in the dialect of Hudhayl, and so forth. Others say that the entire Qur'aan is recited in each of these dialects, thus forming the seven *ahruf*.

This was the opinion of Aboo 'Ubayd al-Qaasim ibn Sallaam (d. 224 A.H.), al-Bayhaqee (d. 458 A.H.), Ibn 'Attiyah (d. 541 A.H.) and others.

2) The seven *ahruf* denote seven ways of recitation (*lahajaat*) such that words are replaced by their synonyms. In other words, the seven *ahruf* have the exact same meanings but different wordings.

This was the opinion of Imaam at-Tabaree (d. 311 A.H.), at-Tahaawee (d. 321 A.H.), Ibn 'Abd al-Barr (d. 463 A.H.) and others.

---

392 For a discussion of the weakness in the above two *hadeeth*, see Itr, p. 138.
393 See the next chapter for further details on the *qira'aat*.
394 Zarzur, p.186.

3) The seven *ahruf* refer to seven different ways that the verse can be changed. In other words, whenever a difference is found between these *ahruf*, this type of difference will fall into one of the following seven categories: [395]

1. Change in wording. For example, in 101:5, *ka al-'ihni il-manfoosh* is changed to *ka as-soof il-manfoosh*, both of which mean the same thing.

2. Differences in wordings or letters such that they conform to the vowelless, dotless script of 'Uthmaan.[396] For example, *fatabayanoo* is changed to *fatathabatoo* in 49:6, just by changing the dots. Also, in *Soorah* al-Faatihah, *maaliki* is changed to *maliki* without any change in the script of 'Uthmaan.

3. Change in word order. For example, in 2:195, *wa qaatalu wa qutilu* is changed to *wa qutilu wa qaatalu*.

4. Addition or subtraction of a letter or word. For example, in 57:24, *fa inna Allaaha hoowa al-ghaniyul hameed* is recited without the pronoun, *fa ina Allaah al-ghaniyul hameed*.

5. The form of the word structure is changed. This change could be from plural to singular or dual (or other variations), or from feminine to masculine. For example, in 23:8, the plural *li amanaatihim* is changed to the singular *li amanatihim*.

6. Differences in inflection points. For example, 2:125, *wa attakhadhoo mim maqaami Ibraaheema musallaa* is read in the command *wattakhidhoo*.

7. Differences in pronunciation. For example, lessening the effect of certain *hamzahs* (called *tas-heel*) or pronouncing certain *alifs* and *yaas* differently (called *imaalah*).

This was the opinion of Ibn Qutaybah (d. 276 A.H.), al-Baaqillaani (d. 403 A.H.), Makkee ibn Abee Taalib (d. 437 A.H.), ar-Raazee (d. 606 A.H.), Ibn al-Jazaree (d.832 A.H.), and others. Some of them give different categories, but their general thesis is the same.

Among these three opinion, the third one seems to have the least weight. Despite the fact that it classifies the differences in the *ahruf* into ingenious categories, it does not explain the essence of what the *ahruf* are. In other words, when Hishaam was reciting a different *harf* from 'Umar, he was probably differing with 'Umar in more than one of these seven categories. Therefore, the third definition does not really answer the question as to the meaning of the *ahruf*.

The first two opinions, on the other hand, have very strong evidences to support them.[397] It seems – and Allaah knows best – that both of these opinions have an element of truth in them, and there does not exist any grounds for rejecting either of them.

---

395 All of these variations, except for the first, are found in the present-day *qira'aat*.
396 The manuscript of 'Uthmaan did not have dots or diacritical marks to distinguish between certain letters and vowels. See Chapter 8, on "The Collection of the Qur'aan."
397 See Itr, pps. 168-177.

Therefore, it is concluded that the seven *ahruf* represent variations based upon, but not limited to, the most fluent Arab tribes of that time. These variations occurred in words, letters, and pronunciations, such that all these variations made it easier for the Companions to memorise the Qur'aan. These variations did not always reach seven different ways of recitation for each verse, but whenever such variations existed, the different ways of recitation never exceeded seven.[398]

IV. Are the Ahruf in Existence Today?

A very crucial question that arises is whether these seven *ahruf* are still present today.

Of course, this question in essence depends upon how one defines the *ahruf*. For example, az-Zarqaanee strongly argues that all the *ahruf* have been preserved, but this goes back to his definition that the *ahruf* represent seven ways that the verse can be changed (opinion (3) above). Thus, since these variations are still present in today's *qira'aat*, he argues that all seven *ahruf* have been preserved.[399] The present discussion will, of course, utilise the definition that was concluded upon in the previous section.

The scholars of Islaam are divided into three opinions with regards to this issue.

The first group of scholars, composed of at-Tabaree (d. 310 A.H.), at-Tahaawee (d. 321 A.H.), Ibn Hibbaan (d. 354 A.H.) and those who follow them, argue that only one *harf* is in existence today. At-Tabaree holds that the recitation of the Qur'aan in seven *ahruf* was a concession given to the Companions at the time of the Prophet (ﷺ), but when 'Uthmaan officially compiled the Qur'aan, he specifically ordered the committee assigned to write the *mus-haf* to preserve only one *harf*. He writes, "The only recitation that the Muslims have today is the one *harf* that their pious Imaam ('Uthmaan) chose for them, leaving the remaining six."[400] He is alluding to the statement of 'Uthmaan to the committee that wrote the *mus-haf*, "... if you differ in (the spelling) of a word, then write it in the script of the Quraysh."[401] This, according to at-Tabaree and those who follow his opinion, shows that 'Uthmaan preserved only one *harf*.

In response to the question, "How could 'Uthmaan and the Companions purposely have left out the other six *ahruf*?" at-Tabaree answers:[402]

> The seven *ahruf* were revealed by Allaah during the time of the Prophet
> (ﷺ) to facilitate the memorisation of the Qur'aan, since the dialects of the
> Arabs were many. This facilitation (i.e., the *ahruf*) was not necessary to pre-
> serve, and eventually there was no need of it. In fact, it became the cause of
> dissension amongst the Muslims, as those people new to Islaam began ar-

---

398 cf. al-Qaaree, p. 79, and al-Hamad's conclusion, p. 144, which is very similar to this one.
399 az-Zarqanee, v. 1, p. 170-172.
400 al-Hamad, p. 147.
401 See Chapter 8 for a discussion of the collection of the Qur'aan.
402 Ubaydaat, p. 162.

guing over the differences in the recitation of the Qur'aan. Therefore, Allaah inspired[403] 'Uthmaan to discard the other six *ahruf* and collect the Qur'aan in one *harf*, so that the *ummah* would be united in its recitation. The Companions agreed to this action of his, and the agreement of the Companions is binding on the *ummah*.

The second group of scholars holds that all of the *ahruf* are in existence today, and the *mus-haf* of 'Uthmaan was written to preserve all seven *ahruf*. This was the opinion of Aboo Bakr al-Baaqillaani (d. 403 A.H.), and a small group of scholars. They claim that the Companions would never abandon a recitation that they used to recite during the lifetime of the Prophet (ﷺ), and that they would not discard any knowledge that the Prophet (ﷺ) had given them.

The third group of scholars is composed of Ibn Taymiyyah (d. 724 A.H.), ash-Shaatibee (d. 790 A.H.), ar-Raazee (d. 606 A.H.), Ibn Katheer (d. 774 A.H.), Ibn al-Jazaree (d. 832 A.H.) and others. They argue that 'Uthmaan preserved the *ahruf* to the extent that the script of his *mus-haf* allowed him to do so. Thus, these scholars hold that a portion of the seven *ahruf* are preserved.

The question then arises: On what basis did 'Uthmaan decide which portions of the *ahruf* to preserve? The answer to this is twofold: First, Zayd ibn Thabit was in charge of the collection of the *mus-haf*. Zayd had been present when the Prophet (ﷺ) recited the whole Qur'aan for the last time, only months before his (ﷺ) death.[404] It can be assumed, then, that Zayd was aware of the portions of the *ahruf* that the Prophet (ﷺ) recited, and he must have chosen those to the exclusion of the others. Secondly, the Companions unanimously agreed to discard all readings that conflicted with the *mus-haf* of 'Uthmaan. Obviously, they would eliminate only that which they knew was not a part of the Qur'aan, and their consensus is binding on the *ummah*.

Ibn al-Jazaree (d. 832 A.H.) writes,[405]

> The majority of the scholars of the *salaf* and the later generations are of the opinion that the 'Uthmaanic *mus-hafs* contains of the seven *ahruf* only that which its script allows. (What is preserved) are the recitations that the Prophet (ﷺ) recited to Jibreel (during the last year of his life). The present *mus-haf* contains all this reading, and not a single letter from it is missing.

The third opinion (i.e., that a portion of the seven *ahruf* have been preserved) seems to be the strongest one, for the following reasons:

1) The Companions were meticulous in preserving the knowledge that they received from the Prophet (ﷺ). They understood their responsibility in transferring

---

403 The Arabic is *ilhaam*, which is the type of inspiration that is given to pious people, and is not the *wahy* that is given to the prophets. The mother of Moosaa received this type of inspiration when she was commanded by Allaah to let Moosaa adrift in the river. Refer to Chapter 3 for more details.

404 Actually, the Prophet (ﷺ) recited the whole Qur'aan twice to Jibreel, and heard it from him twice. Some scholars held the view that these recitations of the Qur'aan occurred in different *ahruf*. See Itr, pp. 263-73.

405 Ibn al-Jazaree, *an-Nashr*, v. 1, p. 31, with changes.

this vast knowledge to the *ummah*. It is because of this concern of theirs that detailed information exists about every topic of Islaam, so much so that the Muslims even know how many white hairs the Prophet's (ﷺ) beard contained![406] Therefore, it cannot be said that the Companions purposely left out six *ahruf* and preserved only one of them in the *mus-haf* of 'Uthmaan without bringing forth some strong, unequivocal proof. Al-Qaaree writes,

> This opinion (that the Companions left out six *ahruf*) is strange, and extremely weak, for it claims that a part of the Qur'aan was removed by consensus of the Companions, since each of the *ahruf* is part of the Qur'aan. Therefore, how could 'Uthmaan, or any of the Companions for that matter, or rather *all* the Companions, discard something from the Qur'aan without a clear proof from the Creator? Even if we say that the Companions were given the concession of choosing one *harf* to recite in, as at-Tabaree (d. 310 A.H.) claims, and they were not accountable for all seven *ahruf* since it was a concession from Allaah, we say: This concession was given so that they could choose to recite the Qur'aan in any one of these seven *ahruf*, whichever was the easiest for him. There was no concession, however, in *preserving* these *ahruf*, rather they were responsible for preserving all of them... that were not abrogated...[407]

2) The 'Uthmaanic *mus-hafs*, as was mentioned earlier, were devoid of dots and vowel points. Since this knowledge was available to the Arabs at that time,[408] it seems likely that the *mus-haf* was purposely written without these dots or inflection points so that it would encompass different readings, and hence the different *ahruf*. Also, as was mentioned in the relevant chapter, the script of the 'Uthmaanic *mus-haf* was written with specific rules in mind, apparently in order to accommodate the various recitations, and this shows that the *mus-haf* was written with the intent to preserve more than one *harf*.

3) If, as at-Tabaree holds, only one *harf* has been preserved, from where then do the differences in the ten *qira'aat* originate from? All scholars are unanimous that these ten *qira'aat* originated from the Prophet (ﷺ) himself; therefore is seems apparent that the *qira'aat* have some integral relationship with the *ahruf* (as shall be discussed in the next chapter). Concerning this issue, Imaam at-Tabaree is forced to contradict his stance, as Makkee ibn Abee Taalib (d. 437 A.H.) pointed out:

> At-Tabaree concedes to the fact that the various *qira'aat* that conform to the *mus-haf* of 'Uthmaan are a part of the seven *ahruf*, and this is what we also believe. However, he also claims... that the *mus-haf* (of 'Uthmaan) has only preserved one *harf*, to the exclusion of the other six. These two positions are contradictory...[409]

---

406 Anas ibn Maalik stated, "I could not count more that fourteen white hairs in the Prophet's (ﷺ) beard and hair." Reported by at-Tirmidhee in his *Shamaa'il*, # 31.

407 al-Qaaree, p. 71.

408 Although there is a strong difference of opinion over this. See al-Hamad, p.151, where he tries to prove that this knowledge did not exist until the Muslims invented it.

409 al-Hamad, p. 140.

4) The different *mus-hafs* that 'Uthmaan ordered to be written were not identical to each other, for in a number of places, the addition or deletion of a word or letter occurred in some of the *mus-hafs*.[410] This change is reflected in the various *qira'aat* in existence today, for within the ten *qira'aat*, there exist word changes and word additions that could not have originated from the same *mus-haf*. It seems apparent this was done with a goal in mind, and the strongest conclusion seems to be that, by these differences in the *mus-hafs*, 'Uthmaan had intended to preserve the differences in the *ahruf*.

These same four arguments, however, cannot be used for the second opinion (that *all* of the *ahruf* were actually preserved), because of the fact that certain variations that the Companions used to recite as part of the Qur'aan are now no longer a part of the Qur'aan (as will be explained in the chapters of *naskh* and *qira'aat*). These variant readings can be explained as having been a part of the seven *ahruf* before the final reading of the Qur'aan by the Prophet (ﷺ) to Jibreel. This reading, which took place before Zayd ibn Thaabit, cancelled the *ahruf* that 'Uthmaan did not preserve.[411] Imaam al-Qistillaanee (d. 923 A.H.) said, "In this (last) recitation of the Prophet (ﷺ) to Jibreel, there were two benefits: First, to strengthen and preserve the Prophet's (ﷺ) memorisation of the Qur'aan, and, second, to affirm those verses that were not abrogated and to indicate which verses were."[412]

v. The Wisdom in the Various Ahruf

Obviously, it cannot be said for certain the exact wisdom behind any Divine act, for the Creator's knowledge is infinite. However, the scholars of Islaam have said that the revelation of the Qur'aan in seven *ahruf* had the following benefits:[413]

1) To facilitate the memorisation of the Qur'aan. This is the only benefit that is explicitly narrated in the *hadeeth*. The Arabs did not all speak Arabic in the same way; each tribe and location had slight variations and peculiarities unique to it. If the Qur'aan had only been revealed in one *harf*, it would have been difficult for the many different Arab tribes to memorise the Qur'aan properly. However, since the Qur'aan was revealed in seven *ahruf*, this greatly eased its memorisation. This was of primary importance in its preservation and propagation.

2) To prove the miraculous nature of the Qur'aan. For despite all of these differences, the meanings of the *ahruf* did not contradict one another, but rather were complementary.

3) To prove the truthfulness of the Prophet Muhammad (ﷺ), for despite the fact that he (ﷺ) was illiterate, the revelation of the Qur'aan occurred in different tribal dialects and different words, all of which consisted of the most fluent and eloquent speech of his time.

---

410 See Ch. 8, 'The Compilation of the Qur'aan,' for further details and examples.
411 Ibn al-Jazaree, p. 31.
412 Uwais, p. 8.
413 cf. Itr, pps. 216-228.

4) To honour the *ummah* of the Prophet Muhammad (ﷺ), and show its superiority over all other nations. No other nation had been given its book in such a manner, in varying *ahruf,* to ease the process of preservation. Thus, the revelation of the Qur'aan showed the unique status that the Prophet (ﷺ), and his *ummah*, occupied over other nations. In one *hadeeth*, the Prophet (ﷺ) remarked, "The earlier books would be revealed from one door (of heaven), in one *harf*, but the Qur'aan was revealed from seven doors (of Heaven), in seven *ahruf.*"[414]

---

414 Reported by al-Haakim, see *as-Saheehah* # 5870.

CHAPTER 11

THE QIRA'AAT OF THE QUR'AAN

I. The Meaning of the Word 'Qira'aat'

The word '*qira'aat*' is the plural of '*qiraa'a*', which comes from the root *q-r-a* meaning, 'to read, to recite.' '*Qiraa'a*' means the recitation of something.

In Qur'aanic sciences, it refers to the various ways and manners of reciting the Qur'aan that are in existence today. As Imaam az-Zarkashee stated, the Qur'aan is the revelation that was given to Muhammad (ﷺ), and the *qira'aat* are the variations in words and pronunciations of this revelation. Thus the *qira'aat* are the verbalisation of the Qur'aan, and the Qur'aan is preserved in the *qira'aat*.

Each *qiraa'a* has its own peculiar rules of recitation (*tajweed*) and variations in words and letters, and is named after the reciter (*Qaaree*) who was famous for that particular *qiraa'a*.

II. The History of the Qira'aat

The primary method of transmission of the Qur'aan has always been and always will be oral. Each generation of Muslims learns the Qur'aan from the generation before it, and this chain continues backwards until the time of the Companions, who learnt it from the Prophet (ﷺ) himself. As 'Umar ibn al-Khattaab stated, "The recitation of the Qur'aan is a *Sunnah*; the later generations must take it from the earlier ones. Therefore, recite the Qur'aan only as you have been taught."[415] This is the fundamental principle in the preservation of the Qur'aan.

In the last chapter, the revelation of the Qur'aan in seven *ahruf* was discussed. As the Prophet (ﷺ) recited the Qur'aan in all of these *ahruf*, the Companions memorised it from him accordingly. Some of them memorised only one *harf*, others more than this. When the Companions spread throughout the Muslim lands, they took with them the variations that they had learnt from the Prophet (ﷺ). They understood the importance of the oral transmission of the Qur'aan. 'Umar ibn al-Khattaab, during his caliphate, sent several prominent Companions to various cities to teach the people Qur'aan; 'Ubaadah ibn as-Saamit was sent to Hims, Ubay ibn Ka'ab to Palestine, and Aboo ad-Dardaa to Damascus.[416]

---

415 Itr, p. 244
416 Wohaibee, p. 46

Likewise, during his caliphate, 'Uthmaan also realised the importance of the proper recitation of the Qur'aan, and sent reciters of the Qur'aan all over the Muslim lands, each with a copy of his official *mus-haf*. He kept Zayd ibn Thaabit in Madeenah; with the Makkan *mus-haf*, he sent 'Adullaah ibn Saa'ib (d. 63 A.H.); to Syria was sent al-Mugheerah ibn Shu'bah (d. 50 A.H.); Aboo 'Abd ar-Rahmaan as-Sulamee (d. 70 A.H.) was sent to Koofah; and 'Aamir ibn 'Abdul Qays to Basrah (d. ~ 55 A.H.).[417]

The Companions, in turn, recited and taught these variations to the Successors (*tabi'oon*), who taught them to the next generation (*atbaa' at-tabi'oon*), and so on. Each generation had in its rank those who were famous for their knowledge of the recitation of the Qur'aan.

Thus, among the Companions, there were many who were famous as having heard from the Prophet (ﷺ) most if not all of the Qur'aan. Included in this category are 'Uthmaan ibn 'Affaan, 'Alee ibn Abee Taalib, 'Ubay ibn Ka'ab, 'Abdullaah ibn Mas'ood, Zayd ibn Thaabit, Aboo ad-Dardaa, and Aboo Moosaa al-Ash'aree. These Companions taught those Companions who were younger or had not had as much exposure to the Prophet's (ﷺ) recitation, such as Aboo Hurayrah and Ibn 'Abbaas, who both learnt from Ubay. Some learnt from more than one Companion, as, for example, Ibn 'Abbaas also learnt from Zayd ibn Thaabit.

These Companions then taught the Successors. Since the Companions spread over the various parts of the Muslim world, each region started developing a specific type of recitation. Again, all of these various recitations had originated from the mouth of the Prophet (ﷺ), and the Companions spread the different variations throughout the Muslim world.

Those famous among the Successors for the recitation of the Qur'aan are: in Madeenah, Sa'eed ibn al-Musayyib (d. 90 A.H.), 'Urwah ibn az-Zubayr (d. 94 A.H.), Saalim (d. 106 A.H.), and 'Umar ibn 'Abd al-Azeez (d. 103 A.H.); in Makkah, 'Ubayd ibn 'Umayr (d. 72 A.H.), 'Ataa ibn Abee Rabah (d. 114 A.H.), Taawoos (d. 106 A.H.), Mujaahid (d. 103 A.H.) and 'Ikrimah (d. 104 A.H.); in Koofah, 'Alqamah ibn Qays (d. 60 A.H.), Aboo 'Abd al-Rahmaan as-Sulamee (d. 70 A.H.), Ibraaheem al-Nakhaa'ee (d. 96 A.H.) and ash-Sha'bee (d. 100 A.H.); in Basrah, Aboo al-'Aaliyah (d. 90 A.H.), Nasr ibn 'Aasim (d. 89 A.H.), Qataadah (d. 110 A.H.), Ibn Sireen (d. 110 A.H.) and Yahya ibn Ya'mar (d. 100 A.H.); and in Syria, al-Mugheerah ibn Abee Shihaab and Khaleefah ibn Sa'ad.[418]

Around the turn of the first century of the *hijrah* appeared the scholars of the Qur'aan after whom the *qira'aat* of today are named. At this time, along with many other sciences of Islaam, the science of *qira'aat* was codified. Thus, members of this generation took from the Successors the various recitations that they had learnt from the Companions, and adopted a specific way of reciting the Qur'aan, and this is what is called

---

417 az-Zarqaanee, v.1, p. 404.

418 It should be kept in mind that this is a partial list and is far from exhaustive. Those who are interested may consult Ubaydaat, p. 164, Qattaan, p. 170, and az-Zarqaanee, v.1, pps. 414-416.

a *qiraa'a*. Each of these persons is called a *Qaaree*, or Reciter. These *Qaarees* were the most famous reciters of the Qur'aan in their time, and people from all around the Muslim lands would come to them to learn the Qur'aan.

To summarise, the *qira'aat* are particular methodologies of reciting the Qur'aan. They are named after the *Qaarees* who recited the Qur'aan in that particular manner, and were famous as being the leaders in this field. They represent the various ways that the Companions learnt the Qur'aan from the Prophet (صلى الله عليه وسلم). They differ from each other in various words, pronunciations, and rules of recitation (*tajweed*). They are *not* the same as the seven *ahruf*, as shall be elaborated upon shortly.

The scholars of the succeeding generations started compiling works on the different *qira'aat* that were present in their times. For example, Aboo 'Ubayd al-Qaasim ibn Sallaam (d. 224 A.H.) compiled twenty-five *qira'aat*, Ahmad ibn Jubayr al-Koofee (d. 258 A.H.) wrote a book on five of the *qira'aat*, and al-Qaadee Ismaa'eel ibn Ishaaq (d. 282 A.H.) compiled his book on twenty *qira'aat* (including the famous 'seven'). Even Muhammed ibn Jareer at-Tabaree (d. 310) compiled a work on the *qira'aat*. However, the most famous of these books is the one by Aboo Bakr Ahmad ibn Mujaahid (d. 324), entitled *Kitaab al-Qira'aat,* in which he compiled seven of the most famous *qira'aat* of his time from the major cities in the Muslim world. He was the first to limit himself to these particular *Qaarees*, for he wanted to combine the most famous recitations of Makkah, Madeenah, Koofah, Basrah, and Damascus, for these were the five territories from which the knowledge of Islaam sprung forth – the knowledge of the Qur'aan, *tafseer*, *hadeeth* and *fiqh*.[419] He wrote in his introduction,

> So these seven (that I have chosen) are scholars from the Hijaaz (i.e., Makkah and Madeenah), Iraq (i.e., Koofah and Basrah) and Syria (i.e., Damascus). They inherited the Successors in the knowledge of the recitation of the Qur'aan, and the people all accepted and agreed upon their recitation, from their respective territories, and the territories surrounding them...[420]

He purposely chose seven *Qaarees* to match the number of *ahruf* that the Qur'aan was revealed in. Unfortunately, this led many people to mistakenly believe that the different *qira'aat* were the same as the *ahruf* that the Prophet (صلى الله عليه وسلم) referred to in the various *hadeeth*. This is obviously false, since Ibn Mujaahid wrote his book four centuries after the Prophet's (صلى الله عليه وسلم) death. Due to this misconception, many of the later scholars took Ibn Mujaahid to task, wishing that he had chosen a different number, so that this confusion could have been prevented. Ibn al-Jazaree (d. 832 A.H.) wrote,

> Many of the scholars disliked the fact that Ibn Mujaahid restricted himself to seven *qira'aat*, and said that he was mistaken in doing so, and wished that he had chosen a number greater than this, or less than this, or at least explained the purpose behind choosing this number, so that those people who have no knowledge would not have been misled.[421]

---

419   Uwais, p. 16.
420   Ibn Mujaahid, p. 87.
421   Ibn al-Jazaree, p. 39.

Another misconception that arose was that some scholars assumed that these seven *qira'aat* were the *only* authentic *qira'aat* of the Qur'aan. Thus, these scholars considered any *qiraa'a* besides these seven to be defective (*shaadh*) *qira'aat*. This, too, is a misconception, as there were other authentic *qira'aat* that Ibn Mujaahid did not compile.

Due to the popularity and excellence of Ibn Mujaahid's book, these seven *qira'aat* became the most famous *qira'aat* of that time,[422] and the students of knowledge left other *qira'aat* to study these seven. Eventually, except for three other authentic *qira'aat*, all the other *qira'aat* were left, and only these ten were studied. This does not imply, however, that somehow a portion of the Qur'aan was lost by preserving only these ten. Many of the *qira'aat* were merely a mixture of others, so that their loss would not mean a loss of certain pronunciations or words. The Muslims are assured of the fact that they have the complete revelation that Allaah revealed to the Prophet Muhammad (ﷺ), for it is Allaah's promise to protect it:

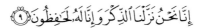

«Verily, it is We who have revealed the Qur'aan, and surely We will guard it» [15:9]

III. The Conditions for an Authentic Qiraa'a

It was mentioned in the last section that, during the first few centuries of the *hijrah*, there were many *qira'aat* that used to be recited. The scholars of the *qira'aat* therefore established rules in order to differentiate the authentic *qira'aat* from the inauthentic ones.

The famous scholar of the Qur'aan, Muhammad ibn al-Jazaree (d. 832 A.H.), said:

> Every *qiraa'a* that conforms to the rules of Arabic, even if by one manner, and matches with one of the *mus-hafs* of 'Uthmaan, even if such a match is not an obvious one, and has an authentic chain of narrators back to the Prophet (ﷺ), is an authentic *qiraa'a*. Such a *qiraa'a* cannot be refuted or denied, but rather must be believed in, and is amongst the seven *ahruf* that the Qur'aan was revealed in. Therefore the people must accept it, whether it be from the seven *qira'aat* (mentioned above), or from the ten *qira'aat*, or even other than these. And whenever any *qiraa'a* fails to meet one of the above mentioned three conditions, then it will be labelled (according to which

---

422 This is very similar to what happened in the history of *hadeeth*. The reason that six particular books of *hadeeth* (al-Bukhaaree, Muslim, Aboo Daawood, at-Tirmidhee, an-Nasaa'ee and Ibn Maajah) are known as the "*Sihaah Sitta*" or the "Six Authentic Books", is because of one book on the 'Names of Narrators', *Asmaa ar-Rijaal,* written by 'Abd al-Ghanee al-Maqdisee (d. 600 A.H.). Due to the thoroughness of this work, people started classifying these six books separately from other works of *hadeeth*, and many considered these six book as authentic (*saheeh*). This description, however, is only applicable to the two *saheeh* collection of al-Bukhaaree and Muslim; the rest of these works contain both authentic and inauthentic *ahaadeeth*.

of the conditions are not met) either weak (*da'eef*), irregular (*shaadh*), or false (*baatil*). And this (i.e., these conditions) is the strongest opinion among the scholars of the past and the present.[423]

Therefore, Ibn al-Jazaree mentioned three conditions:

1) The *qiraa'a* must conform to Arabic grammar. It is not essential, however, that the grammar used be agreed upon by all Arabic grammarians, or that the *qiraa'a* employ the most fluent and eloquent of phrases and expressions. This is the meaning of the phrase, "...even if by one manner." The basic requirement is that it does not contradict an agreed upon principle of Arabic grammar.

Some scholars, however, do not agree with this condition.[424] They argue, "If a *qiraa'a* is proven to have originated from the Prophet (ﷺ), then we cannot apply the rules of grammar to it. If we were to do this, and presumed an error in the *qiraa'a*, then we would be implying that the Prophet (ﷺ) made mistakes (Allaah forbid!). Therefore, an authentic *qiraa'a* overrides a rule of Arabic grammar!"

What this is implying is that it is the Qur'aan, through any of its *qira'aat*, that is given preference over any rule of grammar, for the Qur'aan is the Speech of Allaah, the most eloquent of Speech, and the rules of grammar must be based on this. Among the scholars of the Qur'aan who held this view are Makkee ibn Abee Taalib (d. 437 A.H.) and Aboo 'Amr ad-Daanee (d. 444 A.H.). For them, the conditions for an authentic *qiraa'a* are the last two.

Actually, if the practice of the scholars of the Qur'aan is examined, it is apparent that the above difference is a difference in semantics only, for the first category of scholars (such as Ibn al-Jazaree) will reject a rule of grammar as invalid if it contradicts any of the ten authentic *qira'aat*. Thus, the attempts by some grammarians to invalidate certain *qira'aat* (such as az-Zajjaaj's[425] attempt to invalidate the *qiraa'a* of Hamzah in verse 4:1) have been rejected by all the scholars of *qira'a*, whether they include this condition or not.[426] This point will be discussed in greater detail below.

2) The *qiraa'a* must conform with one of the *mus-hafs* of 'Uthmaan. In the chapter on the compilation of the Qur'aan, it was mentioned that 'Uthmaan sent out between four and eight *mus-hafs* around the Muslim world. All of them were without dots and vowel marks. Also, these *mus-hafs* had minor variations between them.

As long as a *qiraa'a* satisfied any one of these *mus-hafs*, it was considered to have passed this condition, even if it conformed slightly. For example, the word *maaliki*[427] in *Soorah* al-Faatihah is written in all the 'Uthmaanic *mus-hafs* as *m-l-k* (ملك), which allows for the variation found in other *qira'aat* of *maliki*.[428] This is an example where

---

423 Ibn al-Jazaree, p. 9. I have paraphrased from the Arabic.

424 cf. az-Zarqaanee, v.1, p. 422.

425 He is 'Abd al-Rahmaan ibn Ishaaq az-Zajjaaj al-Nihawandee (d. 332), a noted Muslim grammarian.

426 az-Zarkashee, *Bahr*, v. 1, p. 471.

427 The *qiraa'a* of 'Aasim and al-Kisaa'ee

428 The *qiraa'a* of Warsh, Ibn Katheer, Ibn 'Aamir, Hamzah and Aboo 'Amr.

the conformation is "not obvious." An example of an explicit conformation is in 2:259, where one recitation is *kayfa nunshizuha*,[429] but without a dot over one letter becomes *kayfa nunshiruha*.[430] An example of a *qiraa'a* conforming to one of the *mus-hafs* of 'Uthmaan without the others is the *qiraa'a* of Ibn 'Aamir, who read 3:184 as *wa bi zuburi wa bil kitaab* instead of *wa az-zuburi wal kitaab* (i.e., without the *ba*s), since the *mus-haf* that 'Uthmaan sent to Syria had the two *ba*s in it.

An example of a *qiraa'a* that contradicts all the *mus-hafs* of 'Uthmaan is the *qiraa'a* attributed to Ibn 'Abbaas in 18:79, which translates as, "...and there was, behind them, a king who seized every ship by force," whereas Ibn 'Abbaas read it, "...and there was, in front of them, a king who seized every useable ship by force." The two changes in the recitation of Ibn 'Abbaas are not allowed by the *mus-haf* of 'Uthmaan, and cannot, therefore, be considered an authentic recitation.

3) The *qiraa'a* must have an authentic (*saheeh*) chain of narrators back to the Prophet (ﷺ). This is the most important condition, and guarantees that the variations that occur in the *qira'aat* have all been sent down by Allaah as part of the Qur'aan, recited by the Prophet (ﷺ), and passed down to the Muslim *ummah* without any addition or deletion. As was quoted from 'Umar earlier (and this same statement has also been made by Zayd ibn Thaabit, and many of the Successors), "The recitation of the Qur'aan is a *Sunnah*; the later generations must take it from the earlier ones. Therefore, recite the Qur'aan only as you have been taught."

However, an important question is: do these chains of narration have to be *mutawaatir*? The overwhelming majority of scholars claimed that they did. The only notable exceptions were from Makkee ibn Abee Ṭaalib (d. 437 A.H.), and later Ibn al-Jazaree (d. 832 A.H.) (whose definition is being quoted). Both of these scholars are highly respected, classical scholars in the field of *qira'aat*.

Ibn al-Jazaree wrote, "Some of the later scholars have presumed... that the Qur'aan can only be proven with *mutawaatir* narrations! The flaws in this opinion are obvious..."[431]

However, this opinion itself goes against the consensus (*ijmaa'*) of almost all the other scholars. Imaam an-Nuwayree (d. 897 A.H.), a commentator of Ibn al-Jazaree's work, wrote:

> This opinion is a newly-invented one, contradicting the consensus (*ijmaa'*) of the jurists and... the four *madh-habs*... and many scholars, so many that they cannot even be counted, such as Ibn 'Abd al-Barr, Ibn 'Atiyyah, Ibn Taymiyyah, Imaam Nawawee, al-Azraa'ee, as-Subkee, az-Zarkashee, Ibn al-Haajib, and many more besides these. As for the reciters of the Qur'aan, they were agreed on this since the earliest times, and the only ones to con-

---

429 The *qiraa'a* of 'Aasim, and others
430 The *qiraa'a* of Naafi', and others
431 Ibn al-Jazaree, p. 13.

tradict them in the later times are Makkee ibn Abee Taalib[432] and those who
followed him (i.e., Ibn al-Jazaree).[433]

In reality, Ibn al-Jazaree's opinion seems to have more theoretical than realistic value, for even he admits, in another of his works, that the ten qira'aat are all mutawaatir. He states, "Whoever says that the mutawaatir qira'aat are unlimited, then if he means this in our times, this is not correct, for today there are no authentic mutawaatir qira'aat besides these ten; however, if he means in earlier times, then it is possible that he is correct..."[434] Therefore, Ibn al-Jazaree was of the view that it was not necessary for a qiraa'a to be mutawaatir for it to be accepted, but at the same time he did believe that the ten qira'aat were all mutawaatir.

Ibn al-Jazaree's conditions were perhaps applicable in his time, when there existed numerous qira'aat besides the ten that are present today. According to him, such qira'aat could be recited as long as they had an authentic chain of narrators back to the Prophet (ﷺ), even if such chains were ahaad. Most of the other scholars of qiraa'a, however, did not agree with him on this point.[435] However, since in our times, only these ten qira'aat are in existence, this issue becomes more theoretical than practical, as most of the scholars are in agreement that these ten qira'aat are all mutawaatir.

In conclusion, the conditions for an authentic qiraa'a is that it must be mutawaatir, and conform to at least one of the mus-hafs of 'Uthmaan. Any time such a qiraa'a exists, it overrides any rule of Arabic grammar.

It should be mentioned, however, that there has never existed any mutawaatir qiraa'a that contradicted any rule of Arabic grammar.[436] Al-Qaaree writes,[437]

---

432 Makkee ibn Abee Taalib is quoted as having been the first to hold this opinion in all the works that I have come across discussing this topic (also see, al-Qadhi, p. 8). However, I came across another work of his entitled Kitaab al-Ibaanah 'an Ma'aani al-Qira'aat, in which he clearly states that any qiraa'a must be mutawaatir for it to be accepted. For example, on p. 43, while discussing the shaadh qira'aat, he states, "...and the Qur'aan cannot be confirmed with an ahaad narration;" on p. 31, "...and this (i.e., taking a shaadh qira'aat) implies confirming the Qur'aan with an ahaad narration, and this is not allowed by any of the people (of knowledge)." Elsewhere (p. 39), he clearly states concerning this opinion "...and this is the opinion we believe and hold to." I did not see any of the other books that I read mention these quotes, so I do not know whether this was his earlier opinion, or his later one, nor could I ascertain when he wrote the book. In any case, further research must be done to ascertain whether this really was the final opinion of Makkee ibn Abee Taalib.

433 al-Qadhi, p.8.

434 Uwais, p. 12, quoting from Ibn al-Jazaree's Munjid al-Muqreen. Also, see Uwais' discussion on this point, pps. 11-14.

435 Other scholars make a differentiation between the Qur'aan and the qira'aat, and state that, in order for the Qur'aan to be accepted, the narrations must be mutawaatir, but in order for a qira'a to be accepted, an ahaad narration will suffice. However, this differentiation does not seem to solve the problem, for the qira'aat are the Qur'aan, and the Qur'aan is preserved in all of the qira'aat. Therefore, if a qiraa'a is substantiated as authentic, that automatically implies that it is part of the Qur'aan.

436 This is not to say that there have not existed qira'aat that Arab grammarians have not found fault with. There have been numerous attempts to prove various grammatical 'faults' in the qira'aat, but other grammarians have always proven that such readings do have grammatical basis for them. cf. al-Qaaree, Abd al-Aziz: Hadith al-Ahruf as-Saba'ah, in Majalah Kulliyah al-Qur'aan al-Kareem, v. 1, 1983, p. 115, for examples.

437 al-Qaaree, p. 116, with paraphrasing. The addition in brackets are mine.

If we ponder over this issue, and reflect over these conditions, we finds that this last condition (i.e., the *qiraa'a* must conform with Arabic grammar) is, in reality, not a 'condition' in the sense of the word, meaning that if this 'condition' is not met, the *qiraa'a* is rejected, for two reasons:

Firstly, such a case has never occurred, meaning that there is no authentic, *mutawaatir qiraa'a* that conforms to the 'Uthmaanic *mus-haf* that has no basis in Arabic grammar.

Secondly, even if we allow for the possibility that there exists such a *qiraa'a* – an authentic, *mutawaatir qiraa'a* conforming to the script, yet not having any basis that we can discover in Arabic grammar – then this too does not imply the rejection of the *qiraa'a*. This is because our ignorance of such a grammatical basis does not rule out the possibility of such a basis, since no matter how much our knowledge encompasses, it will still be limited. Also, whenever a *qiraa'a* has a *mutawaatir* chain of narrators and conforms with the 'Uthmaanic script, this is unequivocal proof that it is a part of the Qur'aan, and therefore there cannot be any argument against it.

To conclude, therefore, we say: This last condition (meaning the conformation of a *qiraa'a* with Arabic grammar) is in reality a necessary by-product of the other two conditions, and is not a 'condition' *per se*.

As has already been alluded to, there are ten *qira'aat* that meet the above requirements, and these will be discussed below. Taqee ad-Deen as-Subkee (d. 756 A.H.) stated,

> The seven *qira'aat* that ash-Shaatibee compiled[438] along with the other three *qira'aat* are all authentic *mutawaatir qira'aat*. This has been recognised by all, and every letter that any of these *qira'aat* have differed with the others in, is recognised to have been revealed to the Prophet (ﷺ). None can reject this fact except the ignorant.[439]

Theoretically, it is possible for there to still exist other authentic *qira'aat* besides these ten, since there is no divine law regulating that there can only be ten *qira'aat*. Realistically, however, such an existence is impossible, as the scholars of the Qur'aan would have known of them by now.

IV. The Other Types of Qira'aat

If a *qiraa'a* fails to meet any of these conditions, it is classified in a different category. Different scholars have adopted different classifications for defining those *qira'aat* that do not meet the above three conditions. One of the simpler ones is as follows: [440]

1) The <u>Saheeh</u> (Authentic) *Qira'aat*: These are the ten authentic *qira'aat*, and the conditions of acceptance were discussed above.

---

438 Qaasim ibn A<u>h</u>mad as-Shaa<u>t</u>ibee (d. 590 A.H.) compiled the seven *qira'aat* of Aboo Bakr ibn Mujaahid in a poem known as the *Shaa<u>t</u>ibiyah* to facilitate its memorisation.

439 as-Suyoo<u>t</u>ee, v. 1, p. 82

440 Ubaydaat, p. 178

2) The *Shaadh* (Irregular) *Qira'aat*: These *qira'aat* have an authentic chain of narration back to the Prophet (ﷺ) and conform to Arabic grammar, but do not match the *mus-hafs* of 'Uthmaan. In addition, they are not *mutawaatir*. In other words, they employ words or phrases that the 'Uthmaanic *mus-hafs* do not allow. Most of the time (but not all, see as-Suyootee's classification below) this type of *qira'aat* was in fact used by the Companions as explanations to certain verses in the Qur'aan. For example, 'Aa'ishah used to recite 2:238 '...*wa salat al-wusta*' with the addition '*salat al-asr.*' The meaning of the first is, "Guard against your prayers, especially the middle one." 'Aa'ishah's addition explained that the "middle prayer" alluded to in this verse is in fact the 'Asr prayer. There are numerous authentic narrations from the Companions of this nature, in which they recited a certain verse in a way that the *mus-haf* of 'Uthmaan would not allow.

Another explanation for this type of *qira'aat* is that they were a part of the *ahruf* that were revealed to the Prophet (ﷺ) but later abrogated, and thus not preserved in the *mus-haf* of 'Uthmaan.

3) The *Da'eef* (Weak) *Qira'aat*: These *qira'aat* conform with Arabic grammar and are allowed by the *mus-haf* of 'Uthmaan, but do not have authentic chains of narrations back to the Prophet (ﷺ). An example of this type is the recitation of 1:4 as *malaki yawmu deen*, in the past tense.

4) The *Baatil* (False) *Qira'aat*: These *qira'aat* do not meet any of the three criterion mentioned above, and are rejected completely, even as *tafseer*. For example, the reading of 35:28 as *inama yakhsha Allaahu min 'ibadhil 'ulama*, changes the meaning from, "It is only those who have knowledge amongst His slaves that truly fear Allaah," to, "Allaah is afraid of the knowledgeable of His slaves!" (All praise be to Allaah, He is far removed from all that they ascribe to Him!!)

The ruling concerning these last three types of *qira'aat*, the *shaadh*, the *da'eef* and the *baatil*, is that they are not a part of the Qur'aan, and in fact it is *haraam* (forbidden) to consider such a *qiraa'a* as part of the Qur'aan. If it is recited in prayer, such a prayer will not be acceptable, nor is one allowed to pray behind someone who recites these *qira'aat*. However, the *shaadh* and the *da'eef qira'aat* may be studied under the science of *tafseer* (and other sciences, such as the science of grammar, or *nahw*) as long as they are identified as such. The *shaadh qira'aat*, in particular, used to form a part of the seven *ahruf* that the Qur'aan was revealed in, but these recitations were abrogated by the Prophet (ﷺ) himself, and therefore not preserved by 'Uthmaan. Under this category fall many of the recitations that are transmitted with authentic chains of narrations from the Companions, and yet do not conform with the 'Uthmaanic *mus-haf*. These recitations used to form a part of the Qur'aan, and were recited by the Companions, until they were abrogated by the Prophet (ﷺ) before his death.

As-Suyootee,[441] following Ibn al-Jazaree (d. 832 A.H.), classifies the various *qira'aat* into six categories, which are, briefly:

1) *Mutawaatir*: These are the seven *qira'aat* compiled by Ibn Mujaahid, plus the other three.

2) *Mash-hoor* (Well-known): These are some of the variations found within the ten authentic *qira'aat*, such as the differences between the *raawis* and *turuqs* (to be discussed below).

3) *Ahaad* (Singular): These are the *qira'aat* that have an authentic chain of narration, but do not conform to the *mus-haf* of 'Uthmaan, or contradict a rule of Arabic grammar (the same as *shaadh* above).

4) *Shaadh* (Irregular): These are the *qira'aat* that do not have an authentic chain of narration back to the Prophet (ﷺ) (the same as *da'eef* above).

5) *Mawdoo'* (Fabricated): These are the *qira'aat* that do not meet any of the three conditions (same as *baatil* above).

6) *Mudraj* (Interpolated): In this category, as-Suyootee classified those readings that the Companions used to add for the sake of interpretation. For example, the verse,

$$ وَلَهُ أَخٌ أَوْ أُخْتٌ $$

«...and he has a brother or sister...» (4:12)

was recited by Sa'eed ibn Abee Waqqaas as, "...and he has a brother or sister from the same mother."

These types of additions are explained as having been heard by that Companion from the Prophet (ﷺ), either as an explanation of the verse (in which case it was assumed by the Companion to be part of the verse), or that this was one of the *ahruf* of that verse that was later abrogated by the Prophet (ﷺ) during his final recitation to Jibreel.[442]

As-Suyootee stated that the first two types, *mutawaatir* and *mash-hoor*, are considered part of the Qur'aan, and can be recited in prayer, but the last four types are not a part of the Qur'aan.

v. The Authentic Qira'aat and the Qaarees

Now that the various types of *qira'aat* have been discussed in detail, it is time to look at the ten authentic *qira'aat*, and the *Qaarees* whom they are named after.[443] The first seven are the ones that Aboo Bakr ibn Mujaahid (d. 324 A.H.) preserved in his book, and which ash-Shaatibee (d. 548 A.H.) versified in his famous poem known as *ash-Shaatibiyyah*.

---

441 as-Suyootee, v. 1, p. 102

442 cf. as-Suyootee, v. 1, p. 102.

443 All of the biographical information in this section, unless otherwise referenced, was taken from al-Banna, v.1, pps. 19-32, az-Zarqaanee, v.1, pps 456-477, and al-Haashimee, pps. 39-155.

1) Naafi' al-Madanee:

He is Naafi' ibn 'Abd al-Ra<u>h</u>maan ibn Abee Na'eem al-Laythee, originally from an Isfahanian family. He was one of the major scholars of *qira'aat* during his time. He was born around 70 A.H., in Madeenah, and passed away in the same city at the age of 99, in 169 A.H. He learnt the Qur'aan from over seventy Successors, including Aboo Ja'far Yazeed ibn al-Qa'qa' (d. 130 A.H.), who took his recitation from Aboo Hurayrah, who took his recitation from Ubay ibn Ka'ab, who took his recitation from the Prophet (ﷺ). After the era of the Successors, he was taken as the chief *Qaaree* of Madeenah. Eventually, his *qiraa'a* was adopted by the people of Madeenah.

Among his students was Imaam Maalik (d. 179 A.H.). Imaam Maalik used to recite the Qur'aan in the *qiraa'a* of Naafi', and he used to say, "Indeed, the *qiraa'a* of Naafi' is the *Sunnah*,"[444] meaning that this *qiraa'a* was the most liked by him.

The two students who preserved his *qiraa'a* are:

i) Qaloon: He is 'Eesaa ibn Meena az-Zarqee (120-220 A.H.). He was the step-son of Naafi', and lived his whole life in Madeenah. After Naafi' died, he took over his position as the leading *Qaaree* of Madeenah.

ii) Warsh: He is Aboo Sa'eed 'Uthmaan ibn Sa'eed al-Mi<u>s</u>ree (110-197 A.H.). He lived in Egypt, but travelled to Madeenah in 155 A.H. to study under Naafi', and recited the Qur'aan to him many times. Eventually, he returned to Egypt, and became the leading *Qaaree* of Egypt.

2) Ibn Katheer al-Makkee:

He is 'Abd Allaah ibn Katheer ibn 'Umar al-Makkee, born in Makkah in 45 A.H. and died 120 A.H. He was among the generation of the Successors (he met some Companions, such as Anas ibn Maalik and 'Abdullaah ibn az-Zubayr), and learnt the Qur'aan from the early Successors, such as Abee Saa'ib, Mujaahid ibn Jabr (d. 103 A.H.), and Darbaas, the slave of Ibn 'Abbaas. Darbaas learnt the Qur'aan from Ibn 'Abbaas, who learnt it from Zayd ibn Thaabit and Ubay ibn Ka'ab, who both learnt it from the Prophet (ﷺ).

Imaam ash-Shaafi'ee (d. 204 A.H.) used to recite the *qiraa'a* of Ibn Katheer,[445] and once remarked, "We were taught the *qiraa'a* of Ibn Katheer, and we found the people of Makkah upon his *qiraa'a*."[446]

The two primary *Qaarees* who preserved his *qiraa'a* are:

i) al-Buzzee: He is Abul <u>H</u>asan A<u>h</u>mad ibn Buzzah al-Makkee (170-250 A.H.). He was the *mu'adh-dhin* at the Masjid al-<u>H</u>araam at Makkah, and the leading *Qaaree* of Makkah during his time.

---

444 al-Haashimee, p. 39.
445 Hence his opinion of the origin of the word 'Qur'aan'; cf. Ch. 2, 'The Meaning of the Word 'qur'aan'.
446 al-Haashimee, p. 59.

ii) Qumbul: He is Aboo 'Amr Muhammad ibn 'Abd al-Rahmaan (195-291 A.H.). He was the leading *Qaaree* of the Hijaaz. He was also one of the teachers of Aboo Bakr ibn Mujaahid (d. 324 A.H.), the author of *Kitaab al-Qira'aat*.

3) Aboo 'Amr al-Basree:

He is Zabaan ibn al-'Alaa ibn 'Ammaar al-Basree. He was born in 69 A.H. and passed away in 154 A.H. He was born in Makkah, but grew up in Basrah. He studied the Qur'aan under many of the Successors, among them Aboo Ja'far (d. 130 A.H.), and Aboo al-'Aaliyah (d. 95 A.H.), who learnt from 'Umar ibn al-Khattaab and other Companions, who learnt from the Prophet (ﷺ).

The two primary *Qaarees* who preserved his *qiraa'a* are:

i) ad-Doori: He is Hafs ibn 'Umar ad-Doori (195-246 A.H.). He was one of the first to compile different *qira'aat*, notwithstanding the fact that he was blind.

ii) as-Soosee: He is Aboo Shu'ayb Saalih ibn Ziyaad as-Soosee (171-261 A.H.). He taught the Qur'aan to Imaam an-Nasaa'ee (d. 303 A.H.), of *Sunan* fame.

4) Ibn 'Aamir ash-Shaamee:

He is 'Abdullaah ibn 'Aamir al-Yahsabee, born in 21 A.H. He lived his life in Damascus, which was the capital of the Muslim empire in those days. He met some of the Companions, and studied the Qur'aan under the Companion Aboo ad-Dardaa, and al-Mugheerah ibn Abee Shihaab. He was the Imaam of the Ummayad Mosque (the primary mosque in Damascus) during the time of 'Umar ibn 'Abd al-'Azeez (d. 103 A.H.), and was well-known for his recitation. Among the seven *Qaarees*, he has the highest chain of narrators (i.e., least number of people between him and the Prophet (ﷺ)), since he studied directly under a Companion. He was also Chief Judge of Damascus. His *qiraa'a* became accepted by the people of Syria. He died on the day of 'Aashoora,[447] 118 A.H.

The two primary *Qaarees* who preserved his *qiraa'a* are:

i) Hishaam: He is Hishaam ibn 'Ammaar ad-Damishqee (153-245 A.H.). He was well-known for his recitation, and his knowledge of *hadeeth* and *fiqh*, and was one of the teachers of Imaam at-Tirmidhee (d. 279 A.H.).

ii) Ibn Zhakwan: He is 'Abdullaah ibn Ahmad ibn Zhakwan (173-242 A.H.). He was also the Imaam of the Ummayad Mosque during his time.

5) 'Aasim al-Koofee:

He is 'Aasim ibn Abee Najood al-Koofee, from among the Successors. He was the most knowledgeable person in recitation during his time, and took over the position of Imaam of the *Qaarees* in Koofah, after the death of Aboo 'Abd ar-Rahmaan as-

---

447 The tenth of Muharram.

Sulamee (d. 75 A.H.). He learnt the Qur'aan from Aboo 'Abd ar-Rahmaan (who studied under 'Alee ibn Abee Taalib, and was the teacher of al-Hasan and al-Husayn), and from Zirr ibn Hubaysh (d. 83 A.H.) and Aboo 'Amr ash-Shaybaanee (d. 95 A.H.). These learnt the Qur'aan from Ubay ibn Ka'ab, 'Uthmaan ibn 'Affaan, 'Alee ibn Abee Taalib, and Zayd ibn Thaabit, who all learnt from the Prophet (ﷺ). He passed away 127 A.H.

He taught the Qur'aan to Imaam Aboo Haneefah (d. 150 A.H.), who used to recite in the *qiraa'a* of 'Aasim. Imaam Ahmad ibn Hambal (d. 204 A.H.) was once asked, "Which of the *qira'aat* do you prefer?" He replied, "The *qira'a* of Madeenah (i.e., Naafi'), but if this is not possible, then 'Aasim."[448]

His two students who preserved his *qiraa'a* are:

i) Shu'ba: He is Shu'ba ibn 'Iyaash al-Koofee, born 95 A.H. and passed away 193 A.H.

ii) Hafs: He is Aboo 'Amr Hafs ibn Sulaymaan al-Asadee al-Koofee (90-180 A.H.), a step-son of 'Aasim. He was the most knowledgeable person of the *qiraa'a* of 'Aasim.

6) Hamzah al-Koofee:

He is Hamzah ibn Habeeb al-Koofee, born 80 A.H. He met some of the Companions, and learnt the Qur'aan from al-'Amash (d. 147 A.H.), Ja'far as-Saadiq (d. 148 A.H.) (the great-grandson of Husayn), and others. His *qiraa'a* goes back to the Prophet (ﷺ) through 'Alee ibn Abee Taalib and 'Abdullaah ibn Mas'ood. He passed away 156 A.H.

The two primary *Qaarees* through whom his *qiraa'a* is preserved are:

i) Khalaf: He is Khalaf ibn Hishaam al-Baghdaadee (150-227 A.H.). He memorised the Qur'aan when he was ten years old.

He also has his own *qiraa'a*, different from the one he preserved from Hamzah (see below).

ii) Khallaad: He is Aboo 'Eesaa Khallaad ibn Khaalid ash-Shaybaanee. He was born 119 A.H. and passed away 220 A.H.

7) Al-Kisaa'ee:

He is 'Alee ibn Hamzah ibn 'Abdillaah, born around 120 A.H. He was the most knowledgeable of his contemporaries in Arabic grammar, and is considered one of the classical scholars in this field. He authored numerous books, and excelled in the sciences and recitation of the Qur'aan. Students used to flock to him to listen to the entire Qur'aan, and they even used to record where he stopped and started every verse. The Caliph Haroon ar-Rasheed used to hold him in great esteem. He passed away 189 A.H.

---

448 al-Haashimee, p. 116.

His two primary students who preserved his *qiraa'a* are:

i) al-Layth: He is al-Layth ibn Khaalid al-Baghdaadee. He died 240 A.H.

ii) ad-Dooree: He is the same ad-Dooree who is the student of Aboo 'Amr al-Basree (mentioned above), for he studied and preserved both of these *qira'aat*.

These are the seven *Qaarees* whom Ibn Mujaahid compiled in his book *Kitaab al-Qira'aat*. Of these, all are from non-Arab backgrounds except Ibn 'Aamir and Aboo 'Amr. The following three *Qaarees* complete the ten authentic *qira'aat*.

8) Aboo Ja'far al-Madanee:

He is Yazeed ibn al-Qa'qa' al-Makhzoomee, among the Successors. He is one of the teachers of Imaam Naafi', and learnt the Qur'aan from 'Abdullah ibn 'Abbaas, Aboo Hurayrah and others. He passed away 130 A.H.

His two primary students who preserved his *qiraa'a* were 'Eesaa ibn Wardaan (d. 160 A.H) and Sulaymaan ibn Jamaz (d. 170 A.H.)

9) Ya'qoob al-Basree:

He is Ya'qoob ibn Ishaaq al-Hadhramee al-Basree. He became the Imaam of the *Qaarees* in Basrah after the death of Aboo 'Amr ibn 'Alaa. He studied under Aboo al-Mundhir Salaam ibn Sulayman. His *qiraa'a* goes back to the Prophet (ﷺ) through Aboo Moosaa al-Ash'aree. He was initially considered among the seven major *Qaarees* by many of the early scholars, but Ibn Mujaahid gave his position to al-Kisaa'ee instead. He passed away 205 A.H.

His two primary students were Ruways (Muhammad ibn Muttawakil, d. 238 A.H.) and Rooh (Rooh ibn 'Abd al-Mu'min al-Basree, d. 235 A.H.), who was one of the teachers of Imaam al-Bukhaaree (d. 256 A.H.).

10) Khalaf:

This is the same Khalaf that is one of the two students of Hamzah. He adopted a specific *qiraa'a* of his own, and is usually called Khalaf al-'Aashir (the 'tenth' Khalf).

His two primary students who preserved this *qiraa'a* were Ishaaq (Ishaaq ibn Ibraaheem ibn 'Uthmaan, d. 286 A.H.) and Idrees (Idrees ibn 'Abd al-Kareem al-Baghdaadee, d. 292 A.H.)

All of these ten *qira'aat* have authentic, *mutawaatir* chains of narration back to the Prophet (ﷺ). Each *qiraa'a* is preserved through two students of the Imaam of that *qiraa'a*. Of course, these *Qaarees* had more than just two students; the reason that the *qira'aat* are preserved through only two is that Aboo 'Amr 'Uthmaan ibn Sa'eed (d. 444), better known as Imaam ad-Daanee, selected and preserved the recitation of the two best students of each *Qaaree* in his book, *Kitaab at-Tayseer fee al-Qira'aat as-Saba'*. These two students are each called *Raawis* (narrators), and they occasionally differ from each other. Thus, although other *Raawis* also narrated each *qiraa'a,* only the recitation of two main *Raawis* have been preserved in such detail. References to the recitation of other *Raawis* are, however, found in the classical works of *qira'aat*.

These *Raawis* learnt the *qiraa'a* from their Imaam, and each preserved some of the variations of the recitation of the *Qaaree*. Sometimes, the *Qaaree* taught different *qira'aat* to each *Raawi*. Hafs quoted 'Aasim as saying that the *qiraa'a* he taught him was that of Aboo 'Abd al-Rahmaan as-Sulamee (d. 70 A.H.) from 'Alee ibn Abee Taalib, while the one that he taught Aboo Bakr ibn 'Iyaash (i.e., Shu'ba, the other *Raawi* of 'Aasim) was that of Zirr ibn Hubaysh (d. 83 A.H.) from Ibn Mas'ood.[449]

However, typically the variations between the *Raawis* are minor when compared to the differences between the *qira'aat* themselves (though usually there are differences in the rules of *tajweed* of the *Raawis*). For example, Shu'ba and Hafs differ from each other in around forty places in the whole Qur'aan.[450] To preserve even these differences, however, the *qira'aat* are always mentioned including the *Raawis*. So, when someone recites the *qiraa'a* of Naafi', for example, he should mention whether it is through Warsh or Qaloon (for example, by saying, "The *qiraa'a* of Naafi' through the *riwaayah* of Warsh," or, "The *qiraa'a* of Warsh *'an* Naafi' " for short).[451]

Most of the time, these students, who were *Qaarees* in their own right, studied directly under the *Qaaree* whose *qiraa'a* it was. Thus, for example, Warsh and Qaloon both studied under Imaam Naafi', as did Shu'bah and Hafs with Imaam 'Aasim. However, sometimes, there was an intermediary (or even two) between these students and the Imaam. When this occurred, as for example with Ibn Katheer, the intermediary was not mentioned above, so as not to prolong the discussion. The interested reader may consult any of the references mentioned in the beginning of this section.

There are four *shaadh qira'aat* (following the original definition above). These are not considered as part of the Qur'aan, but may be used as *tafseer,* and, according to some of the *madh-habs*, as a basis for *fiqh* rulings as well.[452] The *Qaarees* whom they are named after are:

1) al-Hasan al-Basree: This is the famous Successor, Hasan ibn Abee al-Hasan Yassaar Aboo Sa'eed al-Basree. He passed away 110 A.H.

2) Ibn Muhaysin: He is Muhammad ibn 'Abd al-Rahmaan as-Suhaymee al-Makkee. He was one of the Chief *Qaarees* of Makkah, along with Ibn Katheer. He passed away 123 A.H.

---

449 Wohaibee, p. 106.

450 Meaning that they differ from each other in forty words, but since these words occur a total of around five hundred times in the Qur'aan, it might appear that their differences are many. cf. al-Qaaree, p. 140.

451 Actually, there is a third level of narration, below that of *raawi*, called a *tareeq* (path). Each *raawi* has two *tareeq*s. The differences between the *turuq* (pl. of *tareeq*) are negligible for our purposes, concentrating mainly on where to stop, certain variations in the particulars of pronunciation, etc. However, on some occasions there are noticeable differences. For example, compare a Qur'aan printed in Pakistan (Taj Company, for example) and one printed in Saudi Arabia or Egypt, and see 30:54. The difference in the words *Da'fin* and *Du'fin* are due to the differences in the *turuq* of the *qiraa'a* of Hafs *'an* 'Aasim!

452 cf. az-Zarkashee, *Bahr*, pps. 474-480, for a discussion of this point.

3) Yahya al-Yazeedee: He is Yahya ibn al-Mubaarak ibn al-Mugheerah. He passed away 202 A.H.

4) al-Shamboozee: He is Muhammad ibn Ahmad ibn Ibraaheem al-Shamboozee. He passed away 388 A.H.

These four *qira'aat* contain most of the *qira'aat* that were recited by the Companions and did not conform to the *mus-haf* of 'Uthmaan. Of course, these four *qira'aat* do not contradict the *mus-haf* of 'Uthmaan in every single verse; only occasionally is there a conflict.

VI. The Qira'aat Today

The *qira'aat* were once a vital part of the Muslim *ummah*, and each part of the Muslim world used to recite according to one of the *qira'aat*. Not surprisingly, the people of a particular city would recite in the *qiraa'a* of the *Qaaree* of that city. Thus, for example, Makkee ibn Abee Taalib (d. 437 A.H.) reported, in the third century of the *hijrah*, that the people of Basra followed the recitation of Aboo 'Amr, those of Koofah followed 'Aasim, the Syrians followed Ibn 'Aamir, Makkah took after Ibn Katheer, and Madeenah followed Naafi'.

Eventually, however, most of the other *qira'aat* died out and were replaced by other ones. Thus, the situation today is that the vast majority of the Muslim world recites only the *qiraa'a* of 'Aasim through the *riwaya* of Hafs (Hafs *'an* 'Aasim). However, there are certain areas in the world where other *qira'aat* are prevalent, and a rough breakdown is as follows:

Qiraa'a	Percentage of Muslim World	Area
Hafs *'an* 'Aasim	95%	Muslim world in general
Warsh *'an* Naafi'	3%	Algeria, Morocco, parts of Tunisia, W. Africa and Sudan
Qaloon *'an* Naafi'	0.7%	Libya, Tunisia and Parts of Qatar
ad-Dooree *'an* Aboo 'Amr	0.3%	Parts of Sudan and W. Africa
Ibn 'Aamir	1%	Parts of Yemen
	Total 100%	

Table A   **The *Qira'aat* Today**

This is obviously a very rough breakdown, based on the population in these respective countries.[453]

The *qira'aat* today are as a whole only memorised at specialised institutions of higher learning throughout the Muslim world (or, a student may study privately under a scholar who has memorised these *qira'aat*). A student of the Qur'aan who wishes to memorise the *qira'aat* must, of course, have already memorised the entire Qur'aan in at least one *qiraa'a*. There are two primary ways of memorising these *qira'aat*, and both involve memorising lengthy poems that detail the rules of recitation (*tajweed*) of each *qiraa'a*, and the differences between them.

The first way is to memorise the *Shaatibiyyah* (its actual name is *Hirz al-Amaanee wa Wajh at-Tahaanee*), which is a poem consisting of 1173 couplets, written by Imaam Qaasim ibn Ahmad ash-Shaatibee (d. 548 A.H.), and then to memorise the *Durrah* (short for *ad-Durrah al-Madhiyyah*) by Muhammad ibn al-Jazaree (d. 832 A.H.). The first poem deals with the first seven *qira'aat*. After a student of the Qur'aan has memorised this, he then moves on to the second poem, which deals with the last three *qira'aat*. This is the primary method by which the *qira'aat* are taught throughout the Muslim world.

The second method is to learn all ten *qira'aat* simultaneously, by memorising the *Tayyibah* (short for *Tayyibah an-Nashr fil Qira'aat al-'Ashr*), which is a poem that deals with all ten *qira'aat*, also by Muhammad ibn al-Jazaree.[454]

VII. The Relationship of the Ahruf with the Qira'aat

The relationship of the *ahruf* with the authentic *qira'aat* must by essence depend upon what the definition of *ahruf* is, and whether one believes that the *ahruf* are still in existence today. Therefore, the scholars of Islaam have defined this relationship depending upon their respective definitions of the *ahruf*. The three major opinions on this issue are as follows:[455]

1) The opinion of Imaam at-Tabaree (d. 310 A.H.), Ibn 'Abd al-Barr (d. 463 A.H.), and others, is that all the authentic *qira'aat* are based upon one *harf* of the Qur'aan. This is because, as was mentioned in the last chapter, they hold that the *mus-haf* of 'Uthmaan eliminated the other six *ahruf* and preserved only one *harf*.

However, this opinion does not seem very strong, since, if the origin of all of the authentic *qira'aat* is one *harf*, then where do all the differences between the *qira'aat* originate from? In addition, as was mentioned in the previous chapter, the opinion that only one *harf* has been preserved does not seem to be the strongest.

---

453   This table was taken from al-Habash, p. 50. In this author's opinion, he has greatly exaggerated the predominance of the *qiraa'a* of Ibn 'Aamir; ad-Dooree's percentage should also be less; and Qaloon should be more than 0.7 %. In addition, Hafs is probably closer to 97 than 95%, and Allaah knows best.

454   The *Tayyibah* is more advanced than the *Shaatibiyyah*-plus-*Durrah* combination, since Ibn al-Jazaree recorded more differences between the various *turuq* than ash-Shaatibee did.

455   cf. Itr, pps. 346-357.

2) The opinion of al-Baaqillaani (d. 403 A.H.) and a few scholars is that all of the seven *ahruf* are preserved in the *qira'aat*, such that each *harf* is found scattered throughout the *qira'aat*. Therefore, there is no single *qiraa'a* that corresponds exactly to any one *harf*, but each *qiraa'a* represents various *ahruf* such that, in the sum total of the *qira'aat*, the *ahruf* are preserved.

This opinion also is based upon these scholars' belief that *all* of the *ahruf* have been preserved. This opinion seems like a strong opinion, except for the fact that there exists many narrations in which the Companions used to recite differently from any of the present *qira'aat* (these are today present in the *shaadh qira'aat*). It seems that they were reciting a peculiar *harf* of the Qur'aan, but this was not preserved in the *qira'aat*.[456]

3) The opinion of Makkee ibn Abee Ṭaalib (d. 437 A.H.), Ibn al-Jazaree (d. 832 A.H.), Ibn Ḥajr (d. 852 A.H.), as-Suyooṭee, and others, and the one that is perhaps the strongest, is that the *qira'aat* represent portions of the seven *ahruf*, but not all of the seven *ahruf* in totality. The differences between the *qira'aat*, even the most minute of differences, originate from the seven *ahruf*, but not every difference between the seven *ahruf* is preserved in the *qira'aat*. This goes back to our position on the existence of the *ahruf* today: that they exist inasmuch as the script of the *muṣ-ḥaf* of 'Uthmaan allows them to. In the last chapter, the methodology that the Companions used to decide which *ahruf* to preserve was discussed. Those *ahruf* that were preserved are the ones that are in existence today, through the variations in the *qira'aat*.

To summarise the last two chapters, we quote Makkee ibn Abee Ṭaalib (d. 437 A.H.), who wrote:

> When the Prophet (ﷺ) died, many of the Companions went to the newly-conquered territories of the Muslims, and this was during the time of Aboo Bakr and 'Umar. They taught them the recitation of the Qur'aan and the fundamentals of the religion. Each Companion taught his particular area the recitation that he had learnt from the Prophet (ﷺ) (i.e., the various *ahruf*). Therefore the recitations of these territories differed based on the differences of the Companions.
>
> Now, when 'Uthmaan ordered the writing of the *muṣ-ḥafs*, and sent them to the new provinces, and ordered them to follow it and discard all other readings, each of the territories continued to recite the Qur'aan the same way that they had done so before the *muṣ-ḥaf* had reached them, as long as it conformed to the *muṣ-ḥaf*. If their recitation differed with the *muṣ-ḥaf*, they left that recitation...
>
> This new recitation was passed on from the earlier generations to the later ones, until it reached these seven Imaams[457] (*Qaarees*) in the same form, and they differed with each other based upon the differences of the people of the territories – none of whom differed with the *muṣ-ḥaf* that 'Uthmaan

---

456 See the chapter entitled, "The *Ahruf* of the Qur'aan," for a discussion of the existence of the *ahruf* today.

457 Actually, until it reached the *ten* Qaarees, and not just the seven.

had sent to them. This, therefore, is the reason that the *Qaarees* have differed with each other...[458]

Therefore, the differences in the *qira'aat* are remnants of the differences in the way that the Prophet (ﷺ) taught the recitation of the Qur'aan to the different Companions, and these differences were among the seven *ahruf* of the Qur'aan which Allaah revealed to the Prophet (ﷺ). Thus, the ten authentic *qira'aat* preserve the final recitation that the Prophet (ﷺ) recited to Jibreel – in other words, the *qira'aat* are manifestations of the remaining *ahruf* of the Qur'aan.

VIII. The Benefits of the Qira'aat

Since the *qira'aat* are based on the *ahruf*, many of the benefits of the *qira'aat* overlap with those of the *ahruf*. Some of the benefits are as follows.

1) The facilitation of the memorisation of the Qur'aan. This includes not only differences in pronunciations that the different Arab tribes were used to, but also the differences in words and letters.

2) Proof that the Qur'aan is a revelation from Allaah, for notwithstanding the thousands of differences between the *qira'aat*, not a single difference is contradictory.

3) Proof that the Qur'aan has been preserved exactly, as all of these *qira'aat* have been recited with a direct, authentic, *mutawaatir* chain of narrators back to the Prophet (ﷺ).

4) A further indication of the miraculous nature (*'ijaaz*) of the Qur'aan, because these *qira'aat* add to the meaning and beauty of the Qur'aan in a complementary manner, as shall be shown in the next section.

5) The removal of any stagnation that might exist with regards to the text of the Qur'aan. In other words, there exist various ways and methodologies of reciting the Qur'aan that are different from each other in pronunciation and meaning, and thus the text remains vibrant and never becomes monotonous.[459]

IX. Some Examples of the Different Qira'aat

It is appropriate to conclude this chapter by quoting various verses that demonstrate some of the differences in the *qira'aat*, with a discussion of the various meanings.[460] Four verses were chosen, the first of which deals with belief, the second and third with stories, and the last with laws. In each verse, it will be seen that, far from

---

458 Ibn Abee Ṭaalib, Abu Muḥammad Makkee: *Kitaab al-Ibaanah 'an Ma'ani al-Qira'aat*. ed. Dr. Muḥyi Ramaḍaan. Dar al-Mamoon li Thurath, Beirut, 1979, p. 39.

459 This is not to imply that the Qur'aan would have become monotonous had the *qira'aat* not existed, but rather that the different *qira'aat* are one of the factors that contribute to this miraculous effect. Any person who has dealt with the *qira'aat* knows this feeling.

460 Many of the differences in the *qira'aat* do not affect the meaning of a verse, but rather change only the pronunciation of certain vowels and letters. However, this section discusses only those differences that result in a change in meaning.

contradicting each other, the *qira'aat* taken together add much deeper meanings and connotations than any one of them individually. In fact, the various readings between the *qira'aat* are considered – in terms of extracting rulings from verses – as two separate verses, both of which must be looked into, and neither of which can abrogate the other.

The scholar of this century, Muhammad Ameen ash-Shanqeetee (d. 1393 A.H.), said in his famous *tafseer, Adwaa al-Bayaan*, "In the event that the different *qira'aat* seem to give contradictory rulings, they are considered as different verses..."[461] meaning that both of them must be taken into account for the final ruling to be given. This same principle applies in verses that deal with stories or belief, as the examples below will show.

1) *Soorah* Faati<u>h</u>ah, verse 4.

$$ مَـٰلِكِ يَوۡمِ ٱلدِّينِ $$

The first reading, that of 'Aasim and al-Kisaa'ee, is *maaliki yawm ad-deen*. This is the recitation that most of the readers will be familiar with. The word *maalik* means 'master, owner,' and is one of the Names of Allaah. The meaning of this name when attributed to Allaah is that Allaah is the one who Possesses and Owns all of the Creation, and therefore He has full right to do as He pleases with His creation, and He has the power to do what He pleases with His creation, and no one can stop or question Him.

The verse therefore translates, "The Only Owner of the Day of Judgement." This name (*Maalik*) is also mentioned in,

$$ قُلِ ٱللَّهُمَّ مَـٰلِكَ ٱلۡمُلۡكِ $$

«Say: O Allaah! *Maalik* (Possessor) of (all) Kingdoms!» [3:26]

Allaah is the Owner who Possesses all things, and on the Day of Judgement, He will Own Rulership and Kingship. As Allaah says,

$$ ٱلۡمُلۡكُ يَوۡمَئِذٍ ٱلۡحَقُّ لِلرَّحۡمَـٰنِ $$

«The sovereignty on that day (i.e., the Day of Judgement) will be the true (sovereignty), belonging to the Most Beneficent» [25:26]

If Allaah is the only *Maalik* on the Day of Judgement, this automatically implies that He is the *Maalik* before the Day of Judgement also, since the one who is the *Maalik* on that day must be the *Maalik* of all that was before that Day!

The second reading, that of Naafi', Aboo 'Amr, Ibn 'Aamir, Ibn Katheer and <u>H</u>amzah, is *maliki yawm ad-deen*, without the *alif*. The word '*malik*' means, "king, sovereign, monarch," and is also one of the Names of Allaah. This also has the connotation of the one who has power to judge. A king (*Malik*) possesses not only wealth

---

461 *Adwaa al-Bayaan*, v. 6, p. 680.

and property (like a *Maalik*), but also the authority to rule, judge and command. The verse therefore translates, "The King (and the Only Ruling Judge) of the Day of Judgement." *Malik*, as one of the names of Allaah, is mentioned in the Qur'aan:

«...The King...»[59:23]

and also,

مَلِكِ ٱلنَّاسِ

«The King of Men» [114:2]

The name of Allaah '*Malik*' is a description of Allaah (i.e., *sifah dhaatiyyah*), since He is 'The King'; whereas the name '*Maalik*' is a description of Allaah and His actions (i.e., *sifah fi'liyyah*), since He is 'The Owner' of all of His creation.[462]

It can be seen that the two readings increase the overall meaning of the verse, each giving a connotation not given by the other, and thus increasing the beauty and eloquence of the verse.

> The result of the two *qiraa'as* is that Allaah is the *Maalik* on the Day of Judgement, and the *Malik*. So on that Day, He will be the Owner (*Maalik*) of the Day of Judgement – no other person will be an owner besides Him in Judgement, even though they might have been owners of judgement in this world. And Allaah is the King (*Malik*) of the Day of Judgement, besides all else of His creation, who, in this world, were mighty and arrogant kings...so on this day, these (kings) will know for sure that they are in reality the most humiliated of creation, and that the true Might, and Power, and Glory and Kingship belongs only to Allaah, as Allaah, all Glory and Praise be to Him, has said,

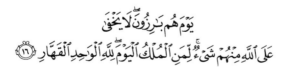

> «The Day when they will (all) come out, nothing of them will be hidden from Allaah. Whose is the Kingdom on this Day?! (Allaah Himself will reply:) It is Allaah's, the Unique, the Irresistible» [40:16]

> So, Allaah has informed us that He is the *Malik* of the Day of Judgement, meaning that He is the only one whom Kingship belongs to, besides all the kings and rulers of this world, and on this day these kings and rulers will be in the greatest humiliation and disgrace, instead of their (worldly) power and glory...

> And, Allaah has informed us that He is the *Maalik* of the Day of Judgement, meaning that He is the only one whom Ownership belongs to. So, there is none that can pass judgements or rule on that Day except Him.[463]

---

462 al-Hamood, p.88.
463 Baazmool, v. 1, p. 403.

2) Soorah al-Baqarah, verse 259.

This verse tells the story of a man who passed by a deserted town, and wondered how Allaah would ever bring it back to life. Thus, as a miracle for him, Allaah caused him to die for a hundred years, then brought him back to life. Allaah also brought the man's donkey back to life in front of his eyes.

The first reading of the relevant part of the verse, by al-Kisaa'ee, Ibn 'Aamir, 'Aasim and Hamzah, is, "*kayfa nunshizuha.*" This is in reference to the resurrection of the donkey. The word *nunshizuha* means, "to cause to rise." The verse therefore translates, "Look at the bones (of the donkey), how We raise them up," meaning, "...how We cause the bones to join one another and stand up again (from the dust)."

The second reading, by Aboo 'Amr, Naafi', and Ibn Katheer, is, "*kayfa nunshiruha.*" The word *nunshiruha* means, "to bring to life, to resurrect." The verse then translates, "...how We resurrect it and bring it back to life."

Again, both readings give different meanings, but put together these readings help form a more complete picture. The bones of the donkey were 'raised up' from the dust and 'resurrected' (meaning clothed with flesh) in front of the man. Each reading gives only a part of the picture, but put together, a more graphic picture is given.

3) In the last portion of the same verse, the readings differ as follows:

The first reading, that of Naafi', Ibn Katheer, 'Aasim, Ibn 'Aamir and Aboo 'Amr, is, "*Qaalaa a'lamu ana Allaaha 'alaa kulli shayin qadeer.*" This translates as, "He said, 'I (now) know that Allaah is indeed capable of all things.'" This shows that, after this miraculous display, the man finally believed that Allaah could bring the dead back to life, and repented of his previous statement.

The second reading, that of Hamzah and al-Kisaa'ee, is, "*Qala'lam ana Allaaha...*" which translates as, "It was said (to him): 'Know that Allaah is capable of all things.'" In this reading, after the resurrection of the donkey was shown to him, he was ordered to believe that Allaah was indeed All-Powerful.

Once again, each reading adds more meaning to the overall picture. After this miraculous display, the man was commanded to know that Allaah is indeed capable of all things. He responded to this command, and testified that, indeed, Allaah is capable of all things.[464]

4) *Soorah* al-Maa'idah, verse 6.

For the last example, it will be seen that even different *fiqh* ruling are given by the differences in the *qira'aat*.

The relevant verse discusses the procedure for ablution (*wudoo*). In the reading of Naafi', Ibn 'Aamir, al-Kisaa'ee and Hafs, the verse reads as follows: "O you who believe! When you intend to pray, wash your faces and your hands up to the elbows, wipe your heads, and (wash) your feet up to the ankles..." The word 'feet' is read

---

464 In this verse in particular, the *i'jaaz* of the Qur'aan can be felt, for the very same verse is the command and response!

arjulakum, and in this tense, it refers back to the verb 'wash.' Therefore, the actual washing of the feet is commanded, according to this recitation.

The remaining *qira'aat* pronounce the word *arjulikum*, in which case it refers back to the verb 'wipe,' so the verse would read, "...wash your faces and hands up to the elbows, and wipe your heads and feet..." According to this recitation, washing is not obligatory, and wiping is sufficient.

This is an apparent contradiction between the *qira'aat*. Does one 'wipe' his feet (meaning pass water over it, similar to how the head is wiped in ablution), or does one actually wash his feet (like the hands and face are washed)? In fact, there is no contradiction whatsoever, for each recitation applies to a different circumstance. In general, the ablution is performed by 'washing' the feet. However, if a person is wearing shoes or socks, and he had ablution before putting them on, he is allowed – in fact even encouraged – to 'wipe' over his feet, and is not obliged to wash them.[465] Az-Zarkashee said, "These two verses can be combined to understand that one reading deals with wiping over the socks, while the second reading deals with washing the feet (in case of not wearing socks)."[466]

Therefore, each of these recitations adds a very essential ruling concerning the ablution, and there is no contradiction between them.

It can be seen from this section that the *qira'aat* are a part of the eloquence of the Qur'aan, and form an integral factor in the miraculous nature of the Qur'aan. For indeed, what other book in human history can claim the vitality that is displayed in the *qira'aat* – the subtle vaiations in letters and words that change and complement the meaning of the verse, not only in story-telling but also in beliefs and commands and prohibitions! To add to this miracle, all of these changes originate from the one script of 'Uthmaan! Indeed, there can be no doubt the Qur'aan is *the* ultimate miracle of the Prophet (ﷺ).

---

465 See *Fiqh as-Sunnah*, v.1, pps. 44-46, for further details on this issue.
466 az-Zarkashee, v. 2, p. 52.

CHAPTER 12

THE CLEAR AND UNCLEAR VERSES- AL-MUHKAM WA AL-MUTASHAABIH

The Qur'aan has been revealed in the most eloquent of Arabic. Therefore, in order for a person to fully understand and appreciate the Qur'aan, he must be knowledgeable of various aspects related to the Arabic language.

Among these aspects is the knowledge of the how words give particular meanings (for example, *'aam* and *khaas*; *mutlaq* and *muqayyad*), how the word or text is used (for example, *haqeeqee* and *majaazee*), and how the text gives the desired meaning (for example, *mantooq* and *mafhoom*).[467] Also essential are other categories of texts (such as the *muhkam* and *mutashaabih*, and the *naasikh* and *mansookh*).

I. Definition of Muhkam and Mutashaabih

The word *muhkam* comes from *h-k-m*, which has the following meanings:

1) 'To judge, to pass a verdict.' One of Allaah's Names is *Al-Hakam*, meaning 'The One who Judges.' This also has the connotation of a standard, such that one has a criterion by which to judge good or evil.

2) 'To prevent, to obstruct.'

A *muhkam* verse is one that it is clear in its meaning, not open to interpretation. Imaam al-Qurtubee (d. 671 A.H.) said, "The *muhkam* is the (phrase or word) whose interpretation is known, its meaning understood and its exposition clear."[468]An example of a *muhkam* verse is,

---

467 This is one of the areas where *'uloom al-Qur'aan* overlaps with *usool al-fiqh*; in fact, it is true to say that these topics are dealt with in much greater detail in works of *usool al-fiqh* than in works of *'uloom al-Qur'aan*. In reality, the detailed explanation of such concepts to a non-Arabic audience is not only tedious, but of relatively little value, as in order to utilise and benefit from these concepts, a strong command of the Arabic language is necessary. However, in order to acquaint the reader with some essential aspects of this knowledge, the more important categories were chosen (the *muhkam* and *muttashabih*, the *'aam* and *khaass*, the *mutlaq* and *muqqayad*, the *haqeeqee* and the *majaazee*, the *mantooq* and the *mafhoom*, and the *naasikh* and the *mansookh*). These categories were not discussed in as much detail as other concepts in this work (an exception was made, however, for the *muhkam* and *muttashabih*, due to the misconceptions prevalent about it, and the *naasikh* and *mansookh*, due to its importance). Those interested in furthering their studies may consult any standard work of *usool al-fiqh*.
468 Ubaydaat, p. 197.

$$\text{ٱلْحَمْدُ لِلَّهِ رَبِّ ٱلْعَـٰلَمِينَ}$$

«All praise is due to Allaah, the Lord of the Worlds» [1:1]

This verse is *muhkam* since there is no ambiguity in it.

The word *mutashaabih* comes from *sh-b-h*, which means 'to resemble, to be similar to.' 'Mutashaabih' has two meanings, the first one is 'resembling,' and the second 'unclear.' The second meaning is related to the first, since those objects which resemble one another are difficult to distinguish, hence 'unclear.'

It is used in both of these meanings in the Qur'aan and *Sunnah*. For example, the Jews say in the Qur'aan,

$$\text{إِنَّ ٱلْبَقَرَ تَشَـٰبَهَ عَلَيْنَا}$$

«...to us, all cows look alike (Ar. *tashabaha*)...» [2:70]

In this verse, the word is used in the first meaning ('resembling'). It is used in the second meaning ('unclear') in the famous *hadeeth* of the Prophet (ﷺ) in which he said, "The *halaal* is clear, and the *haraam* is clear, but between the two are matters which are unclear (Ar. *mutashaabihaat*)...."[469]

Mutashaabih does *not* mean 'allegorical,' as some translators claim.[470]

THE QUR'AAN AS Muhkam AND MUTASHAABIH

On occasion, Allaah calls the entire Qur'aan *muhkam*. For example, He said,

$$\text{الٓرۚ تِلْكَ ءَايَـٰتُ ٱلْكِتَـٰبِ ٱلْحَكِيمِ ۝}$$

«*Alif-Laam-Raa*. These are the verses from the *hakeem* Book »[10:1]

and,

$$\text{الٓرۚ كِتَـٰبٌ أُحْكِمَتْ ءَايَـٰتُهُۥ}$$

«*Alif-Laam-Raa*. (This is a) Book the verses whereof are Perfected (Ar. *uhkimat*)...» [11:1]

In these verses, Allaah is saying that the whole Qur'aan is a clear, perfect Book which acts as a Criterion between good and evil. Imaam at-Tabaree (d. 310 A.H.) said, "Allaah has protected (*ahkama*) His verses from any evil entering it, or any flaw, or any falsehood. Then, He set it forth with commands and prohibitions. This is because to *ihkaam* something means to better it and protect it."[471] As Allaah says of the Qur'aan,

$$\text{لَّا يَأْتِيهِ ٱلْبَـٰطِلُ مِنۢ بَيْنِ يَدَيْهِ وَلَا مِنْ خَلْفِهِۦۖ تَنزِيلٌ مِّنْ حَكِيمٍ حَمِيدٍ ۝}$$

---

469 Narrated by al-Bukhaaree.

470 For example, Yusuf 'Alee. See 'A Review of Some Translations' in Ch. 15 for a more detailed discussion.

471 Zarzur, p. 163.

«Falsehood cannot come to it from before it or from behind it, (it is) sent down by the All-Wise, Worthy of Praise» [41:42]

On other occasions, Allaah calls the entire Qur'aan *mutashaabih*:

$$اللَّهُ نَزَّلَ أَحْسَنَ الْحَدِيثِ كِتَابًا مُّتَشَابِهًا مَّثَانِيَ$$

«Allaah has sent down the best statements, a Book that is *mutashaabih*, oft-recited...»[39:23]

The meaning of *mutashaabih* in this verse is that the verses of the Qur'aan resemble and complement one another in their eloquence and beauty, and in their beliefs and laws, so that there are no contradictions or differences in them.

In one verse in the Qur'aan, however, Allaah describes the Qur'aan as being part *muhkam* and part *mutashaabih*.

The verse in question is,

$$هُوَ$$

$$الَّذِي أَنزَلَ عَلَيْكَ الْكِتَابَ مِنْهُ ءَايَاتٌ مُّحْكَمَاتٌ هُنَّ أُمُّ الْكِتَابِ$$
$$وَأُخَرُ مُتَشَابِهَاتٌ فَأَمَّا الَّذِينَ فِي قُلُوبِهِمْ زَيْغٌ فَيَتَّبِعُونَ مَا تَشَابَهَ$$
$$مِنْهُ ابْتِغَاءَ الْفِتْنَةِ وَابْتِغَاءَ تَأْوِيلِهِ وَمَا يَعْلَمُ تَأْوِيلَهُ إِلَّا اللَّهُ$$
$$وَالرَّاسِخُونَ فِي الْعِلْمِ يَقُولُونَ ءَامَنَّا بِهِ كُلٌّ مِّنْ عِندِ رَبِّنَا وَمَا يَذَّكَّرُ$$
$$إِلَّا أُوْلُوا الْأَلْبَابِ ۝٧$$

«He (Allaah) is the one who has sent down to you (O Muhammad) the Book. In it are verses that are *muhkam* – they are the foundation of the Book – and others are *mutashaabih*. So as for those who have a deviation in their hearts, they follow that which is *mutashaabih*, seeking to cause confusion and chaos, and seeking for its *ta'weel*. But none knows its *ta'weel* except Allaah, and those well grounded in knowledge; they say, 'We believe in it, all of it (both the *muhkam* and *mutashaabih*) is from our Lord. And none receive admonition except those of understanding'» [3:7]

The word *ta'weel* has purposely not been translated above, because its meaning depends upon how one reads the verse. Therefore it is necessary to first explain the meaning of the word *ta'weel*. The word '*ta'weel*' has three meanings:

1) To understand a word in light of one of its connotations, despite the fact that this connotation is not the primary intent of the word. This is done due to some external evidence from the word itself, such as the context in which it occurs. For example, the phrase, "He was a lion in the battlefield," is not understood in its literal sense. The word 'lion' is primarily used to denote an animal, but in this context it does not make sense. Therefore, it is necessary to make *ta'weel* and understand the word 'lion' in this phrase as meaning one of its connotations, namely, 'a brave person.' This meaning of *ta'weel* is the most common one.

2) To explain a word or phrase. This is the same as *tafseer*, in which case something is explained so that it is understood. For example, when Moosaa did not understand the actions of Khidr, Khidr explained to him why he had done these acts,[472] and said,

$$ ذَٰلِكَ تَأْوِيلُ مَا لَمْ تَسْطِعْ عَلَيْهِ صَبْرًا $$

«This is the *ta'weel* (interpretation) of (those) things which you were not capable of being patient over» [18:82]

3) The actuality of an event. In other words, when and how something occurs. It is with this meaning of *ta'weel* that Allaah says,

$$ هَلْ يَنظُرُونَ إِلَّا تَأْوِيلَهُ $$

«Do they (the disbelievers) await for its (the Day of Judgement's) *ta'weel* (i.e., do they await for its fulfilment)...?» [7:53]

Also, Yoosuf tells his family when the dream that he had finally comes true,

$$ هَٰذَا تَأْوِيلُ رُؤْيَٰىَ مِن قَبْلُ $$

«This is the *ta'weel* (i.e., fulfilment) of my dream of old...» [12:100]

With these meanings of *ta'weel* explained, the original verse under discussion is examined. In it, Allaah differentiates the *muhkam* verses from the *mutashaabih*. He calls the *muhkam* verses, or those verses that are clear in meaning, the foundation of the Book. As the authentic *tafseers* of the Qur'aan show, these verses are the verses pertaining to *halaal* and *haraam* and the laws of Islaam.[473] These verses are clear and explicit in their meanings, and none can distort the intent of such verses.

As for the second portion of the verse, there are two ways of reading it.[474] Both of these originate from the Companions (and thus from the Prophet (ﷺ)). The first way is to stop after the phrase, '...except for Allaah.' This was the reading of Ibn Mas'ood. The verse therefore reads, '...and none know its *ta'weel* except for Allaah.' When read in this context, '*ta'weel*' signifies the actuality, such as the time and methodology of a phrase.

The second way of reading this verse is to stop after '...those well grounded in knowledge,' so that the verse reads, '... and none know its *ta'weel* except for Allaah and those well grounded in knowledge.' This is the reading of Ibn 'Abbaas. If one stops at this point, the context implies that the meaning of *ta'weel* is the interpretation. Therefore, 'those well grounded in knowledge' are aware of the interpretation of the *mutashaabih*. Ibn 'Abbaas stated, "I am of those well-grounded in knowledge, who know the meaning (of the *mutashaabih*).[475]

---

472 See the story of Moosaa and Khidr in *Soorah* al-Kahf, verses 60-82, for the various acts that Khidr did.

473 cf. Ibn Katheer, v. 1, p. 370.

474 *ibid.* v. 1, p. 370-372.

475 as-Suyootee, v. 2, p. 4.

Therefore both of these readings are correct, and each changes the meaning of the word '*ta'weel*' accordingly. The *mutashaabih* verses can be understood from one perspective (from the perspective of simply understanding these verses from their linguistic meanings), and cannot be understood from another perspective (from the perspective of the *actuality* of these verses).

THE EXACT MEANING OF Muhkam AND MUTASHAABIH

The scholars of '*uloom al-Qur'aan* have differed over the exact meaning of *muhkam* and *mutashaabih*. As-Suyootee lists almost twenty opinions concerning this issue alone.[476] However, in reality, almost all of the definitions that as-Suyootee quotes have a similar meaning. Az-Zarqaanee states, "If we look at these various opinions, we do not really find contradictions or discrepancies between them, but rather we see that they are all similar and close in meaning."[477]

Some of the meanings that as-Suyootee quotes are:

1) The *muhkam* is that which is clear in and of itself, in contrast to the *mutashaabih*.

2) The *muhkam* are the verses whose meaning is understood, whereas the *mutashaabih* are those verses whose meaning is not understood.

3) The *muhkam* is that which can only hold one valid meaning, whereas the *mutashaabih* has many.

4) The *muhkam* can be understood by itself, whereas the *mutashaabih* must be understood in light of other verses.

5) The *muhkam* does not need any interpretation in order for it to be understood, whereas the *mutashaabih* needs interpretation.

As can be seen, the various definitions have the same theme: the *muhkam* verses are those verses that are clear in meaning, and cannot be distorted or misunderstood, whereas the *mutashaabih* verses are those verses that are not clear in meaning by themselves, and in order to properly understand the *mutashaabih* verses, it is necessary to look at them in light of the *muhkam* verses.

The Prophet (ﷺ) once recited this verse and then said, "So when you see those who follow the *mutashaabih* of the Qur'aan, then these are the ones whom Allaah has mentioned, so beware of them."[478] In this *hadeeth*, the Prophet (ﷺ) warns Muslims against those people who follow the *mutashaabih* without properly understanding them in light of the *muhkam*. The phrase, '...follow the *mutashaabih*..' implies that these people who are being warned against take *only* the *mutashaabih* verses, and interpret them according to their desires. Therefore, those people who interpret the *mutashaabih* verses in light of the *muhkam* verses are not blameworthy. The proof for this is the statement of Ibn 'Abbaas quoted above, who, after reciting this verse, said,

---

476 *ibid*. v. 2, pps. 3-7.
477 az-Zarqaanee, v. 2, p. 295.
478 Narrated by al-Bukhaaree.

"I am of those well-grounded in knowledge, who know the meaning (of the *mutashaabih*)."[479] This shows that the correct interpretation of the *mutashaabih* is possible, and there is no harm if one is qualified to do so. What is blameworthy is the improper interpretation of the *mutashaabih*.

In conclusion, Allaah has called the whole Qur'aan *muhkam*, meaning that it is a clear source of guidance and a criterion between good and evil; He has also called the whole Qur'aan *mutashaabih*, meaning that its verses are similar to one another in beauty and aid one another in meaning; and, finally, He has called part of it *muhkam* and part *mutashaabih*, meaning that part of the Qur'aan is clear and not open to distortion, and part of it is unclear and open to distortion by those 'who have a deviation in their hearts.' The portion that is *muhkam* forms the foundation of the Book, meaning that it comprises all the moral and social laws that mankind needs for its guidance. The *mutashaabih* portion of the Qur'aan is clear in its meaning to 'those well grounded in knowledge,' and it is necessary to understand these *mutashaabih* portions in light of the *muhkam* ones. The actuality of the *mutashaabih* verses, however, is known only to Allaah.

The Attributes of Allaah as Mutashaabih?

One of the issues that has been the subject of great controversy at certain times in Islaamic history is the question: Are the verses pertaining to the Attributes of Allaah from the *mutashaabih*?[480] What is meant by '*mutashaabih*' in this question is that only Allaah knows the true meaning of these Attributes.

The opinion of all the scholars of the *salaf*, without any exception, is that the Attributes of Allaah are *muhkam* from one perspective, and *mutashaabih* from another perspective. The Attributes are *muhkam*, meaning they are understood, in the sense that the linguistic meaning and connotations of these Attributes are known; and the Attributes are *mutashaabih* in the actuality and 'how-ness' of the Attributes. For example, Allaah describes Himself with the Attribute of 'Knowledge'. The meaning of the word 'knowledge' is well-known and understood. When this Attribute is applied to Allaah, we know and understand the meaning of this Attribute, but the *actuality* of this 'Knowledge' can never be understood, since our limited minds cannot comprehend the infinite Knowledge of Allaah.

This agrees with the two recitations of the verse of *Soorah* Aali-'Imraan:

$$وَمَا يَعْلَمُ تَأْوِيلَهُۥٓ إِلَّا ٱللَّهُۗ وَٱلرَّٰسِخُونَ فِي ٱلْعِلْمِ يَقُولُونَ ءَامَنَّا بِهِۦ كُلٌّ مِّنْ عِندِ رَبِّنَا$$

---

479 as-Suyootee, v. 2, p. 4.

480 This point has not been discussed in the detail that it needs, since the detailed explanation of the proper meanings of the Attributes of Allaah is not directly related to the topic being discussed. However, due to the fact that groups such as the *Ash'arees* use the concept of *Mutashaabih* and *majaaz* as a means of denying the Attributes of Allaah, it was decided to briefly discuss this issue. It is hoped that a more detailed discussion of this and other topics related to the Names and Attributes of Allaah may be available in English soon, *inshaa Allaah*.

«...and none know its *ta'weel* except for Allaah, and those well grounded in knowledge; they say, 'We believe in it, all of it (both the *muhkam* and *mutashaabih*) is from our Lord...» [3:7]

As was mentioned in the previous section, if one stops after the word, 'Allaah', this implies that only Allaah knows the *ta'weel* – in this case, the 'actuality' and 'how-ness'. Thus, no one knows the actuality of the Attributes except Allaah. On the other hand, if one does not stop at this place, the verse then implies that Allaah, and those well-grounded in knowledge know the *ta'weel* – in this case, the 'interpretation'. Thus, those well-grounded in knowledge understand the verses pertaining to the Attributes of Allaah. In other words, the Attributes of Allaah are known from one perspective (that of their meanings and interpretations), and unknown from another perspective (that of their actuality and how-ness).[481]

Many of the scholars of the *Ash'arees*, however, claim that some of the verses pertaining to the Attributes of Allaah are all from the *mutashaabih*. What they seek to imply is that the meaning and interpretation of these verses is known only to Allaah. In addition, when the *Ash'arees* see a person of *Ahl as-Sunnah* discuss the Attributes of Allaah, they quote the *hadeeth* mentioned above: "So when you see those who follow the *mutashaabih* of the Qur'aan, then these are the ones whom Allaah has mentioned, so beware of them"[482] implying that the person who mentions the Attributes of Allaah, as found in the Qur'aan, is the one who is following the *mutashaabih*!

Examples that are claimed to be from the *mutashaabih* are the verses pertaining to the Hands (*yad*) of Allaah (48:10), His Eyes (*'ayn*) (11:37), His Face (*wajh*) (55:27), and His Rising over (*istiwaa*) the Throne (20:5). It is claimed by these scholars that the meaning of these verses is known only to Allaah. In addition, they claim that the apparent (Ar. '*dhaahir*') meaning of these verses is definitely *not* the meaning that is desired. After this bold claim, these scholars split into two categories with regards to these verses. The first group claimed that the true meaning of these verses can never be known or understood by mankind, but instead the meanings are 'entrusted' (Ar. '*tafweed*') to Allaah, and are not discussed. This group then attributed this philosophy to the *salaf*, and claimed, "The philosophy of the *salaf* is *tafweed* of the Attributes of Allaah." The second group, on the other hand, claimed that the apparent (*dhaahir*) meanings of these verses can be 'interpreted' to mean other attributes. So, for example, the 'Hand' of Allaah is, in reality, the 'Capability' of Allaah; the '*istiwaa*' over the Throne means the 'Conquering' of the Throne, and so forth.

The detailed refutation of these views may be found in the books of *'aqeedah*; however, since there does not exist any material in English on this topic, a summarised refutation is as follows:

Firstly, their claim that the 'apparent' meaning of the verses is not intended has a number of implications, amongst them:[483]

---

481 Ibn Taymiyyah, *at-Tadmuriyyah*, p. 58.
482 Narrated by al-Bukhaaree.
483 Taken from Ibn al-Qayyim, *as-Sawaa'iq*, v. 1, p. 314-316.

1) That Allaah has revealed in His Book verses which, apparently, seem to mislead and deceive mankind, instead of guiding them.

2) That Allaah did not reveal the truth concerning His Attributes, but rather hinted at them in such couched and vague language that the truth cannot be arrived at except by claiming that the verses pertaining to this topic are not to be understood except after great effort and distortion of their meanings.

3) That Allaah required His servants not to believe in the apparent meanings of what He revealed, but instead believe the exact opposite of what the verses clearly state.

4) That Allaah is always revealing verses concerning His Attributes whose apparent meanings oppose the truth.

5) That the best of this *ummah*, the *salaf*, from the first of them to the last of them, did not understand this important concept properly, for no quotes are found from them that agree with what the *Ash'arees* say. This implies that, either the *salaf* were ignorant of these concepts (in which case the scholars of these *Ash'arees* are more knowledgeable than the *salaf*), or that they knew the truth but did not explain it (in which case the *salaf* were not sincere in spreading the religion of Islaam). Both of these possibilities cannot be true, as the *salaf* are the most knowledgeable and sincere generations of this *ummah*, by testimony of the Prophet (ﷺ).

6) That the *salaf* were ignorant, illiterate people, reading these verses pertaining to the Attributes of Allaah, and not understanding anything from them, nor caring to understand them, or even asking about them.

7) That, if what the *Ash'arees* say is true and all of these implications are correct, it would have been more beneficial and wiser *not* to reveal these verses, since the revelation of these verses has caused nothing but deception and doubts!

All praise is due to Allaah, He is above all that they ascribe to Him! Verily, Allaah, all Praise and Glory be to Him, is more knowledgeable of His Attributes than His creation is, and He is more capable of clearly explaining His Attributes than His creation is!

Secondly, the primary problem with the *Ash'arees*, as was explained in the section on the *kalaam* of Allaah, is they did not understand the verses pertaining to the Attributes of Allaah properly. Instead, they only understood these verses as referring to human-like (anthropomorphic) attributes, and, based on this assumption, they denied the meanings of these verses. So, for example, when Allaah says, "The Ever-Merciful *istawaa* over the Throne" (Allaah has stated seven times in the Qur'aan that He has '*istawaa*' over His Throne, e.g.,

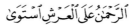

«The Ever-Merciful 'rose over' (*istawaa*) over the Throne» (20:5))

the only understanding that these *Ash'arees* had of this verse is that it implied a body that is in need of another physical object (the Throne) to rest upon! Based on this anthropomorphic understanding, they then negated the meaning of the verse. Likewise, when Allaah says,

$$يَدَاهُ مَبْسُوطَتَانِ$$

«His two Hands are outstretched» [5:64]

the only understanding that the *Ash'arees* had were two human-like physical hands! Had they only realised that Allaah is above their limited imaginations, and that His Attributes cannot be compared or equated with those of His creation, it would have saved them from these serious errors!

Allaah clearly states,

$$لَيْسَ كَمِثْلِهِ شَيْءٌ وَهُوَ ٱلسَّمِيعُ ٱلْبَصِيرُ$$

«There is nothing similar to Him, and He is the All-Hearer, All-Seer» [42:11]

This verse in and of itself is a clear and simple refutation of the *Ash'arees*; after stating that there is nothing similar to Him, Allaah then immediately affirms for Himself two Attributes that are also found in the creation, that of hearing and sight! Why is it that, in this case, the *Ash'arees* understand that Allaah has the Attributes of Hearing and Seeing, but these two Attributes are not similar to the hearing and seeing of mankind; why is it that they understand this properly, yet fall into errors with regards to other Attributes?

The Names and Attributes of Allaah are unique to Him, just like the names and attributes of the created are unique to them.

So Allaah has called Himself with certain Names and Attributes, and these Names and Attributes, when ascribed to Allaah, have unique meanings which none share. And, He has called His servants with names (and attributes) that are peculiar to them... These names are the same when they are separated from their owners... but when they are ascribed to their owners, each one takes on specific characteristics that are unique to it, different from the other...

So, for example, Allaah has called Himself *al-Hayy* (The Ever-Living), for He said,

$$ٱللَّهُ لَا إِلَٰهَ إِلَّا هُوَ ٱلْحَيُّ ٱلْقَيُّومُ$$

«Allaah! There is no deity except Him, the Ever-Living (*al-Hayy*), the Sustainer of all» [2:255]

Likewise, He has also described some of His creation with 'Life' (*hayy*), for He said,

$$يُخْرِجُ ٱلْحَيَّ مِنَ ٱلْمَيِّتِ وَيُخْرِجُ ٱلْمَيِّتَ مِنَ ٱلْحَيِّ$$

«He brings out the living (*hayy*) from the dead, and brings out the dead from the living...» [30:19]

And neither is this *al-Hayy* (i.e., Allaah) like the other *hayy* (i.e., man), since *al-Hayy* is one of the Names of Allaah, particular to Him, and the *hayy* in 'He brings out the living (*hayy*) from the dead' is the name of life that is particular to the created, specific to him....

And Allaah has called Himself *Samee'* (All-Hearing) and *Baseer* (All-Seeing), for He said,

$$\text{إِنَّ ٱللَّهَ كَانَ سَمِيعًا بَصِيرًا}$$

«...truly, Allaah is *Samee'* and *Baseer*» [4:58]

and He has called some of His servants *samee'* and *baseer*, for He said,

$$\text{إِنَّا خَلَقْنَا ٱلْإِنسَٰنَ مِن نُّطْفَةٍ أَمْشَاجٍ نَّبْتَلِيهِ فَجَعَلْنَٰهُ سَمِيعًا بَصِيرًا}$$

«Verily, We have created man from drops of mixed semen... and made him *samee'* and *baseer*» [76:2]

But neither is the *Samee'* like the *samee'*, nor is the *Baseer* like the *baseer*!

And Allaah has called Himself *Ra'oof* (The One Full of Kindness) and *Raheem* (The Most Merciful), for He said,

$$\text{إِنَّ ٱللَّهَ بِٱلنَّاسِ لَرَءُوفٌ رَّحِيمٌ}$$

«Verily, Allaah is, for mankind, the *Ra'oof*, the *Raheem*» [22:65]

and He has called some of His creation *ra'oof* and *raheem*, for He said,

$$\text{لَقَدْ جَاءَكُمْ رَسُولٌ مِّنْ أَنفُسِكُمْ عَزِيزٌ}$$
$$\text{عَلَيْهِ مَا عَنِتُّمْ حَرِيصٌ عَلَيْكُم بِٱلْمُؤْمِنِينَ}$$
$$\text{رَءُوفٌ رَّحِيمٌ ﴿١٢٨﴾}$$

«Verily, there has come to you a Messenger from amongst yourselves... for the believers, he is *ra'oof*, *raheem*» [9:128]

But neither is the *Ra'oof* like the *ra'oof*, nor is the *Raheem* like the *raheem*...!

And He has also described Himself with certain Attributes, and described His creation with these same attributes... (For example) He has attributed to Himself the Attribute of Speech (*kalaam*), for He said,

$$\text{وَكَلَّمَ ٱللَّهُ مُوسَىٰ تَكْلِيمًا}$$

«And Allaah spoke directly (*kallama*) to Moosaa» [4:164]

... And He described some of His creation with the attribute of speech, for He said,

فَلَمَّا كَلَّمَهُ

«...then, when (the king) spoke (*kallama*) to (Yoosuf)...» [12:54]

But neither is this *Kalaam* like the other *kalaam*...!

And He has described Himself as being *istiwaa* over the Throne, for He has mentioned this seven times in His Book. And He has also described some of His creation as being *istiwaa* over objects, for He said,

لِتَسْتَوُۥ عَلَىٰ ظُهُورِهِ

«So that you (mankind) may *istawaa* over their backs (i.e., so that you may ride on the backs of your animals)» [43:13]

...and neither is the one *istiwaa* like the other *istiwaa*![484]

The purpose of this long quote is to show that there are names and attributes of Allaah that have also been given to the creation, but the difference between the *actuality* of the two is as great as the difference *between* the two. Therefore, it is not proper to deny or distort these Attributes merely on the assumption that they give human-like qualities, for Allaah has negated any similarity with His creation:

لَيْسَ كَمِثْلِهِۦ شَىْءٌ وَهُوَ ٱلسَّمِيعُ ٱلْبَصِيرُ

«There is nothing similar to Him, and He is the All-Hearer, All-Seer» [42:11]

The proper methodology with regards to these Attributes is to affirm their linguistic meaning in a manner that befits Allaah, and not to delve into the actuality or 'how-ness' of them, since these are concepts that cannot be grasped by the human mind.

In addition, the presumption of the *Ash'arees* that the apparent (*dhaahir*) meanings of these verses are anthropomorphic necessitates certain facts, including:[485]

1) This presumption of theirs is, in itself, a very mean and low presumption, for how can it be assumed that Allaah would reveal verses in His Book whose apparent, clear meanings are anthropomorphic?

2) In arriving at this presumption, the *Ash'arees* absolutely ignored the verses that negate any relationship between the Attributes of Allaah and those of His creation, such as,

لَيْسَ كَمِثْلِهِۦ شَىْءٌ

«There is nothing similar to Him» [42:11]

In other words, the One Who revealed,

يَدَاهُ مَبْسُوطَتَانِ

---

484 Translated (by meaning) from *at-Tadmureeyah*, pps. 14-19.
485 cf. *at-Tadmureeyah*, p.52.

«Both His Hands (*yad*) are outstretched» [5:64]

is the same One Who revealed,

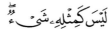

«There is nothing similar to Him» (42:11)

Why do not the *Ash'arees* take the meanings of *both* of these verses, and Attribute to Allaah what Allaah has Attributed to Himself (in this example, that His two Hands (*yad*) are outstretched), while at the same time negating what He has negated (in this example, that these two Hands (*yad*) are not similar in *any* manner to the hands of the creation)?

3) This presumption of theirs led them to deny many Divine Attributes; Attributes that are clearly mentioned in the Qur'aan and *Sunnah*, such as the proper understanding of the *kalaam* of Allaah (as was discussed earlier); the fact that Allaah Loves and Hates, is Pleased with and gets Angry with some of His Creation, and many more Attributes.

4) The net result of all of this was that, in their over-zealousness to remove any resemblance between Allaah and the creation, they ended up comparing Allaah with inanimate objects, or with non-existent objects, or ascribing to Him contradictory Attributes.[486] The example of this with regards to the Attribute of *kalaam* was given previously; in negating the fact that Allaah speaks with a voice, they in essence equated Him with a mute or inanimate object!

Thirdly, there exist numerous quotes from the *salaf* concerning the fact that these verses are to be understood in their literal sense. Perhaps the most famous incident is the response that Imaam Maalik (d. 179 A.H.) gave to the man who asked him,

«'The Ever-Merciful 'rose over' (*istawaa*) His Throne'» [20:5]

how is this 'rising' (*istiwaa*)?"

Imaam Maalik responded, "'*Istiwaa*' is well-known (in meaning), but the 'how' of it is unknown. Yet belief in it is obligatory, and asking questions about such matters is an innovation. Get this man away from me, for I think he is an evil person!"[487] In this very explicit text, Imaam Maalik stated that the meaning of *istiwaa* is well-known in the Arabic language, yet, when this Attribute is applied to Allaah, the actuality of it is

---

486 An example of this is their claim that Allaah is neither above, nor below this world, nor to the left of it, nor to the right of it, nor is He in front of it nor behind it, nor is He inside of it, nor outside of it, nor is He connected to it, nor is He disconnected from it! This, despite the fact that there exists literally *hundreds* of verses and *hadeeth* describing, either explicitly or implicitly, that Allaah is *above* His creation (cf. ad-Dhahabee's *al-'Uloow* for the full proofs). If it were asked to give a definition of something that was non-existent, even the greatest philosopher could not come up with a better description than this description that the *Ash'arees* give to their Creator!!

487 Reported by ad-Daarimee. cf. Ubaydaat, p.204.

unknown. Imaam Maalik did *not* deny the fact that *istiwaa* has a meaning to it (contrary to the philosophy of *tafweed* mentioned above), nor did he deny the fact that it is permissible to attribute this to Allaah (on the contrary, he said, "...belief in it is obligatory"). What Imaam Maalik denied was the fact that mankind has been given knowledge of the *actuality* of the *istiwaa*, thus, "...the 'how' of it is unknown."

Also, the questioner indicated that he understood the verse properly, for he asked, "How is this *istiwaa*?" This shows that the questioner understood what the verse meant, namely that Allaah has 'Risen over' (*istiwaa*) His Throne; his question was not about what *istiwaa* meant, but *how* this *istiwaa* occurred. In response, Imaam Maalik did not criticise or rebuke him for understanding the literal, apparent meaning of the verse (that Allaah has the Attribute of *istiwaa*), but instead criticised him for asking something besides the apparent meaning – for asking the 'how-ness' of the Attribute. In fact, Imaam Maalik told him, "*al-Istiwaa* is well-known," meaning, "Everyone knows what *istiwaa* means!"

Lastly, the phrase, '...and belief in it is obligatory' is another refutation of the belief of the *Ash'arees*. This phrase shows that to believe in this *istiwaa* is obligatory, for the 'it' in the phrase 'belief in it is obligatory' refers back to the *istiwaa*: "*al-Istiwaa* is well-known...and belief in *it* is obligatory..." It must be asked of the *Ash'arees*, who claim that the meanings of these verses are unknown, "Belief in *what* is obligatory?" In other words, what was Imaam Maalik referring to when he said, "...belief in *it* is obligatory"? Imaam Maalik understood that this Attribute had a meaning to it, otherwise he would not have said, '...belief in it is obligatory' (in other words, if this Attribute had no known meaning – the philosophy of *tafweed* – there would be nothing to believe in! Therefore, the fact that '*it*' must be believed in shows that there is *something* to believe in – the Attribute of *istiwaa*!).

It should be understood that all the scholars of the *salaf* agreed in their interpretation and understanding of the Attributes of Allaah. They would take the apparent meanings of these verses (thus believing in what Allaah revealed), without comparing the Attributes found in them with the attributes of the creation (thus rejecting the concept of anthropomorphism). The teacher of Imaam al-Bukhaaree (d. 256 A.H.), Nu'aym ibn Hammaad (d. 228 A.H.), said, "Whoever compares Allaah to His creation has committed disbelief, and whoever denies what Allaah has affirmed for Himself has committed disbelief. And there is no anthropomorphism in what Allaah has affirmed for Himself, or what the Prophet (ﷺ) has affirmed for Him."[488] The famous Imaam and scholar of *hadeeth*, Ishaaq ibn Rahooyah (d. 238 A.H.) said,

> There will only be anthropomorphism if someone says, 'Allaah's hand is like my hand', or 'His seeing is like my seeing', so this is anthropomorphism. As for if a person says, as Allaah Himself has said, '(Allah has the Attributes of) Hand (*yad*), and Hearing, and Seeing' and he does not say how (these are), nor does he give comparisons (based on the attributes of

---

488 ad-Dhahabi, *al-Uluww*, p. 67.

the creation), *then this is not anthropomorphism*!! Allaah has said, 'There is nothing similar to Him, and He is the All-Hear, All-Seer (42:11).'[489]

In conclusion, the Qur'aan has been revealed in clear, lucid Arabic, and Allaah has addressed His creation in the language that they know. To presume that the verses pertaining to the Attributes of Allaah carry no known meanings, or that they carry meanings absolutely contrary to the meanings of their words as known by the Arabs, is in reality a very dangerous and incorrect presumption. Why else has Allaah revealed these concepts, in these clear wordings, except that they be understood in this manner?

Instead of 'reading in' and presuming anthropomorphism in the Speech of Allaah, the *Ash'arees* should instead impugn their own intelligence and understanding of these verses. If the *Ash'arees* claim that the verses pertaining to the Attributes of Allaah are from the *mutashaabih*, they should then understand them in light of the *muhkam* verses, such as,

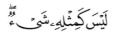

«There is nothing similar to Him» [42:11]

This is the proper methodology of understanding the *mutashaabih* verses.

The statement, "The verses pertaining to the Attributes of Allaah are from the *mutashaabih*," is a vague and imprecise phrase, for it carries a correct meaning, and an incorrect and dangerous one. The correct meaning of this phrase is that the actuality of the Attributes of Allaah are known only to Allaah, and it is impermissible to delve into these concepts. The incorrect meaning of this phrase, and the one that the *Ash'arees* intend, is that the Attributes of Allaah that are mentioned in the Qur'aan and *Sunnah* are not to be understood by mankind by their linguistic meanings; instead, they should either be ignored and not discussed (the essence of the concept of *tafweed*), or reinterpreted until their meanings conform with their desires.

To conclude this section, we quote the famous scholar al-Khateeb al-Baghdaadee (d. 436 A.H.), who wrote,

> As for the Attributes (of Allaah), then all that has been narrated in the authentic *sunnah* – the methodology of the *salaf* is to affirm them, and to take them on their apparent meanings (*dhaahir*), but at the same time to deny any resemblance or 'how-ness' of them. Some groups denied these Attributes, so they ended up denying what Allaah Himself had affirmed. Other groups tried to affirm them in such a manner that they ended up comparing them to the attributes of the creation. And the proper methodology is to take the middle path, between the two extremes, for the religion of Allaah is between the extremes... And the basic principle in this regards is that to speak of the Attributes of Allaah is as if to speak of the Essence of Allaah, so therefore the same methodology is followed. So, as it is well known

---

489 ad-Dhahabi, *al-Uluww*, p. 67.

that to affirm the Creator, all Glory be to Him, is in reality an affirmation of the *Existence* of the Creator, and not *how* He Exists; likewise, the affirmation of His Attributes is an affirmation of their *existence*, and not an affirmation of their *actuality*.

So if we say, "Allaah has a 'Hand' (*yad*), or Hearing, or Seeing," then these are all Attributes that Allaah has affirmed for Himself. *And we do not say, 'The meaning of 'yad' is 'Power', nor that the meaning of 'Hearing' and 'Seeing' is 'Knowledge'; and neither do we say that all of these are physical limbs.* So we do not compare these Attributes with the hands, and ears, and eyes (of the creation) which are physical limbs and organs by which (these attributes) occur. Rather, we say that it is obligatory to affirm these Attributes, since they were found (in the Qur'aan or *sunnah*), and it is obligatory to negate any resemblance between them (i.e., between the attributes of Allaah and the attributes of the creation), because Allaah has said,

$$\text{لَيۡسَ كَمِثۡلِهِۦ شَيۡءٌۖ وَهُوَ ٱلسَّمِيعُ ٱلۡبَصِيرُ}$$

«There is nothing similar to Him, and He is the All-Hearing, All-Seeing.» [42:11]

So when the people of innovations condemned the people of narrations for narrating these *hadeeth*, and confused those who were weak in knowledge that they (i.e., the people of narrations) were narrating things that were not befitting to *tawheed*, and were not permissible in the religion, *and accused them with the disbelief of the anthropomorphists...*[490] they were responded to by saying that there are, in the Book of Allaah, verses that are *muhkam*, whose meaning is understood apparently, and there are also verses that are *mutashaabih*, which cannot be understood except by reverting them to the *muhkam* verses. And it is obligatory to affirm all of these (verses), and believe in both of them (the *muhkam* and the *mutashaabih*). And likewise the *sunnah* of the Prophet (صلى الله عليه وسلم) is understood in a similar manner, and dealt with in the same way – *that the mutashaabih are understood in light of the muhkam, and both are accepted.*[491]

OTHER CATEGORIES OF MUTASHAABIH

Some of the defintions of *mutashaabih* were given in the previous section. These definitions concentrated on one theme: that the *muhkam* verses are clear in and of themselves, whereas the *mutashaabih* verses require external factors to understand them.

There are yet other definitions of '*mutashaabih*' that deal with another meaning of the word: that of 'resembling'. As was mentioned at the beginning of this chapter,

---

490 Is it not as if al-Khateeb al-Baghdaadee is refuting the *Ash'arees* and their accusations against the *Ahl as-Sunnah*.

491 ad-Dhahabi, *al-Uluww*, p. 48.

'mutashaabih' has two meanings: 'to be unclear', and 'to resemble'. Some of the scholars have defined the *mutashaabih* verses as those verses which resemble one another in their wording. There is no contradiction between this definition of *mutashaabih* and between the one that was discussed previously; the previous defintion utilized one of the meanings of the word '*mutashaabih*' ('to be unclear'), and this definition utilises the second meaning of the word '*mutashaabih*' ('to resemble').

It can also be said that the discussion of the previous section involved the *mutashaabih* with regards to *meanings*, whereas this definition involves the *mutashaabih* with regards to *wordings*. Each of these two definitions is a separate science, and it is the second definition that will be elaborated upon in this section.

The definition of this category is quoted by as-Suyootee as: "The *muhkam* are those verses which are not repeated, and the *mutashaabih* are those verses whose wording is repeated."[492] In other words, a phrase or sentence is repeated somewhere else in the Qur'aan, either exactly the same, or with a slight difference.

Az-Zarkashee lists many phrases in the Qur'aan that occur more than once, in exactly the same wording. For example:[493]

1) Those phrases which occur twice (e.g., "...but most of them are not thankful" [10:60 and 27:73])

2) Thrice, (e.g., "Do they not travel through the land..." [30:9, 35:44 and 40:21])

3) Four times, (e.g., "And when We said to the angels..." [2:34, 17:61, 18:50 and 20:116])

4) Five times, (e.g., "Obey Allaah and obey the Messenger" [4:59, 5:92, 24:54, 47:33 and 64:12])

5) Six times, (e.g., "In this are signs for a people who believe" [6:99, 16:79, 27:86, 29:24, 30:37, and 39:32]); and so forth.

As for those phrases which re-occur in other verses with a slight difference in wording, az-Zarkashee also divides them into various categories, classifying them based upon the type of difference between the verses:

1) The difference involves the addition or subtraction of a letter or word (e.g., "It is the same, whether you warn them or not, they will not believe" (2:6), and, "And it is the same, whether you warn them or not, they will not believe"(36:10)); or,

2) the exchange of word order (e.g., "...We will feed them and you..." (6:151) and, "...We will feed you and them..."(17:31)); or,

3) the exchange of a word with its synonym (e.g., "There gushed forth therefrom twelve springs" (2:60), and "There flowed forth therefrom twelve springs" (7:158)); or,

---

492 as-Suyootee, v. 2, p. 3.
493 az-Zarkashee, v. 1, pps. 133-154.

4)   the change from singular to plural.[494]

There have been a number of books written concentrating on these differences, and how they change the meaning of the verse.[495] These subtle changes bring about different meanings, and suit the context within which they occur. Thus, part of the job of the interpreter of the Qur'aan is to analyse why one phrase occurs in a certain manner in one part of the Qur'aan, and in a slightly different manner in another part.

For example, the command prohibiting infanticide occurs twice in the Qur'aan; in one verse, Allaah says,

نَّحْنُ نَرْزُقُهُمْ وَإِيَّاكُمْ

«...We will provide them sustenance and you (also)» [17:31]

and in the other, Allaah says,

نَّحْنُ نَرْزُقُكُمْ وَإِيَّاهُمْ

«...We will provide sustenance for you and for them» [6:151]

At first glance, there does not seem to be any benefit in reversing the order of the pronouns 'you' and 'them'. However, if the two verses are examined closely, the reason and wisdom why each one occurs in a particular order is seen.

The first verse reads,

وَلَا تَقْتُلُوٓاْ أَوْلَٰدَكُمْ خَشْيَةَ إِمْلَٰقٍ نَّحْنُ نَرْزُقُهُمْ وَإِيَّاكُمْ

«And do not kill your children *for fear* of poverty; We will provide them sustenance and you (also)» [17:31]

whereas the second verse reads,

وَلَا تَقْتُلُوٓاْ أَوْلَٰدَكُم مِّنْ إِمْلَٰقٍ نَّحْنُ نَرْزُقُكُمْ وَإِيَّاهُمْ

«And do not kill your children *because* of poverty; We will provide sustenance for you and for them» [6:151]

The two verses cater to different situations. The first verse is addressed to those parents who fear that they will be inflicted with poverty in the future because of their children. These parents are worried that they will not be able to provide enough for their children. Allaah refutes this fear by stating that He will provide for the sustenance of the children, as well as the parents. The second verse, on the other hand, is addressed to those parents who are already inflicted with poverty, presuming that it is their children's fault. In this case, the parents are actually feeling the effects of this poverty, and are not managing to feed themselves properly. Allaah assures them that

---

494 There are more categories of *Mutashaabih* than these, cf. Ubaydaat, pps. 202-204; az-Zarkashee, v. 1, pps. 113-134.

495 One of the classics that is available in print is *al-Burhaan fi Mutashaabih al-Qur'aan* by Mahmood ibn Hamzah al-Karmaanee (d. 500 A.H.), Dar al-Wafa, Cairo, 1991.

they do not have to fear this poverty, for He will provide for them, and for their children. Thus, the exchange of the pronouns in the two verses adds a subtle meaning to each verse.[496]

II. The Haqeeqee and the Majaazee

If a word is used in its literal sense – in other words, its original and primary intent – then this is referred to as its *haqeeqee* meaning. For example, to apply the word 'offspring' to one's children is a *haqeeqee* meaning.

On the other hand, if a word is used in a metaphorical sense – in other words, a meaning or connotation that is not the primary use of the word – then this is the *majaazee* meaning. For example, to apply the word 'offspring' to include grandchildren is a *majaazee* meaning.

Examples that are given of *majaaz* in the Qur'aan are the verses,

$$وَٱخْفِضْ لَهُمَا جَنَاحَ ٱلذُّلِّ مِنَ ٱلرَّحْمَةِ$$

«And lower unto them (one's parents) the wing of submission and humility through mercy...» [17:24]

(the use of 'wing' is *majaazee*, for there is no actual wing);

$$وَسْئَلِ ٱلْقَرْيَةَ ٱلَّتِي كُنَّا فِيهَا$$

«And ask the town where we were...» [12:82]

(the 'town' with its houses and walls is not asked, but rather the 'people of the town' are asked, another example of *majaaz*); and,

$$جِدَارًا يُرِيدُ أَن يَنقَضَّ$$

«...a wall that wished to collapse...» [18:77]

(meaning that the wall was very close to collapsing).[497]

It should be noted that there are a number of scholars throughout history, such as Shaykh al-Islaam Ibn Taymiyyah (d. 724 A.H.), and Muhammad al-Ameen ash-Shanqeetee (d. 1393 A.H.),[498] who denied the existence of *majaaz* in the Qur'aan (and in the Arabic language), and this has been and still is a topic of debate among the scholars.

---

496 al-Karmaanee, p. 178.

497 cf. Ibn Qudaamah, p. 35.

498 These are perhaps the two most famous scholars who have denied the existed of *majaaz* in the Arabic language and the Qur'aan. Some scholars stated that *majaaz* exists in the Arabic language, but is not present in the Qur'aan. The vast majority of scholars, however, (including the sons of Muhammad al-Ameen ash-Shanqeetee!), have conceded to the existence of *majaaz* in the Qur'aan. In fact, the famous Hambalee scholar Ibn Qudaamah (d. 620 A.H.) went to an extreme and stated, "Whoever denies *majaaz* has indeed been arrogant!" (*Rawdah*, p. 35). The topic of *majaaz* and whether it exists in the language or not should not be made a topic of *'aqeedah*, in the sense that if one affirms the existence of *majaaz* in the Arabic language, or =

The Attributes of Allaah as Majaaz?

Perhaps the strongest reason that led some scholars to deny the existence of *majaazee* verses in the Qur'aan is due to the fact that many of the scholars of innovation (such as the *Ash'arees*) have claimed that some of the verses pertaining to the Attributes of Allaah are *majaazee*. This claim, in essence, enabled them to deny many of the Attributes mentioned in the Qur'aan, such as *wajh* (Face), *yad* (Hand), *'arsh* (Throne) and others. These scholars claimed that '*yad*' is *majaaz* for 'Capability', '*'arsh*' for 'Power', and so forth.

However, even if it is claimed that there are *majaazee* verses in the Qur'aan, the Attributes of Allaah can never claimed to be examples of *majaaz* for the following reasons:

1)   All verses and words are always taken in a *haqeeqee* manner unless there is reason or proof to believe otherwise. This fact is agreed upon by all linguists. Thus, in order to say that the 'Throne of Allaah' is *majaazee* for 'Power', one needs to bring clear proof from the Qur'aan or *Sunnah* to prove this point. If there is lack of evidence, the word will be interpreted in a *haqeeqee* sense, viz., that Allaah has a Throne, but it cannot be imagined by humans. Concerning this particular example, the understanding of the 'Throne of Allaah' as being *haqeeqee* is proven by many other verses, such as the verse,

وَكَانَ عَرْشُهُۥ عَلَى ٱلْمَآءِ

«...and His Throne was over the water...» [11:7]

and,

وَتَرَى ٱلْمَلَـٰٓئِكَةَ حَآفِّينَ مِنْ حَوْلِ ٱلْعَرْشِ

«And you will see the angels surrounding the Throne from all sides...» [39:75]

and,

ٱلَّذِينَ يَحْمِلُونَ ٱلْعَرْشَ وَمَنْ حَوْلَهُۥ يُسَبِّحُونَ بِحَمْدِ رَبِّهِمْ

«The (angels) who bear the Throne, and the (angels) around it, glorify the praises of their Lord...» [40:7]

and,

وَيَحْمِلُ عَرْشَ رَبِّكَ فَوْقَهُمْ يَوْمَئِذٍ ثَمَـٰنِيَةٌ

«...eight angels will, on that Day, bear the Throne of your Lord above them» [69:17]

= in the Qur'aan, then he is to be considered an innovator. This is because the existence of *majaaz* is a matter of *ijtihaad*, and is not related to the fundamentals of faith. Therefore, throughout Islaamic history, many scholars of the correct *'aqeedah* (such as Ibn Qudaamah) affirmed the concept of *majaaz*, but stated that the Attributes of Allaah cannot be examples of *majaaz*. It is thus improper to make this concept (i.e., 'Does *majaaz* exist in the Arabic language and the Qur'aan?') a point of difference between the *Ahl as-Sunnah* and the people of innovation, and Allaah knows best...

All these verses clearly show that the Throne of Allaah is a *haqeeqee* throne, for how else was it above water, and how else will the angels surround it, and eight angels hold it, unless it is a *haqeeqee* Throne? Can it be imagined that the 'Power' of Allaah was over water, and that angels will surround the 'Power', and eight angels will carry this 'Power'? In addition, there are numerous authentic *hadeeth* that clearly signify that the Throne is a *haqeeqee* throne. Likewise, all the other Attributes of Allaah can be proven in a similar manner.

2) It is not appropriate that the fundamentals of faith, such as the Names and Attributes of Allaah, be revealed in unexplicit and vague language. Rather, it is essential that these fundamentals of faith be revealed in the clearest and most explicit language; in a manner that leaves no room for doubt, confusion or ambiguity. To claim that Allaah, all Praise and Glory be to Him, revealed His Names and Attributes in *majaazee* form is, in reality, to claim that Allaah did not explain His Names and Attributes properly, but rather hinted at them in vague, couched language; in language that, outwardly, appears to mislead and deceive, rather than guide and instruct (all Praise is due to Allaah, He is above all that they ascribe to Him!). The Qur'aan describes itself in many verses as being a shining light; a revelation in clear, simple Arabic; a Book that guides mankind; that takes him from the darkness to the Light; is it possible that one of the most important topics of faith – that of the Names and Attributes of Allaah – is revealed in such obscure and vague language?

3) The very concept of *majaaz* rests upon the perceived and well-known. In other words, when it is said, "And ask the town...," the only reason that the reader understands, without any doubt, that it is not the actual *town* that is asked, but the *people* of the town, is that it is well-known that *towns* cannot be asked questions – it is the *people* who are asked. Likewise, when it is said, "Zayd was a lion during the battle," the only reason that it is understood that Zayd was not an actual animal during the battle is that Zayd is well-known *not* to be an animal, and thus, it is understood from this that Zayd was a very brave person. The point that is trying to be made is that *majaaz* can only be used when the subject is well-known and understood, and thus there is no danger that a person might be confused between the *haqeeqee* meaning and the *majaazee* one. In matters of the unseen, however, such as the Attributes of Allaah, *majaaz* simply *cannot* be applied, due to the fact that the Attributes of Allaah cannot be perceived or fully understood by the creation. Since there can be no analogical relationship between the Attributes of Allaah and those of His creation, there can be no *majaaz* when it comes to describing the Attributes of Allaah.

4) One of the ways in which *majaaz* is defined is: *Majaaz* is that which is permissible to negate. Therefore, when the phrase, "Zayd was a lion on the battlefield" is heard, it is possible to say, "No, Zayd was not a lion. He was a brave person." If it were claimed that the Attributes of Allaah are *majaaz*, it is as if a person is allowed to deny what Allaah has said (i.e., if a person says that the verse,

يَدَاهُ مَبْسُوطَتَانِ

«...both of His hands are outstretched...» [5:64]

is *majaaz*, in essence this person claims that it is possible to say, "No, both of Allaah's hands are not outstretched," thus clearly and explicitly going against the verse in the Qur'aan).

5) To claim that some of the verses that mention Allaah's Attributes are *majaazee* is, in essence, to claim that *all* of the verses that mention Allaah's Attributes are *majaazee*. What is there that makes these scholars consider some Attributes of Allaah as *majaaz* (for example, the *wajh, yad, 'ayn,* and *istiwaa*) and others as *haqeeqee* (such as the Knowledge, Life, Hearing and Seeing of Allaah)? Just as these scholars acknowledge that Allaah has the Attributes of Knowledge, Life and others, but these Attributes are not similar to those of the creation, they should also acknowledge that Allaah has a *wajh, yad,* and other Attributes, but these are different than the *wajh* and *yad* of the creation. If they claim that some of the verses that mention Allaah's Attributes are *majaazee*, there is no defence if someone were to claim that *all* the verses mentioning Allaah's Attributes are *majaazee*. In fact, some of the deviant groups (such as the *Falaasifa*, or 'Philosophers') did in actuality claim that all the verses pertaining to the matters of the unseen were *majaaz*. They thus denied the existence of Heaven and Hell, and angels and *jinns*, amongst other things! The claim that *majaaz* exists in the verses pertaining to the fundamentals of faith is an extremely dangerous claim, as it opens the door to many extreme deviations from the true religion of Islaam.

Of course, all of these points come after the fact that *all* the scholars of the *salaf* were of the opinion that Allaah's Attributes are *haqeeqee*, and are affirmed as Allaah Himself affirmed them, but that they do not resemble at all the attributes of the creation.

In conclusion, Ibn 'Abd al-Barr (d. 463 A.H.) stated,[499]

> The *Ahl as-Sunnah* have unanimously agreed in affirming those Attributes (of Allaah) that are found in the Qur'aan or *Sunnah*, and believing in them, and understanding them as *haqeeqee*, not as *majaazee*, except that they do not explain the 'how-ness' of these Attributes, nor do they limit them to a particular manner. As for the people of innovations, from the *Jahmiyyah*, and the *Mu'tazilah*, and the *Khawaarij*,[500] then they deny these Attributes, and they do not understand them in a *haqeeqee* manner. And they presume that one who affirms these Attributes is an anthropomorphist (i.e., giving human-like qualities to Allaah)! In reality, those who affirm these Attributes (the *Ahl as-Sunnah*) consider these people to be deniers and negators (of Allaah's Attributes), not affirmers! And the truth in this matter is with those people who say what the Qur'aan and *Sunnah* says (i.e., affirm these Attributes)...

---

499 *Majmoo' al-Fataawaa*, v. 5, p. 198.
500 This author adds: "...and the *Ash'arees*"!

After quoting this, Imaam ad-Dhahabi (d. 748 A.H) stated, "He has spoken the truth – I swear by Allaah!! He who misinterprets all these Attributes, and carries what has been narrated of them upon *majaaz*, will eventually end up negating the Creator of all (His Attributes), and comparing Him to non-existent objects..."[501]

III. The 'Aam and the Khaas

The *'aam* (lit., 'general') is a word that applies to all the members of a specific set, no matter how small or large that set is. For example, Allaah says,

$$كُلُّ نَفْسٍ ذَآئِقَةُ ٱلْمَوْتِ$$

«Every soul shall taste death» [3:185]

This verse is applicable to every soul, be it a human, animal or *jinn*.

Khaas (lit. 'specific'), on the other hand, is a word that is used to denote a limited number of things, including everything to which it can be applied. The primary difference between *'aam* and *khaas* is that *khaas* applies to a single subject or a specified number of objects; in other words, the scope of its application is limited, unlike the *'aam*.[502]

There are three categories of *'aam*:

1) *'Aam* that is totally unspecified. This is rare in the Qur'aan. An example of this is the verse,

$$وَٱللَّهُ بِكُلِّ شَىْءٍ عَلِيمٌ$$

«Allaah is aware of all things» [4:176]

since there are no exceptions to this verse.

2) *'Aam* in wording, but *khaas* in meaning. This is also uncommon in the Qur'aan. An example of this is the verse,

$$ثُمَّ أَفِيضُوا مِنْ حَيْثُ أَفَاضَ ٱلنَّاسُ$$

«Then depart from the place whence the people depart...» [2:199]

The 'people' referred to in this verse are the other tribes of Arabia besides the Quraysh. Even though the wording seems to be *'aam* (i.e., all people), the meaning is in fact *khaas* (i.e., the tribes of Arabia).

3) *'Aam* that has been specified. This is the most common type of *'aam* in the Qur'aan. An example of this is the verse,

---

501 ad-Dhahabi, *al-Uluww*, p. 269.
502 Kamali, p. 105.

$$\text{حُرِّمَتۡ عَلَيۡكُمۡ أُمَّهَٰتُكُمۡ}$$

$$\text{وَبَنَاتُكُمۡ وَأَخَوَٰتُكُمۡ وَعَمَّٰتُكُمۡ وَخَٰلَٰتُكُمۡ وَبَنَاتُ}$$

$$\text{ٱلۡأَخِ وَبَنَاتُ ٱلۡأُخۡتِ وَأُمَّهَٰتُكُمُ ٱلَّٰتِيٓ أَرۡضَعۡنَكُمۡ}$$

$$\text{وَأَخَوَٰتُكُم مِّنَ ٱلرَّضَٰعَةِ وَأُمَّهَٰتُ نِسَآئِكُمۡ}$$

$$\text{وَرَبَٰٓئِبُكُمُ ٱلَّٰتِي فِي حُجُورِكُم مِّن نِّسَآئِكُمُ}$$

$$\text{ٱلَّٰتِي دَخَلۡتُم بِهِنَّ}$$

«Forbidden to you (in marriage) are... your step-daughters... who have been born of your wives with whom you have had intercourse with...» [4:23]

This verse has specified an *'aam* in that only a specific type of step-daughter is forbidden in marriage.

These two complementary categories are primarily used together in deducing the laws of the *Sharee'ah*. The Qur'aan might give a general ruling in one place, yet another verse or *hadeeth* may specify that rule not to apply in certain circumstances.

iv. The Muṭlaq and the Muqayyad

A *muṭlaq* (lit., 'unconditional') verse is one that is absolute in its scope, not limited to what it applies. It differs from the *'aam* in that the *'aam* applies to all members that are included in its meanings simultaneously without exception, whereas the *muṭlaq* can only apply to one member of its meaning. In other words, *'aam* applies to all the members of a specific set, whereas *muṭlaq* only applies to any one member of that set. An example of a *muṭlaq* verse is,

$$\text{فَتَحۡرِيرُ رَقَبَةٍ}$$

«...(the penalty for *dhihaar*[503]) is the freeing of a slave»[58:3]

The condition or quality of the slave has not been specified, so the verse is *muṭlaq*. Since only one slave must be freed, it is not *'aam*; had it applied to all slaves, then it would be *'aam*.

The *muqayyad* (lit., 'qualified') occurs when a *muṭlaq* is specified by an adjective. For example, the word 'house' is *muṭlaq*, but 'a two-story house' is *muqayyad*, since there is a condition attached to the house. An example in the Qur'aan is where Allaah states,

$$\text{وَمَن قَتَلَ مُؤۡمِنًا خَطَـًٔا فَتَحۡرِيرُ رَقَبَةٍ مُّؤۡمِنَةٍ}$$

«Whoever kills a believer unintentionally must free a believing slave...»[4:92]

---

503 This was a practice of the Arabs of *Jaahilliyah*, where a man would tell his wife that she was forbidden for him sexually, by saying that she was like the back of his mother.

This verse is *muqayyad* since it specifies that in this case the slave must be a Muslim.

These categories are also used in interpreting the text and deducing laws. In particular, when one ruling appears in *mutlaq* form, and a similar ruling for another case in *muqayyad*, is the *mutlaq* ruling affected by the *muqayyad* one? For example, with regards to the penalty for *dhihaar*, does the slave that is freed have to be a Muslim, since the exact same ruling (that of freeing a slave), when mentioned in the context of the penalty for involuntary manslaughter, is *muqayyad* that the slave must be a Muslim? So, does the *muqayyad* ruling concerning involuntary manslaughter affect the *mutlaq* ruling regarding *dhihaar*?

According to the majority (the *Shafi'ees, Maalikees* and *Hambalees*), in this case the *mutlaq* is affected by the *muqayyad*, and the slave that is freed in the case of *dhihaar* must be a Muslim. According to the *Hanafees*, on the other hand, the *mutlaq* is not affected by the *muqayyad* in this case, and it is allowed to free a non-Muslim slave in the case of *dhihaar*.[504]

v. The Mantooq and Mafhoom

The *mantooq* of a verse is the apparent meaning that can be understood directly from the words in the sentence. For example, the command to fast a specific number of days in the verse,

$$\text{فَصِيَامُ ثَلَثَةِ أَيَّامٍ فِي ٱلْحَجِّ وَسَبْعَةٍ إِذَا رَجَعْتُمْ}$$

«...then he must fast three days during *Hajj* and seven when he returns...»
[2:196]

is obvious, and is the *mantooq* of the verse.

The *mafhoom* of a verse, on the other hand, is an understanding of the verse that is not explicit in the words of the sentence. There are two main types of *mafhoom*: *mafhoom al-muwaafaqah* and *mafhoom al-mukhaalafah*.

Mafhoom al-muwaafaqah is defined to be the extension of a ruling from a mentioned case to an unmentioned one due to a commonality between the two. For example, Allaah commands believers with regards to their parents

$$\text{فَلَا تَقُل لَّهُمَا أُفٍّ}$$

«And do not say '*uf*' to them» [17:23]

This verse automatically implies that beating or abusing parents is also forbidden. Even though the verse does not explicitly prohibit beating or abusing them, the *mafhoom al-muwaafaqah* of the verse clearly indicates this, since saying '*uf*' to them, beating them and abusing them all share one commonality: that of causing harm and discomfort to them.

---

504 cf. Qattaan, p. 247. Of course, this is a very over-simplified discussion of the topic. In reality, there are a number of different categories where this occurs, and the example given is only of one type.

Mafhoom al-mukhaalafah, on the other hand, is defined to be the application of the opposite ruling of a mentioned case to an unmentioned case, due to the fact that the mentioned case contains a condition that is not found in the unmentioned case. For example, Allaah says,

$$وَمَن لَّمْ يَسْتَطِعْ مِنكُمْ طَوْلًا أَن يَنكِحَ الْمُحْصَنَتِ الْمُؤْمِنَتِ فَمِن مَّا مَلَكَتْ أَيْمَنُكُم مِّن فَتَيَتِكُمُ الْمُؤْمِنَتِ$$

«And whoever amongst you does not have the means to marry free, believing women, they may marry believing girls from among the (slaves) whom your right hands possess..» [4:25]

It can be understood from this verse – the *mafhoom al-mukhaalafah* – that if one is capable of marrying free women, he is not allowed to marry slave girls.

Again, these categories are used in deducing laws from the Qur'aan.

VI. The Naasikh and the Mansookh

Due to the importance of this topic, and its integral relationship to *'uloom al-Qur'aan*, it will be discussed in a separate chapter.

CHAPTER 13

ABROGATION IN THE QUR'AAN
AN-NAASIKH WA AL-MANSOOKH

I. The Definition of Naskh

Both of the words *naasikh* and *mansookh* come from the root *n-s-kh*, which has the following meanings:[505]

1) 'To remove, to abolish, to abrogate'. For example, Allaah says in the Qur'aan,

مَانَنسَخْ مِنْ ءَايَةٍ أَوْ نُنسِهَا نَأْتِ بِخَيْرٍ مِّنْهَآ

«We do not abrogate (Ar. *nansakh*) a verse, or cause it to be forgotten, except that We bring something that is better than it...»[2:106]

and in another verse,

فَيَنسَخُ اللَّهُ مَا يُلْقِى الشَّيْطَنُ

«...but Allaah abolishes (Ar. *yansakh*) what Satan throws in...» [22:52]

2) 'To transcribe, to copy'. This may be used, for example, with reference to recording or copying a written record. Allaah says,

إِنَّا كُنَّا نَسْتَنسِخُ مَا كُنتُمْ تَعْمَلُونَ

«Verily, We were recording (Ar. 'nastansikhu') what you used to do» [45:29]

From this connotation, a scribe is also called '*naasikh*'.

3) 'To replace, to supersede'.

As for its definition in Islaamic sciences, it is: The abrogation of a ruling by a ruling that was revealed after it.

Therefore, at least two rulings must be involved, the *naasikh* and the *mansookh*.[506] The *naasikh* ruling is the ruling that repeals the *mansookh*; *naasikh*, the active partici-

---

505 As for which of these meanings is the primary one, and which are connotations, this is of little consequence to non-Arabic readers. cf. Zayd, pps. 55-61 and ash-Shanqeetee, pps. 18-21 for a discussion of this point.

506 'At least two' because there can be more than one *naasikh* and/or *mansookh* verse. In other words, more than one verse can abrogate a ruling, and one verse can be abrogate more than one ruling.

ple, is the ruling that does the abrogating, while *mansookh*, the passive form, is the ruling that is abrogated.

The Breakdown of the Definition

The phrase: *'The abrogation...'*, implies that the first ruling has been completely repealed. This differentiates it from another phenomenon found in the Qur'aan, that of 'specification' (*takhsees*).'Specification' involves one verse limiting or restricting a general ruling found in another verse, whereas *naskh* involves abrogating the first ruling *in toto* (i.e., it is not applied in any circumstances or conditions). The differences between *naskh* and *takhsees* will be elaborated on later.

This also implies that *naskh* must involve an actual abrogation of a previous Islaamic law, and is therefore different from another phenomenon known as 'initiation'(*badaa'ah*). In other words, in order for *naskh* to occur, there must have previously existed an Islaamic ruling on exactly the same subject which was then abrogated by a later ruling. Therefore, any laws that were revealed without any precedent Islaamic rulings are not considered as examples of *naskh*, but rather of 'initiation' (*badaa'ah*). For example, marriage to one's step-mother was allowed in pre-Islaamic Arab culture. After the advent of the Prophet (ﷺ), a verse was revealed that prohibited marriage to one's step-mother (verse 4:22). Even though this verse repealed the legitimacy of this pre-Islaamic custom, it cannot be considered an example of *naskh*, since there existed no previous Islaamic rulings on the topic. This verse is, however, an example of 'initiation', since this verse abrogated certain pre-Islaamic practices, but not any Islaamic ruling, thus 'initiating' a new Islaamic ruling.

The phrase: *'...of a ruling...'*, implies that *naskh* is only valid in laws, and not in belief (*'aqeedah*). In other words, *naskh* cannot occur with regards to belief in Allaah, His Names and Attributes, the Day of Judgement, and other matters related to the fundamentals of belief. It is concerning these non-abrogated beliefs that Allaah says,

شَرَعَ لَكُم مِّنَ ٱلدِّينِ مَا وَصَّىٰ بِهِۦ نُوحًا وَٱلَّذِىٓ أَوْحَيْنَآ
إِلَيْكَ وَمَا وَصَّيْنَا بِهِۦٓ إِبْرَٰهِيمَ وَمُوسَىٰ وَعِيسَىٰٓ أَنْ أَقِيمُواْ ٱلدِّينَ
وَلَا تَتَفَرَّقُواْ فِيهِ

«He has ordained for you the same religion which He ordained for Nooh,
and that which We have inspired to you (O Muhammad), and that which
we have ordained for Ibraaheem, Moosaa, and 'Eesaa, saying that you should
establish the religion and make no divisions in it» [42:13]

Also, the ruling that is abrogated (the *mansookh*) must originate in the Qur'aan or *Sunnah*; *naskh* cannot occur with respect to *ijmaa'* (consensus) or *qiyaas* (analogy). In other words, no ruling that is derived from *ijmaa'* or *qiyaas* can be abrogated.[507]

---

507 This is due to the fact that *naskh* can occur only during the lifetime of the Prophet (ﷺ), as shall be mentioned shortly, whereas *ijmaa'* and *qiyaas* must occur *after* the Prophet (ﷺ) (as any student of *usool al-fiqh* knows); therefore, these cannot be 'abrogated'.

Lastly, this phrase also implies that the understanding of a verse (*mafhoom*) can also be abrogated, even though its explicit wording (*mantooq*) remains applicable. An example that will help explain this will be discussed later on in the chapter.

The phrase: '...*by a ruling*...', means that the *naasikh* ruling (the one that does the abrogating) must also come from the Qur'aan or *Sunnah*; *ijtihaad* (personal reasoning) or *qiyaas* (analogy) cannot abrogate a ruling from the Qur'aan or *Sunnah*.

The phrase: '...*that was revealed after it*', implies that the *mansookh* ruling (the ruling that is abrogated) must precede the *naasikh* ruling in time. This also implies that *naskh* could only occur in the lifetime of the Prophet (ﷺ), since after his death no new rulings from the Qur'aan or *Sunnah* are going to be revealed.

Naskh is primarily a Madinese phenomenon, since at this stage the laws of Islaam were finalised.

The Salaf and the Term 'Naskh'

It should be pointed out that the *salaf* did not use the term 'naskh' to refer exclusively to abrogation. They also used the term to apply to specification (*takhsees*) and initiation (*badaa'ah*). The first person to limit the meaning of the word *naskh* to apply to abrogation only was Imaam ash-Shaafi'ee (d. 204 A.H.), in his famous treatise on *usool al-fiqh* entitled *ar-Risaalah*.[508]

Therefore, when coming across statements from the scholars of the first three generations that claim that a particular verse was 'abrogated' (*nasakha*) by another verse, this cannot be immediately taken as an example of *naskh*. It is this exact factor which has been one of the greatest causes of confusion with regards to the number of *naasikh/mansookh* verses in the Qur'aan (as shall be elaborated upon shortly). For example, Ibn 'Abbaas stated that the verse,

لَاتَدْخُلُواْ بُيُوتًا غَيْرَ بُيُوتِكُمْ حَتَّىٰ تَسْتَأْنِسُواْ

«Do not enter any houses, except your own, without permission...» [24:27]

was 'abrogated' (*nasakha*) by the verse,

لَّيْسَ عَلَيْكُمْ جُنَاحٌ أَن تَدْخُلُواْ بُيُوتًا غَيْرَ مَسْكُونَةٍ

«And there is no sin on you if you enter uninhabited houses that are of benefit to you (without permission)» [24:29]

This is not an example of *naskh* (in its later definition) in the least, for the second verse specifies that the 'houses' mentioned in the first verse only applies to occupied houses. In other words, this is an example of *takhsees*, and not *naskh*.[509] In the terminology of Ibn 'Abbaas and the *salaf*, *naskh* also meant what is referred to today as *takhsees*.

---

508 an-Nahaas, p. 104.
509 ash-Shanqeetee, p. 15.

Books Written on Naskh

Due to the importance of this topic, there have been a great many books written on the *naasikh* and *mansookh* verses of the Qur'aan. In fact, it would probably be no exaggeration to say that, after the subject of *tafseer*, the topic that has been given the most attention in *'uloom al-Qur'aan* is that of *naskh*.

One of the first to write a treatise concerning this topic is the famous Successor, Qataadah as-Sadoosee (d. 117 A.H.). Some of the more famous authors to have written on this topic are: Ibn Shihaab az-Zuhree (d. 125 A.H.), Ahmad ibn Hambal (d. 241 A.H.), Aboo Daawood (d. 275 A.H.) and at-Tirmidhee (d. 280 A.H.), both of *Sunan* fame, and Aboo 'Ubayd al-Qaasim ibn Sallaam (d. 224 A.H.), whose book is considered to be the best classical discussion of the subject.

After this era, many more authors wrote separate books on *naskh*, such as Makkee ibn Abee Taalib (d. 437 A.H.), Ibn Hazm adh-Dhaahiree (d. 456 A.H.), Ibn al-'Arabee al-Maalikee (d. 543 A.H.), Aboo al-Faraj Ibn al-Jawzee (d. 597 A.H.), and the famous Jalaal ad-Deen as-Suyootee (d. 911 A.H.).[510]

Without a doubt, the most thorough discussion of the topic of *naskh* written in this era is the book *'an-Naskh fee al-Qur'aan'* by Dr. Mustafa Zayd. In it, the author discusses practically every verse that has ever been claimed to have been abrogated, and offers his own conclusions of the validity of each claim. Another excellent work is *al-Ayaat al-Mansookhah fee al-Qur'aan*, by Dr. 'Abdullaah ibn Muhammad al-Ameen ash-Shanqeetee.

II. The Proof of Naskh

The vast majority of scholars have upheld the validity of *naskh*. Only some *Shee'ee* and *Mu'tazilee* scholars (such as Aboo Muslim al-Isfahaanee, d. 322 A.H.), have raised objections concerning *naskh*. Aboo Muslim claims that, while it is not inconceivable that *naskh* can occur, there are no rulings to demonstrate it.[511] However, as Ibn al-Jawzee (d. 597 A.H.) mentioned, Aboo Muslim was the first scholar to deny the validity of *naskh*, and in this he went against the consensus (*ijmaa'*) of all the scholars before him.

Aboo Muslim's view has been aptly refuted, since the Qur'aan and *Sunnah* is very explicit on the occurrence of *naskh*. The Qur'aan says,

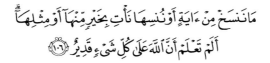

---

510 This list has been summarised from ash-Shanqeetee, p. 8.

511 It should be pointed out that Aboo Muslim did not deny the validity of what has been defined as *'naskh'* above, but rather he did not name it as such. In Aboo Muslim's opinion, all the examples of *naskh* are actually examples of *takhsees*, since, for him, every *'mansookh'* was specified by the *'naasikh'* to have been meant only for a limited time. In other words, Aboo Muslim held the view that *takhsees* was also possible by time – a condition which no other scholar had put. cf. ash-Shanqeetee, p. 66.

«We do not abrogate a ruling, or cause it to be forgotten, except that We substitute in its place something better than it, or similar to it. Are you unaware that Allaah is indeed capable of all things?» [2:106]

In another verse, Allaah says,

$$وَإِذَا بَدَّلْنَآ ءَايَةً مَّكَانَ ءَايَةٍ وَٱللَّهُ أَعْلَمُ$$
$$بِمَا يُنَزِّلُ قَالُوٓاْ إِنَّمَآ أَنتَ مُفْتَرِۭ بَلْ أَكْثَرُهُمْ لَا يَعْلَمُونَ$$

«And when We change a verse (in the Qur'aan) in place of another – and Allaah knows best what he sends down – they say, 'You (O Muḥammad) are but a forger.' Nay, (but) most of them are ignorant!» [16:101]

In these verses, the concept of *naskh* is very explicit.

Apart from these verses, there are numerous instances in the Qur'aan or *Sunnah* where *naskh* has been mentioned explicitly. For example, initially, a Muslim in battle was prohibited from fleeing from the enemy if he were faced with ten enemy soldiers (a ratio of 1 to 10, cf. 8:65). However, Allaah then revealed,

$$ٱلْـَٰٔنَ خَفَّفَ$$
$$ٱللَّهُ عَنكُمْ وَعَلِمَ أَنَّ فِيكُمْ ضَعْفًا فَإِن يَكُن مِّنكُم مِّاْئَةٌ$$
$$صَابِرَةٌ يَغْلِبُواْ مِاْئَتَيْنِ$$

«Now, Allaah *has lightened your (burden),* for He knows that there is a weakness in you. So if there are one hundred of you, they shall overcome two hundred...»[8:66]

The ratio was then reduced to one Muslim for every two non-Muslim soldiers.[512] In this verse, the occurrence of *naskh* is explicit.

With regards to *naskh* in the *Sunnah*, the classic *ḥadeeth* that is quoted is the Prophet's (ﷺ) statement, "I used to forbid you to visit graves, but now you may freely do so, for they remind you of death."[513] Once again, the occurrence of *naskh* is explicit.

III. The Conditions for Naskh

There are a number of conditions that the scholars of *uṣool al-fiqh* and *'uloom al-Qur'aan* have laid down in order to substantiate any claim of *naskh*. One of the reasons for this is that *naskh* is called only as the last-resort, since the very concept of *naskh* implies discarding a ruling for another one. As long as both rulings can be applied, *naskh* is not resorted to.

---

512 cf. ash-Shanqeeṭee, p. 99.
513 Narrated by al-Ḥaakim.

The more important conditions are as follows:[514]

1) The most important condition for *naskh* to have occurred is that the two rulings in question must directly contradict each other, such that both rulings cannot be applied at the same time, and there exists no way to reconcile them. This is because, as just mentioned, *naskh* is only called as a last-resort, when there exists no other way to explain the two rulings. Therefore, if one of the rulings can apply to a specific case, and the other ruling to a different case, this cannot be considered an example of *naskh*.

2) The *naasikh* ruling must have been revealed after the *mansookh*, or else there cannot have been any abrogation. For the claim of *naskh* to be substantiated, a later ruling must have repealed an earlier one. This can be ascertained in two ways: either there is a direct reference in the *naasikh* ruling concerning the previous ruling (e.g., 2:187 and 8:66), or, the relative time-frame of the verses in question is known (by the narrations concerning *makkee* and *madanee* revelations, the narrations concerning *asbaab an-nuzool,* and other narrations). In other words, it must be known for certain that the *naasikh* ruling was revealed after the *mansookh* ruling.

3) Both the *naasikh* and *mansookh* rulings must originate in the Qur'aan or *Sunnah*. This is because *qiyaas* and other forms of *ijtihaad* cannot abrogate a command from Allaah or the Prophet (ﷺ). As for consensus (*ijmaa'*), it is not possible for *ijmaa'* to occur against an explicit command in the Qur'aan or *Sunnah*, therefore this also cannot be the source of *naasikh/mansookh* rulings. In other words, only Allaah has the right to abrogate any command that originated from Him, either in the Qur'aan or through the tongue of His Prophet (ﷺ).

4) Most scholars have also added the condition that the *naasikh* ruling must originate from an equal or greater authority than the *mansookh*. In other words, an *ahaad hadeeth* cannot, according to those who hold this opinion, abrogate the Qur'aan or a *mutawaatir hadeeth*, since it is of a lesser authority. However, this view is not correct, and will be discussed in greater detail below.

iv. The Categories of Naskh

The various legal rulings that have been affected by *naskh* may be classified in different categories. They may be classified with respect to the sources of the *naasikh* and *mansookh* rulings, or with respect to their existence or non-existence in the Qur'aan, or with respect to the rulings of the *mansookh* in comparison with the *naasikh*.

---

514 For other conditions of *naskh*, see Ibn al-Jawzee's conditions (Malbaree, pps. 95-97); Ibn al-'Arabee's (Madgharee, v. 2, pps. 1-6); and ash-Shanqeetee's (pps. 35-37).

A. THE SOURCES OF THE NAASIKH AND MANSOOKH

As was mentioned in the previous section, *naskh* can only occur within the Qur'aan and *Sunnah*; other sources of the *sharee'ah*, such as *qiyaas* and *ijmaa',* do not play a role in *naskh*. Therefore, the *naasikh* ruling can come only from the Qur'aan or *Sunnah*, and the *mansookh* ruling can only be found in the Qur'aan or *Sunnah*. Putting all these possibilities together, there are four logical scenarios of *naskh* with regards to the sources of the *naasikh* and *mansookh*:

1) The Qur'aan abrogating the Qur'aan.

This category is agreed upon by all those who consider the validity of *naskh*. An example of this is the waiting period of a widowed lady; initially she was to be maintained from the wealth of her deceased husband for a period of one year:

$$ وَٱلَّذِينَ يُتَوَفَّوْنَ مِنكُمْ وَيَذَرُونَ أَزْوَٰجًا وَصِيَّةً $$
$$ لِّأَزْوَٰجِهِم مَّتَٰعًا إِلَى ٱلْحَوْلِ غَيْرَ إِخْرَاجٍ $$

«And those of you who die and leave behind their wives should bequeath for them a year's maintenance and residence, without turning them out...»[2:240]

Later on, this ruling was abrogated by the verse,

$$ وَٱلَّذِينَ يُتَوَفَّوْنَ مِنكُمْ وَيَذَرُونَ أَزْوَٰجًا يَتَرَبَّصْنَ بِأَنفُسِهِنَّ $$
$$ أَرْبَعَةَ أَشْهُرٍ وَعَشْرًا $$

«And those of you who die and leave behind their wives, their (wives) should wait four months and ten days...»[2:234]

2) The Qur'aan abrogating the *Sunnah*.

The majority of scholars have agreed to the validity of this type of *naskh*. An example of this is the changing of the *qiblah*; the Muslims used to pray towards Jerusalem by the command of the Prophet (ﷺ) (i.e., the *Sunnah*), but eventually the Qur'aan revealed that the direction of the *qiblah* was to be Makkah,

$$ قَدْ نَرَىٰ تَقَلُّبَ وَجْهِكَ فِى ٱلسَّمَآءِ $$
$$ فَلَنُوَلِّيَنَّكَ قِبْلَةً تَرْضَىٰهَا فَوَلِّ وَجْهَكَ شَطْرَ ٱلْمَسْجِدِ $$
$$ ٱلْحَرَامِ $$

«Verily! We have seen the turning of your face (O Muhammad) towards the heavens. Surely, We shall turn you to a *qiblah* that shall please you! So turn your face in the direction of the *Masjid al-Haraam* (at Makkah)...» [2:144]

The initial *qiblah* was based on the *Sunnah*, and the abrogation came down in the Qur'aan. This incident is clear proof that the Qur'aan can abrogate the *Sunnah*.

3) The *Sunnah* abrogating the Qur'aan.

This category may be further subdivided into two categories:

i) A *mutawaatir hadeeth* abrogating the Qur'aan. This was allowed by Imaam Maalik (d. 179 A.H.), Aboo Haneefah (d. 150 A.H.), and one of the opinions of Imaam Ahmad (d. 241 A.H.). They reasoned that both are forms of revelation from Allaah, and since both give indisputable knowledge (*qat'ee ath-thuboot*), they may abrogate one another.

An example of a *muttawaatir hadeeth* abrogating the Qur'aan is the verse concerning leaving bequest to heirs:

$$\text{كُتِبَ عَلَيْكُمْ}$$

$$\text{إِذَا حَضَرَ أَحَدَكُمُ ٱلْمَوْتُ إِن تَرَكَ خَيْرًا ٱلْوَصِيَّةُ لِلْوَٰلِدَيْنِ}$$

$$\text{وَٱلْأَقْرَبِينَ}$$

«It is prescribed for you, when any of you approaches death and he has
wealth, that he make a bequest to his parents and next of kin...» [2:180]

This ruling was abrogated by the *hadeeth* of the Prophet (ﷺ) in which he said, "There is no bequest to an heir."[515]

ii) An *ahaad hadeeth* abrogating the Qur'aan. Most of the scholars did not allow this type of *naskh*, since, they reasoned, the Qur'aan is *muttawaatir*, and provides indisputable knowledge of authenticity (*qat'ee ath-thuboot*), whereas an *ahaad hadeeth* does not provide indisputable knowledge (*dhannee ath-thuboot*).

This view, although representing the majority opinion, is not necessarily the correct one. Ash-Shanqeetee discusses this question in detail,[516] and concludes that an *ahaad hadeeth* can abrogate the Qur'aan, although such an occurrence is rare. He does give the condition, however, that it must be known for certain that the *ahaad* narration occurred after the revelation of the verse. An example of this, according to ash-Shanqeetee, is the prohibition of the flesh of domesticated donkeys, for it is known that this occurred during the Battle of Khaybar, and as such 'abrogated' the previous ruling that it was allowed (by the understanding of 16:45).[517]

Imaam ash-Shaafi'ee (d. 204 A.H.) did not allow the Qur'aan to abrogate the *Sunnah*, nor the *Sunnah* to abrogate the Qur'aan. He felt the Qur'aan could only abrogate the Qur'aan, and the same with the *Sunnah*.

4) The *Sunnah* abrogating the *Sunnah*.

This was also allowed by all those who upheld the validity of *naskh*. This category may be further subdivided into four categories:

---

515 Reported by Aboo Daawood.
516 ash-Shanqeetee, pps. 36-44. Also see al-Albaanee's comments on this *hadeeth* in *Ahkaam al-Jana'aiz*, p. 7, where he states that an *ahaad hadeeth* can abrogate the Qur'aan.
517 ash-Shanqeetee, p. 39.

i) A *mutawaatir hadeeth* abrogating another *mutawaatir hadeeth*.

ii) An *ahaad hadeeth* abrogating another *ahaad hadeeth*.

iii) An *mutawaatir hadeeth* abrogating an *ahaad hadeeth*.

iv) An *ahaad hadeeth* abrogating a *mutawaatir hadeeth*.

The first three categories are agreed upon by all scholars. The last category, that of an *ahaad hadeeth* abrogating a *mutawaatir* one, is held by those who allow an *ahaad hadeeth* to abrogate the Qur'aan (such as ash-Shanqeetee). The majority, however, do not allow the occurrence of the fourth category.

B. The Verse and Ruling in the Qur'aan

With respect to verses in the Qur'aan, it is possible that either the recitation of the verse, or the ruling, or both, have been abrogated. As was alluded to in earlier chapters, there existed verses that used to be recited as part of the Qur'aan, but whose recitation was later abrogated at the command of Allaah. Some of these abrogated verses dealt with legal rulings.

Thus, (with respect to the Qur'aan only, and not the *Sunnah*) *naskh* may be classified as follows:

1) The Abrogation of the Ruling and the Verse (*Naskh al-Hukm wa at-Tilaawah*).

In other words, neither is the verse present in the *mus-haf*, nor is its ruling applied. An example of this type is the report of 'Aa'ishah, in which she said, "It had been revealed in the Qur'aan that ten clear sucklings (of a baby with a woman) made marriage unlawful (i.e., that the baby would be considered her foster-child). This was later abrogated (and substituted) by five sucklings, and the Prophet (ﷺ) died and it was before that time (found) in the Qur'aan."[518] In this case, neither is the relevant verse found in the *mus-haf*, nor is the ruling applicable.[519]

2) The Abrogation of the Ruling without the Verse (*Naskh al-Hukm doona at-Tilaawah*).

When this occurs, the relevant verse is still recited and is present in the *mus-haf*, but the ruling does not apply. An example of this is the verse prescribing the waiting period of one year for the widow (2:240). Even though this ruling does not apply any

---

518 Reported by Muslim. This does not mean that the verse had been accidentally left out of the *mus-haf*, but rather that it was abrogated only a short time before the Prophet (ﷺ) died (cf. Qattaan, p. 238). Some scholars (such as Mustafa Zayd) have rejected this narration, claiming that it is *ahaad* (since only 'Aa'ishah narrated it), and in order for a verse of the Qur'aan to be accepted, it must be narrated in a *mutawaatir hadeeth*. This may be refuted, however, by saying that the *hadeeth* is *saheeh*, as it is reported in Muslim, Muwatta, Aboo Daawood and at-Tirmidhee; and also that 'Aa'ishah is not reporting a verse from the Qur'aan (which needs a *mutawaatir* transmission) but rather an incident of *naskh*, and this does not need *mutawaatir* transmissions.

519 Although there is a difference of opinion regarding the minimum number of sucklings that are required to prohibit marriage. Some scholars say five, based on this *hadeeth*, whereas others say three or even one. In any case, the verse that initially prescribed ten sucklings can be taken as an example of this category.

more, the verse is still recited as part of the Qur'aan.

Another example is the verse that initially prescribed the punishment for fornication,

$$وَٱلَّٰتِى يَأۡتِينَ ٱلۡفَٰحِشَةَ مِن نِّسَآئِكُمۡ فَٱسۡتَشۡهِدُواْ
عَلَيۡهِنَّ أَرۡبَعَةٗ مِّنكُمۡۖ فَإِن شَهِدُواْ فَأَمۡسِكُوهُنَّ فِى
ٱلۡبُيُوتِ حَتَّىٰ يَتَوَفَّىٰهُنَّ ٱلۡمَوۡتُ أَوۡ يَجۡعَلَ ٱللَّهُ لَهُنَّ سَبِيلٗا$$

> «And those of your women who commit illegal sexual intercourse, take the
> evidence of four witnesses amongst you against them. If they testify, then
> confine them to their houses until death overtakes them, or until Allaah
> ordains for them some (other) way» [4:15]

This verse was abrogated by the verses in *Soorah* an-Noor,

$$ٱلزَّانِيَةُ وَٱلزَّانِى فَٱجۡلِدُواْ كُلَّ وَٰحِدٖ مِّنۡهُمَا مِاْئَةَ جَلۡدَةٖ$$

> «The (unmarried) women and man guilty of illegal sexual intercourse –
> flog each of them with a hundred stripes...» [24:2]

3) The Abrogation of the Verse without the Ruling (*Naskh at-Tilaawah doona al-Hukm*).

In this case, Allaah removed the verse from the Qur'aan but left the relevant ruling. For example, a verse in the Qur'aan used to order those who had committed adultery to be stoned to death. In reference to this verse, 'Umar ibn al-Khattaab said, while giving a sermon in the Prophet's (⿸) mosque, "Verily, Allaah sent Muhammad (⿸) with the truth, and He sent the Book down upon him. The verse of stoning was revealed with it, we recited it, memorised it, and understood it. The Prophet (⿸) awarded the punishment of stoning to death (to the married adulterers), and after him, we also did the same. I am afraid that with the lapse of time, people (may forget it and) say, 'We do not find the punishment of stoning in the Book of Allaah,'[520] and go astray by abandoning this duty prescribed by Allaah. Stoning is a duty laid down in Allaah's book for married men and women who commit adultery when proof is established."[521] In fact, even the wording of the verse of stoning has been preserved in other authentic narrations, "*Wa ash-shaykhu wa-shaykhatu idha zanayaa farjumoohum al-batha nakaala min Allaah...*"[522] meaning, "And the married man or woman, if they commit adultery, then stone them as a retribution of from Allaah." Another narration

---

520 This author recalls a lecture he attended in America a few years ago. The speaker, obviously not very knowledgeable, said in a gathering of Muslims and non-Muslims, "And as for this concept that certain people have that in Islaam you have to *stone* people to death for certain crimes, *hah!* It's not found in the Qur'aan! Its all culture mixed with Islaam!" How true was 'Umar, may Allaah reward him!

521 Reported by al-Bukhaaree and Muslim. In another narration, 'Umar said, "Were it not for the fear that people would accuse me of adding to the Book of Allaah, I would have written the verse with my own hands!"

522 Reported by at-Tabaarani and others. cf. Ibn Hazm, p. 9.

clearly shows the fact that the recitation of this verse was abrogated. 'Umar ibn al-Khattaab narrated, "I once came to the Prophet (ﷺ), and the verse pertaining to stoning was mentioned. I asked the Prophet (ﷺ), "O Messenger of Allaah! Dictate to me the verse, so that I may write it!" The Prophet (ﷺ) responded, "No, I cannot do this anymore,"[523] meaning that he was not allowed to do so anymore. This narration is explicit in the abrogation of the verse.

There are also references to a number of verses not related to commands and prohibitions whose recitation was abrogated. An example of this are those verses revealed with regards to the martyrs of the 'Well of Ma'oonah'.

A group of disbelievers posed as Muslims, and came to the Prophet (ﷺ), requesting him to send them some teachers. The Prophet (ﷺ) sent them seventy Companions to teach them the Qur'aan and other aspects related to the religion. When the Companions left with this group, they were massacred by the disbelievers. In response to this incident, Anas ibn Maalik reported, "Allaah revealed verses of the Qur'aan concerning them (the martyrs): 'Tell our people that we have met our Lord, and He is pleased with us, and we are pleased with Him.' This was then abrogated after we had been reciting it for a while, and (instead) Allaah then revealed,

$$ وَلَا تَحْسَبَنَّ ٱلَّذِينَ قُتِلُوا۟ فِى سَبِيلِ ٱللَّهِ أَمْوَٰتًا $$

«Do not presume that those who have died in the way of Allaah are dead...»»[3:169].[524]

This report is explicit in that there existed verses that were recited in prayer, and whose recitation was later abrogated. This report also shows that the Companions understood and were familiar with the concept of *naskh*.

Another report of this nature is by Ubay ibn Ka'ab. He stated, "We used to consider the verse, 'If the son of Aadam had two valleys of gold, he would wish for a third, for nothing will ever fill the belly of Aadam's son except dust, and Allaah forgives him who repents,' as a part of the Qur'aan. However, (the recitation of this verse was abrogated) by the revelation of *Soorah* at-Takaathur."[525]

Even though the above 'verse' was abrogated as being part of the Qur'aan, it still remained a statement of the Prophet (ﷺ), and is found in many collections of *hadeeth*.[526] Ubay ibn Ka'ab also reported, "*Soorah* al-Ahzaab used to be equal (in length) to *Soorah* al-Baqarah, or even longer."[527] This implies that there existed many verses whose recitation had been abrogated, as the *Soorah* al-Ahzaab that is present in today's *mushaf* is less than a fourth of *Soorah* al-Baqarah.

---

523 Reported by al-Bayhaqee and others. cf. *as-Saheehah*, v. 6, p. 975.
524 al-Malbaaree, p. 113.
525 Narrated by at-Tahaawee in his *Sharh Mushkil Athaar*.
526 For example, in al-Bukhaaree, Muslim, *Musnad* of Ahmad, at-Tirmidhee and others.
527 Reported by Ibn Hibbaan.

Lastly, there are also reports which explicitly show the occurrence of *naskh*, and the total obliteration of the abrogated verse. Aboo Umaamah ibn Sahl reported that a person had memorised a certain *soorah*, so he tried to recite it in prayer one night, but was unable to. In the morning, he went to the Prophet (ﷺ) and found two people also waiting for him. When the Prophet (ﷺ) came, he asked, "O Messenger of Allaah (ﷺ)! I tried to recite such-and-such a *soorah* last night, but could not do so!" At this, the second man said, "I also came because of the same reason!" and the third, "And I too!" The Prophet (ﷺ) explained, "It was abrogated last night,"[528] meaning that they had been caused to forget the relevant verses. In this report, it is clear that divine intervention caused these Companions who had memorised the verses to forget them, thus abrogating even the memory of the verse! This narration also shows that the Prophet (ﷺ) was informed by Allaah whenever a verse was abrogated, since he (ﷺ) knew that these particular verses had been abrogated the night before.

C. The Rulings of the Naasikh and Mansookh

The *naasikh* ruling might be a concession from the *mansookh*, or it might be one that requires more effort. With respect to the degree of difficulty of the rulings, the rulings of *naasikh* and *mansookh* may be divided into four categories:

1) The *naasikh* ruling is more difficult or more constrained than the *mansookh*.

An example of this are the rulings pertaining to adultery. Initially, the punishment for both married and unmarried illegal sexual intercourse was lifelong imprisonment (cf., 4:15). Allaah then revealed the verses of flogging for the unmarried and stoning for the married persons (cf., 24:2).

2) The *naasikh* ruling is equivalent to the *mansookh* ruling in difficulty.

For example, the verses that were revealed concerning the change of the *qiblah* from Jerusalem to Makkah; in this case, the *naasikh* ruling is equivalent to the *mansookh* in effort.

3) The *naasikh* ruling is a concession from the *mansookh*.

In this case, the *naasikh* ruling was easier for the Muslims than the *mansookh*. An example that has already been quoted is with regards to the waiting period of widows; it was reduced from one year to four month and ten days. Another example that was mentioned is with regards to the prohibition of fleeing from the battlefield when the ratio of Muslims to non-Muslims was 1 to 10; this was later abrogated and the ratio reduced to one Muslim for every two non-Muslims.

Another example is the procedure of fasting. Initially, fasting was prescribed

---

528 Reported by at-Tahaawee. There is a difference of opinion whether Aboo Umamah actually narrated from the Prophet (ﷺ). However, since he saw the Prophet (ﷺ), he is considered a Companion, and thus the *hadeeth* is considered authentic (cf. *Tahzeeb al-Kamaal*, v. 2, # 403). In any case, at-Tahaawee also brings another narration (v. 5, p. 272) which mentions a Companion between Aboo Umaamah and the Prophet (ﷺ), so the incident is authentic, *Inshaa Allaah*.

$$كَمَا كُتِبَ عَلَى الَّذِينَ مِن قَبْلِكُمْ$$

«...as it was prescribed for those before you...» [2:183]

This meant, as per the laws of the previous nations, that a Muslim could not eat, drink or have intercourse after he had prayed the evening prayer ('Ishaa), or gone to sleep at night. After this, Allaah revealed,

$$أُحِلَّ لَكُمْ لَيْلَةَ الصِّيَامِ الرَّفَثُ إِلَى نِسَآئِكُمْ هُنَّ لِبَاسٌ لَّكُمْ وَأَنتُمْ لِبَاسٌ لَّهُنَّ عَلِمَ اللَّهُ أَنَّكُمْ كُنتُمْ تَخْتَانُونَ أَنفُسَكُمْ فَتَابَ عَلَيْكُمْ وَعَفَا عَنكُمْ$$

«It is now lawful for you to have sexual relations with your wife on the night of the fast... Allaah knows that you used to deceive yourselves (by having relations with them), so He has turned to you and accepted (your repentance)» [2:187]

Therefore, a Muslim may eat, drink or have sexual relations until dawn.

4) There is no *naasikh* command in place of the *mansookh*.

In other words, Allaah repealed the law *in toto*. An example of this is the command to give charity before going to see the Prophet (ﷺ) privately. Allaah revealed,

$$يَٰٓأَيُّهَا الَّذِينَ ءَامَنُوٓاْ إِذَا نَٰجَيْتُمُ الرَّسُولَ فَقَدِّمُواْ بَيْنَ يَدَىْ نَجْوَىٰكُمْ صَدَقَةً$$

«O you who believe! When you want to consult the Messenger in private, spend something in charity before your private consultation» [58:12]

Allaah then repealed this law totally,

$$ءَأَشْفَقْتُمْ أَن تُقَدِّمُواْ بَيْنَ يَدَىْ نَجْوَىٰكُمْ صَدَقَٰتٍ فَإِذْ لَمْ تَفْعَلُواْ وَتَابَ اللَّهُ عَلَيْكُمْ فَأَقِيمُواْ الصَّلَوٰةَ$$

«Are you afraid of spending in charity before your private consultations? If you do not do it, *and Allaah has forgiven you (for not doing it)*, then (at least) offer prayers perfectly...» [58:13]

Therefore Allaah forgave this charity from them, and they were not required to do it.

v. The Blessings of Naskh

With respect to the Qur'aan, there are two types of *naskh* that occurred. There is a general *naskh*, in which the Qur'aan abrogated the previous scriptures that were revealed to other nations, and there is the specific *naskh*, in which some verses of the Qur'aan abrogated others. It is the second category that has been the discussion of this chapter so far. However, both of these types of *naskh* have benefits behind them.

Benefits of the General Naskh

From the beginning of time, Allaah has revealed to mankind a general code of beliefs and set of laws that would guide them to a better life in this world, and provide for them an everlasting life in the Hereafter. The most important of these messages, and one that has remained a constant theme for all the prophets, is that of the One-ness of Allaah (*tawheed*):

$$وَلَقَدْ بَعَثْنَا فِى كُلِّ أُمَّةٍ رَّسُولًا أَنِ اعْبُدُواْ اللَّهَ وَاجْتَنِبُواْ الطَّاغُوتَ$$

«And verily, We have sent among every nation a Messenger, (saying), 'Worship Allaah alone, and avoid all false deities...'» [16:36]

Included with the belief of *tawheed* was the belief in messengers (*risalaah*), and belief in the Day of Judgement (*aakhirah*). These fundamentals of belief, or *'aqeedah*, remained unchanged for all prophets and messengers, in all times and places.

However, as a manifestation of Allaah's mercy, mankind was not left without guidance in its social and political life. Rather, their Creator provided for them a set of laws that would govern them in their mutual affairs, and instruct them concerning all that was beneficial for them, and warn against all that was harmful to them. These code of laws varied from time to time, and from place to place, for each set of peoples had their own specific problems and peculiar situations that needed to be catered to. Allaah says,

$$وَلِكُلِّ أُمَّةٍ جَعَلْنَا مَنسَكًا لِيَذْكُرُواْ اسْمَ اللَّهِ$$

«And for every nation, We appointed (their) religious ceremonies, so that they may mention the Name of Allaah...» [22:34]

Since each prophet was sent to a different nation, it was possible for one messenger to abrogate the laws of a previous messenger.

$$وَمُصَدِّقًا لِمَا بَيْنَ يَدَىَّ مِنَ التَّوْرَاةِ وَلِأُحِلَّ لَكُم بَعْضَ الَّذِى حُرِّمَ عَلَيْكُمْ$$

«(And 'Eesaa said to his people) I have come confirming that which was before me of the Torah, *and to make lawful for you part of what had been forbidden to you*...» [3:50]

In other words, the laws that 'Eesaa came with were meant to abrogate the laws of Moosaa.

With the coming of the religion of Islaam, however, all previous laws and religions were abrogated:

$$وَمَن يَبْتَغِ غَيْرَ الْإِسْلَامِ دِينًا فَلَن يُقْبَلَ مِنْهُ$$

«And whoever seeks a religion other than Islaam, it will never be accepted from him» [3:85]

The role and status of the Qur'aan with respect to other religions is made clear in the following verse:

$$\text{وَأَنزَلْنَآ إِلَيْكَ ٱلْكِتَٰبَ}$$

$$\text{بِٱلْحَقِّ مُصَدِّقًا لِّمَا بَيْنَ يَدَيْهِ مِنَ ٱلْكِتَٰبِ وَمُهَيْمِنًا عَلَيْهِ}$$

«And We have sent down to you (O Muḥammad) the Book in truth, confirming the Scripture that came before it, and a *muhaymin* over it» [5:48]

The word '*muhaymin*' means that the Qur'aan is a witness over the previous scriptures, so that all that conforms with it from the previous scriptures is accepted, and all that contradicts it is rejected. The Qur'aan, therefore, acts as a *naasikh* agent over the previous scriptures, which are *mansookh* when they conflict with the Qur'aan.[529]

This is one of the greatest blessings of the Qur'aan, for it shows that it is the most complete Book (since nothing can abrogate the Qur'aan after it), and that it is superior to all other Scriptures (since it abrogates all previous Books). It also demonstrates the superiority of the *ummah* of the Prophet (ﷺ) over all other nations, since the set of laws that have been revealed to it are perfect for all and suitable for all nations, at all times. This is in contrast to all other laws, which were only meant for a specific nation, at a specific time.

Benefits of the Specific Naskh

With regards to the specific *naskh* of the Qur'aan, this too has many benefits to it. Makkee ibn Abee Ṭaalib (d. 437 A.H.) stated,

> And this (meaning *naskh*) is from Allaah, and is meant to be for the betterment of His worshippers. So, He commands them with a ruling at a specific time, since He knows that it will be for their betterment for that particular time, but He already knows that this command will be removed from them at a later time, since at this later time that particular ruling will not be for their benefit.[530]

These principles are clearly laid down in the following verse:

$$\text{يَأْمُرُهُم بِٱلْمَعْرُوفِ وَيَنْهَىٰهُمْ}$$

$$\text{عَنِ ٱلْمُنكَرِ وَيُحِلُّ لَهُمُ ٱلطَّيِّبَٰتِ وَيُحَرِّمُ عَلَيْهِمُ}$$

$$\text{ٱلْخَبَٰٓئِثَ}$$

«He (meaning Muḥammad) commands them with all that is honourable and good, and forbids them from all that is evil and immoral; he allows for them all that is pure and beneficial, and prohibits for them all that is evil and harmful...» [7:157]

---

529 cf. *Tafseer Ibn Katheer* on this verse.
530 an-Nahaas, p. 116.

Thus, every case of *naskh* is for the betterment of mankind. As Allaah says,

$$مَا نَنسَخْ مِنْ ءَايَةٍ أَوْ نُنسِهَا نَأْتِ بِخَيْرٍ مِّنْهَا أَوْ مِثْلِهَا ۗ$$

$$أَلَمْ تَعْلَمْ أَنَّ ٱللَّهَ عَلَىٰ كُلِّ شَىْءٍ قَدِيرٌ ۝$$

> «We do not abrogate a ruling, or cause it to be forgotten, except that We substitute in its place *something better than it, or similar to it*. Are you unaware that Allaah is indeed capable of all things?» [2:106]

Each type of *naskh* that was discussed in the previous section has its benefits. As for the abrogation of the ruling without any replacing ruling, or with a lighter ruling, the benefit in this is obvious, in that it lightens the burden of worship, and is a manifestation of the Mercy of Allaah. As Allaah says,

$$يُرِيدُ ٱللَّهُ أَن يُخَفِّفَ عَنكُمْ$$

> «Allaah wishes to lighten (the burden) on you...» [4:28]

and,

$$ٱلْـَٔـٰنَ خَفَّفَ ٱللَّهُ عَنكُمْ$$

> «Now has Allaah made it easier for you...» [8:66]

If the *naasikh* ruling is equivalent to or more difficult than the *mansookh*, this is a means of testing the believers so that

$$لِيَمِيزَ ٱللَّهُ ٱلْخَبِيثَ مِنَ ٱلطَّيِّبِ$$

> «...Allaah may discern the filthy from the pure...» [8:37]

Also, if the *naasikh* is more difficult, the rewards for that particular deed will also multiply. It should be remembered that what might seem like something difficult to us might in fact be beneficial to us or to the Muslims.

$$وَعَسَىٰٓ أَن تَكْرَهُوا$$

$$شَيْـًٔا وَهُوَ خَيْرٌ لَّكُمْ ۖ وَعَسَىٰٓ أَن تُحِبُّوا شَيْـًٔا وَهُوَ شَرٌّ لَّكُمْ ۗ$$

$$وَٱللَّهُ يَعْلَمُ وَأَنتُمْ لَا تَعْلَمُونَ$$

> «And it is possible that you detest something, even though it is beneficial for you. And it is possible that you love something, even though it is harmful for you. And Allaah knows, and you do not know» [2:216]

Thus, the stoning of the married adulterer might be a hardship for him, but it serves as a very severe deterrent for others, and a betterment for society.

As for the abrogation of a ruling without the recitation of the verse, this is a reminder from Allaah to the believers of His blessings, so that they may thank Him for

His Mercy. This verse is also a blessing to recite, for the recitation of each letter gives the reward of ten. If the recitation of the verse was also abrogated, this is another indication of the Mercy of Allaah, since He allowed the believers to implement the *Sharee'ah* in a gradual manner, so that it would not be a great burden on them.

As for the abrogation of the recitation of a verse without its ruling, this is another type of test from Allaah, to see if a believer has faith in the Messenger (ﷺ), since the ruling will then come from the *Sunnah*, and not the Qur'aan. Thus, the believer must truly believe in the Prophet (ﷺ), and follow the Qur'aan and his (ﷺ) *Sunnah* in order to be successful.

VI. The Benefits of Knowing Naasikh and Mansookh

From all the examples that have been given, it is apparent that this knowledge is an essential one. Some of the benefits of knowing *naasikh* and *mansookh* are:

1) To understand and implement the Qur'aan properly.

Without knowing which verses are abrogated, a person might apply those verses that are not meant to be applied. This is why the scholars of Islaam were very concerned in preserving this knowledge. Once, 'Alee ibn Abee Taalib passed by a judge and asked him, "Do you know the *naasikh* from the *mansookh*?" The judge replied that he did not. 'Alee then told him, "You are destroyed (because you are judging between people while you are not qualified to do so) and you destroy other people (because you give them rulings that are incorrect)."[531] And Ibn 'Abbaas explained the verse,

وَمَن يُؤْتَ ٱلْحِكْمَةَ فَقَدْ أُوتِىَ خَيْرًا كَثِيرًا

«And whoever has been blessed with wisdom has indeed been given a great blessing» [2:269],

by saying, " (Wisdom is in knowing) the *naasikh* from the *mansookh*, the *muhkam* from the *mutashaabih*, the earlier (revelations) from the later (ones), and the *haraam* from the *halaal*."[532]

It can be seen from the examples that were given in the previous section that a person is obliged to know the *naasikh* from the *mansookh* if he wishes to derive laws from the Qur'aan and *Sunnah*. It should come as no surprise, therefore, that this knowledge is one of the conditions for a person to be an interpreter of the Qur'aan (*mufassir*), or scholar (*mujtahid*). Imaam ash-Shaafi'ee (d. 204 A.H.) said,

"It is impermissible for any person to give verdicts concerning the religion of Allaah, unless he is knowledgeable of the Book of Allaah, and its *naasikh* from its *mansookh*, and its *muhkam* from its *mutashaabih*, and its interpretation, and its process of revelation, and its *makkee* from its *madanee*,

531 Ibn Hazm, p. 5
532 Qattaan, p.234

and its *asbaab an-nuzool*. In addition to this, he must be knowledgeable of the *Sunnah*..."[533]

2) The knowledge of the gradual revelation of the *sharee'ah*.

Allaah revealed the laws of Islaam gradually, so that it would be easier for the Muslims to implement the new religion. By knowing the *naasikh* from the *mansookh*, a Muslim can appreciate the blessings that were given to this *ummah* in this gradual revelation. Also, it increases one's belief (*eemaan*) in Allaah, as it demonstrates to him some aspects of the infinite Wisdom and Knowledge of Allaah.

3) The defence of the Qur'aan and *Sunnah*.

The concept of *naskh* has been used by the enemies of Islaam (in particular, Orientalists and the 'Muslim' scholars that have been influenced by them) to ridicule and mock the religion, and to try to show contradictions and discrepancies in the *sharee'ah*. Thus, it is essential that Muslims understand and appreciate the concept of *naskh*, so that they are not deceived by the distortions and misinterpretations of those who seek to destroy Islaam.

VII. The Difference Between Naskh and Takhsees

The phenomenon of *takhsees* ('specification') was mentioned at the beginning of this chapter. It is essential that the concept of *naskh* not be confused with that of *takhsees*, and for this reason many scholars of *'uloom al-Qur'aan* included in their works the differences between *naskh* and *takhsees*.

Takhsees is defined to be the specification of a general ruling (*'aam*), such that what seems to be a general ruling only applies in certain cases. For example, the Qur'aan orders the amputation of the hand of the thief,

$$ وَٱلسَّارِقُ وَٱلسَّارِقَةُ فَٱقْطَعُوٓاْ أَيْدِيَهُمَا $$

«And the thief – male or female – cut off their hand» [5:38]

The verse is general (*'aam*), and implies that the hand of every thief must be cut. The Prophet (ﷺ), however, qualified that the thief in this case must steal above a certain monetary value. If he stole below this value, this ruling will not apply to him. Therefore, the Prophet (ﷺ) specified the general ruling of the verse. This, then, is an example of *takhsees*: the hand of every thief will not be cut; only those thieves who steal above a certain monetary value are punished.

Naskh differs from *takhsees* in the following manners:[534]

1) *Naskh* may only occur with regards to laws and rulings (*ahkaam*). *Takhsees*, on the other hand, may occur with respect to other matters. For example, Allaah says,

---

533 an-Nahaas, p. 124.
534 ash-Shanqeetee, p. 34.

$$ وَٱلْعَصْرِ ۝ إِنَّ ٱلْإِنسَـٰنَ لَفِى خُسْرٍ ۝ إِلَّا ٱلَّذِينَ ءَامَنُواْ $$
$$ وَعَمِلُواْ ٱلصَّـٰلِحَـٰتِ وَتَوَاصَوْاْ بِٱلْحَقِّ وَتَوَاصَوْاْ بِٱلصَّبْرِ ۝ $$

«By the time! All of mankind is in a loss. Except those who believe, and do righteous deeds, and exhort one another in truth, and exhort one another in patience» [103:1-3]

The second verse is general (*'aam*), implying that all of mankind will be in loss. The last verse, however, is an example of *takhsees*, since it qualifies those of mankind who are not in a loss.

2) *Naskh* implies a total abandonment of the previous ruling, no matter what the case. *Takhsees*, on the other hand, is defined to be the implementation of a previous ruling in only some of the original cases. In other words, after a *takhsees* occurs, the ruling is not totally invalid, but rather valid in a narrower frame. Therefore, the *mansookh* cannot be applied after the *naasikh* is revealed, but the rulings of *'aam* still apply after the *takhsees*.

3) The *naasikh* must be revealed after the *mansookh*, whereas there is no such time restriction on *takhsees*.

4) *Naskh* only occurs with respect to the Qur'aan or the *Sunnah*. *Takhsees*, on the other hand, may apply to Qur'aan, *Sunnah*, *ijmaa'*, or *qiyaas*. Also, the *naasikh* ruling may only come from the Qur'aan or *Sunnah*, whereas *takhsees* may be based on common sense or *ijtihaad*.

VIII. The Number of Naasikh/Mansookh Verses in the Qur'aan

The scholars of Islaam have differed greatly with regards to the number of verses in the Qur'aan that are *mansookh*. (It should be pointed out that the difference of opinion is concerning those verses whose recitation has *not* been abrogated, and are still found in the *mus-haf*. As for those verses whose *recitation* has been abrogated, there is no means of ascertaining their exact number, since many of them have been abrogated even from memory.)

Some of the various opinions are given in *Table A*.

The names of the scholars are listed according to the number of cases that were considered as candidates for *naskh*. What is meant by 'Candidates for *naskh*' are the number of verses which were discussed by that author as being *possible* to be considered as examples of *naskh*. The second column gives the number of *naskh* cases that were actually concluded by the author as being *legitimate* examples. Thus, for example, Ibn al-'Arabee discusses around three-hundred verses which could be considered as examples for *naskh*. However, of these many verses, he concludes that only a little over a third are actual cases of *naskh*; the rest of the examples are shown by him not to be examples of *naskh*.

Scholar	Number of Verses as Candidates for *Naskh*	Number of Verses Concluded are *Naskh*
Aboo Bakr ibn al-'Arabee (d. 543 A.H.)	297 cases	105 cases
Mustafa Zayd	283 cases	6 cases
Ibn al-Jawzee (d. 597 A.H.)	247 cases	22 cases
Ibn Hazm (d. 456 A.H.)	214 cases	all
Makkee ibn Abee Taalib (d. 437 A.H.)	200 cases	-
Aboo Ja'far an-Nahaas (d. 338 A.H.)	134 cases	20 cases
az-Zarqaani	22 cases	12 cases
as-Suyooti (d. 911 A.H.)	21 cases	20 cases
ash-Shanqeeti	7 cases	all
Walee Allaah ad-Dehlawi (d. 1176 A.H.)	5 cases	all

Table B   The Number of Cases of *Naskh*

It can be seen from this table[535] that there is a very wide difference of opinion regarding the exact number of cases of *naskh* in the Qur'aan. The opinions range from 214 for Ibn Hazm, all the way down to only five for ad-Dehlawee.

The reason that such a diverse opinion exists is that many verses are considered examples of *naskh*, when in fact they are examples of *takhsees*, or do not fall under *naskh* at all. In particular, with regards to those who have over a hundred examples of *naskh*, they all consider the 'Verse of the Sword' as having abrogated dozens of verses.

The 'Verse of the Sword'

The 'Verse of the Sword' is the verse that gave permission for the Muslims to fight the disbelievers wherever they were:

---

535 This table was compiled from ash-Shanqeetee, pps. 93-94; Madgharee, pps. 230-32; an-Nahhaas' work; and al-Malbaaree's work. It should be noted that most authors did not give a specific conclusion for some verses. In those cases, such verses were included in the first column of the table, but not in the second.

$$فَإِذَا ٱنسَلَخَ ٱلْأَشْهُرُ ٱلْحُرُمُ$$

$$فَٱقْتُلُوا۟ ٱلْمُشْرِكِينَ حَيْثُ وَجَدتُّمُوهُمْ وَخُذُوهُمْ وَٱحْصُرُوهُمْ$$

$$وَٱقْعُدُوا۟ لَهُمْ كُلَّ مَرْصَدٍ$$

«Then, when the Sacred Months have elapsed, kill the polytheists wherever
you find them, and capture them, and besiege them, and prepare for them
each and every ambush...» [9:5]

This was one of the last verses to be revealed, and perhaps the last verse that dealt
with the treatment of the disbelievers. According to the scholars that have over a hundred cases of *naskh*, any verse that had commanded any type of treatment with the
disbelievers before this verse was revealed was 'abrogated' by this verse. For example,
with Ibn al-'Arabee, of the 105 cases that he stated are examples of *naskh*, no less than
75 were '*mansookh*' by the 'Verse of the Sword'! The majority of Ibn Ḥazm's cases are
also considered to be *mansookh* because of this verse.

In a masters dissertation specifically on this topic,[536] 'Uthmaan 'Alee discusses 147
verses that have been claimed to have been abrogated by the 'Verse of the Sword,' and
concludes that only five of them can actually be said to be abrogated. He gives a useful
categorisation of the types of verses that have been claimed to have been abrogated by
the 'Verse of the Sword'. The main categories are:

1) Those verses which are statements of fact; for example,

$$وَقُولُوا۟ لِلنَّاسِ حُسْنًا$$

«And say good speech to mankind...» [2:83]

2) Those verses which give warnings and threats to the disbelievers; for example,

$$قُلْ يَٰقَوْمِ$$

$$ٱعْمَلُوا۟ عَلَىٰ مَكَانَتِكُمْ إِنِّي عَامِلٌ فَسَوْفَ تَعْلَمُونَ$$

$$مَن تَكُونُ لَهُۥ عَٰقِبَةُ ٱلدَّارِ إِنَّهُۥ لَا يُفْلِحُ ٱلظَّٰلِمُونَ$$

«Say: O my people! Do your work according to how you do it, surely, I too
am working. Surely, you will come to know for which of us will be the (happy)
end in the Hereafter. Certainly the wrong-doers will not be successful»
[6:135]

3) Those verses which command the believers to turn away from the evil treatment
of the disbelievers, and to deal with them peacefully; for example,

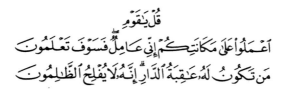

---

536 'Alee, 'Uthmaan Mu'alim Maḥmood: *al-Ayaat al-Muda'ee Naskhuha bi Aayat aṣ-Ṣayf*, Masters Diss.,
Islaamic University of Madeenah, 1992.

«So leave (the disbelievers) to speak nonsense, and play around, until they meet their Day which they have been promised» [43:83]

and,

خُذِ ٱلْعَفْوَ وَأْمُرْ بِٱلْعُرْفِ وَأَعْرِضْ عَنِ ٱلْجَٰهِلِينَ ۝

«Show forgiveness, enjoin what is good, and turn away from the foolish» [7:199]

4) Those verses which command the believers to be patient; for example,

فَٱصْبِرْ عَلَىٰ مَا يَقُولُونَ

«So bear patiently what they say...» [20:130]

5) Those verses which remind the Prophet (ﷺ) that his only duty is to spread the message; for example,

قُلْ أَطِيعُواْ ٱللَّهَ وَأَطِيعُواْ ٱلرَّسُولَ فَإِن تَوَلَّوْاْ فَإِنَّمَا عَلَيْهِ مَا حُمِّلَ وَعَلَيْكُم مَّا حُمِّلْتُمْ وَإِن تُطِيعُوهُ تَهْتَدُواْ وَمَا عَلَى ٱلرَّسُولِ إِلَّا ٱلْبَلَٰغُ ٱلْمُبِينُ ۝

«Say: Obey Allaah and obey the Messenger. But if you turn away, he (i.e., Muhammad (ﷺ)) is only responsible for the duty placed upon him (i.e., to convey the message), and you (are responsible) for that which is placed upon you. If you obey him, you shall be on the right guidance. The Messenger's duty is only to convey (the message) in a clear way» [24:54]

6) Those verses which command the believers to return an evil with a similar evil, and to fight only in self-defence; for example,

وَقَٰتِلُواْ فِى سَبِيلِ ٱللَّهِ ٱلَّذِينَ يُقَٰتِلُونَكُمْ وَلَا تَعْتَدُواْ

«And fight in the way of Allaah those who fight against you, but do not transgress the limits...» [2:190]

7) Those verses which command the believers to respect the treaties that they had with the disbelievers; for example,

فَإِن تَوَلَّوْاْ فَخُذُوهُمْ وَٱقْتُلُوهُمْ حَيْثُ وَجَدتُّمُوهُمْ وَلَا تَتَّخِذُواْ مِنْهُمْ وَلِيًّا وَلَا نَصِيرًا ۝ إِلَّا ٱلَّذِينَ يَصِلُونَ إِلَىٰ قَوْمٍ بَيْنَكُمْ وَبَيْنَهُم مِّيثَٰقٌ

«...but if they turn back, then take hold of them, and kill them wherever you find them, and do not take helpers or allies from them. Except those who join a group, between you and whom there is a treaty (of peace)...» [4:89-90]

It can be seen from the examples and categories quoted that, in reality, most of these verses cannot be considered to have been abrogated in the least. Some of them merely apply to situations other than those that they were revealed for. Almost all of these 'mansookh' verses can still be said to apply when the Muslims are in a situation similar to the situation in which these verses were revealed. Thus, the 'Verse of the Sword' in reality does not abrogate a large number of verses; in fact, az-Zarqaanee concludes that it does not abrogate *any* verse![537]

Another reason why there exists such a difference of opinion is that many scholars failed to understand the meaning of the word 'naskh' when used by a Companion or Successor. As was mentioned earlier, for them, the word 'naskh' did not necessarily mean abrogation. For example, Ibn 'Abbaas stated that the verse,

$$\text{قُلِ ٱلْأَنفَالُ لِلَّهِ وَٱلرَّسُولِ}$$

«The spoils of war are for Allaah and His Messenger» [8:1]

was 'abrogated' by,

$$\text{وَٱعْلَمُوٓاْ أَنَّمَا غَنِمْتُم مِّن شَىْءٍ فَأَنَّ لِلَّهِ خُمُسَهُۥ وَلِلرَّسُولِ}$$

«And know that all war-booty that you obtain – one-fifth is for Allaah and His Messenger...» [8:41]

However, this is a perfect example of *takhsees*, for the second verse clarifies how much of 'the spoils of war' are to be given to the state.

Yet another reason for this difference of opinion is that many verses are understood to be *mansookh* but in reality are not. For example, many scholars stated that the verse,

$$\text{وَلِلَّهِ ٱلْمَشْرِقُ وَٱلْمَغْرِبُ فَأَيْنَمَا تُوَلُّواْ فَثَمَّ وَجْهُ ٱللَّهِ}$$

«And to Allaah belongs the east and west. So wherever you turn (in prayer), you will find the Face of Allaah» [2:115]

was abrogated by the verse which commands the believers to face Makkah (verse 2:149). In reality, the first verse is not abrogated, since it is a statement of fact implying that all directions belong to Allaah, and Allaah has the right to command the believers to face any direction in prayer. As Allaah says,

$$\text{لَّيْسَ ٱلْبِرَّ أَن تُوَلُّواْ وُجُوهَكُمْ قِبَلَ ٱلْمَشْرِقِ وَٱلْمَغْرِبِ وَلَٰكِنَّ ٱلْبِرَّ مَنْ ءَامَنَ بِٱللَّهِ}$$

«It is not piety that you turn you faces east or west, but (true) piety is (found in) one who believes in Allaah...» [2:177]

and,

$$\text{سَيَقُولُ ٱلسُّفَهَآءُ مِنَ ٱلنَّاسِ مَا وَلَّىٰهُمْ عَن قِبْلَتِهِمُ ٱلَّتِى كَانُواْ عَلَيْهَا قُل لِّلَّهِ ٱلْمَشْرِقُ وَٱلْمَغْرِبُ}$$

---

537 az-Zarqaanee, v. 2, pps. 275-282.

«The fools among men will say, 'What has caused them (the Muslims) to turn from their *qiblah* that they used to be upon?' Respond: To Allaah belongs the east and west...» [2:142]

Thus, the verse that is claimed to be abrogated is actually not even commanding anything in the first place; it is merely emphasising that all directions belong to Allaah.

A Last Example

Another example in which there is a difference of opinion are the verses concerning the prohibition of alcoholic drinks. This example is taken by the majority of scholars to be a classic case of *naskh*. Other scholars, however, held the opinion that these verses were not 'abrogated' as such.[538] Since this particular example also helps to define the exact meaning of *naskh*, it shall be discussed in greater detail.

There are two verses that are claimed to be *mansookh*. The first one is,

$$ يَسْـَٔلُونَكَ عَنِ ٱلْخَمْرِ وَٱلْمَيْسِرِ قُلْ فِيهِمَآ إِثْمٌ كَبِيرٌ وَمَنَٰفِعُ لِلنَّاسِ وَإِثْمُهُمَآ أَكْبَرُ مِن نَّفْعِهِمَا $$

«They ask you concerning wine and gambling. Say: There is much harm in them, and some benefit, but the harm is greater than the benefit» [2:219]

and the second one is,

$$ يَٰٓأَيُّهَا ٱلَّذِينَ ءَامَنُوا۟ لَا تَقْرَبُوا۟ ٱلصَّلَوٰةَ وَأَنتُمْ سُكَٰرَىٰ $$

«O you who Believe! Do not approach prayers when you are drunk...» [4:43]

The verse that is considered to be the *naasikh* ruling is,

$$ يَٰٓأَيُّهَا ٱلَّذِينَ ءَامَنُوٓا۟ إِنَّمَا ٱلْخَمْرُ وَٱلْمَيْسِرُ وَٱلْأَنصَابُ وَٱلْأَزْلَٰمُ رِجْسٌ مِّنْ عَمَلِ ٱلشَّيْطَٰنِ فَٱجْتَنِبُوهُ $$

«O you who believe! Verily, intoxicants...are an abomination of Satan's handiworks, so avoid them» [5:90]

Historically speaking, it was this verse that was understood by the Companions to explicitly prohibit wine, as the previous verses had only limited its consumption. There is no difference of opinion that wine is prohibited, but do these verses constitute valid examples for *naskh*?

The first '*mansookh*' verse, according to the scholars who claimed that *naskh* did *not* occur, is not really *mansookh* at all; there is still much harm and some benefit in wine. The same applies for the second '*mansookh*' verse; Muslims are still prohibited from praying while drunk. Therefore, according to these scholars, since the explicit

---

538 cf. ash-Shanqeetee, p. 135.

meaning of the verses (i.e., the *manṭooq*) is still applicable, these verses do not come under *naskh*, since no verse was, according to them, 'abrogated.'

In other words, what these scholars are claiming is that the explicit texts of these verses are not abrogated; wine still contains 'much harm and some benefit' and Muslims still cannot 'approach prayers' while they are drunk. Even though the verse prohibiting prayer in a state of drunkenness can be understood to imply that drinking is not prohibited at other times, or in small quantities, this is only an *understanding* of the verse, and not *explicit* in the text.

In order to refute this view, it is essential to go back to the original definition of *naskh*. According to the majority of scholars, if the understanding (*mafhoom*) of a verse is abrogated, this falls under *naskh*. Az-Zarkashee said, "It is possible for the understanding of a verse to have been abrogated, either with the explicit meaning of the verse, or without it."[539] This was also the opinion of the majority of the scholars.

Therefore, in this case, the explicit text (*manṭooq*) of the verse (i.e., "Do not approach prayers in a state of drunkenness") was not abrogated, but the understanding (*mafhoom*) of the verse (viz., it is permissible to drink, as long as one is not drunk during the time of prayer) was abrogated. This comes under *naskh*.

In the same way, there are many other examples where the scholars are in disagreement over whether to classify certain verses as *naasikh/mansookh* or not. It would not be an exaggeration to say that there is less difference of opinion concerning the *laws* of these verses rather than whether the verses can be considered examples of *naskh*.

Conclusion

This section is concluded by stating that great care needs to be taken when it comes to the number of *naasikh/mansookh* pairs in the Qur'aan. It can definitely be said that there is great exaggeration in some books concerning the number of *naasikh* and *mansookh* pairs in the Qur'aan, but at the same time there is unequivocal proof to show that *naskh* has indeed occurred on several occasions. As as-Suyooṭee wrote, "In reality, it (meaning *naskh*) is rare, despite the fact that many have exaggerated the number of verses of it."[540]

It seems, however, that the number of *naasikh/mansookh* verses in the Qur'aan does not exceed a dozen, and Allaah knows best.[541]

---

539 az-Zarkashee, *al-Bahr,* v. 4, p. 139.
540 as-Suyooṭee, v. 2, p. 28.
541 cf., ash-Shanqeeṭee's work, where he concludes that there are only seven cases of *naskh*.

CHAPTER 14

THE MIRACULOUS NATURE OF THE QUR'AAN – I'JAAZ AL-QUR'AAN

I. Definition of I'jaaz

The word *i'jaaz* comes from *'a-j-z*, which means 'to be incapable of, to be weak'. Therefore, the miracles that the prophets performed are called *mu'jizah*, since mankind is incapable of performing such feats.

This word is not used in the Qur'aan or *Sunnah*, and neither did the Companions use it. However, like many other terms in Islaamic sciences, it was coined by later scholars and accepted among the *ummah*.[542] Probably the first to use this term was Imaam Ahmad ibn Hambal (d. 204 A.H.).[543]

'*Mu'jizah*' are defined to be acts performed by prophets of a miraculous nature that humans are incapable of imitating. *I'jaaz* is the concept; *Mu'jizah* the actual act. An example of a *mu'jizah* is the transformation of the staff of Moosaa into a serpent. The Qur'aanic term for this concept is '*aayah*, or *bayyinah*.

There are a number of conditions that the scholars have given for an act to be considered a *mu'jizah*:[544]

1) It has to occur with the command of Allaah.

2) It must be out of the ordinary occurrences of nature.

3) It cannot be performed again by any person or object.

4) It must occur at the hands of a person who claims prophethood.

5) The act must match the claim of the prophet. For example, if the prophet claims that he will turn a staff into a snake, but instead it turns into another creature, this will not be considered a *mu'jizah*.

---

542 There is no harm in coining new terms to denote acts or concepts that have a basis in Islaam, as the naming of a concept does not necessarily fall into *bid'ah*. However, inventing new concepts or acts of a religious nature is a *bid'ah*.

543 Faqihee, Muhammad Haneef. *Nadhariyya i'jaaz al-Qur'aan 'ind 'Abd al-Qaahir al-Jarjaani*. Masters Diss., Cairo Univ., 1960, p. 13.

544 Itr, p. 25.

6) The act must not refute the prophet's claim. For example, if a prophet claims that a certain stone will speak, and the stone speaks and says that that person is a liar in his claim to prophethood, this will also not be considered a *mu'jizah*.

When applied to Qur'aanic sciences, the term *i'jaaz* is used to denote the inimitable quality of the Qur'aan. In other words, the Qur'aan is set apart from all other books in that it cannot be rivalled or imitated. This is exclusive to the Qur'aan; no other book can claim this. No matter how eloquent the poet, how knowledgeable the scholar, how well-versed the grammarian – none can bring forth anything similar to this, since the Qur'aan is the Speech of Allaah, and the difference between the Speech of Allaah and the speech of His Creation is the difference between Allaah and His Creation.[545]

Other Types of Supernatural Acts

There are other types of miraculous acts, besides *mu'jizaat* (plural of *mu'jizah*). When a supernatural act occurs at the hands of a pious person, this act is called a *karaamah*. Thus, the *karaamaat* (plural of *karaamah*) are miracles given to the believers of a prophet. In general, the miraculous nature of a *karaamah* is inferior to that of a *mu'jizah*. An example of a *karaamah* is the incident in which two Companions returned to their houses from the mosque of the Prophet (ﷺ) during a dark night, and a light shone in front of them, leading the way. When the time came for them to separate paths, the light split into two and led each one to his house.[546]

Ibn Taymiyyah (d. 728 A.H.) wrote, concerning *karaamaat*: "Many of the scholars have mentioned that, in reality, the *karaamaat* of the pious are included in the *mu'jizaat* of their prophets, as they are signs and miracles that prove (the truthfulness) of his prophethood. And this is the correct opinion."[547] In other words, the very fact that a *karaamah* occurs to one of the followers of a particular prophet is proof of that prophet's truthfulness, and thus can be included in the general *mu'jizaat* of that prophet.

When a supposedly 'supernatural' act occurs at the hands of an evil person, such as a magician or an innovator, this is no miracle whatsoever, but rather magic (*sihr*). In fact, these acts have absolutely no miraculous nature to them; they are merely physical feats than can be performed by man or *jinn*. Due to the fact that the *jinn* have different physical capabilities than man (for example, they can carry very heavy objects, and travel at extremely fast speeds), certain people might be deceived into presuming these acts to be 'miracles'. In reality, they are only physical acts of the evil *jinn*, aided by their human counterparts. Therefore, no believer can ever be fooled by the tricks of a magician:

---

545 The last portion of the sentence, 'The difference between...', is a statement of the famous Successor Aboo 'Abd ar-Rahmaan as-Sulamee, although some weak narrations raise it to a statement of the Prophet (ﷺ). cf. al-Laalikaa'ee, v. 2, # 557.

546 Reported by al-Bukhaaree.

547 Itr, p. 33.

$$أَسِحْرٌ هَٰذَا وَلَا يُفْلِحُ ٱلسَّاحِرُونَ$$

"Is this magic? But the magicians will never be successful!" [10:77]

$$فَلَمَّا أَلْقَوْا قَالَ$$
$$مُوسَىٰ مَا جِئْتُم بِهِ ٱلسِّحْرُ إِنَّ ٱللَّهَ سَيُبْطِلُهُ إِنَّ ٱللَّهَ لَا يُصْلِحُ$$
$$عَمَلَ ٱلْمُفْسِدِينَ ﴿٨١﴾$$

«And when (the magicians) cast down (what they had), Moosaa said, 'What you have brought is magic; Surely Allaah will destroy it, for Allaah does not set right the work of evil-doers'»[10:81]

$$وَأَلْقِ مَا فِي يَمِينِكَ تَلْقَفْ مَا صَنَعُوٓا إِنَّمَا صَنَعُوا$$
$$كَيْدُ سَاحِرٍ وَلَا يُفْلِحُ ٱلسَّاحِرُ حَيْثُ أَتَىٰ$$

«And throw (O Moosaa) what is in your hand! It will swallow up all that they have made. That which they have made is only the trick of a magician, and the magician will never be successful, no matter whatever amount (of skill) he may attain!» [20:69]

Thus, the 'miracles' of the magician are the weakest forms of 'miracles', and cannot in any way rival the real miracles of the *karaamaat* and *mu'jizaat*.

II. The Proof for I'jaaz

Part of the *Sunnah* of Allaah is that whenever He sends a prophet, He gives that prophet certain miracles and signs to prove his prophethood to his people. The miracles of Moosaa, 'Eesaa and the other prophets are well-known to all Muslims. Allaah says,

$$وَرَسُولًا إِلَىٰ بَنِى إِسْرَآءِيلَ أَنِّى قَدْ جِئْتُكُم بِـَٔايَةٍ مِّن رَّبِّكُمْ$$
$$أَنِّىٓ أَخْلُقُ لَكُم مِّنَ ٱلطِّينِ كَهَيْـَٔةِ ٱلطَّيْرِ فَأَنفُخُ فِيهِ$$
$$فَيَكُونُ طَيْرًۢا بِإِذْنِ ٱللَّهِ وَأُبْرِئُ ٱلْأَكْمَهَ وَٱلْأَبْرَصَ$$
$$وَأُحْىِ ٱلْمَوْتَىٰ بِإِذْنِ ٱللَّهِ وَأُنَبِّئُكُم بِمَا تَأْكُلُونَ وَمَا تَدَّخِرُونَ$$
$$فِى بُيُوتِكُمْ إِنَّ فِى ذَٰلِكَ لَءَايَةً لَّكُمْ إِن كُنتُم مُّؤْمِنِينَ ﴿٤٩﴾$$

«And We will make him ('Eesaa) a Messenger to the Children of Israa'eel, (saying), 'I have come to you with a sign from your Lord, that I design for you out of clay, as it were, the figure of a bird, and breathe into it, and it becomes a bird by Allaah's leave; and I heal him who was born blind, and the leper, and I bring the dead to life by Allaah's Leave. And I inform you of what you eat, and what you store in your houses.' Surely, therein is a sign for you, if you believe» [3:49]

So many, in fact, are the miracles that were given to certain nations, that Allaah said,

$$\text{سَلْ بَنِىٓ إِسْرَٰٓءِيلَ كَمْ ءَاتَيْنَٰهُم مِّنْ ءَايَةٍۭ بَيِّنَةٍۢ}$$

«And (just) ask the Children of Israa'eel how many miracles We gave them...!» [2:211]

Despite all these miracles, however, the majority of people rejected their prophets.

The disbelievers of Makkah were no exception to the disbelievers of old, and rejected the call of the Prophet (ﷺ). They asked him for miracle after miracle:

$$\text{وَقَالُواْ لَن نُّؤْمِنَ لَكَ حَتَّىٰ تَفْجُرَ لَنَا مِنَ}$$
$$\text{ٱلْأَرْضِ يَنۢبُوعًا ۝ أَوْ تَكُونَ لَكَ جَنَّةٌۭ مِّن نَّخِيلٍۢ وَعِنَبٍۢ}$$
$$\text{فَتُفَجِّرَ ٱلْأَنْهَٰرَ خِلَٰلَهَا تَفْجِيرًا ۝ أَوْ تُسْقِطَ ٱلسَّمَآءَ كَمَا}$$
$$\text{زَعَمْتَ عَلَيْنَا كِسَفًا أَوْ تَأْتِىَ بِٱللَّهِ وَٱلْمَلَٰٓئِكَةِ قَبِيلًا ۝}$$
$$\text{أَوْ يَكُونَ لَكَ بَيْتٌۭ مِّن زُخْرُفٍ أَوْ تَرْقَىٰ فِى ٱلسَّمَآءِ وَلَن نُّؤْمِنَ}$$
$$\text{لِرُقِيِّكَ حَتَّىٰ تُنَزِّلَ عَلَيْنَا كِتَٰبًا نَّقْرَؤُهُۥ ۗ قُلْ سُبْحَانَ رَبِّى هَلْ}$$
$$\text{كُنتُ إِلَّا بَشَرًۭا رَّسُولًۭا ۝}$$

«And they say, 'We shall not believe in you until you cause a spring to gush forth from the earth for us; Or you have a garden of date palms and grapes, and cause rivers to gush forth in their midst abundantly; Or you cause the heavens to fall upon us in pieces, as you have pretended, or you bring Allaah and the angels before (us) face-to-face; Or you have a house of adornable material (i.e., gold and silver), or you ascend up into the sky, and even then we will put no faith in your ascension until you bring down for us a book that we would read!' Answer them (O Muhammad), 'Glorified be my Lord! I am just a man, sent as a Messenger!'» [17:90-93]

In another place, the result of the showing of these miracles has been told,

$$\text{وَلَوْ أَنَّنَا نَزَّلْنَآ إِلَيْهِمُ ٱلْمَلَٰٓئِكَةَ وَكَلَّمَهُمُ ٱلْمَوْتَىٰ وَحَشَرْنَا}$$
$$\text{عَلَيْهِمْ كُلَّ شَىْءٍۢ قُبُلًۭا مَّا كَانُواْ لِيُؤْمِنُوٓاْ إِلَّآ أَن يَشَآءَ ٱللَّهُ وَلَٰكِنَّ}$$
$$\text{أَكْثَرَهُمْ يَجْهَلُونَ ۝}$$

«And even if We had sent down unto them angels, and the dead had spoken to them, and We had gathered together all things before their very eyes, even then they would not have believed, unless Allaah willed, but most of them behave ignorantly!» [6:111]

Allaah then tells the disbelievers the ultimate miracle that the Prophet (ﷺ) has been given:

$$وَقَالُوا لَوْلَا أُنزِلَ عَلَيْهِ$$
$$ءَايَٰتٌ مِّن رَّبِّهِ ۚ قُلْ إِنَّمَا الْآيَٰتُ عِندَ اللَّهِ وَإِنَّمَا أَنَا نَذِيرٌ$$
$$مُّبِينٌ ۝ أَوَلَمْ يَكْفِهِمْ أَنَّا أَنزَلْنَا عَلَيْكَ الْكِتَٰبَ$$
$$يُتْلَىٰ عَلَيْهِمْ ۚ إِنَّ فِي ذَٰلِكَ لَرَحْمَةً وَذِكْرَىٰ لِقَوْمٍ$$
$$يُؤْمِنُونَ ۝$$

«And they say, 'Why are not miracles sent down to him from his Lord?' Say: 'The signs are only with Allaah, and I am only a plain warner.' *Is it not a sufficient (miracle) for them that We have sent down to you the Book which is recited to them? Verily, herein is a mercy and a reminder for a people who believe*'» [29:50-1]

Even this, however, was not sufficient for the disbelieving Makkans. They claimed that the Prophet (ﷺ) was a liar who forged the Qur'aan, or a magician, or one possessed by *jinn*. They even claimed that they could imitate the Qur'aan:

$$وَإِذَا تُتْلَىٰ عَلَيْهِمْ ءَايَٰتُنَا$$
$$قَالُوا قَدْ سَمِعْنَا لَوْ نَشَاءُ لَقُلْنَا مِثْلَ هَٰذَا ۙ إِنْ هَٰذَا إِلَّا$$
$$أَسَٰطِيرُ الْأَوَّلِينَ ۝$$

«And when Our verses are recited to them, they say, 'We have heard this! If we wish, we can say something similar to it. These are nothing but stories of old'» [8:31]

In response to this, Allaah challenged them to fulfil this claim of theirs.

The Challenge!

These verses are called the verses of *tahaddi* (challenge), and this challenge proves the inimitable and miraculous quality of the Qur'aan.

There are five verses that issue the *tahaddi*. They are, in the order that they occur in the Qur'aan, as follows:

1)

$$وَإِن كُنتُمْ فِي رَيْبٍ مِّمَّا نَزَّلْنَا عَلَىٰ عَبْدِنَا$$
$$فَأْتُوا بِسُورَةٍ مِّن مِّثْلِهِ وَادْعُوا شُهَدَاءَكُم مِّن دُونِ اللَّهِ$$
$$إِن كُنتُمْ صَٰدِقِينَ ۝ فَإِن لَّمْ تَفْعَلُوا وَلَن تَفْعَلُوا فَاتَّقُوا$$
$$النَّارَ الَّتِي وَقُودُهَا النَّاسُ وَالْحِجَارَةُ ۖ أُعِدَّتْ لِلْكَٰفِرِينَ ۝$$

«And if you are in doubt as to what We have sent down to Our servant, then produce a *soorah* similar to it, if you are truthful. But if you do not do it – and of a surety you cannot do it – then fear the Fire whose fuel are men and stones, prepared for the disbelievers.» [2:23-24]

2)

أَمْ يَقُولُونَ ٱفْتَرَىٰهُ قُلْ فَأْتُوا۟ بِسُورَةٍ مِّثْلِهِۦ وَٱدْعُوا۟ مَنِ ٱسْتَطَعْتُم مِّن دُونِ ٱللَّهِ إِن كُنتُمْ صَٰدِقِينَ ﴿٣٨﴾

«Or do they say, 'He (Muhammad (ﷺ)) has forged it!' Say: Bring then a *soorah* like unto it, and call upon whomsoever you can, besides Allaah, if you are truthful.» [10:38]

3)

أَمْ يَقُولُونَ ٱفْتَرَىٰهُ قُلْ فَأْتُوا۟ بِعَشْرِ سُوَرٍ مِّثْلِهِۦ مُفْتَرَيَٰتٍ وَٱدْعُوا۟ مَنِ ٱسْتَطَعْتُم مِّن دُونِ ٱللَّهِ إِن كُنتُمْ صَٰدِقِينَ ﴿١٣﴾

«Or do they say, 'He (Muhammad (ﷺ)) has forged it!' Say: Bring then ten forged *soorahs* similar to it, and call upon whomsoever you can, besides Allaah, if you are truthful.» [11:13]

4)

قُل لَّئِنِ ٱجْتَمَعَتِ ٱلْإِنسُ وَٱلْجِنُّ عَلَىٰٓ أَن يَأْتُوا۟ بِمِثْلِ هَٰذَا ٱلْقُرْءَانِ لَا يَأْتُونَ بِمِثْلِهِۦ وَلَوْ كَانَ بَعْضُهُمْ لِبَعْضٍ ظَهِيرًا ﴿٨٨﴾

«Say: If all of mankind and *jinn* gathered together to produce the like of the Qur'aan, they could not produce it – even if they helped one another!.» [17:88]

5)

أَمْ يَقُولُونَ تَقَوَّلَهُۥ بَل لَّا يُؤْمِنُونَ ﴿٣٣﴾ فَلْيَأْتُوا۟ بِحَدِيثٍ مِّثْلِهِۦٓ إِن كَانُوا۟ صَٰدِقِينَ

«Or do they say, 'He has forged it!' Nay! (Rather) they do not believe! Let them, then, produce a recitation similar to it, if indeed they are truthful.» [52:33-34]

These five verses mention different quantities to bring forth: one verse mentions any 'recitation' be bought forth; two verses mention one *soorah*, one verse mentions ten *soorahs*, and one states that a whole 'Qur'aan' must be brought. *Soorah* al-Baqarah is *madanee*, and the rest of the verses are *makkee*, which implies that the verse in al-Baqarah was the last of these verses to be revealed.

The Order of the Verses

Was there a graduality in the challenge? In other words, did the number of *soorahs* that was challenged increase from one to ten to the whole Qur'aan, or decrease? There are four opinions on this matter:[548]

---

548 Ubaydaat, p. 217.

1) The initial challenge was to produce something similar to the whole Qur'aan. This was then reduced to ten *soorahs*, then to finally to one *soorah*. This is the most common opinion, and is the opinion of Ibn Katheer (d. 774 A.H.).

2) The initial challenge was to produce only one *soorah* (10:38). This was then increased to ten *soorahs*, then to the whole Qur'aan. Finally, in the last of these verses revealed (2:24), Allaah reduced the challenge back to one *soorah*.

3) The initial challenge was to produce the whole Qur'aan. When they were unable to do this, the challenge was reduced to ten *soorahs* that would imitate the Qur'aan in prose and syntax, but not in content. Lastly, the challenge was reduced to one *soorah* that matched the Qur'aan in prose and content. This is the opinion of az-Zarkashee in his *al-Burhaan*.[549]

4) There is no graduality in these challenges. In other words, in each verse Allaah is challenging the same thing: to produce something similar to the Qur'aan, be it in one *soorah*, ten *soorahs* or the whole Qur'aan. It is the *quality* of the Qur'aan that must be imitated if the challenge is to be met, and not the *quantity*.

Of these four opinions, the third one (which is very similar to the first opinion) seems to have the strongest proof.[550] This is because the Qur'aan uses the word 'forged' when issuing the challenge to produce ten *soorahs* similar to the Qur'aan, whereas this qualification is not mentioned in any other verse. This hints to the fact that these ten *soorahs* did not have to be as 'authentic' as the other imitations. In other words, the *content* of these ten *soorahs* did not have to have *i'jaaz*; it was only the *prose* that had to be imitated. When the Quraysh were unable to do even this, the challenge was reduced to one *soorah* (10:38), and, lastly, the final challenge and prediction given:

$$ فَإِن لَّمْ تَفْعَلُواْ وَلَن تَفْعَلُواْ فَٱتَّقُواْ $$

$$ ٱلنَّارَ ٱلَّتِي وَقُودُهَا ٱلنَّاسُ وَٱلْحِجَارَةُ أُعِدَّتْ لِلْكَٰفِرِينَ $$

«But if you do not do it – *and of a surety you cannot do it* – then fear the Fire
whose fuel are men and stones, prepared for the disbelievers» [2:23-24]

Another question that must be answered is whether this challenge is still operative, or was it meant only for the disbelievers during the Prophet's (ﷺ) time? The Arabs during the time of the Prophet (ﷺ) used to pride themselves in their skill of poetry and their eloquence, so Allaah issued this challenge to them. However, this does not mean that this challenge was only meant for them, since the Qur'aan is meant to be a miracle until the Day of Judgement. The truth of the matter is that there is still an open challenge to 'all of *jinn* and mankind' to produce something similar to the Qur'aan, and this challenge will continue to be operative until the Day of Judgement.

---

549 az-Zarkashee, v. 2, p. 110.
550 cf. Itr, p. 123.

III. The Qur'aan as the Miracle of the Prophet (ﷺ)

The Qur'aan is *the* miracle of the Prophet (ﷺ). He (ﷺ) was given this miracle as the ultimate proof of his prophethood.

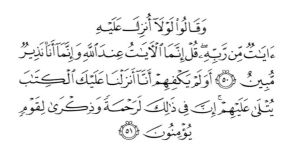

«And they say, 'Why are not miracles sent down to him from his Lord?' Say: 'The signs are only with Allaah, and I am only a plain warner.' *Is it not a sufficient (miracle) for them that We have sent down to you the Book which is recited to them?* Verily, herein is a mercy and a reminder for a people who believe'» [29:50-1]

When the disbelievers asked for miracles from the Prophet (ﷺ), Allaah revealed that the Qur'aan itself is sufficient as a miracle.

The Prophet (ﷺ) also alluded to the status of the miracle of the Qur'aan when he said, "There has not been a single prophet except that Allaah gave him miracles because of which people believed in him. I have been given (as my miracle) the Inspiration (i.e., the Qur'aan) which Allaah revealed to me. I hope, therefore, that I will have the largest number of followers on the Day of Judgement."[551]

The fact that the Prophet (ﷺ) said that he hoped he would have the most number of followers on the Day of Judgement shows that his miracle, that of the Qur'aan, is greater than any miracle that any previous prophet was given. The beauty of this miracle can best be appreciated in the concept of *i'jaaz*.

The Qur'aan is not the only miracle that was given to the Prophet (ﷺ). Among his other miracles was the splitting of the moon in half, the increase of an inadequate amount of food to a very large quantity, the speaking of stones, animals and trees to him, and the sprouting of water from his (ﷺ) hands when the Companions were short of it.[552] However, none of these miracles were permanent – they occurred in front of specific groups of people at specific times and places. There exist detailed narrations concerning these events, and the Muslims must believe in them. The fact remains, however, that later generations must believe in the narrations of those present at the time of the miracle, for they themselves were not present.

---

551 al-Bukhaaree.

552 There are more miracles than these. See al-Waada'ee, Muqbil ibn Haadee, *Saheeh al-Musnad min Dalaa'il an-Nubuwwah*, Dar al-Arqam, Kuwait, 1987, for one of the most authentic lists.

Man being the frail creature that he his, the impact of the written word is much less than the impact of sight. These miracles of a surety occurred, but the effect that these miracles had on those who saw them is much greater than the impact that it will have on later generations who merely read about them. The beauty and the power of the *i'jaaz* of the Qur'aan is that it removes the constraints of time and place upon the miracle – the Qur'aan is a permanent miracle for all generations after the Prophet (ﷺ) to see and appreciate, no matter where they live, or what time frame they are born in.

The famous Muslim historian and sociologist, Ibn Khaldoon (d. 808 A.H.), states in his *Muqqadimah*:

> Know that the greatest of all miracles, and the most sacred and blessed, and the clearest in proof, is the Qur'aan that was revealed to the Prophet (ﷺ). This is because all other miracles, in general, were brought forth separate from the actual inspiration (that the prophet received), as a *means of* proving the truthfulness of the inspiration. As for the Qur'aan, it is the inspiration and the miracle *in one*, and is therefore not in need of any external miracles (to prove itself), unlike all the previous inspirations. It is, therefore, the clearest and most powerful miracle, since it combines the boast and the proof in one (i.e., it combines the boast that it is the truth from Allaah, and the proof for the boast). This is the meaning of the Prophet's (ﷺ) statement, '...I hope, therefore, that I will have the largest number of followers on the Day of Judgement.' This shows that a miracle as clear and powerful as this one – *for it is the inspiration in its essence* – must have the greatest number of believers and followers...[553]

And Shaykh al-Islaam Ibn Taymiyyah (d. 728 A.H.) wrote,

> "The greatest (of all miracles) is the Qur'aan that the Prophet Muhammad (ﷺ) came with, for it is the religion of Allaah and His Speech, and it is the proof of the prophethood of Muhammad (ﷺ)! Its very revelation is one of the most supernatural and extraordinary of acts, for it is the call (to the worship of Allaah), and the proof (of the prophethood of Muhammad (ﷺ)), and the miracle (all in one)!"[554]

IV. The Types of I'jaaz

How is the Qur'aan inimitable? In other words, what aspect of the Qur'aan makes it so miraculous? And what are those aspects of the Qur'aan that cannot be imitated?

There have been numerous responses by the scholars of *'uloom al-Qur'aan*: the Arabic of the Qur'aan; the laws and *sharee'ah* that the Qur'aan came with; the predictions that it gives; the diligence with which it was preserved, and so forth. In reality, the correct opinion is that all of theseaspects, and more, form an integral part of the

---

553 Itr, p. 113.
554 *Majmoo' al-Fataawa*, v.11, p. 324.

i'jaaz of the Qur'aan. In other words, the beauty of the Qur'aan is that it is not just miraculous in one facet, but rather from all facets and angles that one can look at it.

Az-Zarkashee, in trying to answer how the Qur'aan is an example of *i'jaaz*, quotes over a dozen aspects of *i'jaaz*, and then concludes, "...the statement of those who have researched the issue thoroughly is that the *i'jaaz* of the Qur'aan is due to all of the previous factors simultaneously, and not by any one of them only. For (the *i'jaaz*) is in combining all of these facets..." [555]

The scholar Muhammad ibn Juzay al-Kalbee (d. 741 A.H.) divided the *i'jaaz* of the Qur'aan into ten categories:

1) The eloquence of the Qur'aan above that of any human speech.

2) The unique arrangement and organisation of its verses and *soorahs*, and the manner in which the words are arranged.

3) The incapability to produce anything similar to it by the disbelievers during the Prophet's (ﷺ) time and those after them.

4) The stories and accounts of the nations and prophets of old, since the Prophet (ﷺ) had no recourse to such information.

5) The predictions which occurred in the Qur'aan, and which later came true.

6) The Names and Attributes of Allaah, all Glory be to Him, and the attribution of all that Befits Him, and the negation of all that does not Befit Him, and the call of the Creator to the created to worship Him (in other words, the perfect *'aqeedah*). All of this is not possible for a human to bring forth, unless he was inspired by Allaah.

7) The laws and *sharee'ah* that the Qur'aan came with, and the morals and conduct that it called for. All of this leads to the betterment of life in this world and in the Hereafter. The perfection of a set of laws that can be applied to any society at any time and place is humanly impossible, and the *sharee'ah* is the only example of such a set of laws.

8) The fact that it has been protected and remained unchanged over such a long period of time, despite the fact that all other religious books have been distorted.

9) The ease by which it is memorised, and this is known by experience and observance. This is in contrast to all other religious books, for none of them are memorised like the Qur'aan.

10) The deep meanings that are present in it, and the fact that a reader never tires of reading the Qur'aan, no matter how many times he has heard it or read it. This is in contrast to any other book, since a person cannot read it more than a few times without it getting monotonous and mundane.[556]

---

555 az-Zarkashee, v. 2, p. 106.
556 Paraphrased from Darwish, p. 56

Again, the *i'jaaz* of the Qur'aan cannot be limited to one list. There are other aspects of the *i'jaaz* of the Qur'aan that have not been mentioned in this list, including the Qur'aan's stating of scientific facts that were unknown at the time of the Prophet (ﷺ); the impact that it has on those who listen to it; the miraculous nature of the *ahruf*, and what remains of them in the *qira'aat*; the euphonious quality of the Qur'aan, and many more aspects. Some of these aspects will be discussed in greater detail below.[557]

A. THE LANGUAGE AND STYLE OF THE QUR'AAN

The miracles that were given to the prophets were chosen so that they would have the greatest impact on that particular nation. Thus, since the people of the time of Moosaa greatly excelled in the 'art' of sorcery and magic, the miracles that were given to Moosaa were of a similar type, except much stronger and more powerful (for example, the staff, the shining hand, the splitting of the Nile, and others). Likewise, the people at the time of 'Eesaa excelled in the art of healing and medicine, and therefore, the miracles that were given to 'Eesaa were of a similar type (for example, healing the leper, curing the sick, raising the dead, and others).[558]

During the time of the Prophet (ﷺ), the Arabs had reached the peak of eloquence, and this was their most prized art! Poetry was what they valued the most, and each tribe competed with others to see which one could produce the most skilled and eloquent poet. During the annual fair of 'Ukaadh, poets from all over Arabia would compete for the honour of having their poem win the highest praise: that of being posted on the door of the Ka'bah until the next fair.

Due to this pride that was prevalent among the Arabs, the miracle that was given to the Prophet (ﷺ) was of a similar nature; Allaah revealed the Qur'aan in an Arabic that was so emotive and eloquent that the Arabs could clearly see it was a miracle from their Creator. On top of this, Allaah challenged them to bring forth anything similar to the Qur'aan, and told them that such attempts would be futile,

وَإِن كُنتُمْ فِى رَيْبٍ مِّمَّا نَزَّلْنَا عَلَىٰ عَبْدِنَا

فَأْتُواْ بِسُورَةٍ مِّن مِّثْلِهِۦ وَٱدْعُواْ شُهَدَآءَكُم مِّن دُونِ ٱللَّهِ

إِن كُنتُمْ صَٰدِقِينَ ﴿٢٣﴾ فَإِن لَّمْ تَفْعَلُواْ وَلَن تَفْعَلُواْ فَٱتَّقُواْ

ٱلنَّارَ ٱلَّتِى وَقُودُهَا ٱلنَّاسُ وَٱلْحِجَارَةُ أُعِدَّتْ لِلْكَٰفِرِينَ ﴿٢٤﴾

---

557 Some of the aspects of *i'jaaz* have already been discussed, such as the compilation of the Qur'aan, the diligence with which all the knowledge that is essential to understand the Qur'aan has been preserved (such as *asbaab an-nuzool*, *makkee* and *madanee* verses, *naasikh* and *mansookh*, etc.), and the *ahruf* and *qira'aat*. It would, in fact, be no exaggeration to say that every chapter in this book is merely a discussion of one of the many facets of *i'jaaz*!

558 cf. Darwish, p. 55.

«And if you are in doubt as to what We have sent down to Our servant, then produce a *soorah* similar to it..., if you are truthful. But if you do not do it – *and of a surety you cannot do it* – then fear the Fire whose fuel are men and stones, prepared for the disbelievers» [2:23-24]

Some of the aspects of the literary *i'jaaz* of the Qur'aan are as follows:[559]

1) The placement of a particular word in perfect context, over its synonyms. The connotations given by the chosen word are better than those that would have been given by its synonyms.

2) The unique sentence structure and syntax, which does not follow any one pattern but varies throughout the Qur'aan. Each style is unique, and its rhythm clear and resounding.

3) The use of different tenses (past vs. present; plural vs. singular, etc.) to give deeper meanings to a passage.

4) The pronunciation of a word matches its context. In other words, when discussing topics that are encouraging and bearing glad tidings, it uses words that are easy to pronounce and melodious to hear, and vice-versa.

5) The perfect combination of concisement and detail. When the subject requires elaboration, the Qur'aan discusses the topic in detail, and when a short phrase will get the message across, it remains brief.

Al-Azhar University also summarised the various types of literary *i'jaaz*. Their list is as follows:[560]

1) The form of the Qur'aan reflects nether the sedentary softness of the townsmen nor the nomadic roughness of the Bedouins. It possesses in right measure the sweetness of the former and the vigour of the latter.

2) The rhythms of the syllables are more sustained than in prose and less patterned than in poetry. The pauses come neither in prose form nor in the manner of poetry but with a harmonious and melodic flow.

3) The sentences are constructed in an elegant manner which uses the smallest number of words, without sounding too brief, to express ideas of utmost richness.

4) The Qur'aanic words neither transgress by their banality nor by their extreme rarity, but are recognised as expressing admirable nobility.

5) The conciseness of expression attains such a striking clarity that the least learned Arabic-speaking person can understand the Qur'aan without difficulty. At the same time there is such a profundity, flexibility, inspiration and radiance in the Qur'aan that it serves as the basis for the principles and rules of Islamic sciences and arts for theology and the juridical schools. Thus, it is almost impossible to express the ideas of the text by only one interpretation, either in Arabic or in any other language even with the greatest care.

---

559 cf. Itr, pps. 199-280; Qattaan, pps. 264-269; Ubaydaat, p. 224.
560 Taken verbatim from Khalifa, p. 24-25.

6)   There is a perfect blend between the two antagonistic powers of reason and emotion, intellect and feeling. In the narrations, arguments, doctrines, laws, and moral principles, the words have both persuasive teaching and emotive force. Throughout the whole Qur'aan the speech maintains its surprising solemnity, power and majesty which nothing can disturb.

The literary aspect of *i'jaaz*, although the strongest and most apparent aspect of *i'jaaz*, is the most difficult aspect to discuss in a non-Arabic work. The Qur'aan is in "...clear Arabic" (26:195), and in order to understand this concept of *i'jaaz*, a thorough understanding of the Arabic language is essential.

Instead of detailing and giving examples of these various aspects of literary *i'jaaz* – a task which is well-nigh impossible to do in a foreign language – it would perhaps be more prudent to give a few examples of the impact that the eloquence of the Qur'aan had on its first listeners.

Perhaps one of the most famous stories is the story of al-Waleed ibn al-Mugheerah. Al-Waleed was the most eloquent and highly esteemed poet of Makkah at the time of the Prophet (ﷺ). He once passed by the Prophet (ﷺ), and heard him reciting the Qur'aan. This had a visible effect on him, and he went away shaken and startled by what he had heard. The news of this incident spread throughout Makkah. Aboo Jahl, afraid that the people of Makkah might be affected by this news and convert to Islaam, rushed to al-Waleed, and told him, "O my uncle! Say something (against Muḥammad) so that the people will know that you are against him and hate (his message)."

Al-Waleed replied, "And what can I say? For I swear by Allaah, there is none amongst you who knows poetry as well as I do, nor can any compete with me in composition or rhetoric – not even in the poetry of *jinns*! And yet, I swear by Allaah, Muḥammad's speech (meaning the Qur'aan) does not bear any similarity to anything I know, and I swear by Allaah, the speech that he says is very sweet, and is adorned with beauty and charm. Its first part is fruitful and its last part is abundant (meaning that it is full of deep meanings), and it conquers (all other speech), and remains unconquered! It shatters and destroys all that has come before it (of poetry, because of its eloquence)!" Aboo Jahl responded, "Your people will not be satisfied until you speak against him!" Al-Waleed therefore requested Aboo Jahl, "Leave me for a few days, so that I may think of an appropriate response to give to the Quraysh." After the few days were over, Aboo Jahl came back to him and asked him what he had prepared. Al-Waleed, during this time, could not think of any explanation to give except, "This (the Qur'aan) is a type of magic that has an effect on its listeners." In response to this, Allaah revealed,

كَلَّآ إِنَّهُۥ كَانَ لِأَيَٰتِنَا عَنِيدًا ﴿١٦﴾ سَأُرْهِقُهُۥ صَعُودًا ﴿١٧﴾
إِنَّهُۥ فَكَّرَ وَقَدَّرَ ﴿١٨﴾ فَقُتِلَ كَيْفَ قَدَّرَ ﴿١٩﴾ ثُمَّ قُتِلَ كَيْفَ قَدَّرَ ﴿٢٠﴾ ثُمَّ نَظَرَ ﴿٢١﴾ ثُمَّ عَبَسَ وَبَسَرَ ﴿٢٢﴾ ثُمَّ أَدْبَرَ وَٱسْتَكْبَرَ ﴿٢٣﴾ فَقَالَ إِنْ هَٰذَآ إِلَّا سِحْرٌ يُؤْثَرُ ﴿٢٤﴾ إِنْ هَٰذَآ إِلَّا قَوْلُ ٱلْبَشَرِ ﴿٢٥﴾ سَأُصْلِيهِ سَقَرَ ﴿٢٦﴾

«Nay! Verily he (i.e., al-Waleed) has been stubborn in opposing our verses and signs... Verily, he thought and plotted; So let him be cursed, how he plotted! And once more let him be cursed; how he plotted! Then he thought! Then he frowned and was irritated; then he turned back and was proud! Then he said, 'This is nothing but magic from old; this is nothing but the word of a mortal!' I will cast him into the Hell-fire...» [74:16-26].[561]

This, then, is the testimony from the greatest poet alive at the time of the Prophet (ﷺ)!

Yet another incident is that of 'Utbah ibn Rabee'. 'Utbah was once sitting with other members of the Quraysh, and the subject of Muhammad (ﷺ) came up. The elders of the Quraysh began complaining about all the problems that this 'new' message had caused among their people, and started to discuss various ways that they could rid themselves of this irritating problem. 'Utbah suggested that perhaps the Prophet (ﷺ) could be convinced of giving up his message, if only it was explained to him in a gentle manner the problems that his message had been causing. Common sense, 'Utbah argued, would prevail. As proof of his convictions, 'Utbah himself volunteered to be the one to go and talk to the Prophet (ﷺ).

He therefore set out to meet the Prophet (ﷺ), and started to try to convince him (ﷺ) to abandon preaching this 'new' message, and let the Quraysh return to the paganism of their ancestors. After finishing his plea to the Prophet (ﷺ), he (ﷺ) asked, "Have you finished, O Aboo al-Waleed (the *kunya* of 'Utbah)?" When he applied in the affirmative, the Prophet (ﷺ) said, "Then listen to me:

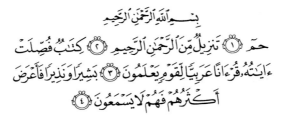

«In the name of Allaah, the Ever-Merciful, the Bestower of Mercy. *Haa Meem*. A revelation from Allaah, the Ever-Merciful, the Bestower of Mercy. (This is) a book whose verses are explained in detail – a Qur'aan in Arabic, for a people who reflect. Giving glad tidings, and warning of (a severe punishment). But most of them turn away, so they listen not...» [41:1-4]

The Prophet (ﷺ) continued to recite, until he finished the *soorah*. 'Utbah sat quietly, entranced by what he was hearing. Then the Prophet (ﷺ) said, "You have heard what you have heard, so do as you please."

When 'Utbah returned to his people, they said to themselves, "I swear by the Lord of the Ka'bah, this 'Utbah is not the same as the 'Utbah that left us!"

---

561 Ubaydaat, p. 225, from *Seerah Ibn Hishaam*, v.1, p.270. Any person who understands even the most basic amount of Arabic cannot help but notice the sheer power and eloquence of these very verses themselves!

And indeed, it was not the same 'Utbah. He said, "O people! I have heard a speech the like of which I have never heard before. I swear by Allaah, it is not magic, nor is it poetry, nor is it sorcery. O gathering of Quraysh, listen to me. Leave this man alone, for I swear by Allaah, the speech that I have heard from him (meaning the Qur'aan) will soon be news (among the other tribes)...,"[562] meaning that the Qur'aan will be the cause of some great event among the Arabs.

Another Companion, Unays al-Ghifaaree, was also one of the many people who clearly saw the beauty of the Qur'aan. Unays was one of the famous poets of Arabia. He once went to Makkah to do some trading, and happened to come across the Prophet (ﷺ), and listened to him recite the Qur'aan. So attracted was he to this recitation, that he was delayed from returning to his caravan. When he finally arrived, he was asked the reason for his delay. He responded, "I have met a person in Makkah who claims to be sent by Allaah. The people claim that he is a poet, or a sorcerer, or a magician. Yet, I have heard the words of sorcerers, and these words in no way resemble those uttered by a sorcerer. And I also compared his words to the verses of a poet, but such words cannot be uttered by a poet. By Allaah, he is the truthful, and they are the liars!"[563]

Yet another story is that of Jubayr ibn Mut'im. Jubayr once heard the Prophet (ﷺ) recite *Soorah* at-Toor in the Maghrib prayer, and he was not a Muslim at that time. He narrates, "I heard the Prophet (ﷺ) recite *Soorah* at-Toor in the Maghrib prayer, and it was the first time Islaam entered and settled in my heart." In another narration, he said, "...and it was as if my heart was about to fly (because of its beauty)!"[564] And the story of 'Umar's conversion is well-known. After listening to *Soorah* Taa Haa, he said, "How beautiful and eloquent is this speech!" and immediately went to the Prophet (ﷺ) to announce his conversion.

In fact, so obvious is the eloquence of the Qur'aan, that even those who have tried to imitate it have miserably failed. After the Prophet's (ﷺ) death, Musaylmah 'the Liar', who had claimed to be a prophet, started to rebel against the Muslim state under the new caliphate of Aboo Bakr. The Companion 'Amr ibn al-'Aas was travelling in the vicinity of Musaylamah, and Musaylamah's people found him and brought him to Musaylamah. 'Amr asked Musaylamah whether he had received any 'revelation'. Musaylamah replied that he had, and started to quote it to 'Amr. After he had quoted three 'verses', 'Amr could not contain his patience anymore, and burst out, "You know as well as I do that you are among the liars!" With that, 'Amr left Musaylamah's camp, and returned to Madeenah. In another incident, two messengers of Musaylamah came to Aboo Bakr, and recited to him some of Musaylamah's 'revelations'. Aboo Bakr replied, "*Subhaan Allaah*!! Woe to you! This speech is not divine! How is he managing to mislead you (with it)?!"[565]

---

562 Itr, p. 142.

563 Narrated by Muslim.

564 Narrated by al-Bukhaaree.

565 Itr, p. 151. Among the 'revelations' of Musaylamah are the following 'verses': "The frog! Daughter of two frogs! We protect what you protect! Your top part is in water, and your bottom part in mud. Neither do you stop the one seeking a drink, nor do you spoil the water! To us belongs half the earth, and to Quraysh the other half, but the Quraysh are a rebellious people." There is not much to comment concerning the 'eloquence' of these verses; for other examples of Musaylamah's literary 'genius', cf. Itr, pps. 150-151.

The eloquence and beauty of the Qur'aan is so great that it is considered to be the ultimate authority and reference work for Arabic rhetoric, grammar and syntax, even by non-Muslim Arabs.[566]

To conclude, it is appropriate to quote the famous scholar Ibn al-Atheer (d. 606 A.H.), who said: "If we begin to investigate into the wisdom and secrets of the eloquence of the noble Qur'aan, we sail into a deep ocean that has no escape from it!"[567]

B. THE PREDICTIONS OF THE QUR'AAN

The Qur'aan contains many predictions of the events to come in the future. Included in this category are all the descriptions of the Day of Judgement, and Heaven and Hell. However, when these events come true,

لَا يَنفَعُ نَفْسًا إِيمَـٰنُهَا لَمْ تَكُنْ ءَامَنَتْ مِن قَبْلُ

«...no good will it do to a person to believe then, if he had not believed before...»[6:158]

Without a doubt, though, the greatest prediction of the Qur'aan is concerning its own i'jaaz. In other words, the Qur'aan has predicted that it will remain unrivalled and unimitated for all of eternity.

قُل لَّئِنِ ٱجْتَمَعَتِ ٱلْإِنسُ وَٱلْجِنُّ عَلَىٰ أَن يَأْتُوا۟ بِمِثْلِ هَـٰذَا ٱلْقُرْءَانِ
لَا يَأْتُونَ بِمِثْلِهِۦ وَلَوْ كَانَ بَعْضُهُمْ لِبَعْضٍ ظَهِيرًا ۝

«Say: If all of mankind and jinn gathered together to produce the like of the Qur'aan, they could not produce it – even if they helped one another!» [17:88]

The futility of trying to imitate the Qur'aan has explicitly been foretold:

فَإِن لَّمْ تَفْعَلُوا۟ وَلَن تَفْعَلُوا۟ فَٱتَّقُوا۟
ٱلنَّارَ ٱلَّتِى وَقُودُهَا ٱلنَّاسُ وَٱلْحِجَارَةُ أُعِدَّتْ لِلْكَـٰفِرِينَ

«And if you are in doubt as to what We have sent down to Our servants, then produce a soorah similar to it..., if you are truthful. But if you do not do it – and of a surety you cannot do it – then fear the Fire whose fuel are men and stones, prepared for the disbelievers» [2:23-24]

Ibn Katheer (d. 774 A.H.), commenting on this verse, said, "'...and of a surety you cannot do it...', meaning that this is a challenge for all of eternity, and this, in itself, is another miracle, since Allaah has predicted, in very certain and sure terms, without any doubt or fear, that nothing will be able to match this Qur'aan, for all of eternity. And this is exactly what has occurred! None have successfully challenged it to this day

---

566 cf. Ubaydaat, p. 224.
567 Itr, p. 200.

of ours, and neither can they do so, for how can they do so when the Qur'aan is the *kalaam* of Allaah...?"[568]

The Qur'aan has also predicted the fact that it will remain uncorrupted and preserved for all of eternity:

إِنَّا نَحْنُ نَزَّلْنَا ٱلذِّكْرَ وَإِنَّا لَهُۥ لَحَٰفِظُونَ ٩

«Verily, it is We who have revealed the Qur'aan, and of a surety We will guard it (from corruption)» [15:9]

There are also predictions related to worldly events. For example, the Qur'aan predicted the outcome of a battle that would occur between the Romans and the Persians. Before the advent of Islaam, the Persians had attacked the Romans, and conquered a part of Syria, which had been under Roman control. A few years before the *hijrah* of the Prophet (ﷺ), the Romans attacked back, and tried to regain their lost territory. The Muslims in Makkah were hoping that the Romans would win, as they were Christians (and thus closer in faith to them), while the disbelievers of Makkah were hoping that the Persians would win, since they were fire-worshippers. During this battle, the Persians won, and this was a cause of great celebration for the disbelievers of Makkah. At this, Allaah revealed,

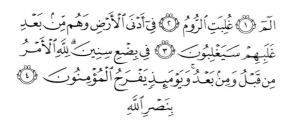

«*Alif-Lam-Meem*. The Romans have been defeated. In a land nearby, and they, after their defeat, will soon be victorious. Within three to nine years,[569] ... and on that day, the Muslims will rejoice with the help of Allaah...» [30:1-5]

Exactly seven years after the revelation of these verses, the Romans attacked the Persians again, and this time they were victorious, and managed to regain their territory. This battle occurred on the same day as the Battle of Badr, when the Muslims were themselves 'rejoicing' because of their victory over the Quraysh. Thus, this verse predicted two events: the victory of the Romans, and the victory of the Muslims.[570]

Other predictions also tell of the victory in the Battle of Badr (54:45), the eventual conquest of Makkah (48:27), and the establishment of Islaam as the ruling authority in the land (24:55). Even though there are not a large number of predictions of this nature in the Qur'aan, they are nonetheless an integral aspect of the concept of *i'jaaz*.

---

568 Ibn Katheer, v. 1, p. 64.

569 The Arabic is *bidi' sineen*, meaning a few years. The word *bidi'* implies any number greater than two and less than ten.

570 Itr, p. 301.

C. THE STORIES IN THE QUR'AAN

The Qur'aan mentions the stories of many prophets and nations of old. The Prophet (ﷺ) had no recourse to such information. He had lived amongst the Quraysh for forty years, and during this time had never studied under any priest or monk, nor had he read any history. Yet, despite his illiteracy, all of a sudden, he started to inform his people of the histories of the previous nations – from the creation of the Heavens and the Earth, to the building of the Ka'bah by Ibraaheem, from the creation of Aadam to the flood of Nooh, from the splitting of the Nile by Moosaa to the virgin birth of 'Eesaa, from the camel of Saalih to the whale of Yoonus... from where did he (ﷺ) obtain all of this knowledge?

قُل لَّوْ شَاءَ
ٱللَّهُ مَا تَلَوْتُهُۥ عَلَيْكُمْ وَلَآ أَدْرَىٰكُم بِهِۦ فَقَدْ لَبِثْتُ
فِيكُمْ عُمُرًا مِّن قَبْلِهِۦ أَفَلَا تَعْقِلُونَ ۝

«Say: If Allaah had willed, I would not have recited (the Qur'aan) to you, nor would He have made it known to you. Verily, I lived amongst you a lifetime before this (revelation started). Have you no sense?!» [10:16]

In other words, the fact that the Prophet (ﷺ) had spent forty years of his life amongst the people of Makkah, during which time he (ﷺ) was not known for any literary activity, was a very powerful factor that proved that his revelation was not from himself, but from Allaah.

The Qur'aan mentions the stories of the people of old as a sign of the Prophet's (ﷺ) prophethood:

ذَٰلِكَ مِنْ أَنۢبَآءِ ٱلْغَيْبِ نُوحِيهِ
إِلَيْكَ وَمَا كُنتَ لَدَيْهِمْ إِذْ يُلْقُونَ أَقْلَٰمَهُمْ أَيُّهُمْ يَكْفُلُ
مَرْيَمَ وَمَا كُنتَ لَدَيْهِمْ إِذْ يَخْتَصِمُونَ ۝

«This is part of the news of the unseen, which We inspire you with. You were not with them (the Israelites) when they cast lots with their pens as to which of them should be charged with the care of Mary, and neither were you with them when they disputed» [3:44]

And also,

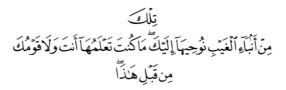

تِلْكَ
مِنْ أَنۢبَآءِ ٱلْغَيْبِ نُوحِيهَآ إِلَيْكَ مَا كُنتَ تَعْلَمُهَآ أَنتَ وَلَا قَوْمُكَ
مِن قَبْلِ هَٰذَا

«This is the news of the unseen which We reveal unto you. Neither you nor your people knew them before this...»[11:49]

Before beginning the story of Yoosuf, Allaah reminds the Prophet (ﷺ),

نَحْنُ نَقُصُّ عَلَيْكَ أَحْسَنَ ٱلْقَصَصِ
بِمَآ أَوْحَيْنَآ إِلَيْكَ هَٰذَا ٱلْقُرْءَانَ وَإِن كُنتَ مِن قَبْلِهِۦ
لَمِنَ ٱلْغَٰفِلِينَ ٣

«We relate to you the best of all stories through Our revelations to you of the
Qur'aan. And before this (revelation), you were among those who knew
nothing of this!» [12:3]

At the conclusion of the same story, Allaah says,

ذَٰلِكَ مِنْ أَنۢبَآءِ ٱلْغَيْبِ
نُوحِيهِ إِلَيْكَ وَمَا كُنتَ لَدَيْهِمْ إِذْ أَجْمَعُوٓا۟ أَمْرَهُمْ وَهُمْ يَمْكُرُونَ

«This is part of the news of the unseen that We reveal by inspiration to you.
You were not present with them when they arranged their plans (nor were
you present) when they plotted together!» [12:102]

Likewise, after mentioning the stories of a number of prophets, Allaah says,

وَمَا كُنتَ بِجَانِبِ ٱلْغَرْبِيِّ إِذْ قَضَيْنَآ إِلَىٰ مُوسَى ٱلْأَمْرَ وَمَا كُنتَ
مِنَ ٱلشَّٰهِدِينَ ٤٤ وَلَٰكِنَّآ أَنشَأْنَا قُرُونًا فَتَطَاوَلَ عَلَيْهِمُ
ٱلْعُمُرُ وَمَا كُنتَ ثَاوِيًا فِىٓ أَهْلِ مَدْيَنَ تَتْلُوا۟ عَلَيْهِمْ
ءَايَٰتِنَا وَلَٰكِنَّا كُنَّا مُرْسِلِينَ ٤٥ وَمَا كُنتَ بِجَانِبِ
ٱلطُّورِ إِذْ نَادَيْنَا

«And you (O Muhammad) were not on the western side (of the mountain)
when We made clear to Moosaa the commandment, nor were you among
those present! But We created generations (after Moosaa), and long were
the ages that passed over them! And (neither) were you a dweller amongst
the people of Madyan, reciting Our verses to them, but We were the ones
sending Messengers! And neither were you at the side of (Mount) Toor when
We called...» [28:44-46]

There are many verses of this nature in the Qur'aan.

The Purposes of the Stories

One of the primary purposes of these stories is to guide the remnants of the previous nations to the truth. The Christians, for example, are told that 'Eesaa preached pure monotheism, and the Jews are told to reflect upon their own religion, and the religion that the Prophet (ﷺ) brought. They are reminded that only Allaah knows the past,

$$\text{أَمۡ كُنتُمۡ شُهَدَآءَ إِذۡ حَضَرَ يَعۡقُوبَ ٱلۡمَوۡتُ}$$

«Or were you present when death approached Jacob?» [2:133]

As Allaah says,

$$\text{إِنَّ هَٰذَا ٱلۡقُرۡءَانَ}$$
$$\text{يَقُصُّ عَلَىٰ بَنِىٓ إِسۡرَٰٓءِيلَ أَكۡثَرَ ٱلَّذِى هُمۡ فِيهِ يَخۡتَلِفُونَ ﴿٧٦﴾}$$

«Verily, this Qur'aan narrates to the Children of Israa'eel most of the (points) over which they differ» [27:76]

Other purposes of these stories is to establish belief in the prophets (as this is one of the fundamentals of faith); to affirm the patience of the Prophet (ﷺ) and the believers (by mentioning how the prophets of old were treated by their peoples); to explain the methodology of calling to the way of Allaah (all the prophets began their call by preaching the true worship of Allaah, *tawheed*); and to guide the Muslims to better morals, since each story of the Qur'aan contains much wisdom and guidance to benefit from.

The stories in the Qur'aan, therefore, are one of the signs of the truthfulness of the Prophet (ﷺ), and another aspect of the *i'jaaz* of the Qur'aan.

D. The Beliefs and Laws of the Qur'aan

The Qur'aan was revealed as a guidance for mankind. The primary purpose of the Qur'aan is to define the true set of beliefs (*'aqeedah*) with regards to the Creator, and to implement these beliefs in a system of laws (*sharee'ah*) that will benefit the creation in this life and the next.

As an indication of the truthfulness of the Qur'aan, the *'aqeedah* and *sharee'ah* of the Qur'aan are perfect. In *'aqeedah*, the topic of primary importance is that of the Creator: His Existence (*Tawheed ar-Ruboobiyyah*), His Names and Attributes (*Tawheed al-Asmaa' wa as-Sifaat*) and His sole Right to be Worshipped (*Tawheed al-Uloohiyyah*). No other religion even comes close to this concept of perfect Monotheism. Jews, Christians, even Hindus, all claim to be monotheistic, but the Trinity of the Christians and the paganism and idolatry of the Hindus make it obvious that such a claim is a false on. The Jews, although perhaps closer than many other religions to monotheism, attribute to their god forgetfulness, weariness and ignorance, amongst other things, and do not have a firm set of spiritual beliefs.

With regards to all other beliefs in the Islaamic *'aqeedah*, they distinctly stand out from all other religions in their purity, and appeal to human rationale. For example, the belief in prophets as recipients of divine revelation, and as the means of communication between God and man, also implies a sense of integrity and honour for the prophets. This integrity of the prophets is denied by the Christians and Jews, who ascribe, amongst other crimes, the crimes of murder, incest and drunkenness to the prophets of Allaah – allegations which Islaam vehemently denies.

The *sharee'ah* is another indication of the *i'jaaz* of the Qur'aan. The *sharee'ah* is the law of Allaah, immutable in its broad aspects.[571] In its final form, it was revealed to the Prophet (ﷺ) over fourteen hundred years ago, in a specific place and time, and amongst a specific people. Yet, these laws, when applied in totality, prove to be for the betterment of the individual and society – irrelevant of the time, place or people. No matter what aspect of the *sharee'ah* is taken, it is found to be perfect in all regards. The laws governing personal hygiene, familial life, societal roles, financial transactions, political dealings – choose what you wish – the *i'jaaz* is apparent.

For an example, let us examine the laws pertaining to marriage in the Qur'aan. Instead of following the path of the Christian priests in forbidding all relations with women, the Qur'aan allows – in fact even encourages – marriage:

$$وَأَنكِحُوا۟ ٱلْأَيَـٰمَىٰ مِنكُمْ$$

«And marry those among you who are single...» [24:32]

It prohibits incest:

$$حُرِّمَتْ عَلَيْكُمْ أُمَّهَـٰتُكُمْ وَبَنَاتُكُمْ وَأَخَوَٰتُكُمْ وَعَمَّـٰتُكُمْ$$

«Forbidden to you are your mothers, your daughters, your sisters, your maternal aunts...» [4:23]

adultery:

$$وَلَا تَقْرَبُوا۟ ٱلزِّنَىٰٓ$$

«And do not approach unlawful sexual intercourse...» [17:32]

and even sexual indecency:

$$وَلَا تَقْرَبُوا۟ ٱلْفَوَٰحِشَ$$

«And do not approach *faahishah* (shameful deeds, debauchery and lewdness)» [6:151]

At the same time, it allows for plurality of wives, thus taking into consideration the biological differences between men and women, and societal needs that vary from time and place:

$$فَٱنكِحُوا۟ مَا طَابَ لَكُم مِّنَ ٱلنِّسَآءِ مَثْنَىٰ وَثُلَـٰثَ وَرُبَـٰعَ$$

«...marry women of your choice, two, three or four...» [4:3]

Instead of the cruel treatment that the women of old were subjected to, the Qur'aan laid down the perfect guidelines for husbands:

---

571 There is room for change in Islam, as long as this change does not go against the Qur'aan, *Sunnah* or *ijmaa'*. The concept of *maslaha mursalah*, for example, takes into consideration public interest when enacting, or not enacting, a law. cf. Kamali, pps. 267-82

$$\text{وَعَاشِرُوهُنَّ بِالْمَعْرُوفِ}$$

«...and treat them (your wives) with equity and kindness...» [4:19]

It clearly defined the roles of men and women, in a manner that is in accordance with the way they were created:

$$\text{الرِّجَالُ قَوَّامُونَ عَلَى النِّسَاءِ بِمَا فَضَّلَ اللَّهُ بَعْضَهُمْ}$$
$$\text{عَلَى بَعْضٍ وَبِمَا أَنفَقُوا مِنْ أَمْوَالِهِمْ}$$

«Men are the protectors and maintainers of women, because Allaah has made one of them to excel the other, and because they (men) spend to support them (women)...» [4:34]

These verses, it should be kept in mind, were revealed in a society where girls were buried alive, women had no rights whatsoever, sexual licentiousness prevailed, and prostitution in all its forms was rampant. Yet, these verses provided – and will continue to provide for all of eternity – a perfect marital and familial set of laws.

The same can be said for every single moral issue that the Qur'aan discusses. In comparison, there is no system of man-made laws that has remained unchanged or provided a perfect set of rules for the betterment of society. If the constitution of any country is examined, one will find discrepancies, absurd laws, and discriminatory and unjust legislations. In addition, such constitutions will never remain constant, but instead change with the passage of time. This is one of the strongest proofs of the inherent deficiency in these laws.[572]

In conclusion, the 'aqeedah and sharee'ah of Islaam are further proofs for the i'jaaz of the Qur'aan, since they provide for a perfect code of beliefs and system of laws for all of humanity.

E. THE SCIENTIFIC FACTS OF THE QUR'AAN

One of the more popular aspects of the i'jaaz of the Qur'aan in these times concerns its comments on aspects of science that the Prophet (ﷺ) and his people could not have known about. There are a number of books written about this topic, perhaps the most popular being Maurice Bucaille's *The Bible, the Qur'an, and Science*.[573]

---

572 The American Constitution, for example, initially equated a black slave to three-fifths of a white man. This strange fraction was decided upon to resolve a conflict between those who wanted black people to equal one white man, and those who claimed that black people were not to be considered men at all; the difference of opinion could only be resolved with this fraction. In 1919, the 18th Amendment of the Constitution prohibited the transportation and manufacture of alcoholic drinks, yet, due to public indifference of this law, it had to be repealed in the 21st Amendment less than fifteen years later.

573 This book is a very useful book in that it details many verses of a 'scientific' nature. Sometimes, however, the author's interpretations are not consistent with the understanding of the verse, such as pps. 167-9. Also, one of the last chapters, 'The Qur'aan, the Hadiths, and Modern Science', presents a very distorted view of *hadeeth*, and shows the author's unfamiliarity with the subject. His stance towards the validity of *hadeeth* and the status of the Prophet (ﷺ) is also not correct.

It should be remembered, however, that the Qur'aan is not meant to be a book primarily devoted to a discussion of 'science', but rather a book that is meant for the guidance of mankind. As such, any references to subjects of a scientific nature are typically brief and not very descriptive.[574] The i'jaaz, however, appears in the fact that even in these limited descriptions, the Qur'aan conforms exactly to modern science, and imparts knowledge that was unknown during the lifetime of the Prophet (ﷺ). These descriptions are free from retroactive ideas that plagued humanity from the earliest of times, such as the concept that the Earth is stationary, and all the other planets and stars rotate about it.

There are numerous examples of such verses, such as the description of the formation of human life. The sperm of man is referred to as a 'mixture of liquids' (76:2), since the sperm is composed of various secretions from the testicles, the seminal vesicles, the prostrate and other glands. From the literally millions of sperms produced and ejaculated, only one sperm is actually used in the fertilisation process – a very small quantity. This is referred to in a number of verses by the word 'nutfah' (cf. 75:37), which signifies a small quantity of mixed fluid. The sperm then joins the female egg, and forms the zygote. This occurs in the mother's womb, a 'safe lodging' (23:13).

The embryo, during its development, is surrounded by three layers: the abdominal wall, the uterine wall, and the placenta, with its choriono-amniotic membranes. These three layers are referred to in the verse,

$$\text{يَخۡلُقُكُمۡ فِى بُطُونِ أُمَّهَٰتِكُم}$$
$$\text{خَلۡقًا مِّنۢ بَعۡدِ خَلۡقٍ فِى ظُلُمَٰتٍ ثَلَٰثٍ}$$

«He created you in the wombs of your mothers, from one stage to another, and all along three veils of darkness surrounded you...» [39:6]

From this,

$$\text{ثُمَّ}$$
$$\text{خَلَقۡنَا ٱلنُّطۡفَةَ عَلَقَةً فَخَلَقۡنَا ٱلۡعَلَقَةَ مُضۡغَةً فَخَلَقۡنَا}$$
$$\text{ٱلۡمُضۡغَةَ عِظَٰمًا فَكَسَوۡنَا ٱلۡعِظَٰمَ لَحۡمًا ثُمَّ أَنشَأۡنَٰهُ خَلۡقًا}$$
$$\text{ءَاخَرَ فَتَبَارَكَ ٱللَّهُ أَحۡسَنُ ٱلۡخَٰلِقِينَ ﴿١٤﴾}$$

«...We made the mixed liquid (zygote) into something which clings (the embryo 'clings' to the womb by means of the umbilical cord), then We made the thing which clings into a chewed lump of flesh, then We made out of that flesh, bones, then We clothed the bones with flesh, and then We brought it forth as a new creature. Se Blessed be Allaah, the best of creators» [23:14]

574 Although this is not always the case – an exception being the evolution of the human embryo, which is described in vivid detail in the Qur'aan.

During the delivery process, the passage of the baby from the mother's womb to the outside world occurs through the birth canal. Typically, this canal is extremely narrow and tight. However, shortly before the birth, certain changes occur, including the release of certain hormones, the contractions of the uterus, and the breakage of the 'bag of water' surrounding the baby, all of which contribute to making the canal loose. This is referred to in 80:20, "Then We made the passage (through the birth canal) easy."

Perhaps the best way to appreciate the beauty of the above verses is to see pictures of the human embryo as it goes through the various stages of development. The reference to a '...chewed lump of flesh' is strikingly similar to the appearance of the embryo after the first month. The embryo, at this stage, is partly out of proportion, for the head is disproportionately larger than the body. This is mentioned in the verse,

$$فَإِنَّا خَلَقْنَٰكُم مِّن تُرَابٍ ثُمَّ مِن نُّطْفَةٍ ثُمَّ$$
$$مِنْ عَلَقَةٍ ثُمَّ مِن مُّضْغَةٍ مُّخَلَّقَةٍ وَغَيْرِ مُخَلَّقَةٍ$$

«We created you from dust, then from a sperm drop, then from a clinging entity, then into a lump of flesh (partly) in proportion and (partly) out of proportion» [22:5]

The vivid yet simple descriptions given in these verses were unknown to the people of the Prophet's (ﷺ) time, demonstrating the *i'jaaz* of the Qur'aan in science.[575]

Other facts that are given in the Qur'aan include the description of the formation of milk (16:66), the notion of orbits for the planets (21:33 and 36:40), and the description of the water cycle (15:22, 35:9 and more). Every verse that discusses nature and the creation falls into this category. In many verses, Allaah Himself commands mankind to ponder over the Creation, and mentions these as an indication of His Existence and Power.

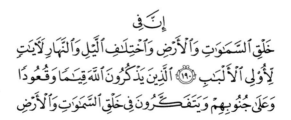

«Verily, in the Creation of the Heavens and Earth, and in the alteration of the night and day, there are signs for men of understanding. Those who remember Allaah standing, sitting and lying down on their sides, and contemplate the creation of the Heavens and Earth...» [3:190-191]

---

575 Perhaps the most detailed study of the verses pertaining to the development of the embryo is the book: *The Developing Human* by Keith Moore, *With Islamic Additions* by Abdul-Majeed Azzindani (Dar al-Qiblah, Jeddah, 1983). Most of the above material was taken from this reference.

One final note on the concept of science as an *i'jaaz* of the Qur'aan: there can *never* be a real contradiction between the Qur'aan and the Laws of Allaah concerning the creation (i.e., actual science). The Qur'aan is the Book of Allaah, and since it is from Allaah,

«there is no doubt in it» [2:1]

Likewise, the laws that govern the creation are also from Allaah. What is studied as 'science', on the other hand, is the *attempt* by man to understand the creation and laws of Allaah. Therefore, it is possible for a scientific assumption to be incorrect, and this is clearly demonstrated by such historically scientific 'facts' as the Earth being flat, or the orbiting of the Sun around the Earth. These concepts were believed in so strongly by the 'scientists' of their time that, on occasion, those who opposed them were harassed and even killed. Yet, later scientists discovered the inaccuracy of these concepts.

Therefore, when there is a conflict between the meaning of a clear, explicit verse (meaning *qat'ee ad-dalaalah*) of the Qur'aan and 'modern' science, a Muslim *must* take the verse of the Qur'aan – without hesitation – over any scientific 'fact'. A rejection of such a verse, or even the apparent meaning of such a verse, would be tantamount to a rejection of Allaah's knowledge. For example, the theory of evolution is, for the most part, agreed upon by the majority of non-Muslim scholars. Whether there is strong proof to back up this theory or not is irrelevant – the Qur'aan is clear that Allaah created Aadam from His own Hands, and

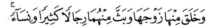

«from him He created his mate, and from these two He spread forth many men and women» [4:1]

Therefore a Muslim can never believe in the theory that men are descendants of apes, no matter what 'proof' might seem to exist.[576] Neither is it allowed, as some Muslim rationalists have done, to try to interpret clear Qur'aanic texts to suit modern theories. Following the above example, to try to interpret the story of the Creation of Aadam and Eve as actually having been the creation of some Neanderthal neo-human species is almost as blasphemous as rejecting the verse in the first place!

It is possible, however, for there to be an *apparent* conflict between a verse and a scientific fact, when no such conflict exists. This occurs when some scholars take one of the possible linguistic meanings of a verse, such that this meaning conforms with the verse, but is not the only meaning that may be derived from it (basically, the verse

---

576 This, despite the fact that the theory of evolution is in itself full of flaws and not without its problems.

is *dhannee ad-dalaalah*). For example, some scholars[577] have understood certain verses of the Qur'aan (e.g., "And it is He who has *spread out* the Earth" (13:3), and (15:19)) to indicate that the Earth is flat, since the phrase '*madd*' occurs, which means 'to spread out'. However, this verse is not explicit in stating that the Earth is flat, and to conclude this from the above verses requires a degree of interpretation. Since there exists clear proof that the Earth is not flat, this interpretation must be rejected. The meaning of the verse, therefore, is that Allaah has created this Earth as a very vast place for mankind, and not that the Earth is flat.

Also, it is essential that scientific facts are not read in where they do not exist. Unfortunately, this has become an all too common trend among 'modernistic' Muslims who have specialised in science, but are not very familiar with the interpretation of the Qur'aan.[578] Once again, the Qur'aan "...is a book of guidance... and not a book of science, nor a mine of cryptic notes on scientific facts."[579]

For example, many people interpret the following verse as a prediction of space travel by man:

«O Assembly of Men and *Jinn*s! If you have power to pass through the zones
of the Heavens and Earth – then pass! But you will never be able to pass
them except with authority (from Allaah)» [55:33]

However, a look at the next verse, and the authentic *tafseer*s of Ibn Katheer and at-Tabaree, will show that this verse is in reference to the *jinn*s listening to the whispers of the angels in the Heaven (or to the Resurrection of the creation on the Day of Judgement), and not to inter-galactic travel!

In conclusion, although the scientific aspect of the Qur'aan is one of the aspects of its *i'jaaz*, it must be put in its proper place, and a proper methodology needs to be followed in order to extract examples of such verses. It does more harm than good when certain verses in the Qur'aan are 'bent over backwards,' so as to say, to seek to prove that they contain certain implied scientific facts. One only needs to read works

---

577   Such as the eminent and esteemed scholar, Shaykh 'Abd al-'Azeez ibn Baaz. This incorrect interpretation does not in any way lessen the stature of such a knowledgeable person, for every single scholar of the Muslim *ummah* had some mistakes. Only the Prophet (ﷺ) is free from error. To quote this opinion as a refutation of Ibn Baaz's scholarship (as many unfortunately do) necessitates the rejection of every single scholar who ever existed, since all of them had a few opinions that were incorrect. In fact, this opinion of the Shaykh's only adds to his status, as it shows his love and concern for the texts of the Qur'aan and *Sunnah*, for he will reject all that appears to contradict it.

578   Such people feel that, in order to prove the veracity of the Qur'aan, they must prove that everything that science talks about must have already been discussed in the Qur'aan. However, the miraculous nature of the Qur'aan does not need such whimsical verification, as this chapter shows.

579   Von Denffer, p. 157. In other words, there are not scientific allusions buried under every third verse in the Qur'aan, waiting to be unearthed by some over-zealous, highly-imaginative Muslim!

in which this methodology was followed to see how ludicrous the conclusions are. (For example, Muḥammad Rasheed Riḍaa (d. 1935), one of the founders of the 'Modernist' movement, claimed that the '*Jinns*' that the Qur'aan was referring to actually alluded to the discovery of disease-carrying microbes!) When such facts are clear and explicit from the verse, they should be mentioned (such as the examples quoted above), but when they go against the intent and meaning of the verse, they should be abandoned.[580]

F. The Effect the Qur'aan has on its Listeners

An aspect of *i'jaaz* that is not discussed in most works is the effect that the Qur'aan has on those who listen to it.[581] No person can remain unaffected after he has listened to the Qur'aan. Is it possible for a person to see a miracle as clear as the Qur'aan and remain indifferent of it? The effect that the Qur'aan had on Jubayr ibn Mut'im, 'Umar ibn al-Khattaab and al-Waleed ibn al-Mugheerah has already been discussed above.

The Qur'aan itself discusses the effect that it has on its listeners in many verses. For the disbelievers, the Qur'aan can only cause them despair, and increase their arrogance, since they must reject what they know to be true. The Qur'aan says:

وَقَالَ الَّذِينَ كَفَرُوا لَا تَسْمَعُوا لِهَٰذَا الْقُرْءَانِ وَالْغَوْا فِيهِ لَعَلَّكُمْ تَغْلِبُونَ ۝

«And those who disbelieve say, 'Do not listen to this Qur'aan, and babble in the midst of its (recitation) so that you may overcome (it)'» [41:26]

وَلَقَدْ صَرَّفْنَا فِى هَٰذَا الْقُرْءَانِ لِيَذَّكَّرُوا وَمَا يَزِيدُهُمْ إِلَّا نُفُورًا ۝

«And surely We have explained in this Qur'aan (Our Signs) so that they may take heed, but it only increases them in aversion!» [17:41]

وَإِذَا ذَكَرْتَ رَبَّكَ فِى الْقُرْءَانِ وَحْدَهُ وَلَّوْا عَلَىٰ أَدْبَٰرِهِمْ نُفُورًا

«And when you (O Muḥammad) make mention of your Lord in the Qur'aan solely, they turn on their backs, fleeing in extreme dislike!» [17:46]

وَيْلٌ لِّكُلِّ أَفَّاكٍ أَثِيمٍ ۝ يَسْمَعُ ءَايَٰتِ
اللَّهِ تُتْلَىٰ عَلَيْهِ ثُمَّ يُصِرُّ مُسْتَكْبِرًا كَأَن لَّمْ يَسْمَعْهَا فَبَشِّرْهُ بِعَذَابٍ أَلِيمٍ
۝ وَإِذَا عَلِمَ مِنْ ءَايَٰتِنَا شَيْئًا اتَّخَذَهَا هُزُوًا

«Woe to every sinful liar – who hears the Verses of Allaah (being) recited to him, yet persists in pride as if he heard them not. So announce to him a painful torment! And when he learns something of Our Verses, he makes of them a jest!» [45:7-9]

---

580 This topic is also discussed in greater detail in Chapter 15, under 'Scientific *Tafseer*'.
581 This is more applicable to those who listen to it and understand in Arabic, as most, if not all, of this *i'jaaz* is lost in translation.

As for the believers,

$$وَإِذَا مَا أُنزِلَتْ سُورَةٌ فَمِنْهُم مَّن يَقُولُ أَيُّكُمْ زَادَتْهُ هَٰذِهِ$$
$$إِيمَٰنًا ۚ فَأَمَّا ٱلَّذِينَ ءَامَنُوا۟ فَزَادَتْهُمْ إِيمَٰنًا وَهُمْ يَسْتَبْشِرُونَ$$

«And whenever there comes down a *soorah*, some of (the hypocrites) say, 'Which of you has had his Faith (*'eemaan*) increased by it?' As for those who believe, it has increased their Faith, and they rejoice!» [9:124]

$$وَإِذَا سَمِعُوا۟ مَا أُنزِلَ إِلَى ٱلرَّسُولِ تَرَىٰ أَعْيُنَهُمْ تَفِيضُ مِنَ$$
$$ٱلدَّمْعِ مِمَّا عَرَفُوا۟ مِنَ ٱلْحَقِّ ۖ يَقُولُونَ رَبَّنَا ءَامَنَّا فَٱكْتُبْنَا مَعَ$$
$$ٱلشَّٰهِدِينَ ۝$$

«And when they listen to what has been sent down to the Messenger, you see their eyes overflowing with tears because of the truth that they have recognised. They say, 'Our Lord! We believe, so write us down among the witnesses'» [5:83]

At the same time, it also increases their fear of Allaah,

$$إِنَّمَا ٱلْمُؤْمِنُونَ ٱلَّذِينَ إِذَا ذُكِرَ ٱللَّهُ وَجِلَتْ$$
$$قُلُوبُهُمْ وَإِذَا تُلِيَتْ عَلَيْهِمْ ءَايَٰتُهُ زَادَتْهُمْ إِيمَٰنًا$$

«The believers are those who, when Allaah is mentioned, feel a tremor in their hearts, and when His verses are recited to them, it increases their faith» [8:2]

$$ٱللَّهُ نَزَّلَ أَحْسَنَ ٱلْحَدِيثِ كِتَٰبًا مُّتَشَٰبِهًا مَّثَانِىَ تَقْشَعِرُّ مِنْهُ$$
$$جُلُودُ ٱلَّذِينَ يَخْشَوْنَ رَبَّهُمْ ثُمَّ تَلِينُ جُلُودُهُمْ وَقُلُوبُهُمْ$$
$$إِلَىٰ ذِكْرِ ٱللَّهِ$$

«Allaah has sent down the best of statements, a Book, its part resembling each other in goodness and truth, oft-repeated. The skins of those who fear their Lord shiver from it (when they recite it or hear it). Then their skin and their heart soften to the remembrance of Allaah» [39:23]

And how could it not have this effect, for does not Allaah say,

$$لَوْ أَنزَلْنَا هَٰذَا$$
$$ٱلْقُرْءَانَ عَلَىٰ جَبَلٍ لَّرَأَيْتَهُ خَٰشِعًا مُّتَصَدِّعًا مِّنْ خَشْيَةِ$$
$$ٱللَّهِ ۚ وَتِلْكَ ٱلْأَمْثَٰلُ نَضْرِبُهَا لِلنَّاسِ لَعَلَّهُمْ يَتَفَكَّرُونَ$$

«Had We sent down this Qur'aan on a mountain, you would surely have seen it humbling itself and crumble out of the fear of Allaah! Such are the parables which We put forward to mankind that they may reflect.» [59:21]

G. The Lack of Contradictions in the Qur'aan

One of the aspects of *i'jaaz* that the Qur'aan alludes to is that it contains no contradictions in it. The Qur'aan challenges,

$$ أَفَلَا يَتَدَبَّرُونَ ٱلْقُرْءَانَ وَلَوْ كَانَ مِنْ عِندِ غَيْرِ ٱللَّهِ لَوَجَدُواْ $$
$$ فِيهِ ٱخْتِلَٰفًا كَثِيرًا ۝ $$

«Do they not ponder over the Qur'aan? Had it been from other than Allaah,
they would have surely found in it many contradictions!» [4:82]

The fact that there are no contradictions in the Qur'aan, despite it having been revealed over a period of twenty-three years, in different circumstances, catering to different problems, is a clear indication of its divine origin. In addition, the lack of contradictions in its *'aqeedah* and *sharee'ah* are further proofs for its origin.

H. The Ease by which the Qur'aan is Memorised

There is not a single practising Muslim on the face of this Earth except that he has memorised some portion of the Qur'aan, verbatim. In comparison, one need only look at other religions and see the number of its adherents who have memorised any portion of their Holy Scriptures. In no other religion is such great emphasis placed on memorising its Holy Scriptures than in Islaam; and no other religion has adherents who have memorised, in totality, its Holy Scripture.

Every Muslim knows by experience the ease with which the Qur'aan is memorised. In contrast, an attempt to memorise a passage out of another work or play is an arduous task. The meanings of such passages may be put to memory, but the actual words and sentences are extremely difficult to memorise, and even harder to keep in memory. And the longer such passages get, the more impossible it becomes to memorise. The memorisation of the Qur'aan, on the other hand, suffers no such obstacles; although perseverance is needed in memorising larger passages, the ease of memorisation still remains the same.

In addition, the memorisers of the entire Qur'aan (*huffadh*) are so common and numerous that there is not a single community of Muslims in the world except that they are present amongst them. Every person in the Muslim community knows of memorises (*huffadh*), and such people are not considered rare or exceptional. It is not too uncommon to meet small children who cannot even communicate in proper sentences, yet have put the entire Qur'aan to memory.[582] Also, it is possible to meet people

---

582 This author mentions the case of one of his friends in the College of Qur'aan at the University of Madeenah. He had memorised the entire Qur'aan before he had completed six years of age!

who, due to old age, have forgotten many facts and experiences of life, but the Qur'aan is still preserved in their memories, as if etched out on stone! Such a person might not even remember the events of yesterday, yet when he recites the Qur'aan, it is as if he is reciting directly from the *mus-haf*.

The fact that the Qur'aan can be memorised is one of the specialities and exclusive blessings of this *ummah*, for no other nation was given the blessing of being able to memorise its Holy Scripture. Ibn al-Jawzee (d. 597 A.H.) wrote in the introduction to his book *al-Hath 'alaa Hifdh al-'Ilm* (The Encouragement of Memorising Knowledge),

> "All praise is due to Allaah, who has favoured us, by His grace, above all other nations..., and blessed us with the memorisation of the Qur'aan...For Allaah has made our *ummah* unique by the fact that it can memorise the Qur'aan, and knowledge. Those who were before us used to read their Scriptures from parchments (i.e., without memory), and were not capable of memorising it... So how can we thank the One who has blessed us to such a degree that a seventy-year old man from amongst us can easily recite the entire Qur'aan from memory?"[583]

v. Intrinsic vs. Extrinsic

The *i'jaaz* of the Qur'aan is a fact that no Muslim can or has denied. However, is the *i'jaaz* of the Qur'aan inherent in the Qur'aan, or is it external to the Qur'aan?

Aboo Ishaaq an-Nadhaam (d. 224), of the *Mu'tazilah*, was the first to claim that the Qur'aan was not inherently miraculous, but rather externally. According to an-Nadhaam, Allaah would prevent any person from imitating it.[584] In other words, according to him, the Qur'aan was capable of being imitated, but if any person tried do to so, Allaah would prevent him and take away his capabilities and powers. This is called '*sarfah*', or 'aversion', since Allaah would avert any such attempts. An-Nadhaam was influenced by Hindu philosophy, for the Hindus believed that the Vedas could be produced by mankind, since it was not miraculous in itself, but if any attempted to produce it, Brahma would destroy such attempts.[585]

An-Nadhaam was later followed in this opinion by Aboo Ishaaq al-Isfaraa'eenee (d. 418 A.H.) of the *Ahl as-Sunnah*, al-Murtadhaa of the *Shee'ah*, and other scholars. The *i'jaaz*, according to these scholars, was not internal to the Qur'aan, but rather external through the Power of Allaah.

This opinion is the incorrect one. As-Suyootee said,

> This opinion is rejected, because of the verse in the Qur'aan:

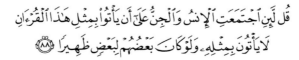

---

583 Ibn al-Jawzee, p. 11.
584 Itr, p. 165.
585 al-Awajee, p. 100.

> «Say: If all of mankind and *jinn* gathered together to produce the like of the Qur'aan, they could not produce it – even if they helped one another!» [17:88]
>
> This verse mentions their incapability to (reproduce the Qur'aan), despite the fact that they still possess their faculties and powers. If (the *i'jaaz* of the Qur'aan) were in the elimination of their power, there would be no benefit in their 'gathering together', for it would be the same as if dead corpses were gathered together. Since the Qur'aan challenges them to 'gather together', this clearly shows that the Qur'aan itself is the source of *i'jaaz*...[586]

In other words, the fact that Allaah is informing them of the futility of their gathering together is a proof that they still possess the power and capabilities that they normally do. If they did not possess their usual faculties, there would be no point to the challenge of 'gathering together'. The miracle is not that Allaah will eliminate their power to imitate the Qur'aan, but rather that the Qur'aan itself is inimitable.

If the opinion of *sarfah* were correct, this would imply that the *i'jaaz* is not in the Qur'aan, but rather with Allaah, which would mean that the Qur'aan by itself has no unique qualities to it. This view cannot be accepted, since the Qur'aan is the Speech of Allaah, and His Speech must be different from the Speech of the creation. Also, a number of different aspects of *i'jaaz* were discussed in the previous section, all of which show that the *i'jaaz* of the Qur'aan is internal to the Qur'aan itself. The eloquence, laws and beliefs, predictions, and the effect that it has on its listeners are all internal to the Qur'aan.

The correct view, therefore, and the view of the majority of scholars, is that the Qur'aan inherently has this quality of *i'jaaz*, without the need for Divine intervention to avert the plans of those who try to imitate it.

VI. The Quantity for I'jaaz

What is the minimum portion of the Qur'aan that qualifies as *i'jaaz*? In other words, what is the minimum portion of the Qur'aan that is capable of proving its miraculous nature?

There are three major opinions on this matter:

1) The *i'jaaz* of the Qur'aan is dependent on the whole Qur'aan. In other words, a *soorah* by itself does not have *i'jaaz* – only the Qur'aan taken in its entirety is a miracle. This is the opinion of some of the *Mu'tazlilah*.

2) The *i'jaaz* of the Qur'aan is present in any *soorah* in its entirety, whether it is a short *soorah* or a long one. By analogy, any group of verses equivalent to a small *soorah* also qualifies as having *i'jaaz*. In other words, a few verses are sufficient to prove the miraculous nature of the Qur'aan. Since the smallest *soorah* is three verses long, those who hold this opinion state that three small verses (or their equivalent) are sufficient to qualify as *i'jaaz*.

---

586 as-Suyootee, v. 2, p. 151. I have paraphrased from the Arabic.

3)   The *i'jaaz* of the Qur'aan is present throughout the Qur'aan, without there being a minimum quantity. Even the smallest portion of the Qur'aan is a miracle by itself, as long as it forms a comprehensible phrase or sentence (but not necessarily a whole verse). As long as a phrase or a sentence can be recognised as the 'Qur'aan', and can be called such, it is considered to be an example of *i'jaaz*.

There is proof for all of these opinions in the Qur'aan, for Allaah challenges to bring forth a whole 'Qur'aan' similar to it (17:88), or one *soorah* (10:38), or even some speech equivalent to it (52:34).

The first opinion was held by some of the *Mu'tazilah*, the second by most of the scholars of *'uloom al-Qur'aan*, and the third by Shaykh al-Islaam Ibn Taymiyyah (d. 724 A.H.), and others.[587] Perhaps the last opinion is the strongest one.

After quoting these various opinions, Qattaan, in his *Mabaahith*, concludes,

> And we do not think that the *i'jaaz* is limited to a certain minimum quantity, for we find it (*i'jaaz*) in the sounds of the letters of the Qur'aan, and in the occurrence of its words, as we also find it in its verses and *soorahs*. The Qur'aan is the Speech of Allaah, and this is sufficient (for it having *i'jaaz* throughout).[588]

Qattaan's remark is convincing, but perhaps a qualification might be added: Any portion of the Qur'aan gives some aspect or aspects of *i'jaaz*, whether it be in its eloquence, or in its laws, or a combination of other aspects. However, a portion of the Qur'aan does not necessarily give every single aspect of *i'jaaz*; only the whole Qur'aan can be taken as an indication of *i'jaaz* in its totality. In other words, a portion of the Qur'aan is miraculous in some aspects, but only the whole Qur'aan is miraculous in every aspect, and Allaah knows best.[589]

---

587   al-Awajee, p. 399.

588   Qattaan, p. 264

589   cf. az-Zarkashee, v. 2, p. 105, where he uses a similar argument for another aspect of *i'jaaz*. Also see al-Awajee's conclusion, p. 113, which is very similar to this one. This does not mean, of course, that a portion of the Qur'aan can be imitated, but only that a portion of the Qur'aan does not substantiate every aspect of *i'jaaz* – only the whole Qur'aan can be claimed to do so.

CHAPTER 15

THE INTERPRETATION OF THE QUR'AAN – TAFSEER

The topic of *tafseer* is the most important topic of '*uloom al-Qur'aan*, since in many ways it is the primary goal of '*uloom al-Qur'aan* – to understand and implement the Qur'aan properly. This has also been the first topic of '*uloom al-Qur'aan* to have been written on, and without a doubt the one in which most of the works in this field have been written about.

I. The Definition of Tafseer and Ta'weel

The word '*tafseer*' comes from '*fassara*', which means, 'to explain, to expound, to elucidate, to interpret.' The word *tafseer* is the verbal noun of '*fassara*', and means 'the explanation or interpretation of something.'

According to another opinion,[590] the word *tafseer* is a transposition from *s-f-r*, which means, 'to expose, to uncover.' Thus, a woman who uncovers her face is called a '*saafirah*', and the act of uncovering her face is called '*sufoor*.' Therefore, according to this definition, '*tafseer*' would mean uncovering the meanings and exposing the secrets of the Qur'aan. However, the stronger opinion is the first one, even though both of these meanings are correct.

In Islaamic sciences, *tafseer* is defined to be: The science by which the Qur'aan is understood, its meanings explained, and its rulings derived.[591]

Another common word that is heard in this subject is the word '*ta'weel*'. What, then, is the difference, if any, between *tafseer* and *ta'weel*?

The word '*ta'weel*' is from *a-w-l*, which means 'to return, to revert,' which implies going back to the original meaning of a word to see what its meanings and connotations are. The meanings of the word '*ta'weel*' were given earlier, and are repeated here.

The word '*ta'weel*' has three meanings:

1) To understand a word in light of one of its connotations, despite the fact that this connotation is not the primary intent of the word.

---

590 az-Zarkashee, v. 2, p. 147.
591 as-Suyootee, v. 2, p. 223.

2) To explain a word or phrase.

3) The actuality of an event.

With these two definitions in mind, there are five main opinions as to the difference between *tafseer* and *ta'weel*, as follows:[592]

1) They are equivalent in meaning. This was the opinion of at-Tabaree (d. 310 A.H.), as his commentary of the Qur'aan uses these two terms interchangeably.

2) *Tafseer* is used in explaining a word which carries only one meaning, whereas *ta'weel* is used in choosing one of the connotations of a word that possesses many connotations.

3) According to al-Maatureedee (d. 333 A.H.), when the interpretation is based on certain knowledge, this is called *tafseer*, whereas when it is based on personal reasoning (*ijtihaad*), it is known as *ta'weel*.

4) Aboo Taalib at-Tha'labee held the view that *tafseer* was the explanation of the literal meaning of the verse, whereas *ta'weel* was the actual intent behind the verse. For example, the *tafseer* of the verse,

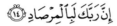

«Verily, your Lord is ever-Watchful» [89:14]

is that Allaah is aware of all that man does, but the *ta'weel* is that the verse is a warning to man not to lapse into sins or to belittle the commandments of Allaah.

5) *Tafseer* is meant to give the meanings of the individual words in a verse, whereas *ta'weel* gives the meaning of the verse as a whole.

There is no one correct opinion amongst these five, since various authors use these two words in all of these meanings. However, the most common understanding in modern usage of the two words is the second one, namely that *tafseer* is used to explain the meaning or intent of a verse which has only one connotation, whereas *ta'weel* is used when one of the possible connotations of a verse or word is chosen over the others due to external factors.

II. The Necessity and Importance of Tafseer

The question arises: Why is there a need for *tafseer*? After all, does not Allaah say in the Qur'aan:

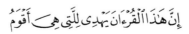

«Verily this Qur'aan leads to the path that is most right» [17:9]

and thus everybody can find the Straight Path through this Book? And is not the Qur'aan a complete source of guidance in and of itself, as it says,

---

592 cf., as-Suyootee, v.2, pps. 221-2, ar-Roomee, pps. 8-9, Zarabozo, p. 14.

وَنَزَّلْنَا عَلَيْكَ ٱلْكِتَـٰبَ تِبْيَـٰنًا لِّكُلِّ شَىْءٍ وَهُدًى وَرَحْمَةً وَبُشْرَىٰ لِلْمُسْلِمِينَ

«And We have sent down the Book to you as an explanation for everything,
a guidance, a mercy and glad tidings for Muslims» [16:89]?

Indeed, it is true that anyone who approaches the Qur'aan with a pure heart, seeking the guidance of Allaah, will find it. As Allaah says,

هَـٰذَا بَيَانٌ لِّلنَّاسِ وَهُدًى وَمَوْعِظَةٌ لِّلْمُتَّقِينَ ﴿١٣٨﴾

«This (Qur'aan) is a declaration for mankind, a guidance and an admonition for those who ward off evil» [3:138]

But this in no way implies that a person who is unaware of the numerous *hadeeth* of the Prophet (ﷺ) in explaining the Qur'aan, and of the reasons behind the revelation of specific verses, and of the intricacies of Arabic grammar and principles of rhetoric, and of the various *qira'aat*, and of the knowledge of the abrogated rulings, and of all of the other topics of *'uloom al-Qur'aan* will benefit from the Qur'aan to the same degree that a person who does know these facts will. For example, an Arabic linguist or grammarian might be able to see a certain wisdom behind the phrasing of a verse that the average person may not. A person specialised in the topics of *'uloom al-Qur'aan* will be better able to grasp the intended meanings of a verse, and derive rulings from it, in contrast to the average layman, who is not qualified to derive rulings from the Qur'aan.

As-Suyootee also discusses the necessity of *tafseer* in his *al-Itqaan*.[593] He begins by stating that it is a known fact that Allaah communicates with man in a way that the will be able to understand. This is the reason that every messenger has been sent in the language of his people. However, there are three basic reasons why *tafseer* is necessary despite these facts. First of all, Allaah uses the most clear, eloquent and concise language, and in doing so the meaning is clear to those who are well-grounded in the Arabic language, but not so clear to those who are not. Secondly, the Qur'aan itself does not always mention the events or references for which each particular verse was revealed, and these must be known in order for the verse to be fully and totally understood. Lastly, some words may have multiple meanings, and it is the job of the person that does *tafseer* to explain what is meant by the word.

It can be said that the purpose of *tafseer* is to elaborate the principles which the Qur'aan came to clarify:[594]

1) The elaboration of a perfect set of beliefs with regards to the Creator, and the relationship of the created with the Creator.

2) The perfection of personal conduct and good morals.

3) The establishment of a set of laws and code of conduct to govern individual and familial relations.

4) The establishment of laws governing societal and political dealings between communities and nations.

---

593 as-Suyootee, v.2, p. 223.
594 cf. Ik, pps. 64-66.

5) The narrations of the history of the previous nations, so that the pious among them may be followed, and the impious to act as a warning.

6) To give the good news of Paradise and the blessings in store for the believers, and the evil tidings of the punishment of Hell in store for the disbelievers.

7) To prove the truthfulness of the Prophet (ﷺ), and this is done by explaining the miraculous nature of the Qur'aan (i'jaaz).

Therefore, the job of a *mufassir* is to explain all of the above points to mankind.

From the above discussion, the importance of *tafseer* should become apparent. The science of *tafseer* is meant to explain to mankind the Book that has been revealed to them from Allaah. The Qur'aan is like a treasure trapped in a glass receptacle; mankind can view and benefit from this treasure, but they are in need of *tafseer*, for *tafseer* acts like the key that unlocks the treasure, so that mankind can benefit from it to the greatest possible extent. Iyaas ibn Mu'aawiyah (d. 122 A.H.) said, "The example of a people who recite the Qur'aan and do not know its explanation is like a group of people who have a written message from their king that comes to them during the night, and they do not have a lamp. Therefore, they do not know what is in the message. The example of one who knows *tafseer* is like a person who comes to them with a lamp and reads to them what is in the message." And the Successor Sa'eed ibn Jubayr (d. 95 A.H.) said, "Whoever recites the Qur'aan and does not explain it, is like an ignorant person."[595]

As-Suyootee said,

> (The science of *tafseer*) is the most honourable of all sciences for three reasons. The first reason is with respect to its topic. It deals with the Speech of Allaah, which contains every kind of wisdom and virtue. It contains pronouncements about what has passed, reports of what will happen and judgements concerning what happens between the people. Its wonders never cease. The second reason is with respect to its goal. Its goal is to lead mankind to the firm handhold of Allaah, and to the true happiness, one that does not end. The third reason is with respect to the great need for this science. Every aspect of this religion and this world, in the near or distant future, is in need of the sciences of the *sharee'ah* and knowledge of the religion, and this knowledge can only be obtained through the understanding of the Book of Allaah.[596]

Apart from these reasons, the Qur'aan itself commands its readers to ponder over it, and to reflect upon its meanings, for it says,

$$\text{كِتَـٰبٌ أَنزَلْنَـٰهُ إِلَيْكَ مُبَـٰرَكٌ لِّيَدَّبَّرُوٓاْ ءَايَـٰتِهِۦ وَلِيَتَذَكَّرَ أُوْلُواْ ٱلْأَلْبَـٰبِ ﴿٢٩﴾}$$

«(This is) a Book which We have sent down to you, full of blessings, so that they may ponder over its verses, and that men of understanding may remember» [38:29]

It is the science of *tafseer* which is the fruit of 'pondering over its verses.'

---

595 Both quotes taken from Zarabozo, *ibid.,* p. 12.
596 as-Suyootee, v. 2, p. 224; cf. Zarabozo, p. 12.

III. The History of Tafseer

A. The Time of the Prophet (ﷺ)

It is no surprise to discover that the science of *tafseer* started during the lifetime of the Prophet (ﷺ) himself. In fact, one of the primary roles of the Prophet (ﷺ), as shall be expounded on later, was to interpret the Qur'aan. Allaah says,

$$وَأَنزَلْنَآ إِلَيْكَ$$
$$ٱلذِّكْرَ لِتُبَيِّنَ لِلنَّاسِ مَا نُزِّلَ إِلَيْهِمْ وَلَعَلَّهُمْ يَتَفَكَّرُونَ$$

«And We have sent down to you (O Muhammad (ﷺ)) the Remembrance,
so that you may clearly explain to mankind what has been revealed to them,
and so that they may give thought» [16:44]

The science of *tafseer* during the Prophet's (ﷺ) life was a relatively easy matter. This was so for a number of factors. Firstly, the Companions were witnessing the revelation of the Qur'aan, and the circumstances during which it was revealed. They were aware of the reason behind the revelation of a verse (*asbaab an-nuzool*), and as such did not need to search for this knowledge as later interpreters would have to. Secondly, the Arabic of the Companions was the Arabic of the Qur'aan, as the Qur'aan was revealed in their dialect. Therefore the Arabic of the Qur'aan was, in general, understood by them without any difficulties. Lastly, and most importantly, the Prophet (ﷺ) was alive, and the Qur'aan was still being revealed, so even if there were any difficulties in understanding any verse, they could turn to the Prophet (ﷺ) for an explanation. An example quoted earlier is with regards to the verse,

$$ٱلَّذِينَ ءَامَنُوا۟ وَلَمْ يَلْبِسُوٓا۟ إِيمَٰنَهُم بِظُلْمٍ$$

«Those who believe and do not mix their belief with injustice...»[6:82]

The Companions asked, "O Messenger of Allaah! Who amongst us does not do injustice (to his soul)?" The Prophet (ﷺ) replied, "Have you not read the statement of Luqmaan,

$$إِنَّ ٱلشِّرْكَ لَظُلْمٌ عَظِيمٌ$$

«Verily, *shirk* is a great injustice?'» [31:13].[597]

In other words, the Prophet (ﷺ) informed them that the injustice referred to in this verse was *shirk*, or the association of partners with Allaah.

The Companions were careful that they understood every single verse in the Qur'aan properly. Aboo 'Abd ar-Rahmaan as-Sulamee (d. 75 A.H.) reported that whenever the people who taught them the Qur'aan, like 'Uthmaan ibn 'Affaan, 'Abdullaah ibn Mas'ood, and others, learnt ten verses of the Qur'aan, they would not proceed further until they had understood whatever ideas and regulations those verses con-

---

597 Reported by al-Bukhaaree.

tained. They used to say, "We learnt the Qur'aan, and studied its ideas and injunctions all together."[598] This narration shows that the Companions were eager to understand Qur'aan, so much so that they would not memorise any verses until they had
already understood what they knew.

The role of the Prophet (ﷺ), and quantity of the Qur'aan that he interpreted, will
be elaborated upon in the next section.

B. The Period of the Companions

After the death of the Prophet (ﷺ), the science of *tafseer* took on a more systematic
approach. Thus it can be considered that the first true *mufassirs* were actually the
Companions. The sources that the Companions used for *tafseer* were the Qur'aan,
the statements of the Prophet (ﷺ), the principles of Arabic grammar and rhetoric,
their own personal reasoning (*ijtihaad*), and pagan and Judaeo-Christian customs
that were prevalent at the time of the revelation of the Qur'aan. These sources will be
discussed in greater detail in the following section.

There were many among the Companions who were well known for their knowledge of the interpretation of the Qur'aan. As-Suyootee wrote, "There are ten who
were famous for their knowledge of *tafseer* among the Companions: the four *Khulafaa
ar-Raashidoon*,[599] 'Abdullaah ibn Mas'ood, 'Abdullaah ibn 'Abbaas, Ubay ibn Ka'ab,
Zayd ibn Thaabit, Aboo Moosaa al-Ash'aree and 'Abdullaah ibn Zubayr. As for the
Khulafaa, 'Alee ibn Abee Taalib has the most narrations amongst them; as for the
other three, there reports are very rare to find, since they died relatively earlier..."[600] In
other words, the *tafseer* narrations of Aboo Bakr, 'Umar and 'Uthmaan are not as
common due to the fact that they were not compiled because of their relatively early
deaths. Also, during their time, there was no great need to interpret much of the
Qur'aan, as the Companions were many and wide-spread. During later times, however, such as during the Caliphate of 'Alee, the need to interpret the Qur'aan was
much greater than before.

There were others besides these ten Companions who were well known for their
knowledge of *tafseer*, such as Anas ibn Maalik, Aboo Hurayrah, Jaabir ibn 'Abdillaah
and 'Aa'ishah, except that they were not in the same category as the ten whom as-
Suyootee mentioned.

The most knowledgeable Companion with regards to the interpretation of the
Qur'aan is considered to be Ibn 'Abbaas. 'Abdullaah ibn 'Umar said, "Ibn 'Abbaas is
the most knowledgeable of this *ummah* concerning the revelation given to Muhammad
(ﷺ)."[601] This is due to the fact that the Prophet (ﷺ) himself prayed for Ibn 'Abbaas,

---

598 Ibn Taymiyyah, p. 12.

599 A term that means 'The rightly-guided caliphs', used to denote the first four caliphs, Aboo Bakr,
'Umar, 'Uthmaan and 'Alee.

600 as-Suyootee, v. 2, p. 239.

601 adh-Dhahabee, v. 1, p. 72 (the reference to adh-Dhahabee, whenever it appears in this chapter, refers
to Dr. ad-Adh-Dhahabee's *Tafseer wa al-Mufasiroon*, unless otherwise specified).

for he (ﷺ) said, "O Allaah! Give him the knowledge of the Book, and of Wisdom!" and in another narration, "O Allaah! Give him the knowledge of the religion, and interpretation."[602] He used to accompany the Prophet (ﷺ) during his youth, as he was his (ﷺ) cousin. Also, his aunt Maymoonah was a wife of the Prophet (ﷺ).

Ibn 'Abbaas was held in great esteem by the Companions, despite his age (he was only thirteen when the Prophet (ﷺ) passed away). 'Umar used to let Ibn 'Abbaas enter into the meetings of the older Companions, so some of them complained, "Why is it that you let him enter, even though we have sons the same age as him (whom you do not allow to enter)?" 'Umar answered, "Since he is amongst the most knowledgeable of you!" So he called them one day, to prove to them this statement, and he asked them, "What do you think of the verse,

$$ إِذَا جَآءَ نَصْرُ ٱللَّهِ وَٱلْفَتْحُ $$

«When the help of Allaah comes, and the Conquest» [110:1]?

Some of them did not reply, while others said, "We have been commanded to thank Allaah and ask for His forgiveness whenever we are helped and aided to victory." 'Umar asked Ibn 'Abbaas, "And do you think the same also, O Ibn 'Abbaas?" He answered, "No!" 'Umar asked, "Then what do you say." He replied, "This is an indication to the Prophet (ﷺ) from Allaah that his life is about to end. The verse means, 'When the help of Allaah comes, and the Conquest' then this is a sign of your approaching death, therefore,

$$ فَسَبِّحْ بِحَمْدِ رَبِّكَ وَٱسْتَغْفِرْهُ إِنَّهُ كَانَ تَوَّابًۢا ٣ $$

«Glorify the Praises of your Lord, and ask for Forgiveness, for verily He is ever-accepting repentance!» [110:3]

'Umar said, "I don't know any other meaning to this except what you have said!"[603]

The narrations of Ibn 'Abbaas, along with those of 'Abdullaah ibn Mas'ood, 'Alee ibn Abee Ṭaalib, and Ubay ibn Ka'ab, are the most numerous narrations from Companions that are to be found in *tafseer* literature. Each one of them established centres of learning during their lifetimes, and left many students among the Successors after their deaths.

The Companions did not leave narrations concerning every single verse in the Qur'aan. This is because the people of their time understood much of what the Qur'aan discussed, and only where the possibility for misinterpretation or ignorance existed did the Companions give their own interpretation of the relevant verse. Such interpretation typically consisted of explaining a verse in clearer words, or explaining a particular phrase or word with pre-Islaamic poetry. Another characteristic of this time is the relatively trivial differences in *tafseer*, as compared to later generations.

---

602 Reported by al-Bukhaaree.
603 Reported by al-Bukhaaree.

C. THE PERIOD OF THE SUCCESSORS

After the generation of the Companions, the students of the Companions took over the responsibility of explaining the Qur'aan. The Successors used the same sources to interpret the Qur'aan that the Companions did, except that they added to the list of sources the interpretations of the Companions. They understood that an interpretation given by the Companions of the Prophet (ﷺ) could not be compared to an interpretation of any person after them. Therefore, the sources for interpreting the Qur'aan during this generation were: the Qur'aan, the statements of the Prophet (ﷺ) that the Companions had informed them of, the Companions' personal reasoning (*ijtihaad*) of the verse, the Arabic language, their own personal reasoning (*ijtihaad*), and Judaeo-Christian tradition.

After the death of the Prophet (ﷺ), the Companions spread out to different Muslim cities in order to teach people the religion of Islaam. Each one taught many Successors, most of whom became scholars in their own right in due time.

Historically, three primary learning centres were established in the Muslim empire: Makkah, Madeenah and Koofah. Each of these areas became leading centres of knowledge during the period of the Successors, including the knowledge of *tafseer*.

In Makkah, where Ibn 'Abbaas had taught, his primary students became the scholars of this area. In particular, Sa'eed ibn Jubayr (d. 95 A.H.), Mujaahid ibn Jabr (d. 104 A.H.), 'Ikrimah (d. 104 A.H.), Taawoos (d. 106 A.H.), and 'Ataa ibn Rabaah (d. 114 A.H.) became leading authorities in this field, and their names are still to be found in many works of *tafseer*.

In Madeenah, the influence of 'Ubay ibn Ka'ab was the strongest in the arena of *tafseer*, and his students Aboo al-'Aaliyah (d. 90 A.H.), Muhammad ibn Ka'ab al-Quradee (d. 118 A.H.) and Zayd ibn Aslam (d. 136 A.H.) emerged as the scholars of *tafseer* in Madeenah during this period.

In Koofah, 'Abdullaah ibn Mas'ood left behind his great legacy to 'Alqamah ibn Qays (d. 61 A.H.), Masrooq (d. 63 A.H.), and al-Aswad ibn Yazeed (d. 74 A.H.). Other Successors from Koofah who were famous for their knowledge of *tafseer* were: 'Aamir ash-Sha'bee (d. 109 A.H.), al-Hasan al-Basree (d. 110 A.H.) and Qataadah as-Sadoosee (d. 117 A.H.)

During this period, greater emphasis was placed on Judaeo-Christian tradition (known as *Israa'eeliyaat*), and because of this, many of these narrations entered into Islaamic literature. Most of the people who narrated these traditions were Jews and Christians who had embraced Islaam, such as 'Abdullaah ibn Salaam (he was a Companion, d. 43 A.H.), Ka'ab al-Ahbaar (he embraced Islaam after the death of the Prophet (ﷺ) and did not see him; he died 32 A.H.), Wahb ibn Munnabih (d. 110 A.H.), and 'Abdul Maalik ibn Jurayj (d. 150 A.H.). Much of the Judaeo-Christian traditions prevalent in *tafseer* literature can be traced back to these scholars.

Also during this time, the differences in interpreting the Qur'aan were much greater than during the time of the Companions. Another characteristic of this period is the increase of forged narrations attributed to the Prophet (ﷺ). This was due to the political and religious strife that was rampant throughout the Muslim territories at that time. Lastly, the quantity of verses for which narrations exist from the Successors is greater than that for the Companions, since more verses needed explanation than during the time of the Companions.

D. The Compilation of Tafseer

After the period of the Successors, the stage of the actual compilation and writing of *tafseer* began. The most important works were by scholars of *hadeeth*, who, as part of their narrations and works of *hadeeth*, also had sections on *tafseer*. Therefore, during this stage, the narrations of *tafseer* were considered a branch of *hadeeth* literature. Some of the scholars of this period that were known for their *tafseer* narrations include Yazeed ibn Haaroon as-Sulamee (d. 117 A.H.), Sufyaan al-Thawri (d. 161 A.H.), Sufyaan ibn 'Uyaynah (d. 198 A.H.), Wakee' ibn al-Jaraah (d. 197 A.H.), Shu'bah ibn al-Hajjaaj (d. 160 A.H.), Aadam ibn Abee Iyaas (d. 220 A.H.), and 'Abd ibn Humayd (d. 249 A.H.). None of their works have survived intact until the present day.[604]

The next stage in the history of *tafseer* saw the separation of *tafseer* literature from *hadeeth*, and the emergence of independent works solely on *tafseer*. Another stride during this stage was that every verse was discussed, so that *tafseer* was not only limited to those verses for which narrations from the Prophet (ﷺ) and Companions existed; rather, these *tafseers* encompassed all the verses in the Qur'aan.

In attempting to answer who the first person to write a comprehensive *tafseer* of the Qur'aan was, the researcher is faced with a rather significant impediment: a lack of almost all manuscripts written during the first century of the *hijrah*. However, there are a number of references in later works to such manuscripts, and among the earliest works referenced is that of Sa'eed ibn Jubayr (d. 95 A.H.).[605] Most likely, this work was not a complete *tafseer* of the Qur'aan, but rather composed of narrations from the previous generations. An interesting narration in the *Fihrist* of Ibn Nadeem (d. 438 A.H.) reads as follows:[606]

> 'Umar ibn Bukayr, one of the students of al-Farraa, was with the governor Hasan ibn Sahl. He wrote to al-Farraa: 'The governor sometimes questions me concerning (the *tafseer* of) a verse in the Qur'aan, but I am unable to respond to him. Therefore, if you think it suitable to compile something with regards to the Qur'aan, or write a book concerning this, I can return to this book (whenever he asks me)'. al-Farraa said to his students, 'Gather together so that I may dictate to you a book on the Qur'aan'...and he told the *mu'adhin* to recite *Soorah* al-Faatihah, so that he may interpret it, until the whole book (i.e., the Qur'aan) was finished. The narrator of the story, Aboo al-'Abbaas, said, 'No one before him every did anything like it, and I don't think that anyone can add to what he wrote!'

604 adh-Dhahabee, v.1, p. 152.
605 ibid., v.1, p. 155.
606 ibid., v.1, p. 154, from the *Fihrist*.

Al-Farraa died in the year 207 A.H., and thus we can say that this is definitely one of the earliest works of this nature.[607] Ibn Maajah (d. 273), of *Sunan* fame, also wrote a *tafseer* of the Qur'aan, but again this was limited to narrations from the previous generations.

One of the greatest classics available is without a doubt the monumental *tafseer* of the Qur'aan by Muhammad ibn Jareer at-Tabaree (d. 310 A.H.). This *tafseer*, although heavily based on narrations, also discusses the grammatical analysis of the verse, the various *qira'aat* and their significance on the meaning of the verse, and, on occasion, Ibn Jareer's personal reasoning (*ijtihaad*) on various aspects of the verse. In many ways, this can be considered to be the first *tafseer* to attempt to cover every aspect of a verse. Other *tafseer*s followed quickly; in particular the *tafseer*s of Aboo Bakr ibn Mundhir an-Naisapooree (d. 318 A.H.), Ibn Abee Haatim (d. 327 A.H.), Aboo Shaykh ibn Hibbaan (d. 369 A.H.), al-Haakim (d. 405 A.H.) and Aboo Bakr ibn Mardawayh (d. 410).[608]

This era also saw the beginning of the specialisation in *tafseer*, with *tafseer*s being written, for example, with greater emphasis on the grammatical analysis and inter-pretation of the Qur'aan. Greater emphasis was also placed on personal reasoning (*ijtihaad*), and *tafseer*s written solely for the defence of sectarian views (such as the *tafseer*s of the *Mu'tazilah*), and even for the defence of one's *fiqh madh-hab* (such as the *tafseer*s of the *Hanafees*, *Shaafi'ees* and *Maalikees*) appeared. Another aspect that started during this era was the deletion of the *isnaad* from *tafseer* narrations, and this led to the increasement of weak and fabricated reports in *tafseer* literature.

A Summary

To summarise, it is possible to divide the history of *tafseer* into five periods.[609] The first period is considered to be the time of the Companions and Successors, and con-sisted mainly of narrations concerning those verses over which there was a difference of opinion or misunderstanding, in addition to the *hadeeth* of the Prophet (ﷺ) deal-ing with *tafseer*. Personal reasoning (*ijtihaad*) from the Companions and Successors was, in general, only resorted to when absolutely necessary.

The second period is the era of the late Successors, and the generation after them. During this time, *hadeeth* literature had begun to be compiled, and *tafseer* narrations therefore become a part of *hadeeth* works. Also during this time, the various *hadeeth* of the Prophet (ﷺ) and narrations from different Companions began to be compiled, whereas in the first period, these narrations were typically limited to a specific area.

The third stage saw the rise of independent *tafseer* works, based on the *hadeeth* works of the previous generation, and thus *tafseer* became an independent science among the Islaamic sciences. This stage, which can be said to begin in the second half

---

607 This work, unlike many others from its era, is available in manuscript form, and part of it has been published by Daar al-Kutub al-Misriyah, 1956.

608 adh-Dhahabee, p. 152.

609 cf. adh-Dhahabee, v. 1, pps. 151-56.

of the third century, also produced the first complete Qur'aanic *tafseer*s, whose commentary was not limited to only those verses concerning which narrations existed from previous generations. However, during this stage, the primary source of *tafseer* still remained narrations from the previous generation.

It was only during the fourth stage where reliance on narrations decreased, and much greater emphasis was placed on personal reasoning, and *tafseer*s were written based on sectarian bias. For example, as-Suyootee narrates concerning the verse,

$$غَيْرِ ٱلْمَغْضُوبِ عَلَيْهِمْ وَلَا ٱلضَّآلِّينَ$$

«...Not the path of those whom You are angry with, nor those who are astray»
[1:7]

that there exist ten different opinions concerning who this verse refers to, despite the fact that the Prophet (ﷺ) has clearly explained that it refers to the Jews and Christians![610] This period also witnessed the increasement of forged narrations in *tafseer* literature, as the *isnaad* disappeared from *tafseer* works.

The final period of the history of *tafseer*, which has lasted from the fourth century of the *hijrah* until today, saw the culmination of the science of *tafseer*, and the emergence of various categories of *tafseer*, such as *tafseer* based on narrations, on personal reasoning, topic-wise interpretation, polemical interpretation, and jurisprudential interpretation (these will be discussed in greater detail below). Other *tafseer*s sought to combine all of these topics into one work, thus giving a broad, all-encompassing approach to interpretation.

IV. The Principles of Tafseer

By the 'Principles of *Tafseer*' is meant the proper methodology in interpreting the Qur'aan, which includes the conditions and characteristics of a *mufassir* (one who interprets the Qur'aan), and the basis and characteristics of a proper *tafseer*.

The science of *tafseer* is one which, similar to the other sciences of Islaam, is based on well-grounded, systematic principles. These principles are derived from the Qur'aan, the *Sunnah* and the statements of the Companions.

As-Suyootee, in summarising the principles of *tafseer*, said,[611]

> The scholars have said: Whoever wishes to interpret the Qur'aan, he should first turn to the Qur'aan itself. This is because what has been narrated succinctly in one place might be expounded upon in another place, and what is summarized in one place might be explained in another...
>
> If he has done that, then he turns to the *Sunnah*, for it is the explainer of the Qur'aan, and a clarifier to it. Imaam as-Shaafi'ee said, 'All that the Prophet (ﷺ) said is based on his understanding of the Qur'aan.' And Allaah said,

---

610 as-Suyootee, v. 2, p. 190.
611 as-Suyootee, v. 2, p. 225.

$$\text{إِنَّآ أَنزَلْنَآ إِلَيْكَ ٱلْكِتَٰبَ بِٱلْحَقِّ لِتَحْكُمَ بَيْنَ ٱلنَّاسِ بِمَآ أَرَىٰكَ ٱللَّهُ}$$

«Verily, We have revealed to you the Book, in truth, so that you may judge between mankind by that which Allaah has shown you» [4:105]

And the Prophet (ﷺ) said, 'Indeed, I have been given the Qur'aan, and something similar to it,'[612] meaning the *Sunnah*.

If he does not find it (the *tafseer*) in the *Sunnah*, he turns to the statements of the Companions, for they are the most knowledgeable of it, since they witnessed the circumstances and situations the Qur'aan was revealed in, and since they were blessed with complete understanding, and true knowledge, and pious actions...

These principles, and others, will now be discussed in greater detail.

1) Tafseer OF THE QUR'AAN BY THE QUR'AAN

The most important source of understanding the Qur'aan is the Qur'aan itself. After all, the Qur'aan is an entire Book that has been revealed by Allaah, and therefore in order to understand any one verse, the entire context of this verse must be looked at. The meanings of the Qur'aan can never contradict each other, as Allaah says,

$$\text{أَفَلَا يَتَدَبَّرُونَ ٱلْقُرْءَانَ وَلَوْ كَانَ مِنْ عِندِ غَيْرِ ٱللَّهِ لَوَجَدُواْ فِيهِ ٱخْتِلَٰفًا كَثِيرًا ﴿٨٢﴾}$$

«Do they not ponder over the Qur'aan? For indeed, had it been from other than Allaah, they would surely have found many contradictions in it» [4:82]

In this verse, the command is given to ponder over the whole Qur'aan, verse by verse, for had it been from any other than Allaah, its verses would have contradicted one another. Therefore, it is essential to turn to the Qur'aan itself in order to interpret any verse in the Qur'aan.

This principle is demonstrated in many verses in the Qur'aan. Sometimes, a question is asked, and then answered in the next verses. For example,

$$\text{وَٱلسَّمَآءِ وَٱلطَّارِقِ ﴿١﴾ وَمَآ أَدْرَىٰكَ مَا ٱلطَّارِقُ ﴿٢﴾ ٱلنَّجْمُ ٱلثَّاقِبُ ﴿٣﴾}$$

«By the Heavens, and the *taariq*. And what will make you know what the *taariq* is? (It is) the star of piercing brightness» [86:1-3]

In other cases, the reference to another verse is not obvious. For example, the reference to

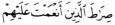

«the path of those whom You have favoured» [1:7]

---

612   Reported by Aboo Daawood, at-Tirmidhee and an-Nasaa'ee.

is explained in 4:69 as:

$$وَمَن يُطِعِ ٱللَّهَ وَٱلرَّسُولَ فَأُوْلَٰٓئِكَ مَعَ ٱلَّذِينَ أَنْعَمَ ٱللَّهُ عَلَيْهِم مِّنَ ٱلنَّبِيِّـۧنَ وَٱلصِّدِّيقِينَ وَٱلشُّهَدَآءِ وَٱلصَّٰلِحِينَ وَحَسُنَ أُوْلَٰٓئِكَ رَفِيقًا$$

«And whoever obeys Allaah and His Messenger, they will be in the company of those whom Allaah has shown favour, of the Prophets, and the truthful followers, and the martyrs, and the pious. And how excellent these companions are!»

Therefore, the second verse explains who 'those whom You have favoured' are.

In some places in the Qur'aan, a story is mentioned in brief, and in another place it is elaborated. For example, in the story of the repentance of Aadam, verse 2:37 states,

$$فَتَلَقَّىٰٓ ءَادَمُ مِن رَّبِّهِۦ كَلِمَٰتٍ فَتَابَ عَلَيْهِ$$

«Then Aadam received from his Lord words, and He relented towards him.»

In this verse, the 'words' that Aadam received are not mentioned, and it is essential to turn to another verse to know what Aadam said:

$$قَالَا رَبَّنَا ظَلَمْنَآ أَنفُسَنَا وَإِن لَّمْ تَغْفِرْ لَنَا وَتَرْحَمْنَا لَنَكُونَنَّ مِنَ ٱلْخَٰسِرِينَ ﴿٢٣﴾$$

«They (Aadam and Eve) said, 'Our Lord! We have wronged ourselves. If you do not forgive us and have Mercy on us, we will be of the lost!» [7:23]

Other verses direct the reader to another passage in the Qur'aan, or tell the reader that the subject has already been mentioned. For example, Allaah says,

$$وَعَلَى ٱلَّذِينَ هَادُوا۟ حَرَّمْنَا مَا قَصَصْنَا عَلَيْكَ مِن قَبْلُ$$

«And unto the Jews, We forbade them such (foods) that We have already mentioned to you before...» [16:118]

In other words, these prohibitions have already been elaborated upon elsewhere in the Qur'aan (cf. 6:146). In another verse, Allaah states,

$$أُحِلَّتْ لَكُم بَهِيمَةُ ٱلْأَنْعَٰمِ إِلَّا مَا يُتْلَىٰ عَلَيْكُمْ$$

«Lawful to you (for food) are all the beasts of cattle, except that which will have been recited to you.» [5:1]

After two verses, the beasts that are forbidden are 'recited':

$$حُرِّمَتْ عَلَيْكُمُ ٱلْمَيْتَةُ وَٱلدَّمُ وَلَحْمُ ٱلْخِنزِيرِ$$

«Forbidden to you are all dead animals, and blood, and the flesh of pigs....» [5:3]

The Prophet (ﷺ) also showed the principle of interpreting the Qur'aan by the Qur'aan when he was asked concerning the verse,

$$ ٱلَّذِينَ ءَامَنُوا۟ وَلَمْ يَلْبِسُوٓا۟ إِيمَٰنَهُم بِظُلْمٍ $$

«Those who believe and do not mix their belief with injustice...»[6:82]

The Companions asked, "O Messenger of Allaah! Who amongst us does not do injustice (to his soul)?" The Prophet (ﷺ) replied, "Have you not read the statement of Luqmaan, إِنَّ ٱلشِّرْكَ لَظُلْمٌ عَظِيمٌ 'Verily, *shirk* is a great injustice?'" (31:13).[613] In other words, the Prophet (ﷺ) quoted them another verse in the Qur'aan to explain to them what the 'injustice' referred to in the verse actually meant – an example of *tafseer* of the Qur'aan by the Qur'aan.

Included in the interpretation of the Qur'aan with the Qur'aan is the knowledge of *asbaab an-nuzool*, the knowledge of *makkee* and *madanee* verses, the *naasikh* and *mansookh* verses, the various *qira'aat*, and the knowledge of the different categories of verses (the *muhkam* and *mutashaabih*, the *'aam* and the *khaas*, the *mutlaq* and the *muqqayad*, the *mantooq* and the *mafhoom*, the *haqeeqee* and the *majaazee*, and other categories which were not discussed). This is because a general ruling (*'aam*) in one verse might be specified (*khaas*) in another verse, and so forth. In addition, all the different *qira'aat* of a verse must be considered to arrive at a proper understanding of a verse. All the relevant verses must be taken into account to form a complete picture, as all the verses of the Qur'aan complement one another.

To conclude, it is essential that every verse of the Qur'aan be looked at in light of its sister verses; no interpretation of any verse can contradict another verse.

2) Tafseer by the Sunnah

After the *tafseer* of the Qur'aan by the Qur'aan itself, the second source of *tafseer* is *tafseer* by the *Sunnah*. It must be mentioned that even though the *Sunnah* is taken to be the 'second' source of *tafseer*, it is in fact of equal importance to the Qur'aan. In other words, a person wishing to understand the Qur'aan *must* turn to the *Sunnah* in order to understand it correctly. The Qur'aan and *Sunnah* must be taken together to arrive at a proper understanding of a verse.

In fact, one of the primary roles of the Prophet (ﷺ) was to explain the meanings of the Qur'aan to mankind. Allaah says,

$$ وَأَنزَلْنَآ إِلَيْكَ ٱلذِّكْرَ لِتُبَيِّنَ لِلنَّاسِ مَا نُزِّلَ إِلَيْهِمْ وَلَعَلَّهُمْ يَتَفَكَّرُونَ $$

«And We have sent down to you (O Muhammad (ﷺ)) the Remembrance, so that you may clearly explain to mankind what has been revealed to them, and so that they may give thought» [16:44]

---

613 Reported by al-Bukhaaree.

Therefore, not only was the job of the Prophet (ﷺ) to convey the literal text of the Qur'aan, he also had to convey its explanation as well.[614]

How Much of the Qur'aan was Explained?

The question arises, then, as to how much of the Qur'aan was actually explained by the Prophet (ﷺ)? In other words, do there exist narrations from the Prophet (ﷺ) concerning the interpretation of every single verse, and if not, then how is the previous quoted verse of the Qur'aan understood?

The scholars of Islaam were divided into two opinions with regards to this issue. Shaykh al-Islaam Ibn Taymiyyah (d. 728 A.H.) was of the view that the Prophet (ﷺ) explained all of the Qur'aan, whereas Jalaal ad-Deen as-Suyootee (d. 911 A.H.) claimed that the Prophet (ﷺ) only explained a small portion of it.[615] In fact, both of these opinions are correct once the intent of both sides is understood. Those who claimed that the Prophet (ﷺ) only explained a small portion of the Qur'aan meant that there do not exist very many verbal narrations from the Prophet (ﷺ) concerning the detailed explanation of every single verse in the Qur'aan. On the contrary, as-Suyootee only managed to find a few hundred narrations from the Prophet (ﷺ) (including weak and fabricated ones) in which he (ﷺ) explicitly interpreted a verse.[616] On the other hand, what Ibn Taymiyyah meant was that the Prophet (ﷺ) left us all the necessary knowledge needed in order to properly understand the Qur'aan. As 'Aa'ishah reported, the Prophet's (ﷺ) character embodied the Qur'aan.[617] Therefore, even though there might not exist many explicit statements from the Prophet (ﷺ) concerning *tafseer*, the Prophet (ﷺ) did leave us with the information and methodology necessary for understanding the Qur'aan. Therefore, it is essential to understand the Qur'aan not only in light of the explicit narrations of the Prophet (ﷺ) on the Qur'aan, but also in light of all of the *hadeeth* of the Prophet (ﷺ), whether they are concerning beliefs or laws, and in light of the actions of the Prophet (ﷺ), since his sayings and actions can be considered to be embodying the laws of the Qur'aan.

This opinion is supported by numerous statements from the Companions. Aboo 'Abd ar-Rahmaan as-Sulamee (d. 75 A.H.), the famous Successor, narrated, "Those who taught us the Qur'aan, such as 'Uthmaan ibn 'Affaan, 'Abdullaah ibn Mas'ood, and others, told us that they would not memorise more than ten verses until they had understood what knowledge it contained, and implemented it. They used to say, 'So we learnt the Qur'aan, (its) knowledge and (its) implementation at the same time.'"[618] It is apparent, then, that the Companions made sure that they understood the meaning of the Qur'aan, and then implemented it. 'Umar narrated, "Amongst the last verses

---

614 al-Albaanee, Muhammad Naasir ad-Deen, *Manzilat as-Sunnah fi al-Islaam* (Dar al-Hayah al-Islaamiyah, Egypt, n.d.), p.5.

615 adh-Dhahabee, v. 1, p. 54. Actually, as-Suyootee clarifies his point of view later on in his *Itqaan*, which agrees in principle with Ibn Taymiyyah's view. cf. *Itqaan*, v. 2, p. 264.

616 cf. *Itqaan*, v. 2, pps. 244-264.

617 Reported by al-Bukhaaree.

618 Ibn Taymiyyah, p. 12.

to be revealed were the verses pertaining to interest, and the Prophet (ﷺ) passed away before explaining them to us."[619] This narration explicitly shows that the Prophet (ﷺ) used to make sure that the Companions understood the Qur'aan, since the only reason that the verses of interest were not explained in great detail was due to the sudden death of the Prophet (ﷺ).

As was mentioned earlier, there are only a small percentage of verses for which explicit narrations exist from the Prophet (ﷺ). The verse concerning the interpretation of 'wrongdoing' (6:82) as *shirk* has already been given above. This example illustrates the necessity of the interpretation of the Prophet (ﷺ), for even the Companions, despite their knowledge of Arabic, could not understand the correct interpretation of this verse until they had asked the Prophet (ﷺ). Another example is the *hadeeth* of the Prophet (ﷺ) in which he explained '...those whom You are angry with,' and '...those who are astray,' (1:7) as the Jews and Christians.[620] He also explained the 'middle prayer' (2:238) as the Aṣr prayer,[621] the 'additional (reward)' (10:26) as the seeing of Allaah by the believers in Paradise,[622] and that *al-Kawthar* (108:1) was "...a river that my Lord has given me in Paradise."[623]

In addition to such explicit examples of *tafseer*, there exist numerous examples from the life and sayings of the Prophet (ﷺ) which explain certain verses of Qur'aan, but are not recorded as explicit statements of *tafseer*. For example, the Prophet (ﷺ) stated, "Hell will be brought forth on that Day (i.e., Day of Judgement). It will have seventy thousand ropes (attached to it), and on each rope, there will be seventy thousand angels dragging it."[624] Although this *hadeeth* does not mention any verse in the Qur'aan, it can be used to interpret verse 90:23, "And Hell will be brought that Day." The *hadeeth* describes how it will be brought. In another example, the penalty prescribed for theft is, "As for the thief, male or female, cut off his/her hand" (5:38). The *Sunnah* of the Prophet (ﷺ) explains that the thief's hand is only to be cut off if he steals above a certain monetary value, and that in such a case the right hand is to be cut off from the wrist joint.[625] These additional details needed for understanding this verse are not present in the Qur'aan itself. In another verse, the Qur'aan proclaims,

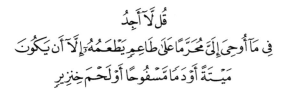

«Say, I do not find in that which has been revealed to me anything which is
forbidden to eat by anyone who wishes to eat it except a dead animal, or
blood poured forth, or the flesh of swine...'» [6:145]

619 Reported by Aḥmad and Ibn Maajah.
620 Reported by at-Tirmidhee.
621 Reported by at-Tirmidhee, and referred to in al-Bukhaaree and Muslim.
622 Reported by Muslim.
623 Reported by al-Bukhaaree and Muslim.
624 Reported by at-Tirmidhee.
625 cf. al-Albaanee, *Manzilat*, p. 6.

However, this verse is not exhaustive, as the *Sunnah* adds to this list all animals with fangs or claws, and excludes from the general ruling of dead animals seafood and locusts.[626]

From these and other examples, it is possible to say that the Prophet (ﷺ) explained the Qur'aan in the following manners:[627]

1) By his implementation of general or vague commands. For example, the Qur'aan orders the believers to pray and perform *Hajj*. The Prophet (ﷺ), by his actions and statements, showed the believers the exact procedure and timings of prayer, and the specific rites of *Hajj*.

2) By explaining unclear concepts in verses. For example, the verse commanding the believers to begin their fasts,

حَتَّىٰ يَتَبَيَّنَ لَكُمُ ٱلْخَيْطُ ٱلْأَبْيَضُ مِنَ ٱلْخَيْطِ ٱلْأَسْوَدِ

«...when the white thread becomes clear from the black thread» [2:187],

was explained by the Prophet (ﷺ) as being the streaks of light in the sky after dawn.

3) By specifying the exact connotation of a word or phrase. The example in which the Prophet (ﷺ) specified that the 'injustice' referred to in 6:82 was *shirk* falls in this category.

4) By constraining a general ruling or verse. The example of the specification of 'thief' and 'hand' by the Prophet (ﷺ) was given above.

5) By generalising a specific ruling or verse. An example of this is when some Companions came to the Prophet (ﷺ) and asked him concerning the verse,

«And if you travel through the land, there is no sin upon you if you shorten
your prayers, if you fear that those who disbelieve may harm you» [4:101]

The Companions could not understand why the Prophet (ﷺ) and the Muslims were still shortening their prayers during travel, despite the fact that there was no longer any fear from enemy attacks. The Prophet (ﷺ) responded, "(The concession to shorten prayers even in a state of security) is a charity which Allaah has given you, therefore accept the charity."[628]

---

626 ibid, p. 7.
627 Based on adh-Dhahabee, pps. 60-62, and others.
628 Reported by Muslim.

6) By explaining the intent of a verse. The example in which the Prophet (ﷺ) explained

$$\text{غَيْرِ ٱلْمَغْضُوبِ عَلَيْهِمْ وَلَا ٱلضَّآلِّينَ}$$

«...those whom You are angry with, and those who are astray» [1:7]

as the Jews and Christians falls under this category.

7) By adding extra commands or prohibitions to the verse. An example of this is the Prophet's (ﷺ) prohibition of joining a woman with her maternal or paternal aunt in marriage (i.e., as co-wives), whereas the Qur'aan only prohibits combining a woman with her sister (4:23).

8) By emphasising the meaning of the verse. In other words, by practising and affirming the laws in the Qur'aan. For example, all _hadeeth_ stressing good treatment to wives merely affirm the verse,

$$\text{وَعَاشِرُوهُنَّ بِٱلْمَعْرُوفِ}$$

«And live with them on good terms (and kindness)» [4:19]

9) By showing that the verse was abrogated. This category has already been discussed.[629]

These few examples should be sufficient to illustrate that the _Sunnah_ is of equal importance to the Qur'aan in deriving laws and understanding the Qur'aan. The Qur'aan can never be understood properly without the _Sunnah_. Even the Companions, whose knowledge of the Arabic language was unparalleled, had difficulty understanding many verses until the Prophet (ﷺ) cleared up the exact meaning for them.

These two sources of _tafseer_, _tafseer_ of the Qur'aan by the Qur'aan, and _tafseer_ of the Qur'aan by the _Sunnah_, are the two ultimate sources for understanding the Qur'aan. Neither is allowed to contradict itself or the other, and both sources must be taken simultaneously in order to arrive at a correct understanding. These two sources are also the final authority on the interpretation of the Qur'aan — no interpretation is allowed to contradict or supersede the interpretation of the Qur'aan by the Qur'aan and the _Sunnah_.

3) TAFSEER BY THE STATEMENT OF THE COMPANIONS

After the Qur'aan and _Sunnah_, the next important source for understanding the Qur'aan is the understanding of the Companions. The statements of the Companions are taken as a fundamental source of _tafseer_ for the following reasons:

1) The primary reason is that the Companions are a generation that was chosen by Allaah to accompany the Prophet (ﷺ), and to pass on the religion and teachings

---

629 See, 'The Categories of Naskh,' in Chapter 13.

of Islaam to later generations. Their character and religious knowledge has been testified by Allaah and the Prophet (ﷺ), for Allaah says in the Qur'aan,

$$مُّحَمَّدٌ رَّسُولُ ٱللَّهِ وَٱلَّذِينَ مَعَهُۥٓ أَشِدَّآءُ عَلَى ٱلْكُفَّارِ رُحَمَآءُ بَيْنَهُمْ تَرَىٰهُمْ رُكَّعًا سُجَّدًا يَبْتَغُونَ فَضْلًا مِّنَ ٱللَّهِ وَرِضْوَٰنًا$$

«Muhammad (ﷺ) is the Messenger of Allaah. And those who are with him (i.e., the Companions) are severe against the disbelievers and merciful amongst themselves. You see them bowing and falling down in prostration, seeking the Bounty of Allaah and His Pleasure...» [48:29]

In more than one verse of the Qur'aan, Allaah mentions the fact that

$$رَّضِيَ ٱللَّهُ عَنْهُمْ وَرَضُواْ عَنْهُ$$

«He is well pleased with them, and they with Him» [99:8]

thus clearly showing the superiority of the Companions over other generations. The Prophet (ﷺ) said, "The best of all mankind are my Companions, then those that will follow them, then those that will follow them."[630]

2) The Companions actually witnessed the revelation of the Qur'aan. Many of its verses were revealed to cater to problems that had risen amongst them. As such, they were familiar with the *asbaab an-nuzool*, with the *makkee* and *madanee* verses, and with the *naasikh* and *mansookh*, and did not need to go searching for this knowledge, as later generations would have to do.

3) The Qur'aan was revealed in the Arabic that the Companions spoke. Therefore, many words and phrases that later generations had difficulty understanding were clear to the Companions.

4) The Companions were the most knowledgeable of generations with regards to pre-Islaamic customs. Therefore, they understood the references in the Qur'aan to such customs.

There is a difference of opinion whether the interpretation of a Companion is of definitive authority. In other words, once a Companions has given an interpretation of a verse, must that interpretation be accepted, as is the case with the previous two sources of *tafseer*?

Al-<u>H</u>aakim an-Naisapooree (d. 404 A.H.), the author of *al-Mustadrak*, considered any interpretation by a Companion to be equivalent to a *hadeeth* of the Prophet (ﷺ), for he believed that all such interpretations must have originated from the Prophet (ﷺ). However, this opinion is not accepted in its generality, and the majority of scholars, such as an-Nawawee (d. 676 A.H.), as-Suyootee (d. 911 A.H.), and Ibn Taymiyyah (d. 728 A.H.), held the view that the interpretation of a Companion is equivalent to a *hadeeth* of the Prophet (ﷺ) only when it concerns matters which are not based on

---

630 Reported by al-Bukhaaree.

personal reasoning (*ijtihaad*), such as reports concerning *sabab an-nuzool*, or the knowledge of the unseen. This is because such knowledge could not have originated from the Companions' *ijtihaad*, and must have come from the Prophet (ﷺ). A report from a Companion not concerning these topics cannot be taken as equivalent to a *hadeeth* of the Prophet (ﷺ); rather, it is given a status below that of a *hadeeth*.[631] However, this does not diminish the status of the *tafseer* from the Companions. The Companions were the most knowledgeable of this nation, and as such their personal reasoning (*ijtihaad*) occupies a status above that of any later scholar.

Az-Zarkashee summarised this point when he said,

> As for the interpretation of the Companions, it is investigated into: if this interpretation was based upon language, then they are the scholars of the language, and there is no doubt that they should be given credence to in this interpretation. If this interpretation relies upon what they saw of *asbaab an-nuzool*, or other circumstances (i.e., of pre-Islaamic customs), then again there is no doubt concerning this type of interpretation.[632]

After the interpretation of the Qur'aan by itself and by the *hadeeth* of the Prophet (ﷺ), the Companions relied upon four primary sources to interpret the Qur'aan:[633]

1) Their knowledge of Arabic language, rhetoric, grammar and pre-Islaamic poetry.

2) Their knowledge of the pre-Islaamic customs of the Arabs.

3) Their knowledge of the habits of the Jews and Christians at the time of the revelation of the Qur'aan.

4) Their personal reasoning and their keen intellect (which, of course, was based upon knowledge).

Another integral aspect of the *tafseer* of the Companions is the *shaadh* and *mudraj qira'aat* which were discussed earlier. It is necessary to take these *qira'aat* into account when interpreting a verse. As mentioned earlier, such *qira'aat* cannot be considered as the Qur'aan, but may be studied as *tafseer*. One of the interpretations of this type of *qira'aat* is that they were added, not as Qur'aan, but for the sake of interpretation by the Companions. For example, in the *shaadh qiraa'a* of Ibn Mas'ood, the verse which told the believers to "fast three days" (5:89) as an expiation of an unfulfilled oath was read by him as: "fast three consecutive days." Due to this *shaadh qiraa'a*, later scholars differed over whether it was necessary to fast three consecutive days, or whether it sufficed to fast any three days if one did not fulfil an oath.

To conclude, if the Companions agreed to an interpretation of a verse, that interpretation must be accepted, since it qualifies as *ijmaa'*. On the other hand, if there exist narrations from one Companion concerning the interpretation of a verse, and there does not exist any narrations to the contrary from other Companions, this inter-

---

631 cf. as-Suyootee, *Tadreeb ar-Raawee*, pps. 156-8.
632 az-Zarkashee, v. 2, p. 172.
633 cf. adh-Dhahabee, v. 1, p. 63.

pretation is also accepted, but is not equivalent in strength to the interpretation given by the Prophet (ﷺ). If there exist various narrations from different Companions which are not contradictory in nature, then all such interpretations are accepted. If there exist contrary narrations from different Companions concerning the same verse, in this case the researcher can choose between the different interpretations, depending on which interpretation seems to have the strongest evidence to support it.

Tafseer by the Statement of the Successors

Before moving on to the next section, a brief note concerning the *tafseer* narrations from the Successors would be useful. Some scholars took the *tafseer* of the Successors to be the next source of *tafseer* after the *tafseer* of the Companions. As proof for this stance, they relied on the statements of certain prominent Successors concerning their knowledge of the Qur'aan. Qataadah (d. 110 A.H.) said, "There is not a single verse in the Qur'aan except that I have heard something concerning it." Mujaahid (d. 103 A.H.) said, "I recited the Qur'aan to Ibn 'Abbaas three times. In each recitation, I stopped at every verse, asking him concerning its interpretation." This is why Sufyaan ath-Thawree (d. 161 A.H.) said, "When you hear an interpretation from Mujaahid, this should be sufficient for you!"[634]

Other scholars, however, rejected this view. They claimed that an interpretation of a Successor could not have originated from the Prophet (ﷺ), as could the interpretation of a Companion, since they never saw the Prophet (ﷺ). Also, they did not witness the revelation, as did the generation before them, and their trustworthiness is not guaranteed specifically for every one of their generation, unlike the Companions (in other words, the trustworthiness of every single Companions is guaranteed by the Qur'aan, whereas this is not the case for the Successors, for they have been praised as a *generation*, and not individually).

Therefore, the correct view in this matter, as Ibn Taymiyyah (d. 728 A.H.) said, is that if the Successors give the same interpretation to a verse, then their interpretation must be accepted, but if they differed among themselves, then the opinion of one group will have no authority over the other group, nor over the generations after them. In such cases, one must resort to the Qur'aan, the *Sunnah*, the Companions, and the Arabic language in order to obtain the correct interpretation.[635]

4) Tafseer BY ARABIC LANGUAGE AND CLASSICAL POETRY

This topic is in reality two topics: *tafseer* by the Arabic language, and *tafseer* by classical poetry.

The relationship of the understanding of the Qur'aan to knowledge of the Arabic language is clear; it is impossible to truly understand and interpret the Qur'aan without knowledge of the Arabic language. Since the Qur'aan refers to it having been

---

634 Quotes taken from Ibn Taymiyyah, p. 58.
635 cf. Ibn Taymiyyah, p. 59.

revealed in 'a clear Arabic tongue' (16:103), the necessity of knowing this language in order to understand it cannot be overemphasised. In fact, the Qur'aan states that one of the reasons that it has been revealed in Arabic is so that it can be pondered over:

$$إِنَّآ أَنزَلْنَهُ قُرْءَٰنًا عَرَبِيًّا لَّعَلَّكُمْ تَعْقِلُونَ ۝$$

«We have sent down to you an Arabic Qur'aan so that you may understand»
[12:2]

The interpretation of the Qur'aan must comply with the rules of the Arabic language, in terms of vocabulary, grammar, rhetoric and principles of discourse.

Imaam Maalik (d. 179 A.H.) said, "If any person is brought to me, having interpreted the Qur'aan while he is ignorant of the Arabic language, I will make an example of him (by punishing him)."[636] The famous Successor and student of Ibn 'Abbaas, Mujaahid (d. 103 A.H.), said, "It is impermissible for any person who believes in Allaah and the Last Day to speak concerning the Book of Allaah if he is not knowledgeable of the dialects of the Arabs."[637] Imaam ash-Shaatibee (d. 790 A.H.) underlined this principle clearly when he said, "Whoever desires to understand the Qur'aan, then it will be understood from the speech of the Arabs, and there is no way other than this."[638]

Therefore, it is essential to have a thorough understanding of the characteristics of the Arabic language, for it is not possible to understand the Qur'aan by only knowing 'dictionary' Arabic. Imaam al-Qurtubee (d. 671 A.H.) warns in the introduction to his *tafseer* against,

> ...rushing to interpret the Qur'aan by the apparent Arabic wording, without researching into its strange and obscure words, its interchangeable phrases, and into the (characteristics) of succinct speech, deletion, and ellipsis. Whoever... rushes to extract meanings based on the apparent Arabic meanings – his errors are frequent, and he enters into the realm of those who interpret the Qur'aan (solely) with their intellects.[639]

For example, the phrasing of a verse might be general, whereas its context shows that it is specific. In other cases, words or even phrases might appear missing, yet this is a characteristic of eloquent Arabic, since the missing words are understood by context. In some verses, it might appear that the logical sequence of words has been reversed, but such a reversal adds subtle meanings that would otherwise not be present. Such characteristics, and others, are well known to the Arabs, and are an indication of the eloquence of the Qur'aan.

The interpretation of the Qur'aan based on the Arabic language must not contradict an interpretation based on the Qur'aan, *Sunnah*, or statement of the Compan-

---

636 az-Zarkashee, v. 2, p. 160.
637 az-Zarkashee, v. 1, p. 293.
638 Ik, p. 137.
639 al-Qurtubee, v. 1, p. 49. See some examples of such errors under the section, 'A Review of some Translations' in Ch. 16.

ions. This is because Allaah and His Messenger (ﷺ) are more knowledgeable of what they wish to express than later scholars of the language are. Likewise, the knowledge of the Companions is greater than the knowledge of any later linguist or grammarian. Therefore, the status of interpreting the Qur'aan based on the Arabic language comes after these three sources, and cannot supersede them.

To give an example of an interpretation that is based on Arabic yet contradicts something stronger than it, the scholar Aboo 'Ubayd al-Mu'tazilee said concerning the verse,

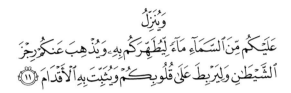

> «...and He caused rain to descend on you from the sky, to clean you thereby
> and to remove from you the whisperings of Shaytaan, and to strengthen
> your hearts and make your feet firm thereby» [8:11]

"This verse is *majaaz*, and it means that Allaah sent down patience upon the Companions, so that they would be firm against their enemies."[640]

This interpretation, although perhaps acceptable from a linguistical point of view, contradicts authentic narrations which show that the verse is to be taken in a *haqeeqee* manner; that it actually rained on the Companions, and that this rain caused the desert sand to become 'firm' and thus made it easier for the Companions to walk. At-Tabaree (d. 310 A.H.), commenting on the view of Aboo 'Ubayd, said, "...and this opinion goes against all the scholars of *tafseer*, from the Companions and Successors. And it is sufficient evidence that an opinion is mistaken when it contradicts those whom we have mentioned."[641]

Linguistic vs. Islaamic

When there occurs a word or phrase in the Qur'aan that gives different meanings based on the linguistic connotation of the phrase, and its Islaamic meaning (i.e., *lughawee* vs. *shar'ee* meanings), in general the *shar'ee* connotation is given precedence, unless there is evidence to suggest otherwise. This is because the Qur'aan was revealed to explain the *sharee'ah* of Islaam, and not to explain Arabic. To give an example, the Arabic word '*salaat*' linguistically means a verbal invocation (also known in Arabic as *du'aa*). However, in its *shar'ee* connotation, the word implies a known set of actions and movements performed at specific times of the day, or for specific occasions. Therefore, in the verses describing the relationship with hypocrites, when the Prophet (ﷺ) is commanded,

---

640 at-Tayyaar, p. 45.
641 at-Tabaree, v. 9, p. 197.

$$\text{وَلَا تُصَلِّ عَلَىٰٓ أَحَدٍ مِّنْهُم مَّاتَ أَبَدًا}$$

«And do not ever perform the *salaat* upon them (the hypocrites who died)»
[9:84]

the word '*salaat*' is taken in its *shar'ee* meaning (i.e., the funeral prayer over a deceased hypocrite is forbidden), since this is the primary and understood meaning of the word. In order to prohibit even verbally asking for their forgiveness, other verses and *hadeeth* must be used. On the other hand, in the verse,

$$\text{خُذْ مِنْ أَمْوَٰلِهِمْ صَدَقَةً تُطَهِّرُهُمْ وَتُزَكِّيهِم بِهَا وَصَلِّ عَلَيْهِمْ}$$

«Take from their money alms, so that they may be purified by it, and sanctified with it, and make *salaat* for them» [9:103]

the word '*salaat*' is understood in its linguistic meaning, i.e., a verbal invocation of blessing and forgiveness, since there exist narrations that the Prophet (ﷺ), when he used to receive such alms, would verbally bless their donors.[642]

An integral aspect of interpreting the Qur'aan by the Arabic language is interpreting the Qur'aan by poetry. This was a practice that originated during the time of the Companions.

Poetry Prohibited?

Certain verses of the Qur'aan and *hadeeth* seem to prohibit poetry. It is therefore essential to discuss them to understand their proper intent. The Qur'aan says,

«As for the poets – (only) the misguided follow them. Do you not see that they speak about every matter in their poetry, and that they say what they do not practice? Except those (poets) who believe, and do righteous deeds, and frequently remember Allaah...» [26:224-7]

Therefore, those poets who versify about matters which are useful, and practice what they preach, and remember Allaah constantly, are not amongst those censured by the Qur'aan. The Prophet (ﷺ) also spoke against this type of poetry, for he (ﷺ) said, "It is better for a man's chest to be filled with pus than to be filled with poetry."[643] This *hadeeth* has been understood to refer to the poet who becomes excessively involved in his poetry, so much so that it 'fills his chest' and turns him away from the remembrance of the Qur'aan.[644] Therefore, poetry in and of itself is not prohibited in

---

642 cf. al-'Uthaymeen, p. 29.
643 Reported by al-Bukhaaree and Muslim.
644 cf. al-Albaanee, *Saheehah*, v. 1, p. 660.

the Qur'aan or *sunnah* – it is only evil and excessive poetry that is censured. In fact, the Prophet (ﷺ) stated, "Indeed, some poetry has great wisdom in it."[645]

It might be asked, "How can we interpret the Qur'aan – the Speech of Allaah – by poetry, which is the speech of men?"

Aboo Bakr ibn al-Anbaaree (d. 328 A.H.), in explaining this concept, said,

> There are numerous narrations from the Companions and Successors concerning their explaining the obscure and rare words in the Qur'aan with poetry. Yet, despite this, some who have no knowledge have criticized the grammarians, and said, "When you do this, you are make poetry a source (of understanding) rather than the Qur'aan!" And they said, "How can you use poetry to comprehend the Qur'aan, when poetry has been condemned in the Qur'aan and *sunnah*?!"
>
> The response to this is that the situation is not as they have presumed; we have not made poetry a primary source over the Qur'aan, but rather we wish to clarify the meanings of the obscure and rare words in it. This is because Allaah has said,

«Verily, We have revealed this as an Arabic Qur'aan» [12:2]

and He says,

«...(the Qur'aan is) in a clear, Arabic tongue» [16:103].[646]

In other words, the purpose of poetry is to explain the Arabic of the Qur'aan, and is not meant to be the basis from which Islaamic laws or beliefs are derived.

Ibn 'Abbaas said, "If you ask me concerning the rare words in the language, then seek it in poetry, for poetry is the recordings of the Arabs," and he also said, "Poetry is the recording of the Arabs. Therefore, if a word of the Qur'aan – that was revealed in the language of the Arabs – is obscure to them, they return to their recordings, and take the meanings from it."[647]

'Umar was once with the other Companions in a gathering, and he asked them the meaning of the verse,

أَوْ يَأْخُذَهُم عَلَى تَخَوُّفٍ

«Or He will take them upon *takhawuf*» [16:47]

At this, an old man from the tribe of Hudhayl stood up and said, "This is from our dialect. *Takhawuf* means attrition (suffering loss little by little)." 'Umar asked him, "Is this something that the Arabs know from their poetry?" He answered, "Yes," and recited to them the line of poetry,

---

645 Reported by al-Bukhaaree.
646 as-Suyootee, v. 1, p. 157.
647 az-Zarkashee, v. 2, p. 294.

'Her saddle *takhawuf* (abraded) from a long and high hump,
As when a piece of skin used for smoothing arrows has *takhawuf*
(abraded) from the back of a tree'

At this, 'Umar said, "Stick to the recordings, and you will not be misled." When asked, "What are the recordings?" he replied, "The poetry of pre-Islaamic times. Therein is the explanation of your Book, and the meaning of your words."[648]

As-Suyootee, in his *al-Itqaan*, quotes a lengthy account between one of the leaders of the *Khawaarij*, Naafi' ibn Azraq, and Ibn 'Abbaas. Naafi' once passed by Ibn 'Abbaas while he was interpreting the Qur'aan to those around him. Naafi' said to his companion, "Come, let us go to this person who is pretending to interpret the Qur'aan even though he has no knowledge concerning it."[649] They went to Ibn 'Abbaas in order to try to outwit him, and asked him, "We wish to ask you concerning the Book of Allaah, and we want you to explain it to us and bring us proofs from the Arabic language (for your statements), for verily Allaah has revealed the Qur'aan in a clear Arabic tongue." Ibn 'Abbaas told them, "Ask me whatever you wish!" So they asked him, "Tell us the meaning of the verse,

«There is no *rayb* in it» [2:2]?"

Ibn 'Abbaas responded, "(This means) there is no doubt in it." They asked, "Do the Arabs know this meaning?" He replied, "Yes. Have you not heard the line by Ibn Zabaree:

'O Umaamah! There is no *rayb* (doubt) concerning the truth,
There is only *rayb* (doubt) concerning what a liar says!'"[650]

Naafi' then proceeded to ask Ibn 'Abbaas the interpretation of a further one hundred and eighty nine verses, in each case trying to show that Ibn 'Abbaas was ignorant of the meaning of the verse. However, for every obscure phrase in each verse, Ibn 'Abbaas was able to explain its proper meaning, and quote a line of classical poetry to prove this meaning.[651] In this incident, not only is the necessity of knowing Arabic poetry to interpret the Qur'aan shown, but also the superiority of the knowledge of the Companions over that of any other generation.

Whose Poetry?

The question arises, however, as to whose poetry may be used to interpret the Arabic of the Qur'aan? The scholars have divided the Arab poets into four categories, as follows:[652]

---

648 adh-Dhahabee, p. 80; cf. Zarabozo, p. 20.

649 This is one of the characteristics of the *Khawaarij*, that they felt themselves to be more knowledgeable than the Companions of the Prophet (ﷺ), and in fact accused most of them of disbelief. It is for this reason and others that the Prophet (ﷺ) said, "The *Khawaarij* are the dogs of the Hellfire." (Reported by Ahmad, cf. *Mishkaat* # 3554).

650 as-Suyootee, v. 1, p. 158.

651 cf. as-Suyootee, v. 1, pps. 158-175.

652 'Abd ar-Raheem, p. 55.

1) Pre-Islaamic poets, meaning those who died before the advent of the Prophet (ﷺ). Examples of this category include Imri' al-Qays, al-'Ayshee and an-Naabighah.

2) Contemporary poets, meaning those who were alive when the Prophet (ﷺ) announced his prophethood. Examples in this category include Labeed, and the famous Companion, Hassaan ibn Thaabit.

3) Early poets, meaning those who appeared after the Prophet (ﷺ) but still relatively early in Islaamic history. Examples in this category are Jareer and Farazdaq.

4) Later poets, meaning those who came after the last category till the present time.

Concerning the first two categories, there is no difference of opinion that their poetry may be used to interpret the Qur'aan. The third category has been the subject of dispute among the scholars, one of the reasons being the lack of any clear time frame to indicate a cut-off point between this category and the last one. However, the strongest opinion seems to be that the famous poets in this category can be used to interpret the Qur'aan, since at this early stage, the Arabic language was still relatively pure and free from the foreign influences that was indicative of later times. As for the last category, the majority of scholars do not allow for the interpretation of the Qur'aan by their poetry, even though some (such as az-Zamakhsharee), allowed the use of their poetry, as long as the poet was of a trustworthy character, and known for his knowledge of the Arabic language.[653]

To conclude, it is essential to have an extensive knowledge of Arabic language and poetry in order to properly understand certain words and phrases in the Qur'aan. Such poetry is only used to obtain a linguistic meaning or interpretation of an obscure word, and is not directly used to form the basis for any Islaamic rulings.

5) Tafseer By Pre-Islaamic Arab Customs

Another integral knowledge that is essential in understanding the Qur'aan is the knowledge of the customs and manners of the pre-Islaamic Arabs. This is because the Qur'aan was revealed in a certain society and time frame, and it addressed many of the issues related to that society. Therefore, in order to understand such verses, it is essential to know the customs and manners that they are referring to, since the actual verses themselves do not allude to them.

A few examples will help illustrate this point. Allaah says in the Qur'aan,

---

653 cf. 'Abd ar-Raheem, p. 56-57.

$$\text{يَسۡـَٔلُونَكَ}$$
$$\text{عَنِ ٱلۡأَهِلَّةِ قُلۡ هِيَ مَوَٰقِيتُ لِلنَّاسِ وَٱلۡحَجِّ وَلَيۡسَ ٱلۡبِرُّ}$$
$$\text{بِأَن تَأۡتُواْ ٱلۡبُيُوتَ مِن ظُهُورِهَا وَلَٰكِنَّ ٱلۡبِرَّ مَنِ ٱتَّقَىٰ}$$
$$\text{وَأۡتُواْ ٱلۡبُيُوتَ مِنۡ أَبۡوَٰبِهَا وَٱتَّقُواْ ٱللَّهَ لَعَلَّكُمۡ}$$
$$\text{تُفۡلِحُونَ ﴿١٨٩﴾}$$

«They ask you (O Muḥammad) concerning the crescent. Say: 'They are signs to indicate fixed periods of time for mankind, and (to indicate) the *Hajj* (pilgrimage).' And it is not righteousness to enter your houses from the back, but true righteousness is (he) who fears Allaah. So (therefore) enter houses through their proper doors, and fear Allaah that you may be successful» [2:189].

A reader of this verse who is unaware of the customs of the pre-Islaamic Arabs will bewilderedly ask, "Of what relationship is the sighting of the crescent to entering houses from the front or back, and of both of these acts to the fear of Allaah?"

The answer to this question lies in knowing one of the superstitions of the pre-Islaamic Arabs. When the moon used to be sighted for *Hajj*, the pagans of old would refrain from entering their houses through their front doors, and instead would jump over their back walls to enter their houses. Thus, Allaah revealed in this verse the prohibition of such superstitions, and told them that true righteousness was not found in any superstition, but rather in the fear of Allaah.[654]

In another verse, Allaah says,

$$\text{وَإِنۡ خِفۡتُمۡ أَلَّا تُقۡسِطُواْ فِي ٱلۡيَتَٰمَىٰ فَٱنكِحُواْ}$$
$$\text{مَا طَابَ لَكُم مِّنَ ٱلنِّسَاءِ مَثۡنَىٰ وَثُلَٰثَ وَرُبَٰعَ}$$

«And if you fear that you shall not be able to deal justly with (female) orphans under your care, then marry women of your choice, two, three, or four» [4:3]

'Urwah ibn Zubair could not understand the relationship of taking care of orphans with marrying other women. He went to his aunt, 'Aa'ishah, to ask her to clear up this confusion. She replied, "O my nephew! This verse is referring to the orphan girl who is in the care of her guardian, and he is attracted by her beauty and wealth. He wishes to marry her, without paying her the dowry that she deserves, so this verse prohibited them (the guardians) from marrying them (the orphans) if they did not think that they would be able to deal justly with these girls in their dowry, but instead to marry other free women."[655] In this incident, 'Aa'ishah's knowledge of pre-Islaamic customs allowed her to understand the intent of this verse.

---

654 cf. Ibn Katheer, v. 1, p. 242.

655 Paraphrased from Ibn Katheer, v. 1, p. 488.

As a last example, the Qur'aan says,

$$\text{مَاجَعَلَ اللَّهُ مِنْ بَحِيرَةٍ وَلَا سَآئِبَةٍ وَلَا وَصِيلَةٍ وَلَا حَامٍ وَلَكِنَّ}$$
$$\text{الَّذِينَ كَفَرُوا يَفْتَرُونَ عَلَى اللَّهِ الْكَذِبَ وَأَكْثَرُهُمْ لَا يَعْقِلُونَ ﴿١٠٣﴾}$$

«Allaah has not ordained the *baheera*, or the *saa'ibah*, or the *waseelah*, or the
haam, but those who disbelieve invent lies against Allaah. And most of them
have no understanding» [5:103]

Once again, it is essential to turn to pre-Islaamic Arab customs in order to understand
what this verse is referring to. The Arabs of old had certain superstitious religious
practices concerning their animals, and in this verse Allaah is informing them that
these practices have no basis in the religion of Allaah, but instead are lies that the
pagans had attributed to Him.[656]

Although this source of *tafseer* is not essential in order to understand every single
verse in the Qur'aan, it is nonetheless one of the necessary knowledges that a *mufassir*
must have.

6) TAFSEER BY JUDAEO-CHRISTIAN NARRATIVES

The Judaeo-Christian narratives are known in Arabic as *Israa'eeliyaat*. These narrations are mostly found in Judaeo-Christian sources, such as the Torah, the Bible
and the Talmud, although some were orally passed down. Although most of the
Israa'eeliyaat deal with the stories of the previous nations, there are also narrations on
aspects of laws, beliefs and the signs of the Day of Judgement.

Hadeeth Related to *Israa'eeliyaat*

There are three primary *hadeeth* that deal with the use and value of *Israa'eeliyaat*,
which, at first glance, seem to contradict themselves. However, as usual in cases in
which *hadeeth* appear to 'contradict' one another, a closer inspection shows that such
is not the case.

The Prophet (ﷺ) said, "Spread knowledge from me, even if it is a sentence (i.e., a
verse of the Qur'aan or *hadeeth* of the Prophet (ﷺ)), and narrate from the Children of
Israel without hesitation, but whoever intentionally forges a lie upon me, then let him
prepare his place of residence in Hell."[657] In this *hadeeth*, it appears that all *Israa'eeliyaat*
narrations can be accepted.

In another *hadeeth*, it is reported that 'Umar once came to the Prophet (ﷺ) with a
copy of the Torah. The Prophet (ﷺ) asked him, "What is this, O 'Umar?" He replied, "It is a book that I had copied so that I can add, to my (present) knowledge,
more knowledge." At this, the Prophet (ﷺ) became so angry that his cheeks appeared
flushed, and he immediately ordered all the Companions to be called to the *masjid*.

---

656 cf. Ibn Katheer, v. 2, p. 121.
657 Reported by al-Bukhaaree.

He (ﷺ) then stood up and said, "O people! Verily, I have been given the most concise and precise of speech... and I have come to you with (the knowledge) that is pure. Therefore, do not be misled. I swear by Him in whose Hands is my life, were Moosaa alive right now, he would have no option but to follow me!"[658] In this narration, the Prophet (ﷺ) appears to be strongly prohibiting even reading *Israa'eeliyaat* narrations.

The third *hadeeth* dealing with the subject mentions that the Jews would read the Torah in Hebrew, and then explain it to the Muslims in Arabic. The Prophet (ﷺ) remarked, "Do not believe the People of the Book, nor disbelieve them, but rather, say, 'We believe in Allaah, and what has been revealed to us, and what has been revealed to you.'" In this narration, the Prophet (ﷺ) told the Muslims that they were not allowed to believe in such narrations, nor could they deny their truthfulness, but could only affirm that Allaah had sent down revelations to both communities.

In combining these three narrations, the following conclusion may be reached: It is permissible to quote *Israa'eeliyaat*, as long as these narrations do not contradict any verses of the Qur'aan or *hadeeth* of the Prophet (ﷺ). However, such narrations cannot be used as a source of knowledge, as their authenticity is unknown – rather, Muslims cannot outright deny their authenticity, nor can they convincingly affirm them.

The permission to narrate from the *Israa'eeliyaat* 'without hesitation' applies to those narrations which do not contradict the Qur'aan or *Sunnah*, but at the same time, the Muslims are warned that such narrations cannot authoritatively be believed in. The Prophet (ﷺ) strongly objected to 'Umar's action of reading the Torah since 'Umar felt that it would increase his knowledge. The Prophet (ﷺ) explained that all the knowledge that was essential to know was available in the Qur'aan and *Sunnah*.

The Qur'aan also makes an allusion to the *Israa'eeliyaat*. In the story of the 'Sleepers of the Cave' (cf. *Soorah* al-Kahf, verses 9-26), Allaah mentions the various opinions that were held by the People of the Book concerning their exact number:

$$سَيَقُولُونَ ثَلَـٰثَةٌ$$
$$رَّابِعُهُمْ كَلْبُهُمْ وَيَقُولُونَ خَمْسَةٌ سَادِسُهُمْ كَلْبُهُمْ رَجْمًا$$
$$بِالْغَيْبِ وَيَقُولُونَ سَبْعَةٌ وَثَامِنُهُمْ كَلْبُهُمْ قُل رَّبِّي أَعْلَمُ$$
$$بِعِدَّتِهِم مَّا يَعْلَمُهُمْ إِلَّا قَلِيلٌ فَلَا تُمَارِ فِيهِمْ إِلَّا مِرَآءً ظَـٰهِرًا$$
$$وَلَا تَسْتَفْتِ فِيهِم مِّنْهُمْ أَحَدًا ﴿٢٢﴾$$

«And they say that they were three, the dog being the fourth among them, and (others) say that they were five, the dog being the sixth – wildly guessing at the unknown. (Others) say that they were seven, the dog being the eighth. Answer (O Muḥammad): 'My Lord knows best their numbers; none knows them but a few.' So do not debate with them except with clear proof. And do not consult any of them (the People of the Book) about the affair (of the People of the Cave)» [18:22]

---

658 Reported by Aḥmad. See *Irwaa*, # 1589, for varying narrations.

In these verses, a number of points may be derived. Firstly, the number of people in this group was seven, since Allaah refuted the first two opinions, but silently approved the last one. Secondly, the verse alludes to the fact that knowing such facts is of no great value – rather one should respond that this knowledge is with Allaah. Thirdly, the Jews and Christians debate amongst themselves and with the Muslims on topics concerning which they have no clear knowledge, wildly guessing at the unknown. This shows that much of the *Israa'eeliyaat* is the product of human authorship. Fourthly, due to the last two facts, there is no great benefit to be obtained by debating with the Jews and Christians, except concerning those matters in which there exists certain knowledge. Lastly, there is no reason for the Muslims to question the Jews and Christians concerning such narrations, since they themselves are only guessing, and if this knowledge were of any benefit, it would have been revealed in the Qur'aan or *Sunnah*.[659]

Since the Prophet (ﷺ) allowed the narration of such literature, it is not surprising to find prominent Companions, such as 'Abdullaah ibn 'Amr ibn al-'Aas and Ibn 'Abbaas, quoting many *Israa'eeliyaat* narrations. During the Battle of Yarmuk against the Romans (13 A.H.), 'Abdullaah ibn 'Amr found two loads of books of the Christians and Jews. These books formed the basis of many of his *Israa'eeliyaat* narrations.[660] However, none of the Companions used these narrations as sources of knowledge. This is because the Qur'aan is explicit that the Jews and Christians tampered with their respective scriptures, and changed the divine revelation. Therefore, it is impossible to ascertain which facts they added and which are still intact.

During the period of the Successors, the *Israa'eeliyaat* literature began playing a more prominent role in *tafseer*. This was primarily due to a number of famous scholars who were originally Jews and Christians, but had converted to Islaam. After their conversion, they used to narrate the *Israa'eeliyaat* that they had learnt in their youth. Famous among them were Ka'ab al-Ahbaar (d. 32 A.H.), Wahb ibn Munnabih (d. 110 A.H.), and 'Abd al-Malik ibn 'Abd al-'Azeez ibn Jurayj (d. 159 A.H.).[661]

Unfortunately, later generations became lax concerning the prophetic prohibition in believing in the *Israa'eeliyaat*, and thus many of these narrations entered into *tafseer* literature and were accepted as fact. Even such prominent scholars such as Imaam Ibn Jareer at-Tabaree (d. 310 A.H.) and Ibn Katheer (d. 774 A.H.) are well-known for including such material in their *tafseer* literature, although these two scholars would usually point out the uselessness of such material.

The Categories of Israa'eeliyaat

As alluded to earlier, the *Israa'eeliyaat* can be divided into three categories:[662]

1) Those narrations which are confirmed in the Qur'aan and *Sunnah*. Most of the stories in the Qur'aan concerning the previous nations are also found in the Bi-

---

659 cf. Ibn Taymiyyah, p. 57.
660 adh-Dhahabee, v. 1, p. 185.
661 *ibid*, v. 1, p. 206.
662 adh-Dhahabee, v. 1, p.189.

ble. The general themes of many stories are common to both books, such as the Flood of Noo<u>h</u>, and the prophethood of Ibraaheem, Moosaa and others. Such narrations in the Bible may be accepted, since the Qur'aan confirms their authenticity

2) Those narrations which contradict the Qur'aan, the *Sunnah*, or Islaamic teachings. For example, the Bible ascribes to certain prophets evil deeds, such as the story of Loo<u>t</u>'s intercourse with his daughter-in-law, and Sulaymaan ordering the death of one of his generals so that he could marry his wife. Such crimes are unacceptable to ascribe to prophets, and as such these narrations must be rejected as false. In other places in the Bible, Allaah is given certain characteristics (such as regret, tiredness, and ignorance) that do not befit Him. These types of *Israa'eeliyaat* cannot be narrated unless one explains their falsehood.

3) Those narrations concerning which the Muslims have no knowledge. The majority of *Israa'eeliyaat* narrations fall under this category. It has been allowed to narrate such stories without actually believing in them. For example, almost all the stories in the Bible are, in general, more detailed than their Qur'aanic counterparts. Names, figures and places which are typically not mentioned in the Qur'aan are mentioned in the Bible and other *Israa'eeliyaat* material.[663] These facts cannot be accepted as truth by Muslims, for it is not known whether they were tampered with or not. Example of such facts are the names of the twelve Children of Jacob, the name of the Angel of Death (known in Muslim literature as *Azraa'eel*),[664] the colour of the dog of the Sleepers of the Cave, the part of the cow that Moosaa hit the dead man with, and the names of the birds which Ibraaheem resurrected.[665]

Ibn Taymiyyah (d. 724 A.H.), in summarising the potential usefulness of the *Israa'eeliyaat*, comments, "They may be quoted, as the *hadeeth* (of the Prophet (ﷺ)) permits it, but let us note that most of them have no value whatsoever so far as religious matters are concerned."[666]

7) Tafseer by Subjective Opinion (Ra'y)

The last source of *tafseer* is *tafseer* by subjective opinion, commonly known in Arabic as *ra'y*. In other words, a scholar uses his personal opinion (*ijtihaad*) to arrive at an interpretation of a verse, and this is called *tafseer* with *ra'y*.

---

663 This is a further indication of the *i'jaaz* of the Qur'aan, for there is absolutely no benefit to be gained by such knowledge, and in fact is more tedious to read than useful to know.

664 This name does not occur in any verse of the Qur'aan or *hadeeth* of the Prophet (ﷺ). Therefore, it is safer not to call the angel of death Azraa'eel, since we do not know for sure the authenticity of this name. For further details, see Ashqar, 'Umar Sulaiman, *'Aalim al-Malaaikat al-Abraar,* (Dar an-Nafais, Kuwait, 1986), p. 18.

665 cf. Ibn Taymyyah, p. 56.

666 Paraphrased from Ibn Taymiyyah, p. 56.

A number of scholars have claimed that there is a difference of opinion over the legitimacy of this type of *tafseer*. They claimed that certain scholars allowed this type of *tafseer*, whereas others prohibited it. In reality, as many researchers have shown, the difference of opinion is only verbal.[667] This is because *ra'y* is of two types: *ra'y* that is based upon knowledge and conforms with the Qur'aan and *Sunnah*, and *ra'y* that is based upon desires and disagrees with the Qur'aan and *Sunnah*. Those scholars that are quoted as prohibiting *tafseer* with *ra'y* in reality are prohibiting the second category of *ra'y*, and not *ra'y* in general.

The Two Types of Ra'y

The evidence that *ra'y* is of two types is found in the Qur'aan, the *Sunnah* and the statements of the Companions. The first type of *ra'y*, which is based upon knowledge, is not prohibited, whereas the second type of *ra'y*, which is not based upon knowledge, is prohibited.

The proofs that *ra'y* based upon knowledge is not prohibited are many, including:[668]

1) The verse,

$$ أَفَلَا يَتَدَبَّرُونَ ٱلْقُرْءَانَ أَمْ عَلَىٰ قُلُوبٍ أَقْفَالُهَآ ۝ $$

«Do they not reflect and ponder over the Qur'aan? Or are there locks on their hearts (that prevent them from understanding it)?» [47:24]

This verse asks mankind to ponder and reflect over the Qur'aan, which shows that there are meanings and interpretations that are to be obtained only after contemplation – *tafseer* with *ra'y*.

2) The verse,

$$ كِتَٰبٌ أَنزَلْنَٰهُ إِلَيْكَ مُبَٰرَكٌ لِّيَدَّبَّرُوٓا۟ ءَايَٰتِهِۦ وَلِيَتَذَكَّرَ أُو۟لُوا۟ ٱلْأَلْبَٰبِ ۝ $$

«(This is) a Book that We have sent down to you, full of blessings, so that they may ponder over its verses, and that men of understanding may remember» [38:29]

Once again, the believers are told to ponder over its verses.

3) The verse,

$$ وَلَوْ رَدُّوهُ إِلَى ٱلرَّسُولِ وَإِلَىٰٓ أُو۟لِى ٱلْأَمْرِ مِنْهُمْ لَعَلِمَهُ ٱلَّذِينَ يَسْتَنۢبِطُونَهُۥ مِنْهُمْ $$

«...If they had only referred it back to the Messenger, or to those in authority amongst them, then those who are qualified to extract interpretations (or rulings) would have known it» [4:83]

---

667 cf. adh-Dhahabee, v. 1, p. 267; at-Tayyaar, p. 48; Ik, p. 171; ar-Roomee, p. 79.
668 adh-Dhahabee, v. 1, pps. 265-274; ar-Roomee, pps. 78-85.

This verse shows that there are people (the scholars) who are qualified to extract some knowledge that others might not be able to, once again proving that *tafseer* with *ra'y* is allowed, if based upon knowledge.

4) The prayer that the Prophet (ﷺ) made for Ibn 'Abbaas, "O Allaah! Grant him interpretation" shows that there are meanings to the Qur'aan that are not obvious to everyone, and that is why the Prophet (ﷺ) prayed that Ibn 'Abbaas be given this knowledge.

5) The Companions and those after them all interpreted the Qur'aan with more than just narrations, and this proves that *tafseer* based upon *ra'y* is allowed. For example, when Aboo Bakr was asked concerning the case of *kalaalah* mentioned in verse 4:176, he replied, "I say with my *ra'y*, so if it is correct, it is from Allaah, and if it is incorrect, it is from myself and *Shaytaan*."[669] This shows that Aboo Bakr interpreted the Qur'aan based upon *ra'y*.

6) The fact that *ijtihaad* is a part of this religion, and with it, any stagnation that might have existed is removed from the religion. *Tafseer* with *ra'y* is one type of *ijtihaad*, and thus allowed.

The proofs that *ra'y* based upon desires is prohibited are:

1) The verse,

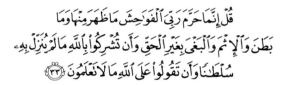

«Say: My Lord has only prohibited evil deeds, the apparent and hidden of them,... and that you say concerning Allaah that which you do not know» [7:33]

2) The verse,

وَلَا تَقْفُ مَا لَيْسَ لَكَ بِهِۦ عِلْمٌ

«And do not follow that which you have no knowledge of» [17:36]

These two verses discourage speaking without knowledge, and included in this is *ra'y* that is not based upon knowledge.

3) The many narrations that exist from the *salaf* that show their caution in interpreting the Qur'aan without any knowledge. Perhaps the most famous quote is that of Aboo Bakr, who said, "What earth would give me support, and what sky would shelter me, if I said concerning the Book of Allaah what I do not know?"[670]

The above evidences prove that *ra'y* is divided into two types: *ra'y* that is praiseworthy, and *ra'y* that is blameworthy. The *ra'y* that is praiseworthy is that which is based upon knowledge, and performed by one who is qualified to do so. Therefore, this type

---

669   at-Tabaree, v. 4, p. 284.
670   ar-Roomee, p. 82.

of *ra'y* does not contradict the Qur'aan, the *Sunnah*, the statements of the Companions and the rules of the Arabic language; rather, such a *ra'y* is *based* on these sources. The *ra'y* that is blameworthy is that which is performed without knowledge, by one who is not qualified to perform it. Such types of *ra'y* typically contradict stronger sources of *tafseer*.

Where is Ra'y Used?

It is obvious that *tafseer* by personal reasoning (*ra'y*) cannot, by its very definition, be explained or confined to a particular methodology. Suffice to say, however, that such interpretations (specifically for those generations after the Companions) are the weakest source of *tafseer*, and as such it is not allowed to contradict any source higher than it. Any time an interpretation based on *ra'y* contradicts any other source of *tafseer*, it must be rejected, since there is no guarantee that it is correct.

Some scholars have classified the areas that *ra'y* might be used as follows:[671]

1)   To uncover meanings in a verse that conform with Arabic, and the Qur'aan.

2)   To discover certain hidden aspects of the Qur'aan within the realm of human limit. An example of this is when a certain linguist sees why one phrase or word has been used in a certain context over its synonyms.

3)   To see the goals of certain verses and understand their perspectives. An example of this is when a scholar puts forth a certain relationship between a set of verses.

4)   To extract and elaborate the morals that are to be gained from Qur'aanic stories.

5)   To demonstrate the literary *i'jaaz* of the Qur'aan.

A Divine Blessing

Perhaps one of the most important factors that is essential in order to arrive at a proper interpretation based upon *ra'y* is a divine blessing from Allaah. This is because *tafseer* based upon *ra'y* requires a keen intellect, and an ability to grasp meanings that are not apparent in a verse. These qualities are from the blessings and mercy of Allaah, and cannot be achieved by book-knowledge alone. It was this type of understanding that the Prophet (ﷺ) prayed for Ibn 'Abbaas when he (ﷺ) said, "O Allaah! Bless him with the knowledge of interpretation."[672]

However, even though this type of knowledge cannot be gained through books, there are certain ways to achieve it. As the scholars of the past said, "Whoever fears Allaah with the knowledge he knows, Allaah will bless him with knowledge of that which he does not know."[673] This is also alluded to in the verse:

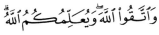

«So fear Allaah, and Allaah will teach you...»[2:282]

---

671 cf. Ik, p. 175.
672 Reported by al-Bukhaaree.
673 Reported by Aboo Nu'aym.

If a person makes his intentions sincere for the sake of Allaah, and practices the knowledge that he knows, and strives to gain more knowledge, it is very likely that he will be blessed with this type of ability.

v. The Qualifications of a Mufassir

A person who wishes to interpret the Qur'aan (a *mufassir*) must fulfill certain conditions and qualities before he is allowed to explain the Qur'aan to people – not everybody can just pick up the Book of Allaah and start interpreting it!

As was quoted earlier from Imaam ash-Shaafi'ee (d. 204 A.H.), "It is impermissible for any person to give verdicts concerning the religion of Allaah, unless he is knowledgeable of the Book of Allaah, and its *naasikh* from its *mansookh*, and its *muhkam* from its *mutashaabih*, and its interpretation, and its process of revelation, and its *makkee* from its *madanee*, and its *asbaab an-nuzool*. On top of this, he must be knowledgeable of the *Sunnah*..."[674]

As-Suyootee, in his *al-Itqaan*, lists fifteen characteristics that a person must have before he is qualified to interpret the Qur'aan. However, these are only a summary of the qualities that a *mufassir* is required to have. Some of these qualities, and others, are listed briefly below. The first four are inherent qualities that are essential in a *mufassir*, and the others are external and acquired.[675]

1) The proper intentions, since the Prophet (ﷺ) said, "All actions are by intentions."[676] The *mufassir* must intend to please Allaah by this action of interpreting the Qur'aan, and he must intend to guide people to the Straight Path to the best of his abilities.

2) The correct Islaamic beliefs (*'aqeedah*). If a person is not a Muslim, or of a heretical or misguided sect, then he cannot be trusted in interpreting the Qur'aan, for his motive will be to defame Islaam, or to defend his particular sect or beliefs.

3) To be free from practising or believing in innovations, and to respect the Qur'aan. If a person is innovating in the religion of Allaah, then he will have no qualms about innovating in the interpretation of the Book of Allaah. Also, the *mufassir* must love and respect the Qur'aan, and have the proper beliefs concerning it. Part of this belief is that he must believe that the Qur'aan is the actual *kalaam* of Allaah (and not an 'expression' of the *kalaam* of Allaah!). Ibn al-Qayyim (d. 758 A.H.) said, "...(a *mufassir*) must witness that it (the Qur'aan) is the *kalaam* of Allaah, which Allaah actually spoke, and which was revealed to the Prophet (ﷺ) by inspiration. And none can grasp its meanings unless his heart is free of misgivings and doubts with regards to the Qur'aan, and if a person does not really believe that the Qur'aan is from Allaah, then there is a disease in his heart (which prevents him from understanding the Qur'aan)."[677]

---

674 an-Nahaas, p. 124.
675 as-Suyootee, v. 2, pps. 225-37; ar-Roomee, pps. 136-42; Zamralee, pps. 11-13.
676 Reported by al-Bukhaaree and others.
677 ar-Roomee, p. 12.

4) Repentance and a pious heart. This condition means that a *mufassir* must fear Allaah to the best of his abilities, and if he falls into a sin, he must immediately repent to Allaah for that sin, and not return to it. This is because, as Ibn al-Qayyim said, "No heart can understand the Qur'aan, or grasp its meanings, except if it is pure, and it is impossible for a heart full of evils and innovations to understand the meanings of the Qur'aan properly."[678]

5) A thorough and proper understanding of the fundamentals of religion ('*aqeedah*), so that a *mufassir* can avoid falling into many of the heresies and innovations that misguided sects did with regards to the understanding of the Qur'aan.

6) Following the proper methodology of *tafseer*. A basic introduction to this methodology was outlined in the previous section.

7) Knowledge of the Arabic language and its vocabulary. Such knowledge must, of course, be on a scholarly level; a person whose primary language is Arabic is not necessarily knowledgeable of Arabic to the level that is required to interpret the Qur'aan.

8) Knowledge of Arabic grammar (*nahw*).

9) Knowledge of Arabic morphology (*sarf*).

10) Knowledge of the basis of Arabic words and word structures (*ishtiqaaq*)

11) Knowledge of Arabic rhetoric, eloquence and manners of oratory.[679]

12) The knowledge of the *saheeh*, *da'eef*, *shaadh* and *baatil qira'aat*s.

13) The knowledge of the principles of *fiqh* (*usool al-fiqh*), so that he can interpret the verses pertaining to laws in a proper manner.

14) The knowledge of *fiqh* itself, so that he is aware of the various interpretations of the verses pertaining to laws.

15) The knowledge of *asbaab an-nuzool*, and related sciences.

16) The knowledge of *naasikh* and *mansookh*, and related sciences.

17) The knowledge of the *hadeeth* of the Prophet (ﷺ), in particular those related to the interpretation of the Qur'aan.

18) The knowledge of all the other branches of '*uloom al-Qur'aan*, including *makkee* and *madanee*, *muhkam* and *mutashaabih*, and the types of *i'jaaz* of the Qur'aan.

19) A divine endowment that is not possible to obtain by one's self. This is a type of gift from Allaah to whomever He chooses. This type of intellect was what the Prophet (ﷺ) prayed for when he prayed for Ibn 'Abbaas, "O Allaah, grant him an understanding of interpretation."

---

678 Zamralee, p. 11.

679 This one point is a summary of three different points in the *Itqaan*, all of which are types of knowledge related to the Arabic language. These are the knowledges of *ma'aani*, *badee'*, and *bayaan*.

From this list, which is far from exhaustive, it can be appreciated that not everyone is qualified to pick up the Qur'aan and start interpreting it, in particular if he is not even familiar with Arabic! Of the fifteen conditions that as-Suyootee mentions in his list, seven – almost half – are directly related to the knowledge of the Arabic language. In addition, the knowledge required for every other condition (in terms of books and scholars) is not available in any language other than Arabic! It is not surprising, therefore, to see Shaykh al-Islaam Ibn Taymiyyah (d. 728 A.H.) saying that, "...the Arabic language is a part of the religion (of Islaam)!"[680]

VI. The Types of Tafseer

Ibn 'Abbaas said, "*Tafseer* is divided into four types: a type that the Arabs know by their language, a type which no one can be excused from not knowing, a type which the scholars are aware of, and a type which none can know except for Allaah."[681] As for the type which the Arabs are aware of because of their speech, this is due to their knowledge of Arabic vocabulary, grammar and the principles of rhetoric. As for the type which no one can be excused from not knowing, this refers to the basic principles of Islaam, such as the Oneness of God (*tawheed*), the finality of the prophethood of Muhammad (ﷺ), and the general laws and commandments in Islaam. As for the type which the scholars are aware of, this is because they are knowledgeable of all the branches of *'uloom al-Qur'aan*, and are capable of *ijtihaad*. They are, therefore, qualified to interpret the verses of the Qur'aan in a manner which others are incapable of. As for the type whose knowledge is known only to Allaah, this is the knowledge of the matters of the unseen, such as the time of the Day of Judgement and the actuality of the Attributes of Allaah.

However, what is meant in this section by the 'types' of *tafseer* are the various methodologies that the scholars of *tafseer* have used while interpreting the Qur'aan. During the history of Islaam, the Qur'aan has been subject to hundreds of *tafseers*, and it is not feasible to discuss all of them. It is possible, however, to divide the *tafseers* that have been written into broad categories, into which almost all *tafseers* can be classified, and discuss the general principles that each category has in common.

The various *tafseers* can, in general, be classified in one of six main categories, each of which has certain commonalties that which will be discussed below. Of course, when a certain *tafseer* is placed in one category, this does not imply that all that is found in that *tafseer* is based upon that one particular methodology, bur rather that the general methodology of the book is as shown.

For each category, examples of the most famous *tafseers* that were written with that methodology will be given, and some will be elaborated upon in the next section.[682]

---

680 Ibn Taymiyyah, Ahmad ibn 'Abd al-Haleem: *Iqtidaa as-Siraat al-Mustaqeem*, (ed. Dr. Naasir al-Aql, Maktabah ar-Rushd, Riyadh, 1994) p. 469.

681 az-Zarkashee, v. 2, p. 164.

682 The primary references for the names, classifications, and short critiques of all of these *tafseers* were: adh-Dhahabee (entire work), ar-Roomee (pps. 144-152), an-Najdee (entire work), and the relevant *tafseers* themselves.

A. Tafseer based on Narrations

This category is known as *tafseer bil ma'thoor*, or *tafseer* based on narrations. In other words, the Qur'aan is interpreted based upon other verses of the Qur'aan, *hadeeth* of the Prophet (ﷺ), and statements of the Companions and Successors. This type of *tafseer* is, of course, the most authentic and proper method of *tafseer*. Typically, the authors of this type of *tafseer* included *isnaads* of the narrations, or at least referenced the work where the *isnaad* was found.

The most important works based on this type of *tafseer* are:[683]

1) *Jaami' al-Bayaan 'an Ta'weel Aay al-Qur'aan*, by Muhammad ibn Jareer at-Tabaree (d. 310 A.H.) (This work will be discussed in greater detail in the next section).

2) *Tafseer al-Qur'aan al-'Adheem*, by Ibn Abee Haatim ar-Raazee (d. 327 A.H.). This work is a compilation of narrations from the Prophet (ﷺ) and the *salaf* concerning *tafseer*. The author is a famous scholar of *hadeeth*, and one of the Imaams of the science of *jarh wa ta'deel* (the science of categorising the people of narrations based upon their acceptance and reliability). In his work of *tafseer*, he kept his own comments to a minimum, and compiled thousands of narrations from the Prophet (ﷺ) and the *salaf*. This *tafseer* was only printed recently, and is one of the classic works in the field of *tafseer bi al-ma'thoor*.[684]

3) *Bahr al-'Uloom*, by Aboo al-Layth as-Samarqandee (d. 375 A.H.). This work was only printed recently, after having existed for centuries only in manuscript form. Although the author quotes from the *salaf*, he does not include the *isnaad*s of the narrations, thus making it difficult to benefit fully from it. On occasion, he ascribes views and interpretations to unknown scholars, by stating, 'Some of them said...'. In addition, after quoting the various opinions concerning a verse, he rarely draws a decisive conclusion between these opinions, thus leaving an average reader confused. Certain *Soofic* tendencies are also to be found in it. However, the work is a useful reference, especially if one wishes to obtain early interpretations of a verse after the time of the *salaf*.

4) *Al-Kashf wa al-Bayaan 'an Tafseer al-Qur'aan*, by Aboo Ishaaq ath-Tha'labee (d. 427 A.H.). Commenting on this *tafseer*, Shaykh al-Islaam Ibn Taymiyyah (d. 724 A.H.) said, "...there are a large number of fabricated *hadeeth* which have been reported by ath-Tha'labee... As a man, ath-Tha'labee was righteous and pious, but he cared little about his sources, and copied from the books of *tafseer* all kinds of things without discriminating between the authentic, weak and fabricated..."[685]

---

683 ar-Roomee, p. 90. Also see adh-Dhahabee's work, v. 1, pps 214-261.

684 There are four primary works in the field of *tafseer bi al-ma'thoor*: the *tafseer* of Ibn Jareer at-Tabaree (d. 310 A.H.), the *tafseer* of Ibn Abee Haatim (d. 327 A.H.), the *tafseer* of 'Abd ibn Humayd (d. 249 A.H.), and the *tafseer* of Ibn al-Mundhir (d. 318 A.H.). It is reported that all narrations of *tafseer bi al-ma'thoor* revolve around these four great works. Unfortunately, only the first two are in print; the other two have not, as of yet, been discovered in manuscript form. It is also reported that Imaam Ahmad ibn Hambal (d. 241 A.H.) authored a voluminous work of *tafseer*, but this too is missing.

685 Ibn Taymiyyah, *Muqaddimah*, p. 40

This *tafseer* contains a large quantity of *Israa'eeliyaat* narrations. Ath-Tha'labee also delves extensively into the grammar of the Qur'aan, and the rulings and opinions concerning the verses related to *fiqh*.

5) *Ma'aalim at-Tanzeel*, by Aboo Mu<u>h</u>ammad al-<u>H</u>usayn ibn Mas'ood al-Baghawee (d. 516 A.H.). The author was a very famous scholar of *hadeeth* (his book of *hadeeth*, *Sharh as-Sunnah*, is his most famous work), *fiqh*, and *tafseer*. Many scholars praised his *tafseer*, and Ibn Taymiyyah said of it, "The *tafseer* of al-Baghawee is a summarised version of at-Tha'labee's *tafseer*, except that he avoided narrating fabricated traditions and the views of the innovators."[686] The *tafseer* mentions the interpretations of the *salaf* without *isnaad*.

6) *Al-Muharrar al-Wajeez fee Tafseer al-Kitaab al-'Azeez*, by Ibn 'A<u>t</u>iyyah al-Andalusee (d. 546 A.H.). The author was a very famous scholar of Andalus, and eventually became its Chief Judge (*Qaa<u>d</u>ee*). Ibn Taymiyyah praised his *tafseer*, but pointed out that it has minor errors in it.[687]

7) *Tafseer al-Qur'aan al-'A<u>dh</u>eem*, by Ibn Katheer ad-Dimashqee (d. 774 A.H.). (This work will be discussed in greater detail in the next section).

8) *Al-Jawaahir al-<u>H</u>assaan fee Tafseer al-Qur'aan*, by 'Abd ar-Ra<u>h</u>maan ath-Tha'aalibee (d. 876 A.H.). The author summarised this *tafseer* from over a hundred works (some of them not extant anymore), primarily basing it on Ibn 'Atiyyah's work. Most of the quotes from other *tafseer*s are verbatim, and referenced.

9) *Ad-Durar al-Manthoor fee at-Tafseer bi al-Ma'thoor*, by Jalaal ad-Deen as-Suyootee (d. 911 A.H.). In this work, as-Suyootee compiled all the narrations he could find from the Prophet (ﷺ) and the *salaf* concerning the interpretation of every verse. The work is voluminous and extremely useful; however, in order to maximise its value, it needs to be critically edited to differentiate the weak narrations from the authentic ones.

10) *Fat<u>h</u> al-Qadeer*, by Mu<u>h</u>ammad ibn 'Alee ash-Shawkaanee (d. 1250 A.H.). The author was a famous scholar of Yemen, and one of the greatest scholars of his time. This *tafseer* is an excellent combination of interpretation based upon narrations, proper *ra'y*, differences in the *qira'aat*, and the language and grammar of the Qur'aan. Ash-Shawkaanee managed to eloquently summarise an interpretation of the Qur'aan based on these various methodologies into five volumes.

11) *Adwaa' al-Bayaan fee 'Ee<u>d</u>ah al-Qur'aan bi al-Qur'aan*, by Mu<u>h</u>ammad al-Ameen ash-Shanqeetee (d. 1393 A.H.). Ash-Shanqeetee has been called by many the scholar of this century, and this work is just one indication of that. In the work, the author conditioned upon himself to interpret the Qur'aan with the Qur'aan (although he did not interpret every verse). No student of knowledge can afford to be without this work. Unfortunately, he passed away before he could complete

---

686 Ibn Taymiyyah, *Muqaddimah*, p. 40.
687 al-Qa<u>tt</u>aan, p. 365.

the work, but his main student (Shaykh 'Atiyyah Saalim) took over from where he left, and completed the last two volumes of the *tafseer*.

Of course, this list is not exhaustive, and neither are all the works mentioned correct in all that they say. However, in general, the works listed followed the methodology of *tafseer* with narrations, and gave this methodology precedence over others.

B. TAFSEER BASED ON PERSONAL OPINIONS

Tafseer ar-Ra'y was defined and discussed earlier. These *tafseer*s are based primarily on *ijtihaad* from the *mufassir*, based on the nuances of the phrasing of a verse, the various linguistic connotations carried by a word, and other factors. Of course, this does not imply that the narrations of the Prophet (ﷺ) and Companions are absolutely ignored in these works, but rather that the primary purpose and source of these *tafseer*s was *ijtihaad*.

Although some of the *tafseer*s written with this methodology are useful works, the problem that arose was that the two primary sources of *tafseer* – *tafseer* of the Qur'aan with the Qur'aan and *Sunnah* – were not given great emphasis by most of these scholars, and secondary sources were used to interpret the Qur'aan. Thus, some of these *tafseer*s (but not all) became well known for contradicting other verses and *hadeeth* of the Prophet (ﷺ), since these were not considered while interpreting a verse. In addition, some of these *tafseer*s were written based upon the type of *ra'y* that is blameworthy; in other words, scholars who did not have the proper *'aqeedah* wrote interpretations of the Qur'aan in which they sought to defend and prove their innovations.

One of the best forms of *tafseer* is one in which *tafseer* by narrations is given precedence, while *tafseer* based on *ijtihaad* (*ra'y*) is only used as long as it does not contradict anything stronger than it. Some of the works mentioned above (for example, the works of Ibn Katheer and ash-Shawkaanee) can be considered as having combined these two types of *tafseer*, with the proper emphasis on each type.

The works that can be classified in this category can be sub-divided into two categories: *tafseer* based upon praiseworthy *ra'y*, and *tafseer* based upon blameworthy *ra'y*.

The works that might be considered as having followed *tafseer* based upon *ra'y* that is praiseworthy are:[688]

1) *Mafaatih al-Ghayb*, by Fakhr ad-Deen ar-Raazee (d. 606 A.H.) (This work will be discussed in greater detail in the next section).

2) *Anwaar at-Tanzeel wa Asraar at-Ta'weel*, by Naasir ad-Deen al-Baydaawee (d. 691 A.H.). The author based his *tafseer* on some narrations from the *salaf*, az-Zamakhsharee's work, and ar-Raazee's work, and also included his own *ijtihaad*. At times, he is influenced by az-Zamakhsharee's opinions in *'aqeedah*, and ar-Raazee's 'scientific' interpretations of certain verses.

---

3) *Madaarik at-Tanzeel wa Haqaa'iq at-Ta'weel*, by Aboo al-Barakaat an-Nasafee (d. 701 A.H.). The author was an ardent *Ash'aree* in *'aqeedah* and *Hanafee* in *fiqh*, and his *tafseer* is a clear indication of this. His *tafseer* is primarily based on al-Baydaawee's and az-Zamakhsharee's works, except that he deletes the *Mu'tazilee* beliefs found in the latter. The *tafseer* summarises az-Zamakhsharee's comments on the literary eloquence of the verses.

4) *Lubaab at-Ta'weel fee Ma'aanee at-Tanzeel*, by 'Alaa ad-Deen al-Khaazin (d. 741 A.H.). The author, as he himself mentions in his introduction, merely summarised some of the *tafseers* written before his time, basing his summary primarily on al-Baghawee's work.

5) *Gharaa'ib al-Qur'aan wa Raghaa'ib al-Furqaan*, by Nidhaam ad-Deen ibn al-Hasan an-Naysabooree (d. 728 A.H.). The author based his *tafseer* primarily on ar-Raazee's work, and added many benefits from az-Zamakhsharee's work. The author was not merely a compiler of quotes, for he frequently gives his own opinions, and critiques the views of ar-Raazee and az-Zamakhsharee. However, the *tafseer* contains some philosophical discussions, certain *Soofic* interpretations, and a defence of the views of the *Ash'arees* against the views of the *Mu'tazilah*.

6) *Al-Bahr al-Muheet*, by Muhammad ibn Yoosuf, otherwise known as Aboo Hayyaan (d. 745 A.H.) This is a very useful work, since the author concentrated on the grammatical analysis of the Qur'aan, and accentuated its literary *i'jaaz*. At first glance, the work seems to be more of a grammatical discussion than interpretation of the Qur'aan, but this is perhaps the most distinctive feature of the work, as the author mentions the various differences that the scholars of grammar have held concerning the analysis (*i'raab*) of certain verses. This work is perhaps the first work to turn to in order to obtain a linguistical analysis of a verse. Another salient feature of this *tafseer* is that Aboo Hayyaan refutes many of az-Zamakhsharee's heretical ideas from the Arabic language itself (in other words, he shows how az-Zamakhsharee is incorrect in deriving certain beliefs based upon Arabic grammar).

7) *Tafseer al-Jalaalayn*, by Jalaal ad-Deen al-Muhalla (d. 864 A.H.) and his student, Jalaal ad-Deen as-Suyootee (d. 911 A.H.). This *tafseer* was started by al-Muhalla, but he died before completing it, so his student, as-Suyootee, completed it after his death. This *tafseer* is perhaps the most famous *tafseer* in this category, and very popular amongst the masses, primarily due to its simplicity and modest size.

8) *As-Siraaj al-Muneer fee al-I'aanathi alaa Ma'rifathi ba'di Ma'aanee Kalaami Rabina al-Hakeem al-Khabeer*, by Shams ad-Deen Muhammad ibn Muhammad, otherwise known as al-Khateeb as-Sharbeenee (d. 977 A.H.). Despite its lengthy title, the *tafseer*'s primary purpose was to simplify and condense the interpretation of the Qur'aan so that the average Muslim could read it. The author benefits from and quotes many works of the *tafseers* (in particular, the works of al-Baydaawee, al-Baghawee, ar-Raazee and az-Zamakhsharee), and includes his own critical comments as well. In addition, he strives to show the relationship between the arrangement of the verses of the Qur'aan.

9) *Irshaad al-'Aql as-Saleem ilaa Mazaaya al-Kitaab al-Kareem*, by Aboo as-Sa'ood Muhammad ibn Muhammad al-'Imaadee (d. 982 A.H.). This *tafseer* is a moderate-sized one, and especially useful for its discussion of the eloquence of the Qur'aan, and certain wisdoms behind its arrangement.

10) *Rooh al-Ma'aanee fee Tafseer al-Qur'aan al-'Adheem wa as-Saba' al-Mathaanee*, by Shihaab ad-Deen al-Aloosee (d. 1270 A.H.). A voluminous work; the author quotes and benefits from many *tafseers*, and also gives his opinions. However, on too many occasions, the author gives bizarre *Soofi* interpretations to a verse, and this is why some scholars use this *tafseer* as an example of *tafseer al-ishaaree* (to be discussed below).

11) *Mahaasin at-Ta'weel*, by Jamaal ad-Deen al-Qaasimee (d. 1332 A.H.). The author was a famous scholar of Syria, and his work earned him considerable praise by the scholars of his time, such as Muhammad Rasheed Rida (d. 1354 A.H.) and others. This *tafseer* is primarily a collection and summary of quotes from other *tafseers*, and the author purposely keeps his comments to a minimum.

12) *Tafseer al-Kalaam al-Mannaan*, by 'Abd ar-Rahmaan as-Sa'adee (d. 1376 A.H.). The author was one of the most famous scholars of Arabia, and a defender of the *'aqeedah* of the *salaf*. His aim in this *tafseer* was to present the meanings and interpretations of the Qur'aan in simple language, without any detailed discussions or evidences from other sources; hence it is included in this category. It is available in five small volumes. This *tafseer* is perhaps the most useful work of *tafseer* for the layman who does not wish to go into any detail about the various interpretations of the Qur'aan; if a person wishes to understand the Qur'aan in plain and simple language, this is the reference that he should obtain.

It must be mentioned, however, that the fact that these *tafseers* followed *ra'y* based upon knowledge does not imply that all that is contained in them is correct; on the contrary, some of them contain grave errors (such as the works of an-Nasafee and ar-Raazee), while others are relatively error-free (such as as-Sa'adee's work).

The *tafseers* that are written with *ra'y* that is based upon desires, and with the intention of defending innovations, are many; in fact, every *tafseer* written by a scholar of one of the heretical sects can be considered an example of this type of *tafseer*. Perhaps the more famous of these *tafseers* are:

1) *Tanzeeh al-Qur'aan 'an al-Mataa'in*, by Qadee 'Abd al-Jabbaar al-Hamadanee (d. 415 A.H.), one of the leading scholars of the *Mu'tazilah*.

2) *Al-Kashaaf*, by Mahmood az-Zamakhsharee (d. 538 A.H.), also of the *Mu'tazilah*. (This *tafseer* will be discussed in the next section).

3) *Majma' al-Bayaan fee Tafseer al-Qur'aan*, by Aboo 'Alee al-Fadl ibn Hasan at-Tabarsee (d. 538 A.H.), a *Shee'ite* scholar.

C. Tafseer of the Jurists

The Qur'aan is, of course, the primary source of *fiqh*, or jurisprudence. Therefore it is no surprise to find that certain scholars have turned to the Qur'aan with this in mind, and written *tafseers* with the primary purpose of extracting laws from the Qur'aan. This type of *tafseer* is known as *tafseer al-fuqahaa*, or *tafseer* of the jurists. In fact, some *tafseers* of this type only deal with those verses that have a direct relationship to *fiqh*, and do not discuss verses primarily related to other matters. However, most of the classics in this field discuss all the verses of the Qur'aan, with particular emphasis on law-related verses.

Some of the famous *tafseers* written with this methodology include:[689]

1)   *Tafseer Ahkaam al-Qur'aan*, by Aboo Bakr ar-Raazee, otherwise known as al-Jassaas (d. 370 A.H.). This *tafseer* is written from a *Hanafee* point of view.

2)   *Ahkaam al-Qur'aan*, by Aboo Bakr al-Bayhaqee (d. 458 A.H.). This *tafseer* is a compilation of narrations from Imaam as-Shaafi'ee.

3)   *Tafseer Ahkaam al-Qur'aan*, by Aboo Bakr ibn al-'Arabee (d. 543 A.H.). Primarily written from a *Maalikee* perspective, and is considered a reference for the *madhhab*.

4)   *Al-Jaami' li Ahkaam al-Qur'aan*, by Aboo 'Abdullaah al-Qurtubee (d. 671 A.H.). To place this *tafseer* in the category of *tafseer bi al-ma'thoor* would not be incorrect, for the author follows the proper methodology in the interpretation of the Qur'aan. However, the *tafseer* emphasises the aspects related to the *fiqh* of a verse. Although al-Qurtubee discusses all the opinions concerning the *fiqh* of a verse, the *tafseer* is considered to be from a *Maalikee* perspective.

5)   *Zaad al-Maseer fee 'Ilm at-Tafseer*, by Ibn al-Jawzee (d. 597 A.H.). Even though this *tafseer* is not primarily meant for *fiqh*, it nonetheless can be considered a *Hambalee tafseer* in its discussion of verses related to *fiqh*.

6)   *Nayl al-Maraam fee Tafseer Aayat al-Ahkaam*, by Muhammad Siddeeq Hasan Khan (d. 1307 A.H.) This *tafseer* only discusses those verses that deal with *fiqh*. The author was one of the scholars of *Ahl al-Hadeeth* in India, and therefore his *tafseer* does not conform to one particular *madh-hab*.

7)   *Rawa'i' al-Bayaan Tafseer Aaytaat al-Ahkaam*, by the modern author Muhammad 'Alee as-Saboonee. He also restricts himself to those verses related to *fiqh*, and does not conform to one particular *madh-hab*.

8)   *Tafseer Aayaat al-Ahkaam*, by Manaa' al-Qattaan (author of *Mabaahith fee 'Uloom al-Qur'aan*). This one also is restricted to verses related to *fiqh*, and is not confined to one *madh-hab*.

---

689 ar-Roomee, p. 94.

D. SCIENTIFIC TAFSEER

Another category of *tafseer* is what has been termed 'scientific *tafseer*', or *tafseer al-'ilmee*. This type of *tafseer*, as can be presumed from its title, seeks to interpret the Qur'aan based upon scientific facts. These *tafseers* concentrate on those verses in the Qur'aan which discuss nature and aspects related to the physical world, and seek to explain these verses in the light of 'modern' science. Therefore, these *tafseers* seek to elaborate upon the scientific *i'jaaz* of the Qur'aan.

However, as was pointed out earlier in the section of scientific *i'jaaz*, it is absolutely essential that the proper methodology for extracting these scientific facts be followed. Unfortunately, almost none of the *tafseers* that are famous for this type of interpretation followed such a methodology; instead, these authors sought to prove that the Qur'aan mentions every type of science and knowledge known to man. Most of these interpretations even went to ludicrous extremes, claiming that the Qur'aan had 'founded' and laid down the sciences and principles of engineering, medicine, astronomy, meteorology, algebra, metallurgy, agriculture, carpentry, sowing, weaving, tanning, baking, precise measuring, and underwater diving![690] As can be seen, most of these topics are not mentioned as such in the Qur'aan at all; on occasion, some basic aspects of these sciences are mentioned or hinted at, but never is any discipline or principle explained. To presume that these sciences are all based on the Qur'aan requires quite a degree of imagination; it is true that the Qur'aan does not condemn these sciences, and encourages knowledge in general, but to claim that it forms the basis for the principles of these disciplines is absurd.

The two most famous *tafseers* in this category are *Mafaatih al-Ghayb*, by Fakhr ad-Deen ar-Raazee (d. 606 A.H.) (also mentioned above), and, *al-Jawaahir fee Tafseer al-Qur'aan al-Kareem*, by the famous Egyptian scholar, Shaykh Tantaawee Jawharee (d. 1359 A.H.). There are other *tafseers* that have been influenced to various degrees by this type of interpretation, perhaps one of the most extreme being *Tafseer al-Maraaghee*, by Ahmad ibn Mustafa al-Maraaghee (d. 1952 CE). In this work, the author denies or distorts almost all the supernatural miracles of the prophets, and denies the existence of angels and *jinns*, on the presumption that these facts are not explainable by science. He even goes to the extreme of claiming that Aadam is not the father of all of creation, since 'modern historical and scientific research does not support this theory'[691]!!

Dr. Muhammad adh-Dhahabee, one of the foremost scholars of comparative *tafseer* of this century, complains of the increasing popularity of this type of *tafseer*, and states,[692]

> This type of *tafseer* – I mean *tafseer al-'ilmee*, which tries to prove that the Qur'aan is composed of all types of disciplines, the modern and the undiscovered – has became increasingly widespread in our times, and very

---

690 For a list of the various verses that have been used to 'prove' these aspects, see adh-Dhahabee, v. 2, pps. 518-522.

691 an-Najdee, p. 69.

692 adh-Dhahabee, v. 2, p. 534. This author has not seen a better refutation of the over-zealousness of this brand of *tafseer* than ad-Adh-Dhahabee's discussion of the topic, v. 2, pps. 511-588.

popular for those who are specialised in science and care for the Qur'aan. The effect that this brand of *tafseer* that has dominated the hearts of these people has had is that we find a plethora of books being released in which these authors try to twist the Qur'aan so that it appears as if all the sciences of the heavens and earth are in it, whether explicitly or implicitly. And this is based upon their presumption, as we mentioned earlier, that these interpretations of the Qur'aan are the most important proof of its authenticity, and its *i'jaaz*, and its permanency (that it can be applied in all generations).

In reality, it seems that the authors of these type of *tafseers* were so impressed and awed with the West and its sciences, that they felt that the only way of proving Islaam was to show that the Qur'aan had preceded the West in the knowledge of all of these sciences. These authors failed to realise, however, that the goal of the Prophet (ﷺ) was not to teach mankind science, but rather to teach them the worship of Allaah! It is *not* of the primary goals of the *Sharee'ah* to provide and elaborate upon the disciplines of modern science, as Imaam ash-Shaatibee (d. 790 A.H.) mentioned over six centuries ago.[693] Ash-Shaatibee further stated that,[694]

> ...the *salaf* of this *ummah*, from the Companions and the Successors and those that came after them, were more knowledgeable of the Qur'aan and its sciences and what was hidden in it; yet none of them spoke of these things that are claimed to exist except for what we discussed (i.e., some basic sciences)... and if they had become engrossed in such subjects, and examined (the Qur'aan in such a light), it would have reached us, and at least the basic *principle* of this issue (i.e., scientific interpretation) would have been proven to us. But we do not find any mention of this, which shows that they did not have this concern with them. And this is clear proof that the Qur'aan was not sent to affirm what these people are presuming (exists in the Qur'aan). Yes, we are not denying that the Qur'aan mentions some science that the Arabs had, and other (sciences) that are well-known; material that astonishes people of intellect... but to presume that it contains matters that it does not, then no!

In other words, if the *salaf* did not place too much emphasis on this type of *tafseer*, this shows that it is not worth holding it in such importance. As ash-Shaatibee stated, it is true that the Qur'aan contains scientific facts – facts that a person living in the sixth century CE would not know, but to presume that this is the primary purpose of revelation, or that the Qur'aan is a reference to *all* the sciences is a gross error.

To conclude, *tafseer al-'ilmee* must be placed in its proper position; too much emphasis should not be given to this topic, and neither should one exert all his efforts in this field. The Qur'aan was sent as a guidance for mankind so that they could properly worship their Creator, and not to lay down principles of science. In addition, the proper methodology should be followed when this type of interpretation is resorted to. *Tafseer al-'ilmee* is an important type of *tafseer*, but only if it is used properly.

---

693 adh-Dhahabee, v. 2, p. 525.

694 *ibid.*, v. 2, p. 526. Is it not as if ash-Shaatibee is addressing the modern authors of these types of *tafseers*?

E. TAFSEER BASED ON INNER MEANINGS

Tafseer al-Ishaaree is a type of *tafseer* in which it is assumed that every verse in the Qur'aan has a certain hidden or inner meaning to it, and this meaning cannot be obtained except by a few chosen people. This type of *tafseer* was prevalent amongst the *Soofis*. Needless to say, such *tafseer* was well-known for its extremely imaginative interpretations, the majority of which had no basis from any verse! It is for this reason that many scholars said, "This type of *tafseer* is not considered *tafseer*!"[695]

However, some scholars allowed this type of *tafseer*, as long as the following conditions were met:[696]

1) That no *fiqh* rulings or *'aqeedah* be derived from such *tafseer*.

2) That the *ishaaree* interpretation does not contradict the apparent meaning of the verse.

3) That the *ishaaree* interpretation is not claimed to be the *only* or primary meaning of the verse, thus negating the apparent meaning.

4) That the *ishaaree* meaning does not contradict other aspects of the *Sharee'ah* or common sense.

5) That this interpretation has some basis for it in the *Sharee'ah*.

6) That it is not presumed that belief in the *ishaaree* interpretation is obligatory.

In reality, it would not be incorrect to say that *ishaaree* interpretations that are acceptable (i.e., that meet the above conditions) are nothing more than interpretations based on correct *ra'y*. Thus, it would probably be safer to refrain from using the term *tafseer al-ishaaree*, due to the fact that this name has been associated with far-fetched interpretations, particularly of the *Soofis*.

Tafseer al-Ishaaree was not used by all those who interpreted the Qur'aan; on the contrary, the majority of works quoted above did not concern themselves with this type of interpretation. Some works, while concentrating primarily on the apparent meanings of the verse, also commented on *ishaaree* meanings. Perhaps the most famous *tafseer* of this type is al-Aloosee's (d. 1270 A.H.) work (quoted above), since, after quoting various opinions concerning the apparent interpretations of a verse, he usually ends the topic by mentioning such *ishaaree* interpretations. Other works totally ignored the apparent meanings of the verse, and concentrated only on *ishaaree* ones. These works were primarily authored by extreme *Soofis*, and are not very popular amongst the masses. An example of such a work is the *tafseer* of Muhee ad-Deen ibn 'Arabee (d. 638A.H.), the famous *Soofi* heretic. This *tafseer* contains such blasphemous interpretations that even al-Azhar University (which is well known for its *Soofi* leanings) issued a decree prohibiting the publication and sale of this work!

To give some examples of what *tafseer al-ishaaree* is like, three *ishaaree* interpretations are quoted, in order of 'extremity'.

---

695 az-Zarkashee, v. 2, p. 170.
696 cf. Ik, pps. 208-209; adh-Dhahabee, v. 2, p. 408.

An example of this type of *tafseer* is concerning the story of Ṭaaloot when he tested his people. The Qur'aan states,

$$
\text{فَلَمَّا فَصَلَ طَالُوتُ بِالْجُنُودِ قَالَ إِنَّ ٱللَّهَ مُبْتَلِيكُم}
$$
$$
\text{بِنَهَرٍ فَمَن شَرِبَ مِنْهُ فَلَيْسَ مِنِّي وَمَن لَّمْ يَطْعَمْهُ فَإِنَّهُ}
$$
$$
\text{مِنِّي إِلَّا مَنِ ٱغْتَرَفَ غُرْفَةً بِيَدِهِۦ فَشَرِبُوا مِنْهُ إِلَّا قَلِيلًا}
$$
$$
\text{مِّنْهُمْ}
$$

«Then, when Ṭaaloot set out with his army, he said, 'Verily, Allaah will test you with a river; whoever drinks from it, he will not be with me, except if he takes (a sip) with his hand.' Yet, they all drank of it, except a few of them...» [2:249]

Some 'scholars' said, in the interpretation of this verse, that the river is meant to be a parable of this world; whoever 'drinks' from it excessively will fail, and whoever abandons it totally cannot survive, but the one who takes the bare minimum of what he needs is the one who will be successful. After quoting this interpretation, Imaam al-Qurṭubee (d. 671 A.H.) said, "And how beautiful is this, were it not for the fact that it involves excessive interpretation, and a distortion of the apparent meanings of the verse."[697]

Another example is the *ishaaree* interpretation of the verse,

$$
\text{وَلَوْ أَنَّا كَتَبْنَا عَلَيْهِمْ أَنِ ٱقْتُلُوا أَنفُسَكُمْ أَوِ ٱخْرُجُوا مِن}
$$
$$
\text{دِيَٰرِكُم مَّا فَعَلُوهُ إِلَّا قَلِيلٌ مِّنْهُمْ}
$$

«And if We had ordered them to kill themselves, or to leave their houses, very few would have done so» [4:66]

One of the famous scholars of the *Soofis* interpreted this verse as, "'To kill your-selves' means to go against all its desires, and 'to leave your houses' means to expel all love of this world from your hearts. Only 'a few would have done it' in quantity, but these (people) are great in quality, and they are the special ones who have reached the true positions,"[698] meaning that they are the 'friends' (*walee*) of Allaah, the title of *Soofi* leaders. As is seen from this interpretation, a certain concept or philosophy is 'read in' to the verse, as the verse makes absolutely no mention of going against one's desires and leaving the love of this world.

As a last example, the first letter in the Qur'aan is *baa* (in the *basmalah* preceding the *Faatiḥah*) and the last letter is *seen* (in, 'min al-jinnat wa an-naas' in 114:6). From this fact, certain 'scholars' derived the word '*bas*', meaning, 'sufficient'; as if the Qur'aan is stating that it is sufficient for all of mankind's needs.[699] Such far-fetched interpreta-

---

697 al-Qurṭubee, v. 3, p. 248.
698 adh-Dhahabee, v. 2, p. 419.
699 cf. Ik, p. 214.

tions have no basis in the proper methodology of *tafseer*. Likewise, all interpretations based on the number of times a word or letter occurs in the Qur'aan are examples of *tafseer al-ishaaree*. Such interpretations are unheard of from the *salaf*, and if there was any benefit to be gained from this type of *tafseer*, they would have discussed it and elaborated upon it.

In conclusion, it is necessary to be extremely cautious if one is reading an *ishaaree* interpretation of the Qur'aan, as such interpretation is usually not in accordance with the proper methodology of *tafseer*.

F. Modernistic Tafseers

What is meant by this category are not those *tafseer*s written in modern times, but rather a type of *tafseer* that is different from the categories mentioned above, with its unique styles, themes, and methodologies that are suitable for modern-day readers. In other words, the authors of these *tafseer*s tried to present the interpretation of the Qur'aan in an unprecedented style – a style that they felt would be more amenable to the generation of present times, that would solve problems that its readers would be facing in their daily lives, that would ignore much of the material found in older *tafseer*s that modern readers would neither comprehend nor find useful, that would incorporate Western thought and philosophy in its interpretation; basically, a *tafseer* that was meant for today's generation.

Although such an idea is admirable, and its goals praiseworthy, many of the authors of this type of *tafseer* did not realise the fact that the proper methodology of *tafseer* does not change with time. It is, therefore, not possible that a person re-interpret the Qur'aan in a manner or methodology not consistent with the methodology of the *salaf* in *tafseer*. In addition, almost all of these authors were influenced strongly by the 'Modernist' school of thought (known as the *Islaahiyyah* movement), founded by Jamaal ad-Deen al-Afghaanee (d. 1897 CE) and his student, Muḥammad 'Abduh (d. 1905 CE) (and by Sir Sayyid Aḥmad Khaan in the Indian subcontinent). Although this movement has some praiseworthy points (it fights against blind-following, *taqleed*; it seeks to re-affirm the importance of *ijtihaad*; in many ways it avoids the superstitions and *shirk* practices of today's societies), at the same time it represents one of the most powerful forces against the true teachings of Islaam. This is because of the fact that its primary goal is to combine Western philosophy with Islaamic thought and teachings; an act that the *Mu'tazilah* before them tried and failed to do; an act that, in essence, goes against the very purpose of the religion![700]

The more famous *tafseer*s of this category are:[701]

---

700 This is not the place to refute the ideas of this movement, which, unfortunately, is probably one of the strongest philosophies alive today, especially amongst the Muslims of the West. For a better discussion and critique of this movement, the reader is referred to Muḥammad Ḥaamid Naaṣir's *al-Aṣraaniyoon* (Maktabah al-Kawthar, Riyadh, 1996) (Unfortunately, no book is yet available in English on the topic. However a good series of audio lectures by Jamaal Zarabozo is available).

701 ar-Roomee, p. 105; adh-Dhahabee, v. 2, pps. 588-668.

1) *Tafseer al-Manaar*, by Muḥammad Rasheed Riḍa (d. 1354 A.H.; 1935 CE). Although the author was not as extreme in his beliefs as his teacher, Muḥammad 'Abduh, he was still greatly influenced by him. In fact, it is narrated that Rasheed Riḍa, while writing this *tafseer*, purposely avoided reading any work of *tafseer*, for fear that he might be 'influenced' by it, and thus possibly affect his own interpretation![702] In reality, the *tafseer* is not without its benefits, but the influence that Muḥammad 'Abduh had on him is very noticeable throughout the work; the author denies *all* the miracles of the Prophet (ﷺ) except the Qur'aan, interprets '*jinn*' as being disease-carrying microbes; denies the reality of magic, and other aspects which are not surprising to find in a 'modernistic' work.

2) *Tafseer al-Maraaghee*, by Aḥmad Muṣṭafa al-Maraaghee (d. 1370 A.H.; 1952 CE). This *tafseer* was commented upon earlier. An-Najdee summarised this and all similar *tafseer*s when he said, "And al-Maraaghee tried to make this *tafseer* of his a 'modern' *tafseer* of the Qur'aan, one that would be appropriate and suit the present Muslim situation. However, he fell into error because of his following certain views and ideas of the West, and his over-exaltation of the physical sciences..."[703]

3) *Tafseer al-Qur'aan al-Kareem*, by Mahmood Shalthooth (d. 1383 A.H.; 1963 CE).

4) *Fee Dhilaal al-Qur'aan*, by Syed Quṭb (d. 1387 A.H.; 1966 CE). Although Syed Quṭb was much less influenced by the *Islaahiyyah* school than the others that are mentioned, he was greatly influenced by the *Ikhwaan al-Muslimeen* movement of Egypt, and died for its cause. To claim that his *tafseer* is the most popular *tafseer* of modern times would not be an exaggeration. The *tafseer* is very simple to read, and aims to prove the superiority of the law of Islaam over all other laws, and the importance of establishing the law of Allaah on earth.[704] However, perhaps due to the fact that Syed Quṭb was not very knowledgeable of the various sciences of Islaam, the *tafseer* has some grave errors in it (in many matters of *'aqeedah*, for he was influenced both by the *Ash'arees* and the 'modernists'; his misconception that the primary purpose of Islaam is to fight tyrannical governments and establish the law of Allaah; his concept that all Muslim societies and governments are representative of *Jaahiliyyah*, etc.). In addition, since he was very much influenced by the arts (literature, poetry, etc.), at times his interpretation seems to be discussing some work of Arabic literature rather than the Book of Allaah, and many phrases of his are not befitting when discussing such topics.[705]

---

702 adh-Dhahabee, v. 2, p. 620.

703 an-Najdee, p. 69.

704 This principle, although in essence correct, was taken to an extreme by the *Ikhwaan* of Egypt, and the *Jaamati Islaami* of Pakistan, until it became the *primary* goal of these movements. For an excellent discussion of this aspect, see Dr. Rabee' Ibn Haadee al-Madkhalee's *The Methodology of the Prophets in Calling to Allaah* (al-Hidaayah Publishing and Distribution, Birmingham, 1997)

705 ar-Roomee, *Ittijahaat*, v. 3, p. 1052. For a critique of the views of Syed Quṭb, see the works of Dr. Rabee' Ibn Haadee al-Madkhalee, in particular, *Adwaa al-Islaamiyah ala 'Aqeedat Syed Quṭb wa Afkaarihi* (Maktabah al-Ghuraba, Madeenah, 1993).

In conclusion, this brand of *tafseer*, although perhaps the most popular amongst the Muslim masses of today, usually contains ideas and perspectives that are alien to Islaam. Although the majority of the contents of these *tafseer*s are acceptable, there are serious and not too infrequent deviations from the beliefs of *Ahl as-Sunnah*, both in *'aqeedah* and in methodology.

It is a very noble and necessary goal to present the interpretation of the Qur'aan in a manner which the people of a particular time and place will appreciate. However, this does not mean that the *usool at-tafseer* of such interpretations needs to change as well. It is possible to present the interpretation of the Qur'aan in a language and style that modern readers will benefit from while still following the proper methodology of *tafseer*, and authors such as as-Sa'adee, al-Qaasimee, al-Jazaa'iree and ash-Shanqeetee have shown and proven this in their respective *tafseer*s.

VII. Some Famous Tafseers

The purpose of this section is to briefly mention some of the most important and famous *tafseer*s in existence, and to mention the general methodology that each *mufassir* followed.[706]

'Jaami' al-Bayaan' of at-Tabaree

Jaami' al-Bayaan 'an Taweel Aay al-Qur'aan (The Comprehensive Explanation of the Interpretation of the Verses of the Qur'aan), by Muhammad ibn Jareer at-Tabaree (224 - 310 A.H.) is one of the earliest and greatest *tafseer*s in existence, and is considered the first reference to turn to among all the works of *tafseer*. This is because at-Tabaree compiled in this *tafseer* many narrations from the Prophet (ﷺ), the Companions, the Successors and those after them concerning the interpretation of the verses and phrases of the Qur'aan. The author was a scholar in almost all fields of Islaamic sciences, for he wrote, in addition to this *tafseer*, a masterpiece of Islaamic history entitled *Taarikh ar-Rusul wal Mulook*, another now-extant work on the *qira'aat*, and many other works in almost all fields of Islaam. He even founded his own *madhhab*!

His work of *tafseer* is one of the classics in the realm of *tafseer bi al-ma'thoor* (*tafseer* by narrations). Typically, at-Tabaree quotes a verse of the Qur'aan, and then states, "The various narrations concerning the interpretation of such-and-such..." and then proceeds to quote up to a dozen narrations from the *salaf*. After quoting the various narrations on a verse, he usually gives the opinion that he thinks is the strongest one, with his evidences. At times, he also discusses the various *qira'aat* of a verse, quotes lines of classical poetry to substantiate the meaning of an obscure word, delves into a grammatical analysis of a verse, and uses his own reasoning (*ijtihaad*). One of the unique features of this *tafseer* is that he quotes all the chains of narration (*isnaad*) for

---

706 These reviews were taken directly from each *tafseer*, and from the relevant portions of ad-Adh-Dhahabee's work.

every statement that he brings, and thus the authenticity of any narration may be verified. He also refutes the heretical beliefs of the *Mu'tazilah* and other sects during his time, and interprets the Attributes of Allaah upon the methodology of *Ahl as-Sunnah*.

Due to these factors – and more – scholars since his time until today have praised this *tafseer* over others. As-Suyootee said, "And his book (meaning at-Tabaree's *tafseer*) is the best and greatest of all *tafseers*"; an-Nawawee (d. 676 A.H.) said, "The *ummah* has agreed (*ijmaa'*) that nothing has ever rivalled the *tafseer* of at-Tabaree"; and Shaykh al-Islaam Ibn Taymiyyah (d. 724 A.H.) said, "As for the *tafseer*s that are in circulation, the most accurate of them is the *tafseer* of Ibn Jareer at-Tabaree, for he mentions the statements of the past generations with *isnaads*, and the *tafseer* is free of innovations..."[707]

Some of the criticisms that have been made of this *tafseer* is that at-Tabaree did not only collect authentic narrations, and thus it is difficult for a beginning student of knowledge to ascertain which narrations are authentic. In addition, at times at-Tabaree quotes Judaeo-Christian narrations (*Israa'eeliyaat*) which are of no value whatsoever. However, these criticisms are trivial when compared to the overall merits of the work. In addition, the *tafseer* has been critically edited by one of the leading scholars of *hadeeth* of this century, Shaykh Ahmad Shaakir (d. 1377 A.H.), and is available in 30 volumes with his commentary on the *isnaads* of the narrations of the first few volumes. Unfortunately, Shaakir passed away before his editing of the *hadeeth* could be completed.

'Tafseer al-Qur'aan al-'Adheem' of Ibn Katheer

Another important *tafseer* is that of 'Imaad ad-Deen Abul Fidaa Ibn Katheer (700 - 774 A.H.), entitled *Tafseer al-Qur'aan al-Adheem*. Ibn Katheer was one of the most famous scholars of his time, having studied under Shaykh al-Islaam Ibn Taymiyyah (d. 724 A.H.), al-Haafidh al-Mizzee (d. 742 A.H.) and other notable scholars. His *tafseer* is considered to be the second reference after that of at-Tabaree. An advantage of this *tafseer* is that it is easier to read than at-Tabaree's, since Ibn Katheer greatly summarises the different opinions that at-Tabaree quoted, usually only giving the strongest opinion. In addition, in many places Ibn Katheer gives his opinion concerning the authenticity of a particular narration. At other times, however, he merely quotes the *isnaad*, and does not comment on the authenticity.

Another advantage of this *tafseer* is that he explains the verses in simple language, so that the reader may understand the intent of the verse. On occasion, he also mentions the various *qira'aat* of a verse, but he does not elaborate greatly on the grammar (*'iraab*) of the Qur'aan.

The main criticism that had been made against this *tafseer* is that Ibn Katheer occasionally quotes *Israa'eeliyaat* which are of absolutely no value. However, his view concerning the usefulness of these narrations is clear, for he writes after quoting one of these stories, "...and it seems that this story is taken from the *Israa'eeliyaat*, and

---

707 Quotes taken from adh-Dhahabee, v.1, p. 218.

therefore it is allowed to quote them, but not to believe in them or reject them. They cannot be relied upon except when they conform with the truth, and Allaah knows best."[708]

In reality, this *tafseer* is the most useful work for a beginning student of knowledge, since it discusses and interprets the verses in sufficient detail to benefit from, without going into extreme details that might bore the reader. Therefore, in this regards, it would be of more benefit than at-Tabaree's *tafseer*. Ibn Katheer successfully summarises the essence of the various interpretations based on *tafseer bi al-ma'thoor*, and occasionally adds other aspects of interpretation related to the verse.

As-Suyootee said of it, "There is no book that has been written like it!"[709]

The *tafseer* is available in four average-sized volumes. Work has already been started by Shaykh Aboo Ishaaq al-Huwaynee to critically edit the *hadeeth* in this *tafseer*, but as of yet only the first volume has been published.

'Mafaatih al-Ghayb' of ar-Raazee

The most famous *tafseer* based upon intellect (*tafseer ar-ra'y*) is that of Muhammad ibn 'Umar ar-Raazee, better known as Fakhr ad-Deen ar-Raazee. He was born in 544 A.H., and became well known for his knowledge of Arabic grammar, and philosophy (*'ilm al-kalaam*). He died of poisoning in 606 A.H.

His *tafseer*, *Mafaatih al-Ghayb*, (The Unlocking of the Knowledge of the Unseen), although apparently seems to be complete, was completed after his death. Therefore, there is some difference of opinion as to who completed this work, and where he took over from ar-Raazee's interpretation. Evidence seems to suggest that ar-Raazee was able to complete this work until *Soorah* al-Ambiyaa, and after his death it was finished by two later scholars.[710] Whatever the case may be, the work is still considered one of the classics in the realm of *tafseer* based upon *ra'y*.

Ar-Raazee was an ardent *Ash'aree* by faith, and a rigid follower of the *Shaafi'ee madh-hab*. Therefore, he does not hesitate to defend his faith against the *Mu'tazilah* wherever he feels that a particular verse gives him the opportunity to do so. Whenever a verse of legal implications is come across, he gives the positions of the different scholars, and invariable 'proves' the superiority and correctness of the *Shaafi'ee* point of view in every case.

One of the benefits that may be obtained from this *tafseer* is that ar-Raazee includes a detailed discussion of the relationship between the various verses and *soorahs* in the Qur'aan, and this is a topic that is generally neglected in other *tafseers*. However, such relationships are, of course, based upon his personal opinion (*ijtihaad*), and therefore cannot be accepted as absolute. Yet another benefit of this *tafseer* is that he pays special attention to the grammatical analysis and commentary of the Qur'aan.

---

708 Ibn Katheer, v. 1, p. 117.
709 adh-Dhahabee, v. 1, p. 257.
710 cf. adh-Dhahabee, v. 1, p. 301.

The main criticism with regards to this *tafseer* is the fact that it is full of philosophical discussions and quotes from different philosophers, and in many places the work seems more like philosophical ramblings than Qur'aanic commentary. In addition, he does not hesitate to quote the 'current scientific' opinions of his day, specifically whenever he interprets a verse dealing with astronomy and nature. Since the scientific views of the eleventh century are considered outdated to say the least, these discussions often seem rather ludicrous and far-fetched. Due to these discussions, many scholars have strongly criticised this *tafseer*. Aboo Hayyaan (d. 745 A.H.) said of it, "Imaam ar-Raazee brought in his *tafseer* many long discussion of topics that have absolutely no value to the science of *tafseer*. This is why some scholars even said of it, 'In this (*tafseer*) you will find everything except *tafseer*!'"[711]

'al-Kashaaf' of az-Zamakhsharee

Among the many *tafseer*s of the *Mu'tazilah*, the most famous one is *al-Kashaaf 'an Haqaa'iq at-Tanzeel wa 'Uyoon al-Aqaaweel fee Wujooh at-Ta'weel* (The Unveiling of the Truths of the Revelation and the Essence of the Opinions Concerning the Perspectives of Interpretation), by Mahmood ibn 'Umar al-Khawarizmee, better known as az-Zamakhsharee (467-538 A.H.). He was one of the leading *Mu'tazilee* scholars of his time, and due to his great knowledge and eloquence, was able to spread the doctrines of the *Mu'tazilah* to a great extent. Far from being hesitant in announcing his heretical doctrines, he was aggressively outspoken concerning the *Mu'tazilee* faith. It is even said that he started his *tafseer* with the phrase, "All praise is due to Allaah, who created the Qur'aan."[712]

Az-Zamakhsharee was extremely proud of his work, and praised it himself on many occasions. In the introduction to the work, he says, after explaining the reasons for writing the work, that he completed it 'during the time-period of the caliphate of Aboo Bakr (i.e., two years and a few months), even though it should have taken over thirty years.'[713] In a separate poem, he versified,

> The *tafseer*s in this world are infinite,
> Yet I swear by my life that none is like my *Kashaaf*.
> If you truly seek guidance, then resolve yourself to read it,
> For ignorance is a disease, and the *Kashaaf* is the cure.'[714]

In reality, it is difficult to deny the *Kashaaf* of its merits, and the praise that az-Zamakhsharee heaped on it. Despite his blatant *Mu'tazilee* bias, and his vehement and fiery attacks against the *Ahl as-Sunnah*, az-Zamakhsharee was nonetheless a scholar of the highest calibre in terms of his knowledge of Arabic vocabulary, gram-

---

711 adh-Dhahabee, v. 1, p.304.

712 adh-Dhahabee, v. 1, p. 438. As was mentioned in Ch. 2, the *Mu'tazilah* believe that the Qur'aan is created, contrary to the belief of the *Ahl as-Sunnah*. For reasons as to why this phrase was eventually changed, see the reference cited.

713 *al-Kashaaf*, v. 1, p. 18.

714 adh-Dhahabee, v. 1, p. 442.

mar, rhetoric and manners of eloquence. In his *tafseer*, he emphasises the grammatical beauty and eloquence of the Qur'aan, and accentuates its literary *i'jaaz*. He discusses the wisdom and beauty behind the particular phrasing of verses and passages, and demonstrates time and time again the literary magnificence and splendour of the Qur'aan. Even subtle sentence structures that a less discerning eye would pass over are minutely scrutinised by az-Zamakhsharee to unearth a panorama of meanings and wisdom that demonstrates over and over again the unrivalled literary miracle of the Book of Allaah.

All of these merits, however, must be put in perspective. At times, az-Zamakhsharee seeks to prove *Mu'tazilee* doctrines by confusing the readers with his knowledge of Arabic. For example, in his *tafseer* of the verse, "Some faces that day will be radiant, looking at their Lord," (75:23) he misinterprets the meaning of the word 'looking' to 'expecting mercy', and even quotes a line of classical poetry to prove this meaning![715] By doing this, he seeks to prove the belief of the *Mu'tazilah*, who deny that the Muslims will see Allaah on the Day of Judgement and in the Heavens, contrary to clear verses in the Qur'aan and *hadeeth* of the Prophet (ﷺ) to this effect. However, given that the line of poetry quoted is authentic, az-Zamakhsharee has overlooked the principle that poetry is used to explain obscure words in the Qur'aan, and is not used to re-interpret the obvious. The above verse in the Qur'aan is explicit in its meaning, as is the *hadeeth*, "Verily, you will see your Lord (as easily) as you see this moon (the full moon)."[716] Therefore, no line of poetry can be used to contradict the explicit meanings of the Qur'aan and *Sunnah*.

In other places in this *tafseer*, az-Zamakhsharee defends the doctrine of the eternal damnation of sinners in the Hellfire, the non-existence of magic, the free-will of humans over which Allaah has no control, the doctrine that man is the creator of his actions, and many other *Mu'tazilee* beliefs.[717]

Therefore, this *tafseer* is a dangerous one, since the reader may be convinced by az-Zamakhsharee's knowledge into believing some of these *Mu'tazilee* doctrines. It is precisely for this reason that most scholars warned against this *tafseer*, such as Shaykh al-Islaam Ibn Taymiyyah (d. 724 A.H.), Ibn al-Qayyim (d. 758 A.H.), as-Subkee (d. 756 A.H.) and many others.

We quote Shaykh al-Islaam's stance on the this issue in its entirety, for – as typical with his writings – it is full of benefit and wisdom:

> What I am saying is that people like the *Mu'tazilah* first form some ideas,
> and then interpret the Qur'aan to suit their purpose. None of the earlier

---

715 cf. *al-Kashaaf*, v. 2, p. 509.

716 Reported by al-Bukhaaree, Muslim, Aboo Daawood, at-Tirmidhee, an-Nasaa'ee, Ibn Majah and others.

717 The *Ahl as-Sunnah* believe that Muslim sinners are not eternally damned to the Hellfire, and all of mankind who testify and believe in *tawheed* will eventually enter Paradise, and that magic is real, and that Allaah has control over man's actions despite the fact that man has free-will, and that Allaah is the creator of man's actions, with the belief that man has free will. For details and proofs of these points, the reader is referred to standard works of theology, such as *Sharh 'Aqeedah at-Tahaawiyah*, and others.

generations – the Companions or the scholars of this *ummah* – are with them in what they believe or how they interpret the Qur'aan. Their interpretations of the Qur'aan can easily be shown to be wrong in two ways: by demonstrating that their views are erroneous, or by showing that their interpretations of the Qur'aan are unjustified...

Some have a lucid and charming style of writing, and introduce their erroneous beliefs so cleverly that many of their readers fail to see them. The author of the *Kashaaf*, for instance, (i.e., az-Zamakhsharee), has succeeded in making his ideas attractive to a great number of people who would hardly look for erroneous ideas in his commentary. In fact, I know some *tafseer* writers and scholars who approvingly quote in their writings and speeches passages from their (the *Mu'tazilee*) commentaries that contain ideas which follow on from the principles which they (the *tafseer* authors) believe and know to be wrong, but are not aware of them (being present in the quote). Since their language is elegant, their erroneous views have entered (other misguided sects) and become much more destructive.[718]

Due to the benefits of this *tafseer*, certain later scholar of the *Ash'arees* tried to clear up the *Mu'tazilee* doctrines of this *tafseer* in critical footnotes. The most well known of these commentaries of the *Kashaaf* is *al-Insaaf min al-Kashaaf* by Ahmad ibn Muhammad al-Iskandaree (d. 683 A.H.). The most widely available edition of the *Kashaaf* has the *Insaaf* as footnotes to the main text.

In conclusion, this *tafseer* should only be read by one who is firmly grounded in the knowledge of the fundamentals of belief ('*aqeedah*) of both the *Ahl as-Sunnah* and the *Mu'tazilah* if one reads the *Kashaaf* without its critical commentaries (and of the *Ash'arees* if he reads it with one of these commentaries!).

VIII. The Dangers of Improper Tafseer

The Prophet (ﷺ) forbade arguing over the Qur'aan, and stated that such argumentation leads to disbelief. Once, he (ﷺ) passed by a group of people arguing over the Qur'aan. He commanded them, "Verily the nations before you were destroyed by this action of yours; they would try to contradict part of the Book of Allaah with other parts. Indeed, the Book of Allaah came to confirm its verses with each other (and not to contradict them). Therefore do not reject its verses due to other verses. When you know something from it (the Qur'aan), say it, and if you do not know it, then leave it to one who does know!"[719] He (ﷺ) also said, "Those before you were destroyed because they argued over their Book."[720] In another narration, he (ﷺ) said, "To argue over the Qur'aan is equivalent to disbelief (*kufr*)."[721] The Prophet (ﷺ) also warned against people who interpret the Qur'aan improperly when he said, "The thing that I fear the most for my *ummah* is the hypocrite with an eloquent tongue who argues

---

718 Ibn Taymyyah, pps. 47-8, with slight changes.
719 Reported by Ahmad and an-Nasaa'ee; cf. *Mishkaat* # 237.
720 Reported by Muslim.
721 Reported by Ahmad and Aboo Daawood; cf. *Mishkaat* # 236.

with the Qur'aan."[722] In other words, the Prophet (ﷺ) is warning against deviants who seek to prove their heresies with verses from the Qur'aan.

There are a number of oft-quoted *hadeeth* on the prohibition of speaking about the Qur'aan without any knowledge. Although the principles and prohibitions outlined in these *hadeeth* are correct, the *hadeeth* themselves are weak. The *hadeeth* in question are as follows: It is reported that the Prophet (ﷺ) said, "Whoever speaks concerning the Qur'aan with his personal reasoning, then even if he is correct, he is mistaken,"[723] and in another *hadeeth*, he (ﷺ) is reported to have said, "Whoever speaks concerning the Qur'aan without any knowledge, then let him seek his place in the fire of Hell!"[724]

The Companions and early generations were very cautious when it came to interpreting the Qur'aan without the proper knowledge. Aboo Mulaykah said, "Ibn 'Abbaas was asked concerning a verse; if some of you were to be asked concerning it, you would have replied, but he refused to say anything." And a person asked the Companion Jundub ibn 'Abdillaah (d. 90 A.H.) concerning a verse in the Qur'aan. He responded, "I must request that, if you are a Muslim, please do not sit with me," meaning that he was not qualified to interpret the verse. And it is narrated that Sa'eed ibn al-Musayyib (d. 90 A.H.) would not speak concerning the Qur'aan except with that which was understood by everyone, without going into any details. And Masrooq (d. 63 A.H.) said, "Beware of *tafseer*, for it is as if you are narrating concerning Allaah!" And Ibraheem an-Nakhaa'ee (d. 96 A.H.) said, "Our companions would be scared of *tafseer*, and fear it out of respect."[725]

It is no exaggeration to say that every single deviant sect that has sprung forth in the history of Islaam has misinterpreted verses of the Qur'aan in order to support its particular beliefs. For example, the very first sect to split from the Muslim nation, the *Khawaarij*, believed that 'Alee and Mu'aawiyah, and the people who followed them, had disbelieved, since they had both agreed to allow arbitrators to judge between them. They felt that 'Alee and Mu'aawiyah had, by accepting the judgement of the arbitrators, rejected the verse in the Qur'aan, "Verily, Judgement is only for Allaah" (12:40). However, the proper interpretation of this verse is that all judgement must be based upon the commands of Allaah (and by extension the commands of the Prophet (ﷺ)), and not that people are prohibited from judging between themselves.

Without relying on the proper methodology of *tafseer*, it is possible to interpret the Qur'aan in any way one desires to. The Qur'aan itself alludes to this when it says,

$$\text{فَأَمَّا ٱلَّذِينَ فِى قُلُوبِهِمۡ زَيۡغٌ فَيَتَّبِعُونَ مَا تَشَٰبَهَ مِنۡهُ ٱبۡتِغَآءَ ٱلۡفِتۡنَةِ}$$

«...and as for those in whose hearts is a disease, they follow that which is unclear in it (i.e., the Qur'aan), seeking thereby to cause dispute and turmoil» [3:7]

---

722 Reported by Aḥmad and al-Bazzaar; cf. Ibn 'Abd al-Barr, p. 493.
723 Reported by at-Tirmidhee.
724 Reported by at-Tirmidhee and Aboo Daawood.
725 All quotes from ar-Roomee, p. 82-83.

In other words, those who desire chaos amongst the Muslims will try to twist Qur'aanic verses that might not be entirely clear to suit whatever concepts and ideas they wish to prove.

It is even possible to misinterpret verses so that it seems that the Qur'aan itself is proving some of the most Islaamically heretical ideas possible! An example of this is the interpretation (or rather misinterpretation) of the Qadianis concerning the finality of the prophethood of Muhammad (ﷺ). The Qur'aan says,

مَّا كَانَ مُحَمَّدٌ أَبَآ أَحَدٍ مِّن رِّجَالِكُمْ وَلَكِن رَّسُولَ ٱللَّهِ وَخَاتَمَ ٱلنَّبِيِّـۧنَ

«Muhammad is not the father of any of your men, but he is the Messenger of Allaah, and the Seal (*khaatam*) of the prophets» [33:40]

This verse is the most explicit indication of the finality of the prophethood. However, the Qadianis try to prove that, by using the word *khaatam* (translated by them as 'seal'), and not *khaatim* ('the last of something'), the Qur'aan is stating that the Prophet (ﷺ) was the best and most perfect of the prophets, but not necessarily the last of them.[726] This interpretation can only be accepted by one who is ignorant of the Arabic language, and of the principles of *tafseer*. This is because, although *khaatam* does signify 'seal,' a look at any of the dozen classical Arabic lexicons will show that it also signifies finality, or the last of something.[727] The interpretation of the Qadianis has absolutely no basis in the Arabic language. An even more blatant indication of the ludicrousness of this interpretation is the fact that, of the ten *qira'aat*, only 'Aasim read the phrase in question as *khaatam*; the rest of the nine *qira'aat* read the phrase as *khaatim*! This is a stark indication of the ignorance of misguided sects with regards to the proper methodology required to interpret the Qur'aan. As was mentioned earlier, it is essential to take *all* the *qira'aat* of a verse into account when interpreting it, and all the different readings must complement one another. With this in mind, the interpretation of the Qadianis is shown to be baseless, even if their unique interpretation of the Arabic meaning of *khaatam* is considered.[728]

Even more ludicrous are some of the interpretations based on forged narrations and presumed inner meanings (*tafseer al-ishaaree*) to a verse. For example, in certain *Soofi tafseer*s, the verse,

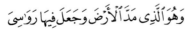

«And it is He who has spread out the earth, and placed therein firm mountains» [13:3]

---

726 cf. Muhamamd Ali's footnote to this verse in his *The Holy Qur'aan*, or any other Qadiani publication on this topic.

727 cf. Zaheer, Ihsan Elahi, *Qadiayaniyat* (Idara Tarjuman as-*Sunnah*, Lahore, 1989) for a more detailed discussion of this point.

728 This is excluding the other verses in the Qur'aan that allude to the finality of the prophethood, the numerous authentic *hadeeth* on this subject, the understanding of the Companions, and the consensus of the Muslim *ummah* on this matter. Due to this grossly heretical belief, the Qadianis have been excluded from the fold of Islaam by all of the scholars of the Islaam.

is interpreted as follows: "Allaah is the one who has spread out the earth, and placed in it His *awtaad* (one of the highest hierarchial levels in *Soofi* doctrine), and the Chosen Ones among His servants. Therefore, it is essential to turn to them, and to seek help from them, and whoever travels in the earth in order to find them, is successful and has been saved!"[729] The verse is clearly referring to the miraculous nature of the creation of the earth and the mountains, yet, by letting their imaginations free, certain *Soofis* have been able to read into this verse the concept of *awtaads*, and of the necessity of asking them for help and aid instead of Allaah! This belief of these *Soofis* is a manifestation of *shirk*, which Allaah has said in the Qur'aan that He would not forgive!

These examples prove the necessity of relying upon the proper methodology of *tafseer*, and of depending upon classical, authentic *tafseers* to obtain the proper understanding of a particular verse or passage.

---

729 Quoted from adh-Dhahabee, v. 2, p. 419.

CHAPTER 16

THE TRANSLATION OF THE QUR'AAN

Among the many miracles and blessings of Allaah is the '...differences of your languages and colours. Verily in this are indeed signs for men of sound knowledge' (30:22). Indeed, the differences in human languages is yet another proof of the existence and power of the Creator. It was Allaah Himself who honoured Aadam by teaching him '...the names of all things...' (2:31), and honoured Adam's progeny and 'taught him eloquent speech' (55:4).

Therefore, with all of the different languages on the face of the Earth, it becomes necessary to translate important texts and books written in one language into other languages so that a greater segment of mankind may benefit from them.

The Arabic word for translation is 'tarjamah'. This word also has the connotation of 'interpretation'; hence Ibn 'Abbaas was called the 'Tarjumaan al-Qur'aan,' meaning 'The Interpreter of the Qur'aan.' However, it is the first meaning of the word 'tarjamah' that we are interested in in this chapter.

I. The Types of Translation

There are two ways of translating a text: a literal, verbatim translation, and a translation by meaning.

1) Verbatim translation: What is meant by this is the word-for-word translation of a text, such that each word of the first language is translated into its equivalent in the other language. In such translations, the word order remains almost the same.

2) Translation by meaning: In this case, the intent or meaning of a text is translated into a different language.

Those who speak more than one language realise that verbatim translation is not successful in imparting understanding of a text. This is because the grammar and syntax of every language is different, and each has its specific procedure and methodology of speech. In addition, not every word has an equivalent in another language.

II. The Ruling on Translations

The Prophet (ﷺ) was sent for all of mankind, as Allaah says,

$$قُل يَٰٓأَيُّهَا ٱلنَّاسُ إِنِّي رَسُولُ ٱللَّهِ إِلَيْكُمْ جَمِيعًا$$

«Say: 'O Mankind! Verily, I am sent to all of you as the Messenger of Allaah...'»[7:158].

He (ﷺ) was also given his message in Arabic, the language of his people, conforming with Allaah's practice,

$$وَمَآ أَرْسَلْنَا مِن رَّسُولٍ إِلَّا بِلِسَانِ قَوْمِهِۦ$$

«And We have not sent any Messenger except with the language of his people» [14:4].

In fact, the absurdity of the Prophet (ﷺ) giving his message in a language other than Arabic has also been explained:

$$وَلَوْ جَعَلْنَٰهُ قُرْءَانًا أَعْجَمِيًّا لَّقَالُوا لَوْلَا فُصِّلَتْ ءَايَٰتُهُۥٓ ءَأَعْجَمِيٌّ وَعَرَبِيٌّ$$

«And if We had sent this as a Qur'aan in a foreign language, they would have said, 'What! (A book) not in Arabic and (the Messenger) an Arab?!'» [41:44].

The question then arises: If the Prophet (ﷺ) was sent for all of mankind, and the Qur'aan is in Arabic, is the translation of the Qur'aan allowed so that the Qur'aan may be spread to all of mankind?

As for verbatim translations, this is forbidden with regards to the Qur'aan. This is because there is no benefit to be gained out of it.[730] The Qur'aan is in Arabic, and any type of translation will not be regarded as the Qur'aan – the Speech of Allaah and the revelation to the Prophet (ﷺ).[731]

As for translations of the meaning, this is allowed and in fact *fard kifaayah*[732] for the *ummah*, as part of its duty to spread the message of Islaam.[733] In fact, there has been no known difference of opinion on this issue.[734] How else can it be expected that non-Arabs encounter the message of the Qur'aan? It is true that the Qur'aan is not translatable, for no translation can do justice to its eloquence and beauty, but perhaps, in the translation, a faint glimmer of the shining splendour of the original may be seen, enough, maybe, to spark in a curious reader an interest that will lead him closer to the truth.

---

730 An exception might be made, however, for a verbatim translation that is meant to help people learn the Arabic of the Qur'aan. An excellent example of this in English is Jamal-un-Nisa bint Rafai's *The Qur'an: Translation and Study* (Abul Qasim Publications). So far, only the first few *juz* have been completed.

731 See Ch. 2 for proof that the Qur'aan is only in Arabic and is the Speech of Allaah.

732 A type of obligatory act such that, if part of the *ummah* does it, the rest are not accountable, but if none does it, then all are accountable.

733 az-Zarqaanee, v.2, p.133.

734 *World Bibliography*, p. XXIII.

The Conditions of Translation

However, a translation of the Qur'aan is only allowed if the following conditions are observed: [735]

1) The translator must be a Muslim with correct Islaamic beliefs (*'aqeedah*). This is because a person who does not believe in the Divine Authorship of the Qur'aan will never be able to do justice to its translation. This point was elaborated on in the previous chapter.[736]

2) The translator must be proficient in Arabic and the language that he is translating in.

3) The translator must be knowledgeable of the grammar and peculiarities of the Arabic language, and specifically the Qur'aan.

4) The translator must be familiar with the other Islaamic sciences to a degree with which he can translate the Qur'aan with the proper interpretation.

5) The translation must conform to the intent of the verse, such that it is a reasonable rendering of the meanings of the original. For this, the authentic, classical interpretations of the Qur'aan must be consulted.

6) The translation must be complete, such that the original (i.e., the Qur'aan) is not needed by the person reading the translation, or else the whole purpose of the translation is lost.

7) Neither the translator nor his audience may believe that the translation *is* the Qur'aan. The translator should include appropriate remarks on this issue, preferably in the introduction. He must clarify to his audience that the Qur'aan is only in Arabic, and that the translation is only a rendering of the meaning of the Qur'aan into a different language. He must mention that the translation can never be substituted for the original (the Qur'aan). It is also incorrect to call such translations, 'The Qur'aan,' or even, 'A Translation of the Qur'aan,' for the Qur'aan cannot be translated. Such works must be called, 'A Translation of the Meanings of the Qur'aan,' or similar such wordings, so that it is clearly understood by the audience that the work in their hands is *not* the Qur'aan.[737] Some scholars have even stipulated that it is mandatory for the Arabic text to be written along with the translation – either side-by-side or above it – so that it is mentally understood that the translation is not the actual Qur'aan.[738]

These conditions, especially the first one, make it imperative that the translation be done by a knowledgeable Muslim. A translation done by a person who excels in the knowledge of Arabic and English, but is not a Muslim, must be rejected for this

---

735 az-Zarqaanee, v.2, pps. 122-124; Ubaydaat, p. 278.
736 See 'The Qualities of a *Mufassir*', points 2-4.
737 az-Zarqaanee, v.2, p.136.
738 cf. al-Uthaymeen, p. 33. However, this author asked Shaykh al-'Uthaymeen (on the 11th of Ramadhan, 1418 A.H., in the *Masjid al-Haraam*) whether the writing of the Arabic script with a translation was mandatory or not. He replied that it was not obligatory to do so, but only encouraged.

reason, no matter how eloquent the English. (An example of such a translation is Arthur J. Arberry's *The Koran Interpreted*.)

It is also permissible to interpret and explain the Qur'aan in a different language, as long as the readers can tell the difference between the interpretation and the translation. For example, in Khan and Hilali's translation of the Qur'aan, verse 2:4 has been translated as, "And those who believe in (the Qur'aan and the *Sunnah*) which has been sent down..." The phrase 'the Qur'aan and the *Sunnah*' is not in the Arabic, but it is the intent of the verse. By including it in parentheses, the translators have indicated that this is not in the Qur'aan but rather it is an interpretation of the verse. This is allowed, and, according to some, encouraged.

The Translation as the Qur'aan

As was mentioned in the conditions for translation, it is not permissible to believe that the translation is the actual Qur'aan. The fact that a translation of the Qur'aan cannot be considered as a substitute for the actual Qur'aan has been agreed upon by all the major scholars of Islaam, and was never seriously a topic of debate amongst the scholars.

However, there have been some modern 'scholars' who have stated that a translation of the Qur'aan may actually be considered as the original! This issue became the topic of serious discussion during the late half of the nineteenth century, and reached its height in the early part of the twentieth century, during which time Kamaal Ata Turk (d. 1929 CE) ordered that the Arabic Qur'aan be substituted for a Turkish translation, which would be read during prayer and outside of it! The Egyptian 'intellectual' Fareed Wajdee (d. 1954 CE) and the then Grand Shaykh of al-Azhar, Muhammad Mustafa al-Maraghee (d. 1945 CE), were also of the opinion that such a translation could take the place of the Qur'aan.[739]

The simplest refutation of this view is by recalling the definition of the Qur'aan: The Qur'aan is the Arabic Speech (*kalaam*) of Allaah, which He revealed to Muhammad (ﷺ) in wording and meaning, and which has been preserved in the *mus-hafs*, and has reached us by *muttawaatir* transmissions, and is a challenge to mankind to produce something similar to it.

Therefore, the fact that the Qur'aan is in Arabic is an integral part of the definition. As was mentioned earlier, there are eleven references in the Qur'aan that it is in the Arabic language, amongst them the verses, "...this (the Qur'aan) is in a clear Arabic tongue" (16:103), and, "Verily, We have revealed this as an Arabic Qur'aan" (12:2), and, "And thus We have inspired you with an Arabic Qur'aan" (42:7).

---

739 *World Bibliography* , p. XXVI. What is meant by 'take the place of the Qur'aan' is that the translation could be used to derive laws, beliefs and be recited in prayer, and not that the Arabic Qur'aan should be neglected. To see a fuller discussion of their precise views, and a refutation of it, see ar-Roomee, *Ittijahaat*, pps. 413-441.

Al-Azhar University, in 1936 CE (1355 A.H.), finally issued a *fatwa* in which it stated that the Qur'aan is only in Arabic, and any translation cannot be considered a substitute for the Qur'aan.[740] This *fatwa* effectively ended the debate that had been raging on before this time.

Another issue that is related to the above one is the recitation of translations of the Qur'aan during the prayer.

The recitation of the translation of the Qur'aan during prayer is forbidden according to the vast majority of scholars, including the *Shaafi'ees*, *Maalikees*, and *Hambalees*. If a person prays with such a translation, his prayer will not be valid. However, Imaam Aboo Haneefah (d. 150 A.H.) allowed the recitation of the Qur'aan in Persian,[741] and based on this, some of the later Hanafees allowed it in Turkish and Urdu. The two students of Aboo Haneefah, Imaam Aboo Yoosuf (d. 182 A.H.) and Muhammad ash-Shaybaanee (d. 189 A.H.), restricted the generality of their teacher's ruling, and allowed it only when a person did not know Arabic, and was forced by necessity to recite it in a foreign language.[742] However, all of these opinions go against the majority opinion, and do not have any proof to back them up.

Qaadee Aboo Bakr ibn al-'Arabee (d. 543 A.H.), the famous *Maalikee* commentator on the Qur'aan, said in reference to the following verse:

وَلَوْ جَعَلْنَهُ قُرْءَانًا أَعْجَمِيًّا لَّقَالُواْ لَوْلَا فُصِّلَتْ ءَايَنتُهُۥٓ ءَاعْجَمِيٌّ وَعَرَبِيٌّ

«And if We had sent this Qur'aan in a foreign language other than Arabic, they would have said, 'Why are not its verses explained in detail (in our language)? What! A (book) not in Arabic and a (Messenger who is) Arab?'» [41:44]

Our scholars (of the *Maalikees*) have said that this verse refutes the view of Aboo Haneefah, may Allaah have mercy on him, that the Qur'aan may be (recited) in its translation, such as Persian. This is because the verse negates the attribute of (the Qur'aan) being non-Arabic.

Ibn Hajr al-Asqalaanee ash-Shaafi'ee (d. 852 A.H.), the famous commentator of *Saheeh al-Bukhaaree*, wrote,

If a person is capable of its recitation in Arabic, then he is not allowed to change it (to another language), and his prayer is void (if he does this). This is the case even if he is not capable of this (i.e., even if he cannot recite the Qur'aan in Arabic, he is prohibited from reciting it in a different language).

Ibn Hajr then went on to mention that the Law-giver provides certain formulas[743] to recite in the prayer for the one who does not know Arabic, until he memorises the necessary *soorahs*.

---

740 *ibid*. p. XXVIII

741 It should be mentioned that some scholars say that Aboo Haneefah never made such a statement, or that he withdrew from this stance later on in his life. cf. az-Zarqaanee, v.2, p.163.

742 Qattaan, p. 318.

743 Such as *subhan Allaah*, or *alhamdulillah*. See Syed Sabiq, *Fiqh us-Sunnah*, v.1, p.122.

Shaykh al-Islaam Ibn Taymiyyah (d. 728 A.H.) said, "As for bringing a word (from another language) to explain the meaning (of another word), such as a word of the Qur'aan, then this in essence is not possible. This is why the scholars of the religion held the view that it is impermissible to recite (the Qur'aan) in a language other than Arabic, whether a person is capable of reading Arabic or not, because this (translation) removes the fact that the Qur'aan is a revelation from Allaah." In another place, he said, "As for the Qur'aan, it is not to be recited in other than Arabic, whether a person is capable of doing so or not. This is according to the majority opinion, and it is the correct opinion, without a doubt."[744]

Imaam an-Nawawee (d. 676 A.H.) said, "It is not allowed to recite the Qur'aan in any language other than Arabic, regardless of whether a person is capable of speaking Arabic or not, and whether such recitations occur during prayer or not."[745]

Therefore, it is concluded by stating that it is necessary to translate the Qur'aan into different languages, since this is part of the duty of spreading Islaam. Such translations, however, may never be taken as substitutes of the Qur'aan, nor is it allowed to recite translations of the Qur'aan in prayer. Such a prayer, if performed, is not valid and must be repeated.[746]

THE IMPORTANCE OF ARABIC

It is imperative that the Muslims in particular are familiar with the Arabic language to a degree that they can understand the Qur'aan. Arabic is the language of Islaam – it has been and always will be. The Muslims who do not understand Arabic must realise the great loss that they are in by not being able to understand and read the words of their Creator. When they read 'translations' they should recognise that these are the words of a human interpreter, and not the words of the Creator. The beauty, the eloquence, the rhythm, the *i'jaaz* – all is lost in translation. Instead of being able to read the Words that Allaah Himself Spoke and revealed to Muhammad (ﷺ), a person instead must rely on the words and speech of a mortal. Can there be a greater loss than this?

The scholars of this *ummah*, from the Companions to this generation, all realised the importance of the Arabic language. Ubay ibn Ka'ab said, "Teach Arabic (i.e., Arabic grammar) like you teach the memorisation of the Qur'aan!" Aboo Bakr said, "That I recite and forget (a portion) is more beloved to me than to make a grammatical mistake!" And 'Umar once passed by a group of archers who missed their targets. He

---

744 All quotes taken from Qattaan, p. 319-20.

745 az-Zarqaanee, v.2, p.160.

746 Concerning writing the Qur'aanic Arabic in another script (what is known as 'transliteration'), this should be avoided as much as possible. In fact, the Committee for Religious Verdicts at Azhar even issued a verdict (*fatwaa*) stating that such transliterations were forbidden. They wrote, "There is no doubt that the Latin script is devoid of a number of letters present in the Arabic script, and so it can never give (the sound) that the Arabic letters give. If the Qur'aan were written in a Latin script...there would occur errors and mispronunciations in its words, which would invariably lead to changes in its meaning..." az-Zarqaanee, v.2, p.134.

reprimanded them, and they responded that they were only beginners, but they made a grammatical mistake in phrasing their response. He told them, "Verily, your mistakes in (Arabic) grammar are more difficult for me to bear than your mistakes in archery!"[747]

Imaam ash-Shaafi'ee (d. 204 A.H.) said, "Therefore, it is imperative that every Muslim should strive to learn Arabic as hard as he can, so that he can testify the *shahada*, and recite the Book of Allaah, and say the invocations that are mandatory upon him, such as the *takbeer, tasbeeh, tashahud*[748] and other prayers. And the more he learns the language that Allaah Himself chose to be the language of him who sealed the prophets, (ﷺ), and to be the language of His Final Revelation, the better it is for him!"[749]

And Shaykh al-Islaam Ibn Taymiyyah (d. 728 A.H.) even went so far as to say that, "...the Arabic language is a part of the religion, and knowing it is obligatory. This is because the ability to understand the Qur'aan and *Sunnah* is obligatory on every Muslim, and yet they cannot be understood without knowing Arabic, and (the general Islaamic principle is that) every act that is an essential prerequisite to perform an obligatory act is also obligatory."[750]

It is for this precise reason that it is seen that those Muslim societies that are ignorant of Arabic are, in general, less Islaamically knowledgeable (and hence more susceptible to deviation) than those societies which are firmly grounded in Arabic. It is not surprising, therefore, that one of the goals of the enemies of Islaam is the destruction of the Arabic language, for they realise that one of the uniting factors of the Muslims is the language of the Qur'aan.

The orientalist Philip DeTrazy wrote, in 1948 CE,

> Due to the power of the Qur'aan, the Muslims have become a united nation in their language, religion, laws and politics. For the Qur'aan has combined all the Arabs, and it is inconceivable that, were it not for the Qur'aan, classical Arabic would have spread among them ... And were it not for the Qur'aan, numerous peoples would not have taken up this language, and learnt how to read and write it, and studied it and worked with it. And were it not for the Qur'aan, every nation among the nations of Muslims would have had their own language...So the Qur'aan has been the source of preserving communication between the Islaamic and Arab nations.[751]

Sir Edward Benson wrote, "The basis of Islaam is the Arabic language. If it is lost, Islaam is lost!"[752] One of the ministers of England, Sir Gladstone, wrote, "As long as the Muslims have the Qur'aan in their hands, Europe can never prevail over the

---

747 Quotes taken from Aboo Ubadah, pps. 15-20.
748 The *takbeer* is to say, '*Allaahu Akbar*,' the *tasbeeh* to say, '*Subhaan Allaah*' and the *tashahud* is the prayer that is said in the last portion of the *salaat*.
749 az-Zarqaanee, v.2, p.152.
750 Ibn Taymiyyah, *Iqtidaa*, p. 469
751 Translated from Aboo Ubaadah, p. 15.
752 *ibid.* p. 59.

East."[753] During the French occupation of Algeria, the French government was advised by its consulate in Algeria, "We will never be able to overpower the Algerians as long as they read the Qur'aan and speak Arabic. Therefore, we must remove the Arabic Qur'aan from their midst, and abolish the Arabic language from their tongues."[754] And this is exactly what Kamaal Ataa Turk, the secular leader of Turkey who abolished the Islaamic caliphate in 1921, did. He ordered for the Qur'aan to be recited in Turkish, even during the prayers, and transposed the Arabic alphabet with the European one, such that even today, the Turkish language, which was once written in Arabic, is now written in Latin.

III. The History of Translation

The first translation of any part of the Qur'aan occurred during the lifetime of the Prophet (ﷺ). The Muslims in Abyssinia, under the leadership of Ja'far ibn Abee Ṭaalib, recited the first few verses of *Soorah* Maryam to the Negus, which were translated to him. These verses led the Negus to convert to Islaam. This incident occurred before the *hijrah* and is probably the first recorded instance of any translation of the Qur'aan.[755]

After the *hijrah*, the Prophet (ﷺ) sent letters to the emperors of Persia, Rome, Egypt, and Bahrain, inviting them to Islaam. Most of these letters included some verses in the Qur'aan, and these verses would had to have been translated along with the letters. In particular, the Prophet (ﷺ) included verse 3:64:

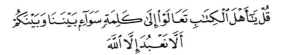

«Say: O People of the Scriptures! Come to terms common between us and you: that we worship none but Allaah...»

These letters were sent out around the sixth year after the *hijrah*.[756]

Reports are also found that state that the Companion Salmaan al-Farsee was requested by some Persian converts to translate some portions of the Qur'aan, which he then sent them.[757] Concerning other early translations,[758]

> There are Syriac translations made by non-Muslims, in the second part of the first century A.H. in the period of Ḥajjaaj ibn Yoosuf (d. 95 A.H.). There is also a possibility of the existence of a Berber translation written in

---

753 ar-Roomee, *Ittijahaat*, p. 416.

754 Aboo Ubaadah, p. 44.

755 See *Raheeq al-Makhktoom*, p. 113.

756 ibid., pps. 414-23.

757 as-Sarakhsee, *al-Mabsoot*, v. 1, p. 37. As-Sarakhsee quotes this as proof for the fact that it is permissible to recite the Qur'aan in another language, as the report mentions that these new Muslims would recite these translations in their prayer. However, this incident is not found mentioned before this time, in any other book, nor is its *isnaad* known. In order to derive any rulings from an incident, it first must be substantiated to have occurred!

758 *World Bibliography*, p. XXVIII.

127 A.H. There was a Persian oral translation made by Moosaa ibn Sayyaar al-Aswaaree before 225 A.H. and a complete Indian translation before 270 A.H. According to T.W. Arnold, a Chinese translation also possibly existed.

The first written Persian translation was done at the command of the Samaanid king, Aboo Saalih Mansoor ibn Nooh (d. 364 A.H.). This translation was accompanied by a translation of Imaam at-Tabaree's (d. 310 A.H.) *tafseer*, part of which is still available in manuscript form. The first Turkish translation was completed in the 5th century of the *hijrah*, but only the mention of this translation is left. The earliest Turkish translation that is still extant was completed in 734 A.H.

The earliest Hindi translation is reputed to be the one ordered by the Raja Mahrook, in 270 A.H., who ordered the Muslim ruler of Sind, 'Abdullaah ibn 'Umar, to translate the Qur'aan for him.

Urdu translations have all been fairly recent, due to the fact that Urdu is itself a relatively young language. The first complete translation of the Qur'aan into Urdu was done by Mawlaana Shah Rafee' ad-Deen (the son of Shah Walee Allaah ad-Dehlawee), in 1190 A.H. (1776 CE). It was published in Calcutta. This was followed by a more popular translation by another of Shah Walee Allaah's sons, Shah 'Abd al-Qaadir. This second translation was completed in 1205 A.H., and published in Delhi. The first Punjabi translation was attempted by Nuwaan Kootee Shah, and published in Lahore in 1885 CE (this translation was not complete, however). The first Gujurati translation was done by 'Abd al-Qaadir ibn Luqmaan, and published in Bombay, in 1879 CE. Concerning Bengali translations, it is claimed that the first partial translation was done by Ghulam Akbar Ali of Mirzapoor, in 1868 A.H., whereas the first complete translation was done by a Brahman, Garish Chandra Sen, in 1886 CE. The first translation of the Qur'aan into Malay was done in the middle of the 17th century by 'Abd ar-Ra'oof al-Fansooree, a famous scholar of Singkel. It was published in Cairo in 1923 CE. The first Swahili translation was printed in 1923 CE, in London. It was done by the missionary Godfrey Dale, and printed under the auspices of the "Society for Promoting Christian Knowledge."[759]

Translations into Western Languages

The first translation of the Qur'aan into a Western language was done in 1143 CE by Robertus Retenesis, who was helped by Hermannus Dalmata. It was translated into Latin under the command of Peter the Venerable, Abbot of Cluny. The Abbot's motive for such an undertaking was to try to defame Islaam, as during this time the Crusades were being fought. This translation was spread in manuscript form, until it was approved by Martin Luther, and printed by Bibliander Press in Basle, Switzerland in 1543. Martin Luther also wrote an introduction to this edition.

---

759   All the material of the last few paragraphs has been summarised from *World Bibliography*, pps. XXVIII-XXXIV.

Alphonse X (1252 - 1284 CE) ordered a certain Abraham of Toledo to translate portions of the Qur'aan, and thus the first Spanish translation of seventy *soorahs* was accomplished.

The first partial translation into English appeared in 1515. It was published in England, and shows the early interest that existed in that country concerning Islaam. It was only 61 pages in length, and entitled, *"Here begynneth a lytell treatyse of the Turkes law called alcoran. And also it speketh of Machamet the Nygromancer."* The translator and other particulars about the translation are unknown.

Perhaps the first 'modern' translation of the Qur'aan was the Italian one by Andrea Arrivabene, published in 1547. This translation served as the basis for the first German translation, done by Solomon Schweigger in 1616, and printed in Nuremburg. This German translation formed the basis for the first Dutch translation, printed in Hamburg in 1641.

In 1647, Andre du Ryer, who was the French Consul in Egypt for some years, translated the Qur'aan (from Arabic, for a change!) into French, and it was from this edition that Alexander Ross translated it into English in 1649. Thus, the first complete English translation was actually a translation from the French, and as such was highly inaccurate. This was the standard English translation for around a century. In his introduction, Ross wrote:

> ...this, his *Alcoran* (sic) (the Ground-work of the Turkish religion), hath been already translated into...Latin, Italian, (and) French, yet never gained any prosletyte, where the Sword, its most forcible, and strongest arguement, hath not prevailed...Thou shalt find it of so rude, and incongruous a composure, so farced with contradictions, blasphemies, obscene speech, and ridiculous fables...Such as it is, I present it to thee, having taken the pains only to translate it out of French, not doubting, though it hath been a poyson (sic) that hath infected a very great, but most unsound part of the Universe, it may prove an Anti-dote, to confirm in thee the health of Christianity.[760]

Ross' spirit for translating the Qur'aan speaks for itself. In addition, Rev. Zwemer said of him, 'He was utterly unacquainted with Arabic, and not a thorough French scholar, therefore his translation is faulty in the extreme.'[761] Similar assessments were made by Savary and Sale.[762]

After Ross, Father Ludovic Maracci, who was a Confessor to Pope Innocent XI, translated the Qur'aan into Latin in 1698. This was published in Padua, and was to form the basis of many other English translations. He dedicated his work to the Holy Roman Emperor Leopold I, and he introduces it by a one volume introduction entitled a "Refutation of the Koran." In his translation, Maracci included '...quotations from various Arabic Commentaries, carefully selected and garbled, so as to give the worst possible impression of Islam to Europe.'[763]

760 Arberry, p. 8.
761 Kidwai, p. 19.
762 Khalifa, p. 65.
763 Yusuf 'Ali, p. xv.

After him, George Sale, a lawyer who had learnt Arabic from a royal court interpreter by the name of Dadichi, completed his famous translation into English in 1734. Since his Arabic was poor, Sale relied heavily on Maracci's Latin version, in addition to the Arabic text of the Qur'aan printed in Hamburg in 1694 (which itself was not free of errors). This translation, though, was undoubtedly the most famous one for over two centuries. It was translated into Dutch (in 1742), German (in 1764), French (in 1750), Russian (in 1792), Swedish (in 1814) and Bulgarian (in 1902), and the original English alone has seen over a hundred and twenty editions.

Sale was no altruist, and he did not hide his intentions for translating the Qur'aan. He writes in the introduction to his translation:

> I imagine it almost needless to either make an apology for publishing the following translation, or to go about to prove it a work of use as well as curiosity. They must have a mean opinion of the Christian religion, or be ill grounded therein, who can apprehend any danger from so manifest a forgery...I shall not here inquire into the reasons why the law of Muhammad has met with so unexampled a reception in the world (for they are greatly deceived who imagine it to have been propagated by the sword alone)...But whatever use an impartial version of the Koran (*sic*) may be of in other respects, it is absolutely necessary to undeceive those who, from the ignorant or unfair translations which have appeared, have entertained too favourable an opinion of the original, and also to enable us effectually to expose the imposture...

With such blatant antagonism towards Islaam and the Prophet Muhammad (ﷺ), it is not surprising that his translation is crude, inaccurate and full of interpolated phrases.

It is on the Sale translation that the famous philosopher Thomas Carlyle based his unfair assessment of the Qur'aan. "It is as toilsome reading as I ever undertook, a wearisome, confused jumble, crude, incondite. Nothing but a sense of duty could carry any European through the Qur'aan,"[764] he wrote. It was also on this translation that Edward Gibbon based his sarcastic remarks on the beauty of the Qur'aan, "...the European infidel...will peruse with impatience the endless incoherent rhapsody of fable, and precept, and declamation, which seldom excites a sentiment or an idea, which sometimes crawls in the dust, and is sometimes lost in the clouds."[765]

The next translation that had a major impact in the English language was that of Reverend J. M. Rodwell, in 1861. More sympathetic then his predecessor, he claimed that the Prophet (ﷺ) '...had worked himself up into a belief that he had received a divine call...'.[766] He also gives 'useful advice' to missionaries so that they can carry out their proselytism among Muslims.

In his translation, Rodwell was probably the first to even attempt to imitate the style of the Arabic. Unfortunately, he rearranged the *soorahs* to, what he thought was,

---

764 Arberry, p. 12.
765 *ibid.* p. 12.
766 Arberry, p. 13.

a chronological order. For this, he relied primarily on Noeldeke's monumental work, *Geschichte Des Qorans* (to be discussed in the next chapter). This meant that, if one wanted to look up a particular verse, he would first have to go to the table of contents, and see where Rodwell had placed the translated verse. Rodwell's unfamiliarity with the Arabic language, and his ignorance of Islaam in general, is seen throughout his translation.

This translation was followed by the translation of Edward Henry Palmer in 1880, which he did for the Oxford University Press's *Sacred Books of the East* series, edited by Max Mueller. He, at least, did not attempt to rearrange the Qur'aan in any bizarre order. However, in common with all other non-Muslim translations of the Qur'aan, there exist many instances of incorrect translation and either omissions or additions into the text.

Richard Bell authored another translation in 1937. He went to measures even more extreme than any of his predecessors in 'critically re-arranging the *soorahs*', and as such is perhaps the most difficult translation to read. He gives his unique perspective on the actual arrangement of the *soorahs* and verses of the Qur'aan, as he wished to 'illustrate alterations, substitutions and derangements'[767] of the text of the Qur'aan. Obviously, the altered arrangement and *soorah* substitutions are based upon little more than his own deranged imagination.

One of the better, and perhaps more sympathetic, translations is the one by Arthur J. Arberry, who completed his translation in 1955. He writes in his Introduction:

> In choosing to call the present work *The Koran Interpreted* I have conceded the relevancy of the orthodox Muslim view, of which Pickthall, for one, was so conscious, that the Koran is untranslatable...the rhetoric and rhythm of the Arabic of the Koran are so characteristic, so powerful, so highly emotive, that any version whatsoever is bound in the nature of things to be but a poor copy of the glittering splendour of the original.[768]

His translation does not contain any explanatory notes or background information on the *soorahs*. As is typical with such translations, though, it is not free from omissions and mistranslations.

N. J. Daawood's translation came out in 1956, in which he also 'critically rearranged' the order of the *soorahs*. He was an Iraqi Jew, and his bias is blatantly shown throughout his translation. For example, he translates the phrase '*banee Aadam*' as 'Children of Allaah' (instead of 'Children of Aadam').

English Translation by Muslims

Among Muslims, one of the first translations into English was Dr. Mu*h*ammad 'Abdul *H*akeem Khan's, published in Patiala (India) in 1905. It has short exegetical footnotes. This was followed by Mirza Hairat Dehlawi's translation, *The Koran: Prepared by Various Oriental Learned Scholars*, published in Delhi, in 1912. During the

---

767 Kidwai, p. 19.
768 Arberry, p. 26.

same year, Mirza Abul Fadl's translation, *The Qur'aan Translated into English from the Original Arabic*, was released in Allaahabad, and dedicated to Sultan Jahan Begum, ruler of Bhopal.

Mohammed 'Ali, the Qadiani,[769] came out with his translation, '*The Holy Qur'aan*' in 1916. This translation, even though by a Qadiani, was to have a profound impact on many later translations (in particular, Pickthall's, Yusuf Ali's, Sarwar's, Daryabadi's and Shakir's).

Hafidh Ghulam Sarwar came out with his *The Holy Qur'aan* in 1929. It was published in the Indian Sub-Continent, Singapore, and England. The translator also included some essays about Islaam, and the *seerah* of the Prophet (ﷺ).

After this appeared two translations that both gained considerable favour among Muslims. The first was by Muhammad Marmaduke Pickthall, an Englishman who had lived in the East, and served the Nizam of Hyderabad. His translation, *The Meaning of the Glorious Qur'aan*, was released in London, in 1930, and was significant in that it was the first translation by an Muslim Englishman. Pickthall wrote:

> The aim of this work is to present to the English readers what the Muslims the world over hold to be the meaning of the words of the Koran (*sic*), and the nature of the Book, in not unworthy language and concisely, with a view to the requirements of English Muslims...The Koran cannot be translated. This is the belief of the old-fashioned Sheykhs and the view of the present writer... (this) is only an attempt to present the meaning of the Koran – and peradventure something of the charm – in English. It can never take the place of the Koran in Arabic, nor is it meant to do so.[770]

The second one appeared in 1938, when 'Abdullaah Yusuf 'Ali came out with his famous translation, *The Holy Qur'aan: Translation and Commentary*. This was followed by a host of others, such as Abdul Majeed Daryabadi's *The Holy Qur'aan with English Translation and Commentary*, in 1941; 'Ali Ahmad Khan Julunduri's *Translation of the Glorious Holy Qur'aan with Commentary*, in 1962; and Hashim Amir Ali's *The Message of the Qur'aan Presented in Perspective*, in 1974. In 1977, Muhammad Taqi al-Din al-Hilali and Muhammad Muhsin Khan, both of the Islaamic University of Madeenah, released a translation of the Qur'aan based on classical *tafseers*, *Explanatory English Translation of the Meaning of the Holy Qur'aan*. Muhammad Asad, a Jew who converted to Islaam, wrote his famous translation, *The Message of the Qur'aan*, in 1980. Thomas B. Irving, an American Muslim, wrote his *The Qur'aan: The First American Version* in 1985.[771]

---

769 The Qadianis were declared non-Muslims in a conference of world-wide scholars hosted in Pakistan in the late 70's. The reason that Mohammed 'Ali is mentioned in this group is that he belongs to a pseudo-Islaamic sect.

770 Pickthall, p. x.

771 The various translations given in this section are not meant to be exhaustive list of all the translations available. There are too many translations to talk about in a work of this nature. There have been over twenty translations (that this author is aware of) by Muslims into English, and another seven by Qadianis, not to mention the works out by other non-Muslims. For further details, see *The Message*, vol. 15, no. 10, pps. 17-20. The historical material for this section (where not explicitly quoted) was taken from Arberry, pps. 7-29; Khalifa, pps. 64-68, and *World Bibliography*.

IV. The Problems with Translations

The greatest problem with a translation of the Qur'aan is, of course, the fact that it transforms the Qur'aan as the *kalaam* of Allaah in Arabic, to the speech of a human in another language. In this destructive process, the beauty and miraculous nature of the Qur'aan is almost completely lost, as the very Words of Allaah are replaced by human substitutions. The perfect choice of wordings, the syntax of the verse, the powerful rhythm of the passages, the manners of eloquence displayed by the Arabic – all are destroyed. Even the famous Orientalist, Professor H. R. Gibb, remarked, "An English translation of the Qur'aan must employ precise and often arbitrary terms for the many-faceted and jewel-like phrases of the Arabic, and the more literal it is, the greyer and more colourless it must be."[772] The Arabic language is an extremely rich and powerful language, and it is simply not possible to convey in another language all the meanings that are conveyed in Arabic.

Perhaps the following few examples will help illustrate this point better.

In verse 76:3, Allah states,

$$\text{إِنَّا هَدَيْنَٰهُ ٱلسَّبِيلَ إِمَّا شَاكِرًا وَإِمَّا كَفُورًا ﴿٣﴾}$$

«Verily, We have shown him (i.e., mankind) the way; whether he be grateful or ungrateful (it is up to him)!»

In this verse, Allaah uses two opposite adjectives: grateful (*shaakir*) and ungrateful (*kafoor*).

Arabic nouns are based upon certain roots and structures (known as *awzaan*). Typically, two opposites would be mentioned with the same root structure, so that an aesthetic parallel is achieved. However, the two structures of the nouns used in this verse are not the same: the first one is based on the root structure '*faa'il*' whereas the second on '*fa'ool*'. The point that is trying to be made is that the Qur'aan uses two different root structures for these opposites, whereas it would appear to make more aesthetic sense to use the same root structure (i.e., either pair '*shaakir*' with '*kaafir*', or '*shakoor*' with '*kafoor*'. The verse in the Qur'aan pairs '*shaakir*' with '*kafoor*').

In actuality, the choice of these two different root structures adds a depth to the meaning that would otherwise not be present in the verse. The root structure '*fa'ool*' is used to indicate a more forcible and efficacious state than the root '*faa'il*'. Therefore, by using the adjective '*kafoor*' (which is in the '*fa'ool*' structure) to describe the ungrateful, and '*shaakir*' (which is in the '*faa'il*' structure) to describe the grateful, the Qur'aan subtly, yet powerfully, conveys the fact that man is easily able to reach a state of extreme ungratefulness, but when he chooses to thank Allaah, he cannot easily reach the equivalent extreme in thanking Him, because the blessings of Allaah are too many and too great to thank. Yet another meaning that is conveyed is that most of mankind will be in the '*kafoor*' state. As Allaah says in another verse,

---

772 *Modern Trends in Islaam*, p. 4.

$$\text{وَقَلِيلٌ مِّنْ عِبَادِيَ الشَّكُورُ}$$

«And (only) a few of My servants are *shakoor* (grateful).» [34:13]

Therefore, only a small percentage of mankind can reach the level of *shakoor*, whereas there will be many who can reach the level of *shaakir*. This is in contrast to ungratefulness, for most of those who are ungrateful will reach the depths of ingratitude – the level of *kafoor*.

By using two different root structures, each of which conveys a slightly different meaning, a whole new meaning is added. This meaning cannot be conveyed into another language by simple translation, and all translators ignored these extra meanings in their translations.

The addition and deletion of certain letters also adds different meanings to a word. In the last verse of *Soorah al-Baqarah*, the Qur'aan states,

$$\text{لَا يُكَلِّفُ اللَّهُ نَفْسًا إِلَّا وُسْعَهَا لَهَا مَا كَسَبَتْ وَعَلَيْهَا مَا اكْتَسَبَتْ}$$

«Allaah does not charge a soul except (with that which is within) its capacity. It will have (the consequence of) what (good) it has gained, and it will bear (the consequences of) what (evil) it has earned.» [2:286]

The first verb, which has been used to express the gain that a person earns in good, is *kasab*, whereas the second verb, which has been used to express the earnings of evil, is *iktasab*. The second verb is from the same root as the first ('kasaba', meaning, 'to earn, or gain'), except that an extra letter has been added (the letter *taa*). This letter gives the verb the added connotation of 'effort'. In other words, the second verb signifies that some effort must be employed in order to earn evil. This extra meaning is not present in the first verb.

The resulting change in meaning is that the earning of rewards from Allaah is a very simple and easy task, whereas the earning of evil is not so easy, and requires effort from the person. It also shows that the earning of evil goes against the nature of man, since he must exert himself in order to 'gain' the consequences of his evil deeds, whereas no such exertion is required in order to gain the rewards for his pious deeds. In addition, the verse also implies that evil *thoughts* which do not lead to any actions will not be punished; only evil *actions* will be punished (since thoughts do not require any effort, in contrast to acts). On the other hand, good intentions will be rewarded, even if not followed up by actions. Thus, if a person *intended* to do evil, but did not do so, he will not be held accountable for such intentions. On the other hand, if a person *intended* to do a good deed, but for some reason did not do so, he will still be rewarded for his intentions. Yet another meaning that is added is that man is the consequence of the evil that he has earned, since he must 'exert' himself in order to obtain it; yet, the rewards of his good deeds do not emanate from him, but from Allaah, since he was not responsible in procuring the good. In other words, the evil is his own doing, whereas the good is from the blessings of Allaah. As Allaah says in another verse,

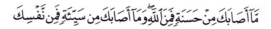

«Whatever good reaches you, is from Allaah, but whatever evil befalls you is from yourself.» [4:79]

All of these extra meanings were gleaned from the one extra letter in the second verb! Such subtle meanings can never be conveyed in translation. In fact, it cannot even be expected of the translators of the Qur'aan to try to express these meanings in translation!

Another example in which the distinction between two derivatives has a subtle change in meaning is the difference between the two verbs 'nazzala' and 'anzala'. These two verbs were translated by all translators by the same word; no distinction was made between them. However, the two words have slightly different meanings. 'Nazzala' signifies the piece-meal revelation (or descent) of something, whereas 'anzala' signifies the revelation (or descent) of something all at once. The revelation of the Qur'aan has been described in different verses by both of these words, thus signifying the two different revelations of the Qur'aan mentioned earlier: the descent of the entire Qur'aan to the *Bayt al-'Izza* on the Night of Decree, and the piece-meal revelation of the Qur'aan after that time. One verse which combines these two verbs is 46:20. The translation given by all translators does not take into account the difference between these two forms:

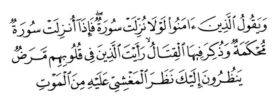

«Those who believe say, 'Why is not a *soorah* revealed (*nuzzila*) (for us)?' But when a decisive *soorah* is revealed (*anzala*), and fighting (*jihaad*) is mentioned in it, you see those in whose hearts there is a disease (i.e., the hypocrites) looking at you with a look of one who has fainted, on the verge of death...»

The fact that the two different forms are used is significant. In the first half of the verse, the believers wish that Allaah reveals (*nazzala*) *soorah*s, one after the other, showing that they earnestly desire and eagerly await the revelation of the Qur'aan. The hypocrites, on the other hand, pretend to share these emotions with the believers, but when Allaah reveals (*anzala*) only one *soorah* which mentions fighting, the hypocrites show their true colours, and become pale out of fear! In other words, the hypocrites ask for many revelations (*nazzala*), but when only one revelation comes (*anzala*), they cannot even fulfil its commands! So they boast for a lot, but cannot fulfil even a little! Once again, this added meaning is absolutely ignored by all translators, and the two different derivatives are treated as one.[773]

773 See al-Isfahaanee, p.800, for more discussion of these derivatives.

An example of where Arabic eloquence (*balaagha*) is lost in translation is verse 19:4. In it, the Prophet Zakariyyah (Zacharias) is praying to Allaah to bless him with a child, and describes his old age:

قَالَ رَبِّ إِنِّى وَهَنَ ٱلْعَظْمُ مِنِّى وَٱشْتَعَلَ ٱلرَّأْسُ شَيْبًا

«He said, 'O My Lord! Indeed my bones have grown feeble, and grey hair
has spread on my head...»

The Arabic of the last portion of the verse is: '*ishtha'ala ar-ra'su shayba*'. This phrase, despite its conciseness (only three words), is indicative of the eloquence of the Qur'aan, and az-Zamakhsharee is able to extract no less than five examples of the usage of various types of Arabic eloquence (some of which cannot even be explained in English!).[774] For example, the primary meaning of the verb '*ishtha'ala*' which is used in the verse is to express the sparks that are emitted by a fire. Therefore, Zakariyyah is comparing the whiteness of his hair to the sparks that emit from a fire, an example of one type of metaphor. Also, the verse translates as, '...(my) head sparks..', thus attributing the sparking effect, not to the hair where it occurs, but to the place and origin of that hair (the head), thus accentuating the severity of his old age. This phrase also gives the impression that the sparks are occurring from many places, thus indicating that, not only are his hairs white, but these white streaks are to be found all over his head. In essence, this phrase of only three words conveys the image of Zakariyyah's old age in such graphic detail that the English equivalent would require a few paragraphs of text! Of course, all such eloquence is completely lost in translation.

In all of the above examples, the only factor that was involved was the actual Arabic of the verse; no knowledge of *asbaab an-nuzool*, or the different *qira'aat*, or any external information was needed. A person well-grounded in the Arabic language would have been able to obtain these benefits and interpretations solely from the wording of the verse. However, in the process of translation, all of these examples, and countless more, are lost, as the very Speech of Allaah - the most eloquent of all speech - is re-interpreted and re-phrased by a human, to be transformed into another language!

As these few paragraphs have illustrated, it is not possible for a perfect translation of the Qur'aan to exist. Any translation of the Qur'aan is bound to be imperfect due to the simple fact that it is a human endeavour, and not Divine.

Despite the fact that a perfect translation of the Qur'aan can never exist, it is possible that a relatively reliable and legitimate translation be produced. Although such a translation could not take the place of the original, and would never be absolutely flawless, it would accurately reflect the basic meanings of the Arabic text in a lucid and clear style. This, then, is the goal of a good translation of the Qur'aan.

English has had its fair share of Qur'aan translations, as the previous section illustrated. Yet, despite the ample number of translations, it is still possible to say that almost all of them are not highly accurate. It is sad to note that most English transla-

<hr>

774 See *al-Kashaaf*, v. 3, p. 6.

tions that are in existence today suffer from very serious flaws and shortcomings. This is because most of these translations suffer from one very basic flaw: the translators were not qualified to undertake the monumental task of translating the Qur'aan!

Perhaps the first disqualification is on the basis of *'aqeedah*; many translators were not Muslim, and even of those that were, almost none were actually knowledgeable of the beliefs of the *Ahl as-Sunnah*. (This is the first condition that was mentioned under 'The Conditions for Translation.') The second disqualification is that most translators were not well grounded in Arabic language and grammar, and thus not qualified to explain or translate the Qur'aan (conditions 2 and 3, above). To further compound this disqualification, most Muslim translators had not seriously studied Islaam and the religious sciences to the level necessary for a translator (condition 4 above). On the contrary, many of them had studied in Western universities, and were greatly influenced by Western sciences and philosophies. And even the few that had undergone rigorous religious training had problems with the language of translation, for English was not their mother tongue! One of the prerequisites for a translator is that he must be fluent in *both* languages: Arabic and the language of translation (condition 2 above). Examples will be given shortly to substantiate these claims. In addition, most translators did not avail themselves to authentic *tafseer*s of the Qur'aan in order to properly understand the intent of the verses. Had they done so, it would have greatly minimised the errors found in their translations.[775]

Some researchers have classified the reasons that errors have occurred in these translations as follows:[776]

1) Nescience of the Arabic word's exact meaning. For example, verse 18:26 utilises a certain tense which signifies amazement and wonder. This tense was apparently not understood by Sale, who translated the verse as: "Do thou make Him to see and to hear" thus understanding the tense as implying a question! Rodwell understood this as a command: "Look thou and hearken to him alone!", whereas Palmer apparently missed the whole point, and translated it as a rather dreary, "He can see and hear." A more accurate translation of the verse is Pickthall's, "How clear of sight is He and keen of hearing!"

2) Awareness of only one shade of meaning. For example, Jeffery translates 17:60 as, "Verily thy Lord is round about the people," and Rodwell has a similar, "Verily thy Lord is round about mankind." The word that they translated as 'round about' in reality means 'encompassed', meaning that Allaah has full control over His creatures and none of them can evade His Judgement.

3) Confusion between different Arabic words. For example, Menezes mistakenly translated Aboo Bakr (the name of the famous Companion) as, "the father of the virgin!" Apart from the fact that this is a proper name, and is not meant to be translated, the word for virgin is *'bikr'*, not *'bakr'*!

---

775 The only exception to this (from the works that this author has come across) is Khan and Hilali's translation, as shall be discussed soon.

776 Khalifa, p. 67. The examples and quotes are also from this source.

4) Limited knowledge of Arabic eked out with figments of imagination. For example, Bell understood the 'Qur'aan' to be different from the '*Furqaan*' and the '*Kitaab*'. As was mentioned earlier, these are merely different names of the Qur'aan

5) Mistaking Arabic for Hebrew or Syriac. Watt concluded that the meaning of '*rujz*' in 74:4 was the same as the Syriac '*rugza*', which means, 'wrath', whereas the real meaning is 'pollution' (which is used in the verse to signify idols).

6) Some confusion with Hebrew traditions. For example, Jeffery confused the Arabic '*sakeenah*' in 48:4 with the Hebrew '*shekinah*'.

These six categories are perhaps more applicable to non-Muslim translators. Perhaps the three most common causes for errors by Muslim translators are:

1) An incorrect understanding of a word.

2) A misunderstanding of the intent of the verse.

3) Unfamiliarity with the rules of Arabic grammar.

An example of where a particular word was translated incorrectly is verse 21:87. In it, Allaah mentions the incident of Yoonus, in which he left his people after they had not responded to his call. The verse uses the word '*naqdira*' which has a number of meanings, including: 'to have power over' and 'to hold responsible for'. Most translators, including Yusuf Ali and Pickthall, took the first meaning of the word, thus translating the verse as, "And remember Dhoo an-Noon (Yoonus), when he departed in anger. He presumed that We had no power over him..." This translation attributes a type of unbelief (*kufr*) to a prophet, for how can any believer believe that Allaah has no power over him? The correct translation, therefore, is: "...and he presumed that We shall not call him to task..."; in other words, he presumed that the act that he had done was not a sinful act and he would not be punished for it, and not that Allaah had no power over him!

Another example is the translation of the word '*burooj*'. In verse 85:1, Allaah swears by the skies, full of *burooj*. Yusuf 'Ali translates this as, "By the Sky; (Displaying) the Zodiacal signs." In classical Arabic, however, the word '*burooj*' is used to denote a constellation of stars. Later Arabic, however, gave it the added meaning of 'the Zodiacal signs', and this is the meaning by which later dictionaries define it. The Zodiacal signs are signs from ancient Greek mythology, and play absolutely no role in Islaam. Thus, the translation of Yusuf 'Ali gives a very dangerous and incorrect implication. The proper translation of the verse is, "(I swear) by the heavens which contain constellations."

An example where the translator does not understand the intent of the verse is Muhammad Ali's translation of verse 32:28: "And they say, when will this victory come, if you are truthful?' Say: On the day of victory, the faith of those who (now) disbelieve will not profit them..." In the footnote, he explains the day of victory as the conquest of Islaam over other religions. What is meant by the verse, however, is the Day of Judgement, or the day of punishment, for that is the day that the faith of a disbeliever will not be accepted. Ibn Katheer (d. 774 A.H.) states,

"Whoever presumes that the intent of this verse is the Conquest of Makkah has strayed far, and fallen into serious error! For, on the day of the Conquest of Makkah, the Prophet (ﷺ) accepted the Islaam of the disbelievers, and if the intent of this verse was the Conquest of Makkah, the Prophet (ﷺ) would not have accepted their Islaam...".[777]

Another mistranslation due to an incorrect understanding of a phrase occurs in verse 37:28. In it, Allaah mentions that the disbelievers will regret the fact that they did not heed the call of the believers in this life.

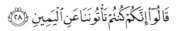

«They will say (on the Day of Judgement), 'It was you (i.e., the believers) who used to come to us 'an al-yameen.'» [37:28]

Now, the phrase ''an al-yameen' literally translates as 'from the right-hand side', and this is how a number of translators, such as Ali and Shakir, translated it. However, what is actually intended in the verse, as ash-Shawkaanee (d. 1250 A.H.)[778] and others point out, is that the believers used to come to the disbelievers with the truth. The 'right-hand side' is used to denote the side of truth and justice, and thus the believers used to approach the disbelievers with the truth, but the disbelievers would reject it. Some translators, however, did not understand the meaning of this phrase, and translated it verbatim, without giving any comment or explanation as to its meaning!

An example that demonstrates lack of knowledge of Arabic grammar is the translation of verse 56:82. The verb 'taj'aloona' that is used in the verse comes from a class of verbs that need two 'objects' (maf'ool) to them in order to form a complete sentence.[779] The first 'object' that is mentioned, however (rizqakum), does not form a comprehensible sentence with the verb unless one adds a noun to it. This fact would be apparent to any linguist at the first reading of the verse. The noun that is missing can either be deduced from the context, or from authentic narrations from Ibn 'Abbaas (found in at-Tabaree, Ibn Katheer, and others. The noun is 'shukr'). However, due to the fact that most translators were, apparently, not aware of the rules pertaining to this class of verbs, they ignored the fact that the sentence could not be translated verbatim. The verse, therefore, was translated as, "And you have made it your means of livelihood that you should declare it false!" by almost all translators (Yusuf 'Ali, Muhammad 'Ali, Pickthall, Shakir, and others). The correct translation of the verse, however, as done by Khan and Hilali, is, "And instead (of thanking) Allaah for the provisions He gives you, on the contrary, you deny him (by disbelief)!" (The noun that was added was 'thanking'). The difference in meaning between the two transla-

---

777 Ibn Katheer, v. 3, p. 512.

778 *Fath al-Qadeer*, v. 4, p. 516. An alternate interpretation is that the 'right hand side' indicates power, or forcefulness. See the reference for further details.

779 As used in this verse. There are certain cases where it would only need one object, but this case does not apply to this verse.

tions is clearly noticeable; in fact, at first glance it seems that the two translations are absolutely unrelated to one another, despite the fact that they are actually the same verse!

Yet another example which demonstrates a lack of knowledge of Arabic grammar is the translation of verses 70:6-7. These verses employ the word, 'ra'aa'. This word has a number of meanings to it, depending on its grammatical actions and context. If it has one 'object' after it, it means: 'to see', whereas if it has two 'objects', its meaning changes to: 'to presume', or 'to firmly believe'. In these verses, the word occurs twice, and each time it has two objects. Most translators (if not all), apparently not aware of these grammatical rules, translated these verses as, "They (the disbelievers) see it (the Day of Judgement) as far away. But we see it as near!" This translation, although not actually incorrect, is at the same time not very accurate. A more accurate translation of the verse would be: "They presume it as far away. But we know for certain that it is near!" In other words, the disbelievers are not sure about the occurrence of the Day of Judgement, and even if it occurs, they think that there is a long time left for it. The believers, on the other hand, know for certain that it will occur, and with this certain knowledge, they know that it is very close by! The difference between the two translations, and the deeper meanings of the second, come only from applying basic Arabic grammar!

As a last, and slightly more complicated, example, let us examine verse 34:28. All translations reviewed – without any exception – translated the verse, with minor differences, as,

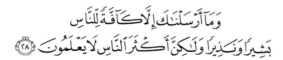

«And We have not sent you (O Muḥammad) except as a bearer of glad tidings, and a warner, to all of mankind, but most of mankind know not.»

The phrase, '...to all of mankind...' occurs in the Arabic as '...kaafath li naas'. According to this translation, the word 'kaafath' means 'all of', and is a conditional adjective, known in Arabic as haal, of 'mankind' (or, 'naas'). In this verse, it can be seen that the conditional adjective occurs before its subject, which is 'naas' (mankind).

Now, according to the majority of classical Arabic grammarians (but not all), it is not allowed for a conditional adjective, or haal, to precede its subject in a number of cases, including the case where its subject was connected to the letter laam (to be more precise, if the subject were preceded by one of the prepositions known as the huroof al-jar, one of which is the laam). In this verse, it can be seen that the subject is indeed connected to the letter laam (i.e., the subject, 'naas', is preceded by the letter laam, which is transliterated above as 'li'). Therefore, according to the majority of Arabic grammarians, it would not be allowed to understand the verse the way that it has been translated above. In fact, both az-Zajjaaj (d. 311 A.H.), and az-Zamaksharee (d. 538 A.H.), two of the most famous scholars of Arabic grammar, called this interpretation of the verse, 'a clear error!'[780] According to these scholars, the word '*kaafath*' must be understood as meaning one of its other derivatives, so that it is not taken to be a conditional adjective (*haal*) of 'mankind'. This alternate meaning is 'a preventor' (from the root *kaffa*, meaning 'to stop'), and the verse would therefore translate as, "And we have not sent you (O Muhammad) except as a preventor for mankind (i.e., to prevent them from wrongdoing and *shirk*), a giver of glad tidings, and a warner." This second translation offers a totally different understanding of the verse.

Although the widespread English translation of the verse cannot be called incorrect (due to the fact that there is a difference of opinion amongst classical Arabic grammarians over this particular grammatical rule, with a minority of them allowing such an interpretation), it must be asked, "How many of the translators who translated this verse were actually even aware of this rule of Arabic grammar, and the difference of opinion over it, and, based on research and analysis, purposely chose one opinion over the other?"

The point that is trying to be made is that it is essential that such detailed rules of Arabic grammar be known and thoroughly understood by anyone who wishes to translate the Qur'aan. Arabic is a highly complex language, and it is not possible that a person with a rudimentary knowledge of Arabic, armed with a few dictionaries and lexicons, can do justice to any translation!

Perhaps the safest and most accurate method to have translated the above verse, as ash-Shawkaanee (d. 1250 A.H.) interprets in his *tafseer*, is to have included both possible translations.[781]

A Review of Some Translations

These reviews are not intended to be exhaustive, but rather to give the reader an insight into the translator's beliefs, and some benefits and faults of the translation. The purpose of this section is not to find every single fault that has occurred, but rather to give a general ruling on the translation. The comments that were made in the previous section must be kept in mind; almost all the translations mentioned here are demonstrative of the three categories of errors mentioned above.

Only the more popular Muslim translators have been reviewed, since non-Muslim translations cannot be relied on, no matter how superb the English, and Qadiani translations invariably inject their doctrines into the Qur'aan. (However, an exception was made for Muhammad Ali's translation, since it had great influence on both Pickthall and Yusuf 'Ali).

Muhammad Marmaduke Pickthall's *The Meaning of the Glorious Qur'aan* is one of the more popular translations. It was released in 1930, and has seen over 27 editions.

---

780 *al-Kashaaf*, v. 3, p. 592
781 For further details on this particular rule and its application on the verse, see *al-Kashaaf*, v. 3, p. 592; *Fath al-Qadeer*, v. 4, p. 432; *Diyaa as-Saalik*, v. 2, p. 205.

Pickthall was an Englishman who had, in the words of Arberry, 'achieved a certain repute as a novelist... and was a man of distinct literary gifts'.[782] He had travelled in the East, and had worked for the Nizam of Hyderabad. For his translation, he relied quite heavily on Muhammad Ali's translation (mentioned below).

The translation is quite literal, and therefore is not smooth reading. Also, his use of Biblical English (*thee, thou*, etc.) does not suit modern readers. There are very few notes or explanations, which makes it confusing for those who are not familiar with the Qur'aan, but at least helps in minimising Ali's influence on him. Overall, though, the translation is a generally acceptable, albeit literal, rendering of the Arabic.

It would be no exaggeration to say that the most popular translation of the Qur'aan in existence today is 'Abdullaah Yusuf Ali's *The Holy Qur'aan: Translation and Commentary*. It has seen over 35 editions since its release in 1936, not counting the revised ones.

'Ali had studied in England in the late 19th century, and was of a *Sunni Bohri* family. He had learnt Arabic from his father. Although well-versed in English grammar and literature, he was not familiar with Islaamic sciences, and depended mostly on Mohammad Ali's translation for his interpretory comments.

The English of his translation is simpler than Pickthall's – and therefore easier to read – but could be better. There are ample footnotes, and, in general, the translation itself is acceptable.

The problem with this translation, however, is Ali's footnotes. These are indicative of his "*Soofi* leanings, and smack of apologia and pseudo-rationalism."[783] The Muslim World League released a pamphlet detailing the errors in these footnotes, but this pamphlet was not exhaustive. There have been 'revised' editions of Yusuf Ali's translation published, but even these are not free from error.

Some of the problems of this translation is his idea of 'analogy' in the Qur'aan. Due to a misinterpretation of verse 3:7, he believes that many of the statements of the Qur'aan are allegorical. According to his footnotes, Heaven and Hell are states of the mind and do not really exist (notes 44, 50, 168, 452, 499, 579); *jinns* are not a separate creation of Allaah but rather an innate force in man (note 929); the *hooris* of Heaven are only for companionship, and not for pleasure (note 44). In addition, 'Ali has an extremely liberal approach to *fiqh*, for he states that insurance and interest are allowed (notes 241, 324) and polygamy is discouraged in Islaam (note 509), to note some examples. Many of these problems have been solved in the 'revised' addition, but some work still needs to be done.[784] Also, most of these concepts are found in Muhammad Ali's translation, and Yusuf Ali's dependence on it is obvious. In fact, he

---

782 Arberry, p. 20.

783 Kidwai, p. 17.

784 For further details, see *Al-Basheer*, vol. 3, no. 4 & 5, *On 'Abdullaah Yusuf 'Alee and Muhammad Asad's commentaries.*

785 Yusuf 'Ali, p. xvi.

states in his introduction that Muḥammad Ali's translation is 'a scholarly work, and equipped with adequate explanatory matter in the notes and the Preface.'[785] Yet another aspect of this translation is that Yusuf 'Ali continually intersperses his *Soofic* thought and philosophy whenever he gets an opportunity to do so.

Also, Yusuf 'Ali was clearly influenced by the 'modernist' school of thought, which sought to explain away everything that they felt 'modern' science could not explain or rationalise. For example, concerning the Prophet's (ﷺ) night journey (*al-Israa wa al-Mi'raaj*), he writes, "The majority of Commentators take this Night Journey literally... Even on the *supposition* of a *miraculous bodily* Journey, it is conceded that the body was almost transformed into a *spiritual fineness*."[786] The implied meaning is obvious, and contradicts the belief of *Ahl as-Sunnah* that the Prophet (ﷺ) was transported in body and soul during *al-Israa wa al-Mi'raaj*. While mentioning the story of the resurrection of the birds at the call of Ibraaheem (2:260), Yusuf 'Ali has difficulty believing that the birds were actually killed by Ibraaheem, as is the clear understanding of the verse, and the view of classical commentators.

Apart from these notes, as was mentioned earlier, the translation – in general – is acceptable, and the English readable.

Taqiuddin Hilali's and Muḥammad Muhsin Khan's *Interpretation of the Meanings of the Holy Qur'aan* was first released in 1977, and has seen a number of editions since. It was initially a mutli-volume work, and has lately been re-released in one summarised volume.

Both of the translators are from the Islaamic University of Madeenah, and perhaps better qualified than all the previous translators mentioned to undertake such a task. The translation relies on classical Islaamic *tafseer*s, such as Ibn Katheer's, al-Qurṭubee's and aṭ-Ṭabaree's works. Therefore, this translation is undoubtedly the finest in terms of being free of inaccurate interpretations. It has copious notes, taken mainly from *Saheeh al-Bukhaaree*, and also many interpolated meanings in brackets in the text. It perhaps might have been more prudent to place these phrases as footnotes, to avoid confusion between the actual text and explanatory notes. It also has very useful appendi.

The English, however, is not as smooth as other translations. The absence of a translator whose mother tongue is English is noticeable in the translation. Also, the translation leaves many phrases in Arabic, and then gives an explanation of the phrase in English. Although this is occasionally useful, at times it makes for tedious reading.

Muḥammad Asad's *The Message of the Qur'aan* was first released in 1980. The translator was a very well known figure, and had written two famous works, *The Road to Makkah* (a highly readable autobiography), and *Islam at the Cross-roads*. He had also translated a portion of *Saheeh al-Bukhaaree*, which is a very good translation.

---

786 ibid, p. 691. Emphasis mine.

His translation of the Qur'aan, unfortunately, contains many unorthodox ideas. It is an English translation with a *Mu'tazilee* perspective. He denies the miracles that the prophets performed (for example, the resurrection of the birds in the story of Ibraaheem, 2:260), believes that *jinn* are not separate creatures, and also has a very liberal approach to *fiqh* (for example, the concept of *hijab* varies with time and place, cf. *Soorah Noor*).

Apart from problems of this nature – and they are numerous in number – the English is one of the best that this author has seen; very lucid and readable. However, it is not to be recommended because of its misinterpretations.

Muhammad 'Ali, came out with his *The Holy Qur'an: English Translation* in 1917, and it has seen ten editions. The author is a Qadiani, and thus this translation is full of heretical ideas. He does not believe in the finality of the Prophet (ﷺ),[787] and twists the meaning of those verses that state this (cf. his footnote to 22:40). He also believes that 'Eesaa died on the cross, and was not raised up to the Heavens, as the Qur'an clearly states (cf. 3:55 and 4:157, and Ali's 'interpretation' of them). He too denies the miracles of the prophets, and claims that Heaven and Hell are not real (cf. his Introduction, p. xx onwards). In fact, he even goes so far as to say Hell is actually a place for the 'treatment of spiritual diseases,' and its 'punishment not meant for torture but for purification'! (p. xx). Due to the fact that this was one of the first translations in English by a 'Muslim,' it had a great influence on future translations, particularly Yusuf Ali's and Muhammad Marmaduke Pickthall's. In fact, Muhammad 'Ali quotes with pride the famous Christian missionary Rev. Zwemer, who wrote:

> A careful comparison of Mr. Pickthall's translation with that of the Ahmadiyya translator, Maulvi Muhammad 'Ali, shows conclusively, that Mr. Pickthall's work is not very much more than a revision of the Ahmadiyya version (p. vii).

This translation was also heavily used by Sarwar and Shakir.

M. M. Shakir came out with 'his' translation, *The Holy Qur'an*, in 1982. Actually, it is based almost completely on Muhammad Ali's translation, except for minor changes. A simple comparison between the two translations shows that Shakir merely revised Ali's translation. Kidwai calls it, 'an example of blatant plagiarism.'[788] Also, Shakir is of the *Shee'ite* faith, and the index clearly indicates this, as he lists 'verses' that refer to *Imaamat*, the martyrdom of Hussayn, the caliphate of 'Alee, and so on.

---

787 Although it should be pointed out that he is of the 'Lahori Qadianis,' who verbally believe in the finality of the Prophet (ﷺ), but in reality exalt the status of Mirza Ghulam Ahmed to that of a prophet. 'Ali writes in his Introduction, p. vii, while discussing his sources, 'And, lastly, the greatest religious leader of the present time, Mirza Ghulam Ahmed of Qadian, has inspired me with all that is best in this work. I have drunk deep at the fountain of knowledge which this great Reformer – *Mujaddid* of the present century and founder of the Ahmadiyyah Movement – has made to flow...'

788 Kidwai, p. 18.

T. B. Irving's translation, *The Qur'an: The First American Version*, was released in 1985. It is meant to be in American English. Apart from the Biblical connotations of the title (there cannot be different 'versions' of the Qur'aan), the translation has no explanatory notes, does not contain the Arabic text, and is not free from translation errors.[789]

---

789 Perhaps the reader will feel that the above reviews have been a bit harsh. However, it should be kept in mind that this is the Qur'aan – the Book of Allaah – that we are dealing with, and thus even 'minor' problems should be considered major ones, especially when such problems concern inauthentic interpretations of the Qur'aan. In reality, despite the more than two-dozen or so translations that exist, there still does not exist one good translation that combines authentic Qur'aanic interpretation and flawless English. Khan and Hilalee's is, as of yet, the best in terms of interpretation, but, at least in this author's opinion, there still exists an urgent need to produce a lucid, highly readable and authentic rendering of the meanings of the Qur'aan in English, and Allaah knows best!

These lines were written based upon the translations that the author had access to at the time of writing. However, slightly before the final editing of this work, Saheeh International released its *The Qur'aan: Arabic Text with Corresponding English Meanings*. Although I have not exhaustively reviewed the work, it is an impressive translation, distinctly superior to all others that have been reviewed. The English is surprisingly smooth, and accurately reflects the Arabic meanings. The footnotes are short and to the point, and greatly aid in the understanding of the verse. This translation clearly shines above the rest with its accuracy and simplicity. Perhaps the primary criticism that must be made against it is the fact that the translator(s) remains shrouded in anonymity! The names and credentials of the translators must be known, so that due credit (and criticism) can be given. It has never been the practice of the scholars of Islaam to write under pseudonyms and hide behind unknown names! Despite this obvious criticism, however, the work is indeed a commendable effort in the field of English translations, and will probably remain unique in its class for some time to come.

CHAPTER 17

The Qur'aan and Orientalists

1. The Authorship of the Qur'aan

Orientalists are non-Muslim scholars who have achieved considerable repute as authorities on Islaam. They have dedicated their lives to the study of Islaam. As such, they must be looked at with extreme caution, for when a researcher studies Arabic and learns more about Islaam than the average Muslim, yet still remains a non-Muslim, his intentions must be questioned. Such people have, by their own testimony, lifted from themselves the veil of ignorance, and have seen and appreciated the beauty and authenticity of Islaam. They have removed any possible excuse that might have existed for not accepting Islaam. For reasons that can only be guessed, they heard and recognised the call of the Creator, but refused to answer and submit to Him!

For example, Arthur Jeffery, author of '*Materials for the History of the Text of the Qur'an*', studied in Egypt and Damascus for a number of years. During these years, he went over all the *qira'aat*, including the *shaadh* ones, with the scholars of al-Azhar, and pored over many of the books on the Qur'aan and its sciences – printed copies and manuscripts. The vast majority of Muslims, even those specialised in the *qira'aat*, have not done as much research as Jeffery did. Can it be imagined that he did not see the *i'jaaz* of the Qur'aan through its many facets?

Another Orientalist, Arthur Arberry, also studied in Egypt. His Arabic was fluent, and he appreciated the beauty of the Qur'aan, '...the rhetoric and rhythm of the Arabic of the Qur'aan are so characteristic, so powerful, so highly emotive, that any version whatsoever is bound by the nature of things to be but a poor copy of the glittering splendour of the original.'[790] Elsewhere, he even admitted that the Qur'aan was a solace and comfort for him:[791]

> During the long months, the dark and light months, of labouring at this interpretation, eclectic where the ancient commentators differ in their understanding of a word or phrase... the radiant beauty of the original is not clouded by such vexing interpolations – all through this welcome task I have been reliving those Ramadhan nights of long ago, when I would sit on the veranda of my Gezira house and listen entranced to the old, white-bearded Sheykh who chanted the Koran for the pious delectation of my

790 Arberry, p. 24.
791 Arberry, p. 28.

neighbour.... It was then that I, the infidel, learnt to understand and react to the thrilling rhythms of the Koran, only to be apprehended when listened to at such a time and in such a place. In humble thankfulness I dedicate this all too imperfect essay in imitation of those magical Egyptian nights.

Yet, despite all these confessions, Arberry, as did Jeffery, died as a non-Muslim. Why then, when they realised the beauty of the Qur'aan, did they reject its call?

The topic of the authorship of the Qur'aan has puzzled Orientalists for a long time. If the Prophet Muhammad (ﷺ) was an impostor, then how was one to explain his austere and magnanimous life? And if he were not an impostor, this would imply that 'Eesaa and Muhammad (ﷺ) were sent by the same God, and this they were not willing to believe. Therefore, they were in a dilemma, and were forced to concoct some explanation as to who the author of the Qur'aan was, and why the Prophet (ﷺ) had claimed to be a prophet. As Rodwell wrote,[792]

> In close connection with the above remarks, stands the question of Mohammed's sincerity and honesty of purpose in coming forward as a messenger of God. For if he was indeed the illiterate person the Muslims represent him to have been, then it will be hard to escape their inference that the Koran is, as they assert it to be, a standing miracle. But if, on the other hand, it was a Book carefully concocted from various sources, and with much extraneous aid, and published as a divine oracle, then it would seem that the author is once open to the charge of the grossest imposture, and even of impious blasphemy...The more insight we obtain, from undoubted historical sources, into the actual character of Mohammed, the less reason do we find to justify the strong vituperative language poured out upon his head...

As Rodwell states, if Muhammad (ﷺ) were the author of the Qur'aan, this would then imply that he was an impostor. But the more one studies the biography (*seerah*) of the Prophet (ﷺ), the less one finds reason to presume this. Material gain; the desire for power and glory; the desire to unify the Arabs; the desire for moral reformation, all of these possible 'motives' are immediately eliminated by an unbiased reader of the Prophet's (ﷺ) *seerah*. In fact, the entire *seerah* of the Prophet (ﷺ) is one of the strongest proofs of his sincerity.

An Example of the Prophet's (ﷺ) Sincerity

Perhaps one of the greatest incidents that demonstrates the truthfulness of the Prophet (ﷺ) is the story of the death of the Prophet's (ﷺ) son. Ibraaheem, the last of the children to be born to the Prophet (ﷺ), died when he was less than two years old. The Prophet (ﷺ) was visibly grieved by this, and tears streamed down his face. Even the Companions were distressed and saddened to see the Prophet's (ﷺ) state. A few hours after Ibraaheem's death, a solar eclipse occured, blocking out the bright light of the sun. Immediately, word spread amongst the Muslims: Even the sun and moon are saddened by the Prophet's (ﷺ) loss!

---

792 Arberry, p. 15-16.

What greater opportunity than this?! What more can possibly be asked by an impostor?! A charlatan would have seized this moment – this golden opportunity that would be heard for generations: Even the skies grieve with the Prophet! Muhammad (ﷺ) could have called the people of Madeenah, and told them, "Yes! Even the heavens are affected by my loss!" In fact, he did not even have to call them; he merely had to remain silent, and let the rumours spread. Already all of Madeenah was marvelling at this clear 'miracle'.

Yet, the true prophet that he was, Muhammad (ﷺ) could not deceive or lie to his people. He issued a general summons to the people of Madeenah, and waited until they all gathered in the mosque. Then, he stood up in front of them, praised Allaah and thanked Him, and said that ever-so-powerful statement, "Verily, the sun and the moon are two of the signs and miracles out of the many miracles of Allaah. They do not eclipse because of the death or birth of any human being."[793] So simple the phrase, yet so full of meaning; so innocent the sentence, yet so powerful in its implications. Can there be any doubt as to the Prophet's (ﷺ) truthfulness?

AUTHORSHIP THEORIES

In general, there are four primary 'explanations' that Orientalists adopt or have adopted to explain the phenomenon of the Qur'aan. Some amongst them even bypass this question, and state with certainty that the Prophet (ﷺ) was the author of the Qur'aan, without giving any explanation as to how an illiterate person could write such a masterpiece, or even the motives behind such an endeavour. Sale wrote, "That Muhammad was really the author and chief contriver of the Qur'aan is beyond dispute; though it is highly probable that he had no small assistance in his design from others."[794]

What is the most surprising aspect of these 'explanations', however, is how remarkably similar they are to the claims of the disbelievers of old – claims that the Qur'aan itself mentions and refutes. The unoriginality of these explanations is a stark indication in itself of the authenticity of the Qur'aan.

A Poet?

The first 'explanation' that is given is that the Prophet Muhammad (ﷺ) was a poet – an extremely eloquent and skilled poet – but a poet nonetheless. This was put forth by Stobart around a century ago, and echoed by Bell and even Rodinson as late as the 1970's. Bell described the Prophet (ﷺ) as a poet, '...but not of the ordinary type'![795] Stobart claims, after reading a translation of the Qur'aan, that anyone who had some knowledge of Jewish history 'and possessed of some poetic fire and fancy'[796] could write the Qur'aan.

---

793 Reported by al-Bukhaaree, and others.
794 Sale, p. 50.
795 Khalifa, p. 11.
796 Khalifa, p. 11.

How reminiscent this is from the cry of the pagans of old!

$$أَمْ يَقُولُونَ شَاعِرٌ$$

«Or do they say, 'He is a poet!'» [52:30].

$$بَلْ قَالُوٓا۟ أَضْغَٰثُ أَحْلَٰمٍۭ بَلِ ٱفْتَرَىٰهُ بَلْ هُوَ شَاعِرٌ فَلْيَأْتِنَا بِـَٔايَةٍ كَمَآ أُرْسِلَ ٱلْأَوَّلُونَ$$

«They say, '(These inspirations are only) muddled dreams; Nay! he has invented it; Nay! he is a poet!' Then let him bring us some miracles like (the prophets) of old (were given)!'» [21:5]

$$وَيَقُولُونَ أَئِنَّا لَتَارِكُوٓا۟ ءَالِهَتِنَا لِشَاعِرٍ مَّجْنُونٍۭ ﴿٣٦﴾ بَلْ جَآءَ بِٱلْحَقِّ وَصَدَّقَ ٱلْمُرْسَلِينَ ﴿٣٧﴾$$

«And they said, 'Are we going to abandon our gods for the sake of a mad poet?' Nay! Rather (Muḥammad) has come with the Truth, and confirmed the Messengers (before him)» [37:36]

Rather,

$$وَمَا هُوَ بِقَوْلِ شَاعِرٍ قَلِيلًا مَّا تُؤْمِنُونَ ﴿٤١﴾$$

«And it is not the words of a poet! Little faith you have!» [69:41]

$$وَمَا عَلَّمْنَٰهُ ٱلشِّعْرَ وَمَا يَنۢبَغِى لَهُۥٓ إِنْ هُوَ إِلَّا ذِكْرٌ وَقُرْءَانٌ مُّبِينٌ$$

«And We have not taught (him) poetry, nor is it befitting for him. Rather, this is only a Reminder, and a clear Qur'aan» [36:69]

A Madman?

Yet another 'explanation' is that he (ﷺ) was an epileptic who was possessed by devils, and thus was able to produce such eloquent speech. This was a common theme of the Orientalists of the Middle Ages, such as San Pedro. Phillip K. Hitti wrote, "The Prophet experienced ecstatic seizures as he received the revelations, giving rise to the charge that he was epileptic."[797]

However, even Orientalists themselves have had to reject these claims as false. Daniel commented, "...epilepsy as applied to the Prophet was the explanation of those who sought to amuse rather than to instruct."[798]

If one looks at the *seerah* of the Prophet (ﷺ), one cannot find any grounds for these claims. Epilepsy is not found mentioned at all in any of the classical works of *seerah*. In addition, the Prophet (ﷺ) lived a normal, sane life throughout his sixty-three years. There are no incidents in the Prophet's (ﷺ) life that can be given as examples of insanity; on the contrary, his whole *seerah* is a refutation of it!

---

797 Njozi, p. 19.
798 Khalifa, p. 13.

Once again, modern authors merely took these same ideas from the disbelievers of old.

$$ أَوَلَمْ يَتَفَكَّرُواْ مَا بِصَاحِبِهِم مِّن جِنَّةٍ إِنْ هُوَ إِلَّا نَذِيرٌ مُّبِينٌ ﴿١٨٤﴾ $$

«Do they not reflect and ponder? There is no madness in their companion (Muḥammad). He is but a plain warner» [7:184]

$$ وَيَقُولُونَ أَئِنَّا لَتَارِكُوٓا۟ ءَالِهَتِنَا لِشَاعِرٍ مَّجْنُونٍۭ ﴿٣٦﴾ بَلْ جَآءَ بِٱلْحَقِّ وَصَدَّقَ ٱلْمُرْسَلِينَ ﴿٣٧﴾ $$

«And they said: 'Are we going to abandon our gods for the sake of a crazy poet?' Nay! Rather (Muḥammad) has come with the Truth, and confirmed the Messengers (before him)» [37:36-37]

$$ لَا تَدْخُلُوا۟ بُيُوتًا غَيْرَ بُيُوتِكُمْ حَتَّىٰ تَسْتَأْنِسُوا۟ $$

«Or do they say: 'There is a madness in him?' Nay! He has brought them the Truth, but most of them are hostile to the truth» [23:70]

Allaah responds to these accusations, in defence of the Prophet Muḥammad (ﷺ),

$$ مَآ أَنتَ بِنِعْمَةِ رَبِّكَ بِمَجْنُونٍ ﴿٢﴾ $$

«You are not, by the Grace of your Lord, a madman» [68:2]

Taught by Others?

The third 'explanation' given by Orientalists is that the Qur'aan was composed by or with the help of Jews and Christians at the time of the Prophet (ﷺ). They differ, though, as to who these sinister figures were. Some claim that it was Baheerah, the monk that the Prophet (ﷺ) allegedly met in Syria when he was a teenager.[799] This was the claim of Sir William Muir, Margoliouth and others.[800] Even giving that this incident is true, would a meeting of less than a few hours – while the Prophet (ﷺ) was a teenager – give him the capability to compose the Qur'aan?

Others, such as Menzes and Gardner, allege that the Prophet (ﷺ) was taught the Qur'aan by Salmaan al-Farsee. Since Salmaan was a Zoroastrian-turned-Christian before he embraced Islaam, it would make sense, they claim, that he fired the Proph-et's (ﷺ) imagination with stories of the Judaeo-Christian prophets.[801] In response to this, from where then did the Prophet (ﷺ) get all of this information before Salmaan came onto the scene? Salmaan, as is well known, came to the Prophet (ﷺ) years after the *hijrah*, whereas most of the Qur'aan was revealed before the *hijrah*. In fact, almost

---

799 Actually, this incident might not be authentic, as Imaam adh-Dhahabee pointed out. In its chain is 'Abd al-Raḥmaan ibn Ghazwan, who is *munkar* (rejected). Also, it has other problems; cf. Numani, p 158. Despite these faults, however, some scholars of *hadeeth* have authenticated this incident, such as al-Albaanee (cf. *Fiqh as-Seerah*, p. 66)

800 Khalifa, p. 14.

801 Khalifa, p. 15.

all the stories of the prophets of old were revealed at Makkah, even before Salmaan embraced Islaam or met the Prophet (ﷺ)!

Other claims are even more preposterous. Both Bodly and Gibb claimed that the Prophet (ﷺ) was taught Christianity by Qiss ibn Sa'eedah, an Arab bishop who used to preach Christianity at the annual Ukadh fairs. Unfortunately, both of them conveniently forget to mention that this individual died over a century before the Prophet's (ﷺ) birth![802]

Lastly, since the Orientalists could not find any figure in the life of the Prophet (ﷺ) who could have influenced him to such a great extent, they claim an 'unnamed source' who helped Muhammad (ﷺ) concoct the Qur'aan. Rodinson wrote, "The long rambling accounts of Jewish patriarchs and prophets correspond in so much detail with the Talmud that of their essentially Jewish origin there can be doubt."[803]

What is so surprising concerning these claims is that they are mostly based upon the stories found in the Qur'aan that are also found in the Bible. This fact, according to these Orientalists, proves that the Qur'aan is based upon biblical sources, either oral or written. This can be refuted in a number of ways. Firstly, the stories appearing in the Qur'aan are always slightly different than their Biblical versions, as any reader of the two books knows. This shows that the Prophet (ﷺ) did not blindly imitate Judaeo-Christian sources. Secondly, there are numerous stories mentioned in the Qur'aan that are not found in the Bible, such as the dialogue between Ibraaheem and his father, and Ibraaheem and the tyrannical king. Likewise, certain prophets are mentioned in the Qur'aan but not in the Bible, such as Hood and Saalih. Thirdly, the general similarities between certain stories in the Qur'aan and Bible can also be explained by saying that they both originated from the same source, namely, divine inspiration. Fourthly, and this perhaps is the strongest refutation, these stories were unknown to the people of the Prophet's (ﷺ) time. The Qur'aan states, concerning these stories,

$$ تِلْكَ مِنْ أَنْبَاءِ الْغَيْبِ نُوحِيهَا إِلَيْكَ مَا كُنْتَ تَعْلَمُهَا أَنْتَ وَلَا قَوْمُكَ مِنْ قَبْلِ هَذَا $$

«This is the news of the unseen which We reveal unto you. Neither you nor your people knew them before this...»[11:49]

This verse claims that the people of the Prophet's (ﷺ) time did not know these stories, which implies that the Prophet (ﷺ) must have received them from inspiration. If any of the claims of the Orientalists were true, and these stories were known to some of the Arabs, then surely some pagan would have stood up and said, "Nay, Muhammad! I knew these stories before you. Your claim is not true!" But throughout the Prophet's (ﷺ) twenty-three years of prophethood, no one claimed this, despite the fact that the disbelievers tried everything to disparage the Prophet (ﷺ). This is a clear sign that the people of Arabia had had no exposure to these stories, and were ignorant of them, until the Prophet (ﷺ) received his revelation.

---

802 *ibid.* There are very weak reports, however, which state that the Prophet (ﷺ) saw Qiss as a young boy, but did not recall anything of what he said. See Ibn Katheer, v.2, p.250.

803 *ibid.*

Once again, the disbelievers during the Prophet's (ﷺ) time mimicked that same call that is heard today by these Orientalists.

وَلَقَدْ نَعْلَمُ أَنَّهُمْ يَقُولُونَ إِنَّمَا يُعَلِّمُهُۥ بَشَرٌ لِّسَانُ
ٱلَّذِى يُلْحِدُونَ إِلَيْهِ أَعْجَمِىٌّ وَهَٰذَا لِسَانٌ عَرَبِىٌّ
مُّبِينٌ ﴿١٠٣﴾

«And indeed We know that they (the pagans) say, 'It is only a human who teaches him.' The tongue of the man they refer to is foreign, while this is in a clear Arabic tongue» [16:103]

ثُمَّ تَوَلَّوْا۟ عَنْهُ وَقَالُوا۟ مُعَلَّمٌ مَّجْنُونٌ ﴿١٤﴾

«Then they turned away from him, and said, 'A (person) taught (by someone else), a madman!» [44:14]

وَقَالَ ٱلَّذِينَ كَفَرُوٓا۟ إِنْ هَٰذَآ إِلَّآ إِفْكٌ
ٱفْتَرَىٰهُ وَأَعَانَهُۥ عَلَيْهِ قَوْمٌ ءَاخَرُونَ فَقَدْ جَآءُو ظُلْمًا وَزُورًا
﴿٤﴾ وَقَالُوٓا۟ أَسَٰطِيرُ ٱلْأَوَّلِينَ ٱكْتَتَبَهَا فَهِىَ تُمْلَىٰ
عَلَيْهِ بُكْرَةً وَأَصِيلًا ﴿٥﴾ قُلْ أَنزَلَهُ ٱلَّذِى يَعْلَمُ ٱلسِّرَّ
فِى ٱلسَّمَٰوَٰتِ وَٱلْأَرْضِ

«Those who disbelieve say, 'This (Qur'aan) is nothing but a lie that he has invented, and others have helped him with it.' So they (the disbelievers) came forth with an unjust evil, and a wicked lie! And they say, 'Stories of the ancient; he has written it, and they are dictated to him (by others) morning and evening.' Respond (to them): 'This has been revealed by He who knows the secrets of the Heaven and Earth...» [25:4-6]

If that is the case, then let them answer the challenge:

أَمْ يَقُولُونَ ٱفْتَرَىٰهُ قُلْ فَأْتُوا۟ بِسُورَةٍ
مِّثْلِهِۦ وَٱدْعُوا۟ مَنِ ٱسْتَطَعْتُم مِّن دُونِ ٱللَّهِ إِن كُنتُمْ صَٰدِقِينَ ﴿٣٨﴾

«Or do they say, 'He has forged it!' Say: Then bring a *soorah* similar to it, and call whoever you wish, besides Allaah, if you are truthful!» [10:38].

In addition, the first verse alludes to a very important fact: all of these 'figures' are non-Arabs, yet the Qur'aan is put forth as a literary miracle in Arabic. How could the Prophet (ﷺ) learn this from a non-Arab?!

Imagination?

The last 'explanation' given is that the Prophet Muḥammad (ﷺ) imagined that he was the prophet of Allaah, and in this imagination, he was able to compose the Qur'aan. In other words, as Rev. Rodwell put it, he '...had worked himself up into a belief that he had received a divine call...'.[804]

In the 1960's, Anderson and Watt repeated these claims. Anderson claimed the Qur'aan was the 'result of wishful thinking', and Watt concluded, "What seems to a man to come from outside himself may actually come from his unconscious."[805] Another modern Orientalist, Kenneth Cragg, wrote, "Such was the ground and meaning of Muḥammad's call, in a brooding wilderness experience, where facts of conscious observation in the contemporary scene became articulate in a personal calling to utterance and warning in the city."[806] R. A. Nicholson also propounded the religious illusion theory, for he stated, "Whether we regard it as 'a pathological case' or a grand example of mystical ecstasy, at the outset of his mission a dominating motive can be discerned in his conviction that the Last Judgement was near and that he must at all costs warn his countrymen of the doom impending...To say that... the Qur'aan is, on the whole, uninspired, does not mean that its author was conscious of fraud when he gave out all sorts of regulations and instructions in the Qur'aan's name."[807] Rodinson, recasting these ideas in modern vernacular, insisted that the Qur'aan was an example of 'auditory visual hallucination'.[808]

In reality, this claim can be considered another example of the claim that the Prophet (ﷺ) was a madman. To claim that the Prophet (ﷺ) believed he was a prophet while he was not is to claim that he was insane. Yet, since these Orientalists knew that the Prophet's (ﷺ) *seerah* clearly disproved any claims of insanity, they brought forth another theme: that the Prophet (ﷺ) was sane in all his affairs, except the fact that he was a prophet! Can it be imagined that one who 'works himself up' into the belief that he is a prophet remains sane in all his affairs; as a father and husband; as a political leader and ruler of state; as a military commander; in fact, in all walks of life?

In addition, the presumption by these Orientalists that the Qur'aan was the product of the Prophet's (ﷺ) subconscious mind is, in reality, an indication of their ignorance of the Qur'aan. Can it be believed that the Qur'aan, with all its laws, commands and prohibitions, beliefs, stories and morals, is the result of a person's subconscious? Can it be believed that, for twenty-three years, a person 'imagined' such a miraculous book and brought it forth from his fantasy?

Again, the disbelievers of old issued the same explanation as their modern counterparts:

---

804 Arberry, p. 15.
805 Quotes from Khalifa, p. 12.
806 Njozi, p. 5.
807 Njozi, p. 20.
808 Khalifa, p. 12.

$$\text{بَلْ قَالُوٓاْ أَضْغَٰثُ أَحْلَٰمٍ بَلِ ٱفْتَرَىٰهُ بَلْ هُوَ شَاعِرٌ فَلْيَأْتِنَا بِـَٔايَةٍ كَمَآ أُرْسِلَ ٱلْأَوَّلُونَ}$$

«Nay, they say, 'These (revelations) are muddled dreams – Nay, he has invented it! – Nay, he is a poet! Then let him bring us some miracles like (the prophets) of old (were given)!'» [21:5]

Bryan S. Turner, in summarising these various views, states,[809]

> Traditional European biographers of the Prophet have either taken the position that Muhammad was psychologically normal but insincere about his supposed message from Allaah, or that Muhammad was insane and believed in the truth of his prophetic mission.

The Qur'aan states, in refutation of all of these views,

$$\text{فَذَكِّرْ فَمَآ أَنتَ بِنِعْمَتِ رَبِّكَ بِكَاهِنٍ وَلَا مَجْنُونٍ ۝ أَمْ يَقُولُونَ شَاعِرٌ نَّتَرَبَّصُ بِهِۦ رَيْبَ ٱلْمَنُونِ ۝ قُلْ تَرَبَّصُواْ فَإِنِّي مَعَكُم مِّنَ ٱلْمُتَرَبِّصِينَ ۝ أَمْ تَأْمُرُهُمْ أَحْلَٰمُهُم بِهَٰذَآ أَمْ هُمْ قَوْمٌ طَاغُونَ ۝ أَمْ يَقُولُونَ تَقَوَّلَهُۥ بَل لَّا يُؤْمِنُونَ ۝ فَلْيَأْتُواْ بِحَدِيثٍ مِّثْلِهِۦٓ إِن كَانُواْ صَٰدِقِينَ}$$

«Then remind and preach (to them, O Muhammad), for, by the grace of your Lord, you are not a sorcerer, nor a madman. Or do they say, 'He is a poet! We await some calamity to befall him by time!' Respond (to them), 'Wait, for I too will wait with you!' *Do their intellects command them with this (i.e., to invent these lies and explanations against you), or are they a people who exceed the limits (in disbelief)?* Or do they say, 'He has forged it!' Rather, they do not believe. *Then let them produce a speech similiar to this, if they are truthful!* » [52:29-34]

Is it not strange how Orientalists try to come up with an explanation for the authorship of the Qur'aan, instead of accepting who the Qur'aan itself claims is its Author? And is it not even more remarkable that they echo and imitate the same concoctions as their predecessors during the life of the Prophet (ﷺ) did?

$$\text{إِنَّ فِي ذَٰلِكَ لَـَٔايَةً وَمَا كَانَ أَكْثَرُهُم مُّؤْمِنِينَ ۝}$$

«Verily, in this there is a sign; yet, most of them are not believers!» [26:67]

---

809 Njozi, p. 21.

II. Some Books by Orientalists

The topic of the Qur'aan amongst the Orientalists has not attracted as much interest as the topics of _hadeeth_ and _fiqh_. This is because it is relatively easier for them to cast doubts on the authenticity of _hadeeth_ and the flaws of _fiqh_. For example, Joseph Schacht, one of the most famous Orientalists of this century, claimed that all _hadeeth_ are forgeries of later generations, attributed to the Prophet (ﷺ) by them for personal motives. He even claimed that the more reliable the _isnaad_, the more later this forgery occurred![810]

With regards to the Qur'aan, it is much more difficult for them to try to find 'facts' that support their claims, and interpret them to suit their needs, as they have done with other topics. Recently, however, Orientalists have turned their attention to attacking the Qur'aan, and have started trying to cast doubts about its authenticity.

Although much has been written in the field, there are three works that stand out above the rest, and have gained considerable repute as authorities in the field. Each of these works will be discussed below.

'Geschichte des Qorans' of Noeldeke

The first work is by Theodore Noeldeke, a very famous German Orientalist. He entitled it 'Geschichte des Qorans', or 'History of the Qur'aan'. The work was written with the help of three other German Orientalists: Pretzl, Schwally and Bergstraesser. It was published over a period of three decades, in three volumes. The first volume was published in 1909, and the last in 1938. It won national awards from the Paris Academy of Inscriptions, and drew great acclaim from Orientalists all over the world.

Von Denffer has a brief, yet superb, review of the work, which is quoted in its entirety: [811]

> The 'History of the Qur'an' produced by four German orientalists, deals in three parts with 'The Origin of the Qur'an', 'The Collection of the Qur'an', and 'The History of the Qur'anic Text'. The complete book naturally reflects the different approaches and types of scholarship of the various authors. Noeldeke's bias against Islaam can still be clearly discerned, although he later renounced some of his views regarding the history of the Qur'an.[812]
>
> The main substance of the first volume is its second part 'On the Origins of the Various Parts of the Qur'an'. Here, on the basis of Noeldeke's earlier works, the _soorahs_ have been arranged in four periods, three Makkan and one Madinan, depending heavily on Muslim sources, especially on Suyootee's _Itqaan_ and Tabari. Due to this, the material presented is, apart from the usual biased comments, a good cross-section of classical Muslim

---

810 For a superb refutation of the Orientalist views on _hadeeth_, see M. M. Azami, _On Schacht's Origins of Muhammadan Jurisprudence_, John Wiley & Sons, 1985.

811 Since the work is in German, this author was unable to review the work personally. The author is grateful to _The Islamic Foundation_ for permission to quote this section. Von Denffer, pps. 158-60

812 He believed, for example, that the _muqatta'aat_ represent the initials for the scribes of the Qur'aan. He later changed his mind on this point.

writings on the subject. Incidentally, Pickthall (the well-known Qur'an translator), relied heavily on this for his remarks on chronology in his translation.

There is a final discussion on 'Revelation not included in the Qur'aan' discussed on the basis of the various *ahadith* and other sources.

The second volume, dealing with the collection, is almost completely based on Muslim sources (again *Itqaan* dominates) and presents a calm discussion of the 'ruling tradition' *vis-à-vis* other reports about the collection of the Qur'an. Schwally, after presenting the material and his reflection on it, comes to conclusions very close to classical Muslim views, namely that 'the shape of the Qur'aan, as we have it now, was completed two to three years after the death of Muhammad, since the 'Uthmanic edition is only a copy of Hafsa's piece, the editorial work of which had been completed under Aboo Bakr, or at the latest under 'Umar. This editorial work however probably only concerned the compositions of the *surat* and their arrangement. As far as the various pieces of revelation are concerned, we may be confident that their text has been generally transmitted exactly as it was found in the Prophet's legacy'.

Volume three is mostly concerned with the written text of the Qur'an and the various readings. It is once more a sober presentation of information derived basically from Muslim sources. Bergstraesser has dealt mainly with the written form of the 'Uthmanic Qur'an, the variant readings, as contained in the *masaahif* of Ibn Mas'ood and Ubay. He then introduces the historical development of the *qira'aat*.

Pretzl presents the various readings, emphasising the famous 'seven readings', describes the Muslim literature on the *qira'at* and finally deals very briefly with the palaeography and decorative designs of old Qur'anic manuscripts. As in volume two, the main sources are classical Muslim authors, especially as-Suyootee, al-Mabanee, al-Jazaree and various writers on *qira'at*. Until today, Noeldeke/Schwally is the most comprehensive – if not the sole – serious attempt by Orientalists to deal with the Qur'an – at least in a descriptive manner. For this is what the later authors – not so much Noeldeke – had in view: to collect the available material on the subject and to present it. While some of the authors' comments and conclusions would not be welcomed by Muslims, the vast area that has been covered and the presentation based on the classical Muslim literature on the topic are of a merit that has to be acknowledged. Especially in the latter two volumes, there is surprisingly little that Muslims might find derogatory in style, and indeed the basic presentation is not unlike classical Muslim literature on the subject."

'Materials for the History of the Text of the Qur'an' by Arthur Jeffery

The next book that is of great importance is that of Arthur Jeffery, entitled *Materials for the History of the Text of the Qur'an: The Old Codices*. This book also includes in its entirety the Arabic original of *Kitaab al-Masaahif* by Ibn Abee Daawood (d. 316

A.H.). It was first published in 1937, in Leiden, and reprinted a number of times since. Jeffery bases his edition of *Kitaab al-Masaahif* on the only available manuscript copy in the famous Zahiriyah Library of Damascus, which he came across by chance.

Therefore the work is actually two books; the first is Jeffery's *Material for the History of the Text of the Qur'an*, and the second is Ibn Abee Daawood's book, edited by Jeffery.

Jeffery's own work is an almost four-hundred page long compilation of the different recitations of certain Companions and Successors who were known to have written *mus-hafs*. He compiled information regarding fifteen codexes from the Companions, and thirteen from the Successors. By a 'codex' he meant a *mus-haf*. He lists all the readings in these *mus-hafs* that do not conform to the present day *mus-haf* (although in reality many of them do conform with the *mus-haf* of 'Uthmaan; they are merely different from the *mus-haf* written in the *qiraa'a* of Hafs).

Jeffery divides the work based on each codex, and under each codex, he lists, in order, all the verses where a different recitation occurs. The most important and longest of them are the codexes of Ibn Mas'ood and Ubay ibn Ka'ab.

Jeffery compiled this information from over thirty classical Islaamic texts, some authentic and some not. The sources range from classical lexicons, to the famous works of *tafseer*, to the works on the *qira'aat*. Unfortunately, for each variant recitation, he did not list the exact reference work that it was obtained from.

To give an example of what Jeffery compiled, we will quote from Ibn Mas'ood's *Soorah Faatihah*. He read, according to Jeffery, with the following differences

1) 'malik' as 'maalik'

2) 'ihdina as-siraat al-mustaqeem' as 'arshidna as-siraat al-mustaqeem'

3) 'siraat alladheen an'amta 'alayhim' as 'siraat man an'amta 'alayhim'

4) 'ghayril maghdoobi' as 'ghayral maghdoobi'.

Jeffery continues in a similar fashion for the rest of the Qur'aan.

Obviously, what Jeffery is trying to prove is that there are variant readings to the Qur'an which were not preserved. He writes, '...it is quite clear that the text which 'Uthmaan canonised was only one out of many rival texts...'; therefore the purpose of Jeffery's book is to, '..investigate what went before the canonical texts.'[813] His supposition is that the 'original' text was tampered with by the Companions, and only one chosen.

There are three points to be made concerning this.

1) On the supposition that Jeffery's theory is absolutely correct – that the text of the Qur'aan as 'Uthmaan preserved it was chosen by him from amongst many variant texts – what are the implications of this from Jeffery's work? Even if we allow for all these readings that Jeffery compiled to be authentic, and representing legitimate vari-

---

813 Jeffery, p. X.

ants from the text of 'Uthmaan, not a single reading actually contradicts another one in meaning. No verse is added, no ruling contradicted, no law repealed. There are literally thousands of differences mentioned in this book, each one of which merely rephrases a certain verse of the Qur'aan.[814] Therefore, the question must be asked, what is gained by substantiating these 'variant' texts? Agreed, if what Jeffery claims is true, this would imply that the actual *text* of the Qur'aan that is present is only one of a number of authentic texts, but what presumption or theory can be advanced based on this claim? Of course, this is supposing that Jeffery's basic premise is true, and to this we do not agree.

2) More importantly – and this is the greatest flaw of the book – the authenticity of these recitations has to be established. In other words, how can the reader be assured that these recitations were actually recited? Jeffery himself admits, "The question arises, of course, as to the authenticity of the readings ascribed to these Old Codices. In some cases it must be confessed there is a suspicion of readings later invented by the grammarians and theologians being fathered on these early authorities in order to gain prestige of their name. The suspicion is perhaps strongest in the case of distinctly *Shee'ite* readings..."[815]

From a Muslim standpoint, we have recourse to the *isnaad*. Jeffery, however, believes the *isnaad*s to hold very little, if any, value. Due to this opinion, he does not quote *isnaad*s for each variant reading. Therefore, in order to find the authenticity of a certain reading, it is necessary to go back to the thirty works from which Jeffery compiled his work, verify which one of them mentions this reading, and then check its *isnaad* for authenticity. (This is supposing that the original work even mentions an *isnaad*, for some of these recitations are merely referenced in later works without any *isnaad*.)

However, from Jeffery's own position on the concept and reliability of *isnaad*, he contradicts himself. If he does not believe in the authenticity of the *isnaad* system, then from where are all of these readings obtained? After all, it is through *isnaad*s that all of the readings of the Companions and Successors has been handed down to us. If Jeffery were to apply his standards and implement his belief of the *isnaad* system, all of these readings should be doubted, just like their _hadeeth_ counterparts! But, not surprisingly, Jeffery concludes, 'On the whole, however, one may feel confident that the majority of readings quoted from any reader really go back to early authority'.[816] This clear double standard on Jeffery's part is not surprising; whenever an Orientalist finds some information that he feels can be used to discredit Islaam and cast doubts on it, then he will use it, no matter what the context, authenticity or actual implications of the text may be. As Jeffery so clearly and unabashedly states, "Much of the

---

814 Actually, this author looked over most of the entries in the book, and could only find one instance where the variant 'reading' clearly goes against the beliefs of Muslim. The 'verse' in question occurs as an addition to 26:215, and mentions that the true believers are only from the family of the Prophet (ﷺ). This is obviously a *Shee'ite* forgery, as Jeffery himself hints. cf. p. 189 of the book

815 Jeffery, p. 15.

816 Both quotes are from Jeffery, p. 15

material given by Ibn Abee Daawood regarding the history of the text of the Qur'aan, though extremely unorthodox, yet agrees so closely with conclusions one had reached from quite other directions that one feels confident in making use of it, however weak orthodoxy may consider its *isnaad* to be."[817] Therefore the reason that these narrations are authentic, according to Jeffery, is because they agree with preconceived conclusions that were arrived at from 'quite other directions'; unnamed and unknown directions, it should be pointed out!

3) The question obviously arises as to the valid interpretation of these variant readings. After all, Jeffery compiled these readings from various books of *tafseer* and *qira'aat*. How, then, are they to be explained?

The explanation of these variant readings is very simple, and relies upon the understanding of the *ahruf* and *qira'aat* of the Qur'aan, as was explained previously. It is noticed that many of these variant readings are found in the *qira'aat* of today – the *saheeh*, *da'eef* and *shaadh* ones. If anything, this actually further strengthens the belief of the Muslims regarding the *qira'aat*, since these differences have come down to this generation from the Companions, who all learnt from the Prophet (ﷺ). The existence of the *saheeh qira'aat* at the time of the Companions is something that does not need to be proven, but in doing so, Jeffery has 'confirmed' that the ten *qira'aat* originated from the Companions (and hence the Prophet (ﷺ)) and not from later authorities. An example of this is Ibn Mas'ood's recitation of '*maliki*' as '*maaliki*'. As was quoted earlier, this difference is still existent in the authentic *qira'aat*, thus merely proving their origin. As for those variants which are considered *da'eef qira'aat*, they cannot be accepted as the Qur'aan, and as such there is no use in quoting such material as 'variant' to the text of the Qur'aan, since the authenticity of these *da'eef qira'aat* is not established. As for the *shaadh qira'aat*, they used to be recited by the Companions before their recitation had been abrogated. These cannot be considered as part of the Qur'aan anymore, as was mentioned earlier, and thus to quote them as having been left out of the Qur'aan is true, but they were left out at the command of the Prophet (ﷺ). Likewise, those recitations that are shown to be authentic but are not a part of the *qira'aat*, such as Ibn Mas'ood's reading of '*ihdina*' as '*arshidna*', are only examples of the *ahruf* of the Qur'aan that were not preserved by the command of the Prophet (ﷺ).

In conclusion, from a Muslim's perspective, Jeffery's collection is only useful insofar as it lists many of the variant readings – the authentic and inauthentic ones. A critical analysis of the authenticity of each and every variant reading must be established before the book can be of any great value. Also, the variant readings quoted in Jeffery's book (at least the authentic ones) are all part of the *ahruf* of the Qur'aan, some of which still exist in the *qira'aat*, and some of which have been abrogated by the Prophet (ﷺ). Obviously, Jeffery absolutely ignores the concept of the *ahruf* and *qira'aat*, for if he were to take this into account, then these readings would be explained without recourse to his theory that the Qur'aan is incomplete. In other words, Jeffery's

---

817 Jeffery, p. VII

work is an example of an Orientalist taking a concept (the concept of the *ahruf* and *qiraʾaat*), distorting it, and then presenting it in a sinister light in order to cast doubts upon Islaam. Had he only understood the correct interpretation of this concept – an interpretation that is claimed by him to be 'largely fictitious'[818] without any explanation why – it would have saved him the trouble of compiling his work.

The second book in Jeffery's collection is his editing of 'Abdullaah Ibn Abee Daawood's (d. 316 A.H.) *Kitaab al-Masaahif*. The author is none other that the son of the famous collector of the *Sunan*, Aboo Daawood as-Sijistaani (d. 275 A.H.). However, he did not enjoy the same prestige as his father, and he has mixed reviews from the scholars of *hadeeth*. Nonetheless, the book is an excellent reference, and it contains the necessary *isnaads* for each narration, so the authenticity of each narration may be ascertained. It deals, as its title indicates, with the *mus-haf*; it discusses the writing of the *wahy*, the various *mus-hafs* of the Companions and their differences; the compilations of Aboo Bakr and 'Uthmaan; the division of the Qur'aan; the writing of the *mus-haf*, and certain aspects of *fiqh* related to the *mus-haf*.

'The Collection of the Qur'aan' by John Burton

The last work that shall be discussed is a relatively recent one: *The Collection of the Qur'an* by John Burton. It was first published in 1977 by Cambridge University Press.

What Burton did was to take the theories of Schacht concerning the validity of *hadeeth* and apply them to the history of the compilation of the Qur'aan. As was mentioned earlier, Schacht (and before him Goldziher) claimed and popularised the theory that all *hadeeth* literature are forgeries of the scholars of the second and third century of the *hijrah*. Burton writes in his introduction that his work, '..seeks to re-open the question of the collection of the Qur'aan as seen by Muslims. Their accounts will be re-examined in the light of studies by Goldziher and Schacht...'.[819]

For Burton's honesty, at least, he must be given greater credit than Jeffery. He states, '...one must either accept all *hadeeth* impartially with uncritical trust, or one must regard each and every *hadeeth* as at least potentially guilty of a greater or lesser degree of inherent bias[820]...We cannot in our arrogance continue to presume that, guided by mere literary intuition, we can safely pick our way, selecting or rejecting *hadeeth*s...'[821]

Actually, Burton has some very interesting and unique theories. He dismisses all the narrations concerning the collection of the Qur'aan, since all these stories, according to Schacht's principles, must be inventions by later generations. Therefore, since he has rejected all these narrations, he is forced to bring forth a totally unique and bizarre history of the compilation of the Qur'aan.

---

818 Jeffery, p. 5.

819 Burton, p. 5.

820 It is amusing how Burton gives an *either-or* argument here concerning *hadeeth*; either naively accept everything or critically reject everything. He does not even bother to mention the fact that there are strict rules of the *muhadeetheen* that enable a scholar to detect what is authentic from what is weak.

821 Burton, p. 234

According to Burton, it was Muhammad (ﷺ) himself who compiled the Qur'aan. However, "Amid his manifold state responsibilities Muhammad could not always himself remember the precise wording in which he had given out certain revelations. This is how different Companions received their slightly differing versions, although all were received direct from the Prophet himself. Certain verses Muhammad forgot outright, others he summarily altered. With his own hand he had cancelled yet other verses."[822] This is Burton's understanding of the concept of the *ahruf*!

In trying to explain why later Muslim authorities claimed that the Companions were the ones who compiled the Qur'aan (since, according to him, these authorites forged the narrations pertaining to the collection of the Qur'aan), Burton comes out with another bizarre theory. After the Prophet's (ﷺ) death, argues Burton, later Muslim jurists forged the concept of *naskh*, so that they could justify certain *fiqh* positions that they held (such as the stoning of the adulterer). These jurists wished to somehow support these positions of *fiqh*, so they decided, according to Burton, to forge certain 'verses' that used to be a part of the Qur'aan. As it was well known what the Qur'aan was, these verses could not be added into the present *mus-haf*, so, somehow, a means of proving that these verses had once formed a part of the *mus-haf* but now no longer did had to be theorised. This was the concept of *naskh*.

In order to justify this theory, Burton continues, these jurists claimed that the Prophet (ﷺ) could not have compiled the Qur'aan in his lifetime, since *naskh* could occur at any time during his life. This, according to Burton, led these jurists to develop the concept of *naskh*, and invent 'verses' that had been left out of the present *mus-haf* that dealt with the *fiqh* positions that they wished to prove. Since the Prophet (ﷺ) could not have compiled the Qur'aan, it must have been the Companions who had done so, and this explains the 'forged' narrations concerning the history of the compilation of the Qur'aan.

Burton states, "This motive (i.e., that of proving the validity of *naskh*) induced the Muslims to exclude their Prophet from the history of the collection of their Qur'aan text. It was a compelling motive. It was their only motive."[823]

Initially, according to Burton, the role of compiling the Qur'aan was given to 'Uthmaan. However, when the popularity of 'Uthmaan declined amongst the masses, the people had to transfer the honour of the initial compilation to Aboo Bakr and 'Umar, and to give 'Uthmaan a lesser role. With all of these jumbled reports appearing on the scene,

> This led to the attempts to harmonise these conflicting attribution: Abu Bakr had initiated the sacred undertaking, 'Umar acquiring the merit of having completed it; 'Umar is credited with initiating the undertaking, 'Uthman is grudgingly allowed the lesser merit of completing the work of his pious and energetic predecessor.[824]

---

822 Burton, p. 234
823 Burton, p. 232
824 Burton, p. 230

This, then, is the summary of Burton's version of the compilation of the Qur'aan. It is an amusing story, if nothing else. The scholars of Islaam were in a dilemma to explain their stance on certain *fiqh* issues. Therefore, they had to invent the concept of *naskh* in the Qur'aan, and back it up by forging 'verses' that were supposed to have been *mansookh*.

If these scholars had so little sincerity that they had no qualms forging verses from the Qur'aan, then why not just forge *hadeeth* to support their points? In other words, why go through the nuisance of inventing the concept of *naskh* and then trying to prove it by backing it up with false narrations, when they could have just as easily concocted a *hadeeth* to prove their positions? After all, this is the whole theory of Schacht and modern Orientalists – that later jurists concocted *hadeeth* as they desired!

In reality, Burton does not substantiate his claims with any strong proof. For example, he only brings two verses to prove his thesis that later scholars invented the concept of *naskh*: the 'verse of stoning' and the 'verse of suckling'.[825] Throughout the whole work, the primary example that is reiterated is the 'verse of stoning'. If what Burton states is true, then there should exist a large quantity of verses which give *fiqh* rulings but were left out of the *mus-haf*. In other words, if the whole concept of *naskh* was propagated with the sole purpose of supporting certain *fiqh* positions that a jurist might hold, then certainly these jurists would have used this concept regularly, and attributed many of their views to 'verses' that had been abrogated. However, as is well known, there exist very few verses of this nature, and Burton can only quote two examples throughout his work. In addition, he gives a very weak interpretation of the Qur'aanic verses that explicitly mention the concept of *naskh*, and of the occurrences of *naskh* during the Prophet's (ﷺ) lifetime.

Another point that Burton absolutely ignores is that the Prophet (ﷺ) was illiterate. The indisputablity of this fact is well-known, and beyond the need for any *isnaad*. Even the Qur'aan refers to the Prophet's (ﷺ) illiteracy a number of times. How is it possible, then, that the Prophet (ﷺ) secretly authored the Qur'aan, edited it, and distributed it amongst the people?

Throughout the work, Burton constantly re-emphasises one theme: that all the narrations concerning the compilation of the Qur'aan are forgeries of later generations. With this presumption in mind, Burton goes to excessive (and in fact ludicrous) extremes in trying to determine the *motives* for these forgeries. It never occurs to Burton that the early scholars of Islaam (the *salaf*) were not so depraved or unscrupulous that they would forge narrations and attribute them to the Prophet (ﷺ) at whim. If Burton's theory (based on Schacht and Goldziher) are true, this implies that the *salaf* were busy propagating lies and forgeries throughout their lives; all the time well aware that these narrations were all forgeries (since they themselves were doing the forging!), but naively studying them; travelling great distances to obtain them; honouring those that had memorised them; and codifying them with great care! The

---

825 Both of these verses were discussed in Ch. 13 'Abrogation in the Qur'aan'

theory that all these narrations are forgeries that occurred on such mass-scales, and the silent approval of all the scholars of that time concerning them, seems so naive and absurd that only one who is blinded in his animosity of Islaam can believe it.

Actually, Burton's whole theory rests, as was stated earlier, on Schacht's conception of *hadeeth* literature. This view has been aptly refuted by M. M. Azami in his superb work '*On Schacht's Origins of Muhammadan Jurisprudence*'.[826] In this work, Azami demonstrates the inconsistencies in Schacht's theories and source material; his unwarranted assumptions and unscientific research methods; his ignorance of the political situation of the time; and his misunderstandings and distortions of the quotations of early scholars.[827] Therefore, with the refutation of Schacht, Burton's theories are automatically disproved.

Burton's conclusion, though, is unusual, coming from an Orientalist. He claims that the '*mus-haf* that we have in our hands today is the *mus-haf* of Muhammad', meaning that Muhammad (ﷺ) had written the whole Qur'aan in one book before his death.

In conclusion, Burton's work represents a very bizarre and highly contradictory account of the collection of the Qur'aan. Burton seems to take a few examples and draw extraordinary conclusions and sweeping generalities with them, absolutely ignoring all other narrations and factors related to the topic. In this author's opinion, in order to come forth with something totally unique, Burton outdid himself.

---

826 Published by John Wiley and Sons, New York, 1985.
827 cf. pps. 115-154. No student of knowledge can be without this work, especially if he wishes to respond to the claims of Orientalists.

EPILOGUE

I. The 'Return' of the Qur'aan

The statement of 'Amr ibn Deenar (d. 126 A.H.) was quoted earlier in which he said, "I have met the Companions of the Prophet (ﷺ), and those that came after them for seventy years, all of them said, 'Allaah is the Creator, and everything besides Him is created, and the Qur'aan is the *kalaam* of Allaah, from Him it came, and to Him it will return.'"[828]

This statement, which was used in the section concerning the *kalaam* of Allaah, mentions the fact that the Qur'aan will 'return' to Allaah. What is the meaning of this phrase which was said by so many Companions and Successors?

Among the signs of the Day of Judgement is the increase of ignorance, and the disappearance of knowledge. The Prophet (ﷺ) said, "Before the Day of Judgement, there will be a time (or 'days') in which Ignorance will be sent down, and Knowledge will be raised up."[829] The 'raising up of Knowledge' has been interpreted by the Prophet (ﷺ) himself to mean the death of scholars. The Prophet (ﷺ) said, "Allaah does not snatch away knowledge from the chests of His servants, but He takes away knowledge by the death of scholars, until, when there are no more scholars remaining, the people take ignorant leaders (i.e., as scholars). And these leaders will be asked (by the people), and they will respond without any knowledge, and they will be misguided, and misguide others."[830]

And as the Day of Judgement comes closer, more and more ignorance will appear, and knowledge will lessen, until, in the very last of time, the Qur'aan itself will be taken away, and raised up from amongst mankind. This will occur after the time of 'Eesaa, when the only people remaining will be the worst of all of mankind; the generation upon whom the Trumpet of the Day of Judgement will be blown while they are still alive.

The Prophet (ﷺ) said, "Islaam will disappear just like the colours of a dress fade away, until people will not even know what fasting, prayer, the rites (of _Hajj_) and charity are. And the Book of Allaah will be lifted up one night, so that not even one verse will remain. And a group of old people will remain, who will say, 'We found our

---

828 Reported by al-Bayhaqee in his *Sunan*.
829 Reported by al-Bukhaaree.
830 Reported by al-Bukhaaree.

forefathers on this *kalimah*: *Laa ilaaha ila Allaah*, so we too say it.'"[831] Ibn Mas'ood said, "Indeed, the Qur'aan will be taken away from your midst; one night it will be raised up, and it will leave from the chests of men, and nothing will remain of it on the earth."[832] 'Abdullaah ibn 'Amr stated, "The Day of Judgement will not come until the Qur'aan returns from whence it was revealed. It will have a sound like the buzzing of bees and it will say, 'O my Lord! From you I came and to you I am returning. I am recited, but not acted upon; I am recited, but not acted upon.'"[833]

Shaykh al-Islaam Ibn Taymiyyah (d. 728 A.H.) stated, in explanation of these narrations, "It will be raised up one night, towards the very end of time, from the *mus-haf* and the chests of men, so not a single word will remain in the hearts, nor will a single letter remain in the *mus-haf*."[834] It appears, therefore, that although knowledge in general will not be taken away from the chests of men, the Qur'aan, towards the end of time, will, and Allaah knows best.

In any case, the *hadeeth* are explicit that the Qur'aan will be raised up from the earth, and this is the meaning of the phrase of the *salaf*: '...and to Him it will return'. The time when this 'raising up' occurs will be the end of time, the time in which the Qur'aan has been abandoned by the people; when they leave the Qur'aan, it is only befitting that the Qur'aan is taken away from them.

II. An Appeal

The present work has been an attempt to present to the reader a glimpse of the power and beauty of the Qur'aan. There can be no doubt that the Qur'aan is the greatest miracle of the Prophet (ﷺ) – a miracle that can be appreciated by all of mankind. Yet, despite the power and status of the Qur'aan, many Muslims are heedless of it.

It is distressing to see that the Muslims of today have turned away from this great treasure that has been revealed to them – the very Speech of Allaah. They have made the Qur'aan a sacred family heirloom; to be treasured in exotic and expensive covers, yet to be uninhabited by the best of all covers – their hearts; to be recited and listened to in the best and most melodious of voices, yet to ignore its meanings; to be placed high above all other objects in any room, yet to occupy the lowest station in their daily lives; to be read when a death has occurred, yet to be ignored by the living; to be written in the fanciest of scripts and on the most expensive of papers, yet to be heedless of its commandments and prohibitions.

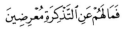

«What is the matter with them, that they have turned away from the Remembrance?» [74:49]

---

831 Reported by Ibn Maajah; authenticated in *Saheeh al-Jaami'*.
832 Reported by at-Tabaraanee.
833 ad-Darimee, *ar- Radd*, p. 189.
834 *Majmoo' al-Fatawaa*, v. 3, p. 198. Also see Waabil, p. 135.

$$\text{يَٰٓأَيُّهَا ٱلۡإِنسَٰنُ مَا غَرَّكَ بِرَبِّكَ ٱلۡكَرِيمِ ٦}$$

«O Mankind! What has made you careless concerning your Lord, the Most Generous?» [82:6]

O Muslims! O Believers of the Qur'aan! Beware that you do not fall into those whom the Prophet (ﷺ) will complain about to his Lord on the Day of Judgement:

$$\text{وَقَالَ ٱلرَّسُولُ يَٰرَبِّ إِنَّ قَوۡمِي ٱتَّخَذُواْ هَٰذَا ٱلۡقُرۡءَانَ مَهۡجُورٗا ٣٠}$$

«And the Messenger (will) say: 'O My Lord, indeed my people took this Qur'aan as something worthy of being abandoned!'» [25:30].

The scholar Ibn al-Qayyim al-Jawziyyah (d. 758 A.H.) said,

> There are various types of 'abandonment' of the Qur'aan:
>
> 1) To abandon listening to it and believing in it.
>
> 2) To abandon acting upon it, and ignoring its lawful and prohibited ordinances (_halaal_ and _haraam_), even if one believes in it and recites it.
>
> 3) To abandon judging by it, and resorting to it as a judge when there are differences in the essence of the religion or other matters.
>
> 4) To abandon pondering over it, and understanding it, and seeking the explanation of it.
>
> 5) To abandon using it as a cure in all types of diseases of the heart, and instead to seek to cure these diseases by other means.
>
> And all of these categories are included in the statement of Allaah,

$$\text{وَقَالَ ٱلرَّسُولُ يَٰرَبِّ إِنَّ قَوۡمِي ٱتَّخَذُواْ هَٰذَا ٱلۡقُرۡءَانَ مَهۡجُورٗا ٣٠}$$

> «And the Messenger (will) say: "O My Lord, indeed my people took this Qur'aan as something worthy of being abandoned!'» [25:30],
>
> even though some of these types of abandonment are worse than others."[835]

How many of these types of abandonments are we guilty of?

O Muslims! Have you not read the outcome of the one who turns away from the Qur'aan?

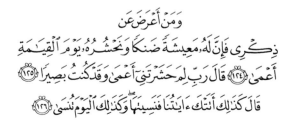

$$\text{وَمَنۡ أَعۡرَضَ عَن}$$
$$\text{ذِكۡرِي فَإِنَّ لَهُۥ مَعِيشَةٗ ضَنكٗا وَنَحۡشُرُهُۥ يَوۡمَ ٱلۡقِيَٰمَةِ}$$
$$\text{أَعۡمَىٰ ١٢٤ قَالَ رَبِّ لِمَ حَشَرۡتَنِيٓ أَعۡمَىٰ وَقَدۡ كُنتُ بَصِيرٗا ١٢٥}$$
$$\text{قَالَ كَذَٰلِكَ أَتَتۡكَ ءَايَٰتُنَا فَنَسِيتَهَاۖ وَكَذَٰلِكَ ٱلۡيَوۡمَ تُنسَىٰ ١٢٦}$$

---

835 Ibn al-Qayyim, p. 113. The five categories have been translated in meaning, not verbatim.

«And whoever turns away from My Remembrance (the Qur'aan), for him is a life of hardship, and We shall raise him up, on the Day of Judgement, blind. He will say, 'O My Lord! Why have you resurrected me blind, when I used to see (in this world)?' (Allaah) will respond, 'Likewise (in this manner), Our verses came to you, but you ignored them. And, likewise, today you shall be ignored'» [20:124-126].

The one who was blessed with sight, but turned away from the light and guidance of the Qur'aan, deserves that his sight to be snatched away from him, for of what use was it? If his sight was blind to the light of the Qur'aan, then, on the Day of Judgement, it shall be blind to all else.

$$ وَمَن كَانَ فِي هَٰذِهِۦ أَعْمَىٰ فَهُوَ فِي ٱلْأَخِرَةِ أَعْمَىٰ وَأَضَلُّ سَبِيلًا ۝ $$

«And whoever is blind in this world (to the Qur'aan), then he will be blind on the Day of Judgement, and even more astray!» [17:72]

The Prophet (ﷺ) said, "Indeed, Allaah will honour people (i.e., in this world and the Hereafter) by this Book, and He will debase others by it."[836] There are only two categories of people when it comes to the Qur'aan; those that will be honoured because of it, and those that will be humiliated because of it. The Prophet (ﷺ) also said, "Whoever puts (the Qur'aan) ahead of him, it will lead him to Paradise; and whoever throws it behind him, it will drag him into Hell."[837]

Which of these two categories do you wish to be in?

---

836 Reported by Muslim.
837 Reported by at-Tabaraani.

APPENDIX

PICTURE PLATES

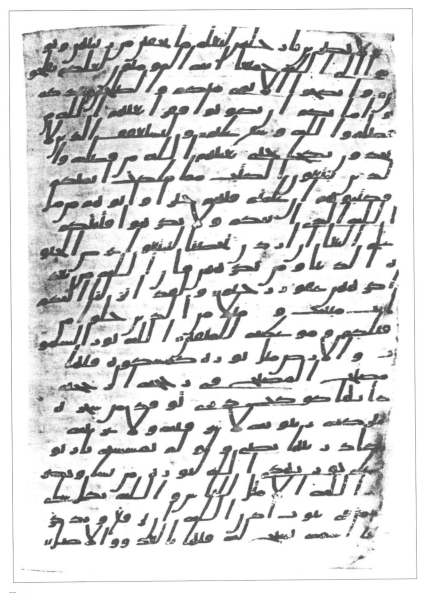

PLATE ONE

Soorah Noor, last portion of verse 31 to end of verse 36. This is one of the oldest extant manuscripts of the Qur'aan, written in the 2nd century of the *hijrah* (around 150 A.H.), probably in Makkah or Madeenah. It is written on vellum, in an old and rare script known as *maa'il*. It is devoid of diacritical marks (*taskheel*) and dots (*nuqat*). There are circular marks to indicate the endings of the verses. A characteristic that is typical of extremely early manuscripts such as this one is the fact that, at the end of a line, the writer might break a single word into two parts, with a portion of it on the first line, and the rest on the second. (For example, see the end of the first line and the beginning of the second. The word '*tooboo*' is split up, with the first part '*too*' written on the first line, and the rest of it, '*boo*', on the second line.) Later, as the art of writing evolved, each word was written together, and not split up at the end of a line.

(British Library, London)

PLATE TWO

Soorah as-Shu'araa, last word of verse 193 to middle of verse 205. This manuscript dates back to the 3rd century of the *hijrah*, and is a classic example of early Kufic script. Small dots are present to distinguish between similar letters. The *tashkeel* system is that of Aboo al-Aswad's. Not all letters have a diacritical mark on them (unlike later *mus-hafs*). Instead, only those letters which would typically be problematic to a new reader are marked with *tashkeel*. This phenomenon is character-istic of the *mus-hafs* of the first few centuries of the *hijrah*. In this plate, the *tashkeel* markings are in red, and the *nuqat* written with a finer pen in black, so that the actual text of the Qur'aan can easily be distinguished from the other additions. Each verse ending is marked by three dots in a triangle, and the large circular design that can be seen on this plate is used to indicate the passage of ten verses. There are no *hamzahs*, *shaddahs*, *sukoons*, or signs indicating stopping places (*wuqoof*). All words are written together, and not split between lines. The *mus-haf* is written on vellum, in Iraq.

(British Library, London)

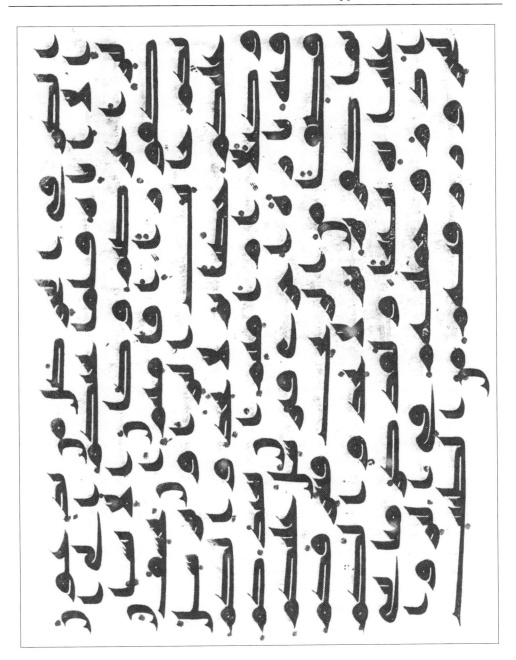

PLATE THREE

Soorah al-Israa, verse 67 to verse 70. Another example of Early Kufic, from the 4th century. Notice that more letters have the *tashkeel* on them (compared with plate two). However, the letters are not dotted (*nuqat*). This disparity between manuscripts is common, for each writer would take into account the purpose (and sometimes even person) for which the Qur'aan was written, and cater to the specific situation. More 'advanced' reciters of the Qur'aan would not need as much *tashkeel* and *nuqat* as others might. This manuscript is written on vellum, probably in North Africa.

(Chester Beatty Library, Dublin)

PLATE FOUR

Soorah al-Anfaal, verse 41. This manuscript is written by 'Uthmaan ibn H̲usayn al-Warraaq (d. 466 A.H.), in Iraq. It is written in Eastern Kufic script, on paper (all later plates are also on paper). It is noticed that all the letters have the appropriate *tashkeel* on them, all letters are dotted, and *h̲amzahs*, *shaddahs* and *sukoons* can be seen. In addition, the *taskheel* system of Aboo al-Aswad has been replaced with the 'modern' version. However, all these signs, along with the dots, are written with gold-coloured ink, and the *taskheel* in red, so that the Qur'aanic script is clearly differentiable from other additions. The top of the page has written on it 'The Tenth *Juz*', since at this verse the tenth *juz* starts.

(Mashhad Shrine Library, Iran)

PLATE FIVE

The first three verses of *Soorah at-Tawbah*. Another example of Eastern Kufic, written in Persia, in the 6th century. Once again, all letters have appropriate *nuqat* and *tashkeel* marks, and *hamzahs*, *sukoons*, and *shaddahs* can be seen. However, only the *taskheel* (in Aboo al-Aswad's system) is in a different colour than the text; the rest of the *nuqat* and additions are in black, as is the text. The top line, which is in golden ink, states, "*Soorah at-Tawbah*, One hundred and thirty *ayaahs*", and the word '*Madaneeyah*' is seen in the right column, before the beginning of the soorah, signifying that this soorah is a *madanee soorah*. Earlier manuscripts did not mention these details.

(Chester Beatty Library, Dublin)

Soorah Ibraaheem, verse 27 to the middle of verse 37 Another example of Eastern Kufic, written by 'Alee ibn Muhammad ibn Muhammad (d. 620 A.H.), in Persia. Not only are all the *tashkeel* and *nuqat* present, along with *hamzahs*, *sukoons*, and *shaddahs*, but occasional symbols indicating stopping places (*wuqoof*) can be seen. The *tashkeel* system used is the 'modern' one. The verse endings are indicated by four dots in a square structure; after every five verses, a circle with a triangle is drawn, and, after every ten verses, an ornate circle. Almost all extra markings are in the same colour as the text.

(Mashhad Shrine Library)

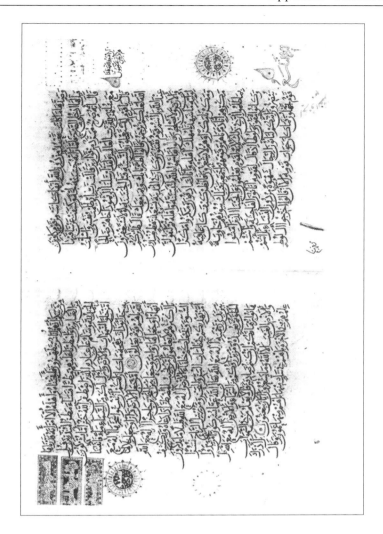

PLATE SEVEN

Soorah an-Naml, verse 43 to 66. A classic example of the *Naskhee* script. This is probably the only extant manuscript written by the famous 'Alee ibn H̲ilaal, otherwise known as Ibn al-Bawwaab (d. 413 A.H.). This manuscript was written in 391 A.H., in Baghdad. Although it was Ibn Muqlah (d. 327 A.H.) who introduced the *Naskhee* script with which this Qur'aan is written, it was Ibn al-Bawwaab who aided in popularising it. Unfortunately, none of Ibn Muqlah's writings have been preserved, and this plate is one of the earliest examples of *Naskhee*. Ibn al-Bawwaab also helped popularise the 'modern' version of *taskheel*, dropping the older system of Aboo al-Aswad. All *taskheel*, *nuqat* and other punctuation signs are written in the same colour as the text. The bottom of the left column indicates the start of the ninth *juz*. The two lines of text in the upper portion of the right column is the ending of verse 45, the beginning portion of which is in the main text. It seems as if the writer accidentally forgot to complete the verse and moved on to the next one; by the time he realised his error, it was too late to do anything about it except write the remaining portion in the column (typos were not that easily rid of as they are today!) Even the greatest of calligraphers are only human!

(Chester Beatty Library, Dublin)

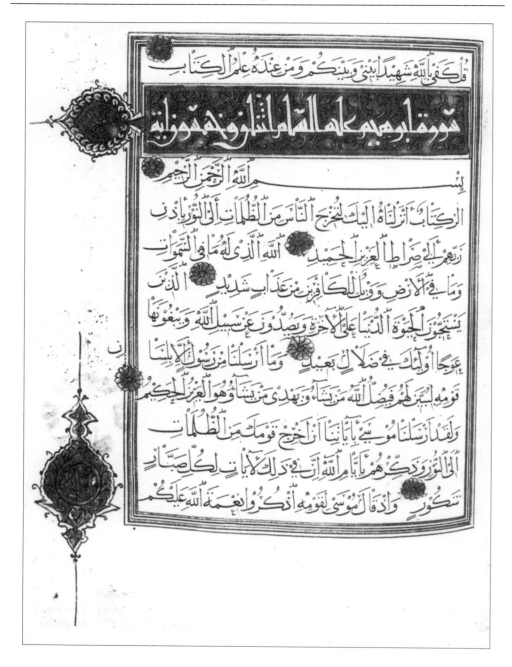

The last verse of *Soorah al-Hijr* and the first five of *Soorah Ibraaheem*. This is one of the works of Yaqoot al-Musta'simee (d. ~ 700 A.H.), one of the most famous calligraphers of Islaamic history. He was nicknamed 'The Sultan of the Calligraphers'; this plate shows us why. This script, known as *Rayhaanee*, is an off-shoot of *Nashkee*. The *soorah* heading is written in Eastern Kufic.

(Iran Bastam Museum, Tehran)

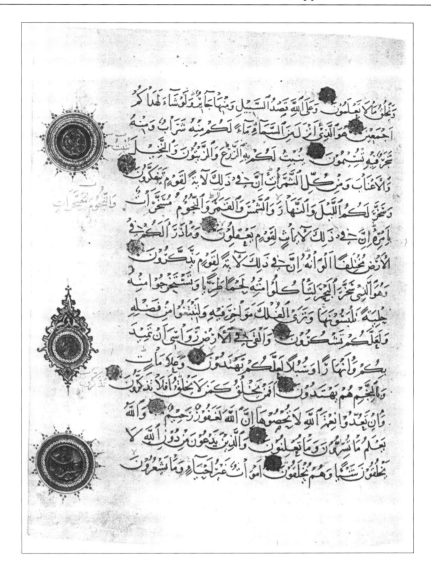

PLATE NINE

Soorah an-Nahl, the last portion of verse 8 to the middle of verse 21. Another example of *Naskhee*, by Yaqoot al-Musta'simee, written in 693 A.H. in Iraq. The signs for stopping (*wuqoof*) are more numerous and detailed than in earlier manuscripts. The large circle in the upper left column indicates the completion of ten verses; after every five verses appears the symbol in the middle of the column. After yet another five, the same circular symbol appears, but written inside is the verse number, 'Twenty', which is the number of verses since the beginning of the *soorah*. A common feature of many *mus-hafs* of this era is the fact that alternate *qira'aat* of the verse would be written in the margin. Typically, the Qur'aan would be written in the common *qiraa'a* of the locality, while other *qira'aat*, less commonly recited than the primary one, would be written in the margin. In this example, the Qur'aan is written in *Hafs*, and the alternate readings (three examples of which can be seen in the margin) are for the *qiraa'a* of *Shu'bah*.

(Istanbul, Topkapi Saray Library)

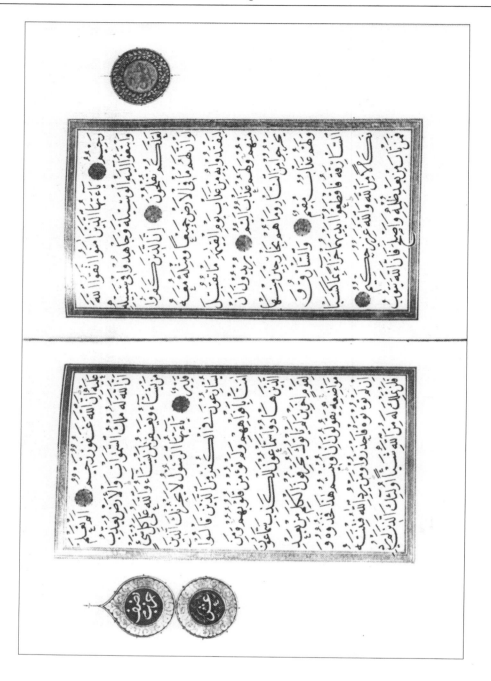

PLATE TEN

Soorah al-Maa'idah, verse 34 to 41. This *Naskhee* example is written by Hamd Allaah Ibn ash-Shaykh, one of the teachers of the Ottoman Sultan Bayazeed II, in 897 A.H., in Turkey. The markings indicating five and ten verses are present in the margin, as well as an indication for half of the *hizb*.

(Istanbul, Topkapi Saray Library)

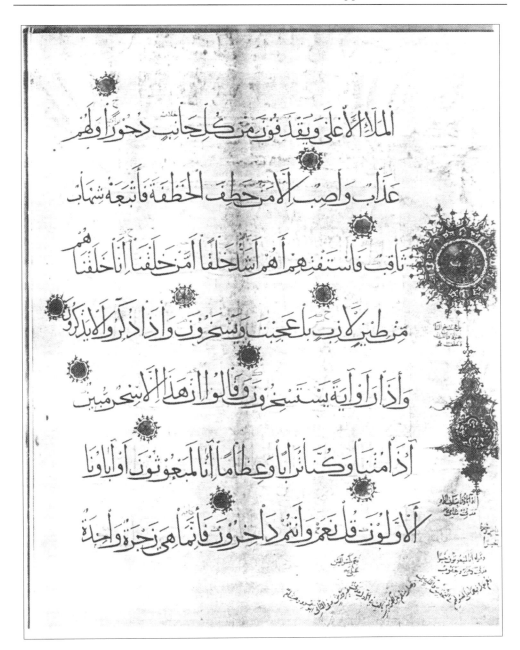

PLATE ELEVEN

Soorah Saafaat, verses 8 to 30. This example of the *Muhaqqaq* script was written by 'Umar ibn 'Alee ibn Muhammad in 600 A.H., in Iraq. Of particular interest is the fact that the margins contain the variant readings of all ten *qira'aat*.

(Turkish and Islamic Museum, Istanbul)

PLATE TWELVE

Soorah ash-Shu'araa, verses 59 to 63. This is a classic example of the *Maghribee* script. Written in the 6th century in Spain, it is in the *qiraa'a* of *Warsh*. Notice the slightly different system of *nuqat*; in the second verse, the first letter is a *faa* (written with one dot below the letter), and the second word in the same verse has a *qaaf* in it, represented by one dot above the circle. The system of *tashkeel* is also slightly different.

(Turkish and Islamic Museum, Istanbul)

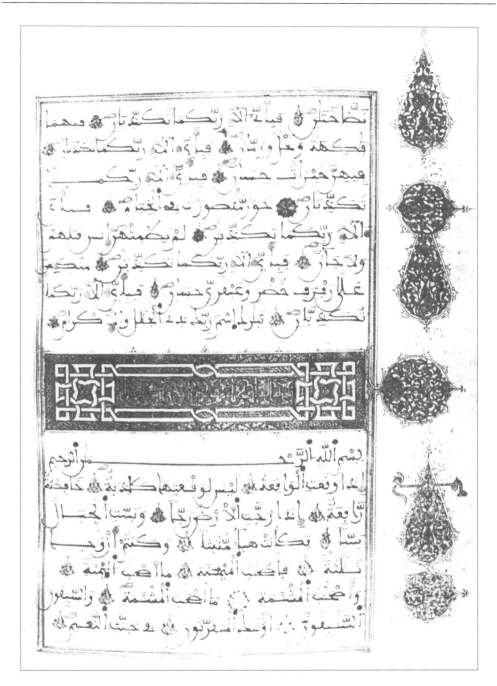

PLATE THIRTEEN

The last ten verses of *Soorah ar-Rahmaan*, along with the first few of *Soorah al-Waaqi'ah*. Another example of *Maghribee* script. This particular manuscript was written for the Shareefee Sultan Moolay Zaydaan, in 1008 A.H. However, it was captured along with the rest of his library by looting Spanish pirates in 1611 CE (1020 A.H.).

(San Lorenzo del Escorial Library, Spain)

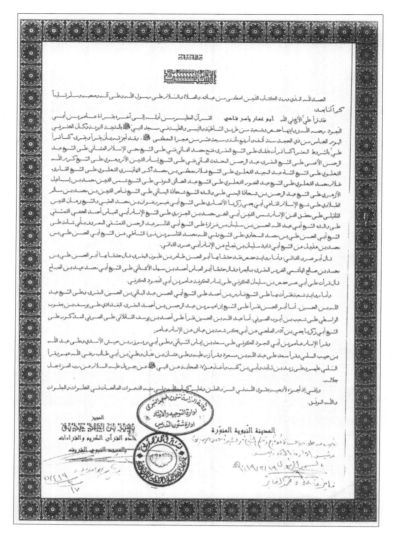

PLATE FOURTEEN

An example of an *ijaaza*, or *sanad*, which is awarded to a student of the *qira'aat* by a Shaykh. The *ijaaza* signifies the fact that the Shaykh is satisfied with the student's recitation of the Qur'aan, and that the student has perfected the recitation of the *qiraa'a* that the *ijaaza* was awarded it. (*Ijaazahs* are awarded in all ten *qira'aat* through all of their *turuqs*). This one was awarded in 1419 A.H., in the Prophet's (ﷺ) Masjid in Madeenah. It is for the *qiraa'a* of 'Aasim, through his two students Shu'bah and Hafs. This simple list of names represents one of the most powerful proofs of the complete preservation of the Qur'aan. It is a continuous, direct and unbroken chain of narrators, from the present day to the Prophet (ﷺ), to Jibreel, to Allaah, all Praise and Glory be to Him. This in essence implies the fact that the correct transmission of the Qur'aan is *guaranteed* and *documented*; every single person whose name is present in an *ijaaza* was awarded the *ijaaza* by his Shaykh (the name before him), all the way back to the age of the famous *Qaaris*, who studied under the *taabi'een,* who studied under the Companions, who learnt the Qur'aan directly from the Prophet (ﷺ). This particular *ijaaza* contains 34 people between the recipient and the Prophet (ﷺ); higher *ijaaza*s are available, though, and in all ten *qira'aat*. Can any other religious book claim such a rigorous proof of preservation?

BIBLIOGRAPHY

Qur'aans

Al-Qur'aan al-Kareem:

H̲afs̲:   1) Calligraphy by 'Uthmaan Taha. Printed by Dar al-Fajr 'Uthmaaniyah, Beirut. 1984

2) Calligrapher not mentioned. Printed by Taj Company, Karachi. 1982

Warsh: 1) Calligraphy by Ah̲mad ibn Hamyi. Official *mus̲-h̲af* of Morocco.

2) Calligraphy by 'Uthmaan Taha. Printed by 'The King Fahd Complex for the Printing of the Holy Qur'aan', Madeenah. 1991

Qaloon: Calligraphy by Aboo Bakr Saasi al-Maghribi.Official *mus̲-h̲af* of the Re public of Libya, 1989.

Al-Qira'aat al-Asharath al-Muttawaatirah min T̲ariqay al-Shat̲ibiyyah wa al-Durrah, written besides the text of the Qur'aan. Compiled by Kharoof, Muh̲ammad Fahd and Rajih, Muh̲ammad Karim. Dar al-Muhajir, Madeenah. 1994.

Books and Dissertations

Aajurree, Aboo Bakr Muh̲ammad. *as-Sharee'ah*. ed. by Waleed ibn Muh̲ammad. Mu'asasah Qurtubah, Cairo. 1996.

Aboo Shahbah, Muh̲ammad. *Al-Madkhal li Dirasaat al-Qur'aan al-Kareem*. Dar al-Liwaa, Riyadh. 3rd ed., 1987.

Aboo Ubaadah, Ibraaheem ibn Muh̲ammad. *Lughat al-Qur'aan*. Daar al-Watan, Riyadh. 1993.

'Abd ar-Rah̲eem, Muh̲ammad. *Tafseer as̲-S̲ahaabah: Mumayizaatuh, Khas̲aa'is̲uh, Masaadiruh*. Maktabah at-Turaath al-Islaamee, Cairo. 1991.

Ah̲mad, Abdullaah. *as-Sunnah*. Ramaadee li an-Nashr, Riyadh. 1995

al-Awaji, Muh̲ammad. *I'jaaz al-Qur'aan 'ind Shaykh al-Islaam ibn Taymiyyah*. Masters Diss., Islaamic Univ. of Madeenah, 1984.

al-Albaanee, Muh̲ammad Naas̲ir al-Deen.

Ah̲kaam al-Janaa'iz. Maktab al-Islaami, Beirut. 1986.

Da'eef al-Jami' as̲-S̲agheer wa Ziyadah. Maktab al-Islaami, Berut. 1991.

Da'eef Sunan at-Tirmidhee. Maktab al-Islaami, Beirut. 1991.

Footnotes to Muh̲ammad Ghazali's *Fiqh as-Seerah*. Dar al-Qalam, Damascus. 1989.

Manzilat as-Sunnah fi al-Islaam. Dar al-Hayah al-Islaamiyah, Egypt, n.d.

Saheeh al-Jaami' as̲-S̲agheer wa Ziyaadah. Maktab al-Islaami, Beirut. 1988.

Silsilah al-Ah̲aadeeth ad̲-D̲a'eefah. Maktabah al-Ma'aarif, Riyadh. 1995

Silsilah al-Ah̲aadeeth as̲-S̲aheeh̲ah. Maktabah al-Ma'aarif, Riyadh. 1995.

'Ali, Maulana Mu<u>h</u>ammad. *The Holy Qur'aan*. Speciality Promotions Co., Chicago. 1985.

'Alee, 'Uthmaan Mua'alim Ma<u>h</u>mood. *al-Ayaat al-Muda'ee Naskhuha bi Aayat as-<u>Say</u>f*. Masters Diss., IUM, 1992.

Aleeway, Aleeway Khaleefah. *Jami' an-Nuqool fi Asbaab an-Nuzool*, Matabi al-Ashaa', Riyadh. 1984.

Arberry, Arthur J. *The Koran Interpreted*. The MacMillan Company, New York. 1955.

Azami, M. M. *Studies In Early Hadith Literature*. American Trust Publication, Indianapolis, Indiana. 1992.

Banna, A<u>h</u>mad ibn Mu<u>h</u>ammad. *Itihaaf al-Fudhala al-Bashar fi al-Qira'aat al-Arba'atha Ashr*. Alim al-Kutub, Beirut. 1987.

al-Barbahaaree, al-<u>H</u>asan. *Shar<u>h</u> as-Sunnah*. Maktabah as-*Sunnah*, Cairo. 1996.

Baazmool, Mu<u>h</u>ammad ibn 'Umar ibn Saalim: *al-Qiraa'aat wa Atharuhaa fee at-Tafseer*, Daar al-Hijrah, Riyaadh. 1996.

Bucaille, Maurice. *The Bible, the Qur'aan, and Science*. American Trust Publications, Indiannapolis. 1978.

Bulayhee, <u>S</u>aali<u>h</u> ibn Ibraaheem. *Al-Huda wa al-Bayaan fi Asmaa al-Qur'aan*. [?]. 1977.

Burton, John. *The Collection of the Qur'an*. Cambridge University Press, Cambridge. 1977.

Curtis, Roy Young Mu<u>h</u>ammad Mukhtar. *Authentic Interpretation of Classical Islamic Texts: An Analysis of the Introduction of Ibn Katheer's 'Tafseer al-Qur'aan al-Azim.'* Ph.D. dissertation, University of Michigan. 1989.

Damishqee, <u>T</u>aahir Jazariy. *Tibyaan li ba'ad al-Mabaa<u>h</u>ith al-Muta'aliq lil Qur'aan ala <u>t</u>areeq al-Itqaan*. Edited by Aboo Ghuzza 'Abd al-Fatta<u>h</u>. Maktabah al-Mathbua'at al-Islaamee, Beirut. 4th ed., 1992.

ad-Daani, Aboo 'Amr Mu<u>h</u>ammad ibn Sa'eed.

> *al-Bayaan fi 'ad aay al-Qur'aan*. ed. Dr. Ghanem al-<u>H</u>amd. Markaz al-Makhthoothat, Kuwait. 1994.

> *Kitaab al-Tayseer fi al-Qira'aat as-Saba'*. Dar Kutub al-Arabiyya, Beirut. 1984.

> *al-Muqni' fi rasm Ma<u>s</u>aa<u>h</u>if al-Amsaar*. Maktab al-Kuliyat al-Azhar, Egypt. 1978.

ad-Daarimee, 'Uthmaan ibn Sa'eed. *ar-Radd ala al-Jahmiyyah*. ed. Badr al-Badr. Darr ibn al-Atheer, Kuwait. 1995.

Daraz, Mu<u>h</u>ammad 'Abdullaah. *an-Naba al-'A<u>dh</u>eem; Nadaraat Jadeedah fi al-Qur'aan*. Dar al-Ilm, Kuwait. 1970.

Darwish, 'Abd al-Mun'im Faraj. *Lulu wa al-Marjan fi Tanbeeh ala i'jaaz al-Qur'aan*. Markaz al-Dawah wa al-Irshad. Dubai. n.d.

adh-Dhahabee, al-Imaam Shams ad-Deen Muḥammad ibn Aḥmad.

Ma'arifat al-Quraa' al-Kibaar 'alaa ath-Tabaqati wal Aathaar. ed. Shu'ayb al-Arna'oot, et. al. Muasasah ar-Risaalah, Beirut. 1988.

Siyar A'laam an-Nubalaa. ed. Shu'ayb al-Arna'oot, et. al. Muasasah ar-Risaalah, Beirut. 1996.

al-Uluww. ed. by Muḥammad Naaṣir ad-Deen al-Albaani. al-Maktab al-Islami, Beirut. 1991.

adh-Dhahabee, Dr. Muḥammad Ḥusayn. *at-Tafseer wa al-Mufassiroon*. Maktabah Wahbah, Cairo.1995.

al-Fanaysaan, Sa'ood 'Abdullaah. *Ikhtilaaf al-Mufasireen*. Maktabah Daar ar-Rush, Riyaadh. 1997.

Faqihee, Muḥammad Ḥaneef. *Nadhariyya i'jaaz al-Qur'aan 'ind 'Abd al-Qaahir al-Jarjaani*. Masters Diss., Cairo Univ., 1960.

al-Ghazalee, Aboo Ḥaamid: *Iḥyaa 'Uloom al-Deen*, Ashraf Publishers, Lahore, n.d.

al-Ḥaqq, Ikraam Allaah Imdaad. *Imaam 'Alee al-Madeenee wa Manhajuhu fi Naqd ar-Rijaal*. Masters diss., Umm al-Qurra Univ., Makkah. Published by Dar Bashair, Beirut, 1984.

al-Ḥamad, Ghanim Qadoori. *Rasm al-Maṣaaḥif; diraasat lughawiya wa tariḳhiya*. Masters diss., Cairo Univeristy, 1976.

al-Ḥamood, Muḥammad ibn Ḥamad. *al-Manhaj al-Asmaa fee Sharḥi Asmaa Allaahi al-Ḥusnaa*. Maktabat al-Imaam adh-Dhahabee, Kuwait, 1993.

al-Harbee, Aḥmad ibn Awad. *al-Maatooreediyya: Diraasat wa Taqweem*. Daar al-'Aaṣimah, Riyadh. 1413 AH.

al-Ḥaashimee, 'Abdul Mun'im. *Qurraa al-Qur'aan*. Daar Ibn Katheer, Damascus. 1993.

Ibn 'Abd al-Baar, Yoosuf. *Jaami' Bayaan al-'Ilm wa Faḍlihee*. ed. by Aboo al-Ishbaal az-Zuhayree. Maktabah Ibn Taymiyah, Cairo. 1996.

Ibn Abee Ṭaalib, Aboo Muḥammad Makkee. *Kitaab al-Ibaanah 'an Ma'anee al-Qira'aat*. ed. Dr. Muhyee Ramaḍaan. Dar al-Mamoon li Thurath, Beirut, 1979.

Ibn 'Abd al-'Izz al-Ḥanafee, Muḥammad. *Sharḥ Aqeedah al-Ṭaḥaawiyyah*. al-Maktab al-Islaamee, Beirut. 1988.

Ibn al-'Arabee, al-Qaḍee Aboo Bakr. *an-Naasiḳh wa al-Mansooḳh fi al-Qur'aan al-Kareem*. See under al-Madgharee.

Ibn al-Atheer, Mubaarak ibn Muḥammad al-Jazaree. *al-Nihaayah fi Ghareeb al-Hadeeth*. Maktabah al-Islaamiyya, Cairo. 1965.

Ibn Hajr, al-Haafidh Ahmad ibn 'Alee.

al-Isaabah fi Tamyiz as-Sahabah. Dar al-Kutub al-Ilmiyyah, Beirut. 1995.

Taqreeb at-Tahdheeb. ed. Aboo al-Ishbaal al-Pakistaanee. Daar al-Aasimah, Riyadh. 1996

Ibn Hazm al-Andaloosee, Aboo 'Abdillaah Muhammad. *al-Naasikh wa al-Mansookh fi al-Qur'aan al-Kareem*. Dar al-Kutub al-Ilmiyyah, Beirut. 1986.

Ibn al-Jawzee, Aboo al-Faraj Abd ar-Rahmaan.

al-Hath alaa Hifdh al-Ilm wa Dhikr Kibaar al-Huffadh. Dar al-Kutub al-Ilmiyyah, Beirut, Lebanon.1986.

Nawasikh al-Qur'aan. See under al-Malbaree.

Ibn al-Jazaree, Muhammad ibn Muhammad. *an-Nashr fi al-Qira'aat al-'Ashr*. Dar Kutub al-Ilmiyyah, Beirut. n.d.

Ibn Katheer, 'Imaad ad-Deen Ismaa'eel. *Tafseer al-Quraan al-'Adheem*. Daar al-Khayr, Beirut. 1991.

Ibn al-Qayyim, Shams ad-Deen.

Fawaa'id al-Fawaa'id. ed. by 'Alee al-Halabee. Daar ibn al-Jawzee, Dammaam. 1996.

as-Sawaa'iq al-Mursalah. Daar al-Aasimah, Riyaadh. 1988.

Ibn Qudaama, 'Abdullaah ibn Ahmad.

al-Burhan fi Bayaan al-Qur'aan. Matabah al-Huda, Pt. Said. 1989.

Rawdat an-Naadir. Maktabah Daar al-Baaz, Makkah. 1994.

Ibn Taymiyyah, Ahmad ibn 'Abd al-Haleem.

Iqtidaa Siraat al-Mustaqeem, ed. Dr. Naasir al-'Aql, Maktabah ar-Rushd, Riyadh. 1994.

Majmoo' al-Fataawa. Compiled by 'Abd ar-Rahmaan ibn Muhammad. n.p. 1997.

An Introduction to the Principles of Tafseer. al-Hidaayah Publishing and Distribution, Birmingham. 1993.

at-Tadmooriyyah. Al-Maktab al-Islaamee, Beirut. 1988.

Ik, Khaalid 'Abd ar-Rahmaan. *Usool at-Tafseer wa Qawaa'idih*.Dar an-Nafees, Beirut. 1986

Itr, Hasan Diyaa ad-Din.

al-Ahruf as-Saba' wa manzil al-Qira'aat minha. Dar al-Bashair al-Islaamiyyah, Beirut. 1988.

al-Mu'jiza al-Khaalidah. Dar al-Bashair al-Islaamiyyah, Beirut. 1994.

al-Isfahaanee, ar-Raaghib. *Mufradaat al-Qur'aan*. Daar al-Qalam, Damascus. 1997.

James, David. *Qur'ans of the Mamluks*. Alexandria Press, London, 1988.

Jeffery, Arthur. *Materials for the History of the Text of the Qur'an,* along with *Kitaab al-Masaahif of Ibn Abee Daawood.* Leiden, 1937.

Juday', 'Abdullaah Yoosuf. *Al-Aqeedah as-Salafiyyah fee Kalaam Rab al-Bariyyah.* Daar al-Imaam Maalik, Riyadh. 1995.

Kamali, Mohammad Hashim. *Principles of Islamic Jurisprudence.* Islamic Texts Society, Cambridge. 1991.

al-Khalaal, Aboo Bakr Ahmad ibn Muhammad. *As-Sunnah.* Edited by Dr. Atiyya Zahranee. Dar ar-Rayah, Riyadh. 1994.

Khalifa, Mohammad. *The Sublime Qur'an and Orientalism.* Longman, London. 1983

Khaatir, Muhammad Ahmad. *Qira'aat 'Abdallaah ibn Mas'ood: makaanatuha, masadiruha, ihsauha.* Dar al-'Itisam, Cairo. 1990.

al-Khamees, Dr. Muhammad ibn 'Abd ar-Rahmaan. *'Itiqaad al-A'immah al-Arba'ah.*

Khayyaat, Khaleefah. *Taareekh.* ed. by Dr. Akram Umari. Daar Tayibah, Madeenah.1985.

al-Laalikaa'ee, Abul Qasim Hibat Allaah. *Sharh usool 'Itiqaad Ahl as-Sunnah wal Jama'ah.* Ed. by Dr. Ahmad Sa'ad al-Ghaamidee. Dar at-Tayibbah, Riyadh. 1995.

Ma'abad, Muhammad Ahmad. *Nafahaat min 'uloom al-Qur'aan.* Maktabah at-Tayibah, Madeenah. 1987.

al-Madgharee, Dr. Abdul-Kabeer al-Alawee. *an-Naasikh wa al-Mansookh fi al-Qur'aan al-Karim li al-Qadee Aboo Bakr ibn al-'Arabee.* Ministry of Religious Affairs, Morrocco. n.d.

al-Malbaree, Muhammad Ashraf 'Alee. *Nawasikh al-Qur'aan li al-Alaamah Ibn al-Jawzee.* Masters Diss., IUM. 1984.

al-Mizzee, Jamaal al-Deen Yoosuf, *Tahzeeb al-Kamaal fi Asmaa ar-Rijaal.* ed. by Dr. Bashaar Awwaad. Muasasat ar-Risalah, Beirut. 1980.

Moosaa, 'Abd ar-Razaaq. *Murshid al-Khalaan ilaa Ma'rifat 'ad Aay al-Qur'aan,* IUM Press, Madeenah, 1990.

al-Mubaarkafooree, Safee ur-Rahmaan. *ar-Raheeq al-Makhtoom.* Maktabah as-Sahaabah, Jeddah. 1990.

Muslim, Mustafa. *Manaahij al-Mufassireen.* Daar al-Muslim, Riyadh. 1995.

an-Najdee, Muhammad. *al-Qawl al-Mukhtasar al-Mubeen fee Manaahij al-Mufassireen.* Maktabah adh-Dhahabee, Cairo. 1992.

an-Nasaa'ee, Ahmed ibn Shu'ayb. *Fadail al-Qur'aan.* Dar Ihyaa al-'uloom, Beirut. 1992.

an-Nahaas, Aboo Ja'afar Ahmad ibn Muhammad. *an-Naasikh wa al-Mansookh fi Kitaab Allaahi 'Azza wa Jal.* ed. by al-Laahim, Sulayman 'Abdullaah. Muassasah ar-Risaalah, Beirut. 1991.

Njozi, Hamza Mustafa. *The Sources of the Qur'aan: A Critical Review of the Authorship Theories*. WAMY, Saudi Arabia. n.d.

Noor, Khaalid. *Manhaj Ahl as-Sunnah wa Manhaj al-Ashaa'irah fee Tawheed Allaah Ta'aala*. Ph.D., IUM. al-Ghuraba Publications, Madeenah. 1995.

Numani, Allama Shibli. *Sirat-un-Nabi* (Engl.). Kazi Publications, Lahore. 1981.

Patton, Walter M. *Ahmed ibn Hanbal and the Mihna*. Librairie et Imprimerie, Leiden. 1897.

al-Qadee, Abdul Fattah. *al-Budoor adh-Dhaahiriyyah wa yaleehi, al-Qira'aat as-Shaadah*. Dar Kutub al-Ilmiyyah, Beirut. 1981.

Qattaan, Manna'. *Mabahith fi 'uloom al-Qur'aan*. Muasasat al-Risalat, Beirut. 1983.

Qurtubee, Muhammad ibn Ahmad. *Al-Jaami' li ahkaam al-Qur'aan*. ed. by Dr. Muhammad Ibraaheem al-Hafnawee, Dar a-Hadeeth, Cairo. 1994.

ar-Raazee, Muhammad ibn 'Umar Fakhr ad-Din. *Ahkaam al-Basmalah*, ed. Majdee Ibraahim, Maktabah al-Qur'aan, Cairo, n.d.

Rodwell, J. M. *The Koran*. Everyman Publications, London. 1994.

ar-Roomee, Fahd ibn 'Abd al-Rahmaan ibn Sulayman.

    Dirasaat fi 'uloom al-Qur'aan. Maktabah at-Tawbah, Riyadh. 1994.

    Ittijahhat at-Tafseer fee al-Qarn ar-Rabi' Ashr. Muasasah ar-Risaalah, Beirut. 1997.

    Usool at-Tafseer wa Manaahijih. Maktabah at-Tawbah, Riyadh. 1993.

Sabbagh, Muhammad ibn Latifi. *Lamahath fi 'uloom al-Qur'aan*. Maktab al-Islaamee, Beirut. 3rd ed., 1990.

as-Sabt, Khaalid. *Kitaab al-Manaahil al-Irfaan: dirasat wa taqweem*. Daar Ibn 'Affaan, al-Khobar. 1997

as-Sakhawee, 'Ilm ad-Din.

    Jamaal al-Quraa wa Kamaal al-Aqraa. Matba' al-Madanee, Madeenah. 1987.

    al-Maqaasid al-Hasanah fee Bayaan Katheer min al-Ahadeeth al-Mushthahira alaa al-Alsinah. Daar al-Kutub al-Arabi, Beirut.1996.

Sale, George. *The Koran*. Frederick Warne and Co., London. 1887.

Saleh, Subhee. *Mabahith fi 'uloom al-Qur'aan*. Dar al-Ilm lil Malayeen, Beirut. 1979.

Shakir, M. H. *The Qur'aan Translated*. Tahrike Tarsile Qur'an, New York.1997.

ash-Shaatibee, Qaasim ibn Feeruh. *Hirz al-Amaani wa Wajh al-Tahani fi al-Qira'aat al-Saba'*. Dar al-Mathbuath, Jeddah. 1990.

as-Suyootee, Jalaal al-Din 'Abd al-Rahmaan.

    al-Itqaan fee 'uloom al-Qur'aan. Dar al-Marifah, Beirut. n.d.

    Labaab al-Nuqool fi Asbaab an-nuzool. Dar Ihyaa al-'uloom, Beirut. 1983.

Shuroot al-Mufassir wa Aadabih. Taken from *al-Itqaan*. See under az-Zamralee.

Tanasiq ad-Durar fi Tansub as-Suwar. Alim al-Kutub, Beirut. 1987.

Tadreeb ar-Raawee fee Sharh Taqreeb an-Nawawee. Dar al-Kutub al-Arabi, Beirut. 1993.

at-Tabaree, Muhammad ibn Jareer. *Jaami' al-Bayan 'aan Ta'weel al-Qur'aan*. Edited by Muhammed Shakir. Dar al-Ma'arif, Cairo. n.d.

at-Taahawee, Aboo Ja'far Ahmad. *Sharh Mushkil al-Athaar*. ed. by Shu'ayb al-Arna'oot. Muasasah ar-Risalah, Beirut. 1994.

Tarhoonee, Muhammad ibn Rizq. *Mawsoo'ah Fadaa'il Suwar wa Aayaat al-Quraaniyah*. Maktabah al-Ilm, Jeddah. 1994.

at-Tayyaar, Musa'id. *Fusool fee usool at-Tafseer*. Daar an-Nashr ad-Duwalee, Riyadh. 1993.

Ubaydaat, Mahmood Saalim. *Diraasaat fi 'uloom al-Qur'aan*. Dar Ammaar, Jordan. 1990.

Umayrah, 'Abd ar-Rahman. *ar-Rijaal Anzal Allaahu fihim Qur'aanan*. Dar Jeel, Beirut. 1990.

Uwais, Ahmad Taahir. *Kitaab al-Mustaneer fi al-Qira'aat al-'Ashr*. Doctoral Diss., Madeenah Univ. 1993.

al-Uthaymeen, Muhammad ibn Saalih. *Usool fi at-Tafseer*. Dar Ibn al-Qayyim, Dammam. 1989.

Von Denffer, Ahmad. *'Uloom al-Qur'aan: An Introduction to the Sciences of the Qur'an*. The Islamic Foundation, Leicester. 1983.

al-Waadi'ee, Muqbil ibn Haadee. *Saheeh al-Musnad min Asbaab an-nuzool*. Matabi' al-Hadaf, no city, n.d.

al-Waahidee, Abee al-Hasan 'Alee ibn Ahmad. *Asbaab an-nuzool*. Ed. by Assaam al-Humaidaan. Dar as-Salah, Dammam, 1992.

Waabil, Yoosuf. *Ashraat as-Saa'at*. Daar ibn al-Jawzee, Dammaam, 1993.

Wehr, Hans; Cowan, J.M. *Arabic-English Dictionary*.

World Bibliography of Translations of the Meanings of the Holy Qur'an Research Centre for Islamic History, Art and Culture (under the OIC). Istanbul. 1986.

al-Wohaibi, Saleh Sulaiman. *Qur'aanic Variants ('Ilm al-Qira'aat): An Historical-Phonological Study*. Ph.D. dissertation, Indiana University, 1982.

Zaid, Mustafa. *an-Naskh fi al-Qur'aan*. Dar al-Fikr, Beirut. 1971.

Zamralee, Fawwaaz Ahmad. *Shuroot al-Mufassir wa Aadaabih li as-Suyootee*. Dar Ibn Hazm, Beirut. 1994.

az-Zarkashee, Badr al-Din Muhammad ibn 'Abdullaah.

al-Burhaan fi 'uloom al-Qur'aan. Maktabah al-Asriyyah, Beirut. 1972

al-Bahr al-Muheet, ed. Muhammad Sulayman al-Ashqar, no city, n.d.

az-Zarqaanee, Muhammad 'Abd al-Adheem. *Manaahil al-Irfaan fi 'uloom al-Qur'aan*. Dar al-Fikr, Cairo. n.d.

Zarzoor, Adnan Muhammad. *'Uloom al-Qur'aan; Madkhal ila Tafseer al-Qur'aan wa Bayaan 'Ijazihi*. Maktab al-Islaami, Beirut. 1981

Magazines and Periodicals

Majalah Kulliyah al-Qur'aan al-Kareem . Vol. 1, No. 1

al-Badawee, Muhammad Sibawaih. *al-Masaahif al-'Uthmaaniyyah, al-Mus-haf al-Koofee*.

al-Qaaree, 'Abd al-'Azeez 'Abd al-Fattah. *Hadeeth al-ahruf as-Saba'ah*.

The Message . Vol. 15, No. 10

Kazi, Yasir. *The Documentation of the Qur'aan*.

Kidwai, A.R. *English Translations of the Holy Qur'an: An Annotated Bibliography*.

Al-Basheer .

Vol. 3, No. 5 & 6: Zarabozo, Jamaal al-Din, *On Yusuf Ali's and Muhammad Asad's Commentaries*

Vol. 5, No. 6: Kazi, Yasir, *The History of the Qur'an and Related Matters*

Unpublished Works

Sideeq, Basheer Ahmad.

Siraaj al-Mu'alim min Qira'aat sayidana al-Imaam Aasim min riwayat Shu'bah.

al-Usool li qira'aat Warsh.

(Both photocopies of original, in handwriting of author).